GILLES
Deleuze
&
Félix
Guattari

EUROPEAN PERSPECTIVES

EUROPEAN PERSPECTIVES

A Series in Social Thought and Cultural Criticism

LAWRENCE D. KRITZMAN, EDITOR

European Perspectives presents outstanding books by leading European thinkers. With both classic and contemporary works, the series aims to shape the major intellectual controversies of our day and to facilitate the tasks of historical understanding.

For a complete list of books in the series, see pages 653–55.

GILLES Deleuze & Félix Guattari

Intersecting Lives

François Dosse

Translated by **Deborah Glassman**

Columbia University Press   New York

Columbia University Press
Publishers Since 1893
New York   Chichester, West Sussex
Originally published as *Gilles Deleuze et Félix Guattari. Biographie croisée*
Copyright © Editions La Decouverte, Paris, 2007
Translation copyright © 2010 Columbia University Press
All rights reserved

Columbia University Press wishes to express its appreciation for assistance given
by the government of France through the Ministère Français de la Culture with
the preparation of this translation.

This work, published as part of a program providing publication assistance, received
financial support from the French Ministry of Foreign Affairs, the Cultural Services of
the French Embassy in the United States and FACE (French American Cultural Exchange).
www.frenchbooknews.com.

French Voices Logo designed by Serge Bloch

Library of Congress Cataloging-in-Publication Data

Dosse, François, 1950–
   [Gilles Deleuze et Félix Guattari. English]
   Gilles Deleuze and Félix Guattari : intersecting lives / François Dosse.
      p. em.—(European perspectives)
   Includes bibliographical references and index.
   ISBN 978-0-231-14560-2 (cloth : alk. paper)—ISBN 978-0-231-51867-3 (e-book)
   1. Deleuze, Gilles, 1925–1995.   2. Guattari, Félix, 1930–1992.   I. Title.   II. Series.

B2430.D454D6713 2010
194—dc22
[B]

2009047835

Columbia University Press books are printed on permanent and durable acid-free paper.
This book is printed on paper with recycled content.
Printed in the United States of America

c 10 9 8 7 6 5 4 3 2 1

Contents

Acknowledgments

I would like to thank all those who generously contributed their time during the interviews that I carried out between 2004 and 2006. Their help was essential for making this biography possible: Alfred Adler, Éric Alliez, Dudley Andrew, Bernard Andrieu, Manola Antonioli, Alain Aptekman, Olivier Apprill, Philippe Artières, Zafer Aracagök, François Aubral, Danièle Auffray, Jacques Aumont, Kostas Axelos, Alain Beaulieu, Raymond Bellour, Thomas Bénatouil, Réda Bensmaïa, Denis Berger, Giuseppe Bianco, Pierre Blanchaud, Pascal Bonitzer, Julian Bourg, Christian Bourgois, Constantin Boundas, Christine Buci-Glucksmann, Bernard Cache, Michel Cartry, Pascal Chabot, Pierre-Antoine Chardel, Noëlle Châtelet, Jean Chesneaux, Michel Ciment, Pascale Criton, Andrew Cutrofello, Fanny Deleuze, Christian Descamps, Marc-Alain Descamps, Juacques Donzelot, Jean-Maris Doublet, Jean-Claude Dumoncel, Élie During, Corinne Enaudeau, Jean-Pierre Faye, Pierrette Fleutieux, François Fourquet, Daniel Franco, Gérard Fromanger, Maurice de Gandillac, Roger Gentis, Fernando Gonzales, Frédéric Gros, Lawrence Grossberg, Bruno Guattari, Emmaneulle Guattari, Jean Guattari, Alain et Danièle Guillerm, Nicole Gullet, Suzanne Hême de Lacotte, Eugene Holland, Michel Izard, Eleanor Kaufman, Lawrence Kritzman, Christina Kullberg, David Lapoujade, Claude Lemoine, Jean-Louis Leutrat, Sylvain Loiseau, Sylvère Lotringer, Yves Mabin, Norman Madarasz, Robert Maggiori, Josée Manenti, Jean-Paul Manganaro, Patrice Maniglier, Michel Marié, Jean-Clet Martin, Hervé Maury, Philippe Mengue, Alain Ménil, Catherine Millot, Olivier Mongin, Pierre Montebello, Liane Mozère, Lion Murard, Jean-Pierre Muyard, Stéphane Nadaud, Jean Narboni, Toni Negri, Miguel Norambuena, Jean Oury, François Pain, Dominique Païni, Jo Panaget, Thierry Paquot, André de Souza Parente, Giorgio Passerone, Paul Patton, Florence Pétry, Richard Pinhas, Rafaël Pividal, Jean-Claude Polack,

Matthieu Potte-Bonneville, Daniel Price, John Protevi, Olivier Querouil, Anne Querrien, David Rabouin, Jacques Rancière, Francois Regnault, Olivier Revault D'Allonnes, Judith Revel, Alain Roger, Jacob Rogozinski, Suely Rolnik, Élisabeth Roudinesco, Jean-Michel Salanskis, Elias Sanbar, Anne Sauvagnargues, René Schérer, Dominique Séglard, Guillaume Sibertin-Blanc, Danielle Sivadon, Gérard Soulier, Hidenobu Suzuki, Jean-Baptiste Thierrée, Simon Tormey, Serge Toubiana, Michel Tournier, Michel Tubiana, Guy Trastour, Kuniichi Uno, Janne Vehanen, Paul Veyne, Arnaud Villani, Tiziana Villani, J. MacGregor Wise, Frédéric Worms, Chris Younès, Dork Zabunyan, and François Zourbachivili.

I would also like to thank Virgine Linhart profoundly for having very generously provided the interviews she conducted for her study of Felix Guattari's life with the following: Éric Alliez, Raymond Bellour, Franco Berardi Bifo, Denis Berger, Jacky Berroyer, Novella Bonetti-Bassano, Jack Brière, Michel Butel, Michel Cartry, Gaby Cohn-Bendit, Marie Depussé, Gisèle Donnard, Jean-Marie Doublet, Hélène Dupuy de Lôme, Mony Elkaïm, Patrick Farbias, Jean-Pierre Faye, François Fourquet, Gérard Fromanger, Gervaise Garnaud, Sacha Goldman, Bruno Guattari, Emmanuelle Guattari, Jean Guattari, Tatiana Kecojevic, Jean-Jacques Lebel, Sylvère Lotringer, Pierre Manart, Lucien Martin, Ramondo Matta, Ginette Michaud, Gian Marco Montesano, Yann Moulier-Boutang, Lion Murard, Toni Negri, Jean Oury, Pierre Pachet, François Pain, Jo Panaget, Jean-Claude Polack, Anne Querrien, Jacques Robin, Michel Rostain, Dominique Seglard, Gérard Soulier, Isabelle Stengers, Massaki Sugimura, Paul Virilio, and Claude Vivien.

I would also like to thank my friend Jean-Christophe Goddard very much for having invited me to speak during the exciting two-day workshop on *Anti-Oedipus* that he organized at the University of Poitiers on December 2–3, 2005.

Thanks also to Anne Sauvagnargues and Guillaume Sibertin-Blanc for having allowed me to come to their seminar, "Reading Deleuze and Guattari's *A Thousand Plateaus*," at the Working Group on Deleuze, Spinoza, and the Social Sciences at the Center for the Study of Rhetoric, Philosophy, and the History of Ideas (CERPHI) in 2005–2006.

My thanks also go to Emmanuelle Guattari, for her early support for this project, and to José Ruiz Funes, for having facilitated my access to the Guattari collection at the IMEC Archives.

Thanks also to Fanny Deleuze and Emmanuelle and Bruno Guattari for having spoken with me and for giving me permission to publish their personal photographs.

Finally, and with the deepest gratitude, I would like to thank my first readers, who helped me substantially improve the first draft. I obviously owe them a great debt for innumerable corrections, information, and suggestions: Manola Antoniolli, Raymond Bellour, François Fourquet, Hugues Jallon, Thierry Paquot, Guillaume Sibertin-Blanc, and Danielle Sivadon. And of course, my thanks to Florence Dosse, for having given up her own research so that I could benefit from her indispensable skills as a reader.

GILLES
Deleuze
&
Félix
Guattari

Introduction

Betwixt or Between

Four-handed. The work of Gilles Deleuze and Félix Guattari remains an enigma, even today. Who was the author? One or both of them? How could two such different men, with such distinct sensibilities and styles, pursue their intellectual agenda together for more than twenty years (1969–1991)? How could they have been so close—yet so distant that they used the formal *vous* to address each other (though both used the informal *tu* quite easily with others)? How do we describe the propulsive energy of this unique adventure? How did the collaboration between these two writers function? It is often difficult to determine what belongs to whom in their writing, but at the same time it would be somewhat of an exaggeration to suggest a hypothetical "third person," since both writers maintained their own identity and went in distinctly different directions, even as they collaborated on a common enterprise.

In 1968, Gilles Deleuze and Félix Guattari inhabited very different worlds, and there was little chance that they would ever meet. Deleuze was a recognized philosopher who had by then already published a large body of work; Guattari was a militant psychoanalyst, the director of a psychiatric clinic, the author of several articles, and a social scientist. While we might agree with Robert Maggiori that they were destined to meet,[1] there was no historical necessity in the meeting. How their two worlds came into contact with each other remains an open question. As we shall see, the tremendous intensity of May 1968 made such an unlikely encounter possible. More prosaically, we know that Dr. Jean-Pierre Muyard, who was practicing at La Borde, was the mercurial and important middleman who brought the two together. Félix Guattari dedicated *Anti-Oedipus*, the first joint publication of the two authors: "To Jean-Pierre, the true culprit, the leader, the initiator of this perverse undertaking."

In the late 1950s, Jean-Pierre Muyard was a medical student in Lyon and a militant member of the left wing of the National French Students' Union (UNEF), which vigorously protested the war in Algeria. He became president of the Lyon section of the UNEF in 1960 and that same year met Jean-Claude Polack, the president of the General Association of Parisian Medical Students. Muyard was specializing in psychiatry but was also taking sociology courses at the Lyon University Humanities Division, and he was particularly interested in the courses given by the philosopher Henri Maldiney. In 1965, Muyard became vice president of the National French Students Mutuelle (MNEF) and got involved in creating an office to provide psychological counseling to university students (BAPU). He first met Guattari during a seminar organized by the Left Opposition in 1964 in Poissy, to which Jean-Claude Polack had invited him. Muyard recalls:

> I remember the impression that I had, I'd describe it as something physiological, the impression that Guattari immediately made on me felt like a startling vibration, a process of connection. The connection took place then and there and I accepted the energy more than the personality or the man himself. He was exceptionally intelligent, like Lacan, devilishly brilliant. Lucifer was, of course, the angel of light.[2]

In 1966, Nicole Guillet asked Muyard to move into the clinic at La Borde, as the influx of long-term patients required more doctors. He moved there that year and stayed until 1972. "Doc Mu's commitment and professional work at La Borde made him a real member of 'Félix's gang.' "

As a student in Lyon, Muyard kept in touch and on occasion visited other friends in the Lyon University Humanities Division. They described Deleuze's courses with enthusiasm. In 1967, Deleuze's book on Sacher-Masoch won him over.[3] The two men became friends, and Deleuze began a running discussion with Muyard so as to better understand the world of psychotics. "He said, I discuss psychosis and madness, but I don't know anything about it from the inside. But he was also phobic about deranged people and couldn't have spent even an hour at La Borde."[4]

By 1969, Muyard had wearied of Guattari's unbridled activism at La Borde, where he was constantly breaking up established groups to create new ones. "He needed something like Ritalin, which we give to hyperactive children today. We had to find a way to calm him down. Although he claimed that he wanted to write, he never wrote."[5] Muyard decided to arrange for

Deleuze and Guattari to meet. In June, he put Félix Guattari and François Fourquet in his car and drove them to Saint-Léonard-de-Noblat, in Limousin, where Deleuze was living. Guattari and Deleuze immediately connected. Guattari's conversation was full of topics that interested Deleuze, such as mental illness, La Borde, and Lacan—he had just finished a lecture entitled "Machine and Structure"[6] that he was to give at the Freudian School of Paris. For his demonstration, he drew from Deleuze's arguments in *Difference and Repetition* and *The Logic of Sense*.[7]

The text is important. Guattari had been a disciple of Lacan until then, and he was beginning to position himself as Lacan's interlocutor, hoping that the master would anoint him as a preferred partner. But Lacan's attitude toward him was ambiguous; he preferred the Maoist-Althusserian clique from the rue d'Ulm, which included Jacques-Alain Miller and Milner. Guattari was left out in the cold. "When I met Deleuze in 1969, I really seized the opportunity. I'd made headway in arguing with Lacan on two different issues: Oedipal triangulation and the reductiveness in his thesis on the signifier. Step by step, the rest dissolved like a rotten tooth, like a saltpetered wall."[8]

At the time, Deleuze was at a turning point in his professional life. He had been working on the history of philosophy—Hume, Kant, Spinoza, Nietzsche—and in 1969 had published two more personal books, *Difference and Repetition* and *The Logic of Sense*. This was the period when philosophy was coming under fire from structuralism and from Lacanian thinking, which was at the vanguard of structuralism. Ambient "psychoanalysis" and the general infatuation with Lacan were challenging philosophy. When Deleuze met Guattari, he had an excellent opportunity to respond.

Meeting Guattari revitalized Deleuze. He received Guattari at his home in Limousin, where he was convalescing after a serious operation a year earlier: his tubercular lung had been removed; from then on he suffered from chronic respiratory difficulties. He was also becoming an alcoholic, which he discussed in an interview with Claire Parnet.[9]

To continue the discussion about psychiatry that Guattari had begun with Deleuze, Muyard suggested that the two meet again at Dhuizon, in a chateau located near La Borde, where Guattari lived. There, Gilles Deleuze, Jean-Pierre Muyard, and Félix Guattari discussed what was eventually to become *Anti-Oedipus*. A letter dated August 19, 1969, from François Fourquet to his friend Gérard Laborde, describes the ambience at Dhuizon:

It's pretty strange here. Having Deleuze at Dhuizon has triggered a series of events that I think will continue for a long time. Many people are here besides Félix and Arlette: Rostain, Liane, Hervé, Muyard, Elda, etc.; they're all buzzing around the daily primal scene, in which Félix and Deleuze create intensely, Deleuze takes and then adjusts notes, critiques, links Félix's work to the history of philosophy. In a word, it's working. That's not to say that it's easy going in the little family (which includes Geneviève and me). One of the younger siblings has the privilege of watching the battle of the gods: Muyard, who was responsible for having Guattari and Félix meet.[10]

Muyard still played middleman for a while before leaving the scene: "I had done my job; Mephisto withdraws. I had the feeling that I was no longer useful even though Deleuze wanted to work with me and wanted me to be at the meetings, but I felt that I was bothering Félix. The alchemy had worked and would continue to do so for a very long time."[11]

During the spring of 1969, before they had ever met, Deleuze and Guattari had exchanged a few letters that attested to their nascent friendship. On April 5, 1969, Guattari wrote to Deleuze, alluding to his writer's block and his inability to take the time he needed because of his activities at La Borde. "Dear friend, I must find a way to express how deeply I am touched by your attentiveness to the various articles that I've sent you. I am reading *The Logic of Sense* very carefully and coming to the conclusion that our viewpoints are profoundly similar. Meeting when it is convenient for you will be, for me, an event with several origins that is already retroactively present."[12] By contrast, he felt that he was communicating with Deleuze by extrasensory means, through *The Logic of Sense*. In an earlier letter that Deleuze had written to his former student Ayala, he suggested that it might be interesting to assemble all the texts that he had sent to Guattari. Félix remained doubtful: "Isn't all that something of an amazing swindle?"[13]

In May 1969, Deleuze wrote to Guattari.

I also feel that we've become friends before meeting one another. So please forgive me for insisting on the following: it is clear that you invent and use a certain number of very new, complicated and important ideas that have been developed in relationship to the practical research at La Borde. For example, group fantasy, or your notion of transversality, which I think makes it possible to get beyond the old but still powerful duality between personal and collective unconscious.[14]

Deleuze felt that these ideas needed to be worked out theoretically and disagreed with Guattari's argument that the current situation was not the most propitious; this amounted to saying that "we can only really write when things are going well instead of seeing writing as a modest but active, effective way of leaving the battle for a moment and feeling better oneself."[15] Deleuze tried to convince Guattari that the moment had come to work out the theory. Finally, "the other solution of publishing the articles in their current state becomes the best and most desirable one."[16] This became *Psychoanalysis and Transversality*, published in 1972 with a preface by Deleuze.[17]

On June 1, 1969, Guattari acknowledged his weaknesses and the reasons for his "extreme confusion" to Deleuze.[18] His writer's block resulted from the fact that he neither worked nor read theory in any sustained way and from his fear of picking up something that he had left hanging for too long. There was also his complicated personal history, his pending divorce, the three children, the clinic, a variety of conflicts, and his affiliation with militant groups and the Federation of Study Groups and Institutional Research (FGERI).[19] With respect to theory, he considered that "ideas are conceptual tools, things."[20]

Deleuze wrote to Guattari immediately after their first meeting in June 1969, describing how they should proceed. "Of course we have to drop all forms of rhetorical politeness but not, of course, the forms of friendship that make it possible for one of us to say to the other, 'you will see,' 'I don't understand,' 'that's wrong,' etc. Muyard has to be involved in this correspondence. Finally, there can be no imposed regularity."[21] Of their first meetings Deleuze recalled that

> the forms of psychosis do not evolve in an Oedipal triangulation, or at least not necessarily and not in the way that is claimed. That's essentially it, it seems. . . . It's hard to get beyond the *familialism* of psychoanalysis with its daddy-mommy (the text of mine that you are still reading adopts this approach). So the issue is to show how, in psychosis, for example, socioeconomic mechanisms can bear directly on the unconscious. I don't mean the mechanisms per se—profit margin, benefit—it's much more complicated and you addressed this

once when you said that madmen don't simply create a world, they also create a political economy, or when you and Muyard were discussing the relationship between a capitalist crisis and a schizophrenic break.[22]

He added that two of Guattari's ideas, with which he was not yet sufficiently familiar—"about machines and about antiproduction"—made it possible to understand how social structures have an unmediated effect on the psychotic unconscious. Deleuze also agreed with Guattari's criticism of *familialism*:

> I think that you are proposing a very rich line of reasoning, for the following reason: we attribute a moral image to the unconscious either so that we can say that the unconscious is immoral or criminal, etc., even while adding that that is OK, or in order to say that morality is unconscious (superego, law, transgression). I once told Muyard that that didn't work, and that the unconscious was not religious, that there was neither law nor transgression, which are both idiotic notions. . . . Muyard said that I was going too far and that law and transgression as Lacan understands them have nothing to do with any of that. He was right, of course, but that doesn't matter, it's still the whole theory of the superego that seems wrong to me and the entire theory of guilt.[23]

Written just before the long periods of work at Dhuizon during August 1969, the letter reveals that *Anti-Oedipus*, published three years later, would dispute "Oedipal triangulation" and that the reductionism regarding the family was already clear to the two men. Guattari quickly replied. In his letter of July 19, he described his idea of a machine that "metonymically expresses the machine of industrial society."[24] On July 25, Guattari sent Deleuze some notes that established an equation between capitalism and schizophrenia: "Capitalism is schizophrenia, insofar as the society-structure cannot support the production of 'schizo.'"[25]

From the start, their relationship centered on theoretical issues; their immediate complicity was personal and intellectual, but they never became profoundly close. They came from two very different worlds, and each respected the other's network of relationships. The success of their common intellectual work depended on mobilizing and using everything that made them different, rather than pretending that they worked in osmosis. Each had an exalted idea of friendship. "They had retained the distance that Jankelevitch called the 'amative distance,' meaning that you are not restricted to a specific position. Contrary to a gnosological distance, an *amative* distance has to do with a rapprochement or distancing."[26] Guattari was anxious about meeting with Deleuze. He had always worked in groups and would have preferred that his friends at the Center for Institutional Study, Research, and Training (CERFI) be involved.[27] The first CERFI group came together at Dhuizon and wanted nothing more than to participate, but François Fourquet made it very clear that there was to be no discussion. Deleuze hated endless group discussions and could or would only work with two or three people at most.

Guattari's companion Arlette Donati told him about Deleuze's concerns. Their first book was written primarily through letters.[28] This approach to writing completely upset Guattari's daily life, because it forced him to work alone, which was not his habit, as he had been used to directing his groups. Deleuze expected Guattari to wake up and get to his desk right away, to outline his ideas on paper (he had three ideas per minute), and, without rereading or reworking what he had written, to mail his daily draft. He imposed what he considered to be a necessary process for getting over writer's block. Guattari followed the rules faithfully and withdrew into his office, where he worked slavishly until four o'clock in the afternoon every day, after which he went to La Borde to quickly make his rounds before returning to Dhuizon, generally around six o'clock. Jean Oury felt abandoned: Guattari had been omnipresent in the daily life of La Borde but was now devoting himself to his work with Deleuze. Arlette Donati even brought him his lunch every day because he did not stop working to eat.

For the most part, the writing plan for *Anti-Oedipus* was that Guattari sent his texts to Deleuze, who then reworked them for the final version. "Deleuze said that Félix was the diamond miner and he was the polisher. So he needed only to send him the texts as he wrote them and he would work on them; that's how it went."[29] Their common endeavor relied far more on epistolary exchange than on dialogue, although they did meet at Deleuze's house every Tuesday afternoon, the day that Deleuze taught his morning course at Vincennes. On good days, Deleuze came to Guattari, but he avoided the unbearable madness at La Borde. "One day, Félix, Arlette Donati, Gilles, and I were eating at Dhuizon and we got a call from La Borde saying that a guy had set fire to the chateau chapel and run off into the woods.

Gilles blanched, I froze, and Félix called for help to find the guy. At that point, Gilles said to me, 'How can you stand those schizos'? He couldn't bear the sight of crazy people."[30]

Deleuze and Guattari have described their work together on several occasions, but they did so somewhat discreetly. Describing their writing together when *Anti-Oedipus* first came out, Guattari remarked:

> This collaboration is not the result of a simple meeting between two people. In addition to the particular circumstances leading up to it, there is also a political context. At the outset, it was less a matter of sharing a common understanding than sharing the sum of our uncertainties and even a certain discomfort and confusion with respect to the way that May 1968 had turned out.[31]

Deleuze remarked:

> As regards writing together, there was no particular difficulty and both of us realized slowly that this technique had some clear function. One of the very shocking aspects of books about psychiatry or psychoanalysis is their duality in the sense of what an ostensibly sick person says and what the healer says about the patient. . . . Curiously, however, we tried to get beyond this traditional duality because two of us were writing. Neither of us was the patient or the psychiatrist but we had to be both to establish a process. . . . That process is what we called the *flux.*[32]

In 1991, when *What Is Philosophy?* was published,[33] Robert Maggiori had a lengthy discussion with Deleuze and Guattari, once again recalling how they met and worked together. "My meeting with Félix centered around issues in psychoanalysis and the unconscious. Félix brought me a new field and allowed me to discover a new area even if I had previously spoken about psychoanalysis, which is what interested him about me."[34]

Jean-Pierre Muyard, the person who brought them together, does not figure in their description. Deleuze agreed: "Félix sought me out." Guattari confirmed Deleuze's remark. "I went to find him, but after that meeting, he was the one who suggested that we work together."[35] They did not spend much time discussing how the manuscript was actually written—Deleuze said it was a "secret"—but they spoke at length about working together.

Deleuze referred to Kleist to describe what had happened with Guattari. Working out an idea through dialogue includes stuttering, ellipses, and inarticulate sounds. "It's not that we know something, it's first a certain state of ourselves," Deleuze claimed. "It's easier when there are two of you 'to put yourself in this state.'"[36] They met to speak, and at their meetings, after having distilled the discussion, they selected the themes that they would work on, and then each wrote successive versions of what they had discussed. "Each of us worked like an inlay or quotation in the other's text, but at a certain point, we no longer knew who had written what. It was writing and variation."[37] This way of working clearly presupposed a community of being, of thinking, and of reacting to the world. "The condition for being able to work as a pair effectively was a shared, implicit, but inexplicable foundation that made us laugh or worry, be repulsed or excited by the same things."[38]

Guattari also discussed the meetings and their exchanges of different versions of their texts. For him, their dialogue remained a conversation between two very different people. "We are very different. As a result, our rhythms for agreeing on a theme or on an idea are different. But we are complementary, of course. I'm more attracted to adventurous things; let's call it a conceptual commando who likes to visit foreign lands. Gilles, on the other hand, is a philosophical heavyweight, he has a whole bibliographic administration."[39] Deleuze had always loathed discussions that were sterile exchanges of opinions, preferring conversations where the speaker spoke only after engaging in an internal polemic. Their dialogues were something like a "purification ritual: while one spoke, the other listened silently, not only so that they could understand one another and come to some agreement, but also because it meant that one was always at the service of the other."[40] Even if one of them put forth an idea that seemed preposterous to the other, the other's job was to understand rather than discuss the foundations of the thought. "If I told him that the center of the earth was made of raspberry jam, his role would be to find out how to make that idea work (if we can call such a thing an idea)."[41] Their exchanges produced a true "work machine" that made it impossible to know who wrote what precisely.

As Deleuze explained it, the important thing was to transform "is" (*est*) into "and" (*et*) not in the sense of any particular, purely conjunctive relationship but in the sense of an implication in a whole series of relationships. The "and" was assigned to the possibility of creation, to the creative stuttering, to multiplicity. "AND is neither one thing nor the other, it's always

in-between, between two things; it's the borderline, there's always a border, a line of flight or of flow, only that we don't see it because it's the least
perceptible of things. And yet it's along this line of flight that things come
to pass, becomings evolve, revolutions take shape."[42] Their books are
entirely unique as a result.

To embark on a quest for the paternity of this or that idea would be, as
Stephane Nadaud has written, to "miss the idea of *arrangement*, which is
fundamental to their work."[43] Their writing is organized so as to put into
place a collective *arrangement* of utterance, which is the true father of invented ideas. Does this mean that it gave birth to a third man, the sum of
their coalescence, a Félix-Gilles or "Guattareuze," as the illustrator Lauzier
put it? Reading Deleuze, we might think so: "But we didn't collaborate like
two different people. We were more like two streams coming together to
make a third stream, which I suppose was us."[44] But this was not really the
case—the two men remained at a respectful distance and maintained their
differences. "There is a true politics of dissent between us, not a cult but a
culture of heterogeneity that makes each of us acknowledge and accept the
other's singularity. We're doing something together because it works;
something greater than ourselves carries us along. Gilles is my friend; he's
not my pal."[45]

It is essential to understand the notion of *arrangement* to appreciate
how unusual this situation was. As Deleuze said to his Japanese translator
Kuniichi Uno, "Utterance does not refer to the subject. There is no subject
of the statement, only an arrangement. Which means that in the same arrangement, 'subjectification processes' will assign different subjects, some
as images and others as signs."[46] With Uno, a former student who became
a friend, Deleuze was the most candid about how he and Guattari worked
together. Guattari was the group's star, and Deleuze used the evocative
metaphor of the ocean breaking on a hill to describe their relationship.

> He [Guattari] would have to be compared to the ocean, endlessly
> moving with reflections of light constantly breaking on the surface;
> he can jump from one thing to another, he does not sleep much, he
> travels, he never stops, never ceases. He has extraordinary gears. I
> would be more like the hill, very little movement, unable to do two
> things at once, my ideas are stable and whatever occasional move-
> ment there is is internal. Between the two of us, Félix and I could have
> been a good Japanese fighter.[47]

In addition, Deleuze remarked, "It's only if you watch Félix very closely that you realize how alone he is. Between two different activities or in the midst of a group, he can retreat deeply into solitude."[48] Deleuze described Guattari as the inventor of unusually creative and versatile ideas. "His ideas are designs or even diagrams. I'm interested in concepts."[49]

Guattari's idea of a machine replaced the idea of structure and provided Deleuze with a possible way out of structuralist thinking, something that he had already explored in *The Logic of Sense*. In his criticism of Lacan's notion of the unconscious being structured like a language and in terms of a political unconscious, Guattari was well ahead of his friend when they met in 1969. Deleuze was ahead of Guattari with respect to the history of philosophy, but in 1972, he acknowledged that in many major areas he trailed Guattari. "But I was working solely with concepts, rather timidly in fact. Félix had talked to me about what he was already calling 'desiring machines': he had a whole theoretical and practical conception about the unconscious as a machine, of the schizophrenic unconscious. So I myself thought he'd gone further than I had."[50] There was the pleasure of working together, mutual enrichment, humor, and moments of hilarity, and, as their mutual friend Gérard Fromanger said, "they were proud of one another; each felt honored by having the other one listen to him. They were unbelievably trusting of one other, like two paternal twins who became a whole together. Jealousy never entered the picture, they were unreservedly open whenever they met, which is what made for the quality of their writing, this sort of complete openness and the gift of trust."[51]

The two men created a veritable laboratory for testing their ideas, thanks to the transversal nature of their work. Guattari's contribution to Deleuze was above all a breath of fresh air in a rarefied universe. "You felt that he rejoiced in his meetings with Félix. They seemed happy to be meeting, although they didn't see each other much because they knew how delicate human relations can be."[52]

The differences in their personalities produced a two-speed machine: "Our rhythms were always different. Félix complained that I didn't respond to his letters, but I could not answer immediately; it took me one or two months, by which time Félix had already moved on."[53] By contrast, however, when they worked together, each would force the other into taking firm positions, and this would go on until both fighters were exhausted and the idea they were discussing and arguing about had taken off; something like a "setting" or foundation for the idea arose from their work of proliferation and dissemination: "I considered that Félix had real insights, whereas I was a kind of lightning rod stuck in the ground so that the idea could take a different shape, and then Félix corrected it, etc. That's how our work developed."[54]

In August 1971, they organized a final long working session at Toulon Bay in Brusc-sur-Mer to finish *Anti-Oedipus*. The two men, accompanied by their families, rented a house near the beach, and both men continued their discussion, alone. The final manuscript was completed on December 31. "Our book delicately concluded on 31 December, clearly indicating that endings are also beginnings. It's good, and bears witness to your creative energy and to my inventive effort."[55]

In March 1972, however, when the book was actually published, Guattari was going through a difficult stretch. His hyperactivity and the immense effort he had put into the book led to something of a collapse, a feeling of emptiness. Completing a work is never as satisfying as the many imagined possibilities and ongoing pleasures of a work in progress. "I feel like curling up into a tiny ball and being rid of all these politics of presence and prestige. . . . The feeling is so strong that I resent Gilles for having dragged me into this mess."[56] In his diary, he described feeling overwhelmed when he compared his desultory work habits to Deleuze's efficient tendencies. "Deleuze works a lot. We're really very different. . . . I'm a sort of an inveterate self-taught man, a putterer, a character from a Jules Verne story."[57] Above all, during a momentary halt in their arrangement, in the interregnum between the conclusion of a manuscript's writing and the book's publication, Guattari voiced his anxiety:

> Keep my pen, my own way. But I don't really see myself in the *A-O*. I needed to stop trying to run behind Gilles' image and the finished perfection that he gave to the book's final possibility. . . . He's suddenly overcome by feeling like he's drowning, losing his identity. He's always thinking about the *work*. And for him [Gilles], it couldn't merely be notes, the initial material that disappears in the final 'arrangement.' That's why I feel a bit overcoded by *Anti-Oedipus*.[58]

Thanks to his collaboration with Guattari, Deleuze was able to write a new, experimental kind of book, something that in *Difference and Repetition* he said that he wanted to do. "The time is coming when it will hardly be possible to write a book of philosophy the way it has been done for so long: 'Ah! the old style. . . .' This search for a new means of philosophical expression begun by Nietzsche must be pursued today with respect to the renewal of certain other arts."[59] As Arnaud Bouaniche has noted,[60] when Deleuze spoke at Cerisy during the decade devoted to Nietzsche on the topic of nomadic thinking, he announced his intention of producing a new style. With respect to Nietzsche, he defined a new type of book that diverged from traditional codes. "We are familiar with the important instruments of codification and the three major examples: the law, contracts, and institutions."[61] Yet Nietzsche resisted all codification efforts, and that was how Deleuze and Guattari thought of their writing, as well. "It is difficult to scramble all the codes, even at the level of the most basic writing and language."[62] The authors sought a means of escaping all forms of codification, by letting external forces inveigle them into producing unduly unconventional forms. This they achieved in *A Thousand Plateaus*, the second volume of *Capitalism and Schizophrenia*, which was published in 1980.

In the meantime, Guattari got his rhythm back with Kafka, who offered him a universe that corresponded to both his anxiety and tremendous desire to create, a creative disorder much like his own. "There is a conjunction between the two machines—the literary machine in Kafka's work and my own Guattari machine."[63] Guattarian writing took a detour through Kafka so as to better return to Deleuze and, in the process, write a book with him about Kafka.[64] This was the book for which Guattari and Deleuze laid out an idea that they developed later of "collective *arrangement* of utterance." "We don't believe that an utterance can be attributed to a subject, regardless of whether or not the subject is doubled, split, or conceptualized.[65]

The "two-speed" machine started working again for *A Thousand Plateaus*, where the central notion was *arrangement*. This time Deleuze and Guattari wrote together somewhat differently. "The composition of this book is far more complex, the areas that it addresses far more varied; our habits were such, however, that one of us could guess where the other was going."[66] The intense discussions at the outset of this new project and the complicity that grew out of them suggest that *A Thousand Plateaus*, which also involved a great deal of back and forth among the different versions, was largely the product of a common effort during oral work sessions.

When it came out in 1980, *A Thousand Plateaus* drew to a close something that had begun in 1969. In 1984, Deleuze wrote, "At that point, Félix and I both really needed to work alone again to catch our breath. But I am certain that we will work together again."[67] He plunged into a book on cinema; Guattari returned with vigor to his cultural and political activism. But Guattari once again suffered from a sense of absence, of void, of isolation and solitude, and wrote to Deleuze about it. Deleuze answered:

> I've read and reread your letter where you say that since our work together has faded, you no longer know what it meant for you or where you are at now. For me, however, things are very clear, I know that you are a prodigious creator of "wild" ideas. That's why I found the British empiricists so charming, it's you who had that. . . . In any case, I really believe that the two of us will work together again.[68]

These were not empty words of consolation. When Deleuze began his lecture course on cinema in the early 1980s, he never lost sight of his work with Guattari. Very early on he spoke about the theme of *What Is Philosophy?*—their last work together—which was published in 1991:

> Here's my work plan for the year. On the one hand, I will be giving a course on "Cinema and Thought" in relation to Bergson's *Matter and Memory*, which is inexhaustible, I think. But on the other hand, I'd like to continue this categorical table that coincides with your work. There, the center, for me, would be to find a clear and simple answer to the question of what is philosophy? So, there are two questions. First, the one you were asking, I think: why call that "categories"? What exactly are the ideas of contents, expression, singularity, etc., etc.? Pierce and Whitehead make modern tables of categories: how has this idea of categories evolved? And second, if we start with the most simple of these categories, contents and expression, I repeat my question: why do you privilege the expression from the point of view of the arrangement? You have to explain this to me, patiently.[69]

What Is Philosophy? was written somewhat differently than the earlier books. "Guattari is in it throughout, in the way that aspirin dissolved in water is everywhere," as Robert Maggiori remarked about what he considered a fundamental work.[70] Guattari worked from the manuscript that Deleuze sent him, making suggestions, corrections, and defining new directions:

> I'd like to suggest the theme of opposition between mixture and interaction. . . . About the brain's operation on itself: see Francisco Varela's autopoetic systems. . . . I talked about this a little bit in "Machinic heterogenesis." . . . The esthetic passage is the intersection between the infinite movement of concept and the finite movement of function. There is a simulation of infinity, a refined artifice of infinity that brings the paradigm of creation to a hysterical conversion point.[71]

The tendency today is to forget Guattari's name and remember only Deleuze's. Yet *What Is Philosophy?* cannot be read as a return to "true" philosophy by Deleuze without Guattari. Its contents, style, and concepts make it impossible to imagine how the book could be "de-Guattarized" to make Deleuze its sole author. This would be to ignore the way the two authors worked together, similar to what they described in their *Rhizome*, of branching, of the *arrangement* between a wasp and an orchid.

> The orchid leaves its own territory by forming an image, by imitating a wasp; but the wasp returns to its territory in this image while leaving its turf at the same time and becoming part of the orchid's reproduction apparatus; the wasp reterritorializes the orchid by carrying pollen . . . capture code, surplus-value code, increase of valence, a true becoming, becoming-the-wasp of the orchid, becoming-the-orchid of the wasp.[72]

Why does a wasp get involved in a sexual relationship with an orchid, knowing that there is pollination but no reproduction for it? Entomologists explain this as a relationship between two different registers of codes in the parallel evolution of two species, which have nothing to do with each other but in their meeting changing both their destinies.

For Deleuze, this arrangement could only work on the condition that everything else be closed out. If there was a chance that it could be dissipated, Deleuze reacted strongly, reminding Guattari of their initial rules and conditions. Their friendship was generally serene, and they had very few quarrels or tensions, but, with respect to the arrangement they created, on one occasion in 1973 Deleuze felt compelled to remind Guattari of "the rules," because he did not want to get caught up in someone else's activities. The disagreement arose because Deleuze and Michel Foucault were being considered by the Ministry of Public Works as the two intellectual authorities who could represent the CERFI. Deleuze refused to let himself be bound by the CERFI.

> Félix, oh Félix, dear Félix, I love you and nothing could affect our relationship. So I am telling you what is worrying me externally, in a flash. I already told you recently that at the beginning of our friendship I had told Arlette—this will complicate matters, that I want to take something from Félix that he'll never want to give me, and he wants to take me somewhere I would never want to go. From the beginning, in fact, you had suggested that we include others in our work, some members of the CERFI. I had said, absolutely not as far as I'm concerned and for a long time, we completely respected each other, you respected my solitude and I, your groups, without interfering.[73]

All of their close friends were aware of the intensity of this friendship. "I have rarely seen two people truly love and value each other as much as Gilles and Félix. They are entirely trusting of each other; their intellectual bond is totally human and moving."[74] Certainly, there were a few difficult moments, especially toward the end of the 1980s. "Speaking to each of them, I felt a moment of coolness. Talking to Félix about something that Gilles was supposed to do, he said, 'Oh yes, poor old guy.' Gilles asked, 'Marco, do you see Félix? 'Yes.' 'Oh, he's a good guy Félix, a very good guy . . .' Sudden coolness."[75] Something from their first period seemed to have broken somewhat. There were longer periods of silence, fewer meetings, and at the end of the 1980s, the consecration of Gilles Deleuze somewhat at the expense of Guattari, whom some would have even wanted to expunge from the texts—to "de-Guattarize" them, as mentioned earlier.

During Guattari's long depression in those dark years, Deleuze remained present. Michel Butel recalls:

> Exhausted, Deleuze, gasping for air, called to ask me what I was doing that evening. I said that I was going to watch the European Cup Championship because I was nuts about sports. Deleuze said, "I'm

going to a party at Félix's house, he needs someone there." I went. . . . Félix was completely <u>sacerdotal,</u> sitting on the floor watching the final soccer match, in fact. And there was Gilles sitting next to him. He would have probably given his right arm not to be at that party watching soccer on TV since, for him, two people were already a crowd.[76]

PART

RT

FOLDS
PARALLEL BIOGRAPHIES

1

Félix Guattari
The Psychopolitical Itinerary, 1930–1964

Little Pierre, as he was called at home, was born on March 30, 1930, the third of three sons: Jean, Paul, and Pierre-Félix. His family quickly realized that he was surprising and strange, although they certainly did not anticipate his intellectual career. "Félix was the little duckling in the nest," remarked Jean, nine years his elder and somewhat of a father figure to Félix.[1] In this rather traditional, conservative family, the last-born child enjoyed more freedom than his brothers and was more independent at an earlier age. His oldest brother had to go to work when he was seventeen; Pierre-Félix, who turned fifteen in 1945, was able to go to the university thanks to the Liberation.

The Guattaris were not intellectuals, but the parents had their passions. Félix's mother was an avid reader and frequently went to museums; his father was a natural musician who could play anything on the piano even though he had never learned to read music. Above all, his father, who had been gassed in the Great War and was trepanned, loved to gamble, and because salt air was good for his health, he moved the family to Monte Carlo, where he went to the casino the way other men went to work at the factory to earn money.

BANANIA YUM YUM

During the war, Félix's father had become friendly with Pierre Lardet, a well-known artisan who, in 1912, had discovered a delicious drink in Nicaragua made of banana flour, crushed seeds, cocoa, and sugar. In 1914, when he returned to Paris, Lardet began to produce the drink on an industrial scale. The brew became quite popular, thanks in part to the "Banania Yum Yum" marketing campaign. The ad worked in part because it used images of Senegalese artillerymen, who had become popular in 1915. Lardet got rich, bought racing horses, dressed in a grand bourgeois style, and became a regular at the Casino de Paris. When one of his friends suggested that he take the company public and sell shares, he decided to buy a chocolate factory in Epinay. The business collapsed, however, and Lardet was forced to declare bankruptcy. During the dramatic trial that followed, Lardet drew a revolver and fired a shot in the middle of the courtroom.

Félix Guattari's father was promoted to run the factory, which up to that point he had managed, but he chose instead to move to La Rapouillère, a tiny town in the Orne, to raise sheep. The sheep venture failed, and next he moved to the Oise to raise angora rabbits, angora being very popular after the war. Pierre Félix was born among the rabbits in Villeneuve-les-Sablons (now Villeneuve-le-Roi), next to Méru. The modernization of the textile industry quickly led to the collapse of the traditional angora industry, and the Guattaris were forced to eat their rabbits. As Jean, the eldest of the three children, put it, "My father wasn't made to raise rabbits either."[2]

The family moved back to the Paris area, where, after all the failures, it was hard to start anew. They moved into public rent-controlled housing in Montrouge (*La Cité des Oiseaux*), a suburb just outside Paris proper. The father started a few small, unsuccessful businesses selling coffee pots and then potatoes but did not earn enough to support his wife and three children. At the end of his rope, he contemplated suicide. In 1934, however, he managed to borrow some money and went back to chocolate, creating a new company called Monbana. He set up a factory in La Garenne-Colombes and ultimately became the director of a fairly prosperous business, the management of which took up all of his time. Jeanne Paoli, Félix's mother, took care of the family, with "a certain sense of sacrifice."[3] Corsican by origin, when she married at age seventeen, she reconnected with her Italian roots, as Guattari's family came from Bologna. "They got married in 1919; he was a war hero and it was more out of admiration for a boy like that than anything else."[4] Mrs. Guattari had artistic and literary sensibilities and influenced her youngest child considerably, especially by projecting her regret at having only sons. Pierre-Félix seems to have been a particularly shy and withdrawn child, "almost feminine."[5]

In 1952, when Guattari was twenty-two, he left home to live with his girlfriend, Micheline Kao, who lived with her family down the street from his parents' home. In his diary, he described a fight between Micheline and his mother, revealing his mother's jealousy. "My mother's insistence on controlling where I spend my nights makes me anxious . . . (it's worth pointing out that my father just observed the whole thing)."[6] Somewhat later he wrote, "I never dared to love my mother. . . . When you lack the courage to love your mother you're condemned to wait endlessly at life's threshold. . . . I'm constantly fleeing the world. I don't feel it, I don't take the plunge. I'm both too close and too far from maternal objects. . . . It's killing me."[7] Three years later, he wrote in his diary:

> The rigor that gives me great logical strength in reasoning and which, with regards to feelings, quickly turned into rigidity, this mind for systems which means that without my own system, I'm at a loss, in despair, deteriorated, I think this rigor is something that came from my mother. She moved to Montoire, she criticized me for having abandoned her. She was temperamentally exclusive. Surely my need for a clan comes from her. . . . I'm so much like her because she gave birth to me . . . what a mess. She had too much of a hand in shaping me and co-existence was no longer possible.[8]

One of Guattari's earliest memories of his father dates to 1933. Félix was three and his father announced, "I have to tell you that we're going to start a business." Born of the despair of the early years of crisis, the remark reflected his father's absolute determination to make it; it became something of a lifelong principle for little Félix, who was very impressed by it. "I think that I've started businesses and had his my whole life."[9] The success of the undertaking had some negative effects on the very young boy: his parents had far less free time to attend to him and he quickly felt abandoned by them. He became unwell but was unable to express himself in words. His pallor and reserve worried his parents, and they took him to a doctor, who prescribed a visit to the country to restore his health: "so from one day to the next, I, who was so attached to my life with my brothers and everything, found myself banished to Normandy to my very austere grandmother, cut off from everything."[10] The separation was a very bad experience: he felt that his mother had no time for him and had shunted him off. "I cried when they came to see me and when they left. I was completely miserable."[11]

THE TRAUMATIC SCENE

In 1939, at his grandparents' house in Louviers, nine-year-old Félix witnessed a scene that was surely the cause of a radical change in his behavior.

Victor, Félix's step-grandfather and a former miner at Montceau-les-Mines, was listening to his favorite radio series, *The Stuttgart Traitor*. He brought his radio into the toilet, leaving the door ajar.

> At his feet there is a box of cut-outs: the little paper dolls for which I made the dresses. Grandpa's head is drooped on his knees, his arms are dangling. Is he touching my toys? I wanted to yell at him. Silence. I turn my head, slowly—forever—toward the *light* on the radio. There's an incredible noise. He falls down. Grandmother is yelling. A stroke.[12]

The grandmother arrived, panicked, and cut the ends of his ears to try to get his heart beating. When that did not work, she put a newspaper over her husband's head to keep the flies off him.

This brutal encounter with death had a profound effect on Félix Guattari's personality. When he was fifty-four, he reiterated that it took him a long time to free himself of this trauma, which provoked severe anxiety attacks and a pronounced sense of mortality, people's fatuousness, and the general futility of things. "It was like something that exploded on me, horrible anxiety attacks that literally floored me with fright."[13] His parents, who did not want to leave his grandmother alone, decided that Félix should stay with her for a while, especially since he was now going to school in Louviers. His sense of abandonment grew, aggravated by the anxiety provoked by his grandfather's sudden death. Finally, his grandmother understood. "Yes, you're afraid that the same thing will also happen to me,"[14] and she decided to call his parents to come and retrieve their son.

Soon thereafter, young Félix changed radically. He had been reserved, shy to the point of being almost fearful, letting others take his toys from him, dominated by his brothers and especially the younger Paul, who used him as his whipping boy, but he now quickly became a group leader. "And, then, as if it weren't enough to organize a gang, I organized the enemy gang."[15] He quickly earned a reputation in La Garenne-Colombes, and when it came time to register him in the local high school, the principal refused. His mother was forced to find another school sufficiently far away so that her son's reputation would not dog him.

At this high school, Félix met an extraordinary social-science teacher named Fernand Oury, a disciple of Célestin Freinet. Oury, whose course Félix was taking, would later become famous in institutional pedagogy.[16]

Their first meeting was very brief. After three weeks of classes, Fernand disappeared: the Germans imprisoned him in 1943. But the memory of the meeting was so intense that when the fifteen-year-old Guattari learned after the Liberation that Fernand Oury was in charge of recreational activities in the Student Hostel organization, he immediately joined. A world of fraternal sociability opened up for Guattari, one very different from his mother's rigid views. Guattari was fascinated by Oury's personality and his pedagogical skills. "I was taken by a great desire to see Fernand. I started to love and to miss his very special way of looking at things, the way things became enveloped in a mysterious, quasi-poetic veil when you were in his presence."[17]

Thanks to the hostel networks of the Liberation, adolescents from families of modest means could go on organized vacations. For the group leader that Félix had become, the hostels were above all a place where he discovered girls; until then he had lived exclusively among boys. On one of these trips, he met another young man named Pierre. "I said, no point in calling me Pierre, just call me Félix."[18] His father's brother-in-law, Uncle Félix, had been killed at Verdun. A passionate admirer of Vlaminck, Uncle Félix had made a strong impression on his nephew. "He was a little like an idealized me."[19] After his parents' professional problems, the need to be ready to "start a business" at every moment, and his grandfather's dramatic death, Guattari remade himself and became Félix, or happiness.

His yearning to be happy in the moment and his exceptional vitality were born of his precocious awareness of mortality and of the very real presence of death. Recognizing that he faced an unavoidable finitude, "start a business" became the byword for dispelling anxiety and the deathly forces. Young Félix had encountered death even before the death of his grandfather; in July 1971, he wrote in his diary that at six or seven, he suffered from a recurring nightmare. "A woman in black. She came near the bed and I was very frightened. It woke me up. I didn't want to go back to sleep. And then one night, my brother loaned me his air rifle and told me that all I had to do was to shoot her if she returned. She didn't come back. But what surprised me the most, and I still remember this quite well, is that I hadn't loaded the gun."[20] This woman in black, the eponymous heroine of G. Leroux's novel, also evoked Aunt Émilia, the widowed sister of Félix's father, whose husband, Félix, had died in the Verdun trenches. "But of course, of course, the armoire, the woman in *moiré*, the Black Army, *armoise*, my arms, the *mouise* of the thirties, my father had gone broke when he started raising angora rabbits, with the help of this same Aunt Émilia . . ."[21]

WAR'S END

Guattari was precociously politically aware at the time of the Liberation. In 1945, at the same time as he joined the Student Hostels organization, he started to attend Communist Party meetings. His father had been a member of the *Croix de Feu* in the 1930s and a stalwart Gaullist during the war. When he found out that his son was selling the Communist Party newspaper *Humanity* under the bridge at the train station in La Garenne-Colombes, he was not at all happy. Paul, the eldest brother, derided Félix, expressing the family's disapproval by mocking him with "Get your copy of *Humidity*, the main organ of the Frigidaire Party."

The atmosphere in the postwar youth hostels was particularly intense. Many young singers—Francis Lemarque, the Jacques Brothers, the Barbus, Pierre Dudan—and actors, such as Yves Robert, got their start there, in the all-night sessions. Others were trained as cultural-activity directors and as political or union leaders. Guattari had his first romantic encounters, but when he brought his girlfriend Annick home to his parents, she wasn't to his mother's taste (she was older than Félix) and was quickly sent away, never to get a second chance.

In 1944, young Félix started to write stories and poems and describe his dreams. He was obviously gifted intellectually. "I had learned to write almost all at once, to read all at once. . . . The kids in the class were hemming and hawing and I was reading quite well."[22] He did well at Paul-Lapie Junior High in Courbevoie and went on to do his final year at Condorcet High School; he passed the *baccalauréat* examination in philosophy-science in 1948. He was passionate about philosophy and hoped that his professor, whom he considered excellent, would encourage him to pursue his studies in the field, but despite his good score on the "*bac,*" he was unable to bring himself to discuss this with his professor and remained unsure about his choice. His brother Jean managed to convince him to study pharmacy, despite a profound reluctance. He did his first internship in pharmacy in July 1948 in Bécon les Bruyères and found it immensely dull. He failed the first-year exams. Under the watchful eye of his older brother, he repeated the year but did not do much better the second time around. What he wanted above all was to leave home and get a job in the civil service so that he could be financially independent. He considered taking the student-inspector examination given by the Post-Telephone and Telegraph.

At the same time, he seems to have found a soulmate in Micheline Kao, a young Chinese girl whom he met when he was sixteen and she was fourteen. They were neighbors on the rue de l'Aigle in La Garenne-Colombes and had met in 1946 during a vacation trip organized by Fernand Oury to Aubier-le-Vieux in the Alps. "I remember a boy who wanted to give the impression of being an adult and who was smoking a pipe."[23] Micheline Kao was intrigued by Félix and found him somewhat curious; he declared eternal love, but she felt little more than friendship toward him. They played cat and mouse until 1951. "I didn't want him, and then suddenly one day, I ended up 'giving in,' so to speak."[24]

In 1951, they decided to live together at the home of Micheline Kao's working-class parents, who were very welcoming. They moved their things out of the first floor of the house so that the young couple could be comfortable and have some privacy. Félix moved his piano in along with his books. Micheline's father adopted Félix as a son. Félix's family members accepted his departure but were both surprised and displeased to see him move in down the street with a family who was very attentive to him. "Mr. Kao brought him his breakfast in bed!"[25] Félix's parents feared that the Kaos wanted to steal their son away from them.

This affective reconstruction occurred against a background of tremendous professional confusion. Guattari realized, with horror, that by studying pharmacy he was cutting himself off from writing, which was for him an existential necessity. "I was quite upset to find that I couldn't write any more, that I was no longer reading, so I copied books to get back in touch with writing. I remember that I copied a whole book by Camus."[26] No longer speaking to his father also helped Félix find his professional path, but he was increasingly sure that he was choosing the wrong profession. He decided to stop studying pharmacy and to register at the Sorbonne in philosophy. His father, who barely spoke, had not really paid much attention to his son's distress. One day, while shoveling snow in front of the house, the father suddenly asked his son, "'But Pierre, why do you want to stop studying?' I said, 'Because I don't like it, it's not at all right for me.' 'But, what would you want to study?' Everyone had known this for ages. 'I would like to study philosophy.' 'Oh, um, so, then just go do philosophy.'"[27] During those years, the paternal figure was certainly lacking, despite the fact that Félix wrote in his diary in 1953 that his moral structure was based on the paternal *imago*. He considered this father figure "both very moral, nationalistic, *Croix de feu*, no trafficking with the Germans, listens to the English, respectful of family, and at the same time, gnawed at by freedom, a medium, liar, voyeur, gambler, businessman, intelligence."[28]

In the early 1950s, Guattari was so strongly influenced by Sartre that he started using Sartrean language in his diary, which contains easily identifiable existential themes. "This objectification (of time) contributes by antithesis to making us feel time, which is to say, to removing it from the world."[29] Time and nothingness, death, and the necessity of freeing himself from the morbid anxiety that gripped him prompted Guattari to practice phenomenological exercises on himself the way others practiced Loyola's spiritual exercises—to better understand himself and to eliminate any bad faith.

> I dove in. I was living something like permanent anxiety. In the train, I found the method, if there is a method, for seeing oneself as inauthentic: enumerate, clarify all the objects of which one makes oneself the involuntary subject . . . until there is a kind of void. It's easier to be a phenomenologist for things than for people. . . . The whole issue is that the other person sees you, has an overall view of your being. Everything depends on the intentionality with which he makes you exist for him. The Sartrean battle continues. . . . There is no time *in* the world; we project it onto the world. To think that I only understood that last night.[30]

Félix Guattari even commented on *Being and Nothingness* in his diary. About the "On Determination as Negation" chapter, he wrote, "The for-oneself establishes the world as a totality. There is nothing that is being. This totalization is of *nothing* over *being*; *it totalizes and fragments at the same time*. I can't manage to destroy this notion of everything and I'm working hard at it."[31] The result was an existential theme that gave rise to a desperate, lifelong quest for immediate happiness, in the intensity of the present moment and the commitments that it elicits: "I felt that finding happiness was something of a necessity. . . . This 'primary consolation' cannot be found in either the past or the future. They have to be found in the most immediately present being. You have to become being *in the world*, give the world an image of happiness, even the most simple, the least hopeful."[32] "B.N. [*Being and Nothingness*] magnificent. Magnificent. I read and circled whole paragraphs with a green pencil and I'm delighted, it wakes me up."[33]

Guattari never repudiated his taste for Sartre. In 1990, toward the end of his life, he wrote:

> For me, Sartre is an author like Goethe and Beethoven, it's all or nothing. I spent fifteen years of my life completely immersed in Sartre's work and actions. . . . Everything I said or did was obviously affected by him. His reading of annihilation, of detotalization, which became becoming for me, deterritorialization, his idea of seriality, of the pratico-inert, which informed my idea of the group-subject, his understanding of freedom, and of the commitment and responsibility of the intellectual, which he embodied, all of these remained imperatives or at least immediate givens for me. I prefer having been wrong staying with Sartre than to have been right and agreeing with Raymond Aron.[34]

Félix was a member of the French Communist Party even though temperamentally he was initially more of an anarchist. In the suburban world of the hostels, he met militant Trotskyites in 1948 and became a political activist in the French section of the Fourth International of the International Communist Party, which, at the time, was little more than a small group of dissidents that the French Communist Party considered the worst enemies of the working class. Guattari even became the head of one of the four Trotskyite units in the Parisian Student Hostel groups.

In Garenne, an especially dynamic group of young workers were organized in the Hispano-Suiza factory, which was famous for building the French version of Rolls-Royces and for having manufactured all the planes used in World War I. Garenne was a working-class community that was divided between the Peugeot and Hispano factories, a breeding ground for jobs in these two large companies, and a proletarian hotspot. Raymond Petit, a charismatic militant working at Hispano, attracted young workers and quickly became their spiritual father. His influence was such that he managed to persuade the management and local workers' committee to create a youth group of Hispano workers so that they could take vacations and ski trips and take advantage of the hostel network. Petit's contagious enthusiasm made him suspect in the eyes of the management, who saw him as an agitator. He was offered the position of permanent member of the workers' committee to take care of vacations for young factory workers. Petit was aware that he risked cutting himself off from his original milieu but could not refuse the promotion. In his new position, he was able to push Hispano to become the first company to send workers under twenty-one on winter ski vacations, which amounted to getting them a third week of paid vacation: this was in 1950.

TROTSKYITE COMMITMENT

Raymond Petit was a libertarian communist who fought ferociously against every form of bureaucracy, which was not at all to the taste of the French Communist Party leaders. Dropped by the FCP, he returned to the base and his workshop pals, including the young Roger Panaget, who had started working at Hispano in 1947 and who held weekly meetings to organize weekends and vacations. With the Young Workers Group, he decided to organize museum visits, song fests, folk dancing, spelunking trips, cinema outings, theater visits, study circles, and even volleyball teams. "During the road trips, the teams shared the work: gathering and cutting wood, sweeping, and peeling vegetables."[35] Group living eliminated the hierarchies that separated people, and strong friendships developed between the young women and men.

Their enthusiasm radiated beyond the confines of the Hispano factory, and other young people in the area joined in. Félix Guattari found the experience compelling, and he participated in the group activities, where he made friends with Raymond Petit and Roger Panaget. For Félix, Petit was a model of engagement. "Last night with Raymond, I saw that my studies were now directly becoming part of the framework of my revolutionary ideal."[36]

When Guattari moved to La Borde in 1955, he suggested that Roger Panaget move into his bedroom at Micheline Kao's parents' house. Guattari belonged to the Young Revolutionaries Movement, a preliminary to joining the International Communist Party and being admitted to the elect of the proletarian avant-garde. His Trotskyism remained "subterranean," however: the style at the time was to infiltrate communist movements. He participated in a series of initiatives such as the brigade parties in Yugoslavia to support Tito, who was being denounced by the FCP. He volunteered to be the head of a workers' brigade, and in 1949 helped dig the foundations of the future university of Zagreb. As a militant leader, he confiscated the meal tickets of any recalcitrant workers who complained or dragged their feet when it came to carrying stones or digging trenches.

Maintaining good relations with the communists in Paris's western suburbs while being a militant Trotskyite was not always easy. When pro-Tito propaganda was being disseminated in 1950, Félix and his Trotskyite group were attacked by some thugs from the FCP in a particularly violent battle that lasted the entire night. The FCP leadership had begun to notice Guattari and considered him a dangerous pro-Tito propagandist. One day, he was even called in to justify his anti-Party activities to his comrades. Fearing the worst, Guattari's Trotskyite pals tried to dissuade him from going to this meeting, where there was every reason to fear that he would be beaten. This was during the period when the Cominform was denouncing Tito supporters as lubricious snakes. Tito was considered an imperialist agent who had created a fascist dictatorship. The night before the meeting, Guattari was once again involved in a violent confrontation in Paris, where a meeting was supposed to be held to prepare the brigades' trip to Yugoslavia. "Sections of the Paris Federation surrounded us. We were under attack for hours by waves of Party militants. . . . At the end, a bunch of wild Stalinists chased us in the metro. I had accompanied a young Yugoslav woman named Mileva who was working at the Embassy to her home, she was so beautiful it took your breath away."[37] Paulo, Guattari's Trotskyite pal, was wounded and wore a bandage on his head. He insisted on going with Félix to the next day's meeting, which could have easily led to further violence. Guattari dissuaded him from coming to keep things cool and attended the meeting alone. He managed to extricate himself thanks to his reputation with the student hostels. "The redhead from the SH was there. I had gone in, we had a discussion and shouted at each other but there were no fistfights."[38] His popularity with youth groups saved him from what might have been a serious settling of accounts.

Guattari's political family was split in 1951 between the Pablo-Franck group, which he ended up joining and which favored joining the FCP, and the Lambertist group, which was against joining. Félix had registered as a philosophy student at the Sorbonne and couldn't infiltrate, as he was too well known as a Trotskyite. Cultivating the networks of militants at the Sorbonne, he took refuge in the Franco-Chinese Friends. Hope became a banner that was rising, since Mao's victory in 1949, in the Far Eastern sky.

In 1953, Raymond Petit, from the Hispano group, was one of the first to visit China. A year later, a delegation of forty-nine Frenchmen, including

Jean Eiffel, René Dumont, Michel Leiris, Claude Roy, and two students, went to Beijing. Félix was part of the group. His brother recalled still with some surprise that, "One day, he said to me, 'Can you drive me to Le Bourget tomorrow? I'm going to Beijing.'"[39] The brief trip was exhilarating and disorienting, as he noted in his diary. "What stays with me from my trip to China is the impression of a dream. Where was I? With whom? What character was I playing?"[40] When he decided to get involved in the Franco-Chinese Friends, Guattari met Jean Chesneaux, a China historian who connected French intellectuals with militants from the Chinese Communist Party.

As he was shifting his political work toward the Sorbonne's FCP's "philo group," Guattari suggested to Denis Berger, a member of the International Communist Party and its political bureau, that they launch a mimeographed newsletter called *Discussion Tribunal* immediately after the 1956 Twentieth Congress of the U.S. Communist Party. The fifth-column strategy had reached its limits, and there was an urgent desire to express oneself and to be heard. The publication of Khrushchev's report was useful for raising a certain number of questions, but it was not yet the right moment for suggesting an alternative political organization; what was needed was to provoke questions and encourage discussions about ideas. Félix brought the future anthropologists Lucien Sebag, Michel Cartry, and Alfred Adler, as well as Philippe Girard and Anne Giannini Monnet (related to Jean Monnet, considered the founder of modern Europe), into the International Communist Party, which was only a small group of eighty. The circulation of *Discussion Tribunal* quickly extended beyond the Sorbonne student world and was supported by François Châtelet and Henri Lefevre, two famous intellectuals. Jean-Paul Sartre also supported the plan and was among the donors as (he was listed as HK, for "Heidegger/Kierkegaard") up to 1958, when he stopped supporting the paper, believing that France was at risk from the fascism engulfing certain neighboring countries and thus it was more important to close ranks with the FCP.

When the Soviets invaded Hungary in the fall of 1956, the need for critical discourse within the communist movement became even more urgent. The *Discussion Tribunal* group drew closer to another small group of communist intellectuals who were putting out another newsletter, *L'Etincelle* (*The Spark*). That group included the well-known philosopher Victor Leduc, Jean-Pierre Vernant, Yves Cachin (the nephew of Marcel Cachin, the founder of the FCP), Jean Bruhat, Anatole Kopp, and a very active core of militants from the eleventh arrondissement of Paris organized around Gérard Spitzer, who had joined the French Workers' Party in 1943 and the FCP during the Liberation. They together issued a radical critique of Stalinism and denounced the FCP's inadequate protest against the war in Algeria, specifically its support for the vote giving the army special powers. On March 12, 1956, SFIO Secretary General Guy Mollet, who had become president of the Council when the socialists won the legislative elections, proposed a law granting the army special powers and significant latitude in its actions. Most parliamentary groups, including the communists, voted in favor of the law. At Hispano, there was an immediate protest against mobilizing recruits for the war. Petit, Panaget, Levildier, and Brivette organized the first demonstration, which led to violent clashes with the police at Bois-Colombes and made the headlines of *Humanity*, the FCP paper. The association between the two groups was short lived, however, because the FCP leadership denounced them as a Troskyite group. This frightened most of the *L'Etincelle* militants, who toed the party line, with the exception of Spitzer's group (Simon Blumenthal, Paul Calvez), who continued to associate with the former *Discussion Tribunal* group.

These shifting groups gave rise to a new mimeographed *Communist Opposition Newsletter*, which in 1958 became *La Voie Communiste* (*The Communist Path*). Denis Berger, a member of the International Communist Party political bureau, led the battle against Pierre Franck, to force him to accept this publication, which brought different groups together and was intended to be more than a simple internal newsletter. Berger thought it should be publicly distributed in newsstands, but he failed to persuade the International Communist Party leaders. "I was excluded, I'd joined in 1950."[41] At that point, Raymond Petit and Guattari decided to quit the International Communist Party. *La Voie Communiste* was more than a publication; it was a small organization on the margins of Trotskyism. The first issue raised the question of who we are and what we want. The answer was: "To find the Communist Path for our country."[42] The publication was born amid protests against the Algerian war, which became the primary battleground until 1962. The third issue proclaimed "Algeria First,"[43] as the crisis being created by the Algerian war was shaking the foundations of the Fourth Republic.

The leaders met weekly. Guattari was actively involved in writing articles under the penname Claude Arrieux. In February 1961, he, Claude Deville, and Jean Labre interviewed Sartre,[44] and in early 1962, he was involved in writing a critical account of the evolution of the FCP. He wrote several papers about how the Sixteenth Congress was prepared and organized, denouncing its Stalinist loyalties. The Hispano Group figured heavily in the publication, but it was referred to as the Simca Group to protect their undercover work and to undermine the Stalinist leadership. Guattari held the financial lifelines of *La Voie Communiste*, since the clinic at La Borde was the source of most of its funding.[45] Given the mobilization against the Algerian war, *La Voie Communiste* very quickly made about two or three hundred contacts. "That was how Félix had conceived of the work. We didn't bring people into a program; we worked with them. His work at La Borde was immediately useful to him and he began to theorize it."[46] The idea was to create a nonsectarian group rather than a classical party, an organization conceived more along the lines of the youth group at Hispano.

Three of *La Voie Communiste* leaders, Denis Berger, Gérard Spitzer, and Roger Rey, were more specifically involved in clandestine work supporting the struggle for Algerian independence. In 1959, Spitzer, the editor, was found guilty of posing a threat to national security and sent to prison, where he started a hunger strike lasting from February 27 through March 20, 1960. He was freed after eighteen months, thanks to a massive information campaign undertaken by *La Voie Communiste*, which had created a defense committee headed by Élie Bloncourt.[47] In the meantime, Berger had become a specialist in organizing escapes. The French intelligence services had arrested him on December 5, 1958, and imprisoned him for ten days, during which time he learned that he had been expelled from the International Communist Party. In February 1961, he managed to organize the escape of six women members of Algeria's National Liberation Front support network from the Roquette, a Parisian prison. Between 1958 and February 1965, forty-nine issues of *La Voie Communiste* came out and were read by a remarkably broad audience, given its lack of institutional support. As soon as the Manifesto of the 121 "regarding the right to insubordination in the Algerian War" was issued, the paper published it and was immediately seized.[48]

La Voie Communiste's two different groups of students and workers were located at the Sorbonne and at Hispano, respectively. Guattari shuttled between these two worlds and recruited Michel Cartry, whom he had met and befriended during a pedagogy course in June 1952. Michel Cartry quickly joined Félix in the FCP philosophy group, which met on the place de la Contrescarpe in Paris. "Félix initiated us into Trotsky."[49] They stuffed their comrades' mailboxes with copies of the *Discussion Tribunal*, took pseud-onyms, and scandalized the orthodox FCP militants, who were shocked to find people in their own ranks betraying the cause of the working class. "In a meeting of the Party's philosophy cell, someone shouted, 'there are some bastards here,' it was one of my best friends who said that."[50] When he started working on the *Discussion Tribunal*, however, Michel Cartry was unaware that Félix was an organized militant Trotskyite. It was only after that first experience that Félix asked him and Lucien Sebag to go a step fur-ther and to join the Fourth International. In 1958, denouncing the vote of special powers in the Sorbonne courtyard, Lucien Sebag, Michel Cartry, and Philippe Girard were expelled from the Communist Student Union.

Michel Cartry and Alfred Adler, friends from Condorcet High School, were both Sartrean enthusiasts. "I would have walked barefoot and naked through the snow to get *Les tempes modernes* [*Modern Times*] when it came out."[51] When Sartre closed ranks with the communists, Adler decided to join the FCP in 1953, as did Michel Cartry, Pierre Clastres, and Lucien Sebag. Guattari was responsible for putting some distance between Adler and Sar-tre, by showing him some of Lacan's writings. "That's when I started to wa-ver."[52] Politically, however, Adler still considered himself an untainted communist. "I was practically hanging a portrait of Stalin on the wall at home."[53] Things changed in 1956. Adler and his friends joined *La Voie Com-muniste*, whose members at the time included the future writers Pierre Pachet and Michel Butel as well as many other Sorbonne students from Guattari's gang. Among the famous recruits was Daniel Cohn-Bendit's brother Gaby Cohn-Bendit, who, in 1956, was also studying philosophy at the Sorbonne.

In 1956, Claude Vivien, a friend of Gaby Cohn-Bendit and Pierre Pachet, was also a member of the philosophy group. "It was the most extraordinary group I'd ever met in my life."[54] Vivien was the youngest member, and he took part in all the discussions and the communal life the group lived in the Latin Quarter. This was during a period of tensions with fascist groups and frequent antiwar demonstrations. Using his tried-and-true method for getting people to break away from Stalinism, Guattari invited Vivien to spend a weekend at La Borde. "It was extremely important in my life. I met crazy people and realized that they weren't very different from me."[55] Like many others, Vivien planned a two-day visit but ended up living at La Borde for four years, working as a monitor while continuing his philosophy stud-ies and his political activities. He was also involved in the protest work of the *Discussion Tribunal*. Félix had him read Trotsky and join the Fourth International. In 1956, when the French Communist Party expelled the philosophy cell and created the UEC, Viven was its secretary. He joined *La Voie Communiste* with Guattari and Gérard Spitzer, for whom he had considerable respect,[56] and with Denis Berger and the future lawyer Simon Blumenthal.

Until 1962, *La Voie Communiste* had effectively contested the misdeeds of the colonial war in Algeria, but once the Evian Agreement was signed, it was just marking time. There were still some moments of engagement, as when Mohammed Boudiaf's Socialist Algerian Revolutionary Party met in its offices on rue Géoffroy-Saint-Hilaire. Guattari felt close to Boudiaf,[57] who was in contact with *La Voie Communiste*. Things very quickly fell apart, however, and *La Voie Communiste* disappeared in 1965. Certain members had already been leaning toward Maoism, urged on by Simon Blumenthal and Benny Levy, while others were singing the praises of Ben Bella. In 1961, *La Voie Communiste* had published the theses of the Chinese communists about peaceful coexistence,[58] but in 1963, after the end of the Algerian War, it took on a Maoist hue and published the twenty-five points of the Chinese Communist Party's political program.[59]

This shift was not to Guattari's taste, and in 1964, he wrote critical studies of the Soviet regime. He felt increasingly detached from the journal's orientation and ended up walking out quite suddenly. "I dropped them all from one day to the next. . . . In 1964, I was fed up."[60] Gérard Spitzer was particularly unforgiving about Guattari's decision and blamed him for cutting off vital funding for *La Voie Communiste*. However, when Guattari felt that an institution continued to exist in a vacuum by doing little more than playing on its small cultural capital, he had no qualms about moving forward and destroying it in order to create other possibilities elsewhere. In 1964, the student movement was becoming more radical and drew him in.

FÉLIX: AN EARLY LACANIAN

In the 1950s, Guattari was known both for his political militancy and for being a specialist in Lacanian ideas. At the Sorbonne, he elicited considerable interest. He distributed completely unknown texts by Lacan and enjoyed a certain prestige as a theoretician able to make Lacan's very obscure work accessible to neophytes. He was also running a clinical practice at

La Borde. "At that point at the Sorbonne I was known as Lacan. I was bugging everyone about Lacan."[61]

For this reason, the meeting between Guattari and the psychiatrist Jean Oury was decisive. Guattari was still a young boy in 1945; he was only fifteen when he was a student of Fernand Oury, who at the time was organizing frequent meetings with his Student Hostel youth groups. Jean, Fernand's brother, was twenty-one at the time and first met young Guattari in La Garenne-Colombes, where they both lived. Oury's departure for Saint Alban created a temporary hiatus in his friendship with Félix, who was studying pharmacology at the time and was profoundly bored and uninterested. In December 1950, at a loss to help Félix, Fernand proposed that Félix visit his brother Jean, a psychiatrist and, at the time, the director of the Saumery clinic in the Loir-et-Cher. "Fernand said to me, 'above all, don't destroy him.' He didn't need me for that."[62] Guattari became fascinated by Jean Oury's psychiatric work.

Jean Oury strongly urged Guattari to read Lacan and to keep him informed about Lacan's research, since his psychiatric responsibilities left him too little time to go to Paris, where Lacan was teaching. Jean Oury was six years older than Guattari and played the role of moral confessor, becoming another substitute father figure. In 1952, Guattari wrote something in his diary that he called "The JO (Jean Oury) line: No protection, let things take their course so long as there are no attacks (blows, wounds). . . . For that, you need silence and little emotivity. Be simple."[63] At the age of twenty-six, Jean Oury was already an experienced psychiatrist, and some practical advice came out of the endless discussions with Guattari about his choice of career.

Jean Oury supported Guattari's desire to quit pharmacology, encouraged him to start studying philosophy, and made some suggestions about whom to read in addition to Lacan, Sartre, and Merleau-Ponty. This bespeaks the role that Oury played in Guattari's life and the strength of the relationship that grew between them, the indestructibility of the bicephalic machine that they created at La Borde and that weathered significant storms. Guattari drove between Paris and Jean Oury's clinic in Saumery on his motor scooter. "We spent entire nights talking, we made concrete music and we recorded bird calls and did what was called 'mint and water,' which meant taking objects and making sentences around them to create a new syntax."[64]

Thanks to Oury, Guattari read Lacan's texts on the mirror stage, aggression, and the family earlier than the rest of the intellectual world. He was so affected by them that he learned them virtually by heart, and, in 1951 and 1952, he would recite them to anyone who would listen. In 1953, Guattari went to a lecture on Goethe that Lacan gave at the Collège de Philosophie on rue de Rennes in Paris. Lacan fascinated him. At the end of 1954, Lacan invited Guattari to his seminar at the Sainte-Anne psychiatric hospital in Paris. This was before an appearance by Lacan would pack a lecture hall. "I was the first nonpsychiatrist, nondoctor"[65] to take the master's seminar; Lacan had not yet become the toast of Parisian intellectuals. During the same period, Guattari discovered linguistics, a field in which he later became extremely interested. This was also the year of Lacan's famous Rome lecture, where he established the importance of linguistic methods for psychoanalysis. Lacan was not Guattari's only introduction to linguistics, however. "For the first time, I was thinking about the problem of language, which became an issue for me because of Lacan and his invectives against Blondel. Because of Izard and his love of poetry, above all else. Because of Roudant, to whom I had explained how much I was now starting to understand his project. There is no thought that is not embodied in language."[66]

Beyond his interest in how language functions, during the period when linguistics was increasingly in vogue, Guattari wanted to express himself, to create an opus, a recurrent obsession for him. On September 1, 1953, he wrote in his diary "I WANT TO WRITE A BOOK"; at the end of the month, he wondered what he would write about.

> Write. I want to write. It's become an imperious need. . . . But write what? Maybe start with my problems writing. . . . Can I make a philosophical literature? Write about death, for example? But I haven't read anything. Not for a long time, I haven't read anything about anything. Childhood memories? Yes, of course, but they come when they want to. You have to work on them. DIG a first hole. That supposes a poetic deepening of the situation. Having excluded things poetic and anything philosophical, my options are a novel or a diary. I'm afraid of novels and diaries bore me. Couldn't I write a novel, writing every day, with *me, Micheline, JO.* An *ideal* girl, etc. Something that would communicate and crystallize my being stuck. Writing a book was the great myth of my youth.[67]

At the time, Guattari was speaking the Lacanian "language" and was writing to his guru, who answered and arranged times to meet and talk.

Finally, Guattari got "on the couch," the first of the La Borde staff (all of whom followed), paying fifty francs a session, a considerable sum at the time. After having converted Claude Vivien politically and getting him to move to La Borde, he brought him to Lacan's seminars at Sainte-Anne, in 1956. "That impressed me tremendously because someone was breaking with the Sorbonne professors that I knew, no small matter: Vladimir Jankelevitch, Jean Wahl, Ferdinand Alquié. I was fascinated, and then Félix had me go into analysis with Lacan."[68] In 1954, Guattari focused almost exclusively on Lacan. "Am I a philosopher? Am I just a philosophy student? The only sign of any concern with philosophical issues lately has been Lacan's lectures."[69]

Guattari's notes reveal the emergence of his idea of the machine, a theme that he systematized later in his life and that was already manifest in Lacan's courses in late 1954 and early 1955. "There are unconscious manifestations of the subject as an individual-machine that require special treatment if they are to be reintroduced into reality."[70] "Descartes: the machine is the clock. These machines are basically human (Aragon salutes the clock)."[71] "If the machine integrates degraded forms of knowledge like Maxwell's demon, it will accomplish miracles. That's where there is an inversion of entropy."[72] The machine as opposed to structure later became one of Félix Guattari's favorite themes—and then one of the favorite themes of Deleuze-Guattari.[73]

2

La Borde
Between Myth and Reality

Set in the heart of the Sologne in the Loir-et-Chair, the La Borde chateau was a mythical place, an unorthodox psychiatric clinic where mental illness was treated unconventionally. Over time, it became a real utopia where the psychiatric movement both proved itself and continued to evolve. Rejecting the traditional approach of isolating people with psychiatric disorders, La Borde took the preclinical approach of mixing patients and their pathologies with normal people—without forgetting that psychotic patients needed medical treatment.

Located in the Centre Region's commune of Cour-Cheverny, not far from two well-known Loire River chateaus—Chambord and Blois, which was barely ten miles away—La Borde was a world apart. The nineteenth-century chateau stood in the middle of an enormous park overlooking a few outbuildings; it had first-floor offices, a kitchen, living rooms, an infirmary, a laundry room, and patients' rooms on the second floor. The greenhouse and vegetable garden were somewhat farther away, and an equestrian center, chicken coops, and pigpens were set in the neighboring woods. A hundred-year-old cedar tree grew next to the chateau until it was toppled by a storm, and a vast pond nearby served as a reminder that this was the Sologne. A hall set close by could accommodate about a hundred people; a small chapel had been converted into a library. Here, a collective experiment sought to reinvent the world while remaining remote from its turbulence.[1]

THE LEGACY OF INSTITUTIONAL PSYCHOTHERAPY

An 1838 law defining the legal standing of public establishments for the insane was crucial in establishing the policy of locking up and abusing people suffering from psychiatric disorders, although it could also serve to prevent administrative arbitrariness. "Benignly applied, the '38 law could protect a person against maltreatment by his or her family or the local authorities."[2]

The story of La Borde began in 1921, with a psychiatric sanctuary established by Dr. Tissot in Saint-Alban en Lozère. Changes in psychiatric practice had crystallized at the end of World War II into a very distinct kind of hospital that benefited from its isolation. An entire network of Resistance fighters had taken refuge here during the war, and the legacy of protest remained strong. Resistance fighters and conscientious objectors, along with a few important intellectuals, also came for brief periods. Paul Balvet's reforms had turned nurses into actual health workers, thus providing patients with more humane care. Lucien Bonnafé, a communist and the head of the underground in the upper Lozère, became the director in 1942 and made it a practice to allow hospital patients to come and go from the asylum and to develop relationships with the local population.

In 1939, the arrival of the Catalan psychiatrist François Tosquelles shook things up at La Borde. Tosquelles was a militant in the Trotskyist Marxist Unification Workers' Party and had been the director of the psychiatric service of the Spanish Republican Army. He had fled Franco's Spain, crossing the Pyrenees on foot to reach a Spanish refugee camp in Sept-Fons. Angels Vivès, another Catalan psychiatrist, told Paul Balvet that Tosquelles was in the camp; Balvet knew the "Red psychiatrist's" reputation and went to the camp to bring him to Saint-Alban.

Tosquelles had started working in psychiatry at the age of sixteen. He was twenty-four when the Spanish Republicans were forced to react to General Franco's *pronunciamiento* and had already been practicing psychiatry for four years at the Pere Mata Institute, in Reus, where, for more than a century, the work had focused on reading centers. Early in his career, he had taken part in an innovative experiment at the Catalonia General Hospital, where Professor Mira y Lopès organized the health services in an unusual way, inspired largely by German psychiatric practices. When Tosquelles crossed into France, he was carrying Hermann Simon's *Psychotherapy in the Asylum* with him and had it translated into French. The book described Simon's experience in Guttersloch and addressed both the psychiatric institution and the patients by providing stimulating creative and professional activities for the entire hospital community.[3]

The intellectual energy that had gathered during the war made Saint-Alban Hospital a propitious place for Tosquelles' avant-garde views. Most of the psychiatrists were under thirty and able to reinvent the world. When a patients' club was created at Saint-Alban, Tosquelles joined the intense collective undertaking that led to the creation of the Société du Gévaudan, a professional group. "To prepare a joyful future, we discussed psychiatry, we made critical changes in the basic concepts and the different possible types of therapy."[4] In 1952, when Bonnafé was appointed to a job in Paris, Tosquelles became the hospital's medical director.

The Resistance had a considerable impact on Saint-Alban Hospital. The overall context, the wait for weapons drops for the Resistance fighters hiding on the premises, and the relationships that had been forged with the neighboring populations all contributed to making the hospital an open place integrated into local life and involved in what the Société du Gévaudan called "geopsychiatry," which coordinated psychiatric and traditional local activities. The hospital and the town were so well integrated that doctors would go to patients' houses to fetch them and continue to monitor them when they returned home.

The interweaving of the Resistance and the hospital was so tight that the recruitment of interns was closely linked to the local Resistance network. Clinic director Lucien Bonnafé had brought in Paul Eluard, who created a clandestine publishing house, as well as other people who were closely connected to the Resistance, including Georges Sadoul and Gaston Bissette. He sought out the philosopher Georges Canguilhem, who was in medical school in Toulouse and an associate commissioner of the Republic in Clermont-Ferrand. Involvement with the war and everything about it—the local resistance, the Auvergne Resistance, the Mont Mouchet, intellectual resistance, clandestine publications—were all very important for Saint-Alban[5] and ultimately shaped how La Borde was run, defining, as Jean Oury noted, its "matrix" or melting pot.[6]

Immediately after the war, many young interns wanted to work at Saint-Alban. Jean Oury arrived in 1947 with a whole new generation who had come to train there,[7] and he immediately connected with Tosquelles. At eighteen, Oury had conceived a project to create a working group among his liberal friends. Like Guattari, he was deeply involved in La Garenne-Colombes activities, in the Student Hostel movement, and in youth groups that were very active after the war's end. His father worked as a polisher at La Garennes' prestigious Hispano-Suiza company.

When Jean Oury came to Saint-Alban, he brought Lacan's May 1947 lecture—a text that would become the theoretical foundation of his long career as a psychiatrist. The psychiatrist Ajuriaguerra, his colleague Georges

Daumézon, and the sociologist Georges Gusdorf had organized a series of lectures at the Ecole Normale Supérieure[8] after the 1946 Bonneval meeting where Lacan had developed his ideas of psychic causality. "I saw several guys come and give talks, but when I heard this guy, I said to myself, finally someone smart; it was Lacan, and it was a relief."[9] He had hesitated between studying physics-chemistry or psychiatry, but Lacan's lecture clarified his choice. Years passed, however, before he had any personal contact with his master. "It was only in October 1953 that I went to see him as an analyst and that lasted until 1980—twenty-seven years! Twice a week, because I'm incurable."[10] Jean Oury was part of the Lacanian adventure: the schism in 1953, the creation of the Freudian School of Paris in 1964. For four years, he oversaw the certification commission alongside Lacan, Serge Leclaire, and Mustafa Safouan.

JEAN OURY: A NEW VISION

Jean Oury stayed at Saint-Alban until 1949, when he was asked to replace Tosquelles' friend Solanes, who was leaving to take over a hospital in Caracas. Oury went to Saumery in the Loire-et-Cher for a month and stayed until 1953. At the time, the seventeenth-century Saumery chateau was the sole private psychiatric clinic in the region. It had only twelve beds and barely functioned.[11] The future La Borde team took shape at the La Source clinic, and, in many ways, the years between 1950 and 1953 were the high points of La Borde's history.[12]

With its tiny patient population, the microcosm at La Source defined itself as a specific type of community. "The people in this very tight-knit group had met in the Student Hostels movement and in La Garenne-Colombes, Oury's suburb; other friends joined them."[13] Jean Oury's entire network came to spend time at the clinic, helping with the patients and with the activities organized on weekends or during vacations; it was a real tribe. "The Saumery period was what I would call the 'no exit' period."[14] Oury's psychiatric practice at Saumery developed using Saint-Alban's experience. "Without this contextualization, psychiatry is smoke and mirrors. Tosquelles talked about polycentric heterogeneity and at the same time about transdisciplinarity. You can't care for a patient unless you also consider his job, his childhood, and the material conditions of his life."[15] When the clinic owners said that they were going to take things in hand and rejected any proposals to modify the building, Oury decided to go elsewhere.

Oury had managed to create a forty-bed clinic at Saumery, but he was the only person in the region with the authority to make psychiatric decisions, and he felt isolated. He also longed to create his own institution elsewhere. In April 1953, he heard that the La Borde chateau, some six miles away, was for sale. It was relatively isolated; the closest village was about 2.5 miles away and the nearest city was about eight miles away. The building was also in serious disrepair: only the ground floor was habitable, and the various outbuildings were in ruins. Oury bought La Borde and brought with him almost all of his Saumery patients and his eight assistants. He opened the clinic in April 1953. The psychiatric world immediately hailed its creation. As of 1954, psychiatrists including Louis Le Guillant, Evelyne Kestemberg, and Georges Daumézon came to consult Oury and to send their patients to him.

La Borde was the beginning of a new phase. Oury baptized his clinic as soon as it opened in April 1953, writing a constitution that he dated Year I (a tongue-in-cheek reference to the French Revolution) and that defined the three guiding principles for this collective therapeutic undertaking. The managers were protected by democratic centralism, reflecting the Marxist-Leninist ideal that was still popular in the year of Stalin's death. The second principle reflected the idea of a communist utopia whereby each staff member would alternate between manual labor and intellectual work, which effectively made any status temporary. Tasks were assigned on a rotating basis: everyone in the clinic switched from medical care to housekeeping, from running workshops to preparing theatrical activities. The last principle was antibureaucratic, so things were organized in a communitarian way whereby responsibilities, tasks, and salaries were all shared. Although the term "institutional psychotherapy" had not yet been coined, many of its themes were already in evidence: spatial permeability, freedom of movement, a critique of professional roles and qualifications, institutional flexibility, and the need for a patients' therapy club.[16]

An ironic text defining these trends, *Ontology for a Nondeductive Phenomenology*, bore a less pompous subtitle: *A Refreshing Drink*. The idea was to have La Borde define new approaches as creatively as possible, letting chance and spontaneity play an important role, as the surrealists had done. Oury referred to Lacan and to Ponge. "Francis Ponge's approach is to get beyond the object to what Lacan called the Thing. We touched a certain surface, a semantics that directly reflects the way we treat psychotics."[17]

In addition to his passion for the therapeutic aspect of psychiatry, Oury had always been extremely interested in creativity, on which he had written his thesis. By linking creativity with madness, he argued against a purely negative perception of mental illness. "I was presenting creativity as something like a biological defense, an attempt to reconstruct or replace the world."[18] In his thesis, he identified the split created by the psychotic's psychic lesion with autoproduction. "Delirium is productive. . . . I talked about an aesthetic impulse."[19]

For Oury, a clinic was not to be mistaken for a "shoe factory." The therapeutic group at La Borde was not organized by specialties or arranged in a functional hierarchy like traditional hospitals, where specialized ergotherapists and sociotherapists were encapsulated in their specific work and isolated from the rest of the staff. The permanent revolution also included evaluating each project to see how well it was working and for its potential productivity.

Salaries were one of the most delicate issues at La Borde. Initially, there was a very complex principle that defined salaries as a function of a preliminary weighting coefficient linked to the difficulty of the task or the level of competence. When La Borde was created, Oury established a club, based on the Saint-Alban experience. "The first thing that Dr. Odin [*sic*; it was in fact Dr. Oury] did was to look for a place with tables and chairs to sell bars of soap and ballpoint pens, to play cards or read magazines."[20] The goal was the same as at Saint-Alban: create a nonhierarchical social club where patients and doctors, nurses, monitors, and any medical staff could mix. The club was central to life at the clinic and was considered the very heart of the chateau. It occupied the large first-floor living room; there was a smaller side room where soft drinks and tobacco were sold at a bar. A biweekly general meeting was supposed to take place to designate a board and president. In the early days, only the monitors were eligible to serve on the board, but it later became clear that many patients were quite able to handle administrative responsibilities, and they began to be included on the board as well. Many workshop committees and all sorts of meetings kept this sociability alive at La Borde. The club committee organized workshops that oversaw the institutional newspaper, *La Borde Éclair* (*La Borde Brief*), pyrographic activities, a chorus, a puppet theater, and so on. The club committee also oversaw the budget and was financially independent from the clinic, "thus establishing a formal, democratic representative structure."[21] To ensure that the entire staff was involved with the patients, a menu commission was created seven months after La Borde opened to get the cook out of the kitchen and to involve as many people as possible in preparing the meals, to keep the group well integrated and prevent locking people into specialized jobs,

Not everyone favored diluting specializations this way. Creative tensions were supposed to engender permanent attentiveness to difference in a place where psychosis was always challenging rational logic in various ways. The exchanges among the community members were designed to bring people out of their isolation and morbid compulsions, including the repetition compulsion, by constantly creating new group-subjects. The goal of practicing institutional psychotherapy like this was not to create relationships per se but "to develop new forms of subjectivity."[22]

Félix Guattari kept Jean Oury informed about his political activities and above all kept him updated on Lacan's seminar, which he had been attending on a regular basis since the 1950s. Guattari accepted the invitation to come work at La Borde and moved there with his partner, Micheline Kao, in 1955. Guattari and Oury shifted the shared responsibilities somewhat: Guattari continued to be responsible for external relations, for running the therapeutic club, and for planning. La Borde quickly became a "two-headed machine." The close friendship between Guattari and Oury made it possible to surmount the difficult moments and keep La Borde creatively imbalanced in order to remain receptive to innovation.

What attracted Guattari was more the intellectual aspect of the work at La Borde than psychosis. "It's strange but true that I wasn't very interested in mental illness."[23] His experience as a political activist made him good at organization and management. "My behavior toward staff was rigidly militant, and they were very surprised to see the growing discipline in the operations, the meeting style, and the oversight of tasks."[24] Daily life was busy at the clinic: prior to the use of narcoleptics and drug therapy, conflicts between patients often erupted into fights, and it was not unusual for people to get beaned by coffee pots or tools.

Already a recognized group leader, Guattari was determined to use his judo, if necessary, to quell any violent tendencies. He set up spaces where he could speak with the staff and resolve problems through discussion. When he began monitoring some of the patients, he was quite authoritarian and especially firm with patients who refused to get out of bed. They were told to get out of their rooms and get involved in some of the scheduled activities. Between Lacan's seminar and La Borde, Guattari acquired real psychiatric training.

Guattari relaxed his methods after he experienced what it was like to be a patient. In 1957, Oury sent him to Tosquelles at Saint-Alban for temporary hospitalization, so that he could avoid military service in Algeria. There, Guattari discovered how difficult a patient's life could be under the iron rule of overbearing nurses. In the 1950s, Sartre and existentialist positions were coming under question. In his discussions with Oury about the relationship between doctors and nurses, Guattari was obviously concerned about defunctionalization. "The central intention is to abrogate various roles and stereotypes: to behave like a madman, a doctor or a nurse, to promote human relationships that no longer lead automatically to lesser roles and stereotypes."[25] La Borde nurses did not wear white smocks and were indistinguishable from the patients. Oury had a sense of humor, reversing the dogma that once a patient was hospitalized he or she was never released. For him, the medical staff was stable and permanent, and the patients came and went. Ever since the Saint-Alban period and from the moment that La Borde opened its doors, Oury felt that a mad person's words held some truth. Delusional behavior was not fetishized, "but there was a real effort to seek out the creative element, to have the clinical observer be attentive to what we called the madman's transcendental dimension."[26]

Guattari very quickly began personally supervising many patients, including Jack Brière. Guattari was Brière's receiving doctor when he came to La Borde on January 29, 1959, and he saw him in individual therapy until 1967, when Brière left the clinic. Brière suffered from phobic anxiety and his treatment was very traditional. "Félix Guattari didn't speak. I lay on the couch and he sat behind me listening."[27] For four years, Brière served as the secretary and treasurer for the pensioners; he kept the books and oversaw the bank account in Blois. Guattari also managed to get him the money he needed to buy books about metallurgy, in which he was very interested and which later proved to be useful when he took courses at the Conservatoire des Arts et Métiers. Guattari earned the nickname "Speedy Guatt,"[28] because he moved at a pace that amazed Brière. When asked what Guattari had taught him, Brière replied: "To live. He pushed people to realize their desires and he encouraged me to do sculpture."[29]

Jacques Besse was a particularly important patient for Guattari. A great artist, poet, and musician, Besse came to La Borde in 1955 and stayed until his death on May 30, 1999. Born in 1921, Besse had been a brilliant high-school student who was admitted to the competitive, prestigious two-year university preparatory courses. He had studied philosophy and, in 1943, had become the musical director of the Charles Dullin Company. After the

Liberation, he wrote some film music for Yves Allégret and Alain Resnais and composed a piano concerto. In 1950, however, when he returned alone by foot from a trip to Algeria, his life collapsed. He bounced between prisons and psychiatric hospitals until Oury and Guattari brought him to La Borde, where they even published some of his work in their journal, *Recherches* (*Research*).[30]

Besse often wanted to leave the clinic to walk around Paris to draw inspiration. "As I was walking back on automatic pilot to Saint-German-des-Prés, I wondered about the weight or tax of Love but not the blood we will have to pay to the most poetic of Alliances for our prosaic acts, we, the most absurd of people."[31] Guattari would give him a five-hundred-franc bill whenever he went to take a stroll; Besse would spend the money on alcohol and once was committed to the psychiatric hospital at Ville-Evrard, after which he was brought back to La Borde.

Besse participated in all the cultural evenings at La Borde and was persuaded to write an hour-long play entitled *The Exotic West*, which was produced as it was being written. His friend the filmmaker Jacques Baratier visited Besse regularly at La Borde and in 2004 co-wrote and made a beautiful film about him. Laurent Terzieff played Besse, speaking the lines: "Seek the poet, not the patient, behind the words."[32]

To create an alternative to therapeutic groups that were either overly large or one on one, small groups were created at La Borde. "We had six or seven groups with bizarre names, including one from after 1970 called 'the lost.'"[33] Subsequently, basic therapeutic units including patients and medical staff of a size deemed appropriate for modifying a patient's subjective makeup were created and the number ultimately set at fifteen. There were rules; the groups were supposed to stand in for the subject to help individuals overcome the difficulties they had focusing their speech and behavior. The small groups had the unintended effect of creating and reinforcing a sense of hyperfamiliarity and closeness. "I remember one patient who came here in 1971, we told him 'you're going to be in this unit' and the next day he came to see me, saying, 'I have some problems with my family.' I found the money to help him leave."[34]

THE "BARBARIAN" INVASION

When Guattari came to La Borde, he invited several young militant students to spend some time there with him to be in direct contact with the world of mental illness. Oury called them the "invaders" or the "barbarians," but they were useful because the clinic had grown from forty-eight patients in 1955 to ninety in 1958. Mostly political militants and humanists, the first group included philosophers from Félix's gang: Lucien Sebag, Michel Cartry, Alfred Adler, Claude Vivien, and the future psychiatrist Ginette Michaud, virtually all of whom were in the humanities. They met with Félix in the Sorbonne library, well known for its political sociability and for its extremely knowledgeable librarian, Mr. Romeu, who was immensely helpful to students both for their studies and by initiating them into Communist Party activism. La Borde was where he renewed his political convictions and invited his "gang" to involve themselves in political activities.

Michel Cartry was invited to La Borde in the spring of 1953; the clinic had just been created. "La Borde was a great utopia for us. I remember that Oury came to meet us at the Blois train station. We spent a whole night in his office discussing Kierkegaard's *Diary of a Seducer*."[35] Cartry, who later became an anthropologist, was assigned to a young schizophrenic patient with whom Guattari was working and who wrote poems, kept a diary, and attended Lacan's seminar. Guattari sent him to Paris occasionally, relying on Cartry to take care of him.

The "barbarians" came to La Borde whenever they had school breaks, and they got involved in the full gamut of activities: printing, pottery and ceramics workshops, and meetings with doctors, nurses, and patients. "Refusing to consider madness as a simple illness and linking it to intellectual development, to language and to poetry was all very new. It wasn't common at the time."[36] Cartry decided to study anthropology, and his wife Christiane began working as a monitor at La Borde, where they lived for two years and where their son was born.

Cartry's high-school friend, Alfred Adler, who later became an anthropologist, had the same fascinating experience at La Borde. He considered Guattari his "guru." Indeed, the barbarians were called Guattari's "little soldiers." Like the others, Adler was trying to avoid the draft and deployment to Algeria, and he submitted a request to Dr. Lebovici at the University Hospital in Paris, who sent him to a clinic located about six miles from La Borde run by Claude Jeangirard, a friend of Guattari. Adler could therefore visit La Borde every day and work alongside Guattari in his various activities. It was also at La Borde that Claude Vivien first wrote about Freinet. "We slept in sleeping bags up in the attic."[37]

Ginette Michaud was a student in medicine and psychology, but La Borde proved to be a turning point for her decision to become a psychologist. "I was the one who came up with the idea of transversality and discussed it with Félix so that he could work on it."[38] At the time, Ginette Michaud was living with Lucien Sebag, a young philosopher who had switched to anthropology and was considered a potential successor to Lévi-Strauss. Sebag also got involved at La Borde and brought along his brilliant mathematician brother Robert.

In 1962, at the end of the Algerian war, a second wave of "barbarians" came to La Borde, encouraged in part by Guattari's having reinvolved himself with the unionized students of the National Union of French Students and the National French Student Movement (MNEF) groups. Between 1962 and Algeria's independence and before the upheavals of 1968, many students became passionately committed to clinical work thanks to the time they spent at La Borde. Given their strong political ideals, they saw La Borde as representing the psychiatric world and as a genuine social utopia. "I came to La Borde on a summer day, I was twenty at the time, I think. The war had ended; my boyfriend was getting out of prison. It was a lovely day."[39] This was how Marie Depussé, a literature student at the ENS in Sèvres at the time and a future writer, began her description of her first encounter with La Borde. She went regularly to Lacan's seminars with her philosophy-student boyfriend, who had just been released from a three-month prison sentence for having demonstrated against the war in Algeria in a protest that had turned violent. Having decided to celebrate his release by going to the country, they went to La Borde and immediately fell in love with the place. "I stayed at La Borde because I was amazed by the patients and how they were treated."[40] Marie Depussé became an intern at La Borde in 1962, before there were any official interns, and never really left.

During a discussion about a violent patient who seemed to need a series of electroshock treatments, a therapy used at La Borde and requested by many patients to calm their anxiety, Depussé suggested that the patient was trying to start a dialogue through her provocations and violence. "Félix came over to me, smiled, and very quickly told me to stop my studies because my future was at La Borde. This was the period when Félix would say, 'The world is at La Borde.' Which was pretty much true."[41] Marie Depussé hesitated and then began dividing her time between Paris and the ENS during the week, preparing for the *agrégation*, the highest national teachers' examination, and La Borde on the weekends, doing whatever had to be done, including dishwashing and house cleaning. Her father, an architect, built her a beautiful wooden house in the park surrounding the chateau, and she put down roots.

Depussé was also fascinated by Oury, a tireless purveyor of hope who could persuade even the most reluctant patients to get back on their feet. At teatime every day, the utopian tension relaxed. "People are so graceful when they're still, standing around tables, holding a cup of linden-blossom tea at 4 p.m. at La Borde. At this time, they are chosen. Silent conviviality. . . . An hour when time is suspended and we internalize our stay."[42]

During a suicidal episode, Depussé particularly appreciated Guattari's analytic perspicacity. Félix had been notified by her brother, who was alarmed by her state. "One day, stupefied, I ran into Félix not far from the La Borde offices and he said, 'So it seems that you want to die. OK, I'm going to tell you something: croak!' and I laughed. It was the way that he said it, at the right time and place. That's how Félix worked, he truly had therapeutic powers."[43] Marie Depussé stayed at La Borde and wrote two books about the clinic.[44] She was a gifted writer and edited Guattari's texts, trying to dissuade him from trying to write fiction. "He had an exaggerated lifelong obsession with Joyce. He was born and died with Joyce. Joyce has destroyed a lot of people."[45] But when she edited his texts about transversality, she was stunned by the quality and complexity of his thought.

In March 1963, Michel Butel, a writer and militant activist in the Leftist Student Union, visited La Borde for the first time. His sister was in bad shape psychologically, and his friend Jean-Claude Polack suggested that he bring her to see Oury and Guattari. Michel Butel did not expect much from the meeting and attended unenthusiastically, out of a sense of family obligation. He was asthmatic and had a serious attack in the middle of the night. As he looking for his medication, Guattari showed up. "That meeting changed my life. We started talking. He had an amazing way of channeling his desire to get to know people by going right to the heart of things. He could talk about anything."[46] Guattari was ten years older than Butel, and the breadth of Guattari's intellectual curiosity fascinated the younger man. They shared an interest in political activity, which put them on immediate common ground. A lifelong friendship developed between them: Butel came several times to La Borde to work as an intern and was amazed by the omnipresence of his friend Félix. "He was God at La Borde. He was always there. At the time, he was living in a sort of annex abutting the clinic. Whenever anything serious happened, even if it was at three in the morning, you could count on him. He ran extremely demanding meetings; he was the soul of the clinic! Oury was the tutelary figure, but Félix was the one who kept things going every daily."[47]

Jean-Claude Polack, a psychiatrist by profession, arrived in 1963 and later became a pillar of the clinic at La Borde. Polack had begun his medical studies in 1954 and finished his university training in 1962. While he was an intern in psychiatry, he was also a very well-known student leader who, in 1961, headed the medical students' branch of the National French Students' Union, which had twelve thousand members and whose leadership was radically opposed to the war in Algeria. When Polack got to La Borde, he had just been defeated in the elections for NFSU president. The group's leftist current, nominally a minority but in fact a majority in the NFSU, supported him, but during the days preceding the national meeting in Talence, he was interviewed about his program, which was ultraleftist, aggressive, and modeled on the very violent Japanese student groups known as the *Zengakuren*. That program destroyed his chances for election and the minority had to scramble to find a more palatable candidate.

Polack was thrilled about his internship at La Borde, organized by a mutualist group of which he was a member. "It was love at first sight; this was the first place where I sensed that psychiatry was really happening."[48] He returned to the clinic to have himself be declared ineligible for the army, and he started working there as a psychiatrist in 1964. Later, he co-authored a book on La Borde with the psychiatrist Danielle Sivadon, his partner.[49] When Polack discovered La Borde, he was involved in a network of student leaders, union militants, and revolutionaries to whom he described his new passions and the incredible, "little myopic guy" with whom one spent entire nights talking about everything—life, death, love. He urged his friends to come to La Borde as soon as possible. In 1965, in the meantime, he organized a meeting with Guattari at Marie Depussé's house, where they came up with a plan for the Leftist Opposition and its program. In addition to Michel Butel and Jean-Claude Polack, the future sociologists Liane Mozère and Hervé Maury, François Fourquet, Pierre Arutchev, Georges Préli, and a few others were at the meeting. "I was twenty-six at the time and we all fell in love with the crazy people."[50]

Some of the interns who had come during the summer of 1965 remained, including François Fourquet, who had moved to La Borde in the fall of 1966. "I asked to work at La Borde. Félix looked at me surprised: 'What's going on? You have a university career ahead of you. He was right.

I later became a professor.'"[51] But Fourquet felt compelled to work at La Borde, and after finishing his studies at the Institut des Sciences Politiques, he found a way—the clinic needed a manager. Guattari was thrilled to be able to rely on Fourquet, who oversaw the long process of getting the clinic integrated into the national health system, so that patients could get insurance coverage, and of systematizing the management of the hundred patients, monitors, interns, nurses, and doctors. Fourquet rose to the challenge, working until ten o'clock at night during his first months to put the files in order. In addition to working in the office, he also worked as a nurse when needed, alongside his wife Geneviève, a professional nurse. "I was so in love with La Borde that I fell in love with a nurse and we had a daughter."[52] Fourquet was also actively involved with different groups and workshops, but he was primarily the administrative secretary under Guattari until 1972.

In 1964, Michel Rostain, a friend of Jean-Claude Polack, was a member of the CERFI group and the NFSU secretary. Rostain was also thrilled when he discovered La Borde in the 1960s. A Latin Quarter intellectual, he had finished his studies in philosophy and was teaching philosophy to high-school seniors but wanted something beyond a regular daily routine. He called Félix, who invited him to spend some time working at La Borde. "He said, 'come, but you're going to have to work, do the dishes, speak with the patients, learn how to give shots, do night duty, sell flowers with the mentally ill and discuss the organization chart.' "[53] Rostain was deeply attracted to the freedom of speech at La Borde and the interest in going into depth about Marx, Freud, and Lacan while remaining firmly anchored in the reality of a clinic. He came to La Borde every year from 1966 to 1973, for three to twelve months at a time. Lion Murard, another member of Félix's gang and a friend of François Fourquet, with whom he was working on a degree from the Institut des Sciences Politiques, also came to La Borde in 1966 and was immediately charmed by the clinic, "which was working to distinguish the person from the function so as to prevent any kind of hierarchy."[54]

In 1966, François Pain, the brother-in-law of psychiatrist Tony Laine, came to La Borde from Poitiers for a month-long internship. He stayed for seven years. He had just finished high school, had taken the baccalaureate exam, and enrolled in medicine in Tours so as to remain close to La Borde, where he was assigned to Fernand Deligny. His liaison with Danielle Rouleau, a student who had quit Jussieu University to study medicine and who was in analysis with Guattari, kept him involved with La Borde for a long time. From his first internship, he was enthusiastic about living with a group of fifty people who had come from all over France and reinvented the world every day. Pain and Guattari quickly became close, unwavering friends. Oury and Guattari sent Pain to begin analysis with Tosquelles, the clinic's spiritual father. "Once, after I'd been on the couch criticizing Oury for about five minutes, Tosquelles interrupted me and began a long diatribe against Félix. At the end of the session, he asked me how much he owed me. I owed him for a lot of sessions that I hadn't yet paid for, so I just said that my debt was cancelled."[55]

3

Daily Life at La Borde

Life at La Borde was scheduled around innumerable meetings that organized all the groups—the "locals," the "barbarians," the medical staff, and the patients. A new meeting could be created at the drop of a hat, but one meeting in particular became an institution: the Daily Activities Commission. Created in 1955, the DAC met like clockwork every day after lunch in the large living room to organize every detail of daily life.

MULTIPLE INSTITUTIONAL LINKS

When he arrived at La Borde, Guattari immediately took over the DAC. In addition to the myriad kinds of information and activities that had to be organized, the DAC meeting served as an airing ground for grievances and irritations: running it was a delicate task. Above all, the DAC gave disconnected patients an opportunity to reestablish some degree of social life by engaging in harmless verbal sparring. "I am absolutely sure that this was the mainspring of the patients' local resocialization."[1] Guattari did not see the exchanges as power plays but rather considered that they were based on arbitrary exchanges that helped the patients get out of themselves.[2] As a machine producing meaningless words, these somewhat imaginary exchanges served to better integrate the symbolic order. "This daily meeting eliminated the dross to focus on what remained."[3] It worked like a vast machine that assigned people to tasks in a way that achieved maximum mobility.

In 1957, La Borde was flourishing. And much like medieval religious orders that expanded by creating new houses, a decision was made to spread the mission. Claude Jeangirard, a friend of Jean Oury, started a new clinic nearby in La Chesnaie, and Guattari led a team from La Borde to help set it up. Jeangirard had worked in Paris at Sainte-Anne Hospital and at Ville-d'Avray, where La Borde's innovations were starting to elicit some interest. He had visited Oury in August 1955, with the idea of buying a chateau and starting a clinic like La Borde. "He arrived in a magnificent Hispano-Suiza, which impressed me a lot because I had dreamed about Hispano-Suizas throughout my childhood."[4] By November of that year, Oury had found La Chesnaie Chateau, a beautiful place in some disrepair; the La Borde team helped with the renovation and the clinic opened in July 1956.

La Chesnaie functioned much like La Borde except that it organized daily life using a technique called "the grid." The La Borde staffmembers who had come to paint La Chesnaie used the grid when they had too few volunteers for all the tasks; it helped rotate assignments and became something of a regulatory instrument for the entire community. It also helped integrate the staff. The two houses were occasionally embroiled in arguments. "A puerile war broke out between La Chesnaie and La Borde, and as in all primitive societies, there were raids. They wanted to keep a nurse there whom we needed and we went to get her back under cover of darkness."[5]

Oury thought that Jeangirard was not sufficiently involved in the various clinical meetings and, consequently, on July 1, 1957, the La Borde volunteers at La Chesnaie returned to La Borde, led once again by Guattari. "We couldn't pretend that nothing had happened and simply continue with business as usual at La Borde."[6] Starting in July 1957, therefore, a new meeting was scheduled at six o'clock in the evening that quickly became the epicenter of the clinic. At this meeting, the grid method was employed to dole out people's tasks and responsibilities. The assignment of these tasks caused tempers to flare. Initially, work was assigned on the basis of the general schedule and people's willingness to take responsibility for a particular activity. "There were nightly negotiations. We called it the grid"[7] after the grid at La Chesnaie.

Nicole Guillet had always lived in a world close to psychiatry. Her father had been the bursar at the Saint-Alban psychiatric hospital since 1934. She came from an observant Protestant family, but when she was eleven, she skipped the Sunday service to attend meetings of Tosquelles' Gevaudan Society. "We were already discussing how to cure patients and keep them from withdrawing again, how to integrate them with the staff. In this area, Balvet was a precursor of liberalized psychiatry."[8] At seventeen, Nicole

Guillet met Jean Oury when he came to the Lozère. Later, when she was a university student, she met Frantz Fanon and brought him to Saint-Alban to meet Tosquelles. "I remember the first discussion between Tosquelles and Fanon in my mother's living room. The issue was whether or not nurses had to have a primary school diploma [*certificat d'études*]."[9] Nicole Guillet had not quite finished her medical internship in Lyon when Oury asked her to help his friend Claude Jeangirard start an insulin service at La Chesnaie. She came in November 1956 and stayed until July 1957, when the La Borde group returned from La Chesnaie. As there was no position for a full-time doctor at the time, Félix asked Nicole Guillet to help out in the administrative office. "Félix really liked declassifying people, like having a doctor come work in the office. He had the psychologists doing the dishes."[10]

For nearly a decade, Guattari oversaw work schedules at La Borde, and he constantly assigned people to work outside their areas of specialization. "The grid is a double-entry table that lets you collectively manage individual assignments and responsibilities. It's a sort of necessary regulatory instrument for deregulating an institution."[11] The idea was to create a sense of equality by assigning staff to several different kinds of tasks, but the method was authoritarian, and people were quite nervous while awaiting their assignments. Although the grid was efficient, it created considerable tension. "I was motivated by a sort of militant centralism like when a political organization decides to put up posters the next day."[12] Some staff members were thrilled to be living in a group where the manual/intellectual distinction no longer held sway, but many people, including the medical staff, felt housekeeping to be beneath them, and many of the service personnel were afraid to get involved in medical tasks.

The grid was set monthly and updated daily. Employees' names were listed on the x-axis and the time of day was plotted on the y-axis; on the chart, everyone could read their short-term assignments—"dishwashing," "housecleaning," "the chicken coop," "night duty," "pottery workshop"—and long-term assignments. No one disobeyed. For some, the grid embodied the director, the supreme "grid maker," a realization of the utopia; for others, it was a destructive steamroller crushing individuals and their desires in the name of some common interest. Those who were subjected to the work assignments typically overinterpreted them; they saw the grid as a way for Guattari to attack and test this or that inhibition or phobia. "The

gridmaker's decisions were meted out like prison sentences."[13] Over the
years, the somewhat rigid system came increasingly under fire.

> Things are cracking up everywhere. Monitors who want to do dishes!
> A night-watch woman sick of doing twelve hours straight and wants
> her watch to end after five hours! A cleaning woman who helps the
> doctor treat patients and then splits . . . and returns! Another woman
> who leads patients to the chicken coop! A washerwoman monitoring
> the insulin! Everything is topsy-turvy.[14]

In addition to rotating tasks, there was also the delicate question of salaries and how to calculate them. People soon started talking about weighting
jobs with a disagreeability coefficient, which was obviously hard to calculate scientifically. Some activities evolved rather naturally, such as bringing meal trays to patients' room when they could not or would not get out
of bed. The service staff was responsible for setting up the trays for the
monitors to bring upstairs, but the monitors eventually forgot that this was
part of their job. "It's the service staff's job in fact. Slippery trays, slippery
functions."[15]

Oury suggested an adjustment that he called a "temperament," after
Bach's *Well-Tempered Clavier*. He needed more and more staff because the
clinic was growing. In 1959, he called Brivette Buchanan to work as the
medical secretary, and she became a pillar of the institution and a member
of the spiritual family. Like Oury, Brivette had grown up in La Garenne-
Colombes. The two had met during Student Hostel activities, on workers'
caravans, and in the Hispano-Suiza youth group. Brivette and Raymond
Petit, Hispano's leader, became a couple. Brivette worked as a medical secretary at Foch Hospital in the Paris suburb of Suresnes and came to Saumery during her vacations, joining the clinic's collective life. She worked at
La Borde until she retired.

By 1958, La Borde was on the verge of bankruptcy. The manager, Madame Fichaut, ran the place disastrously: she never made a budget, always
bought retail, and was utterly incapable of overseeing the accounts. Her
chaotic office was home to her many cats and was a smelly mess. In April
1958, in something of a "coup d'état," Guattari fired Madame Fichaut. "I
went to that woman and said, 'that's it! Enough is enough!' "[16] He took over
the administration and finances. He had no specific management training,
so he learned on the job. When he started looking into the books, he discov-

ered that La Borde was thirty million francs in debt. Exerting all of his charm, he managed to convince a banker in Blois, Mr. de Querotret, to pay the clinic's most pressing debts. At the age of twenty-five, Guattari saved La Borde from the abyss.

Among the many institutions created at La Borde, the Rotunda became the clinic's political lungs. The Rotunda had previously been a laundry room where people got together every week to discuss politics and current events. Nicole Guillet, who worked as a doctor at La Borde until 1974, oversaw several committees: the kitchen committee, the cultural committee, the household committee, and the menu committee, each of which required a weekly meeting. "For the kitchen committee, I brought the cooks and everyone who worked in the kitchen together. We decided on the menus, we looked at the orders and the complaints. For the cleaning committee, we tried to avoid segregating nurses and cleaning women."[17] In addition, there was the big Friday night meeting to discuss the work of the clinic in general. It started at about 8:30 p.m. and rarely ended before one in the morning. "This was a group where we discussed the life of the clinic. Félix was always suggesting new lines of flight. It was both an institutional law and an exploration of new possibilities. Making the impossible possible."[18] Later, small groups met to discuss theory in Oury's office, usually talking about Lacan's ideas. This later evolved into Oury's seminar.

Félix Guattari and Nicole Guillet ran the big group meeting in Oury's office, the symbolic seat of medical power, on Wednesdays at four o'clock in the afternoon, when Oury was out. This was the meeting for the seriously ill patients who could not manage to participate in discussions or in the various clinic activities. The nondirective group therapy meeting began in silence, but everyone was required to speak during the course of the meeting, which became so important to the participants that the fifteen regular patients insisted on knowing when the next one would take place. Unlike the many ephemeral groups at La Borde, this one, created in February 1961, lasted through the 1970s. Marie Depussé remembers going to one of these meetings, during which, after a long silence, one voice seemed to express something fundamental about the horrors of birth, and a leaden silence fell on the group. Then, "five minutes later or five yards away, [there was] another voice that didn't seem to be answering the first in the way we understand conversation, but was answering all the same. The voice was able to respond to birth by talking about hunger, and death; it was a fantastic ricochet."[19]

The Institutional Psychotherapy
and Sociotherapy Working Group

In 1960, Jean Oury and Hélène Chaignau, François Tosquelles, and Roger Gentis, who worked at Saint-Alban from 1956 to 1964, along with Jean Ayme, a former Trotskyite who was the secretary of the Hospital Psychiatrists' Union, and a few others, created a task force on psychiatric practices called the Working Group for Institutional Psychotherapy and Sociotherapy (GTPSI). The group resurrected Tosquelles' 1955 idea of creating a kind of French Psychiatric Party, but the PPF (for *Parti de psychanalsytes français*) acronym would have been infelicitous, in that it recalled Jacques Doriot's fascist party (the *Parti populaire français*). The initial group, constituted in 1960, included a dozen psychiatrists.[20] In November 1961, after its fourth meeting, Guattari and some of the other La Borde psychiatrists, including Jean-Claude Polack, Renée Bidault and, soon thereafter, Nicole Guillet, joined the group, which continued to function until 1965. At that point, the Society for Institutional Psychotherapy (SIP) was created to discuss institutional psychotherapy outside of the institutions where it was practiced.[21]

The group met regularly, twice a year, for weekend retreats, each time in a different hotel. Brivette Buchanan, Oury's secretary, took notes during the discussions. The group sought to define the unique nature of a group of psychiatrists who agreed on a certain number of postulates specific to their discipline and who, therefore, could not be assimilated by any of the various antipsychiatric currents.[22]

These psychiatrists defined a theoretical field and practice that came to be known as "institutional psychotherapy." One of its major tenets was that mentally ill patients could only be treated in an institution that had reflected on how it operated itself. The second principle was that psychosis could not be treated by any supposedly direct access to a strictly individual, socially disconnected pathology, an approach that reduced treatment to a simple interaction between two individuals: the patient and the doctor. Institutional psychotherapy, by contrast, saw treatment as the introduction of new arrangements and social connections. These ideas, worked out in the early 1960s, extended Sartre's notion of the subject who must free himself or herself from alienation in order to allow his own personal liberty to emerge. The GTPSI wanted to see a group-subject emerge and to deconstruct subjected groups "whose law is imposed from the outside, unlike other groups claiming to establish themselves by assuming an internal law."[23]

Guattari was virtually the only nonpsychiatrist in the room, and when he first addressed the group, he was measured and largely in agreement. Soon, however, he began to develop his own ideas and to include more than purely psychiatric references to broaden the discussion to other areas and to society in general. The way that the group operated clearly reflected "the complicity between Oury and Félix, their habit of discussing things together and of handling ideas in ways that often brought the other participants up short. The discussions demonstrated how Oury and Félix could suddenly veer off in stimulating ways when they spoke together, and the very lively, funny, aggressive or defensive reactions of the others in the group."[24] The duo soon found itself at the core of the group in their familiar roles. Oury, as the recognized psychiatric expert, used Guattari's remarks to jog the discussions out of ordinary categories, and other members of the group tested the wild incursions before Oury addressed them as much as was feasible.

The group gave Guattari an opportunity to arrange his various political and psychoanalytical activities. "Félix's ideas were very 'Labordian' in their expression, the ease of the retorts and challenges, the frequent references to clinical experiments with organizing work, an irritation with the prevailing cautious approach, the still palpable influence of Lacan and structural linguistics."[25] Indeed, during the first half of the 1960s, the ambient structuralism in which linguistics was the lead science continued to influence the GTPSI's theoretical work deeply: Ferdinand de Saussure, Roman Jakobson, and Nicolay Trubetzkoy were cited to support the touted practices. The desire to distinguish between people and their established roles and functions therefore drew inspiration not only from Sartre but also from structuralism and, in this way, extended phonological linguistic analyses into psychiatry.

This was the period when the Saint-Alban psychiatrist Claude Poncin argued for *situemes* linking intrainstitutional relationships and phonemic relationships. In June 1960, Oury showed that La Borde was structured like phonemes were, just as Lacan was claiming that the unconscious is structured like a language. Oury distinguished the different signifying units at La Borde, demonstrating how certain connections, like the symbiotic relationship between the chateau's laundry room and its insulin unit, were so strong that the two places risked becoming isolated from the rest of the clinic. "We called that 'linguistics' as a pun."[26] "We said, you aren't in the laundry, you're doing linguistics and yet you are nonetheless doing the laundry."[27] This did not mean, however, that the reigning structuralist paradigm was being embraced lock, stock, and barrel.[28] Institutional psychotherapy was, from the outset, a part of the general energy in the humanities, but it distinguished itself from structuralist thinking to avoid lending support to the notion that structure develops independently of the subject and is overvalorized with respect to it.

Transversalities

Transversality, the other important "Labordian" idea that Guattari developed in 1964 and presented at the first International Psychodrama Meeting in Paris, was based on a suggestion made by Ginette Michaud.[29] The objective of transversality was to unsettle binary structural oppositions and help set the machine in motion. Starting with an analogy between the way that meaning slips for psychotics and the mechanism of growing social discord, Guattari systematized the opposition between group-subjects and subjected groups, claiming that every group was at risk for this double temptation. Guattari wanted to use "a new concept: transversality in the group" to replace the overly vague notion of institutional transfer.[30] Transversality challenged both the vertical axis of a pyramidal organizational chart and the notion of a horizontal juxtaposing different sectors without establishing a relationship among them. "So long as people remain stuck on themselves, they only see themselves."[31] Some degree of transversality makes it possible to start the analytical process of getting out of oneself and the necessary shift in confronting the group. "Transversality is the site of the group's unconscious subject, the beyond of the objective laws that establish it, the underpinning of the group's desire."[32]

La Borde was also quite festive. Great events, galas, and celebrations were among the high points of Labordian life, making it possible for the entire community to step out of the psychiatric world into something larger. In early summer, the widely attended celebrations organized under the patronage of the Federation of Aid to Mental Health, the Marine Cross, were the most important gatherings in the region. The festivities included theatrical productions put on by the patients and typically organized around themes like "1900," "The Sologne," "The French Revolution," "Western," and "Pleasure Gardens."

The most intense period of cultural activities predated 1968. La Borde got the neighboring towns quite involved and even organized a culture month during which a new show was performed nightly in conjunction with the Blois Cultural Center. During these weeks, the clinic buzzed. Costumes were made, songs and dialogues were learned, and people blanketed the area selling lottery tickets for a car. Some teams even set out at night to put up posters. The celebration of the French Revolution with all the patients dressed as *sans-culottes* and singing "The Carmagnole" was memorable; Jean Renoir even came to introduce his film *La Marseillaise*. That year, as many as five thousand people converged on La Borde. The Blois town hall echoed with calls to "hang all the bourgeois." During one of the celebrations for the "La Sologne" theme, organizers brought in local hunters, storytellers, and musicians and traditional instruments. A tent was set up for Johnny Hallyday to sing his "Long Hair, Short Ideas." In the winter, the clinic also organized galas with stars such as Jacques Brel, who came on two different occasions.

La Borde also gave birth to a circus through Guattari's meeting with Jean-Baptiste Thierrée, a militant Maoist who performed his magic show regularly at the Écluse, a Latin Quarter cabaret on Boulevard Saint-Michel, near the Seine. Guattari's friend François Pain had seen the show and enjoyed it so much that he invited Thierrée to perform at La Borde, at which point Thierrée met Guattari, who suggested that the two work together on a regular basis. Thierrée started spending two days a week at La Borde, mingling with the patients and giving performances. Like the others, he became part of the clinic's daily life and took on different jobs. Thierrée was psychologically unwell at the time, and Guattari got him back on his feet. "I got better as soon as I met Félix. He influenced my work a lot indirectly, by his conviction that everything you want is possible."[33]

Thierrée's dream was to create a new kind of circus, and Guattari encouraged him, giving him the confidence to contact celebrities. He had found a photograph of Victoria Chaplin, one of Charlie Chaplin's daughters who, besides being beautiful, also loved circuses, and wrote to her. "I didn't know her address in Switzerland so I just wrote Victoria Chaplin on the envelope. The letter got there and a month later, she was here."[34] The story ended like a fairy tale, with an elaborate wedding on May 15, 1971, at La Borde. Guattari's companion Arlette Donati was the witness for Victoria, and Michel Rocard, an active member of the Socialist Party at the time, was the witness for Jean-Baptiste. The wedding distressed Charlie Chaplin, however, as he had just written *The Freak* and had planned to have his daughter Victoria play the role of the bird woman.

The Thierrée-Chaplin couple created particularly intense activities at La Borde with their circus tents, horses, wild animals, and snakes; the patients were invited to participate. "Sometimes we were successful. I am thinking especially about Claude Farci, a catatonic. I had this idea of masking him from head to toe and when he was like that he did whatever I wanted him to do. I always asked him, 'Why do you move when you are masked?' He never answered me, and one day he said, 'Because it's not serious.'"[35] In the summer of 1971, before Thierrée and Victoria Chaplin's Bonjour Circus had been created officially, Jean Vilar invited them to the Avignon Festival. When he came back to La Borde, Thierrée and Guattari discussed creating a human menagerie of social cases instead of animals.

THE GUATTARI FAMILY BREAKUP

In 1955, Micheline Kao, Guattari's companion, left her parents' home in La Garenne, with some regret and reluctance, to move to La Borde. She was, however, willing to try living there and to work as the clinic's medical secretary. The couple took up residence in a small bedroom above the chateau's kitchen. In addition to her official duties, Kao got involved in all of the various activities at the clinic, especially the secretarial workshop, which functioned well, and she oversaw the insulin prescriptions from time to time and had night duty. She also continued to type Félix's articles. During this period, Guattari became particularly interested in a profoundly withdrawn autistic patient; after trying different approaches, Guattari managed to communicate with him, got him to speak again, and cured him after having devoted himself virtually exclusively to this case.

The promiscuity in the La Borde community wore on the couple.[36] After a year there, the couple split up and Micheline left. This was the end of a long relationship, although the two remained friends and, a few months later, briefly reconsidered living together again when Félix was looking for a small apartment in Paris and suggested to Micheline that they move in together. In 1957, Micheline met Pierre Guillet, Nicole's brother, whom she ultimately married. The breakup was hard on Félix, who even wrote that Micheline had not wanted to come with him to La Borde and had forced him to choose between her and the clinic, which is what ultimately led to their breakup. When Micheline told Félix that she was going to marry Guillet, his sadness turned to anger. "If you want to get married, you should be marrying me and nobody else."[37] She hesitated since she was still attached to Félix and asked for some time to think it over.

In the meantime, Félix had met Nicole Perdreau, whom he later married and with whom he had three children. She was a young, beautiful woman who had just arrived at La Borde to work as a monitor and was totally lost and depressed. "The young girl was ravishing, what my grandmother called a little Tanagra, a young slender, radiant, perfectly built brunette. The first time I saw Félix with her, she was not yet his wife, but he was distracted by the exquisite young woman who was lying with her head on his knees. I thought, well, that little bespectacled guy sure doesn't waste any time."[38]

Nicole came from a peasant family that lived in Tour-en-Sologne; her alcoholic mother worked as a chambermaid; her father was a former test pilot and mechanic who had just died after an accident in which his ribcage had been crushed. Félix was asked to care for Nicole; his devoted caretaking turned into marriage. Their son, Bruno, was born on December 12, 1958; Stephen was born in 1961, and their daughter Emmanuelle in 1964. "Nicole was very fragile. She was a sweetheart, but she was a little bird. He helped her, he gave structure to her life, and made her very happy by marrying her."[39] After Nicole Perdreau became a part of La Borde, virtually the entire Perdreau family showed up at the clinic.[40]

Nicole and Félix set up house in a small apartment; she was an immaculate housekeeper. "There was only one door and behind it were the slippers that you had to put on if you didn't want his wife shouting at you."[41] To avoid the slipper ritual, Félix's friends climbed through the window to his tiny office.

Félix was a rather absent father who divided his time between La Borde and Paris, where he rented an immense, magnificent apartment on rue de Condé. His son Bruno remembers going with his mother to the Blois train station every Thursday at five to pick up his father, who left for Paris again every Monday. Guattari tried to compensate for his absences by lavishing attention on his children. He brought them all sorts of educational toys from Paris and taught his oldest son to read and to do math in his head at a very early age. "At four and a half, I could read and write, and at six I knew my multiplication tables."[42] Félix was authoritarian; he forced six-year-old Bruno to keep a diary, which caused him great consternation—but he had to do what he was told, since his father locked him in the study with a notebook and a pen.

Overwhelmed by his many activities, Félix quickly stopped devoting much time to his children and leaned on his wife. After their breakup, he delegated this responsibility to Bruno, his eldest son. "I haven't got the time, you take care of everything."[43] When their father was at La Borde, the children's lives were organized on a separate schedule; they ate alone because Guattari worked late and went to bed late. Félix was not particularly interested in taking vacations, so when his wife and children went to spend the month of August on the Atlantic coast at Sables-d'Olonne, he joined them for barely a week. Bruno suffered the least from his father's absence because, as the eldest child, he had experienced his father's very intense albeit fleeting presence, whereas the two younger siblings, Stephen and Emmanuelle, suffered the full brunt of their parents' breakup.

In 1967, Arlette Donati, a young nurse who had been working at a psychiatric clinic in Marseille, came for a ten-day internship at La Borde. It was love at first sight with Félix. "In 1967, an extremely beautiful woman came to La Borde. Her name was Arlette. A far more serious relationship developed this time, because Arlette had an extremely rich personality."[44] Arlette was initially quite disoriented at La Borde and rather unsure about what she was supposed to be doing, for which she was roundly criticized by Oury. "There were common showers and sinks at La Borde, so in the morning everyone ran into their analyst while going to wash, toothbrush in hand. . . . I made a couple of remarks to Oury who literally threw a bunch of books at me, saying, 'Go read, you're an idiot. You don't understand a thing.'"[45]

Guattari defended Arlette at the meetings despite the fact that he was not particularly interested in her initially. But when she left to return to Marseille, he called her constantly to woo her back. Slowly, the liaison led Félix to leave his wife, Nicole. When Arlette returned to La Borde, the two only saw each other in local hotels when Nicole was away. Arlette soon found this tiresome and went to the Tourism Office in Blois to find a house and put an end to the itinerant trysting. While looking for a summer place, she found a magnificent, enormous chateau in Dhuizon, near La Borde, where Félix could also rent rooms and where the couple ended up spending seven years. Arlette's status as Félix's official mistress gave her entry into the clinic's activities.

In Dhuizon, Félix's living quarters were very spacious, unlike the cramped accommodations that he had shared with his wife. Arlette renovated the space, taking down walls and designing modern, sunny bedrooms and an office. Dhuizon quickly became a meeting place for Félix's gang, and his friends from the CERFI regularly came to spend time in a little house close to the chateau. They were becoming a couple, somewhat to Félix's surprise. "I was naïve when I thought that I was done once and for all with this type of conjugality. I was getting involved in conjugal life again, and this time it was my own doing."[46]

For Guattari's wife and children, the separation was disastrous. Nicole and the three children had to leave La Borde—although Nicole continued to work there—and move with her extended family into a working-class neighborhood in Blois. "Our whole world fell apart when our parents separated. It was a total catastrophe. It made us all sick. Stephen bit his nails and even his toenails. Emmanuelle had fungus growing all over her head. Things were awful."[47] Life at La Borde had been rather idyllic: the Guattari children, like the other psychiatrists' children including Oury's, led a communal life, took part in the many different workshops at the clinic, and got involved in things as varied as carpentry, pottery, and drawing, not to mention being close to nature and enjoying the pleasures of building birdhouses. Suddenly, the children were spending weeks with their mother and weekends at Dhuizon, where they drowned in the sea of friends surrounding and isolating their father. The situation continued to be difficult for Félix. "The children were gone. Feeling that something is missing. This was the first time since the separation that I could have them for a whole month. The three of them together form a collective personality."[48]

Not only did Félix suffer from his family breakup, but his parents also blamed him unequivocally. Divorce was not common in the 1960s, and his parents strongly disapproved. Their moral reprobation, as well as that of his brothers, extended to Arlette Donati, who was not welcomed by the family. She upset Félix's sartorial habits. He'd always dressed with great indifference and wore a cardigan all year long, whereas she wanted him to be more elegant and worked on dressing him differently. "When I met him, he looked like an old man except for his eyes. He was dressed like an old man, he had a crew cut, and wore thick-rimmed glasses that probably weighed a ton."[49] Arlette felt that Félix was massively inhibited despite his apparent ease with other people. "He was incredibly ill at ease with himself, as if he had never been able to experience pleasure."[50] She was amazed to learn that he avoided the sun because it caused blisters (she loved the sun) and could not believe that he never did anything physical or engaged in sports. "He had never swum in the ocean, he didn't have nice table manners, didn't know which glass to use at the table."[51]

While living with Arlette, Guattari had increasing numbers of affairs. His psychiatrist friend Jean-Claude Polack, an inveterate womanizer, encouraged him in this and considered Félix to be rather timid in this area. Under Polack's influence, Guattari became an impenitent womanizer. The late 1960s was, of course, a great period of sexual freedom, when the future of the revolution depended in some way on newly defined relationships between the sexes freed of moral constraints and closer to unbridled desire. This lent itself to general libertinage: a good revolutionary often measured himself in terms of his ability to break things off, and in this respect, Guattari was virtually unrivaled.

At a time when free unions rather than marriage were being advocated, when sexual exchanges became frequent, and when women's liberation flourished, it even became common practice to hunt down overly tight couples. Jean Oury observed these "erotic kamikazes"[52] with a critical eye. "These kamikazes had their headquarters in Dhuizon. When any couple got together, they sent in a kamikaze within a week to break them up because love was capitalistic. Erotic power was also very destructive, and when schizophrenics were involved, it became criminal."[53] At Guattari's initiative, a group was created to root out couples representing "horrible conjugality."[54] The psychiatrist Danielle Sivadon arrived at La Borde in 1972 and managed to get together with Jean-Claude Polack, a veritable triumph. "We barely got away with our lives. We had a child, but it was considered very bad form."[55]

Arlette Donati did not find this explosion of sexuality to her taste and was rueful that she and Félix spent only Thursday evenings alone at Dhuizon. Félix protected himself with his network of friends, and his close friend François Pain attended to Arlette during his absences. Emotionally and politically, Guattari had an incredible ability to break off relationships, which can be linked to his anxiety about death and his quasi-phobic rejection of anything resembling a repetition compulsion, recalling his phobia about mortality and death. To banish his fears, he constantly needed to find something or someone new, to try new things and spring into new situations and people.

The Arlette-Félix couple divided its life between Paris and rue de Condé from Monday to Thursday afternoon and Dhuizon the rest of the time. But an endless procession of friends came to both places, and on nice weekends, there could be as many as fifty visitors. "Félix's life at Dhuizon was something like the court of Louis XIV. He had his first, second, and third favorites and merciless battles were sometimes waged among them."[56] Oury saw Dhuizon as the Garden of Adonis. The couple went through serious crises. "Arlette fell in love with a guy from Aix whom I had met long ago at *La Voie Communiste*. They immediately begin making wedding plans . . . I can't stand it."[57]

Félix encouraged Arlette to continue her studies and to enroll in philosophy in Paris; she later became a psychotherapist. His many relationships and the general atmosphere of sexual liberation at La Borde slowly destroyed the couple, and Arlette was less and less able to tolerate the constant invasions of friends. In 1974, she left Félix, although she continued to live at La Borde, moving in with friends who lived in a large house near Dhuizon. She also stayed in the Paris apartment, to which Félix only came once in a while. The breakup was brutal and difficult. "My separation from Arlette sometimes put me into a state of raw despair."[58]

Generally speaking, the second "barbarian invasion" in the mid-1960s of protesting UNEF students at La Borde helped accelerate sexual exchanges and weaken couples. Michel Rostain came to La Borde in 1965 and lived at Dhuizon with Félix as of 1969. He cohabitated with Arlette Donati and the two started an affair; when she moved out, he moved out with her to the house across the way. Michel Rostain had lived with his former high-school student Catherine until 1969, at which point she fell in love with Lion Murard, one of his close CERFI friends. Félix was also involved with Catherine, while Rostain became Donati's lover.

Guattari, who actively opposed the traditional family, was very close to his parents and especially his mother, whose hold on him was considerable. His parents had moved closer to him in 1967. His mother's recurrent ophthalmologic problems brought her to La Borde regularly to consult a doctor, and she became close to Oury, who cared for her as if she were his own mother. During one of these visits, Félix's father and brother Jean were looking for a summer rental in the Loir-et-Cher, in Montoire, the famous site of the handshake between Pétain and Hitler. They went to the first notary they found, who showed them a magnificent stone house, surrounded by a huge park with a towering cedar, on the banks of the Loire, where they could canoe. Félix's parents stayed there for thirteen years. As the house was close to La Borde, it became the family's vacation home for the grandchildren and friends, including Jean Oury. Guattari's parents even tried to relocate the Monbana factory to Montoire, renting the local train station for six months (there was only one train a day), but the plan failed.

The situation reflected Guattari's attachment to his mother. In public speeches, Guattari claimed that parents were meaningless, and he teased Arlette when she invited her parents to Dhuizon. It is noteworthy, therefore, that when his mother died at La Borde in 1969, he "repeated over and over 'I am an orphan.'"[59]

TRIAL BY LACAN

Life at La Borde was also organized around Jacques Lacan's Paris seminars at the Sainte-Anne psychiatric hospital and later on at the ENS on rue d'Ulm. As Jean Oury put it, not without some humor, "Wednesdays at La Borde were deader than Sundays. Why? Not because Wednesday is a day off for school children. It's Lacan's fault. Wednesday is the day of the master's seminar. At La Borde, this created a hemorrhage of staff and money. With Félix, the invasion; with Lacan, the hemorrhage."[60] Oury and Tosquelles had first connected over a text by Lacan whose effect on Oury was so dramatic that he switched from biology to psychiatry and shortly thereafter went to work at Saint-Alban. "Tosquelles tested interns by having them read Lacan and asking them a month later what they thought about his ideas."[61] Oury devoured everything that Lacan wrote, attended his seminar regularly, and became his patient, which he couldn't do while he was living in La Lozère, which was too far from Paris. But once he moved to La Borde, he could realize his dream. The schedule of the clinic and the managing team never missed a Wednesday seminar at Sainte-Anne for anything. Oury took notes scrupulously, which evolved into work topics for the GTPSI meetings.

Oury became an interesting partner for Lacan because he was connected with a famous avant-garde psychiatric clinic, which could be both a source of inspiration and a clinical extension of Lacan's approach to psychosis. In fact, La Borde's entire medical team spent time on Lacan's couch. "Whenever anyone came to La Borde, the first thing that we said was that they should start an analysis and it went without saying that we meant with Lacan. We even forced some people to give up their analyst to see Lacan."[62] Oury's entire approach to psychosis was affected by Lacan's teaching, even if he did not consider himself to be a disciple but rather a peer who often discussed things with Lacan directly while driving him from his country house in Guitrancourt to Paris. "I have absolute respect for this guy, I haven't changed my opinion. For me, there is an absolute coefficient of stability."[63]

Many monitors at La Borde were ordered to start an analysis with Lacan if they wanted to keep working at the clinic. On the weekly train from the clinic to Lacan's seminar and to his couch, they practically filled an entire car. Guattari always maintained that his analysis with Lacan made it possible for him to talk about his subjective experience. The sessions were always of varying lengths, from three or four minutes to, most often, a half-hour divided over the course of a single day, interspersed with interminable moments in the waiting room. For a fee, Lacan occasionally prolonged the sessions to include the car ride from his office to his home on rue de Lille, where Guattari dropped him off after the seminar. "That's part of the analysis,"[64] Lacan would say.

Guattari was one of the founding members of the Freudian School of Paris, established in 1964, and he suggested when it started that the school should publish a letter to counterbalance its tendency toward sectarian isolation. Lacan considered Guattari to be a brilliant young intellectual and raised his hopes of becoming the preferred interlocutor of the guru of the Parisian scene, and Guattari was dismayed to watch the Maoist group around Jacques-Alain Miller gain favor with Lacan. The competition was fierce.

In 1969, before the definitive end of their friendship, Lacan played a characteristic trick on Guattari, who had written an important text that was a crucial response to the reigning structuralist paradigm. In the paper, "Machine and Structure," written initially as a presentation for the Freudian School of Paris, Guattari used categories developed in Deleuze's 1968 *Difference and Repetition* and which became the fundamental basis of their earliest discussions and eventual collaboration. The paper particularly impressed Roland Barthes, who asked Guattari to let him publish it in *Communications*. Guattari talked to Lacan about it while he was on the couch, but the master was indignant: What? Why not publish it in his journal, *Scilicet*? Lacan ordered his patient to choose his camp. Guattari was forced to comply and asked Barthes to remove his text from the issue. Lacan never published Guattari's text, which eventually came out in Jean Pierre Faye's *Change* in 1972.

ERRANT LINES

One night in 1965, a truck stopped at La Borde carrying Fernand Deligny; his companion Any Durand; Josée Manenti, Michel Durafour's ex-wife of twelve years; Yves, the autistic boy of the film *The Slightest Gesture*;[65] Guy, a peasant who later became a nurse; and Yves' wife Marie-Rose. The group had come from the Cévennes with neither money nor a place to go. Fernand Deligny was seeking refuge at La Borde to be able to continue treating his autistic patients. Oury let them settle in while making it clear that Guattari's final approval was needed if they were to stay. The group awaited Félix's return for an entire day. "He stopped and looked at me. 'Are you Josée Manenti?' 'Yes.' 'I'm going to talk to you.' I was immediately struck by his vivacity, his brilliance, his very dry tone and his incredible, well-concealed kindness, fragility and sensitivity. It was something like a treasure trove."[66] Deligny was immediately given a drawing workshop to oversee, and his whole group took up residence at La Borde, where he treated psychotics but primarily autistic patients. He already acquired considerable psychotherapeutic experience and although he had a different perspective from Oury and Guattari, he was equally innovative. His arrival at La Borde had not happened by chance; like Oury and Guattari, he had grown up in the Parisian suburbs, been active in the Student Hostel movement, and protested against institutional powers.[67]

After World War II, Deligny had created the Grande Cordée, the first experiment in outpatient treatment designed to keep adolescent delinquents out of psychiatric hospitals. The experiment was born of his meeting with Huguette Dumoulin, the former director of the National Communist Youth, who was also active in the Student Hostel network. "The offices of the Grande Cordée, which had started in a theater in Montmartre, resembled something like the waiting room of a train station, full of weird, nervous, noisy travelers arriving in waves throughout the day, from morning to night, in a state of constant need."[68] The Student Hostel members from the Paris region who had transformed their summer internships into communal life provided the recruitment grounds for Fernand Deligny's trainers and group leaders. Just as at La Borde, these unstructured cures reflected some measure of political protest against the reigning powers. Deligny was a communist, and he rejected all forms of proselytism. As a therapist, he did not want to be part of the national health system bureaucracy. As a teacher, he remained very critical of professional educators.

Deligny invented an entire poetic language to describe the behavior of young autistic patients. A child who spins is considered to be making a *shadow*; a child shifting from one foot to the other is making a *cloud balance*.

After spending some time in the Vercors in 1954, Deligny and his small group moved first to the Upper Loire from 1955 to 1956, then to the Allier from 1956 to 1959. At that point, he moved to Thoiras, in the rocky Cévennes, an area that was becoming increasingly deserted, where he lived until 1965. Huguette Dumoulin, with whom he had two daughters, and Josée Manenti left Paris with him. Deligny had brought with him the profoundly autistic boy Yves, whom he had been treating since 1956.

Deligny deliberately remained pleasant, nonconformist, and aloof from all institutions. He paid dearly for his rejection of institutional life and its laws. The Grande Cordée never developed as it might have and, in 1965, the small group was utterly penniless. They left the Cévennes and headed toward La Borde, where Deligny worked for a long time: "He was in his workshop all day long. It was great for the patients."[69] Despite their friendship, Josée Manenti and Guattari disagreed vehemently about a patient's treatment. "[Félix] made a deal with me: 'Either you do what I tell you or you get out,' and I answered, 'That's easy, I'm leaving.' We were used to teasing each other a lot."[70] Josée Manenti left La Borde for Paris, where she planned to become a psychoanalyst. Deligny stayed for two years in the "greenhouse" where he had set up his workshop. "He was phobic about groups, he hated them and stayed in his corner."[71] Oury respected Deligny tremendously and considered his writing to be quite poetic. "He has magnificent expressions like the 'seventh side of the dice' or 'what will happen to the fingers without the palm?'"[72] His writing was the first published work of Saint-Alban.

In 1967, after two years at La Borde, Deligny had a chance to return to the Gard, where Guattari had bought a large, thick-walled house at the base of the Cévennes Mountains, in a place called Gourgas in the commune of Monoblet. Initially, the house was to be a vacation spot for La Bordians. But after 1968, Gourgas became a gathering place for people who had been involved in the national protest movement. It was an important spot for meetings and internships that welcomed CERFI researchers and a base for activists who had fallen afoul of the law after May 1968: Jean-Luc Godard even rented it for a short time. Guattari suggested that Deligny move in with his group, and he hired Louis Ohrant, known as Mimir, the former leader of the Blois Communist Youth organization, to manage the place. Mimir resembled Raymond Petit from Hispano; he was a militant of unusual stature who had spent two years in prison for desertion during the Algerian War. He and Félix had become friendly at La Borde.

Louis Ohrant moved into Gourgas with his wife and three children and took care of the house and grounds, raised sheep, and cultivated the fields. Guattari also sent his filmmaker friend François Pain to help Deligny edit the miles of film that he had shot subsequent to the Grande Cordée. But Pain left very soon thereafter. "Deligny wanted me to stay with him, but the monastic life there was not for me."[73] For Deligny, Gourgas was too porous: it was a place that welcomed people too indiscriminately, which was not to his taste. "I'm almost sixty-four, every experiment needs its own space, and it's a real waste to see these different guests invited to live on top of one another in the same place whereas, had the space been respected, they would all get along so well."[74] The fact that Gourgas was open to anyone from the far left created a few peculiar situations, such as when the Trotskyite Youth Alliance for Socialism came for some political training and decided to leave precipitously because its leaders could not stand being in the same place as mentally ill patients. Claude Ségala suggested that Deligny open up Gourgas to disaffected young people, but Deligny refused. He remained in Monoblet with his young autistic wards, however, in a house nearly a mile away from Gourgas.

Deligny's letters to Guattari give some insight into their different positions. Deligny was shocked by Guattari's description of his patients in his 1977 book, *The Molecular Revolution*. "Why do you refer to them as *idiots* when you talk about this place? They are children who refuse to speak."[75] He also acknowledged his surprise at seeing that they were both waging the same battle despite different passions and sympathies. As Deligny said humorously, "you need a bit of everything to disturb/destroy the 'THEM' of this world."[76] Deligny corrected Guattari's final "molecular" declaration of the revolution.[77] "If the molecules were particles and not individual people, your revolution might have a chance of happening."[78] Deligny insisted on using the word "autism" for his patients, as it was the only term that integrated the refractory dimension of their behavior, which he liked because it also took language apart. He rejected Lacan's notion that the unconscious was structured like a language, thereby agreeing with Guattari's critiques: "A consciousness doesn't utter itself, it isn't a language effect."[79]

In the fall of 1979, Deligny was planning to shoot a film at Gourgas when he learned that Guattari wanted to sell the property because he needed money. Deligny did not hide his anger, and the argument eventually destroyed their friendship. It had been very hard to find a balance, for the more than ten years that Deligny lived at Gourgas, between the two men's very different desires: for Guattari, anyone wanting to come to Gourgas should be able to come, whereas Deligny wanted to lead a reclusive life there. "I'm a bit surprised by your letter. If we are to continue writing to each other, I prefer that you adopt a different tone . . . I don't see why La Borde people shouldn't be able to come to Gourgas. Why? In the name of what? So just keep your friendship. It's really too precarious."[80]

4

Testing Critical Research Empirically

When Félix Guattari created the Federation of Institutional Study Groups and Research (FGERI) in 1965, he was at a strategic turning point and clearly leaving *La Voie Communiste* and its Trotskyite associations behind. He wanted to transform intellectual work into a nonacademic research program by bringing together specific competencies from the independent groups composing the federation and organizing things such that individual contributions circulated as much as possible. All of this was done out of a desire to shake up entrenched habits of mind and received ideas in each established discipline.

TRANSDISCIPLINARITY IN ACTION

The FGERI adopted Guattari's principle of transversality[1] in those professional areas that depended on institutional affiliations: psychiatry, anthropology, psychoanalysis, psychology, and nursing. Guattari had starting using this approach at La Borde, and others now joined—teachers and professors, urban planners, architects, economists, filmmakers, alternative military service teachers, and so on. In October 1965, a dozen groups joined together, all affiliated with institutional analysis inspired by Fernand Oury's pedagogy or François Tosquelles' psychotherapy, both of which had already proven their merit. The federation's flexible structure made it possible to bring together over a hundred researchers. It was particularly popular among psychiatrists.

To enable the FGERI to "sign contracts with public or private entities for research on problems that could stimulate and enrich its work,"[2] Guattari led the creation of a Center for Institutional Study, Research, and Training (CERFI), which had considerable influence in the humanities. The CERFI reached its zenith in the 1970s and managed to get sizable government subsidies to finance several substantial research projects in health, train-ing, and public works.

To increase its visibility, the FGERI started a journal whose maiden issue came out in January 1966. A year earlier, Félix and a small group had spent an entire evening trying to find the right title for it: Michel Butel sug-gested a new name every fifteen minutes; a weary Guy Trastour recalled finally suggesting *Recherches* (*Research*),[3] which recalled the title of the MNEF journal *University Research*, co-edited by Trastour's wife Renée Trastour-Fernass, who passed the baton at that point to ensure that the review would be well anchored and embraced in the student milieus. *Re-cherches* was initially run and managed by Josée Manenti, Fernand Del-igny's former companion. Guattari and the others who were interested in creating the FGERI wanted to test the ideas of Marx, Freud, and Lenin against current practices and concerns using cutting-edge work in the humanities. "Repetition is death. To repeat Marx or Freud is to fall prey to a sort of morbid idolatry."[4] The FGERI sought to promote transdisci-plinarity, which they saw not as a disciplinary war about boundaries but as a fresh way of challenging the orientation of various disciplines to ar-ticulate the vectors of research "such that their ideas create 'distinctive oppositions' rather than remaining antagonistic structures of mutual misunderstanding."[5]

To claim that the humanities could benefit from empirical studies was extremely innovative in 1965 and 1966, a time when the intellectual scene was dominated by Althusser: *Reading Capital* and *For Marx* were extremely popular and part of the return to Marx after the epistemological break. A detour via social and institutional practices and empiricism opened the way for promising studies that suggested a way out, lines of flight in an am-bience that was scientific and purely conceptual. Transversality remained marginal, running counter to the fascinations of the day, but the FGERI was nonetheless able to benefit from work on institutional analysis that drew from the contributions of Marxism and Freudian thinking to put the libido at the center of the research process rather than at a remove from serious intellectual work.

From his first presentations in 1966 to the FGERI's "theoretical com-mission," Guattari clearly indicated his distance from Althusserian posi-tions and used Lacan to develop his critique. To those who favored ideas for ideas' sake, he emphasized reality. "There is a threshold beyond which you can't go in derealizing history; history has a residual realism; the inexpugnable reality is the contingent fact that we and no one else make and discuss history."[6] Beyond the philosophy of history, his critique also made it possible to reconnect research, knowledge, and lived experience, actors' representations and their words. Guattari was in no way proposing a full subject in control of itself as a counterpoint to Althusser's subjectless process: what was in question was the split subject. "In truth, the schizo subject will remain in the background and be the subject of the unconscious, the hidden key of repressed utterances. . . . That subjectivity is accountable neither to the law nor to history."[7]

Guattari intended to continue working toward the revolutionary transformation that he had always championed, this time informed by his considerations from within society. It was no longer a question of awaiting the "great day"; the issue was to prepare the revolution by effectively transforming institutions. The FGERI was primarily an intellectual organization, but its members kept their ties with industry and especially with the prestigious Hispano network run by Roger Panaget, who created a Workers' Movement Study and Research Group (*Groupe d'étude et de recherche du mouvement ouvrier*, or GERMO) that was part of the FGERI. There were other groups as well, including a feminist group, the *Groupe des bonnes femmes de gauche* (GROBOFEGA), which became active in 1965 and combined historical and ethnographic research with a specifically feminist activism, particularly in the struggle for free contraception, legalized abortion, and sexual liberation. Its members included Nicole Guillet, the sociologists Liane Mozère and Anne Querrien, the writer Annie Mignard, and Brigitte Maugendre, who later became a psychoanalyst.

The first issues of *Recherches* suggested the FGERI's diversity and its rejection of all forms of centralization. Issue 1 included an article by Félix Guattari on institutional psychotherapy, an indication of the federation's true mainspring, as well as articles about theater, architecture, and the economy. In the second issue, the editorial reasserted the journal's independence from any particular party line, which distinguished it from other publications. "No editorial committee defines a party line or selects articles. There are no theories or ideas to defend. *Recherches* gives voice to a group working in the social arena that is interested in analyzing the institutions where everyone works and is receptive to questions from other established groups in other disciplines."[8] The FGERI had no management; its groups met only during the annual festival at La Borde. Rather than promoting soft interdisciplinarity, the FGERI invited researchers to use the language of their disciplines without making concessions to current fashions or vulgarization.

LEFT OPPOSITION

At the same time as the FGERI was being created, a new political organization was taking shape, with Guattari as its pivotal figure, that crystallized the new forces recruited from among students—the Left Opposition (*Opposition gauche*, or OG). The two groups had been conceived as complementary, the OG being the politically active wing of the FGERI network of professionals that emerged thanks to Guattari's meticulous work on "coat buttons," as was said at the time.

The end of the Algerian war in 1962 spurred Guattari's activity and influence among students in the MNEF and the UNEF. Universities were becoming more radical: the UNEF shifted left in 1963, and the Communist Students' Union (*Union des étudiants communistes*, or UEC) was becoming independent of the French Communist Party (FCP) and its leadership. The Algerian war had mobilized students, but after it ended, the UNEF languished; students made up half of the union members, but there was some disaffection, and the Gaullist government created a union that was attracting growing numbers of student members. The veterans' lassitude led to a crisis. When the UNEF congress opened in Dijon in the spring of 1963, the time was ripe for an *aggiornamento*. UNEF leaders were dismayed that students formed only about one-quarter of their ranks. At this point, a new, more outspoken and engaged student generation emerged, largely from the General Federation of Literature Students (FGEL), which had been run by Jean-Louis Péninou starting in 1963, and from the General Association of Medical Students (AGEMPT), presided by Jean-Claude Polack. The spokespersons for these left-wing student union groups proposed to radicalize the struggles and felt that the UNEF should integrate its demands into a general social critique on behalf of a sweeping program of change. UEC militants led the leftist union, and independence from the FCP apparatus was finding an echo, increasingly, in the student world among literature and medical students. the twin pillars of the unionized left.

FCP leaders had created the UEC in 1958 in order to destroy the philosophy cell of the Sorbonne, which in their eyes had become overly agitated and protesting too much. The UEC leaders Alain Forner, Pierre Kahn, and

Jean Schalit all drew inspiration from Italy to encourage de-Stalinization and were therefore nicknamed the "Italians." Their journal, *Clarity*, reflected their desire for change by including less obviously political articles on artistic creation and intellectual life by such people as Alain Resnais, Maurice Béjart, and Samuel Beckett. They sold twenty-five thousand copies.[9] Internally, UEC leftist groups that were even more radical than the "Italian" leaders were beginning to take shape, especially in the literature section; students were reading the works of Victor Serge, Lenin, Trotsky, Rosa Luxemburg, and André Gorz, inspiring revolutionary aspirations in ways where student protest played an important role. Marc Kravetz, a FGEL leader, summed things up: "The university's strict conditioning (by *Capital*) lends a national dimension to its actions."[10] This group was seeking something other than the pure corporatist form of union activity to lead the student movement to deal with the social and existential questions they were facing, particularly because they felt that they had no place in a society whose dominant values were capitalist consumerism.

The MNEF ran the national student health system and was therefore critically important for Guattari, who wanted to connect politics and psychotherapeutic practice. The MNEF wanted to understand the various specific student pathologies linked to the generalization of tertiary education, and it created special university offices for psychological aid (BAPU), which published *University Research*. This journal inspired the FGERI journal and led to the creation of a national university committee on mental health. The MNEF director Jean Pierre Milbergue wanted to organize the student movement around psychosociological methods, which meant breaking with traditional forms of political activism. He organized a series of internships and meetings between students and specialized professionals. In late 1963, as part of one of these internships, Milbergue arranged a meeting with people from La Borde—Oury, Guattari, and a few others leaving Lacan's seminar on rue d'Ulm—to come to MNEF headquarters, which was located nearby, on the place du Panthéon. Guy Trastour, the new permanent BAPU office member who had been recruited as a technical attaché for mental hygiene, attended and was captivated by what was to him a new perspective on mental illness. "They were framing problems, relationships with others, with mental illness, in a completely new way that I found entirely persuasive."[11] Guy Trastour immediately decided to create, with Guattari, plans for a day hospital that would treat adolescent students and young workers. Guattari's network played a special role in this, in a context of people already familiar with psychological discourse, and Guy Trastour, who was running the BAPU offices, traveled throughout France to establish links between psychologists and students.[12]

Another sign of radicalization occurred in March 1964 at the UEC. The FCP leadership hoped to take advantage of the dissent among protesters of all stripes, including the "Italians," "Trotskyites," and "Maoists," to regain its control of the student organization. It prepared a party meeting carefully, assigning Jean-Michel Catala and Guy Hermier to head the troops assembled by the leadership into the brewing fray. The national office was dominated by the "Italians," who were very much in the minority and leaning toward a compromise with the FCP leadership to retain their leadership. Alan Forner's presumed successor, Pierre Kahn, prepared a report denouncing the various leftist wings. But the "Italians," who had no more than 20 percent of the votes, found themselves voting with the OG on the final motion, and amassed 180 votes, the same number as the partisans of the FCP's orthodox leadership. With this tie vote, tensions ran extremely high. The session resumed on Sunday morning, but as soon as it started, Marie-Noelle Thibault rushed to the microphone, announcing in a strained, emotional voice that the pro-FCP group and the "Italians" had secretly agreed the night before on a plan. She described having inadvertently overheard a conversation between Roland Leroy and Alain Forner, in which they had divided up the positions in the national committee, giving each major faction five seats but reserving thirteen seats for the left. The stupefied audience listened in dead silence for several seconds.[13] Pierre Goldman and Yves Janin then started cursing Roland Leroy and created such a ruckus that the leaders, fearing that their scheme was about to come to naught, closed the session. The curtain thus fell on the first act of the plan to resume leadership; Guy Hermier and Jean-Michel Catala, the two erstwhile leaders of normalization, moved to the national office and took over *Clarity*, leaving Pierre Kahn to play the figurehead role of UEC secretary general.

During this turbulent period, Guattari forged his "band" and established friendships among organized MNEF students, UEC members, and anti-Stalinist revolutionaries. The 1963 "minority" candidate Jean-Claude Polack had come to La Borde as a psychiatric intern and immediately became Guattari's "lieutenant." Michel Rostain, another leader and, in 1964, the secretary general of the student union, was studying philosophy at the Sorbonne and was involved with *La Voie Communiste*, but the divergence between the organization's preaching and its practices made him uncomfortable. In 1964, during a meeting near the Pantheon attended by Antoine Griset, Jean-Louis Peninou, Marc Kravetz, and Guattari, Michel Rostain expressed his views about *La Voie Communiste* and was surprised to see Guattari's delighted response to his remarks. The next day, Guattari invited him to La Borde. Michel Butel was also part of Guattari's inner circle, having met him at La Borde in 1963. He was involved in the UEC, devoting himself to political agitation in the Latin Quarter. At the Sorbonne, Michel Butel met up with his childhood friend Yves Janin, who was even more of a firebrand. They joined up with Pierre Goldman, the most activist of the activists, who was overseeing the UEC's security forces. The trio had every intention of keeping control of the Latin Quarter and of warding off the constant threats from extreme right-wing organizations.

But the Sorbonne and the School of Medicine were not the only turfs where the radical-left union was gaining ground. There were breakaway groups in the law school, where the environment was generally hostile, and at the Paris Institute for Political Science Studies (the *Institut des études de sciences politiques*, or "Sciences Po"). In the early 1960s, Assas Law School had been occupied by right-wing organizations, with none other than Jean-Marie Le Pen serving as honorary president of the Corpo, which speaks volumes about the political environment there. A small axis of resistance calling itself the Cujas Association was starting to take shape, attracting young radicals, leftist Catholics, socialists such as Pierre Guidoni, and UEC militants. Liane Mozère and Hervé Maury, who were to become close, loyal friends of Guattari, were part of this mix. This group of far-left students had to show real mettle, but they also got significant support from Gabriel Le Bras, dean of the Cujas Law School and an expert in canon law, and from Georges Vedel, another prominent jurist, among others.

Sciences Po was a less conservative environment than the Assas and Cujas law schools, and Guattari made some important contacts there. In 1964, at a UEC congress, he met François Fourquet, a left-wing UEC militant and Sciences Po student. Lion Murard, who was somewhat younger than his classmates (he was born in 1945), had enrolled at Sciences Po in 1963, where he became friends with Fourquet, after the two had worked together in the UNEF and UEC minority in 1964 and 1965. Anne Querrien, another important recruit from Sciences Po, enrolled primarily because her father, a government advisor, wanted her there. She immediately got quite involved in the left wing of the UNEF and was elected president of the

Paris section of the MGEN; in 1965, she went on to the national headquarters. Querrien, together with Liane Mozère, François Fourquet, and Hervé Maury all belonged to the UEC law group, where she got involved in the Student Center for Union Research (*Centre étudiant de recherche syndicale*, or CERS) and came across Guattari's name while reading *University Research*. The CERS surveys made it possible to link politics with sociopsychological approaches and also had the advantage of taking a transversal approach: the studies considered students, workers, and peasants all at the same time. The action-research drew conclusions that shed some light on the ambient student malaise and were useful for redefining the demands of the student movement by taking the measure of its needs and aspirations.

The leftist shift orchestrated by the UNEF in Dijon led to a strengthened left wing in the unionist organization. The MGEN president at the time, Antoine Griset, was a member. The UNEF literature group mobilized ten thousand students for a demonstration in Paris, where they clashed with the police. The federation forbade the minister of education, Christian Fouchet, from setting foot in the Sorbonne. When the government raised rents at the international student dorms (the Cité Universitaire), it slammed into a solid wall of refusal. There were some victories during the turbulent final months of 1963. In January 1964, the government withdrew its rent increase for student housing and announced the construction of a new university in Nanterre to reduce the overcrowding at the Sorbonne. These concessions, however, did not quell the student movement but rather encouraged further demands and greater pressure on the government.

In 1965, a new front opened. The UEC was supposed to meet in Montreuil, a Parisian suburb and Stalinist fief. This was the second act of the pro-FCP leadership's putsch, which had begun in 1964, and it was an attempt to assert full control over the student organization. The "Italians" had been subdued and had no illusions about being crushed in the upcoming elections. The 344-to-145 vote on Guy Hermier's motion was clear, and Hermier became the new head of the UEC. Jean-Michel Catal, nicknamed "Dracatala" for his intransigence, was the most hardened pro-FCP member, and he took a seat on the stage.[14] The FCP leadership did, however, acquire an unexpected albeit unnecessary ally: the ENS Maoist group, which constantly denounced revisionism and social traitors. The leaders of this group, buoyed by the prestige of the ENS and Althusser's intellectual authority, decided to ally themselves with Guy Hermier and Jean-Michel

Catala to eliminate every other group from the UEC, and they found themselves meeting with the pro-FCP factions in the national offices that had been purged of anti-FCP groups. The purge ended all illusions of UEC independence from the FCP. In 1965 and 1966, the disciplinary actions spawned new organizations, the Trotskyite Revolutionary Communist Youth group and, later, a Maoist Union of Marxist-Leninist Communist Youth. Guattari's network of leftist groups no longer sat among the power brokers.

In Search of a Program

Excluded from the UEC leadership, the "left" needed to continue to exist, and this time it focused on those outside. This was Guattari's plan when, in 1965, he invited several activists to Marie Depussé's home in Paris to create the Leftist Organization and give it a platform. A large group including François Fourquet, Michel Butel, Pierre Aroutchev, Liane Mozère, Hervé Maury, Georges Préli, and his wife Nicole moved to Godeline to work on a platform. Godeline was located between Cour-Chevery and Bracieux, near enough to La Borde to enable Guattari to continue working with his patients and to visit his friends to see how they were progressing.

The UEC survivors found that defining the rules and political program for an organization seeking to be innovative weighed heavily on their shoulders. "We were supposed to be writing the theses, which became the *Nine Theses of the Leftist Opposition*, but in fact, we were mainly playing a game called *la mano*, where people have to guess what someone is holding in their hand."[15] Guattari was disappointed in how little progress they were making, but he used the time to learn to drive: he would circle around and around the house as Michel Butel watched him, amused. Finally, Guattari lost his patience, stopped paying the rent on the Godeline house, brought the group to La Borde, and put them to work: Guattari, François Fourquet, and Jean Médam wrote up the *Nine Theses*. "Félix wrote in a horrible, incomprehensible jargon and he thought that I could fix up what he wrote but I couldn't. He was absolutely clear when he spoke, by contrast."[16] Guattari was basically the voice of these *Nine Theses*; Fourquet expanded and completed the proposals concerning political economy while encouraging Guattari to develop the psychoanalytic aspects and relate them to the political dimension of protest. That was Félix Guattari's first experience in a co-writing situation.

As concerned the *Nine Theses*, Guattari intended to create a new type of political organization that broke with democratic centralism as it operated in Stalinist and Trotskyite organizations. He also planned to draw some political lessons from the experiment at La Borde and felt that it was up to him to consider people's subjective dimension, their desires, and therefore their unconscious. This supposed, however, a way of organizing things substantially different than *La Voie Communiste*, which had stopped operating in February 1965. Guattari and Fourquet spent the entire summer and fall of 1965 working on the platform. Not only did they have to rewrite the history of the world, but they also had to define future directions and link the traditions of the workers' movement to Freudian-Lacanian knowledge. Guattari urged them to prepare the platform as quickly as possible: by Christmas 1965 it was written, and in February 1966, a brochure came out with a preface by Gérard Spitzer.

The first thesis suggested that a global rather than the more typical national framework be adopted in order to better expose what was considered to be a new contradiction, specific to capitalism, between a global logic and the specific interests of the monopoly capitalist state. The second thesis was a denunciation of reformist Stalinist integration of the workers' movement into the logic of capitalism. The third and fourth theses analyzed the interimperialist contradictions and the emergence of the Third World as a new force to better affirm the international dimension of the workers' movement. "The class struggle is universal."[17] The fifth thesis, a classical critique of the inability of socialist governments to get beyond the rules of the world market, drew heavily on Trotsky while also pointing out certain divergences. "We find Trotsky's economic analyses irrefutable, but we find the political and social consequences that he deduces from them problematic."[18] In the sixth and seventh theses, Guattari tried to give an overall assessment of the situation in France in the mid-1960s regarding the relationship between the state and the imperatives of economic and political modernization. The eighth and ninth theses explored the problem of revolutionary organization and the establishment of a period of regrouping, starting with the necessity of creating a new political organization to change the social relationships of capitalist production while at the same time recognizing the impasse of the centralism of the communist parties. "It is no denial of the Party's role as a leader to argue that leading the struggles of the masses has to be decentralized effectively to the various sectoral levels."[19] The small energetic groups of the far left did not provide a solution to these problems, and the last thesis raised the question of whether or not a new party should be created. The authors acknowledged repeated failures and concluded that the time was not yet ripe. It was therefore a question of regrouping and of a powerful determination to avoid degenerating into impotence.

The Leftist Opposition was thus created with a platform and a journal, the *Leftist Opposition Bulletin* (BOG), which used the mailing list of the network that Guattari had created in the left wings of the UNEF, the MNEF, and the CSU. About a hundred copies were sent bimonthly or monthly, connecting activities in the student movement with those in the workers' movement, thanks to the Hispano group.

In 1966, two complementary reviews, born under Guattari's direction, emerged simultaneously: *Recherches* from the FGERI and the *Leftist Opposition Bulletin*, also known as *Red Square*. *Recherches* was redefined at this point: The early issues had been heterogeneous, reflecting the diversity of the FGERI groups, but, starting in June 1967, they became thematic, resembling something like collective thinking about particular subjects.

The first issue in the series "Programming, Architecture, and Psychiatry" addressed psychiatry from the standpoints of architecture and city planning, bringing together the work of two of the most dynamic groups in the federation: the psychiatrists and the city planners. Initially, consultants from the Ministry of Health and Social Services did a study on the La Borde clinic, which had 150 beds but cared for as many patients as did hospitals with two thousand beds. The methods of institutional psychotherapy starting to interest people beyond the small circle at La Borde, and that this model could offer substantial savings made it even more intriguing. The ministry decided, therefore, to undertake a broader survey as the basis for a report on a plan for construction norms for psychiatric hospitals. The FGERI members Guy Ferrand and Jean-Paul Roubier, both doctors, headed up this project. "The results of the discussions were quite positive, no doubt because they put unconscious mechanisms into play rather than simply transmitting information or comparing opinions."[20] The issue reflected a real interest in the government about modernizing asylums where currently patients were crowded into sites that were a legacy of the imprisonment model. The government's Fifth Plan sought to improve the flagrantly outdated approach to mental-health care by providing thirty thousand beds for public psychiatric services by 1975. This issue of *Recherches* drew modest conclusions, as it was seeking primarily to shed light on the various major choices. "We wish to propose more exact definitions and clarifications to enable the well-meaning decision makers who have some responsibility in this area to make well-informed decisions."[21]

Liane Mozère ran *Recherches* from 1967 until 1970. Born in 1939, she had grown up in Beijing, where her father worked for the *Beijing Journal*; her maternal grandfather was a minister. When Mao came to power in 1949, her family left China for France, and she changed her surname from Tchang and adopted her grandmother's name, Mozère. Her legal training and her specialization on China led her to join the CNRS, but she then quit her job for a more collective approach to research that better corresponded to her militant positions. The CERFI, established in 1967, included an inner circle of leaders who called themselves, disparagingly, the "Mafia"[22] The Mafia wanted to bring together various independent groups and use Marx and Freud as their two pillars: they would merely keep an eye on the problems. Above all, the CERFI wanted to become a group-subject, meaning that the members led a communal life: in the name of the refusal of the separation between public and private lives, they risked unbridled passions and emotional tensions. The interest in unconscious phenomena and desire "also meant that the general assemblies of the Collective often turned into collective analytic sessions; you had to take responsibility for your desire by asking for the salary that you thought you could justify."[23]

When Liane Mozère took over *Recherches* in 1967, Latin American revolutions were proliferating: Fidel Castro, Che Guevara, and the Bolivian guerillas. To expand the small OG Mafia, Guattari and his friends founded the Organization of Solidarity with Latin American Revolution; each decentralized group concentrated on one country in Latin America. This organization made it possible to mobilize a wider circle and enabled Guattari to meet up again with Alain Krivine, an old Trotskyite pal.

In the late 1960s, the generation of French youth involved in protest adopted the vogue for communal living imported from the United States. "We'll pool the strength of our labor, negotiate its value and sell it. As for the money that we make, well, we'll share it, it will help us propagate our ideas, the strength of our labor, our movement as a movement."[24] The CERFI hoped that this experience would enable another form of subjectivity to emerge from the "collective arrangement of enunciation" or from a new "group subjectivity" starting with spatial multilocalization. "It was an urban community."[25]

5

Gilles Deleuze
The Hero's Brother

It is the summer of 1928, at the Deleuzes' vacation spot in Deauville. Five-year-old Georges is standing with his hand on his younger brother Gilles' shoulder. Both boys are dressed in clown costumes. Again in Deauville, we see them again; it is 1934, and nine-year old Gilles is pretending to smoke a rolled paper cigarette. The next year, the two brothers are posing for the camera once again, both dressed in tennis clothes and holding rackets. Georges' hand is still on Gilles' shoulder. After that, nothing: the older brother disappears without a trace.

This older brother played a major role in shaping his younger brother's identity, if only as an absence. Schooled at Saint-Cyr to become a military officer, Georges Deleuze joined the Resistance during the war. He was caught by the Germans and deported to a concentration camp. He died en route. For his inconsolable parents, Georges was a martyr. Gilles suffered doubly from his brother's death. Nothing he could do could compare with his older brother's heroism; Gilles Deleuze was insignificant in his parents' eyes.

Deleuze confided in his friend Michel Tournier, who says that Deleuze rejected family life very early on as a result of his parents' attitude. "Gilles always had a complex about his brother Georges. His parents created a veritable cult around Georges, and Gilles couldn't forgive them for admiring only his elder brother. He was the second child, the mediocre son, while Georges was the hero."[1] No hint of this resentment emerges in any other account. Jean-Pierre Faye, who is related by marriage to Deleuze, recounts a strange childhood event that he found incomprehensible. "During the war, my mother went to the funeral of a young man who had died upon arriving at Buchenwald. Young Deleuze [Gilles] was there, completely distraught, his face contorted with pain."[2] After the war, the trauma was quickly repressed or alluded to only ironically. In 1951, Gilles Deleuze was teaching philosophy at Amiens and told his student Claude Lemoine that he had had a brother "but the dope stabbed himself with his Saint-Cyrien sword during a hazing. It made him laugh. He made him out to be an idiot."[3]

Deleuze tirelessly denounced family ties and the stultifying world of the bourgeoisie. Born on January 18, 1925, in the seventeenth arrondissement of Paris, he found the mere mention of his childhood unbearable. But during his recorded interviews and discussions with Claire Parnet, he recalled certain important moments from his youth.[4]

Gilles' father, Louis Deleuze, was an engineer whose small company—he had a single employee, an Italian worker—was developing a way to make roofs watertight. He was forced to close during the 1930s and was hired by another company that made airplane fuselages. The Popular Front's victory in the 1936 elections distressed Louis Deleuze, who was a right-wing sympathizer of the Croix-de-Feu: he and his friends all hated the Jewish president, Léon Blum. Unlike his father, Gilles, who was eleven at the time, remembered the election as something extraordinary and was thrilled to see the first workers come to the Deauville beaches during their newly declared paid vacations. "It was grandiose."[5]

Louis Deleuze's wife, Odette Camaüer, was a housewife and mother who sympathized with her husband's political values and ideas; she was outraged by the invasion of working-class vacationers on the nearby beaches. "My mother, who was surely the best of women, said that it was impossible to go to a beach with people like that on it."[6] In reaction, doubtless, to his family milieu, Gilles Deleuze later liked to say that his family came from the south and was named *De lyeuse*, meaning "of the oak tree" in Occitan. "A tree whose only concern, like that of my family, was to detach itself by escaping and taking the 'line of flight' of going completely adrift."[7] During his lecture on Pierre Janet, a contemporary of Freud who defined memory as "telling a story," Deleuze recalled a vivid childhood memory of his father trying to help him with algebra during a school vacation. "We knew what would happen. I was panicked. Things turned out just as I had imagined. My father thought that he had a gift for being clear but everything quickly went awry. Within five minutes, he was shouting at me and I started crying."[8]

EARLY LESSONS

When the war broke out, Gilles Deleuze was fifteen and at his parents' vacation rental in Deauville. His parents decided to leave him in a boarding school in Brittany, where he lived in a hotel that had been transformed into a high school. The separation was the first decisive personal rupture for Deleuze, who described himself as having been a mediocre student until then and who had taken up stamp collecting out of boredom. But a particular encounter in Deauville awakened his extraordinary intellectual curiosity.

Deleuze was completely fascinated by his young literature professor, Pierre Halbwachs, whose poor health had led him to be declared unfit for the draft, although he could teach in this hotel-school because he had a degree. Halbwachs introduced Deleuze to French literature, and Deleuze was tremendously excited. He couldn't get enough of literature, and after school he accompanied Halbwachs to the dunes. "I was his disciple. I had found a master."[9] Halbwachs recited Gide, Baudelaire, and Anatole France. Deleuze's landlady became suspicious of their relationship and warned Deleuze against Halbwachs' putative homosexuality. Deleuze told his professor about his landlady's warnings, and Halbwachs went to see her to clear things up. Their conversation ended up worrying her so much that she called Deleuze's parents to warn them. Paris was inaccessible at the time, however: the Germans had crossed into France and were advancing rapidly on the capital. So Gilles and his brother Georges rode their bicycles to Rochefort, where their parents had moved the factory to escape the advancing Nazi troops.

After the Armistice, Gilles Deleuze returned to occupied Paris and enrolled at Carnot High School. In 1943, his last year of high school, he ended up—even though Maurice Merleau-Ponty was also teaching there—in a philosophy class taught by Monsieur Vial, who immediately communicated his passion for philosophy. "From the very first philosophy classes, I knew that that was what I'd do."[10] Deleuze once again flouted institutional boundaries, taking every opportunity to discuss philosophy with his professor, becoming a particularly brilliant student for whom the introduction to speculative philosophy was something akin to a revelation. "When I learned that there were such things as concepts, the effect on me was something like the effect of fictional characters on others. They seemed just as alive and lively."[11]

At the beginning of Deleuze's final year in high school, his friend Michel Tournier, who was just a month older, had already aroused his interest in philosophy. In 1941, Tournier was majoring in philosophy at Pasteur High School and brought Deleuze to his class; his teacher was Maurice de Gandillac. Jean Marinier, who later went to medical school, had introduced Tournier to Deleuze, who was living with his parents on rue Daubigny and starting his penultimate year at Carnot High School. Tournier recalled with some pride that he had introduced Deleuze to philosophy, referring to the class taught by de Gandillac, but he quickly acknowledged that "when Deleuze started studying philosophy, he was head and shoulders above the rest of us."[12] Michel Tournier recalled the conversations in 1941 and 1942 with his new friend. "We fired off words like cotton or rubber balls, and he shot them back, hardened and heavy, like lead and steel cannon balls. We were quickly awed by his gift for pointing out the banality, stupidity, and flaccidity of our thinking with a single word."[13] In 1943, during his final year of high school, Deleuze went with Tournier, who had been invited by de Gandillac, to an event organized by Marie-Magdeleine Davy in her large estate near Rosay-en Brie outside of Paris. Davy had transformed the Fortrelle chateau into a sanctuary for Jews, Resistance fighters, those who had refused to go on the forced labor convoys, and British and American pilots. Her cultural events provided a cover for her political work, and she invited Michel Leiris, Jean Paulhan, Léopold Sédar Senghor, Paul Flamand, Gaston Bachelard, Robert Aron, Jean Wahl, Jean Burgelin, Jean Hyppolite, Maurice de Gandillac, and many others.

Marie-Magdeleine Davy was an unusual woman. Born in 1903 near Paris, "she was a tomboy, she hated dresses, and as early as 1908 wore only shorts or pants. Her mother scolded her for not using feminine adjectives and for speaking about herself in the masculine."[14] She developed an intense love of nature and would climb down from her bedroom window at night using a knotted rope in order to stroll in the huge park and along the river on her grandmother's estate. At the age of eighteen, over her family's objections, she registered at the Sorbonne in philosophy and history, learned Latin, Greek, Hebrew, Sanskrit, and about a dozen modern languages. She met Étienne Gilson, who introduced her to medieval Latin, and she went to salons, particularly those of Marcel Moré, a leftist Catholic and militant personalist who later joined the *Esprit* team, where she met the hoi polloi of philosophy. During this same period, she earned a degree in theology from the Paris Catholic Institute and then a doctorate in theology in 1941, after which she started working at the National Center for Social Research (CNRS) as a twelfth-century specialist, where she translated the works of Guillaume Saint-Thierry, Pierre de Blois, and Bernard de Clairvaux.

A "New Sartre"

When still a high-school senior, young Deleuze immediately drew attention when he arrived at Marie-Magdeleine Davy's estate. He was at ease discussing Nietzsche with Pierre Klossowski; observers whispered, "He'll be a new Sartre."[15] During those years, Deleuze and de Gandillac attended gatherings on the last Saturday of each month at Marcel Moré's large apartment on the quai de la Mégisserie in Paris, which was frequented by well-known intellectuals and university professors. On June 23, 1943, the topic was "Christian Civilization," and Jean Grenier, Brice Parrain, Marie-Magdeleine Davy, Michel Butor, Maurice de Gandillac, and Gilles Deleuze were all in attendance. On March 5, 1944, the subject was "Evil and Sin" in Georges Bataille's work; participants included Jean Daniélou, Alexandre Kojève, Jean Paulhan, Roger Caillois, Georges Bataille, Pierre Klossowski, Jean Hyppolite, Arthur Adamov, Jean-Paul Sartre, Maurice de Gandillac, and the young Deleuze. In 1944, Michel Tournier also brought Deleuze to the public lectures by the psychiatrists Alajouanine and Jean Delay at the Salpetrière Hospital.

Tournier was already dazzled by Deleuze's ability to make the dusty philosophical tradition appear contemporary. Their conversations took place against the somber background of the Nazi occupation. Deleuze, who was eighteen during his last year of high school, was protected and did not join the Resistance, although he was in the same class as Guy Môquet, the militant communist murdered by the Nazis. Deleuze recalled his shock upon learning about the massacre at the village of Oradour-sur-Glane on June 10, 1944.

Deleuze did not enlist during the war; with Tournier and others who shared the same nonacademic notion of philosophy, he created a small group. Under Alain Clément's leadership, the group published a single issue of *Espace*, a philosophy journal, in which they openly expressed their hostility to the idea of interiority, illustrating the cover of this first and only issue with a toilet and the caption: "A landscape is a state of mind." The review attacked the "malodorous brine of the mind," as Sartre had described interior life, and warned the reader: "While the attractions of spiritualism decline daily, we would be wrong to ignore the current success of the various modern humanisms."[16]

In his 1946 article "From Christ to the Bourgeoisie," Deleuze denounced the unbroken historical link between Christianity and capitalism, which are both trapped in the same delusional cult of interiority. He dedicated the article to Marie-Magdeleine Davy, his high priestess who, paradoxically, was a fervent spiritualist. The article was clearly influenced by Sartre, who Davy hated. "Today, many people no longer believe in the inner life"[17] and dwell in a technical world that leaves us empty and reduces us to pure exteriority. The article tried to establish a dialectical relationship between internalization and externalization in order to favor the latter. Deleuze contrasted Pétain's appeal to the French to internalize with de Gaulle's act of externalization by joining the Resistance. He considered that the modern success of the bourgeoisie extended and emphasized the process of internalization. "Nature, in becoming private life, has spiritualized itself as the family and benevolent nature; and the Spirit, by becoming the State, has naturalized itself as the fatherland."[18] Deleuze was ironic about this link, by punning on the comparison between inner life (*vie intérieure*) with home life (*vie d'intérieur*). The supreme paradox, however, was that the bourgeoisie managed to finish off the movement initiated by Christ by internalizing property, money, and possessions, things he had detested and replaced with the values of Being. By naturalizing itself, Christian spiritual life had deteriorated. The initial yearning for Spirit had taken on a "bourgeois nature."[19] A vast secular movement had transformed Spirit into State, God into an impersonal subject, and the Social Contract into an expression of Divinity, and all of this made it possible to conclude that "the relationship linking Christianity and the Bourgeoisie was no accident."[20]

In the fall of 1943, as Deleuze was starting his senior year in high school, the publication of Sartre's *Being and Nothingness* thrilled him and Tournier. "Gilles was calling me daily to tell me what he'd read that afternoon. He knew it by heart."[21] The book was a philosophical comet unlike anything else, and it reenergized philosophy in the deadly climate of the Occupation. "We spent that cold dark winter of the war wrapped in our blankets with rabbit skins tied around our feet but with our minds afire, reading aloud the 722 compact pages of our new bible."[22] Deleuze became familiar with Sartre's work before the general French public developed its taste for him at the Liberation. Sartre not only breathed new life into philosophy but was also a writer and playwright who embodied the possibility of combining speculative thinking and literary creation. This was an early lesson for young Deleuze, who never recanted Sartre.

Deleuze devoured *Being and Nothingness* over the course of the week, and on Sunday, he and Michel Tournier went to the Sarah Bernhardt

Theater to see a production of Sartre's *The Flies*. They were forced to leave the theater when a bomb alert sounded, but while the crowd rushed to the underground bomb shelter, the two friends decided to ignore the warning and enjoy the lovely sunny afternoon.

> We strolled along the quays in a totally deserted Paris. The city was completely empty. Night in mid-day. Then the bombs began raining down. The RAF was targeting the Renault factories in Billancourt. . . . We have nothing to say about this mediocre event. We were only concerned with Orestes and Jupiter struggling with the "flies." The sirens sounded, the bomb alert was over a half hour later, and we returned to the theater. The curtain rose. Jupiter-Dullin was there, shouting for a second time, "Young man, do not blame the gods."[23]

Deleuze's very first publication was a pastiche of Sartre entitled "Description of a Woman: For a Philosophy of the Gendered Other."[24] The send-up was a tongue in cheek phenomenology of lipstick that pointed to the exteriority of interiority, showing what was hidden, and it concluded by saying that the woman is not, but that she temporalizes herself. "Makeup is the formation of this interiority."[25] For the young Deleuze, the urgency of the article, which addressed Heidegger's reproach to Sartre for having described humanity as asexual, was to assign a philosophical status to woman. But the disciple wanted to go further than the master who, in his eyes, did not take his critique to its logical conclusion by describing a universe that was distressing precisely because of its asexuality. With women, the Other appears and an interior world expresses itself through her. "Woman is a concrete universal, a world, not an external world, but the underside of the world, the warm interiority of the world, a distillation of the internalized world. Whence the prodigious sexual success of woman: to possess a woman is to possess the world."[26]

The first fissure in Deleuze's Sartrean passion occurred when existential philosophy came into vogue at the Liberation. On October 29, 1945, Sartre gave his famous speech "Existentialism Is a Humanism." Everyone who was anyone in Paris was there. People were jostling each other for a spot; the audience was packed. The press reported on this as an unprecedented cultural event: a philosopher had caused "fifteen people to faint" and "thirty broken chairs." Deleuze was in the crowd. He had just passed his baccalaureate exam, as had Tournier, and both were disturbed by their guru's performance; they never forgave him for trying to rehabilitate the old notion of humanism. "We were floored. So our master had had to dig through the trash to unearth this worn-out mixture reeking of sweat and of the inner life of humanism."[27] After the speech, the two friends discussed their feelings of betrayal. Despite his disappointment, however, Deleuze long remained influenced by Sartre, as his articles of 1946 and 1947 showed, although he later repudiated them.[28] Deleuze chose another path but always acknowledged his debt to Sartre, as an article written a month after Sartre refused the Nobel Prize in 1964 shows.[29] The article deplored the rudderless generation and acknowledged that Sartre had something to say about modernity and was able to establish himself as the master of the entire Liberation generation. "After long nights, we learned the identity of thought and of freedom."[30] Deleuze did not feel like a part of the spirit of the 1960s, which considered Sartre to be old hat. On the contrary, he denounced the conformity of his era and praised the *Critique of Dialectical Reason* as one of the most beautiful and most important books of recent years.[31]

After his baccalaureate, Deleuze was admitted into the two years of preparatory courses (*hypokhâgne* and *khâgne*) for humanities students at Louis Le Grand High Schools, one of the best in Paris, where he quickly became friends with his classmate Claude Lanzmann. Deleuze was a serious student in his classes, which were taught by Ferdinand Alquié and Jean Hyppolite, but, after having emerged from their profound influence, described them rather sarcastically. Alquié "had long white hands and stuttered; we didn't know if this was something that he had acquired as a young man or that he used to hide his native accent and Cartesian dualities." Jean Hyppolite "had a strong face with rugged features and pounded out his Hegelian triads with his fist, attaching words to them."[32]

Jean-Pierre Faye, another classmate, recalls their first days. "Someone in Alquié's *khâgne* class was sitting and speaking virtually from the first row about the *cogito* in Husserl—it was Deleuze."[33] Even as an apprentice philosopher, Deleuze's exceptional capacity was already obvious, and his peers were attentive when he spoke.

At Henry IV, the other elite Parisian high school, Deleuze took a few courses with Jean Beaufret, who was introducing Heidegger's work in France. Fascinated by his master, Beaufret, like Heidegger, claimed that one had to speak and think in German to truly understand his work. The following week, Deleuze proposed a sarcastic contradiction, claiming that

Alfred Jarry was the French poet who not only understood but also preceded Heidegger. Beaufret asked him to be quiet. Some years later, when Kostas Axelo's book was published,[34] Deleuze twice reiterated this surprising comparison,[35] claiming, "we can consider the work of Heidegger to be a development of pataphysics."[36] Heidegger's particular language, which played with classical Greek and Old German in a modern language with abundant agglutinations, had its equivalent in Jarry's playing off modern French, Latin, Old French, slang, and even Breton. "People think it appropriate to say that these are merely word games," observed Deleuze.[37]

Despite his exceptional abilities, Deleuze failed the entrance examination for the ENS, even though his lectures drew large audiences and were considered must-see events, including his presentation on "Barbarians and Civilized People" assigned by Georges Canguilhem. Deleuze got a good grade, which should have gotten him into the ENS, but he had ignored another exam subject and was failed. Given his good scores, however, Deleuze received a scholarship to prepare for the aggregation examination and, as a fallback, enrolled at the Sorbonne, where he took courses with Canguilhem, Bachelard, and de Gandillac, who later became his thesis director.

As a Sorbonne student, Deleuze was one of a small group that included his longtime friend Jean-Pierre Bamberger, François Châtelet, Olivier Revault d'Allonnes, Claude Lanzmann, Michel Butor, and, of course, Michel Tournier. Not all of them were philosophy students: Jacques Lanzmann, Serge Rezvani, and Pierre Dmitrienko started painting and set themselves up in a former laundry on rue de Vaugirard, where they had their girlfriends pose as models. The constant flow of novice philosophers, including Gilles Deleuze, Claude Lanzmann, Jean Cau, Jacques Houdart, René Guillonnet, Pierre Cortesse, and Jean Launay, would stand silently contemplating the lovely naked models. The Sorbonne students, unlike their bohemian artist friends, obeyed a strict dress code: suits, white shirts, and ties. "Gilles Deleuze was already quite original in his discourse then. The others, especially Claude, merely reproduced the pedantic rhetoric."[38] At the time, Lanzmann and Deleuze were quite close, and Lanzmann spoke about his friend with great fervor and admiration. Gilles Deleuze "was very gentle, very ill at ease, he wore a scarf even in the summer; he looked like a child whose anxious mother had been overly protective. Claude was utterly fascinated by Deleuze's intelligence. He drank in every word by Deleuze and tried to appropriate him in every possible way."[39]

During their second year at the Sorbonne, Deleuze and Olivier Revault d'Allonnes never missed a class with Gaston Bachelard, whom they deeply admired. They also took Jean Wahl's courses on British philosophy and prephenomenological existentialism. They admired Martial Guéroult for his particularly methodical readings. "I always found Gilles to be a great student of Guéroult."[40] Guy Bayet taught a class on Spinoza, who was also on the aggregation reading list.

François Châtelet recalls a particular moment with Alquié and Deleuze concerning Malebranche:

> I recall a lesson . . . by Gilles Deleuze, who was supposed to discuss I don't know what classical theme of Nicolas Malebranche's doctrine in front of one of our deepest and most meticulous historians of philosophy. He made a solid demonstration that he supported with peremptory quotations solely on the principle of the irreducible nature of Adam's rib. When he heard Deleuze's theme, the master blanched and clearly had to exert considerable control not to interrupt him. As the presentation developed, indignation turned to incredulity and then, by the conclusion of the presentation, into admiring surprise. And he had just concluded . . . that he wasn't in the habit of taking problems like the one that had just been treated with such mastery and that in any case, as far as he was concerned, hypothetical explanations of this sort were undeniably interesting.[41]

Those who had passed the written part of the aggregation examination still had to tackle the four-part Great Oral exam, which included a Greek text, a Latin text, and two French texts. To prepare themselves, a group of five students met at Olivier Revault d'Allonne's apartment on rue Méchin, near the Cochin Hospital. The group included Pascal Simon, who died of brain cancer four years after the examination; Alain Delattre, a cousin of the famous General de Lattre de Tassigny; François Châtelet; Gilles Deleuze; and Olivier Revault d'Allonnes. This "club of five" was very disciplined in studying the French philosophical texts on the 1948 program, which included Bergson's *Matter and Memory* and Emile Durkheim's *Rules for a Sociological Method*. Revault d'Allonnes recalls that he and Châtelet, who had Marxist leanings, had no trouble whatsoever appropriating Durkheim's theses but considered Bergson to be a dusty and uninteresting spiritualist. "At the Biarritz Café where we frequently meet, we told Gilles that Bergson sort of irritated us. He answered, 'No, you're mistaken, you've read him badly. He's a very great philosopher.' "[42] Then Deleuze pulled *Matter and Memory* out of his briefcase and starts reading, commenting, and explaining a long passage to his pals. "He had this expression on his face, 'What! you don't like Bergson! I'm really disappointed.' "[43]

As of 1947, Deleuze was already seeing Bergson as a first-rate philosopher, and Bergson's work was always with him and continued to inspire all of his philosophy. Marxism and Sartrean existentialism were the two dominant philosophical influences of the period, and it was unusual to see Bergson as a major philosopher, yet Deleuze, ever interested in thinking against the reigning *doxa* of the period, held his ground. The small study group asked the judges, Alquié, Gandillac, and Lacroze, to give them the written subjects in a sealed envelope. The results of the exam did not disappoint their hopes. Deleuze, doubtless weakened by his rejection from the ENS, did not want to make an oral presentation, and Châtelet had to force him by the strength of his conviction. Deleuze was ranked second among all the candidates.

Deleuze's health was already sufficiently poor that he did not receive the medical certificate required for taking the aggregation examination. He had missed courses during the year, and his worried friends went to visit him at his home on rue Daubigny, where he lived alone with his mother (his father had died soon after his brother). Deleuze was recovering from a violent asthma attack and was unable to get out of bed. "We went to see him and as I recall, it was like visiting Marcel Proust in his bedroom with his mother, a little pink lamp, and Gilles, who was having trouble breathing."[44] Deleuze wanted to escape the confines of this world and passing the aggregation (which he was allowed to take even without the medical certificate) made it possible for him to become financially independent. The vestiges of his conflicted family relationships manifested in a phobia of all milk products, which surprised his friends. "We often invited Gilles to dinner. He always asked the hostess if there was any milk in the dish and if there was, he couldn't eat it."[45]

ILE SAINT-LOUIS

In 1949, Michel Tournier returned from the University of Tubingen, where he had gone to study philosophy, and decided to study for the aggregation a year after his friends had. He failed the exam and became embittered against what he considered to be "an overgrown, fat, Ubu-like student and our most dishonest, destructive educational institution."[46] When he got to Paris, Tournier rented a room in the Hotel de la Paix at 29 rue d'Anjou on the Ile Saint-Louis. In 1950, when Deleuze decided to move out of his mother's house, he rented a room at the same hotel, which is wonderfully situated in the heart of Paris, on the famous island of poplar-lined quays, galleries, and booksellers. The hotel was home to a few stars, including the writer Yvan Audouard and Georges de Caunes, the TV newscaster on France's only station. "He was better known than Brigitte Bardot and De Gaulle."[47] Deleuze, like Tournier, rented his room on a monthly basis and lived in that modest, affordable hotel for seven years. From central Paris, he commuted to Amiens every morning, where he taught philosophy at the high school. He felt that philosophy teachers were indulged because they were looked upon as court jesters, which gave him the leeway to be eccentric on occasion. For example, when he felt tired, he played the musical saw for his students. Alain Aptekman, a great friend of François Châtelet, whom he had met in Tunis, where Châtelet was appointed to the French high school, recalls visiting Deleuze often at his small hotel. "I went to his room several times. It was frightening; there was absolutely no space on the wall that wasn't covered. He'd pinned up tons of reproductions of paintings and the shutters were barely open. The place was totally closed up."[48]

Michel Tournier and Deleuze often met Jacques and Claude Lanzmann, Serge Rezvani, François Châtelet, and Kostas Axelos at their favorite bistro on the island, the Monade, whose name placed the group under the patronage of Leibniz. Tournier and Deleuze, who had neighboring rooms, usually went for dinner to the La Tourelle restaurant on rue Hautefeuille. During these years, Deleuze had a brief love affair with the actress Evelyne Rey, the sister of the Lanzmann brothers. Serge Rezvani recalls her arrival at the Lanzmanns' stepfather's house:

> A young, thin girl with long dark bangs suddenly came in. It was Evelyne, Jacques's sister. . . . She had thick hair and a strange night bird's face, a small, beakish nose (she was crazy enough to have it redone later), very thin, sensitive lips, a rather broad jaw, and above all, shining through the shadows in which she was trying to hide them, her eyes, big eyes of stained-glass blue, as light as beaches in the sun.[49]

Deleuze continued writing in the late 1940s. In 1946, he wrote an introduction to an esoteric work (he used a pseudonym), a job that he got through his connections to Marcel Moré's circles, to make a little money.[50] Deleuze claimed that the work was "extremely interesting" for trying to reunify the distinct languages of science and philosophy and thereby realize the Cartesian ambition of constructing a *mathesis universalis*. Underlying the apparently circumstantial introduction, we can discern Deleuze's view of a monism based on a philosophy of life that subsumes all subdivisions, a position that he always defended. "Unity, hierarchy beyond any anarchical duality, that's life itself, which sketches a third order that cannot be reduced to the two others. Life is the unity of the soul as the idea of the body, and of the body as an extension of the soul,"[51] he wrote, strictly adhering to a Spinozist definition. Deleuze's reading allowed him to elude the mystical element in order to emphasize his own themes: the *mathese* was neither scientific nor philosophical yet something that, by transgressing boundaries, presents itself as an "understanding of life."[52] Sartre's influence is clear in this introduction, where Deleuze claims that every existence finds its own essence outside itself, in the other.[53]

In 1947, Deleuze published an introduction to *The Nun*, a major work of Diderot.[54] He was very interested in the character of Suzanne, because she embodied both nature and freedom to the point that Diderot was mystified by his own novelistic tale. Deleuze insisted on the tension of the heroine's personality, caught between two different styles: the first, a style specific to the eighteenth century, referring to nature, eloquence, and sentimentality; the other, an exclamatory free style, in which minds oppose each other in short sentences and stubborn negations.

For Deleuze, the late 1940s and early 1950s were, above all, the beginning of his teaching career. He taught philosophy at Amiens High School from 1948 through 1952, arriving on Tuesday mornings and returning to Paris on Friday evenings or Saturday mornings. At Amiens, his colleagues included Jean Poperen and Max Milner. For his first class in 1948–1949, he dressed in the very classical, strict white shirt and tie appropriate to a provincial high school professor, but his hat distinguished him and became legendary. He set it atop the desk when he mounted the podium. He chain smoked straight through class.

INSPIRING PHILOSOPHICAL VOCATIONS

Deleuze's interest in promising, talented philosophy students was deep and remained intact beyond the school year. From the very start of his teaching career, Deleuze was a "fantastic inspiration,"[55] according to his student Michel Marié. Born in 1931 into a peasant family, Marié had not signed up for philosophy courses in the high school since he was preparing his baccalaureate in experimental science, but Deleuze fascinated him so much that his life was changed forever.

> Gilles Deleuze, my philosophy teacher, was one of the teachers who had the greatest influence on me. His mental grace and agility, the apparent facility of his teaching, the interest he showed in life (sports, clothing, food, the history of technology). I trusted this young man of twenty-four or twenty-five who was more like an older brother than a father. With him, philosophy wasn't the severe discipline that I feared but an encounter, a fusion between a conceptual apparatus, a culture and its languages and learning techniques, its commentaries and links that you learn by reading generations of thinkers on one hand, and on the other hand, a sort of secret thrust, a mental attitude to perceive, to conceive of the simplest, most ordinary and yet most basic elements of existence.[56]

Deleuze immediately adopted an idiosyncratic teaching style, addressing the most concrete problems facing his adolescent students—sports, flirting, animals—with humor, in order to move quickly to serious reflection using the traditional philosophical repertory of classical authors. During the first year, he talked most about Spinoza, although Bergson was also a major figure in class lectures. After class, Michel Marié often walked his teacher home. Deleuze insisted that Marié study philosophy, but Marié confessed that he wanted to become a worker-priest. "I could feel how strongly he was reacting and that I was paining him. He wasn't anticlerical but rather aclerical."[57] Michel Marié did in fact become a worker-priest and worked for more than two years in a factory, but the papal bull condemning this approach ended his career. Later, in 1954, he took Deleuze's advice and registered at the Sorbonne. He became an urban planner and, subsequently, an anthropologist.

Another of Deleuze's students from Amiens, Claude Lemoine, later became the director of the TV station FR3. He recalls the 1951–1952 school year, which he spent studying philosophy with Deleuze, as decisive for his career. "He immediately made me understand the need for philosophy."[58] The son of a lawyer from the provincial bourgeoisie, Lemoine's future was well defined: he would follow in his father's footsteps and assume his clientele when he retired. "Deleuze said to me, 'No way are things going to happen like that.'"[59] He asked to meet Lemoine's father, who agreed, unenthusiastically, and was finally persuaded that his son would study philosophy in Paris. Claude Lemoine got a score of 19/20 in philosophy on the baccalaureate exam and received a congratulatory telegram from Deleuze. When Claude Lemoine moved to Paris and felt lost in the big city, Deleuze suggested that if he had nowhere else to crash, he move into his mother's apartment on rue Daubigny. Claude Lemoine started his *hypokhâgne* at Louis-le-Grand High School and studied philosophy at the Sorbonne. Since he did not want to teach, he planned a career in journalism, to the despair of his former teacher, and started working in the Société Générale de Presse. In homage to Deleuze and the importance of philosophy, Lemoine and his wife named their eldest son Gilles and their daughter Sophie; putting the names of the two children together created the term "Gillesophie."

At the end of 1952, Deleuze was assigned to Orleans High School, where he taught until 1955. He most often started his *hypokhâgne* class with an anecdote he claimed was true. Things always happened to him during his commute from Paris, and most of the stranger misadventures took place during the ten-minute shuttle ride between the Orleans train station and the Aubray station:

> Someone stole my suitcase. . . . A mistake . . . a terrible mix-up . . . in the shuttle from Aubray. . . . So, imagine, I open my suitcase at the hotel and what do I see? Colgates, Palmolives, all of that, the bag belonged to a traveling salesmen. . . . I can still see him, so rushed . . . a big guy, probably a Belgian. . . . They're all fat, in little houses. . . . How could I teach with toothpaste and shaving cream? And when the fat man opened my suitcase . . . in front of his clients . . . what was he going to show them? The *Critique of Pure Reason* . . . and my class on the transcendental? . . . that wasn't anything that he could sell. . . . He's going to lose his job, I'm sick about it. Well, I'm still going to try and teach you something anyway.[60]

After this preamble, the course began with Deleuze taking a piece of paper out of his pocket, slowly unfolding it, keeping it in his hand without ever looking at it. He gave the impression of improvising, but in fact he prepared his courses meticulously. Giving the sense that he was on the same level as his public, with nothing prepared and being caught unawares, Deleuze feigned being disconcerted by his own questions: "Ah! Transcendental, what does that mean? Kant tells us that it is the conditions of possibility. . . . But why call that transcendental? I don't know, I really don't know at all." Little by little, things decanted, the problem took shape, the articulations made the remarks luminous. "He worked by repetition from different angles, practicing a form of spiral digging."[61] As he had done in Amiens, Deleuze spoke most often in Orleans about Spinoza. "He discussed the opening of the *Ethics* for three or four months."[62] But he also spent a considerable amount of time on psychoanalysis and even Lacan, with a class on "The Opposition Between Lagache/Lacan."

Alain Roger was a boarding student in *hypokhâgne* during Deleuze's last year at Orleans. Deleuze's course load included the final year of high school, two hours of *khâgne*, and one *hypokhâgne* class. The class was full of young women, good students for the most part who were there to prepare for the university rather than for the ENS. Deleuze was so charismatic that he changed Alain Roger's life. At the end of 1954, Roger was entirely demoralized; his parents had forced him to register in *hypokhâgne* after he got an honorable mention in philosophy on the exam, but he had just received several disastrous evaluations, and to top it off, his Latin professor had just failed him, giving him a negative grade of −7/20! This confirmed his conviction that he was in the wrong place and that his parents had made a big mistake. Bicycling was his passion, and he wanted to be a professional. His faithful Stella racer awaited him at his parents' home in Bourges, and he was determined to leave the stultifying *hypokhâgne* world, get back to the open air and roads in Berry, and sign up at the local professional racing club. Louison Bobet was Roger's hero (Roger was born in 1936), and he dreamed of one thing only: winning a leg of the Tour de France after having left Fausto Copi in the Tourmalet—"a dream that never happened because of Deleuze."[63]

Roger was prostrate during his last class of the week. He'd dropped his pen, was gazing into space, tired, his bike on the brain. Deleuze had observed his student's torpor, and when he saw him hurrying out at the end of the class, he caught up with him in the hall and asked him what was wrong. Alain Roger explained his discouragement, and Deleuze tried to raise his spirits. "Is it any better in my class?" He had passed his philosophy examination with an 11/20. "So," Deleuze replied, "+11 and −7 add up to what? 4, that's what it adds up to, that's already less awful." Roger explained that he planned to become a professional cyclist. Deleuze took him to the school's library and Roger followed him somewhat abashedly, not daring to contradict him but still determined about his plans. Deleuze took out three books—Epictetus's *Discussions*, Spinoza's *Ethics*, and Nietzsche's *Genealogy of Morals*—chose a few chapters from each, and asked Roger to prepare a presentation for the following Tuesday. "You are going to look for the center of gravity in this triangle, the intersection of the three medians, it's easy." Instead of escaping home to his bicycle, Roger had to spend the next few days preparing his presentation; Deleuze was not someone to be contradicted. The three works did the trick: In 1967, Roger became a professor of philosophy at Blaise-Pascal University in Clermont-Ferrand, where he remained until 2004. He still wonders "how Deleuze was able to foresee that those three names were going to become my preferred authors for half a century."[64] The ethical triangle that he discussed in his presentation for more than an hour became the core of his new vocation.

Roger was bombarded with assignments to give presentations throughout the year, and he never left the boarding school, a tribute to the confidence that Deleuze had showed in him. Deleuze was more than a professor; he became a spiritual guide, giving Roger a four-year reading program and regularly monitoring his progress. "So, how is *The Sophist* going?" "So, how do you like Bergson's theory of pure perception?" The "therapy" worked, and the would-be cyclist raised his grade of 9/20 in philosophy at the beginning of the year to 16/20 by summer vacation. The first paper of the year, which had earned him a modest 9/20, was a response to the question, "What is desire?" and the comments demonstrated his master's determination to free his student from his dependence on Sartre:

> Obvious philosophical quality. Lots of hope, but you're going to have to give up Sartre, at least for a year, if you want to have your talents bear fruit. You will go back to him but in a different way. You have to read Plato and Kant and understand Sartre after reading them, rather than the reverse. Otherwise you will be stuck and you won't be able to make any headway. In a certain way, this is the moment for starting anew, not that you don't already know a lot, but this is the condition for having what you know about philosophy make sense and evolve.[65]

Teacher and student left Orleans together in 1955. Deleuze was posted to Louis-le-Grand High School in Paris, where he taught until 1957, and

Roger started his *khâgne* at nearby Henri IV High School. The two became friends. Since Deleuze knew that Roger was painfully poor, he often invited him out to eat, but as he himself didn't have much money in the mid-1950s, he would announce, "We're going to have fried eggs."[66] In 1956, Deleuze's support once again saved Roger, who had fallen ill. "During the winter of 1956, I got pneumonia, which kept me bedridden for several long weeks in the school infirmary, where I tried to work despite being sick. Gilles came to see me and I don't know how I would have managed without him, I would have given up."[67]

During the 1955–1956 academic year, Michel Ciment, the future director of *Positif*, was one of Deleuze's *hypokhâgne* students, along with François Regnault, a future Althusserian philosopher. Michel Ciment was keeping a diary at the time and recalls having written on several occasions: "What an extraordinary class." He could not understand the reactions of the students of the other teachers, who worried about Deleuze's less-than-classical approach. Deleuze's students never protested. "Everyone adored him."[68] He gave a class on the question of foundations: "What does it mean to establish something?" in which he used Heidegger and Leibniz, both of whom are particularly difficult authors for students who have just passed their baccalaureate exam; the theme also made him draw from Greek antiquity. "He had made us read a book that profoundly affected me, Xenophon's *On Tyranny*, published by Gallimard with a preface by Kojève and containing the correspondence between Kojève and Leo Strauss."[69] He also gave a long commentary on Plato's *Phaedo*.

Deleuze's *hypokhâgne* students were also surprised that Deleuze discussed literature so much—Proust, Rousseau, and Claudel, whose *Satin Slipper* was on the literature program. He commented on *Protea*, Claudel's play, which he considered to be a very beautiful work; he also mentioned Ambrose Bierce's *Oil of Dog*. Ignoring the boundaries between different literary genres, Deleuze urged his students to read certain mystery novels published in Gallimard's Black Series. Later, he wrote, "A book of philosophy should be in some small measure a very particular variety of detective novel."[70] Besides literature, Deleuze was also crazy about cinema and commented on several films in his classes; he was always particularly fascinated by films in which monsters appeared, and he invited his students to go see them. Deleuze invited Michel Ciment, who was already a cinephile who ran back and forth between Louis-le-Grand and the movie theater on rue d'Ulm, to dinner at the Balzar brasserie nearby. "I was eighteen at the time and I went to watch the Keaton, Bergman, and Stroheim retrospectives . . . and we were talking about cinema. He was already a real cinephile and liked Jerry Lewis a lot. He also liked Stroheim."[71] Everything in his discourse demonstrated his desire to eliminate boundaries between taste and knowledge. He was already talking about animals, saying that rhinoceroses fascinated him. As for music, he claimed to adore Edith Piaf as much as Mozart, "telling us that we had the right to find that just as beautiful."[72]

Deleuze had a kind of natural authority and was always calm, never allowing himself to lose control in the face of any provocation. Given his long fingernails and his affected tone, once one student yelled out "fag!" to which he answered, "Yes, and so?" In a philosophy paper, a very Marxist, very "Stalinized" student named Fussmann had written, "the philosophy professor is the servant of the bourgeoisie, bankrolled by capitalism." As Deleuze was passing back the papers, he read the passage aloud to the class, saying, "At first, I blushed. Then, I grew pale . . ." Another student, François Regnault, was fascinated and clearly understood how much it made Deleuze laugh. To break the tension in the class, he occasionally had his students play the famous Surrealist exquisite cadaver game. Each student wrote a word on a bit of paper, folded it, and passed it to the next student, and Deleuze wrote everything on the blackboard. The poem was called "The Civil Turnip" and began, "The reddish one. She . . . big fly. . . ." "We were a bit immature and Deleuze had amazing things to say about the poem. At the same time, that liberated us from the idea of knowing what an author wanted to say."[73] Sexuality was a taboo topic at the time, and Deleuze was rather bold in discussing Freud and psychoanalysis in his philosophy class, something highly unusual in 1955. Addressing the issue of male-female relations, he commented on the "desire to find a sexual partner," which was far from the sentimental notion of a great love. When discussing homosexuality in ancient Greece, contrary to the Sorbonne's commentary on Plato that avoided the question, Deleuze said, "'Don't be shocked, Greek homosexuality was not at all what you think. It was entirely normal in the Greek world. That's the main difference with Proust, whose homosexuals are closeted.' Nobody had the nerve to say that in those days."[74]

In 1956, Deleuze's private life changed dramatically. Through Michel Tournier, he met Karl Flinker, an art dealer, through whom he met Fanny Grandjouan, who worked at Pierre Balmain's fashion house. He and Fanny were marred in August 1956. A religious ceremony was held in the Saint-

Léonard of Noblat basilica in Limousin, where his wife's family owned property; Poulidor became Deleuze's preferred work place. Deleuze wrote a note to his thesis director, Maurice de Gandillac. "It was a great party. Marriage is marvelous; it was time for me to discover that. Under Fanny's severe eye, Balmain has cut loose. Madame Alquié has helped us through this trial in a delicious way."[75] After living for a short time in rather depressing public housing in Champigny, Deleuze and his wife moved into a small apartment, furnished by the Grandjouan family, in the fifteenth arrondissement in Paris on rue Morillons, near the police lost-and-found and the slaughterhouse. Deleuze also visited Maurice de Gandillac quite often during that year, discussing more than pure philosophy with him. Both of de Gandillac's daughters adored Deleuze, who described the increasingly extravagant adventures of a "Mr. Idiot" to them, claiming that he had been his neighbor at the hotel on the Ile Saint-Louis. Deleuze's sense of humor was already one of his distinctive qualities and surely masked his physical and psychological suffering.

6

The Art of the Portrait

Deleuze discussed his philosophical work on several occasions. Initially, he wrote monographs about well-known philosophers. Typically, his work is divided into two periods: his classical publications on the great authors in the philosophical tradition, including Hume, Bergson, Nietzsche, and Spinoza; and his later, personal work. Deleuze himself suggested this way of reading his work in his discussions with Claire Parnet, when he compared the acts of a philosopher and a painter. Just as Van Gogh began painting portraits before undertaking landscapes, so too the philosopher should begin by trying to recreate the singularity of his predecessors so that, once he is prepared by others' thinking, he can begin his own work. Before becoming a colorist like Van Gogh or Gauguin, a painter should work through "potato colors and earth tones, not at all bright."[1] Deleuze cautioned anyone trying to bypass this initiation: "You have to do this work on the history of philosophy, it's a work of humility. You have to paint portraits for a long time."[2]

Deleuze objected quite violently to this depiction of the two complementary periods of his work, however, as having evolved tranquilly. In 1973, he was barely able to muster terms harsh enough to describe his rejection of the history of philosophy. "I belong to a generation, one of the last generations, that was more or less bludgeoned with the history of philosophy. . . . Many members of my generation never survived it."[3]

The paradox is hard to reconcile, particularly since his remarks of 1973 and those made in 1988 came after his emancipation from the history of philosophy. We might consider that Deleuze avoided the contradiction by making himself the apparent servant of the history of philosophy while stashing bombs beneath the pedestals of each master thinker. "I suppose the way I coped with it at the time was to see the history of philosophy as a sort of buggery or (it comes to the same thing) immaculate conception.

I saw myself as taking an author from behind and giving him a child that would be his own offspring, yet at the same time monstrous."[4] Specialists on the authors whom Deleuze revisited and fathered, including many of his friends, were skeptical about his attitude. For those who considered that Deleuze was betraying the authors on whom he had written monographs, he had hidden his positions until 1969, when he described his own philosophical system in *Difference and Repetition* and *The Logic of Sense*. However, it seems more that Deleuze elevated what he considered to be the best and most authentic in the authors for whom he became the spokesperson, staying as closely as possible to the internal logic of their thinking, much like the way that Martial Guéroult worked, whose rigor Deleuze greatly admired. At the same time, Deleuze always maintained something of a distance so as to shed a particular light on the author at issue. This tension infused new life into the philosophical traditions that he renewed and metamorphosed through his readings.

During this first phase, through 1969, Deleuze's major concern was to respect authorial originality and discern the problems that the authors were attempting to resolve. These interweavings turned him into a philosopher who cultivated at one and the same time an art of distinction, a thirst for personal creation, and a desire to break with ready-made thinking. He also became part of a French tradition that distinguished itself by the singularity of each interpretation and by an approach that was "more problematic than doxographic, more conceptual than erudite."[5] Many people, including some of his friends, tagged him a "dandy," not because of his hat or his long fingernails but because he went against the flow and continued to develop his original thinking, which never embraced the thinking of the time. "Deleuze's originality was . . . to have established himself very early as breaking with all the contemporary trends that excited us students— foremost among them being Marxism and phenomenology. Against the current, with his dandyism—intellectual, behavioral, and sartorial— that everyone recognized."[6] It was absolutely clear that reviving Hume in the intellectual climate of the 1950s, during the reign of the three Hs (Hegel, Husserl, Heidegger), was a consummate act of counterpoint. In 1961, Deleuze repeated the same feat when he published a Sadist reading of Sacher-Masoch, a trendy figure at the time. His article became a milestone.

Upon closer examination, we might concur with Giuseppe Bianco that Deleuze essentially wrote about the authors whom his professors had taught. In fact, at Strasbourg University, Jean Hyppolite gave his 1946–1947 course on Hume; his 1947–1948 course was on Kant, and his course in 1948–1949 was on Bergson. In 1949 and 1950, Hyppolite wrote four articles on Bergson,[7] in which he minimized the psychological dimension of Bergson's work and emphasized its ontological nature, something that Deleuze later adopted. Similarly, Ferdinand Alquié, who had directed Deleuze's secondary thesis on Spinoza, had given two classes on Spinoza in 1958 and 1959.

Jean Wahl was receptive to British philosophy and the person primarily responsible for its dissemination in France; he was also certainly the person who convinced Deleuze to disinter Hume. In addition to his receptivity to writers from other countries, Jean Wahl gave courses on Nietzsche in 1958–1959 and in 1960–1961.[8] He also played a seminal role for Deleuze in rehabilitating Bergson's work; Wahl had been a student of Bergson and had dedicated his thesis to him. He also introduced Bergson to the university by giving several courses on him. Jean Wahl's influence on Deleuze was therefore quite substantial, having introduced him to Bergson, Hume, and British literature. A letter written much later, in 1972, confirms the point:

> You ask if you can use my opinion of Jean Wahl in your book. Absolutely. My opinion is complete admiration. For my generation, Jean Wahl was important first because he introduced us to an enormous number of thinkers—Kierkegaard and Whitehead among them—brought them to life, introduced them in France. It's striking that Jean Wahl's books dominated everything that came *afterward*. He unsettled *French* philosophy completely. Second, his tone, his humor, his irony and above all his style. He really tore down the boundaries between philosophy and poetry, much more than Bachelard, who limits himself to commentary on poetry or dreaming, which is an extension of poetry. Jean Wahl emerges like a philosopher-poet who cannot be reduced to philosophy. Third, his very thinking, and the very contemporariness of his thinking: he was the one who led the reaction against the dialectic when Hegel was in full vogue at the university. It was he who wanted to ascribe some importance to the weight of the construction of "AND." It was he who was the thinker of intensities and of the critique of totality. In everything that was important before and after the war, there are signs of Jean Wahl.[9]

HUME REVISITED

Deleuze got the opportunity to publish his first book in 1952 in the collection of his friend André Cresson, a *khâgne* professor who was producing series of short introductory books to philosophy on the order of "The Life and the Work of . . ." Deleuze had been intrigued by Jean Laporte's empiricist reading of Descartes and his long 1933 article on Hume; together with Cresson, he wrote a book introducing Hume: the man and the work.[10] They claimed that the principle of causality and his reflections on probability were the core of Hume's doctrine. "He observes that probability has rules, and that there are more and less probable propositions."[11] If we cannot reach any absolute, the realm of probability enables us to take a few steps forward with respect to knowledge.

At the same time, Deleuze was preparing for the publication of his doctoral thesis on Hume, which he had worked on under Hyppolite and Canguilhem. Since he did not know how to use a typewriter, he prevailed upon Michel Tournier, his friend and neighbor at the Hotel de la Paix, to do his typing. "He was always bugging me to translate something from German or to type his manuscripts."[12] When Deleuze read the typed manuscript, he did not recognize what he had written and suspected that something had been deleted. His personal dedication on the copy that he gave to Tournier read, "For Michel, the book that he typed and criticized, roundly protested, and may have even shortened since I'm sure that it was longer, but which also belongs to him somewhat as I owe him a lot (not for Hume) in philosophy."

In 1953, the work came out under the title *Empiricism and Subjectivity* and was dedicated to Jean Hyppolite, Deleuze's former professor and the founder and director of *Epiméthee*, the collection in which the book was published.[13] It was wholly out of step with current fashion: Hegel, who was on the 1946 aggregation program, had strongly denounced empiricism, as had Husserl. Deleuze's study drew heavily on Jean Wahl's critical thesis against Hegelianism.

Underlying the discussion of Hume's ideas, Deleuze's particular approach was already clear: to start by locating the problem that the author is attempting to resolve, which is to say, to start by asking the right question. "In fact, a philosophical theory is a developed question and nothing else: by and of itself, it consists not in resolving an elaborately developed question, and nothing else; by itself and in itself, it is not the resolution to a problem but the elaboration, *to the very end*, of the necessary implications."[14] What became Deleuze's constant method is already discernible: in a letter dated 1986 to Arnaud Villani defining what he thought was a useful philosophical book, we can see that the outlines of his method were already clear decades earlier:

> I believe that a worthwhile book can be represented in three quick ways. A worthy book is written only if (1) you think that the books on the same or a related subject fall into a sort of general *error* (polemical function of a book); (2) you think that something essential about the subject has been *forgotten* (inventive function); (3) you consider that you are capable of creating a new *concept* (creative function). Of course, that's the quantitative minimum: an error, an oversight, a concept. . . . Henceforth, for each of my books, abandoning necessary modesty, I will ask myself (1) which error it claims to correct, (2) which oversight it wants to repair, and (3) what new concept it has created.[15]

If we apply Deleuze's criteria to his own work, his book about Hume's empiricism is justified for several reasons. First, he corrects the traditional philosophical misreading that considers the subject to be a natural given and that poorly distinguishes atomism and associationism. Second, with respect to repair, he corrects the oversight regarding the essential notion of construction, which is the institution. Third, with respect to proposing something new, his contribution "would be the possibility of *a science of human nature*, replacing a psychology of the mind with a psychology of affections of the mind."[16]

For Hume, the question is *"How does the mind become human nature?"*[17] Deleuze restored the originality of Hume's answer that the mind does not preexist its contents but depends significantly on experience. A second important question immediately follows from the first: *"how does the mind become a subject?"*[18] For Deleuze, Hume made it possible to displace the classical question of explaining everything by the subject, whereas the job of the philosopher should be to clarify how the subject operates.

Deleuze defined Hume as a thinker of things practical, a moralist, a political thinker, and a historian. Yet, for Hume, the foundation of morality is "sympathy."[19] This affective leap carries a partiality that must be assumed. "One of Hume's simplest but most important ideas is this: humans are far less egotistic than they are *partial*."[20] In addition, Hume introduces a subject that is never simply given but is always constructed, a subject that is not the source of the explanation but is that which must be explained. "Hume's philosophy is always a *theory of practice*."[21] Reason is in the sphere of passion and thus remains dependent on contingency, on the variety of situations, fundamentally variable depending on the moment. Hume insists that the individual is rooted in a social universe, anchored in this belonging, the source of his passion. "Deleuze finds the essence of empiricism in the problem of subjectivity and the subject in Hume is his capacity *to believe and to invent*: believing is the foundation of the knowing subject, invention is the foundation of the moral subject and of politics."[22]

Hume also dissociates himself from the overly formalist abstract social contract as Rousseau, for example, defines it. The question for him is less one of taming selfish ardor than of extending solidarity. "The moral and social problem consists in going from real sympathies that exclude one another to a real whole that would include the sympathies. The problem is how to *extend* sympathy."[23] What results is a theory of institutions specific to Hume, who wanted to give rules priority over the law. "The main idea is this: institutions rather than laws comprise the essence of society."[24] Hume's theses therefore imply a new conception of law and a new definition of the vocation of the human sciences, one more open to the psychological and social dimensions of humans.

Deleuze was particularly interested in this redefinition of a philosophy of law, and he continued to develop an idea of law that is closely articulated with the social realm, as a codification of jurisprudence. He revisited this idea in his 1988 discussions with Claire Parnet, where he defined law not as a canonized limitation beyond the *socius* but rather as a permanent process of invention. "In this respect, the idea that Hume forms of society is very strong. He presents us with a critique of the social contract which not only utilitarians but also the majority of the jurists opposed to 'natural law' would have to take up again."[25] When Dominique Séglard asked Deleuze why he had written his thesis on Hume, Deleuze answered: "Because of the law. My true vocation is law, philosophy, and the law."[26] The jurist Maurice Hauriou agreed with Deleuze, because he also considered the institution to be more important than the contract. For Hauriou, this reference is supremely important in order to be part of the heritage of the internal criticism of republican thinking, which limits the principle of sovereignty. Deleuze added, "I was looking for my man in the preparatory classes. Alquié was Descartes and Hyppolite was Hegel. But I hated Descartes and Hegel."[27]

In the same year that he published his monograph on Hume, Deleuze also published a collection of sixty-six texts that he had selected and introduced on the theme of *Instincts and Institutions*,[28] in a small series directed by Canguilhem. Here, Deleuze explained his interest in the institutional dimension, which, as he saw it, depends, like instinct, on the principle of satisfaction. "There is no doubt that the tendency satisfies itself in the institution: sexuality in marriage, greed in property."[29] In his introduction to the book, Deleuze also discusses the difference between the law and the institution, using Hume's argument on the positivity of an institution rooted in the social world as opposed to theories of natural law relegating this regulatory positivity to somewhere beyond the social realm and restricting law to its negative, limiting dimensions. "Tyranny is a regime with many laws and few institutions; democracy is a regime with many institutions and very few laws."[30] Before law existed, the institution imposed its models on the physical individual and on social bodies that allowed for actions to evolve, and that leads one to think that "man has no instincts, he makes institutions."[31] Deleuze credited Hume with the intuition that the entire debate about human nature has to do with the difference between instincts and institutions. There is nothing natural whatsoever in humans: everything is a construction and is in the process of being constructed. A human being is not born a subject but becomes a subject.

Humans are thus thrust toward a future and a specific inscription in the singular realm of practice. Even habits and repetition are part of this productive process. The subject and subjectivity are always located along the axis of creativity. "In short, believing and inventing is what makes the subject a subject."[32] In terms of method, Deleuze praised Hume for having distinguished transcendental criticism, which emerges from an essential certainty in his own immanent perspective. Here again, Deleuze always adhered to Hume's lesson of remaining in the realm of immanence.

So what becomes of the subject? In the first place, it is a duration, a habit. "Habit is the constitutive root of the subject."[33] One of the important rules of practice is to be found in this temporal condensation that social conventions and customs constitute. Hume conceives of relationships as always external to their terms. With respect to the association of ideas, it merely clarifies the thin film of conscience, of habits of mind, of considerations of common sense, the *doxa*, but it does not elucidate the differences, which can only be understood when the circumstances are taken into consideration. "This notion of 'circumstance' appears constantly in Hume's philosophy. It is at the center of history and it makes possible a science of the particular and a differential psychology."[34] At the heart of Hume's empiricism, Deleuze finds the principle on which he wrote his thesis: difference. "Therefore, experience is succession, or the movement of separable ideas, insofar as they are different, and different insofar as they are separable. We must begin with *this* experience because it is *the* experience. It does not presuppose anything else and nothing else precedes it."[35] His thesis originated here, with his determination to think difference for itself and to reconsider the givens of his monograph on Hume.[36]

Hume's empiricism is integral to a philosophy of practice, an involved subject that is inseparable from a circumstantial given. It is these circumstances that affect human passions and make it possible to restore singularity in the various realms of economy, law, and morality. For Deleuze, Hume is falsely accused of having pulverized or atomized the given. His atomism, like his associationism, is the correlate of his notion of the subject as constituting itself in the given.

Later, in 1972, Deleuze resumed his reading of Hume to write an article for the *History of Philosophy* that was being compiled by his friend François Châtelet.[37] He again emphasized the originality of Hume's empiricist approach, which seems almost like "science fiction,"[38] whereas the enquiry underpinning the approach leads to the practical world and thus to daily life. Hume's merit, in Deleuze's eyes, was to have known how to perceive the externality of relationships with respect to their terms and to have thereby broken with the judgment of attribution. Reading Deleuze's 1972 description of Hume makes one wonder if he isn't describing his own philosophical ambitions. Did he, as he said, betray Hume? Deleuze's Hume is at the very least the child of the philosophical system conceived in the eighteenth century and of some provocative questions raised in the twentieth century that revived its contribution. We could consider that Hume's problematic as formulated by Deleuze is "a stranger to the vocabulary of the historical Hume."[39] Deleuze's contribution was to organize some of Hume's propositions into a coherent, systematic ensemble in order to show that the given of experience constitutes the subject.

Deleuze's empiricism was not limited to Hume: Hume was his first effort, but his critique of subjectivity grew more radical over time. Arnaud Villani saw this as an attempt to make empiricism and metaphysics indistinguishable. "Without twisting things inordinately or playing any games, we can say that Deleuze is a metaphysician and a neoempiricist."[40]

A PERIOD OF LATENCY

Between his 1953 work on Hume and his 1962 book on Nietzsche, Deleuze published a few studies and reviews but no real books. When asked about this period by Raymond Bellour and François Ewald in 1988, he described it as a period of latency.

> If you want to apply the biobibliography criteria to me, I see that I wrote my first book rather early on and then wrote nothing for eight years. Yet I know what I was doing, where and how I lived during those years, but I know it only abstractly, somewhat as if someone else were telling me memories that I believe but don't really have. It's like a hole in my life, an eight-year hole. That's what I find interesting in people's lives, their holes, the gaps, sometimes dramatic, but sometimes not dramatic at all.[41]

Yet it is during these periods of absence that essential changes take place, that the forces at work in the movement of thought exert their pressures, whose effects generally become clear only later. There is a necessary moment of distillation that makes one's own path clearer.

What was happening to Deleuze during this period? From 1953 to 1955, he was a philosophy teacher at Orleans High School, then at Louis-le-Grand High School in Paris from 1955 to 1957. He also became an assistant professor of history at the Sorbonne, where he taught from 1957 to 1960. He was overwhelmed by preparing his classes, to which he devoted enormous time and care. At the Sorbonne, he was immediately spectacularly successful. A very young professor for this venerable institution, his course in Cavailles Hall on Wednesdays from two to three in the afternoon was packed. "Not only was the hall full, but students sat on the little platform where the professor's desk was placed. Others had to stand in the corridor and the door was left open so that they could hear. At three o'clock, when the course was over, everyone left, and the next professor, Raymond Polin, who taught in the same room, had six students. Utterly furious, he hated Deleuze."[42] Deleuze also gave a course on Saturday mornings from ten o'clock to noon. According to one of his former students, Marc-Alain Descamps, who came from Bordeaux to continue his studies in philosophy in Paris, "it was spellbinding, I was completely fascinated. He had answers for everything and they had surprising twists; he had a total vision of Plato, Spinoza, Kant, and Hegel."[43] For Descamps, Deleuze was already starting to talk about the importance of iris roots as a metaphor of networking; Deleuze later wrote about this with Guattari when they described the new paradigm of the rhizome. In 1954–1955, he gave a course at the Sorbonne on Aristotle and Hume. Rafaël Pividal, who later became a writer and friend, took the course. "It was absolutely remarkable and even though he was very young, he already had a reputation among the very numerous students who were taking his course."[44]

Deleuze gave a course in 1957–1958 that demonstrated how important Jean Wahl was for him; he addressed Wahl's principal themes of diversity, pluralist philosophies, the irreducibility of the many, and "a philosophy of AND."[45] In 1959–1960, Deleuze's course focused on chapter 3 of Bergson's *Creative Evolution* and on Rousseau.[46] The last course on Rousseau made clear Deleuze's interest—already mentioned with respect to Hume—in the social contract and in natural law in their relationships to the *socius*. The practical and political dimension of Deleuze's thinking, which constantly asserted itself later, was already apparent in embryonic form. On the occasion of Rousseau's 250th birthday, a publication came out in which Deleuze affirmed that Rousseau's most important work was his *Social Contract*.[47] Deleuze's central point was that for Rousseau, the separation of powers is a trap and that the legislative, the power of the law, alone dominates.

But during these eight years of relative silence, what was happening for Deleuze that was essential? The period seems to be a major turning point in his relationship to the history of philosophy and in his emancipation from his former teachers. He still had institutional links with his early training insofar as Jean Hyppolite, his former professor, was his DES director,[48] who was supposed to supervise his thesis. As Hyppolite had been appointed to run the ENS on rue d'Ulm, Deleuze replaced him at the Sorbonne, teaching the history of philosophy. Deleuze already felt what he later called his "detestation" of Hegelianism and of his dialectic, but he was still reading the huge tomes of the philosophical corpus and manifested a certain "philosophical timidity"[49] that led him, for example, in his course on Hume, to omit mention of the central thesis of his DES, which he had defended in 1947 and published in 1953 as *Empiricism and Subjectivity*.

Above all, Deleuze was slowly freeing himself, in a blend of appreciation and rupture, from his two professors, Ferdinand Alquié and Jean Hyppolite.

Alquié had directed his secondary thesis on Spinoza, which was practically finished in the late 1950s. He was a great Descartes specialist and a fervent partisan of dualism against every monist temptation that he identified in Spinoza, Bergson, Hegel, and Marx. For Alquié, dualism alone makes it possible to develop metaphysics around the subject/object distinction. During this period, Deleuze shared Alquié's view of a common metaphysical goal: both thought that reality could in no way be reduced to its representation. In a 1956 review of a work of Alquié on Descartes, Deleuze congratulated his professor for having more than improved the understanding of Descartes' work and for having shown that his thinking "expresses the very essence of metaphysics."[50] Deleuze also concurred with Alquié's presentation of Descartes' philosophical vocation in a movement of singularization "that leads him to break with the habits of those around him, the lessons of his teachers, the traditions of his family, his country, the objective world itself."[51] Deleuze clearly recognized in this an uncharted direction that he took upon himself to explore.

Deleuze dedicated his 1963 book on Kant to Alquié, but their relationship deteriorated quickly after that. In 1967, Alquié reproached his former student for having lost himself in the meanderings of a structural methodology that turned its back on the very essence of philosophy: metaphysics and the question of the subject. On January 28, 1967, during a presentation before the members of the French Philosophical Society on "The Method of Dramatization," Alquié chastised Deleuze for having condemned the question, "what is?"

> I regret the slightly hasty rejection of the question, *What is?* and I disagree with his remark at the outset, which intimidated us somewhat, that no philosopher except Hegel has asked himself this question. . . . When he got to the truth, I said to myself: finally, here's a philosophical example! But the example quickly went wrong because Deleuze told us that we had to ask ourselves: who wants truth? why does anyone want truth? is it the jealous man who seeks the truth? etc., very interesting questions surely but they do not get at the very essence of truth and may therefore not be strictly philosophical questions.[52]

Deleuze's answer suggests how very deeply he was hurt by Alquié's critical assault. After having acknowledged that in fact many philosophers had raised the question of "what is?" (albeit more in terms of "how?"), he said that he was affected by being reproached for having abandoned strictly philosophical questioning, "Because I entirely believe in the specificity of philosophy, and this conviction is something that I got from you."[53] The break between Alquié and his former student was consummated.

During the same period, Deleuze also slowly detached from Jean Hyppolite. After having co-directed Deleuze's DES on Hume with Canguilhem, Hyppolite was chosen to be the director of Deleuze's major thesis on "the idea of the problem." A great Hegel specialist and the translator of the *Phenomenology of the Mind*, Hyppolite also confronted Hegel's ideas with philosophical modernity. Hyppolite had been Deleuze's professor in *khâgne* and had the greatest esteem for his pupil. When Deleuze did not apply for the ENS, Hyppolite suggested that he accompany him to the University of Strasbourg, where he had just been appointed. Deleuze did not go to Strasbourg but did have Hyppolite arrange a university scholarship for him so that he could take the aggregation exam. In 1954, Deleuze reviewed Hyppolite's *Logic and Existence*, published in 1953 by PUF,[54] and he praised the critical distance from humanism and the sketch of an ontology, contrasting it to Kojève's overly anthropological reading of Hegel.

This rereading of Hegel was linked to Heidegger's reception in France during this period, particularly after his 1946 *Letter on Humanism*. Deleuze agreed with Hyppolite's definition of Being as meaning rather than as essence. "In a certain way, absolute knowledge is the closest, the most simple, it *is there*."[55] If ontology abandons essence, there is no second world, and by this fact, absolute knowledge cannot be distinct from empirical knowledge.

Yet Deleuze did not fully embrace all of Hyppolite's ideas and in fact distanced himself radically when Hyppolite, in a very Hegelian manner, averred that Being can only be identical to difference when carried to an absolute—meaning contradiction. In contrast, as of 1954 Deleuze was expressing the major idea that would be at the core of his future thesis, *Difference and Repetition*: it was a matter of constructing an "ontology of difference that wouldn't have to go as far as contradiction, because contradiction would be less rather than more than difference."[56] For Deleuze, the issue was to replace Hyppolite's reading of Hegel, which seeks to shift ontology toward Being, with an ontology entirely oriented toward life.

In 1967, when the break was consummated, the relationship between Hyppolite and his former student had already been deteriorating for quite some time. Deleuze had already refused to have Hyppolite be his thesis advisor and switched to Maurice de Gandillac. According to Alain Roger, one of the reasons for the irreparable break between then, besides their theoretical differences regarding Hegel, seemed to be the rumor that Deleuze had homosexual leanings. "Madame Hyppolite, Marguerite, a very prudish woman, supposedly practically ordered her husband to get rid of him."[57]

In 1959, when François Regnault started at the ENS at the rue d'Ulm and went to the first lectures on Marx around Althusser, he and some friends—Pierre Macherey, Roger Establet—asked that Deleuze be invited. "I clearly remember that Hyppolite asked us who we wanted to invite and when we told him that we wanted to invite Deleuze, he said, 'No, I don't want to.' We never knew why."[58] In any case, their brutal rupture was clearly irreversible. Deleuze did not contribute to the collective *Homage to Hyppolite* published in 1971, organized by Michel Foucault, with whom Deleuze was quite close at the time, nor did he write anything for the volume dedicated to Alquié, which came out somewhat later, in 1982.

Between 1960 and 1964, Deleuze was on sabbatical from the CNRS and thus had more time to explore the books outside the classical philosophical corpus that corresponded to his desire to link criticism and clinical work. Literature became an object—and even his preferred object—for philosophical reflection. He got the opportunity to publish on these topics in the early 1960s. His friend Kostas Axelos was preparing an issue of *Arguments* on "Problematic Love" and had received many contributions on Sade but none on Sacher-Masoch, so he suggested that Deleuze write something. The text, published in 1961, was Deleuze's first study of a literary work, preceding his book on Proust and well before his study of Kafka.[59] He was all the more thrilled to be able to accept Axelos's proposal, because it gave him an opportunity to break with the intellectual taste for Sade, which effectively reduced Masoch to a secondary ingredient of sadism in what was called sadomasochism.[60] With this study, Deleuze killed two birds with one stone: he immersed himself in literature and began studying psychoanalysis at a time when Lacan was increasingly popular among French intellectuals. As of 1961, long before he met Guattari, Deleuze was drawn toward analytical categories. As he explained to Arnaud Villani, a book owes its utility to several imperatives. As for his 1967 *Presentation of Sacher-Masoch*, Deleuze explained why his book met these criteria. "The error is to have neglected the importance of the contract (and, for me, the success of this book is that, after its publication, everyone talked about the masochistic contract, whereas before it was published, this was a very secondary theme); the new concept is the dissociation of sadism and masochism."[61] Deleuze's commentary recalls his emphasis on the question of a concrete social contract in Hume and his vision of the institution as being anchored in the *socius*. For Deleuze, Sacher-Masoch similarly distinguished between the institution and the contract, and his relationship to the contract was absolutely essential.

Refuting the usual assimilation of sadism and masochism, Deleuze contrasted the masochist's contractual practice of alliance to the act of institutionalized possession sought by the sadist. The masochist ensures his relationship with his partner through a contract that gives him free rein for a limited period. By contrast, Sade's thinking belongs to the institutional realm and, as such, is profoundly political, refusing the contractual framework that it completely overruns.

Deleuze also had a second goal, which was to restore Masoch to his rightful place, since he had been completely effaced by Sade. Masoch was no longer read, and in terms of psychotherapeutic practices, he had become a simple variant of sadism in the sadomasochistic entity, whereas "one feels clearly that his universe has nothing to do with Sade's universe."[62] Deleuze therefore decided to retrace the route leading from literary criticism to the clinical practice underlying the syndrome and to disentangle specifically masochistic symptoms from specifically sadistic symptoms. In doing so, his study restored the veritable inventor of the term "masochist"— not the medical psychiatrist Krafft-Ebing, as was thought, but the novelist Sacher-Masoch himself. "Literature is not secondary; it's not an imaginary account of some real perversion. It does indeed contribute and by its own means to the clinical picture of sexuality."[63] At the beginning of Deleuze's introduction to Sacher-Masoch, he asks the Sartrean question, "What's the purpose of literature?" According to Anne Sauvagnarges, this question is to be taken seriously.[64]

In his 1961 article, Deleuze drew above all from Theodor Reik,[65] whom he presented as a major theoretician for having accurately described the symptoms of masochism despite his omission of the contract. Reik showed that "a masochist only feels pleasure after having been punished: which is not to say that he takes his pleasure (unless it's secondary pleasure) from the punishment itself."[66] When *Presentation of Sacher-Masoch* was published in 1967, Freud became the fundamental theoretical reference. Deleuze adopted Freud's distinction between the death wish and the death drive to explain the sadistic tendency to be on the side of pure negation and to draw closer to the death drive. Freud and Lacan both insisted on resistance and on the processes of denial, and Deleuze used Freud's analysis of fetishism to turn it into an attribute of masochism. "Masoch's principal fetishes and those of his heroes include furs, shoes, the whip itself, and strange hats with which he liked to decorate women."[67] The confusion between the two symptomatologies, which led to a single sadomasochism, was not the fault of Freud, who had always distinguished between the two different kinds of behavior. Even before meeting Guattari in 1969, Deleuze was already disputing analytical theory in his critique of the Oedipal structure and the status of castration in Freudian theory. Deleuze viewed analysts as being singularly reductive in their quest to find the paternal image beneath the masochistic ideal at all costs. It was not that he disagreed that the father played a major role in sadism, which develops on the basis of the negation of the maternal figure, but he found it inappropriate to extend this to masochism. On the contrary, the masochist lives in an intermaternal symbolic world in which the types of feminine ideal compose a symbolic order from which the figure of the father is absent, eliminated. In this respect, Deleuze uses Lacan's theory of the foreclosure of "the name of the father." "Lacan articulated a fundamental law according to which whatever is symbolically abolished returns in reality in a hallucinatory form."[68] Deleuze also drew from what he considered to be Freud's masterpiece, *Beyond the Pleasure Principle*, which he praised as a brilliant incursion onto the philosophical continent. The pleasure principle governs everything, without exception, but tolerates complications, sources of externality, of the production of an irreducible residue of a beyond that opens again onto philosophical reflection. This externality pushes Freud to propose a transcendental principle. Eros is thus trapped in the principle of repetition. "You have to understand that repetition, as Freud defines it in his brilliant work, is itself a synthesis of time, a 'transcendental' synthesis of time. It is at one and the same time the repetition of what happened before, during, and after."[69] But Deleuze abandons Freud to disentangle the pleasure principle from the masochist's principle of desire. This unlinking leads the masochist to a double process of desexualization and of resexualization around the repetition principle. Deleuze was proclaiming a central theme of *Anti-Oedipus* when he argued against Freud's views on castration and guilt. "They become too easy, insofar as they serve to reverse situations and to make truly foreign worlds communicate in the abstract."[70]

KANT, UNAVOIDABLY

In 1963, Deleuze wrote a study on Kant, even though Kant was not a member of Deleuze's philosophical pantheon.[71] Deleuze said that he had written this book against an "enemy," even though it was clear that Kant fascinated him: "When you find yourself reading the work of such a genius, there can be no question of saying that you don't agree. First you have to know how to admire, then you identify the problems that he raises, his particular machinery. Admiration leads you to the real critique."[72] In addition to this book, in 1963 Deleuze also published an article on Kant's aesthetics,[73] and he taught several courses on Kant, first at the Sorbonne in the late 1950s and then at the University of Vincennes in 1978. In 1986, he published a long article on the theme of a Kantian "poetic."[74]

Kant's genius, as Deleuze saw it, was to have discovered that man is composed of two faculties that are different in nature: intuition, or receptivity, on the one hand, having to do with experience whose source is sensitivity, and, on the other hand, the concept whose source lies in understanding, which defines the form of knowledge, its *arrangement* in the sentient being. Kant perceives a gap between these two different dimensions and was the first to define human beings on the basis of it: this is his fundamental contribution to modernity. Whereas in the seventeenth century, thought was reflected in infinity, as in Descartes and Leibniz, with infinity taking precedence over finitude, with Kant, intuition and understanding become incommensurable, and the principle of finitude is made into a constitutive principle. This was a profound revolution: experience and the concept no longer overlap each other; the gap cannot be filled or overcome. As he observes the difference in their nature between space-time and the "cogito," Kant questions the conditions of knowledge. Clearly unable to dispense with the gap, he then introduces a third faculty, whose function is to put the first two into relationship; this third faculty Kant calls the "schematism of the imagination." The Cartesian cogito was fissured, well before the advent of psychoanalysis.

In *Kant's Critical Philosophy*, which Deleuze dedicated to his teacher Ferdinand Alquié, Deleuze traces the evolution of the idea of the faculty in the three "Critiques." Kant's Copernican revolution was to submit the object to the subject rather than to presuppose that subject and object were harmonious. "The first thing that the Copernican revolution teaches us is that we are the masters. . . . Kant contrasts wisdom with the critical image:

we, the legislators of Nature."[75] In the *Critique of Pure Reason*, phenomena are subjected to categories, which, as concepts produced by understanding, become the object of a transcendental deduction. Reason legislates, but under the impulse of the desiring faculty, which is to say, under the reign of practical reason, of free will. Yet this independent exercise can only be carried out under a regime of freedom. At the very heart of the transcendental approach, therefore, Kant locates a use of immanence that becomes one of his preferred themes. "The transcendental method is always the determination of an *immanent* use of reason, in accordance with one of its interests."[76] Deleuze always argued for transcendental criticism while believing that Nietzsche, more than Kant, had achieved the fundamental exigency of immanence.

The quest for immanence becomes part of Deleuze's philosophical concern without satisfying it, because Kant stopped midway, by reducing the transcendental dimension to the conditions of a possible experience. Kant thus condemned himself to recognition, to a copy of the authenticated real, and, as Deleuze saw it, fell back into the meanderings of psychological consciousness. To the contrary, Deleuze argued in his thesis on the receptivity to other, more creative, modalities of thought than that of the simple recognition of the same, which can only be reached by insisting on difference for itself.[77] In this, he changed the understanding of the very notion of "faculty," which is always understood as an attitude or a general cognitive function awaiting its specific "possible" contents but which becomes a specific force each time, a force that can affect or be affected by an equally singular phenomenon. "There are therefore multiple modes (in the Spinozan sense) of thinking, of feeling, of remembering, of fantasizing, of speaking . . . that constitute as many distinct faculties, created each time through contact with phenomena or singular works."[78]

Deleuze's relationship to Kant was not simply negative. Vincent Descombes even presents it as pursuing Kant's critical work on ideas of soul, world, and God. "Gilles Deleuze is first and foremost a post-Kantian."[79] Kant is the philosopher to have reached certain limits, like that of time, the subject, and thought, "without ever having dared to breach them."[80] Deleuze tried to go from the Kantian mold to a construction of his own map of Kantian theses. He takes leave of the Kantian duality, where multiplicity is ordered by time that Kant sees as uniform, homogenous, and irreversible, contrary to an approach wherein time is the expression of unplumbable depths. Deleuze, by contrast, argues for a "*heterogeneous temporality* whose fragments can no longer be reassembled according to the idea of a restored totality."[81] Using an approach that he calls transcendental empiricism, he can thus liberate the event's explosive power and specificities. "Only when the world, teeming with anonymous and nomadic, impersonal and preindividual singularities, opens up, do we tread at last on the field of the transcendental."[82]

PROUST IN SEARCH OF TRUTH

In 1964, a year after publishing his book on Kant, Deleuze turned once again to literature and published a book on Proust.[83] He was in this way affirming his determination to bring philosophical reflection to bear on realms ignored by the academic tradition; this was his way of liberating himself from the classical history of philosophy.[84] *Proust and Signs* was his effort to correct the very common error among literary critics of viewing Proust's masterpiece as a work about memory. "What is the unity of *In Search of Things Past*? We know at least what it does not consist in. It does not consist in memory, in recall, even involuntary memory."[85] For Deleuze, Proust's work used memory not as a tool but as a means for reaching truth. "*In Search of Things Past* is, in fact, the search for truth."[86] The quest can only be set into motion by a constraint or violent situation that calls it forth, and for Proust, jealousy is the essential trigger. For Deleuze, the Proustian hero falls in love in order to be able to express his desire to be jealous. In this respect, as a *Bildungsroman*, the novel looks not to the past but rather to the future.

The second correction that Deleuze made to Proustian criticism was to repair a major oversight in the analysis of Proust's work: the universe of signs, which he felt constituted the very unity of Proustian writing. "The word "sign" is one of the most frequent words in the *In Search of Things Past*."[87] Each social segment is compartmentalized, and members recognize one another by their common signs. The Verdurins' signs have little in common with those of the Guermantes, and these are therefore a plurality of incommensurable worlds comprising the narrator's social and sentimental universe. We can discern some coherent subsets among the signs, including signs indicating that one belongs to a particular sophisticated class, signs specific to being in love, or the sign designating sensitive qualities. But the world of Art subsumes the whole; Art plays the role of the ultimate world of signs that are "dematerialized," which "find their meaning in an ideal essence. Thenceforth, the revealed world of Art reacts on all the others."[88] Art is thus given a privileged position insofar as it is the mediation without which the interpretation of signs could not get beyond their apparent opacity.

For Deleuze, a useful book is one that invents a new concept. His work on Proust elucidates the fertility of the notion of "capture." Deleuze takes the capture between two elements: the one, animal—a wasp—and the other, vegetal—an orchid—to a conceptual level; the wasp fertilizing the orchid by transgressing the rules of division between the two worlds. Deleuze rereads the first chapter of *Sodom and Gomorrah* conceptually, where Proust devotes no fewer than thirty pages to the metaphor of the wasp and the orchid, and turns it into a way for philosophy to fertilize literature and vice versa. Moreover, Deleuze concludes his book by observing that the search for truth in Proust's work rivals philosophy's ambition. The image of thought, as Proust understood it, "takes on that which is most essential in classical philosophy of the rationalist type."[89] By signifying that truths belong neither to the arbitrary nor to abstraction, Proust's work has some philosophical import. These truths are to be sought within the zones of opacity where the forces at work in the movements of the mind operate. Underlying the conventions of regulated communication, these subterranean forces are the veritable triggers of thought. The connectors setting thought into motion are the signs themselves that are to be "always interpreted, which is to say, explained, developed, deciphered."[90]

It is noteworthy that whereas Deleuze was innovative in treating literature as a symptomatology, making a clinical examination in line with what he had done with Sacher-Masoch, he still adhered to an entire tradition for which thinking is interpreting. Robert Mauzi, a specialist of French literature, points out the originality of Deleuze's reading of Proust by paying attention to the narrator's temporality rather than to the less important and ignored temporality of the writer; Deleuze does not examine Proust's intentionality; he merely deciphers his universe of signs. "The idea of addressing Proustian subjectivity had to be abandoned, and we have to acknowledge that it is refreshing to read an essay on Proust from which all psychoanalytic or psychological themes have been eliminated."[91]

The philosopher Jean-Claude Dumoncel sees Deleuze's reading of Proust as the key to his thinking, and he claims that what later emerges as an abstract personal thesis—*Difference and Repetition*—finds its most legible expression and veritable thread in the Proustian narration, which amounts to considering that "difference is what gives repetition its object. Repetition only ever receives its degree of difference. It's difference that must be repeated and Proust recounts only this for hundreds of pages."[92] Jean-Claude Dumoncel finds Deleuze's philosophical reading of Proust all the more valid in that Proust claimed Gabriel Tarde and Henri Bergson as his two philosophical sources of inspiration.

In Search of Things Past unfolds between what Deleuze calls "free differences," which make things vibrate, and "complex repetitions," which show themselves as vibrating waves that relate to each in a way that recalls the relationship between thunder and lightning. The waves, however, are not simple repetitions: "Undulation, unlike iteration, is a way of *not* repeating."[93] Vibrating repetition bears within itself potential differences in time. Proust examines the way in which reminiscences that seem to belong to the register of associations emerge into consciousness, like "the taste of the madeleine resembles that of the madeleines that we used to have at tea in Combray, and it resuscitates Combray, where we tasted it for the first time."[94] In this way, he likens his notion to the Bergsonian conception of memory where two "presents" coexist: the present that calls forth another present that was but is no longer and that is evoked only by the presents that recompose it without ever reaching the being of the past being. "The essence of time escapes us."[95] Involuntary memory internalizes the old context that becomes inseparable from the present moment; what is essential therefore is not resemblance but, to the contrary, *"the internalized difference become immanent."*[96] Deleuze entitles his conclusion "The Image of Thought," and we can take the measure of the permanence of this theme of quest throughout his writings, as it is also the title of the very important third chapter of *Difference and Repetition*, where "the image of thought" is the boundary of his exploration of the cinematographic universe in the 1980s.[97] In 1968, when Nietzsche's complete works were published, Deleuze affirmed this fundamental axis in his thinking, which runs through all of his monographs. "Hume, Bergson, and Proust interest me because there are profound elements for a new image of thought in their work. There is something extraordinary in the way that they say to us: thinking does not mean what you think. . . . Yes, a new image of the act of thinking, of the way thought operates, of its genesis in thought itself, that is what we are looking for."[98]

At the same time, the various editions of *Proust and Signs* vary slightly. Originally published in 1964, the 1970 and 1976 editions were somewhat modified. Between the first and second editions, Deleuze met Guattari, whose influence is discernible, and Deleuze, who adopted his theme of transversality, acknowledges his contribution. "With respect to psychoanalytic research, Félix Guattari has created the very productive concept of 'transversality' to take into account the communication and relationships of the unconscious."[99] Transversals were fundamental for understanding the transition from one closed world to another, which does not destroy the specificity of either world but which, without there being any possibility of totalization or confusion, makes it possible to go from one universe of signs to another. These transversals lead the transition from one Albertine to another for privileged passers such as Swann. The transversalities make encounters possible; they make it possible to produce a new flux without endangering the existence of plurality, "without ever reducing the multiple to the One, without ever grouping the multiple into a whole."[100] There are all sorts of transversals: jealousy for amorous multiplicity, a trip for the multiplicity of places, and sleep for the multiplicity of moments.

7

Nietzsche, Bergson, Spinoza
A Trio for a Vitalist Philosophy

NIETZSCHE: ONE OF THREE MASTERS OF SUSPICION

Nietzsche was fundamental for Deleuze as he was formalizing his own philosophical positions. He read Nietzsche as he read other philosophers. First, he repaired the error of interpreting the eternal return as a simple return of the same in obedience to a cyclical law. Then, he and others helped restore the critical, corrosive, progressive aspect of Nietzsche's thinking, which had been primarily used, until that point, to comfort reactionary and elitist positions. Finally, he drew his major concept of difference from Nietzsche as resulting from the liberation of the will to power.

The Germanist Jacques Le Rider aptly described Nietzsche's generally very conservative reception in prewar France. During World War II, however, things became very different: the small group around Marcel Moré, including Georges Bataille, Jean Wahl, Jean Hyppolite, and a very young Deleuze, proposed an entirely different reading of Nietzsche. Canguilhem's influence was also important: in the thesis that he defended in 1943, *Essay on Some Problems Concerning the Normal and the Pathological*, he rejected any evolutionary vision of reason that continued to progress, arguing instead for a resolutely Nietzschean perspective. Deleuze found in him above all a reformulation of the will to power as a "vital normativity," of life as an act of creation or of the institution of new norms.

In 1946, the French Society for Nietzsche Studies was created (and remained active until 1965) "with no political objective or intention to proselytize whatsoever, to help make Nietzsche's work better known by retrieving it from the level of tendentious propaganda to that of thoroughgoing objectivity and informed critique."[1] Deleuze was an active member of the group, whose president, Jean Wahl, gave two courses on Nietzsche

in 1958–1959 and 1960–1961.[2] During the 1950s, Nietzsche's work was starting to be translated, published, and edited, and on the fiftieth anniversary
of Nietzsche's death, the society produced an inventory of the situation.[3]
In addition, an ambitious project to publish his complete works was
launched under the supervision of Deleuze and Maurice de Gandillac. This
places Deleuze's 1962 *Nietzsche and Philosophy* in this tremendous resurgence of interest in Nietzschean studies.[4] However, the reader of Deleuze's
work is immediately aware of the novelty of the approach and perspective
emerging from it.

With Nietzsche, Deleuze was not simply exhuming a vast philosophical
enterprise sandwiched among successive layers of commentary that had
perverted its message. He gave a polemical twist to his work, challenging
the Hegelian dialectic to show how forcefully Nietzsche's ideas attacked
the entire history of philosophy. Nietzsche's philosophy, a "philosophy of
suspicion," according to Paul Ricoeur, functioned by "hammer blows" to
lay out a philosophy of concepts of sense and value, relegating the question
of truth to a secondary level. Nietzsche offered a specific, "genealogical"
approach that did not depend on any particular tribunal of values: "Genealogy means both the value of origin and the origin of values."[5] With respect
to this, Nietzsche rejected any effort to make values absolute; the meaning
of every phenomenality was always to be linked to various viewpoints
bearing them and to the active forces comprising their dynamic. Philosophy's job was to locate this play of forces in what Deleuze called a "symptomatology" or "semeiology."[6] This reevalution of meaning was not meant
to lead to taking refuge in hermeneutics in order to discover some imagined
lost, veiled, or eradicated original meaning. From a Nietzschean perspective, meaning is not part of an already present reservoir but is rather a
produced effect, and the proper undertaking is to discern the laws of production. The history of a phenomenon is first and foremost the history of
the forces having captured it and modified its meaning.

By emphasizing the affirmative "yes," Deleuze presented Nietzsche as
the anti-Hegel and antidialectician. Canguilhem had already considerably
weakened the Hegelian notion of continuity, and Deleuze extended his critique by challenging his concepts of negation and contradiction, which run
philosophy into a dead end because it remains fundamentally a prisoner of
an initial identity whose negation is no more than its double. In this, Deleuze
proposed the concept of difference, which became the core of his thesis
and the line running through all of his thinking. A philosophy of the will

affirms difference, and Deleuze set out to valorize the "differential" in Nietzsche's ideas. Rather than the Christian culture of resentment and guilt, Nietzsche proposes a sovereign individual freed of the morality of customs, "the man who can promise."[7] In this, Nietzsche saw a superior form of responsibility. And, as he usually did, Deleuze "betrayed" Nietzsche, changing this lesson into an exaltation of mankind freed from morality and thus irresponsible. "Irresponsibility, Nietzsche's most noble and beautiful secret."[8]

The pole of reactivity contrasts with that of activity, of the will to power, and can lead to the figure of the superman addressed in book 4 of *Thus Spoke Zarathustra*. Here again, the totalitarian or merely conservative manipulations of Nietzsche's ideas were based on a misinterpretation of the meaning of this superman, which Nietzsche never linked to an exaltation of any kind of power over anyone. His superman attempts less to convert reaction into action than to change negation into affirmation, the very being toward which all humanity tends, according to Nietzsche. This reading of Nietzsche clearly seems to take its source from Spinoza, the other great inspiration of Deleuze's vitalist philosophy.

As for the eternal return, with respect to Nietzschean doctrine, Deleuze's interpretation resembles no other. Arguing against the notion that everything that is produced returns in cyclical movements, Deleuze sees the eternal return as the result of a selection of the strong and an elimination of the weak. "It makes of will something whole. The thought of the eternal return eliminates from will everything which falls outside the eternal return, it makes of will a creation, it carries out the equation 'to will = to create.'"[9] Only differences return; the return is not that of the same but of the other.

What emerges from reading Nietzsche is a new task for philosophy, which should no longer reflect its time but should venture into a more radical critique of its time, raising contentious, untimely questions allowing creative forces to surge forth. The method of choice is "dramatization," which consists in shifting the traditional metaphysical question of "what is?" to "who?" to restore the forces operating in the phenomenon being examined. The concept is therefore to be linked to will so as to account for the concrete universe of life. Philosophy thus takes its distance from its Platonic inspiration by abandoning the question of essence—what is righteousness? what is beauty?—that leads to a dualism opposing the essence of a phenomenon to its appearance. In 1967, the "dramatization method" that Deleuze discussed beyond Nietzsche's theses led to a possible typology of forces according to their active or reactive qualities.[10] This is added to a symptomatology that interprets phenomena on the basis of the forces that produce them and a genealogy that evaluates forces as a function of their will to power—in other words, philosophy with three functions: an artistic function, thanks to the typology; a clinical function, because of the symptomatology; and a legislative function, through its genealogy.

Jean Wahl, who shepherded the return to a favorable view of Nietzsche, lengthily reviewed Deleuze's book in the *Review of Metaphysics and Morality*: he recognized it as a great book and among the best readings of Nietzsche. But with respect to the "originality" of Deleuze's reading, Wahl was somewhat reticent about the polemical tone targeting Hegel, which he attributed to "some sort of resentment,"[11] since he saw Nietzsche as not so far from Hegel in many ways. While Wahl viewed the pages on the dialectic to be among the finest in the book, he also considered Deleuze's criticisms of Hegel to be as superficial as those of the Marxist thinkers, although he agreed on the need for a critical examination of Hegel. At the same time, Wahl paid tribute to the book's conclusion, urging a "new image of thinking" that continued Nietzsche's work by insisting on the forces required to make thinking active and creative. But Wahl thought that Deleuze's interpretation was risky. "There are two dangers or at least two difficulties in this profound and interesting interpretation: the difficulty of having the negative disappear entirely, and another difficulty that would arise were the positive to no longer appear as much as it should."[12]

Just after his book was published, Deleuze organized a colloquium on Nietzsche at Royaumont Abbey from July 4 through July 8, 1964. He submitted the list of participants to Jean Wahl and Martial Guéroult.[13] As David Lapoujade points out, this was the only time that Deleuze organized such an event. That he was able to surmount his profound aversion to colloquia speaks volumes about how important the renewal of Nietzschean studies was to him. During the colloquium, Michel Foucault offered for discussion his comparison of the three "masters of suspicion": Nietzsche, Freud, and Marx.[14]

As the organizer of the colloquium, Deleuze respected the usual protocol of summarizing the meetings' major lessons at their conclusion.[15] He emphasized the lack of sufficient critical editions of Nietzsche that fed persistent misreadings of all sorts and wondered how much of Nietzsche's late-life madness should or should not be part of his philosophical oeuvre.

But the real reason for the opacity in reading Nietzsche's work, as Deleuze saw it, was methodological, having to do with the fact that in Nietzsche meaning is not univocal and does not depend on what it designates. "Every interpretation is already the interpretation of an interpretation, *ad infinitum*. . . . In place of logic, there are a typology and a topology."[16] The notion of value transforms the quest for truth: behind the uncoupling of true and false, the quest should be for some more profound authority, that of the will to power.

In 1965, Deleuze wrote another book on Nietzsche as part of a collection of introductions to philosophy.[17] In it, he showed the striking unity in Nietzsche between thinking and life in a dynamic affirmation of its uniqueness. This existential unity is rooted in the pre-Socratic tradition but has enormous potential for renewing the entire history of philosophy, as it prefigures the future of thought with its innovative style, adding poems and aphorisms to the classical corpus of philosophical texts as privileged interpretative instruments.

Two years later, Deleuze and Foucault wrote an introduction to a French edition of the complete works of Nietzsche,[18] as part of an ongoing systematic examination and chronological publication of Nietzsche's archives begun by Giorgio Colli and Mazzino Montinari. Deleuze and Foucault also indicated that they intended to correct the many changes made by Nietzsche's authoritarian sister and legal heir, Elisabeth, and to unearth what she had kept from the public while cultivating an image of Nietzsche as an anti-Semite and forerunner of Nazism. "The anti-Nietzsche par excellence."[19] In their return to Nietzsche, Deleuze and Foucault offered a new Nietzsche. "We can recognize 'condemned' authors from without, thanks to three qualities: an oeuvre that is brutally interrupted; abusive relatives who meddle heavily in posthumous publications; a book-mystery, something like 'the book' whose secrets are endlessly anticipated."[20]

Discussing his edition of the complete works just before May 1968,[21] Deleuze attributed a large part of this return to the rediscovery of untimeliness and therefore of history as the return of the new and unexpected. Deleuze presents Nietzsche as the example of what contemporary philosophy should accomplish, a radical critique and quest for forms other than the "ego" or "I," for forms of impersonal individualization or preindividual singularities. To illuminate the path of the quest, Deleuze identifies a lineage of philosophers. "It's Lucretius, Spinoza, Nietzsche, a prodigious philosophical lineage, a broken, exploded, and entirely volcanic lineage."[22]

For Nietzsche's reception in France, the early 1970s were particularly intense. Publications proliferated: Pierre Klossowski dedicated his essay on Nietzsche "to Gilles Deleuze,"[23] and a whole new generation was reading Nietzsche in new ways.[24] The fervor reached its apogee in a moment that crystallized all of the energy: July 1972, on the occasion of a decade of Cerisy-la-Salle. Everyone who had ever read Nietzsche came to discuss and debate their interpretations.[25] Deleuze presented a talk entitled "Nomadic Thought."[26] He was only forty-seven at the time, but he opened by emphasizing generational differences. "What a young man discovers when he reads Nietzsche today is certainly different than what my generation discovered."[27] At this point, Deleuze had already met Guattari. Recourse to Nietzsche had taken a very political turn, and he had become a weapon of the most radical critique, confirming the shift toward the far left during the 1960s. Deleuze's new reading was an important spur for this shift. In his talk, Deleuze distanced himself from Foucault's grouping of the triad of Nietzsche, Marx, and Freud as the dawn of our modernity. According to Deleuze, unlike Freudianism and Marxism, Nietzsche comprised a counter-culture irreducible to any institutional recuperation. "Nietzsche pursues an attempt at decoding."[28] Deleuze did, however, think that Nietzsche and Kafka could be compared. Nietzsche embodied a possible philosophy against the philosophical institution, always in relationship to an outside, as Blanchot had shown. The journal *Acephalus*, which published the work of Jean Wahl, Georges Bataille, and Pierre Klossowski, had managed to free Nietzsche from the distorting, fascist mold into which he had been cast. In the early 1970s, the issue, as Deleuze saw it, was to put Nietzsche's aphorisms into a relationship with the outside that gave them their liberating meaning. The specific intensity of these "lived states" had to be rediscovered, the nomadism to which the intensity leads and their humor. "Anyone who reads Nietzsche without laughing, without laughing often and hard and occasionally bursting into uncontrollable laughter, it's as though they weren't reading Nietzsche at all."[29]

A war machine for nomadism and against all forms of recoding, Nietzscheanism became a possible path of liberation from servility and bureaucratic restrictions, a real school of life. It was possible, in the post-1968 years, to talk about a "Nietzsche moment" when Nietzsche's work had a very broad and appreciative audience.[30] This élan found in *The Genealogy of Morals* a lynchpin, particularly when Nietzsche refers to the founders of original civilizations who "arrive, like destiny, without cause, reason, concern, or excuse, with lightning speed, too terrible, too sudden, too convincing, too *other* to even be an object of loathing."[31] Nietzsche was a major source of inspiration for Deleuze's own theme of "nomadology,"[32] which was already present before 1968 but which took on a revolutionary dimension in his work with Guattari, as Manola Antonioli points out,[33] a dimension that continued to expand.[34]

Bergson: The *Élan Vital*

Deleuze was teaching at the Sorbonne from 1957 through 1960 and requested and received a sabbatical to work at the National Center for Scientific Research (CNRS) between 1960 and 1964, making it possible for him to orchestrate his return to a revisited Nietzsche. From 1964 through 1969, he was posted to the University of Lyon,[35] to teach a course on morality; the assignment was not one he embraced with any enthusiasm. "Here I am in Lyon, e-lyonized, e-moved in, e-moralized, professor of morality, etc. I was very happy to see you both, you and Madame Wahl, before my departure."[36] He describes, not without humor, to his friend François Châtelet how hard it was to prepare his thesis: "Oh, my thesis, everything is swimming in this soup (the best must be at the bottom, but it's the least visible)."[37]

He was elected after the college of teachers had eliminated Jules Vuillemin and Henri Lefebre, two rivals whose ideological choices were notorious. "Deleuze was young, he had no label and couldn't be categorized, despite the diabolism of Nietzsche which shone on him."[38] In the philosophy department, Deleuze rubbed shoulders with the well-known phenomenologist Henri Maldiney. "Everything opened with a lecture on reason where the colleagues were slightly out of their element but where Maldiney was utterly at home, which sealed the beginning of a friendship between the two men."[39] Deleuze was quite sensitive to the fact that despite Maldiney's intellectual reputation he had no secure institutional position. His work was internationally influential, yet he was in the precarious situation of being hired to teach individual courses and was thus marginalized in the philosophy department. "Deleuze defended Maldiney against the university authorities," confirms Chris Younès.[40] They were friendly at the time, and Maldiney even managed to drag poor Deleuze along with him on his alpine excursions, where Deleuze could barely breathe!

By contrast, François Dagognet, a former student of Canguilhem, held a powerful position in the philosophy department and nationally as the president of the National Council of Universities (CNU) starting in 1967. The relationship between the two men quickly fell apart; when Deleuze arrived in Lyon, Dagognet welcomed him warmly since he was planning to have him participate in university life, but Deleuze remained aloof and even disdainful, which Dagognet deeply resented. The relationship quickly degenerated into open warfare over Maldiney, whom Deleuze defended vigorously.

Deleuze also spent time with other colleagues, including Geneviève Rodis-Lewis, a famous academic in the history of philosophy, who taught Plato, Malebranche, and, above all, Descartes. In May 1968, Rodis-Lewis could not understand the protests against her and others: "I teach Plato!" Deleuze, by contrast, was thrilled by the protests and mocked his frightened colleagues, particularly Rodis-Lewis, who was working at the time on Descartes' disciples, known as the "little Cartesians." When Deleuze's friend Alain Roger asked him what was going on in Lyon in May 1968 and whether things were violent, Deleuze answered, "The students are very violent, they're marching in the streets against Madame Rodis-Lewis carrying posters saying, 'Enough little Cartesians.'"[41]

In Lyon, Deleuze become friends with the philosopher Jeannette Colombel, a communist intellectual sympathetic to Sartre who taught preparatory classes. Fanny and Gilles Deleuze and Jeannette Colombel and her husband benefited from Lyon's cultural life, going to plays by Roger Planchon and Michel Auclair at the City Theater and quite often to the movies, rushing to see Jean-Luc Godard's *Pierrot le Fou* and *La Chinoise* as soon as they premiered. "During that period, I saw just about every film mentioned in *L'Image-temps*. Ah, Monica Vitti and Antonioni, the first Fellinis, Bergman."[42]

Chris Younès, a student of Deleuze in Lyon for four years, remembers that Deleuze used the history of philosophy very differently than his colleagues. "We really lived Nietzsche, Spinoza, Bergson, Leibniz with him."[43] Between 1964 and 1969, Deleuze progressively liberated himself from the canonical history of philosophy, and although he always taught his preferred authors in his classes, he was already developing more personal themes. In particular, the idea of the event as the explosion of the unexpected was fundamental for him; he adopted from stoicism the necessity of proving oneself worthy and being able to embody this worthiness. He was fascinated by all of the thinking going on about the notion of the event during those years. "Deleuze was always talking about Joë Bousquet,"[44] and the reprint of Bousquet's *Translated from Silence* in 1967[45] gave him the chance to reverse the temporal relationship between man and his wound.[46]

While he was in Lyon, Deleuze developed another important theme from his work on Nietzsche: the eternal return as the return of difference, implying a valorized affirmation and a critique of the logic of resentment and negativity. "That's the heart of what he transmitted to us in Lyon and which took a somewhat different shape later."[47] His students in Lyon were dazzled at how scrupulous he was about remaining close to the texts he was reading and how profoundly he examined their particular logic. Deleuze kept apart from most of his colleagues in Lyon, but he attracted the very largest student audiences for his classes. He lectured to two hundred students, and when he spoke, "he was so charismatic that you could hear the flies buzzing."[48] Even then, many students from other disciplines were coming to his classes and, as was his habit, he gave the impression of improvising. In fact, he had prepared so carefully that he never had to refer to his notes during his classes. "We were all holding our breath because he was such a great storyteller. He was both very intimate and very distant, very much the dandy. He never played favorites and he never changed his bearing."[49]

During this period and before his thesis was published, Deleuze published a work on Bergsonism[50] in 1966; it had had a long gestation period. Bergson had been an important author for Deleuze in the 1940s, even though his friends François Châtelet and Olivier Revault d'Allonnes had serious reservations because they found him too idealistic. From the Liberation until the 1950s, when the three Hs (Hegel, Heidegger, Husserl) reigned, there was no room for Bergson. But Deleuze remained loyal, and he finally got his chance when, in 1956, Merleau-Ponty asked him to write the chapter on Bergson for the collection he was directing entitled *Famous Philosophers*.[51]

Deleuze opened his presentation by stating that we recognize a great philosopher through his capacity to invent concepts. In Bergson's case, the notions of "duration," "memory," "*élan vital*" (vital impetus, vital force), and "intuition" are deeply linked to his contribution. Bergson was a philosopher whose first imperative was to correctly pose the problem to be resolved and suggested that intuition was a productive method for eliminating false problems. Deleuze saw two aspects in Bergson's intuition. It makes the appearance of the thing possible and at the same time presents its appearance as a return. The major implication of such a concept is that it goes beyond the dualism of a material and intelligible world that, according to Bergson, both depend upon the same movement. "Bergson replaced the differentiation between two worlds with the distinction between two movements."[52]

This 1956 text already contained the prolegomena of Deleuze's future thesis of difference as absolute, and it drew its inspiration from Bergsonian positions. According to Deleuze, Bergson shifted the classical and unanswerable question of "why something rather than nothing" to "why this thing rather than that thing?" which leads to the question of difference and to a true metaphysics of difference. "Which is to say that being is difference and neither the immutable or the indifferent, or the contradiction, which is merely a false movement."[53] The possible exit from the aporia, which amounts to opposing in binary fashion the one and the many, is to valorize difference as difference. Bergson was particularly concerned with dividing things appropriately, to distinguish the various heterogeneous elements composing hybrid realities. Here he used Plato's comparison of the philosopher to a good cook who cuts at the natural joints. Intuition is the philosopher's tool, his method of dividing and building pertinent dualisms that cut tendencies rather than things, their moving inscriptions in the duration according to the differentiating lines of matter. It is therefore in this effectuation of virtuality that we find the *élan vital*. Here again Deleuze saw in Bergson this primacy of difference, which became his thesis. "The *élan vital* is difference insofar as it becomes an action."[54]

Between virtuality and its actualization, the link in time is made by memory, which allows the past to continue into the present. It is memory that preserves the "having-been" and its potentialities that survive into what is current. Deleuze insists on Bergson's major contribution of delinearizing the traditional notion of time and breaking with its simple logic of a succession of separate moments: "The past does not constitute itself *after* having been present, *it coexists with itself as present*."[55] Valorizing the virtual in what is actual makes the past and present coexist in the same moment and leads Bergson to argue in favor of a creative *élan*, leaving habit behind. "A lyrical theme courses through Bergson's work: a veritable hymn in honor of the new and unpredictable, of invention and freedom."[56]

The year 1956 was decidedly Bergsonian for Deleuze. In addition to the chapter he wrote for Merleau-Ponty's collection, he also published a long study that he had already presented in 1954 to the Association of Friends of Bergson about the "conception of difference in Bergson."[57] Deleuze freed

Bergson from the hold of the psychologism in which some had hoped to enclose him and insisted instead on the ontological dimension of his work. On this essential point, he used Hyppolite's reading of Bergson, where he contrasts him with Hegel on the question of difference.[58] The article describes the fundamental connection between life and the principle of differentiation. "Life is the process of difference."[59] The processes of differentiation are at the heart of the emergence of the multiplicity of species in the vegetable, animal, and human realms. Bergson took a fundamentally monist and not dualist perspective, but he still considered that human history was distinctive because of the dimension of consciousness. "If difference itself is biological, consciousness of difference is historical."[60] Bergson represented an alternative to the Hegelian dialectic valorizing negation and contradiction by arguing for a conception of difference without negativity. This allowed Bergson to dispatch all causal finality or historical teleology and to emphasize the play of embedded temporal series, which open onto a becoming of indetermination. Indetermination is neither a flabby nor vague notion. Concluding his intense study, Deleuze writes, "Bergsonism is a philosophy of difference, and of the realization of difference: there is difference in person that realizes itself as something new."[61] The same could be said for him as well.[62]

As Anne Sauvagnargues points out, "Bergson orients Deleuze toward a philosophy of difference as a vital operation."[63] And it is precisely in *Creative Evolution* that he achieves the realization of this program. "The *élan vital* is duration that differentiates itself."[64] But Deleuze did not simply reprise Bergson's theme; he made a decisive shift from vitalism to differentialism. In his 1960 class, he compared Freud and Bergson, both of whom assign liberty to novelty and memory to a function turned toward the future. "The greater the past = the greater the future, and therefore freedom. Memory is always a contraction of the past in the present."[65] Deleuze was not interested in reverting to dualism; rather, he wanted to emphasize the lines of difference according to the movements of differentiation. Rather than traditional philosophy's classic duality of the subject of representation and the represented object, which was later adopted by phenomenology, Bergson and then Deleuze propose a different, monist approach in which consciousness *is* something rather than being "consciousness of something." As for experience, it is made only of mixes in which the subject evolves, which implies that the philosopher must appeal to intuition as a method. "The role of intuition is to discern the mixtures and to find the 'pure' things."[66]

When he published *Bergsonism* in 1966, Deleuze was teaching at the University of Lyon.[67] The very title of the book had a provocative ring, as it went against the currently reigning doxa regarding Bergson, which had been defined by Georges Politzer before the war, when he gave an ultracritical and pamphleteering interpretation. Politzer's vitriolic book against Bergsonism was written in 1929 under the anticlerical pseudonym François Arouet.[68] A militant communist who was shot at Mont-Valerien, Politzer became a postwar figure whose view of Bergsonism prevailed in most intellectual circles. He reduced Bergsonism to a form of backward psychologism and turned it into an expression of bourgeois ideology. "During his [Bergson's] entire life, like the indications that he gave about his morality that has not yet and will never be born, we can understand that he gave himself over completely to bourgeois values."[69] Regis Jolivet points out that the philosophical avant-garde of the 1940s and 1950s considered Bergson a "dead dog." Bergsonism in the 1960s was therefore still suspected of being the fig leaf of a vengeful bourgeoisie. That Deleuze took up the *-ism* of Bergsonism was an extraordinary feat. "Deleuze started a process of resurrecting Bergsonism from an ideology to a philosophical doctrine. At the same time, by entitling his book *Bergsonism* he was also thumbing his nose at the Bergsonians, stigmatizing them for having created a kind of church. The title of that book itself was really brilliant."[70]

From the opening lines of his book, Deleuze attacked the commonplace notion that Bergson considered intuition to be a form of intrareflexive spontaneity. To the contrary, he saw in it the very method of Bergsonism and "one of the best developed methods of philosophy."[71] Deleuze adopted this doctrine. It demanded the greatest precision, and its first rule, repeatedly noted by Deleuze as the essential task of philosophy, is to correctly pose problems, as he had already said in his book on Hume. With Bergson, we take one more step toward denouncing false problems; true and false should no longer be tested by examining the proposed solutions but instead should be dealt with at the level of the questions being asked. However, posing the right problem depends not on the ability to reveal what is but on the ability to invent.

One of Bergson's major rules follows from the imperative of discerning true articulations among inherently different categories. Bergson and later Deleuze constantly used dualisms not because they preferred a binary philosophical system, as Bergson's doctrine and Deleuze's are resolutely monist. The entire Bergsonian method is about restoring the inherent differences in nature in the mixtures that experience gives us; intuition guides us in this process of discernment. Perception thus places consciousness fully within the material world, whereas memory situates us firmly in the realm of the mind. Moreover, intuition becomes a method of discernment that lends greater importance to time than space, because duration for Bergson is the very site of the process of differentiation and change. Bergsonian intuition is therefore a rigorous method thanks to its capacity to problematize, differentiate, and temporalize.

One of the major changes that Deleuze affected in the traditional interpretations of Bergson's work was to consider the core of his doctrine to be neither the *élan vital* nor memory but the logic of multiplicity. By contrast with other Bergsonians, Deleuze devotes considerable time to a forgotten 1889 essay by Bergson, "On the Immediate Givens of Consciousness," in which he found the basis of the theory of multiplicities. "For Bergson, the issue is not to contrast the many and the one."[72] The idea of multiplicity offered a way of leaving the Hegelian dialectic, which Bergson considered too abstract and estranged from experience, and to replace it with a subtle perception of singularities.

The more classical theme that Deleuze developed in his book had to do with memory as it leads to a conception of the past that is not amputated from the present but is rather embedded time or coexisting degrees of duration. The present has to do with psychology, but the past has to do with pure ontology: "Pure memory has only ontological meaning."[73] In this, Deleuze agreed with his teacher Hyppolite's rejection of a psychologistic interpretations of Bergson. Bergson disagreed with Ranke's notions of German historicism and with those of the French school (Langlois, Seignobos, and Lavisse) and proposed instead a very innovative idea that the past is never entirely truly past, since it persists into the present, from which it cannot be dissociated.

The philosophy of life that Bergson defines seeks to transcend the limits of mechanistic causality. "The rules of actualization are difference, or divergence, and creation, and no longer resemblance and limitation."[74] Deleuze discerned a line of flight for the creative flows of life in Bergson. To start the movement once again, to sideline the forms in order to focus on the forces, required the capacity to conceive of discontinuity and possible ruptures. Here again, Deleuze found support in Bergson, because "the mind can only clearly represent discontinuity to itself."[75] What counts is the action in the process of occurring, innovative and liberating becomings.

"There is *more* in a movement than in the successive positions attributed to the mobile, *more* in becoming than the successive forms that it takes."[76] This process is life itself in its *élan* and it conjugates both matter, which represents necessity, and consciousness, representing freedom. This advance toward creativity also involves a method of subtraction, something that Deleuze later used, when he was working on cinema in the 1980s, from the first chapter of Bergson's 1896 *Matter and Memory*. Consciousness does not add itself to the world but casts its nets to capture the world; it is the world itself, by subtraction. Here we have a definition of consciousness not as luminous beams that increase in number but as something less, which subtracts. "This is a radical change in the metaphorical register. We're no longer talking about holding a steady light on things or about the phenomenological harpoon; we're in the black screen on which we're projecting the matter of less."[77]

Deleuze appropriates Bergson's theses but, as was his wont, reads them in a unusual way. Even if Bergson had a special place in Deleuze's pantheon, he is no exception to the rule that Deleuze describes as returning to his authors and somehow betraying them. As Frédéric Worms, a Bergson specialist, put it, "whatever you might say, Bergson is a spiritualist, even if I protest this label."[78] But Deleuze's Bergson is a Bergson without consciousness from whom consciousness has been subtracted, no small thing. For Bergson, a thing exists only if memory makes a temporal synthesis of it. Not even the body can support itself alone in Being; it can only support itself by subjectivity, by an action that is immanent to time and to experience, but there exists an act.

However, Deleuze leaves this fundamental aspect of Bergson's ideas completely in the shadow of his commentary and thus ignores an entire part of his work. "He doesn't discuss Bergson's *Two Sources of Morality and Religion* in his book, which is surprising since even the book's title addresses the issue of a distinction by nature. This surprising omission is certainly due to the taboo against consciousness."[79] Duration, for Bergson, is a subjective act, whereas for Deleuze, the movement is reversed; it is the subject that is an effect of duration. Consciousness presents itself as a simple contraction of moments. Deleuze selects one part of Bergson's work and abandons another, because he considers it inessential. That being said, his reading was a major impetus for Bergson's return to the philosophical center stage and to being legitimated by a new generation of philosophers. "Deleuze's 'betrayal' of Bergson was fantastic, something we all need. I adopted the 'bastard,' fed and housed him, and sent him to school, that's what I tried to do."[80]

SPINOZA: THINKING AS AFFIRMATION

Spinoza had a special place in Deleuze's work. In 1977, Deleuze cited him as a significant author, on whom he had worked more than on any other. "I worked most seriously on Spinoza according to the norms of the history of philosophy—but he more than any other gave me the feeling of a gust of air pushing you from behind every time you read him, of a witch's broom which he makes you mount. We have not even begun to understand Spinoza, and I no more than others."[81] Much later, in 1991, when *What Is Philosophy?* was published, Deleuze paid vibrant tribute to Spinoza as "the prince of philosophers. He may be the only philosopher never to have compromised with transcendence and to have hunted it down everywhere."[82]

> Thus Spinoza is the Christ of philosophers, and the greatest philosophers are hardly more than apostles who distance themselves from or draw near to this mystery. Spinoza, the infinite becoming-philosopher: he showed, drew up, and thought the "best" plane of immanence— that is, the purest, the one that does not hand itself over to the transcendent, or restore any transcendent.[83]

Deleuze wrote a complementary thesis on Spinoza, "The Idea of Expression in the Philosophy of Spinoza," under his director Ferdinand Alquié and defended it in 1968.[84] He had begun working on it much earlier and was in fact almost finished by the late 1950s. Deleuze disagreed radically with Alquié's strenuous defense of Cartesian dualism against Spinoza's monism, but he did find some of Alquié's suggestions important, such as the idea of considering "common ideas" as "biological ideas" rather than as abstract, geometric essences.[85] In 1970, Deleuze published an anthology on Spinoza,[86] and in 1978 he wrote an article about Spinoza's relevance.[87] A few years later, he published an essay that revisited these two texts partially.[88] In 1980–1981, he gave a course at Vincennes University on Spinoza, to which he returned in 1993 in *Critique and Clinic*.

Deleuze's exploration of Spinoza's universe, to the very heart of the issues and the foundation of the controversies in which he was engaged, already indicated a decisive break with Spinoza's academic reputation as the master of a disincarnated, inaccessible system. Deleuze gave new life to Spinoza and, at the same time, this gift of revivifying was possible thanks to him. An entire philosophical tradition had transmitted the image of Spinoza as a pure metaphysician to be shunned for not having considered the question of liberty. "Spinoza was decried to the point of making 'Spinozism' an insult if not an incendiary label because the atheological and amoral implications of his metaphysics (deformed and caricatured) were immediately obvious."[89] Hegel considered Spinoza to be the author of a purely theoretical system; Kojève claimed that nothing could be done with Spinoza, whose philosophy was built on a moribund system that excluded freedom as much as it excluded subjectivity. Deleuze freed Spinoza from this imprisonment: "by making him the great "descendent" of the great living Nietzsche, Deleuze reversed things completely."[90]

"The philosopher can live in different countries, frequent various milieus, but like a hermit, a shadow, a voyager, someone who rents furnished lodgings."[91] Throughout his life, Spinoza was concerned about protecting his independence and never requested anything more than tolerance from the authorities; this became a rule Deleuze followed in his own life. However, even in lively seventeenth-century Amsterdam, liberty was no simple matter, as Spinoza bitterly learned. *Ethics*, his great work of fifteen years, could not be published during his lifetime because of its unconventionality. Spinoza died in 1677 without having been able to make it public, and his fears were confirmed when the Presbyterian Council of Leyden, against which there was no possible appeal, judged that: "no book, since the beginning of the world and perhaps until now, has equaled this one in its impiety." Because he refused to submit, Spinoza was transformed into an anchorite, a sort of disincarnate specter. For Deleuze, this representation was quite far from the reality of Spinoza, through whom "Life itself" flowed.[92] Spinoza was, first and foremost, a philosopher of the force of life and of the triumph of joy over sadness, the aspect that Deleuze constantly emphasized. "For Spinoza, life is not an idea or something theoretical, it's a manner of being, the same eternal manner in all of its aspects."[93]

Spinoza was fully a man of his time, and his system was therefore in no way disembodied. He pushed to their limits the questions specific to a modernity that had shifted from a classical relationship to a closed universe to a relationship with a universe become infinite. The great question in the seventeenth century was how to think the infinite. Spinoza's ideas carried the question to its limits, by refusing the opposition between finitude and infinitude, thanks to the invention of a new category of the infinitely small, which could be perceived through series. Spinoza put forward an unusual notion of the individual as composition, power, and degrees. The individual is no longer considered to be a substance but as a relationship independent of its terms. In the second place, the individual is above all power, and not form. Here, Spinoza was proposing the idea of *conatus*, whereby "each thing tends to persevere in its being." The individual therefore tends toward its limit. "That's power: effort insofar as it is tending toward a limit."[94]

In his complementary thesis, Deleuze examined the issue of expression, which he considered central for Spinoza, who used it in his first book of *Ethics*, which Deleuze took as his starting point. "By God, I mean an absolutely infinite being, that is, a substance with an infinity of attributes, each of which *expresses* an eternal and infinite essence."[95] According to Deleuze, the problem of expression condenses the difficult unitary relationship between a substance and the diversity of its attributes. It is through expression that Spinozism is a monism. By contrast to the dimension of "explaining," "expressing" covers an ontological dimension whose impact is to oppose the potentialities of a philosophy of nature to Cartesian thinking. "Expression is not required, therefore, to be the object of a demonstration; it is what sets the demonstration in the absolute."[96] Spinoza had not truly thematized this notion of expression in his work, as Deleuze acknowledges. "The idea of expression in Spinoza is the object neither of a definition nor of a demonstration."[97] Attributes could only be affirmations and were therefore expressive: "Spinoza's philosophy is a philosophy of pure affirmation. Affirmation is the speculative principle on which the entire *Ethics* depends."[98]

The theme of power is central to Spinozism. Power is at work everywhere, and understanding has no special privilege in this realm with respect to its objects, which use the same power to exist. Power is the equivalent of essence. All beings are moved by the power of existing, which is, for mankind, "a part of infinite power, that is, of essence, of God, or of Nature."[99] This divine power is mirrored by a power of existence and of action, of thought and of knowledge. Yet this divine nature is based *"at one and the same time* on necessity and on possibility."[100]

Deleuze showed how Spinoza distanced himself from Descartes and his dualism, which is based on the adequation between an idea and the thing that it represents. In this way, Cartesian thinking condemns itself to remain at the level of the form, thus missing power. For Spinoza, the adequate idea does not signify a correspondence between an idea and the thing but "is precisely the idea expressing its cause."[101] Deleuze created a link between Spinoza and his work on Hume by calling Spinoza's method "empirical" from the moment he shifts the Cartesian questioning of the clear and distinctive and replaces it with a method that no longer asks whether we have inadequate ideas but rather how we manage to formulate adequate ideas. "In this, the Spinozist inspiration is profoundly empirical."[102]

Deleuze often returned later to a major issue that Spinoza raises about a body's power in being able to affect and being affected. "We don't know what the body can do or what we can deduce solely from a consideration of its nature."[103] The capacity of specifically human power cannot be predetermined, since the pole of activity corresponds its passive corollary of being-affected. This power that pushes existence to its extreme limits is named *conatus*—the effort to persevere in being. Deleuze calls this force "desire" and insists on the fact that it is determined by affections. The theme later became important when Deleuze came into contact with psychoanalytic discourse, initially to appropriate it and later to challenge it, by proposing another philosophical direction that takes desire into consideration differently than does Freud. According to Spinoza, the *conatus*/desire is relaunched by encounters that either make us more active, decoupling in this way our power and eliciting joy, or, to the contrary, bear sad feelings condemning us to impotence and passivity, blocking our ability to act. As an affected being, man has a capacity to discern what makes him sad or joyful; he is therefore able to discriminate good from bad encounters. This lucidity about one's self can shed its light in the practical realm. "We triumph if we manage to separate the feeling of sadness, thereby destroying the body affecting us."[104] The result is an ethic that invites us not to descend into hatred, polemic, or any other sad affect in order to always give the upper hand to the specific force for action and creation.

When Spinoza notes the inability to conceive of what a body can do, it was, for Deleuze, a real "war cry,"[105] because Spinoza reverses the priority that had prevailed until then of actions and reactions of the soul over those of the body. For Spinoza, the body goes further than the knowledge that we might have of it, because it incarnates a way of being of one of the two attributes, extension, comprising speeds and slowness arranged among themselves. That which moves the body depends only on immanence.

Spinoza locates himself on a level that is not the moral opposition between Good and Evil but rather on an ethical level, regarding the type of affections that determine the *conatus*. "It's possible that the free, strong, and reasonable man will define himself entirely by the possession of his power to act."[106] There is where the encounter—that Deleuze will later describe as the break in the flux, after meeting Guattari—is fundamental for persevering in being, because "I can" is tied to the capacity to be affected, which depends on encountering another insofar as the other can change the identity of the Same.

In 1977, nearly a decade after the publication of his complementary thesis, Deleuze was invited to a conference organized by the International Center of Synthesis on the occasion of the three hundredth anniversary of Spinoza's death. The title of his talk was "Spinoza et nous" ("Spinoza and Us"). This formulation expresses Deleuze's style of starting in the middle of a philosophical work to intensify the connection between the current reader and the philosopher being read. "Entering through the middle" also made it possible to understand Spinoza better: until then, commentators had focused on thought and extension, which Spinoza considered to be two attributes of substance. Indeed, we can only know these two of the attributes, extension and thought, of the substance that belongs to the divine by virtue of its infinite character. "Deleuze put himself in the middle of the system and located substance, the attributes that express themselves, and recomposes Spinoza's entire system from the notion of expression."[107] What is is not substance but expresses it without any hierarchical quality, making Spinoza a thinker of immanence who breaks with all emanative thinking. Being leads to the One, to univocity, when all the attributes are in a situation of perfect equality.

Deleuze's 1977 lecture adumbrated this shift, which was confirmed in 1981 when he published another book on Spinoza, in which he argued that the lesson of the *Ethics* is essentially practical, since it is an ethological essay rather than a treatise on morality. "Ethology is first of all the study of the relationships between speed and slowness, the powers of affecting and of being affected that characterize everything."[108] This question of differential speeds was important for Deleuze, who uses Spinoza not to define a thing or an individual by its form, organs, or functions nor as a substance or a subject but rather by its longitude and latitude. Deleuze borrows Spinoza's distinction between these two modes of individuation: existence as a divisible ensemble in extensive parts and essence as an intensive part.

He conceived of bodies as kinetic, opposing relationships of speed and slowness in each element. This distinction later served Deleuze and Guattari for thinking in terms of a cartography of bodies.

Deleuze's 1981 publication on Spinoza does not really diminish his 1968 reading, although we can concur with François Zourabichvili's observation that his vision of Spinoza changed, making him "the philosophical hero of the second Deleuze."[109] Deleuze published his second work on Spinoza after 1968 and after his major publications with Guattari, *Anti-Oedipus* and *A Thousand Plateaus*, and consequently insisted on the practical dimension of Spinoza's philosophy and on his affinities with Nietzsche's philosophy. As revisited by Deleuze, Spinoza is the philosopher of an art of living, of a manner of being, making it possible to harmoniously combine the solicitations of affect and concept to intensify the coincidence of greater reason and more joy. To triumph, this way of living must overcome three challenges: power and its interdictions, transcendence with its abyss between thinking and its potentialities, and "a ruinous conception of the relationships between *theory and practice* (the eminence of theory over practice)."[110] Spinoza becomes the major reference for a fully immanent thinking.

After briefly describing Spinoza's life, Deleuze addresses the difference between morality and ethics that earned Spinoza, during his time, the reputation of being scandalous. Spinoza's practical philosophy had in fact challenged the reign of consciousness, values, and passions, which provoked a trio of accusations against him as being immoral, a materialist, and an atheist. Deleuze was struck by the parallel with Nietzsche and argues for this rather explosive comparison. "Everything was tending toward the great identity Nietzsche-Spinoza."[111] Deleuze uses Spinoza as a weapon against structuralism and psychoanalysis. Spinoza makes it possible to exalt the forces of life against a culture of guilt and against any form of thinking that begins with a lack or an absence. "Ethical *joy* is the correlative of speculative *affirmation*."[112]

Everything plays out in existence as an experimentation with good or bad combinations, the only things that can level good and bad. "This is, therefore, the final difference between the good and the bad man: the good or strong man is the one who exists so fully or so intensely that he conquers eternity during his lifetime, while death, always extensive, always external, is for him, rather unimportant."[113] Externalizing death, which Spinoza considers to be a mere accident, is a notion that Deleuze always championed and contrasted to Heidegger's "being-for-death." As Spinoza saw it, death involves only the extensive parts; "the reality of the intensive part remains."[114] This creates a double eternity: of the relationships that define each individual's specificity and of the particular essence characterizing the person who has died. Spinoza can argue therefore that during our lifetimes we experience a form of eternity, which he contrasts to the immortality proclaimed by theologians. Under these conditions, Deleuze claims, "Spinoza considers the idea of a death wish grotesque."[115] Deleuze is also targeting Freudian thinking with his remark.

In 1993, Deleuze returned to Spinoza to distinguish three levels, or three rhythms, corresponding to three kinds of knowledge in the *Ethics*, which, upon first reading, could give the impression of a continuous flow. "Signs or affects; Notions or concepts; Essences or percepts."[116] The book employs different and more or less intense, contracted or dilated rhythms that develop according to their own continuous logic, making the world of "postulates," "demonstrations," and "corollaries" follow upon each. Whereas the world of the "scholies" flows in the lower strata and produces the passions and violence of the secret affects of the book, in a discontinuous order, book 5 follows a completely different rhythm and progresses by luminous flashes of lightning. The demonstrative mode thus changes radically in book 5, contracting to give free expression to a superior speed.

Having paid tribute to the corporation of professional philosophers by publishing these monographs, all the while consolidating the vitalist foundations on which he later drew, Deleuze started publishing his own philosophical ideas in 1968 and 1969. He claims what he is rejecting in his own name. He asserts as he does so his singular thinking, writing, and style.

8

An Ontology of Difference

When Deleuze defended his doctoral thesis in 1968–1969, the time had come for him to show his colors publicly. The author of *Difference and Repetition* distanced himself from the dominant philosophical tradition by arguing for an overthrow of Platonic thinking. His remarks occurred during the 1960s, a decade during which Hegelianism, the reigning force in the history of philosophy, was coming under fire. This was clearly a time of change: in literature with the New Novel, in the social sciences, and in the growing appreciation of Heideggerian thinking; it was an era of "generalized anti-Hegelianism."[1]

OVERTURNING PLATONISM AND HEGELIANISM

Plato held the front line against which Deleuze had to do battle to argue for his positions. "The task of modern philosophy has been defined: to overturn Platonism."[2] Plato poses a very concrete problem: to select from among a growing number of claimants to truth in Athens by subjecting the rivals to a philosophical test that would separate the wheat from the chaff, "'the thing itself' and its simulacra."[3] To make his choice, Plato argues for the concept of the Idea, the essence of the phenomenon. In the name of this essence, Plato can claim to separate the rivals and eliminate imperfect things, falsifiers, and simulacra. Yet Deleuze points out an extraordinary moment at the end of the *Sophist* when Plato finds that the simulacrum is not a simple false copy but that it puts in question the notions of the copy and the model. The simulacrum provides the means of challenging *both* the notion of the copy *and* the model. "The model collapses into difference, while the copies disperse into the dissimilitude of the series they interiorize, such that one can never say that the one is a copy and the other a model."[4] Thus Plato was the first to suggest how to overturn his own method. The irony of destiny and the supreme paradox is that the sophist, whether he takes the form of a satyr or a centaur, attacking Plato for embodying the untrue and the simulacrum, may have ultimately been the true philosopher.

Until that point, Plato would have been reduced to the univocal theses that he develops in the *Theaetetus*, where he appears to initiate an ethical order oriented toward truth, according to the immutable model of recognition. We must follow Plato along the path that he perceived for an instant but was unable to pursue. "Overturning Platonism, then, means denying the primacy of the original over the copy, of the model over the image; glorifying the reign of the simulacra and its reflections."[5] In *The Logic of Sense*, when Deleuze distinguishes the three possible stances of philosophy, he somewhat radicalizes his critique of Platonic thinking, which he envisions as the tradition that has paralyzed us with the belief that the philosopher's destiny is to leave his cave and rise toward the heavens of the ideal world in search of a truth that is inaccessible to the common mortal. Deleuze, like Nietzsche, considers Platonic philosophy to be like the expression of a pathology, a constant flight toward unreality marked by the rhythm of ascensions propelled by "the beating of the Platonic wings."[6]

Making historical virtualities accessible once again, reenlivening the potential of transformation and of revolution, requires recourse to "difference and its power of affirmation."[7] Deleuze is already arguing for this point, well before he began constructing a true philosophy of the virtual,[8] which he contrasts not with reality but with actuality. *"The virtual is fully real insofar as it is virtual."*[9] Difference resists explanation, just as an event risks being subsumed or eradicated by explanatory structures. This allows Deleuze to address the true problematics of philosophy, of thinking the paradox, the great figure and major trope of the 1960s, against the illusion that it is possible to move beyond contradictions. "Paradox is the pathos or the passion of philosophy."[10]

Whereas Gilles Deleuze and Paul Ricoeur took two very different approaches, they both define the philosophical act as a response to paradoxes and tensions created by aporias at the same time. Like Deleuze, Ricoeur never claims one can get beyond contradictions to achieve a totalizing synthesis. He asserts the necessity of thinking incommensurable endpoints together, and he proceeds in fact to invent imperfect mediations by managing a series of flights from the tensions of the aporia. Deleuze seeks a more direct access to pure differences. Another common point between Ricoeur and Deleuze is the metastabilization of the philosopher's questioning stance. Both agree that the question takes priority by dissymmetry, in the relationship between question and answer. "We are led to believe at one and the same time that problems present themselves ready-made and that they disappear in the responses or the solution."[11] For Deleuze, this belief is rooted in childhood prejudice that must be overcome.

DIFFERENCE FOR ITSELF

Deleuze denounces the veritable curse that has stricken all thinking about difference in the Western philosophical tradition, where it is identified with the forces of evil, the fall, sin, and monstrosity. Deleuze sets out to rehabilitate difference, which has been banished to the shadows of the history of thought. Using Plato's metaphor for his own project, Deleuze seeks to bring difference "out of its cave."[12]

But how can one manage to grasp difference? Neither through phenomenology nor dialectics, because to think difference itself presupposes that difference manifests itself as affirmation, and indeed Deleuze argues, "seen the right way up, from top to bottom, difference is affirmation, difference is an object of affirmation."[13] To consider the essence of difference supposes a radical break with the thinking of representation as always subordinated to the identical, to the model to be re-presented, and replaces it with experimentation in the manner of Nietzsche. "Difference must be shown *differing*."[14] The eternal return would thus be the "for itself" of difference, not a return of the same but of the different. Yet aren't we inevitably led to the Same or to some mediations that can reduce differences in order to think them? Deleuze uses the example of lightning, which explodes when intensities in the air become too great. Before the lightning, a precursor indicates its direction in the sky, which would be the "in itself" of difference. "We call this dark precursor, this difference *in itself*, or difference in the second degree which relates heterogeneous systems and even completely disparate things, the *disparate*."[15]

The philosophical tradition would thus have imprisoned itself by conforming to a model considered to be iterable. From Plato's *Theaetetus* to Kant's *Critique of Pure Reason*, a model of recognition oriented philosophy toward what became a *doxa*, an orthodoxy, a source of conformity, and a prisoner to the ideas of the time. Deleuze wonders about the value of thinking that discomforts no one. Philosophy had operated until this point only as the recognition of established values and institutions, as a twin of legitimation, their spiritual surplus.

In 1968, Deleuze's project was to lay out an ontology. As he conceived it, the question-problem dyad should lend new dynamism to an ontological program that starts with the gaping hole that cannot be filled. To do this meant returning to the problem and asking the right question. Ontology thus becomes a challenge rather than a foundation upon which to lean or rest, an aleatory becoming and a possibility. "The specific points are on the die; the questions are dice and the imperative is to throw. Ideas are the problematic combinations that result from throws."[16] These throws of the die have a relationship with the subject, the "I," but the "I" is always broken, fissured, and the throws of the dice displace the line of this fissure in temporality.

The goal of an ontological repetition is to distribute difference between physical and mental repetition and to produce the illusion that affects them. Repetition would create ontology itself not as an analogy, as in representation, because "the only realized Ontology—that *is* the univocity of being—is repetition."[17] For his philosophical program, Deleuze draws essentially from Spinoza and Nietzsche. In his *Ethics*, Spinoza defines attributes as irreducible, since they are formally distinct from genres and ontologically one as substance. Deleuze adds a twist from Nietzsche, who made it possible to realize this univocity by reinvigorating it *"in the form of repetition in the eternal return."*[18] Deleuze traces the radicalization of univocity from Spinoza to Nietzsche, which led to a radical critique of all substance, including Spinoza's substance. "Whence his thesis making substance secondary like the principle of *ipseity*, of identity in and for itself derived with respect to the becoming-other, an effect of the eternal return."[19]

At the end of the book, Deleuze concludes with something of a lyrical song, a fundamentally ontological philosophical cry. "A single and same voice for the whole thousand-voiced multiple, a single and unique Ocean for all the drops, a single clamor of Being for all beings."[20] This unequivocal stance for the univocity of being did not mean that the multiple was somehow diminished, however, but rather the contrary. In *The Logic of Sense*, Deleuze explains: the univocity "of Being does not mean that there is one and the same Being; on the contrary, beings are multiple and different."[21] This gives rise to that paradoxical entity linking incommensurable elements in a disjunctive synthesis.

In radicalizing difference, Deleuze takes a path close to but different from Husserl's phenomenological approach. Deleuze's entire career takes into account the contributions of phenomenology, which are so close to his own positions that, as Alain Beaulieu puts it, Deleuze did not fight phenomenology, he fought "*with* it."[22] Deleuze was ambivalent toward phenomenology, keeping his distance and at the same time using several Husserlian notions, such as "passive synthesis" and "transcendental empiricism," for his own purposes. His friend Paul Virilio, who emphatically proclaims his ties with the phenomenological program, says that Deleuze greatly appreciated Merleau-Ponty's last book, *Visible and Invisible*,[23] and also drew from Husserl, for whom sense is what is expressed or the expression and who questions the sense of perception that cannot be reduced to the physical object or to psychological experience. Ultimately, he wonders, "Could phenomenology be this rigorous science of surface effects?"[24]

Husserl is rather close to Deleuze when he claims that consciousness surpasses itself in a targeted direction, but Husserl misses his target by starting from "an originary faculty of *common sense*, responsible for accounting for the identity of the object in general."[25] The phenomenological project is doomed by its inability to break with common sense. While Husserl clearly understood that necessity of a momentary break with *doxa*, favoring an eidetic reduction, he preserved the basics of common sense by seeking to elevate the empirical to the transcendental. Husserl clearly understood that sense was somewhat independent, but what "prevents him from conceiving sense as a full (impenetrable) neutrality is his concern with retaining in sense the rational mode of good sense and a common sense, as he presents incorrectly the latter as a matrix."[26] Deleuze, by contrast, sought a preindividual, impersonal dimension—not to be mistaken for a formless depth or the efforts of consciousness—located on the surface of the emergence of singularities, "the true transcendental events."[27]

Another tradition that Deleuze exhumes is that of the Stoics, from whom he draws extensively to develop his idea of "disjunctive conjunction." This notion of conjunction was in fact essential for the Stoics, including the nonlogicians. These thinkers reasoned by making obvious the implications of an act. It goes without saying, for example, that going to the baths implies being splashed and that knowing this means that there's no basis for complaint, since this is an integral part of going to the baths. This was a way of strangling judgments and ethics using logic: the important thing was to follow the conjunctions that worked best and were closest to one's will.

Remaining close to one's desires reduces the risks of unexpected and disagreeable things. Ethics thus finds itself in an in-between space. In an analogy used by Diogenes Laertius to define the Stoics' philosophy, "the shell is Logic, next comes the white, Ethics, and the yolk in the center is Physics."[28]

The Stoics' concept of the event suits Deleuze because it maximizes the power of the link between event and logic and promotes the event over the attribute. The Stoics considered that everything was potentially an event, including the tiniest, least remarkable phenomenon; Deleuze adopted this idea as a major tenet of the natural distinction that he makes between "representation" and "expression," in favor of expression. The Stoic sage remains at the surface, enlivened by the logic that makes the pure event accessible. "The sage waits for the event, that is to say, *understands the pure event* in its eternal truth, independently of its spatiotemporal actualization."[29] Following the analyses of the philosopher Victor Goldschmidt, Deleuze sees the Stoic stance as the expression of the desire to embody the pure event in the flesh of the sage, his will to "give body" to the incorporeal effect.[30] When he defines the philosopher's three possible figures, he eliminates two of them: the one seeking truth in the heavens and the one believing that truth that can be found in the depths of the earth's crust, the former using wings and the latter a hammer. He contrasts these with the Stoic attitude, which implies a complete reorientation in thinking: *"there is no longer depth or height."*[31]

For the Stoics, the world of Ideas lies on the surface, and whoever asks a question is shown the most apparently insignificant ordinary event. This world of paradox and contrasts is elucidated by Diogenes the Cynic and Chrysippus the Stoic, as far as we can gather from the writings of Diogenes Laertius. Their philosophical stance gives birth to a method that Deleuze calls the practice of perversion, "if it is true that perversion implies an extraordinary art of surfaces."[32] François Zourbachvili provides a pertinent definition of Deleuze's method of perversion, which has little to do with the little perverse machines scorned by psychoanalysis. "There is a joyful pervert in him."[33] Similarly, Deleuze describes Melville's Captain Ahab as a sublime pervert and, commenting on Michel Tournier's popular *Friday ou les limbes du Pacifique*, celebrates an unpeopled perverse world.[34] Deleuze provides many philosophical uses of perversion that consist "sometimes in reversing the bits of all sorts of theories to use them to other ends, sometimes in relating a concept to its true condition, that is, to the forces and intuitive dynamics that underpin them, sometimes in directly critiquing a theme or notion, approaching it laterally using a "thoroughly twisted conception."[35]

Deleuze takes a concrete situation and points out the places where there is an excess of energy or a line of flight, in contrast to the dialectic, which transcends contradictions through synthesis. And in the name of this perspective, Deleuze seeks the line of flight that maintains the paradoxical tension. By so doing, he renounces the critical position of an overview in the name of which one chooses this rather than that line, adopting the position subtended by Melville's Bartleby's enigmatic sentence, "I would prefer not to."[36]

Deleuze observes the experimentation with the Stoic position above all in literature, in the works of Herman Melville, Lewis Carroll, F. Scott Fitzgerald, and Charles Péguy, among others. But at the end the 1960s, he was particularly fascinated by the poet Joë Bousquet and the wound he suffered during World War I. "Joë Bousquet must be called Stoic. He apprehends the wound that he bears deep within his body in its eternal truth as a pure event."[37] Joë Bousquet was wounded on May 27, 1918, at Vailly, and remained bedridden until his death in 1950. During those years, he lived as a recluse, shuttered up in a room in Carcassonne, where he devoted himself to writing poetry. "My wound existed before me, I was born to embody it."[38]

Deleuze adopts the Stoic's triple challenge. "No one better than Deleuze waged these three battles, against the mathematization of logic, the naturalization of physics, and the technocratization of ethics."[39] On logic, Deleuze agrees with the Stoics but takes radical exception to them by rejecting the dialectical art of speaking the truth and by minimizing the importance of rhetoric as the art of speaking well. He agrees with the Stoics' questioning of attributes that became infinitives (to intensify, to green) and indefinite articles (a life, a becoming, it rains, one dies) and integrates the paradoxes, the disjunctive propositions. The event became identified with an adequation between form and the void.[40]

The second phase of Stoicism was the refusal of the naturalization of physics. In 1988, Deleuze declared this intention to pursue the work begun with Guattari and write a book on "a sort of philosophy of Nature at the moment when the difference between nature and artifice disappears."[41] Indeed, *A Thousand Plateaus* approaches the philosophy of nature that underlies all of Deleuze and Guattari's work, where conceptual personae hobnob with the feelings of ticks, the becoming-animal of the hero of Kafka's *Metamorphosis*, the relationships between wasps and orchids in Proust, and even the relationship to the earth and its dynamic twins of de- and re-territorialization. But the Stoic's world offers a model of plenitude within and of an externalized void with respect to the world. That which prevails no longer comes from elsewhere but from nature in its most diverse forms. Lack is no longer a spring, because "Deleuzean Nature is only immanent to itself, it is perfectly realized in itself."[42] Removed from all transcendence, nature in all its forms is legible in immanence, starting with the connections that even call into question the distinction between the natural and the artificial. The outside that Deleuze adopted from Blanchot and Foucault is indeed present, but as an "outside more distant than any external world."[43] He thus destroys all distinction between internal and external by its distance and its indeterminacy. This universe has the appearance of an ensemble of more or less connected singularities, articulated among themselves, forming something of a "wall of free, loose stones in which each element has its own value and yet also takes its value from its relationship to the others."[44] This multicosmic and plural universe responding to the most varied of logics of assemblage results in a "symphony of Nature"[45] that recalls the Stoic's theme of universal sympathy between things terrestrial and celestial.

The third battle common to the Stoics and to Deleuze involves the refusal to make ethics technocratic. Once the stones of the wall are freed from the cement holding them in place, the world appears fundamentally disparate, and this allows for the most surprising connections in a "chaosmose" in which no hierarchical universe of ethical values can be anchored. What does the wish for the good life correspond to, according to Deleuze's *Logic of Sense*, when it appeared in 1969? What ethics are to be adopted? Once again, the Stoics provide the inspiration, offering an ethic that gives precedence to the event. "Stoic ethics is concerned with the event; it consists of willing the event as such, that is, willing that which occurs insofar as it occurs."[46] Deleuze's entire philosophy of the event is here in this conception, where neither the present nor revolutionary eschatology nor any nostalgia for the past is privileged to preserve the dynamism specific to the singularity of each being and respectful of living beings. Ethics is conceived as a "higher ethology."[47]

THE FRACTURED COGITO

Working out an ontology of difference requires a critique of all thought that overvalues the cogito and any conception focused on a supposed interiority that creates some harmony between man and his surroundings. Despite their very different perspectives, Deleuze adopted Ricoeur's expression in his 1965 essay on Freud, *On Interpretation*. "This active but fractured *I* is not only the basis of the superego but the correlate of the passive and wounded narcissistic ego, thereby forming a complex whole that Paul Ricoeur aptly named the 'aborted cogito.'"[48]

The search for the processes of individuation, of affirmation of singularity, cannot be reduced to a Deleuzean concept of an ego. On the contrary: "Individuality is not a characteristic of the Self but . . . forms and sustains the system of the dissolved Self."[49] No longer considered to be an irreducible, indivisible entity, an individual ceaselessly divides itself and changes its nature, making itself multiple from preindividual singularities according to lines of intensity. It is in the structure of the other and its mode of expression—language—that difference, finally rediscovered, is situated. The philosophical tradition has typically underestimated the force represented by the body, whose basis is difference. Spinoza was already surprised in the seventeenth century by the general ignorance about the power that the body could express. "Spinoza opened up a new direction for the sciences and philosophy. He said that we do not even know what a body *can do*."[50]

The issue, then, is to liberate the forces of affirmation hidden in the body in order to "avoid living separated from our immanent modes of existence."[51] The body is unique; its composition allows for none of the reductionism used by neuroscience to locate genes and neurotransmitters, claiming to reduce human behavior to a simple transposition of the underlying materiality of the human body. For Deleuze, the body does not depend on interiority. "No demonstrative linearity encompasses subjectivity because the living subject traverses the body."[52] This is the rift that produces the decisive shift in the philosophical demonstration that Deleuze attempts in the thirteenth section of *The Logic of Sense*, when he subjects the formal surface logics of Lewis Carroll to those of Antonin Artaud, which belong to the depths and express schizophrenic suffering confronted with life and death.

What the schizophrenic experiences is the absence of the body's surface. "The primary aspect of the schizophrenic body is that it is a sort of body-sieve."[53] The absence of a surface allows proliferating bodies to emerge from the depths. "Everything is body and corporeal. . . . A tree, a column, a flower or a duck grows through the body."[54] The schizophrenic body has three characteristics: it is a sieve, it is fragmented, and it is dissociated. Artaud can be contrasted to Carroll on every point, since Artaud discovered the prodigious language of the vital body. In the thirteenth section of *The Logic of Sense*, Deleuze finds in Artaud the "body without organs," which becomes central to his philosophy and which he later called the CsO, the *corps sans organes*. As Anne Sauvagnargues points out, this organless body is not a body without organs but rather a body "beneath organic determination, a body with undifferentiated organs, a body in the process of differentiation."[55]

Section 13 of *The Logic of Sense* is a nodal point in the evolution of Deleuze's thinking, since the discovery of the power of the forces at work in the body is later superseded by the possible psychotic pathologies that can break into language games. When Deleuze wrote this chapter, he had not yet met Guattari and the psychiatric world was entirely foreign to him, but the questions he asks anticipate that meeting. It also seems that from this point on, the book that Deleuze was writing no longer responded to academic imperatives, from which he had freed himself, but became a way of expressing his own body. "It's a rather Nietzschean attitude, this sort of idiosyncrasy that leads to talking about one's body. Aren't his work and the various objects it envisages so many ways of modeling corporal movement? The living body is dynamic and in motion and the issue is to find objects making it possible to describe that."[56]

Deleuze was deeply interested in psychoanalysis, an area to which he had already devoted his much-remarked study on Sacher-Masoch. The psychotic represents a blind spot in psychoanalytic practice, which cannot account for psychosis or heal those affected by these serious illnesses. Deleuze considered that psychoanalysis, in its realism, materialism, and individualism, remained a prisoner of repetition. Its theory of repetition was based on a philosophy of simple representation, starting from a principle of identity and of divergences from an initial model. Of course, the repetition operating in psychoanalysis did take on different faces at different times, but there again, Deleuze differs from Freud's notion of causality when he sees a process of repression at work that provokes misrepresentations of the same: "We do not repeat because we repress. We repress because we repeat."[57]

Just as Deleuze criticized the mechanism of contradiction in the Hegelian dialectic, so too he criticizes the underlying dualism in Freud's thinking, which, in his theory of drives, favors the conflictual model over the simple form of direct opposition, whereas "conflicts are the result of more subtle differential mechanisms (displacements and disguises)."[58] Deleuze acknowledges the importance of Melanie Klein's exploration of the theater of terror, in which babies spend their first year of life, lost among a whole series of introjected and projected partial objects that, given the depth mediated by these simulacra, make communication among bodies possible. "Melanie Klein describes it as the paranoid-schizophrenic position of the child."[59] Klein describes this attempt to achieve identity corresponding to these partial objects as resembling an understanding of the schizophrenic's position, which, far from substituting the good object for the bad object, proposes instead an organism without parts, or a body without organs.

In *The Logic of Sense*, Deleuze was already taking aim at the importance of the Oedipus complex in Freudian theory. Far from seeing Oedipal incest as leading to depressive frustration or schizoid aggression, Deleuze sees Oedipal desire as an attempt to destroy these risks in a salutary spirit. He even goes so far as to present Oedipus as "Herculean . . . a peacemaker."[60] Oedipus had the best intentions in the world, but the story ended badly. Contrary to the claims of Freudians, Oedipus is merely a "tragedy of Semblance [*Apparance*]."[61] In terms of the Stoic tradition, the story is something that happens, a pure event projected to the plane of immanence.

In 1969, Deleuze still recognized psychoanalysis as a promising discipline and a true "science of events,"[62] not because it could unveil the meaning of events but because the event is the meaning. Here, Deleuze agrees with Freud in trying to distinguish the event from the state of things where it occurred. The second merit of psychoanalysis is, thanks to its theory of fantasy, its decentering of the subject. Deleuze, like most intellectuals during the late 1960s, considered psychoanalysis to be a preeminent science, and he read Jacques Lacan and Serge Leclaire's efforts to explain bodily logics with particular attention.

REHABILITATING THE VANQUISHED

With his consummate ability to think against the times, Deleuze looked critically at the peremptory affirmations of triumphant traditions and chose instead to rehabilitate some that were forgotten and possibly unacknowledged. He revisited and corrected past controversies by examining those losers whose futures were often more interesting than the quickly institutionalized winners. In the late nineteenth century, Émile Durkheim embodied French sociology, and his ideas, along with those of his school, dominated; indeed, the structuralist triumph of the 1960s was an extension of Durkheim's dominance. In a long note in his thesis, Deleuze unearthed Gabriel Tarde, whose sociological theories lost out to Durkheim's, noting, "Gabriel Tarde's philosophy is one of the last great philosophies of nature, in the tradition of Leibniz."[63]

We can understand Deleuze's interest in Tarde's sociology, which drew inspiration from Leibniz, given that for Tarde, "difference [was] its own goal."[64] Tarde wrote that "to exist is to differ," and at the turn of the century, he attempted to restore the specific dynamic of difference. Tarde refused to reify the social world and see it as a thing, because he saw collective representations as constructed rather than as given, as being shaped by currents of imitation and movements of invention.[65] "Tarde was in fact interested in the world of detail or the infinitesimal: the small *imitations, oppositions, and inventions* comprising a whole subrepresentative material."[66] Durkheim and his school accused Tarde of wanting to reduce sociology to psychology or interpsychology and of presuming to explain the social through the individual. "Tarde never recovered from their attack."[67] He was eliminated from the humanities because of a misunderstanding that was used in a polemic against him, although he had never intended to claim that imitation depended on individual logic but rather that it "belongs to a flow or to a wave but not to the individual. *Imitation is the extension of a flow.*"[68] For Tarde, infinitesimal calculations and statistics in general are important for grasping the molecular status of the tiniest transformations in beliefs and desires. To practice microsociology as Tarde invented it "is to study the spread of the waves propagating belief and desire that run through the social realm."[69]

Tarde was a jurist and he disagreed with Lombroso's biological theories of criminality, seeking instead a social explanation for criminal acts, but he also diverged from Durkheim's notion of criminality as a "normal" social phenomenon that could not be attributed to individuals. Tarde's battle on two fronts in no way helped make his ideas well known. He refused reductionism of any type and instead relied on biological knowledge and statistical competence.

As Eric Alliez has pointed out, Tarde's project had a Leibnizian perspective. "It would be impossible to project any other than a Leibnizian starting point."[70] Indeed, Tarde drew inspiration from Leibniz to develop a form of panvitalism of the infinitesimal. Durkheim managed to present Tarde as a psychologist who was arguing for a purely individualistic method influenced by biological naturalism, whereas Tarde was trying to develop a universal sociology based on an approach that allowed for differences and multiplicities of living things, in keeping with Leibniz's principle that the world in its entirety is contained in any given monad. From the outset, Tarde took a sociological perspective. He emphasized a vector at work in society, a sort of desire to be specific to each monad, "a sense as close as possible to *force*."[71] A logic of the power of being of a Spinozan order was at work and oriented desire toward an act of "having." "There's a constitutive power of the *socius* in Tarde."[72] It is easy to see how Deleuze was attracted to vitalist materialism oriented toward freeing the plurality of forces and changing Durkheim's conception of society as a thing into social vitalism. In his 1968 thesis and again with Guattari in 1980, Deleuze emphasizes Tarde's contribution: his words fell on deaf ears. Deleuze's reappropriation was prophetic, however: a "Tarde effect" took hold in France in the late 1990s and was all the more striking for having been delayed for so long.

Deleuze viewed one of his own contemporaries, Gilbert Simondon, as an important thinker. Simondon was a solitary thinker who was interested in phenomena of individuation at the crossroads of technical, scientific and philosophical cultures. Deleuze found in Simondon a quest for the processes of individualization, which began with the encounter of two orders of magnitude, which unleashed a wave, intensity, and potentials. "Individualization is the act by which intensity determines which differential relationships are realized."[73] Simondon explored this preindividual stratum as a reservoir of singularities.[74] For him and for Deleuze, an individual is not a stable being but the result of an encounter of processes, operations, and forms and of differential energies "between affects, percepts, and emotions."[75]

In himself, Simondon constituted "an amazing world, that of a 1960s encyclopedist who marvelously linked physics, biology, and philosophy."[76] An expert who understood the inner workings of the technical world, he worked in a laboratory on rue Serpente, where he carried out his experiments. Simondon despaired of his epoch's failure in its encounter with technical innovation because most users of technology were entirely ignorant of how technology worked and of the stakes involved.

In 1966, Deleuze wrote a review of the publication of a portion of Simondon's doctoral thesis, which he had defended in 1958.[77] Deleuze was struck by Simondon's originality, feeling that he had finally found a thinker for whom the individual "is not only the result but the *milieu* of individuation."[78] He also found some support in his battle with Hegel in the notion of *disparation* (a technical term—dephasing), which was adopted from the psychophysiology of perception. Deleuze found disparation more appropriate and profound than Hegel's notion of opposition.

Deleuze adopted Simondon's theory of individuation through intensive differentiation. "Individuation appears to be the arrival of a new moment in Being, the moment of the phased *being*, coupled with itself."[79] Deleuze discerned an ontological dimension here that was an ontology of difference and of multiplicities. "Simondon worked out an entire ontology according to which Being is never One."[80] Deleuze used this effectively against the Hegelian dialectic: the idea of disparation led to Deleuze's concept of *dispars*, of constituent disparity and of difference in itself. "This theory of *dispars* prepares the heterogeneous synthesis and defines difference as difference of difference."[81]

Simondon also helped Deleuze consolidate the notion of the body without organs by giving it some biological basis. In Simondon's work, Deleuze finds the art of limits removed from the duality of internal/external, which made it possible to say "the skin is what's deepest": "The living being lives at its limits, on its limits. . . . The polarity that characterizes life is at the level of the membrane."[82] Such an approach to living beings also skirts all mechanistic explanations of causality and substitutes the notion of processes with multiple variations of intensity.

Deleuze resurrected another vanquished scientist, the biologist Étienne Geoffroy Saint-Hilaire, who had lost his battle against Cuvier. Here again, as in the confrontation between Durkheim and Tarde, Deleuze is interested in the temporal element, the introduction of a dynamic and the attention to an open process, as opposed to Cuvier's static typology. At the time, however, Cuvier was the modernist who had laid the foundations for new approaches to biology and had studied the coordination of various functions for each species. By contrast with this functional approach, Geoffroy Saint-Hilaire saw that "the introduction of the temporal element is essential."[83] Deleuze drew on Geoffroy Saint-Hilaire as he did on Simondon to buttress his ontology of difference. The body must free itself from the yoke of its functions; Deleuze evoked "Geoffroy's genius"[84] because, unlike Cuvier, Saint-Hilaire addressed the differential relationships among pure anatomical elements.

In 1837, Geoffroy Saint-Hilaire claimed to dream of being the Newton of the infinitely small, to "discover 'the world of details' or 'very short distance,' ideal connections beneath the cruder play of sensible and conceptual differences and resemblances."[85] These differentiations were also about speed, intensity, and slow moments in "the actualization of an essence."[86] Contrasting the arguments of Cuvier and Saint-Hilaire, Deleuze introduced the concept of the fold for the first time in his thesis and used it as the title of his 1988 essay on Leibniz. "The discussion finds its poetic method and test in *folding*: is it possible to go from Vertebrate to Cephalopod by folding?"[87] Deleuze made Geoffroy Saint-Hilaire into the exponent of a monist, Spinozan concept affirming a compositional arrangement like pure multiplicity. Geoffroy's ideas let him argue for the faculty of variations of differentiating actualization. "The Spinoza/Geoffroy Saint-Hilaire relationship should get a special place in the organization of the composition that provides the starting point for Deleuze's conception of immanence."[88]

Deleuze also found some support for his ontology of difference in Raymond Ruyer's work, whose objective, as he described it in 1938, is to create a philosophy of differentiation.[89] Ruyer, like Tarde, viewed existence as difference, because creation operates through differentiations. In his 1938 lecture, Ruyer contrasted the mechanical relationships of animals propelled as if by a powerful motor, as, for example, when an animal goes straight for his food, with behavior observed when the animal is in the presence of some apparent danger. In this latter case, several factors will come into play with respect to the "animal geodesic," and the animal will avoid the danger and stay away. According to Ruyer, this avoidance has to do with creation. The animal creates when it encounters an obstacle, an idea clearly appealing to Deleuze, for whom true thought is not a spontaneous, natural operation but rather a reaction to an external necessity, an encounter, a break in the flow that forces you.

Raymond Ruyer wanted to integrate the lessons of the quantum revolution in physics with the vital realm of biology. He distinguished two levels that Deleuze and Guattari later adopted for other purposes, the "molar" level of large, static ensembles and the "molecular" level of psychological and biological microphysics. The level of individualizing interactions and phenomena were most important for Ruyer, concurring with the results in biology regarding the mode of molecular operations.

To reassert the ontology of difference as a philosophical program, Deleuze has to revisit what had remained unspoken in several works in the repressed tradition of the history of thought. Deleuze and Guattari did not want to transpose these works per se, however, but to translate and transform them into logical operators judged by their own philosophical construction.

THE OTHER METAPHYSICS

When Arnaud Villani asked, "Are you a nonmetaphysical philosopher?" Deleuze answered, "No, I feel like a pure metaphysician."[90] At a time when calling yourself a metaphysical philosopher was akin to being archaic, was this a provocative answer? The answer is unclear; Deleuze certainly thought about building an antisystematic system and was determined to work out a new metaphysics adequate to the logic of multiplicities. In a 1990 letter to Jean-Clet Martin, he explained, "I believe in philosophy as a system. What I don't like is when the idea of system is related to the coordinates of the Identical, the Same, and the Analogous. I feel that I'm a very classical philosopher. For me, the system should be in constant heterogeneity, it should be a *heterogenesis*, which, it seems to me, has never been attempted."[91]

His metaphysics is located in a paradoxical tension between the One and the multiple, never yielding on univocality or on the plurality of singularities that are all located at a level of immanence around the oxymoron that he called "surface metaphysics" in the purest Stoic tradition. "In fact, the metaphysics that Deleuze claims to belong to is less a name (an 'essence'), than an adjective (a 'manner of being')."[92] For Deleuze, the starting point is and can only be univocity: "Being is univocal,"[93] which does not mean, contrary to Alain Badiou's interpretation, that Deleuze's univocity refers to the primacy of the One.[94] In fact, immediately after having claimed this univocity, Deleuze adds, "In effect, the essential in univocity is not that Being is said in a single and same sense, but that it is said, in a single and same sense, of *all* its individuating differences or intrinsic modalities."[95] Deleuze's metaphysics is that of the unfolding of the figure of paradox or tension pushed to the extreme against *doxa*, common sense ever caught between alternatives forcing a choice between this or that term and thereby easily enclosing itself in what Deleuze stigmatizes as the true enemy of philosophy: stupidity. This is in fact the most important meaning of the philosophical discourse. "If thinking only thinks when it is forced and constrained to do so, if it remains stupid unless forced to think, isn't the existence of stupidity also what forces it to think, which is to say that it does not think unless forced to do so?"[96]

Even if it seemed that the structuralist paradigm dominant in the 1960s had dispatched metaphysics, Deleuze nonetheless pursued the issue, which was essential for him, in two books published in 1968 and 1969. Yet "we shouldn't make Deleuze into some UFO of philosophy. He belongs to a tradition and invents his own tradition,"[97] as Pierre Montebello pertinently observes. Deleuze revisits all of the classical philosophers, particularly the vitalist trio of Bergson, Spinoza, and Nietzsche. But there is also a striking concordance with what Pierre Montebello describes as being "the other metaphysics."[98]

Every aspect of the modern rupture, such as the Copernican-Galilean revolution, establishes a break between our earthly world and celestial authority, opening onto infinity and a mathematization of nature, a retreat of the sentient subject. It makes time and space external, which the Cartesian cogito and Kant's critique both reinforce. This evolution led to a crisis in metaphysical thinking and gave pride of place to the properly scientific realm, which made itself independent on the strength of its new conquests but became increasingly cut off from the previously postulated unity between man and the cosmos. At the transition from the nineteenth to the twentieth century, several thinkers tried to reestablish the unity between human experience and original unity. "It was an extraordinarily creative philosophical period."[99] The questions about the unity of Being reemerged, thanks to a profound renewal of metaphysical questioning. Far from seeking to reestablish this unity by means of the thinking subject's greater interiority or the primacy of the cogito, the issue became one of emphasizing pure heterogeneity and the primacy to the relationship between these differences in an "ontology of relationship."[100]

We can see how much this early twentieth-century search established precursors for the ontology of difference that Deleuze later championed. Indeed, the issue for these thinkers was to further decenter "Man" in order to better plunge him into his real environment, to dehumanize him to better humanize nature, in what Pierre Montebello calls "the most human of the metaphysics of the cosmos and the most cosmic of human metaphysics since the Copernican revolution."[101] The issue was not to revive the old metaphysics that granted too much importance to the same, to the identity of the model, but rather to construct a new metaphysics that returns to a philosophy of Nature that permits differences to unfold, because "Being is, in fact, on the side of difference, neither one nor multiple."[102]

Indeed, the major problem raised by these metaphysicians was the inability of science and rationalism in general to think the multiplicity of our world. Tarde is extremely important for Deleuze; he wants to understand the genesis of the smallest differences. "Tarde's hypothesis is that nature is the cosmic constellation of small monadic differences."[103] The issue is not to repudiate science, because its discoveries are essential for better understanding this dispersion of differences; it is to link science to the infinite universe. In this respect, the physical explanation quickly encounters its own limitations insofar as its laws do not take into account the lateral and transversal relationships of monads and their interpenetration. "Each atom is a universe in the making," Tarde wrote.[104] Seeking once again this unity and access to the univocality of the world, these thinkers attacked every form of dualism, and in this respect they share Deleuze's concern with overcoming the polarity between matter and mind and with replacing it by acclaiming life in all of its forms. "If being in itself is ultimately the same as our being, and no longer unknowable, it becomes affirmable."[105] As Nietzsche said, the world is "a world of relationships."[106]

As Deleuze conceives it, ontology should always be indexed to the becoming-being. It is for this reason that he willingly describes himself as a "transcendental empiricist," which makes him close to Whitehead. "Categories belong to the world of representation, and philosophy has often been tempted to oppose notions of a very nature, truly open, attesting to a pluralist, critical sense of the Idea, existentials, percepts, and the list of empirico-ideal notions that we find in Whitehead, which makes *Process and Reality* one of the greatest books of modern philosophy."[107] Later, in *The Fold*, Deleuze relies even more heavily on Whitehead's ideas with respect to the nature of an event as a vibration containing an infinity of harmonies. In Whitehead as in Bergson, Deleuze once again finds an exploration of how subjective production is capable of creativity. "For Whitehead, the individual is creativity, the creation of a New."[108] Deleuze was a transcendental empiricist in the manner of Whitehead, convinced that abstraction does not explain but should be explained and that the issue is not to ascertain the laws of the universal but rather to discern the conditions for the production of newness, which implies starting from the states of things that can only be multiplicities. There is a lot that is similar between Whitehead, this adventurer of plural becomings who claimed that "to establish the limits of speculation is to betray the future,"[109] and Deleuze, the great "immobile" traveler, whose journeys were speculative. Deleuze also concurs with Whitehead in his critique of Cartesianism, that it isolates reason from the rest of the world, separating it from the soul and from matter. Both thinkers were metaphysicians, and in each there is an "insistence on the importance of the full reality of the virtual, even if it is not actual."[110]

This surprising similarity has to do with this other metaphysics that privileges relationships, the conjunction, the "and" that becomes the source of arrangements, of the most diverse connections. The analogy stops, however, with the religious realm, because Deleuze's metaphysics refuses the relevance of any theological discourse, which he views absolutely outside the bounds of philosophical investigation. His problem is to embody the philosopher to the greatest extent possible, by separating these two incommensurable realms in a just manner and by asking questions unique to philosophy. With respect to this fundamental issue, as Arnaud Villani shows, Deleuze and Whitehead took separate routes: Deleuze refused all transcendence, while Whitehead's philosophy became a doctrine of salvation through redemption, otherwise known as "soteriology."[111]

Deleuze's last work, published a few weeks before his death and therefore something of a testament, is another metaphysical affirmation. "We would say of pure immanence that it is A LIFE, and nothing else."[112] On this final occasion, Deleuze mobilized the late work of Fichte, a philosopher whom he had not quoted much to that point, particularly his *Initiation Into the Life Well-Lived*, in which Fichte managed to get beyond the aporias of the split between object and subject. Jean-Christophe Goddard, a Fichte scholar, points out that it might be surprising to see Deleuze use Fichte, who is considered to be the thinker par excellence on the subject, but that would be to ignore the readings of Fichte by Jean Hyppolite and Victor Goldschmidt, Deleuze's first teachers, who understood Fichtean transcendence as a subjectless field of the production of sense, "complete immanence positioned as the foundation, an a-subjective field: 'In rediscovering Fichte just before his death, Deleuze was simply returning to the starting point of his philosophical undertaking.'"[113] Substituting the intellective and formative intuition of the mediating image for intentionality brings Deleuze and Fichte closer in their shared rejection of objectivism and of representational thinking by substituting another metaphysics: "What the image-fantasy, the dreamed image with neither dreamer nor dreamed world, shows is for Fichte and for Deleuze, being in itself, the true being, the Being-One as life and limitless activity."[114]

9

The Founding Rupture
May 1968

In May 1968, the March 22 Movement was meeting daily to plan expanded and increasingly combative demonstrations. When Anne Querrien, a student in Nantes, active CERFI researcher, and friend of Guattari, arrived on the evening of May 8 at the home of Evelyne July, Serge July's wife, she found a note on the locked door: "We are at Félix's house." The movement's militants were meeting at the CERFI office, at 7, avenue de Verzy, in the seventeenth arrondissement.

LIKE A FISH IN WATER

The CERFI dissolved fortuitously into the March 22 Movement at a critical point during the May demonstrations. On this May 8 evening, the CERFI planned to prepare an issue of its review on the student protests.

> So we had planned to meet with Cohn-Bendit and a few others at avenue de Verzy on the evening of the eighth and we were all at the demonstration at the Wine Halls. The demonstration wasn't breaking up easily and we said that we'd meet at avenue de Verzy, but Cohn-Bendit was with twenty-five people and we agreed that we'd all meet there with July, Sauvageot, and Geismar.[1]

Daniel Cohn-Bendit and the student-movement leaders were somewhat dismayed by the latest attempts to check the growing protests. Representatives from the National Union for Higher Education, along with Alain Geismar and Alain Sauvageot from the National Union of French Students, spent the entire day negotiating with the government's representatives, who were trying to quell the protests after the big demonstration on May 7 that ended at the Champs-Elysées.

At 7, avenue de Verzy, the assembled group was making a desperate attempt to get the movement going again. At about three o'clock in the morning, Alain Geismar arrived. He was exhausted from trying to juggle his union responsibilities, which meant that he had to negotiate, and his revolutionary convictions, which made him want to stand fast. "He wanted to jump right away into the fray so much that he came to explain himself to the March 22 crazies."[2] With tears in his eyes, Geismar explained how he had to accept the unacceptable in order to obtain the liberation of the students who had been arrested, with the exception of the foreign students. This prompted the general assembly of the March 22 group to mobilize on May 10 and insist on two demands: the liberation of all the students who had been indiscriminately arrested and the immediate reopening of the Sorbonne. At four o'clock in the morning, they wrote a tract calling for a big demonstration on May 10; four hundred thousand copies were printed.

Félix Guattari was largely uninvolved during the long night of barricades on rue Gay-Lussac. He rode in on a motorcycle at about four o'clock in the morning, disappointed, searching for his CERFI friend François Fourquet, finally finding him near Jussieu, slightly dazed by the tear gas. The street fights fascinated and frightened Guattari, who was no lover of battles. "I remember driving around. There were fireworks everywhere. On some nights it was really something."[3] What excited him were not the physical fights but the general proclamations: "for those who lived it firsthand, the experience was unforgettable."[4]

When the protests expanded beyond the university, Guattari was in his element. He watched as the revolutionary hopes for which he had worked since his thesis on the Left Opposition shifted toward the student movement, the spearhead of the social struggle and the only group able to get around the bureaucracy. But he was also amazed and stupefied by the spontaneity of the events. "When '68 broke out, I had the impression of walking on air. It was a completely strange feeling. I saw myself in the Richelieu lecture hall at the Sorbonne, where I'd been bored to death. . . . Amazing, it was an amazing experience. I hadn't seen it coming at all and hadn't understood at thing. It took me a few days to realize what was happening."[5] Guattari's group had kept him updated on the events over the last few months at Nanterre. Anne Querrien was enrolled in the doctoral program in sociology at the time under Henri Lefebvre and had been involved in the initial actions of the March 22 group. "I had told Félix that what was happening at Nanterre was a lot more fun than the CERFI meetings."[6]

Guattari was intrigued, and he started visiting Nanterre University in April 1968, to see for himself the movement led by the charismatic Daniel Cohn-Bendit, a talented orator with a devastating sense of humor and an innate sense of timing. Guattari returned to La Borde but called out the troops: doctors, monitors, interns, and patients were invited to join the ranks of the revolution in Paris. Jean Oury, the clinic director, was sympathetic to the movement but found Guattari irresponsible in encouraging patients to join the demonstrations.

During the month of May, Guattari and his gang were involved in several militant activities, including the occupation of the ENS on rue d'Ulm Street, an action the FGERI teachers had decided on. Thanks to Fernand Oury, Guattari was familiar with the pedagogical issues, and his FGERI friends often worked with ENS researchers, but the militants at the base had no idea that the ENS even existed and thus found its occupation somewhat surprising.

There was a more spectacular takeover at the Odeon Theater. Jean-Jacques Lebel, a former member of the Socialism and Barbarianism group, had begun practicing revolutionary art, staging happenings, and joining the counterculture, and he called for this occupation. Guattari and the FGERI were not far away and became the vanguard. Lebel had met Guattari through Jean-Pierre Muyard, a professional networker. In 1966, Muyard invited Lebel to a show at the Modern Art Museum in the Tokyo Palace, an evening organized by the La Borde clinic and at which the patients performed. Lacan had invited them all. "Félix was Lacan's heir apparent at the time. He was considered one of the two or three most brilliant guys in Lacan's entourage."[7] Jean-Jacques Lebel and Guattari had an immediate, warm, and intense connection; they were both seeking an antiacademic radicalism. When Lebel met the patients from the unusual psychiatric hospital, having just witnessed them crossing the theatrical boundary between madmen and actors, he was transported. He was particularly amazed when a La Borde patient sat down at a piano and played like a virtuoso. Then the pianist got up, shot the audience a look resembling Antonin Artaud's, and shouted, "Finally I am someone." When this patient bared his inner abyss to the public, was it performance or therapy? "I was overcome and everything corresponded exactly to what we were trying to do, in the line of John Cage and Marcel Duchamp. They came to the same point, taking a different road. They transformed their anxiety into art."[8] At the end of the show, Jean-Jacques Lebel introduced himself to Guattari, who said that he was already aware of his happenings and had been inspired by them; Guattari ultimately invited him to join the FGERI to open a new poetic and theatrical front. Although Lebel was unable to persuade his artist friends to work with the psychiatrists, he and Guattari became inseparable.

At the heart of the May 1968 movement and just after the Sorbonne had been reopened and immediately occupied by protesting students, Lebel wanted to occupy the Odeon Theater, preferring that to getting mired in student radicalism. André Malraux, the minister of culture, frequented this theater, a bastion of official French culture. Once the occupation had been decided on, Guattari agreed without fully evaluating the risks of a direct attack on a symbol of the State. The university was a different matter, as its status protected it against police incursions, but Jean-Louis Barrault's government-subsidized theater was a different matter! Guattari put all the wherewithal of the FGERI, his doctors, and the various militant networks to work. "Many were working in hospitals. We loaded the cars up with bandages, mercurochrome, and antibiotics."[9] Others stockpiled food for a possible siege. "We had visited the theater while pretending to be journalists and had figured out that we could climb onto the roof and bring up the mattresses. We had also scoped out spots where we could stash the medicine and food."[10] The demonstration took place on May 13, and the Odeon was occupied on May 15, with little damage; artists and intellectuals, Julian Beck, the Living Theatre, and above all an anonymous crowd of people gave speeches on the Odeon's stage. In the foyer, the head commando wrote in red: "When the national assembly becomes a bourgeois theater, all the theaters should turn into national assemblies!" Jean-Jacques Lebel, Daniel Cohn-Bendit, and Julian Beck spoke to an enthusiastic audience; people had taken seats in the orchestra and balcony, reiterating that the issue was not to confiscate the Barrault-Renaud Theater but to make it public.

Workers slowly joined the protests, particularly after the May 10 barricades, paralyzing the entire country and occupying most factories. The FCP and the General Workers' Union had kept students and workers separated, with the exception of May 13, when the Young Workers of Hispano Group, which had already upset the union hierarchy, demonstrated openly under the leadership of Jo Panaget, a good friend of Guattari. Panaget asked the CERFI militants to lend a hand at Hispano in La Garenne-Colombes, where the factory, like others elsewhere in France, was closed off by the FCP and the CGT, just as it had been in 1936. In front of the entrance, in a large area used as a permanent forum, the March 22 militants distributed their tracts, led debates, and informed people about what was happening on the campuses. "They had to display the March 22 flag, which was better accepted than the flag of the smaller groups. The March 22 group was so powerful that the CGT was obliged to work with it."[11]

Guattari's group of friends helped the workers. "We were bringing in goods from the Loir-et-Cher to Hispano, although we were somewhat concerned because we were supposed to be bringing in eggs that were all the same size."[12] The young Hispano workers asked their supervisors to organize a discussion in a more institutional setting in the factory. The compromise was to let a few students from the movement into the factory annex in the area used by the workers' committee. Representatives of the factory's management were frightened by how freely the workers spoke about particularly radical forms of revolt. "They started to talk quite violently, saying, 'what the Hell are we doing here? We should all go into the street to demonstrate.' It was so intense and violent that the guys representing the management were totally freaked out."[13] The union leaders had learned their lesson. The next day they arranged the meeting so that they could monopolize the discussions, and they quickly closed the factory doors to outsiders.

In late May, General De Gaulle's stunning speech upon his return from Colombey and Baden-Baden and the big Gaullist demonstration on the Champs Elysées turned the tide. Guattari denounced the attempts to co-opt the event, which had been launched by movements of the extreme left of every stripe. He hoped to save the March 22 movement, its spontaneity, transgressive creativity, and all the committees that had formed in workplaces and neighborhoods during the mobilization. The March 22 group "should claim the right for the committees of the base to remain independent of all the structures claiming to represent them."[14] For Guattari, the March 22 group was what he had called for ever since he had created the Left Opposition. "The March 22 group is exceptional not because it has remained true to its discourse as a free association but because it could be an 'analyzer' of a large mass of students and young workers."[15]

On the morning of June 6, 1968, the confrontations shifted to Flins-sur-Seine in the Yvelines. At three o'clock in the morning, one thousand special and mobile police entered and surrounded the Renault factory. The workers had been striking for nineteen days and refused to resume work, despite the Grenelle agreements. Seeing this massive police offensive, some isolated workers took off their armbands and went to Paris for help.

They went to the Beaux Arts and contacted the March 22 group and the Parisian Action Committees. A general mobilization was declared for the next day, and a meeting was planned for June 7 at five o'clock in the morning, near the factory. Police barricades were set up at the various entrances to Paris to prevent the Parisian militants from getting to Flins. Many managed to elude the police, and numerous confrontations took place on the city's edge. Chases occurred on both sides of the Seine. The day ended with the first, tragic death of the uprising, a young high-school student named Gilles Tautin.

Félix Guattari drove to Flins. "In Flins, I picked up some very young hitchhikers. We were talking, 'What do you do?' 'We are students.' 'Studying what?' They hesitated. Umm . . . at the Sorbonne. They were very young workers, maybe they were apprentices who said they were students because they couldn't imagine having the dignity to go fight unless they were students, which would justify them."[16] In June 1968, Guattari considered that the two most important events of the movement were the radical confrontations in Flins and Sochaux, because both broke sham agreements. "In Flins and Sochaux, both the CGT and the crazed cops denounced the uncontrollable crowd."[17] In Sochaux, on June 11, the police raid on the occupied factory led to the deaths of two workers, including one who was shot. The shift of students to the site of the workers' struggles was a transgression against what had traditionally been the well-guarded borders between these two worlds.

The shock waves of May '68 necessarily affected the patients and employees at La Borde. Many of them continued to shuttle back and forth between the Parisian demonstrations and the clinic. The antiauthoritarian protest was so radical that it thoroughly took over their universe, whose foundation was the protest against all forms of institutional paralysis. This small avant-garde world could not lag behind the movement that it had so carefully prepared. A strike committee was created at the clinic and connections were made among the psychiatric institutes in the Val de Loire region. Nearby factories in Blois, Vendôme, and Romorantin were contacted, and the interns Guattari had recruited linked up with the capital by making their cars available to supply the clinic with food purchased from local farmers. During the month of May, the patients were busier with the tasks at the clinic, since the professionals were often gone. "The movement was raising hard questions. What are you doing at Cour-Cheverny? Do you think that madness is a political phenomenon? Why psychiatry? What rights and powers do the patients have? What does it mean to be cured?"[18] La Borde was moving from institutional psychotherapy to the limits of antipsychiatry, along the lines of Laing, Cooper, and Basaglia, who claimed that the institution itself should be destroyed.[19] Although he was politically sympathetic to the period, Jean Oury, La Borde's director, felt that the protests forming against institutions such as his to be irresponsible and fatal for the future of psychiatry. He hated seeing the interns get up at noon, when they were supposed to start at nine o'clock, denouncing everyone who was already at work as being "alienated by capitalism." Jean Oury thought that everything had been temporarily destroyed. "I said that it was like being bombed."[20] Oury accused Guattari of being ultimately responsible for the denunciation of La Borde as the "Saint Tropez of the Sologne." "It was too much; I threw them out."[21] May '68 put a definitive end to their cohabitation. "At La Borde, if you were on Félix's side you could not be on Oury's side. You had to choose your camp, especially since 1968 traumatized Oury."[22]

Before 1968, during the Vietnam War, Guattari managed to regroup the former proletarian *franc-tireur* (FTP) network of the Loir-et-Cher in the region's bistros to show films on the war. Resuming his practice of infiltration, Guattari and his La Borde group joined the local branch of the FCP; this massive addition of fifteen experienced militants was used as official cover for taking over many small associations, women's movements, cultural movements, film clubs, and so on. The fight for abortion rights very quickly became a major platform for action. Women's liberation and doctor's movements, including members from La Borde, such as Jean-Claude Polack, got involved in the issue. "We had established a very clean abortion method at La Borde largely designed by Jean Oury."[23] But at the time, the FCP was hostile toward any liberalization of abortion, believing that the more proletarians there were the better they would be able to build the foundations of a popular democracy. The FCP leadership eventually grasped that rather unorthodox things were going on in the Loir-et-Cher and sent their inspirational leader, Jeannette Vermeersch-Thorez, the wife of Maurice Thorez, to restore things by reminding them of the party's official positions.

"Comrade Jeannette" had already proven her hostility toward the birth-control pill. Her trip to the region was organized by the French Women's Union, the official front for an organization "of the masses" for FCP women. The meeting, which was supposed to be calm, as it was totally controlled by the leadership, became more confrontational than expected. Vermeersch-Thorez was assailed by questions, and she started shouting that she had no intention of discussing politics with lesbians. "The women started to insult her and she had to leave by mid-afternoon under their jeers."[24] This was too much for the FCP leaders, who excluded the Loir-et-Cher group.

DELEUZE AND 1968

Unlike Guattari, Deleuze was not a revolutionary militant during the two months of protests. The two had not yet met, and their concerns at the time were quite different. Yet the protests, which each of them experienced in their own way, paved the way for their meeting. In May 1968, Deleuze was teaching at the University of Lyon and quickly became quite sympathetic to the student protests. He was one of the rare professors at Lyon, and the only one in the philosophy department, to publicly declare his support for and attend the events of the movement. He was sympathetic and he listened. His student Chris Younès recalls a well-attended general assembly. Next to her, a student was complaining about students on government grants, like herself, having to take the exams, as she was already overburdened with a child and had a poorly paying job as a monitor. "Deleuze was standing next to her and got rather irritated. He said, 'But it's clear that you shouldn't stop the movement. The movement has to happen. You can see that what's happening is important!' "[25]

Deleuze completely agreed with the movement. On May 10, when his thesis advisor Maurice de Gandillac came to his home in Lyon, he found posters, red flags, and scrolls attached to the balcony by Deleuze's children, Julien and Émilie. One evening in May when Jeannette Colombel and her husband were visiting the Deleuzes, a student dropped in unannounced to tell them that the extreme right was preparing to strongarm the student pickets. "Gilles and I raced down the stairs to meet our students."[26] At the end of June, a former student from 1951, Claude Lemoine, who had become a member of Alain Peyrefitte's cabinet and was the head of the French Radio and Television (and thus in the opposing camp), saw a group of demonstrators arrive at the radio station, in the middle of which he recognized Gilles Deleuze. " 'We want to see Lemoine!' So I showed them the neighboring office, which they occupied for four hours. Gilles had recognized me and had a good laugh. For my part, I took the opportunity to get out of there."[27]

Deleuze's priority was to finish his doctoral thesis and defend it in the fall of 1968. He spent the summer working on it at the family property in Mas Révery in Saint-Léonard-de Noblat, in Limousin. He was often extremely tired, however, and consulted a doctor, who diagnosed the return of his tuberculosis, which had resisted antibiotics and made an enormous hole in one of his lungs. He was hospitalized immediately in order not to compromise his thesis defense, which was rescheduled for January 1969. Deleuze defended his thesis at the Sorbonne in early 1969; it was one of the first defenses after May, despite the fact the protests were far from over. Knowing that Deleuze was quite ill, the jury decided to abridge his defense somewhat so as not to tire him unduly; they were fully aware of his exceptional work. Above all, they feared that uninvited guests might arrive and wondered if the defense was going to proceed normally. They

> had only one fear: how to avoid the gangs who were at the Sorbonne. I recall that the president of the jury had told me that there were two options: "either we do your thesis on the ground floor, which has the advantage that there are two exits but the disadvantage that the gangs are hanging around down there, or we do it on the first floor, which has the advantage that the gangs rarely go upstairs but the disadvantage that there is only one entrance and exit." So when I defended my thesis, the jury president stayed posted at the door to see whether the gangs were coming, and I never saw his eyes.[28]

After the defense, Deleuze told his friend François Châtelet that he wanted a position in a Paris university. "Ah, what can I say about the defense, there's nothing amusing to remember, the abyss, the abyss. Saw Alquié the next day and felt that he was breaking with me. So much the better. But I have to find a job next year at Vincennes or Nanterre. I would rather dig another cave than go back to Lyon."[29]

After his defense, Deleuze had to undergo another serious operation, a thoracoplasty, which left him with a single lung and respiratory problems for the rest of his life. The operation required a full year of convalescence, which he spent with his wife in the calm of their house in Limousin. It was during this period of profound weakness and forced retreat that he first met Guattari.[30]

Without May '68, Deleuze and Guattari would never have met. The events had created something like a "founding rupture," as Michel de Certeau might put it. According to Joë Bousquet's teaching, to which Deleuze referred often in 1967, their first common publication, *Anti-Oedipus*, was rooted in the May movement and bore the stamp of the intellectual ferment of the period. When he commented on the publication of their first endeavor, Guattari confirmed, "May '68 shook me and Gilles up as it did many other people. We didn't know one another but this book is still an effect of May."[31]

PART 2

UNFOLDING
INTERSECTING LIVES

10

"Psychoanalysm" Under Attack

In the 1950s, Guattari would stroll through the halls of the Sorbonne swearing strictly by Lacan, the teacher who had inspired him. He knew Lacan's work virtually by heart and encouraged his friends to read him. He was a loyal celebrant at the weekly ceremony of the Seminar. In fact, Lacan so inspired him and he imitated him to such a degree that his friend Philippe Girard referred to him as "Lacan" in the Sorbonne halls. When Lacan created the Freudian School of Paris in 1964, Guattari was one of his lieutenants and even suggested creating a school newsletter, which later became *La Lettre de l'École*.

In 1964, Lacan started his seminar at the prestigious ENS on rue d'Ulm, a beacon of Parisian culture and an intellectual hotspot largely under the aegis of the Althusserians. Lacan became close to a new generation, including Jacques-Alain Miller and Jean-Claude Milner, who later became his personal guard.[1] During this period, Althusser was helping make psychoanalysis a centerpiece of French intellectual life and was squelching the last vestiges of communist resistance to Freudian ideas.[2] For Althusser, the return to Freud took the form of a recourse to Lacan, whom he considered to be an objective ally in his opposition to the centralized FCP bureaucracy, just as Lacan challenged the International Psychoanalytic Association, the official Freudian group.

Lacan managed to convince Guattari to submit a paper for his journal *Scilicet* but ultimately never published it.[3] However, when Lacan learned that his loyal follower was working on a book on psychoanalysis with Deleuze, whom he admired, he saw Guattari in a new light. Lacan was worried about the Deleuze-Guattari collaboration and feared the power and strength of conviction of their potential criticism. "He started calling on me during meetings: 'Guattari, what do you think about that?'"[4] As his concerns grew, he asked Guattari to show him the manuscript of *Anti-*

Oedipus, which was to be published in 1972. "That was clearly not an option! Deleuze mistrusted Lacan like the plague."[5] Guattari politely refused, protecting himself behind Deleuze's preference to show only a finished manuscript. He tried to reassure his former mentor of his loyalty, explaining that he simply felt the need to explore some areas into which he, Lacan, had not yet ventured. But having heard through the grapevine what Deleuze was saying in his Vincennes courses, which, in 1971, included the groundwork of *Anti-Oedipus*, Lacan was all the more worried. Without access to the manuscript and wanting to avoid future misunderstandings, Lacan asked to meet Deleuze, who felt that a phone call sufficed. Rebuffed, Lacan redoubled his efforts to seduce Guattari, inviting him to an expensive restaurant on the quays of the Seine so that Guattari could divulge the mysterious contents of the upcoming book. Guattari did indeed describe the major arguments of *Anti-Oedipus*, all the while fearing the worst, and was amazed by Lacan's entirely positive reaction: he was extremely interested in the book and added that he had created a school where different and divergent opinions could be exchanged. "He said something to me that became famous, like, 'What counts for me is that analysis exist.'"[6]

Lacan's remarks were deceptively reassuring. Lacan's question, "What's this schizoanalysis?" made Guattari uncomfortable, to say the very least.

I got confused and made reference to some sacrosanct Lacanian formula but managed to extricate myself as best I could. Incredibly authoritarian with the *maître d'hôtel* at the restaurant. I was hot and not very hungry. I explain the *o* [the "*petit a*" or "little other"] as a desiring machine, deterritorialization, history. I said whatever came into my head about anthropology and political economy. "I am listening to you. Very interesting. So, Deleuze went overboard at Vincennes after being egged on by students. I don't know if things are already set in stone for you, but I think that it would be interesting if an analyst were involved." It was an emotional moment. But it was too late. Something had been destroyed. Maybe it had always been broken between us. And then, had he ever had access to anyone or ever truly spoken to anyone? He'd established himself as a despotic signifier and maybe he'd long ago condemned himself to irremediable solitude? It was late. It was time to take leave of each other and go our separate ways. Our discussion had satisfied him; he was reassured. Finally! He said as much. Somewhat hunched, a tinge of exhaustion, he limped very slightly and his shadow melted into the darkness of rue de Lille. The front door shut with a bang.[7]

When Lacan discovered how aggressive the book was with respect to his ideas, all the bridges were definitively burned. Not only would the two never see each other again, but Lacan and his friends also started circulating a series of rumors about Guattari's practice to discredit him in psychoanalytic circles.

Guattari had not set out to attack Lacan but rather to go further than Lacan had in his thinking. At the time, *Anti-Oedipus* was conceived as a way of advancing Lacanian ideas. Guattari was well known as a Lacanian analyst and member of his school. In 1975, three years after the book was published, he still had thirty to thirty-five patients in analysis with him.

When Deleuze met Guattari in 1969, he was less conversant with Freud and Lacan but had already begun working on psychoanalysis. In 1961, he published his first work on Sacher-Masoch,[8] which he had developed in his *Presentation of Sacher-Masoch*.[9] Lacan himself acclaimed the book in his seminar, challenging his acolytes to carry out an equally intense analysis of their own. In his class on January 23, 1973, the psychoanalyst Jean Laplanche concurred that Deleuze had indeed attacked Freud's weak points—the manifest perversions: "He easily shows (and how could we disagree with him?) that sadism is not reverse masochism and vice versa."[10]

LACAN DOES LYON

In the fall of 1967, Lacan went to Lyon, where Deleuze was teaching. Deleuze met him at the train station with great deference. Lacan was already a celebrity, everyone who was anyone in Paris attended his seminar, and his *Écrits*, published in 1966, was a bestseller. Jean-Paul Chartier, the dean of the Vinatier Boarding School, had invited Lacan, and Deleuze, delighted by his visit, suggested a cocktail at his home, near place Jean-Mace. "At that time, Deleuze was completely fascinated by psychoanalysis and especially by Lacan. He was captivated by the game of the lost object, for example. His next books included a rewrite of his short *Proust and Signs*, in which he showed how the lost object played out among several scenes."[11] Lacan arrived at Deleuze's home but refused all alcohol. Ten minutes later, claiming fatigue, he said he wanted to rest. Embarrassed by Lacan's abrupt announcement, Jean-Paul Chartier brought him back to his hotel. A meal was planned at the Auberge Savoyarde restaurant in Montplaisir, where the guru Lacan greeted the guests, including Chartier, Deleuze, the philosopher Maldiney, and the psychoanalyst Fédida. Having just arrived at the restaurant, Lacan ordered a bottle of vodka and downed half of it. "Deleuze flattered him, 'Your visit to Lyon is really a great day and will be remembered.' After a moment, Lacan answered churlishly, saying something rather enigmatic: 'not like that.' So Deleuze didn't say another word even though he was about the only one to make any conversation."[12] The small group then set off for the Social Center hall, where Lacan was to speak. He was slightly drunk, threw his coat down on the floor, and grabbed the microphone to start his talk. "Place, Origin, and Goal of My Teaching," the title of his lecture, consisted in transforming *sa vie sexuelle* ("his/her sex life") into its meaningless homonym *ca visse exuelle* ("it screws") and to shed light on "certain things that might in any case ignite a small spark in some minds."[13]

When Lacan finished speaking, Maldiney was the only person who dared ask the master a question and point out a few contradictions. At the end of their exchange, Maldiney talked about an impossible dialogue or, rather, a double, interwoven monologue, to which Lacan answered, "This is not unique to what goes on between philosophers; the same thing goes on between husbands and wives."[14]

A small reception had been planned after the lecture. There, the psychoanalyst Henri Vermorel told Lacan that the lecture had confused him and that he found it incoherent. Unused to such impertinence, Lacan's face reddened with anger. "I felt my Lacan was getting worse and worse. Not even alcohol had any effect. But Lacan himself found the solution to the tensions of the moment: 'I want to finish the evening at Deleuze's house.' I sent someone to find Deleuze who, as a good disciple, agreed."[15] At 11 p.m., the diva demanded a cigar, and Maldiney ended up chasing all over Lyon looking for cigars while Chartier accompanied Lacan to Deleuze's house. "Deleuze received him very kindly; Maldiney came back empty-handed. There were a few students. Probably Fédida. But there was no conversation. Lacan had launched into paranoid recriminations against everyone wanting to steal his ideas and he enumerated all of his grievances, everything of which he was a victim."[16] Deleuze was the only person with the patience to engage in discussion with Lacan and transform what he was saying into something poetic while ignoring the polemical dimension of his monologue. "This little game went on forever. Lacan was tenacious.

Finally he had a servile audience that would stay till the end. He may not have been avenging himself, but this gave him the outlet he needed. Deleuze was immensely patient."[17] It is not particularly surprising that this Lyon visit was not one of Deleuze's fondest memories, and, for his part, Lacan left Lyon somewhat disappointed at not having generated more excitement; his reception had paled in comparison with the electric atmosphere of his Parisian seminar.

LACAN-DELEUZE IN PROXIMITY

For Deleuze, Freud's decisive moment came when he stopped focusing on real childhood events as the only significantly effective events and started working on fantasies. "In short, repetition is in its essence symbolic; symbols or simulacra are the letter of repetition itself."[18] When he established the analytic relationship in order to provoke transference from the patient to the analyst, Freud was still in the realm of strict repetition. "If repetition makes us ill, it's also what cures us."[19] Freud had already shown that infantile sexuality expressed itself in partial drives, and Deleuze saw a continuation of this hypothesis in Lacan's theorization of the object o. Unlike a real object that is or is not somewhere, a partial object as a virtual object "has the property of being *and* not being where it is, wherever it goes."[20] Deleuze drew from Lacan's famous seminar on the purloined letter published in the *Écrits* of 1966: "we find the pages where Lacan likens the virtual object to Edgar Allan Poe's purloined letter to be exemplary."[21]

Lacan observed Deleuze's reference to his work with great interest, and in his 1968–1969 seminar he insistently praised "the elegance of Gilles Deleuze . . . our friend."[22] He contrasted the reigning imbecility in psychoanalysis to Deleuze's demonstration of how masochistic pleasure establishes a contract with the Other. In his March 12 lecture, Lacan encouraged his audience to read *Difference and Repetition* and *The Logic of Sense*. "It so happens that Mr. Gilles Deleuze, as he pursues his work, has published two very important books in the form of his theses."[23] Lacan also implied how deeply his own ideas had influenced Deleuze. "It's his good fortune to be able to take the time to bring together in a single book not only the central tenet of my discourse—and there's no doubt that this discourse is central to his books since he says as much in his book, and that the *Seminar on* The Purloined Letter is his initial point of entry."[24] But Lacan also recognized the philosopher's contribution, particularly of having included the Stoics in his analysis. He congratulated Deleuze for being the one who best defined the structuralist paradigm. "You will see that he says somewhere that the essence of structuralism, if this word has any meaning . . . is a blank, a lack in the signifying chain, and that which results from errant objects in the signified chain."[25] Commenting on this praise, the psychoanalyst Sophie Mendelsohn suggests that Lacan admired Deleuze's ability to go further than he had in making a radical critique of structuralism: "and it seems to me that that's what fascinated Lacan as a reader of Deleuze in 1969."[26]

For Deleuze, repetition in psychoanalysis belongs to three registers: that of realism, that of materialism—where it is subjected to an internal mechanical principle—and that of unrefined, individualistic repetition—where the subject's representations determine the relationship between the new and old present. Despite his discoveries, Freud did not manage to break with the classical notion of representation that makes repetition a principle of identity. Deleuze also criticizes the overemphasis in Freudian theory on dualism, which privileges the conflictual model, which Deleuze replaced with an approach of disguises and displacements based on mechanisms of greater, multiple differentiations that are more "molecular" than "molar." Freud, however, was not imprisoned in a post-Hegelian dialectic; he moved beyond the dualism by proposing a subtler notion of differential displacements, which he expressed by claiming that the unconscious is unaware of negation and by valorizing partial objects. "The unconscious is differential, involving little perceptions, and as such is different in nature from consciousness."[27] According to Freud, the unconscious does not recognize negation, death, or time. Yet, as Deleuze said, these are the things with which psychoanalysis is constantly concerned.

In his conclusion, Deleuze refers to the way that schizophrenics repeat, in gestures and words, and he observes a contraction that destroys the differentiated levels, which has to do with a specific problem between two repetitions. In this respect, Deleuze was interested in Lacan, who had written his thesis on psychosis.[28] He saw psychoanalysis as a step toward getting beyond the limitations of classical reflective thinking, which proceeds from a hypothetical unity that constitutes representation; he already found this inadequate for a philosophy of multiplicity.

In the twenty-ninth series of *The Logic of Sense*, Deleuze uses the pertinent Freudian notion of the castration complex with respect to Oedipus[29] but shifts the forces at play, which, he posits, are to be sought neither in the depths of the unconscious nor in the heights of a superego but at the surface of the ego, in the universe of appearances. "We have to interpret the famous mechanism of 'denial' (that's not what I wanted . . .) and its importance with respect to the formation of *thought*, as expressing the passage from one surface to another."[30] Deleuze wanted to be done with the underlying notion of psychoanalysis as a psychology of the depths and to return it to the plane of immanence. We can see this shift being suggested in his conception of the phenomenon of fantasy. Deleuze considered fantasy to be a pure event, which, as such, is distinct from experience and logic and belongs to "an ideational surface on which it is produced as effect."[31] At this level Deleuze defends psychoanalytic discourse as the expression of pure events: murder-incest-castration.

Psychoanalysis would be the grand science of events on the condition that it not argue that the meaning of the event had to be sought out—the event embodies the sense that emerges in it as it happens. Here, Deleuze still agrees with Freud and Lacan in their analysis of the phallus as fundamentally marked by excess or lack, a veritable point of imbalance always separated from its own origin, a floating signifier, an empty site acting on the pregenital and Oedipal series. But Deleuze again relates this to a source phenomenon whose effect is to transform one series into a signifying series and the other into a signified series. That which is deepest is located on the surface, and *The Logic of Sense* presents an explanation of the paradoxes in the theory of sense. "This book is an attempt at a logical psychoanalytical novel."[32]

At the end of the 1960s, when psychoanalysis was the reigning discipline of structuralism, Deleuze seemed to be borrowing the language and approach of his contemporaries. But this adherence to the language of the moment was in appearance only: he wanted to reveal the psychoanalytic claim to having the inside line on unveiling truth assumed to be deeply hidden and elusive because always blocked. He makes his position quite clear in the eighteenth series, in his discussion of the "three images of philosophers."

In this chapter, Deleuze condemns two attempts to lead the philosopher astray. On the one hand, ever since Plato, there has been the belief that truth can only be elevated, outside the cave, in a sky purified of earthly illusions, in the supralunar universe. "The philosopher's work is always defined as an ascent and a conversion, as the movement of turning towards the lofty principle from which the movement proceeds."[33] In contrast to this tendency to define philosophy as a soaring flight toward the heights, the opposite perversion amounts to looking in the basement, digging as deeply as possible to unearth a hidden truth: the position defined by the pre-Socratics. "The pre-Socratics located thought inside the caverns and life in the depths. They wanted to plumb water and fire. And, like Empedocles smashing the statues, they philosophize with a hammer, the hammer of the geologist and the speleologist."[34] From this arose an entire hermeneutic tradition tirelessly tracking truth beneath its mask; psychoanalysis joins in this quest that Deleuze considered vain.

To these two other traditions Deleuze compares a third initially expressed by the Greek Stoics; awaiting neither heavenly nor autochthonic salvation, they looked laterally, from the event eastward to where the sun rose. The end of the staff offers the solution, on the very surface of immanence. The Stoics' great discovery was to reconsider the surface as an autonomous field, as opposed to the illusions being sought, erroneously, above or below it. This is what Deleuze calls "the staff-blow philosophy,"[35] which should replace the philosophy of hammer blows that includes psychoanalysis, among other things. This immanent perspective made Deleuze's philosophical project quite unique and kept him at a critical remove from psychoanalysis—until he met Guattari. The connections between the vertical logics are on the surface; the plane of immanence should therefore be the privileged realm of investigation from which the echoes of the deep drives and idealized images are made to resonate. This is the experience of a schizophrenic, for whom there are only surfaces, whose body becomes a body-sieve, something expressed magnificently well by Antonin Artaud, who became Deleuze's guide to the realm of schizophrenia when he was writing *The Logic of Sense*. Deleuze borrowed from him a metaphor, which he turned into his essential concept of the body without organs. "No mouth No tongue No teeth No larynx No esophagus No stomach No belly No anus I will reconstruct the man that I am." (The body without organs is fashioned of blood and bones alone.)[36]

In 1969 and 1970, Deleuze was working on schizophrenia. In 1970, he wrote the preface to Louis Wolfson's *The Schizo and Languages*.[37] Deleuze was interested in *how* Wolfson strained language to its limits in a way that recalled Raymond Roussel, in whom Foucault was very interested. The process of schizophrenic proliferation places words in phonically similar but meaningless combinations. But unlike Roussel,[38] who considered that he was working on the poetic dimension of literary creation, Wolfson wanted to liberate himself in every possible way from his mother tongue, which he found oppressive. He wanted neither to make art nor to undertake a scientific experiment but simply to give free rein to his pathogenic inspiration.

Wolfson's goal was to destroy in order to create, to kill his mother tongue so that a new language could be born. Rejecting his mother tongue meant rejecting imposed knowledge, and it recalled his aversion to eating. Only knowledge made life worthwhile, but life was linked to rot, so he had to find another combination of life and knowledge, by disseminating words according to other signifying series. Here Deleuze agreed with Lacan's evaluation of partial objects as preeminent. "The partial object implies an essential phenomenon of *displacement* in which each bit, inseparable from the multiplicity that defines it, nonetheless distances itself from the others and divides itself into itself."[39] Deleuze also adopted Lacan's idea of paternal foreclosure to signify the symbolic absence of the father for Wolfson, who was caught between his real father and his stepfather. "All of the symbolic is real. This Lacanian proposition is well illustrated in *The Schizo and Languages*. Yet, it's always the reference to Klein that is cited."[40] This path led to an improvement in the psychotic who, at the end of his inventive linguistic experience, understands that life is unjustifiable because it needs no justification. The only viable possibility is the adventure of words. "Knowledge is no longer signified, but is instilled in the word; the thing is no longer designated, but overlaps with and is encased in the word."[41]

As Deleuze and Guattari began working on *Anti-Oedipus*, Lacan was drawing away from structural linguistics and increasingly formalizing his thinking, using topological figures and mathemes. Lacan created a symbiosis between Lévi-Strauss's notion of the matheme, the Greek word *mathema* (knowledge), and the world of mathematics. He hoped to break definitively with the overly descriptive nature of what he called, from that point onward, "linguistery" and to be entirely formal so as to reach the pure Signifier, the initial void from which arose the knots that he started calling "borromean" in 1972. Having temporarily cobbled together the fate of psychoanalysis and the social sciences, he fled toward the hard sciences. "Mathematics was the only thing that remained, the sole nourishment of the hermit in the desert."[42]

In his seminars, Lacan was using more and more topological figures: graphs and tori. He made borromean knots on stage with bits of rope or strips of paper that he cut and recut to show that they have neither an inside nor outside. For Lacan, the world is fantasy; located outside intraworldly reality, its unity is only accessible through what discourse lacks. "Only mathematization gives access to the real that has nothing to do with what traditional knowledge has claimed that it is, but it is not what it believes it to be, it is not reality, but fantasy."[43] In attempting to conceive of the totality and the interiority of the lack of what is, Lacan thought about the interior of a space that eliminates categories of inside and outside, internal and external, and all spherical topology.

As he approached a mathematical notion of structure, Lacan was taking one more step toward abstraction and the idea of a free object linked to an operation of specific ideation, which would make it possible to deduce the general properties of a set of operations and to define the area in which demonstrable enunciations determine the operations' properties. Lacan's embrace of formalism was already moving him away from Oedipus, whose importance he judged to be relative, before *Anti-Oedipus* was published. He had already begun to criticize the Freudian use of the Oedipus myth, to demythologize this tutelary figure and to argue for the signifying structure of the Symbolic, particularly in his seminars in the late 1960s. "Lacan focused on the signifying structure and the Oedipus question comes at a place that ostensibly completes the function of the father, we could almost say that this place is something like the hole in the structure."[44]

A Duo's Work Plan

We have already seen the very unusual way that Deleuze and Guattari organized their writing of *Anti-Oedipus*. We already know that the issue is not to identify who wrote what, since the two authors defined their ideas together through their letters and collaboration. Before they began working together and before his first trip to Dhuizon, Deleuze wrote a long letter, dated July 29, 1969, to Guattari, reminding him that he had his article "Machine and Structure"[45] and his notes on Schreber. In answer to the question that Deleuze raised about the mechanisms capable of directly affecting the unconscious, Guattari answered that the unconscious is a machine.[46] When we read the copious notes that Guattari took, we have some sense of how important his contributions were, particularly with respect to psychoanalysis and militant political activism, the areas where Deleuze wanted Guattari's competence, which was greater than his own.

We also have to include Guattari's work on the Danish linguist Hjelmslev. Lacan was criticized for having repressed all forms of polyvocality in the name of the "subject of knowledge," which is the symbolic order. "Lacan is mistaken in having identified, at the level of the primary processes, displacement and condensation with Jakobson's metaphor and metonymy. He linguistifies, diachronizes, and destroys the unconscious."[47] For Guattari, the unconscious is not structured like a language, as Lacan tried to demonstrate. In contrast to the static structure, system, and taxonomy, Guattari argued for the production of flows, of deterritorialized dynamics, preferring to turn to biology rather than to linguistics for useful models. "Cerebral writing is in direct contact with that which, from the outside, is diagrammatic. *It is the organ of machinic affiliation.* Cerebral writing is in direct contact with the body's mechanical systems: perception, the motor system, neuro-vegetative, etc."[48]

Guattari also disputes Lacan's famous claim that "a signifier represents the subject for another signifier," arguing rather that the signifier in no way represents the subject but instead "the *represented* of the 'incestuating' repression." We can always call that the subject, but it is the "subject of repression" and not the "subject of desire." There is in fact no "subject of desire, there is the *production* of desire by a *sign machine*."[49] In his preparatory notes, Guattari preferred a cluster of ideas that appear, with a few exceptions, in the final version of the book, such as "transduction," which he borrowed from Simondon, and "transcursion" and "transcursivity," all of which can be grouped under the already old theme of "transversality."

Guattari also drew on his analytic practice, describing to Deleuze his patients' dreams and their possible interpretation beyond Oedipal categories. Among many other cases, there was that of the thirty-something former militant Science Po student who got a job with the journal *Detective*. "I yelled at him before vacation. . . . And I refused to continue the analysis (to which he was strongly albeit ambivalently attached) if he continued this way. After vacation, he relinquished everything: his job, his maternaloid and sororal girlfriends, etc."[50] As soon as things changed, the patient recounted a dream that seemed to be about parental figures, cadavers, and a monstrous sister. Everything seemed to fit into the Oedipal context, but, for Guattari, the interpretation needed to get beyond the family unit.

> This dream was an answer to the intuition I'd had before vacation: loyalty to the mother (he is incapable of leaving the family home) is

loyalty to the territoriality of the three children (a garden divided into three). Its object is *the hole*, his sister's and his own, which will be filled with the flux of mixed earth. It's *the hole* for the dead produced like a transfinite flux of corpses. . . . Oedipus has nothing to do with any of that![51]

On November 14, 1970, Guattari even sent Deleuze a confidential letter from one of his female patients on feminine sexuality to help them reflect on the differences between male and female homosexuality.

It is absurd to claim, as some did when *Anti-Oedipus* was published, that its authors had no relationship to psychoanalytic practice and were merely promulgating some disconnected "delirium." La Borde and its practices are omnipresent in Guattari's thinking. For example, in a note from October 1, 1970, he claims that it is not unreasonable to "schizophrenize" neurosis, because there is no true neurosis that does not lean on a psychosis. While classical psychiatry tends to make psychosis into neurosis, schizoanalysis should do the reverse. "It seems to me that it is far easier to care for a schizophrenic than a neurotic. Easy, that is, on the condition that you work at it full time."[52] Guattari provided Deleuze with a real-life example of transforming a medical setting, with the creation of artificial families at La Borde, which were baptized as "basic therapeutic communities" or "units of responsibility" to capture the imagination of patients and staff and move them away from Oedipal-familial folds that induce the classic patient-doctor relationship. Guattari described his first case of schizophrenia at La Borde: he would spend as many as five hours a day with the patient, who identified with his therapist's favorite writer, Kafka. Guattari had the patient recopy *The Castle*, and Guattari recorded his readings until he readopted his proper identity. Once cured, the patient left for Israel hoping to make a real contribution to Israeli-Arab peace.

As an analyst, Guattari conceived of schizoanalytic practice by favoring existential breaks, sometimes shattering factitious bonds in a somewhat brutal way. This led, for example, to his heartfelt plea, "Don't mix things up. I'm neither your father nor your mother. . . . Go to hell! If you want, implicitly, I'll adopt your expression, so to speak: 'I am only interested in people insofar as they produce something.'"[53] Guattari reacted when a situation became unbearable, as, for example, in the case of a female patient, a doctor by training, who lay on the couch describing her life as if it were a novel. He got up, picked up a book, and began reading it ostentatiously. In the next session, the patient apologized: "It's true, it was idiotic, I was talking . . . like a book."[54]

Politics, insofar as it transforms collective practices, is the other altogether fundamental aspect of the working relationship between Deleuze and Guattari. In 1973, in an interview with Michel-Antoine Burnier, who was the director of the journal *Actuel* at the time, the two authors emphasized that *Anti-Oedipus* was rooted in May '68. The twin logic of deterritorialization and reterritorialization was not a simple binary opposition between good and evil, since either side could betray the politics of desire. "On the one hand, deterritorialization lacks the arrangement of the desiring machine, and on the other, reterritorialization alienates them, Oedipifies them, archaizes them."[55] Confronted with this twofold risk, how did Guattari conceive of emancipatory struggles? He conceived of them by articulating a reterritorialization compatible with a revolutionary plan based on a level of self-managed subjective consistency, in other words, new processes of subjectivation. Guattari was always concerned with expressing the forms of collective struggles as new forms of subjectivation.

Indeed, *Anti-Oedipus* was first and foremost a violent return of the Lacanian repressed. Lacan's return to Freud had given predominance to the Signifier, the Symbolic, the idea of an unconscious emptied of its affects. Deleuze and Guattari attack this approach radically, opposing Lacan's cherished Law of the Master with the necessary liberation of desiring production. Rather than "I think," they substitute a more originary "I feel" that was nothing other than the production of a becoming. They do nonetheless credit Lacan for having shown how the unconscious is woven of many signifying chains, and in this respect they accept a Lacanian breakthrough allowing for a schizophrenic flux able to subvert the field of psychoanalysis, particularly thanks to the object *o*. "The object *o* erupts at the heart of the structural equilibrium like an infernal machine, the desiring machine."[56] Lacan's major contribution was to shift psychoanalysis from the Oedipal apparatus to a paranoid machine. A major signifier subsumes the signs, maintains them in a mass system, and organizes their network: "That seems to me to be the criterion of paranoid delusion, it's the phenomenon of the network of signs, where the sign sends us back to the sign."[57]

The book took aim less at Lacan than at his disciples and at psychoanalysis in general. Lacan had begun to demythologize the Oedipus complex but he had not crossed the Rubicon, and Deleuze and Guattari ridiculed the way that he had landed on his feet. "'Fantastic and brilliant regression: what an achievement . . . I did it by myself,' as Lacan says, to loosen the yoke of the Oedipus complex and lead it to its own self-critique. But it's like the history of the Resistance fighters who want to destroy a pylon and balance the explosives so well that the pylon shoots up and lands back in its hole."[58] Deleuze and Guattari were as caustic as Michel Foucault was about psychoanalysis. They used his *Madness and Civilization*[59] to link nineteenth-century psychiatry and twentieth-century psychoanalysis: both reduced madness to a "parental complex," and both considered that the avowal of guilt resulting from the Oedipus complex important. "So, instead of being part of an effective liberation, psychoanalysis belonged to the general bourgeois repression that consisted in keeping European humanity yoked to mommy-daddy instead of having finished with this problem."[60]

For Deleuze and Guattari, psychoanalysis progresses by reductions and systematically beats desire back onto a closed system of representation. "Psychoanalysis only raises Oedipus to Oedipus squared, the Oedipal transfer, the Oedipus of Oedipus. . . . It's the invariant of a diversion of the powers of the unconscious."[61] They establish a break between capitalism, which is linked to psychoanalysis, and revolutionary movements that progress alongside schizoanalysis. For them, there is no Signifying Subject, no room for any kind of transcendence; there are only processes.

Above all, Deleuze and Guattari criticize Claude Lévi-Strauss, the father of structuralism, who was fundamental for the very definition that Lacan gave of the unconscious as being structured like a language. They propose instead two divergent logics, the one embodied by the desiring machine and the other by the anorexic structure. "What do we do with the unconscious itself, if not reduce it explicitly to an empty form where desire itself is absent and evacuated? This kind of form might define the preconscious, but certainly not the unconscious."[62] However, Lévi-Strauss finds favor in the authors' eyes for their definition of schizoanalysis, when it comes to minimizing Oedipus. They make use of the myth of reference in Levi-Strauss's first volume of *Mythologies, The Raw and the Cooked*,[63] where the truly guilty party in the story of the incestuous son is the father who wants to avenge himself and who is punished and killed. Deleuze and Guattari conclude, "Oedipus is first of all an idea of a paranoid adult before being a neurotic's childhood feeling."[64]

From the Lacanian theory of desire, they kept only one of the two poles—that of the partial object, the object *o*—and rejected the "capital *o*

Other," which is based on lack. For them, nothing lacks in desire, "it's rather that desire lacks a subject or that a stable subject is missing from desire."[65] They recognize Lacan as having a special status for calling into question the relevance of psychoanalytic discourse and for trying to get beyond the blind spots of psychoanalysis, although they accuse him of continuing to promote the failing family function, of derealizing the production of desire masked as a belief, of an imaginary of representation, and of using Oedipus as a form of reterritorialization, as castration.

Guattari's mark in the work of the two authors is also palpable in the concern to anchor the quest for the unconscious in the collective social fabric. "We must draw a parallel between desiring production and social production."[66] Classical Marxists had juxtaposed these two dimensions, but their approach was unsatisfying. One could begin with the idea that there would be social production on the one hand and a production of desire on the other. "In truth, *social production is solely the desiring production itself under specific conditions*."[67] The social arena and the field of desire are therefore coextensive, a theme developed in *Anti-Oedipus*. The difference between technical machines of production and desiring machines is not a difference in nature but a difference of register, relationship, and size.

Deleuze and Guattari make the notion of the unconscious as a machine of production into the centerpiece of their demonstration. "The basic idea may be this: the unconscious 'produces.' Saying that it produces means that you have to stop treating it, as has been done until now, as a kind of theater where a special drama—the Oedipus drama—is performed. We consider the unconscious to be a factory rather than a theater."[68] The foundations of desire would no longer lack or the Law but rather the will to produce, to affirm one's singularity and power of being. However, *Anti-Oedipus* was not an attempt to restore Marxism or to encourage a "return to Marx," as some claimed at the time.

In his lectures at Vincennes, Deleuze was explicit. "Our work belongs neither to Marxism nor to Freudian-Marxism."[69] He pointed out three important differences with respect to the Marxist approach. The first was that Marx started from a theory of needs, whereas "our problem, to the contrary, is posed in terms of desires."[70] The second difference had to do with the fact that Marxism opposes infrastructure and superstructure, whereas, according to Deleuze and Guattari, no ideological sphere is cut off from the rest of society; there are only organizations of power. "What we call ideologies are utterances of power organizations."[71] The third difference was to avoid the Marxist will to recapitulate seeking a kind of recollection of memory, of a unitary development of productive forces.

> Our perspective is entirely different. We conceive of the production of utterances, not at all like a development or recollection of memory but rather based on the power of forgetting. . . . I think that these three practical differences mean that our concerns have never been to return to Marx but are much more about forgetting, including forgetting Marx. In forgetting, some small bits stay afloat.[72]

As for Deleuze, he contributes the notion that he borrowed from Artaud, the body without organs, which serves as the plane of immanence for recapitulating the entire process of desire. Deleuze insists on the important opposition between the levels of consistency of the desire of the body without organs and the three layers linking it together: the first is organization, which consists in making a body without organs into an organism; the second is signification.[73] Here "we will discuss an angle of signification," and, at their intersection, the final level of subjectification, or subjectivity in the making. It is only in *Anti-Oedipus* that the body without organs joins the considerations about immanence, and its position is fundamental in the conceptual machinery. Deleuze and Guattari do not limit its use to the theory of desire but extend it to the social and historical realms. With *Anti-Oedipus*, this entirely immanentist conception of the body without organs became the source of the life-giving energy for words and things. It was a critical, clinical, anti-institutional weapon and a new tool for defining a political philosophy. Guattari's contribution was to expand this notion, which Deleuze was already using, by enriching it and applying it to new areas at the crossroads of desire and power: the body without organs took on a dimension that it did not have in *The Logic of Sense* and becomes part of the polemic in the critique of Lacan's ideas. He contrasts the position of the Signifier, which is essential in Lacan, to the play of forces of variable intensity in the body without organs, whose field of application is not programmed according to defined functions, as is the case in an organism.

Deleuze and Guattari are fundamentally taking aim at the Oedipal triangle, the lynchpin of the Freudian demonstration, and denouncing its familial fold. "How does psychoanalysis manage, this time, to reduce the neurotic to a poor creature endlessly consuming only mom-dad?"[74] Psychoanalysis is predicated on a terribly impoverishing monocausality that leaves the patient listening to the therapist tell him or her, "Say that it's Oedipus or you'll be slapped."[75] Oedipal organization has not apparently resolved the question of neurosis and it is even less able to resolve psychoses, be they paranoia or schizophrenia. Since Oedipus cannot explain schizophrenics—those who have fled the paternal universe they no longer believe in—it relegates them to somewhere beyond analysis. "Freud didn't like schizophrenics and their resistance to Oedipization; he tended rather to treat them like animals."[76]

Contrary to what some overly hasty readings might suggest, Deleuze and Guattari were not writing a defense of schizophrenia. They wanted to schizophrenize the unconscious to rid it of the Oedipal, familialist scaffolding of psychoanalytic practice. To get beyond the Oedipal triangle, they referred to the institutional psychotherapy being practiced at La Borde where subject and subjected groups were distinguished and where the very idea of individual fantasy came under fire. The schizoanalysis that Deleuze and Guattari were promoting did not try to resolve Oedipus but to "de-Oedipalize the unconscious to get to the real problems."[77] It's not mom and dad who cause the delirium but rather the world: "Every delusion has an historical-global, political, racial content."[78] Schizoanalysis was an argument for a social and political psychoanalysis open to all flows and all signifying ruptures.

The schizophrenia that Deleuze and Guattari were brandishing was not the illness of the same name. It was a universalizing program, a limitless process, a constantly reiterated ability to transgress limits, to carry out a release. They believed that this process was at work in Anglo-American literature, which Deleuze in particular appreciated. Authors such as Hardy, Lawrence, Lowry, Miller, Ginsberg, and Kerouac all carried the world within themselves and could be delusional; they could break their moorings and scramble codes to facilitate the flux. Similarly those who could make language stutter were able to engage in inventing a new style of language that disregarded grammaticality and syntax to let the flux of desire flow and be expressed, like Artaud: "Artaud is the culmination of literature, precisely because he is a schizophrenic and not because he is not. He long ago broke the wall of the signifier: Artaud the Schizo."[79]

AN ATTEMPT AT HISTORICAL ANTHROPOLOGY

The second component of *Anti-Oedipus* was an attempt at anthropology that could bolster the idea that schizophrenic processes are historically rooted. Deleuze and Guattari defined three successive phases: Savage, Barbarian, and Civilized. While Deleuze had very carefully limited the preparation of the book to his discussions with Guattari, he broke his own rules by seeking the advice of several anthropologists who were close to Guattari. By the late 1960s, some anthropologists were making the Oedipus complex less important and culturally relative. For example, the Ortigues couple were doing fieldwork in Dakar directed by Henri Collomb, the ethnopsychiatrist who tried to apply the methods of institutional psychotherapy in Africa. They published a widely discussed *African Oedipus* in 1966.[80] Its argument outraged Guattari and Oury, who considered it inappropriate to fabricate an Oedipus in Africa. Guattari encouraged his friends Alfred Adler and Michel Cartry to dispute the book's central tenets. Michel Cartry, who was very close to Guattari, also knew Deleuze, having taken his philosophy courses on Hume when Deleuze was teaching at the Sorbonne in 1957. When Guattari was working on *Anti-Oedipus*, he asked Cartry as well as his friends Alfred Adler and Andras Zempléni to elucidate the anthropological questions. These ethnologists were particularly well informed about psychoanalytic issues: Michel Cartry had been in analysis with Serge Leclaire, Alfred Adler had been in analysis with Jean Laplanche, and both regularly attended Lacan's seminar.

When Michel Cartry returned from Africa, where he had been doing his research, he was invited to Dhuizon, where Guattari briefed him on the project. In the early 1970s, Cartry went two or three times a month to Guattari's apartment on rue de Condé to work either alone or with Alfred Adler and Andras Zempléni. Cartry and Adler were friends and Africanists, and in 1971 they had just published an important article in the review that Lévi-Strauss directed, *L'Homme*.[81] The article was about an important Dogon myth that relegated the Oedipus complex to almost nothing, and it contested the tenets of structuralism so profoundly that Lévi-Strauss summoned its authors for a discussion. Adler and Cartry showed that in the Dogon myth, the mother plays a very minimal role in kinship structures: she is either excluded or merely an object of lateral marriages. "We reason as if the myth put people in roles defined as father, mother, son and sister, whereas these parental roles belong to an order created by prohibition . . . *incest does not exist*."[82]

According to Adler and Cartry, Lacan's ideas already included the anti-Oedipus, at least according to their reading of his work. Moreover, Lacan was a good friend of Marcel Griaule, who had already exploded the Oedipus myth in the 1950s.[83] When Adler and Cartry's booklike ninety-page article in *L'Homme* "came out, we were like kids waiting for Deleuze's verdict."[84] The major discussion centered around Guattari, but Deleuze also agreed to be involved. "As soon as possible, I'll be quite happy to see A., Z., Cartry."[85] Somewhat later, Deleuze wrote to Guattari: "Adler and Cartry's remarks are very important for us." Deleuze and Guattari submitted their ideas about historical anthropology to their ethnological friends for a critical reading, which led them to rectify their arguments in certain places, as Deleuze acknowledged in his correspondence with Guattari. "I am extremely happy that you feel that our text is working well. And about Cartry's opinion, which will be increasingly important for us (his remarks are already making me correct some details, but will even more so later, so we have to keep in touch with him). Which doesn't change the fact that it's our agreement that's fundamental."[86]

This exceptional involvement of ethnologists, despite Deleuze's intransigence about excluding the CERFI sociologists, was essentially tactical. Structuralism still reigned during this period, and Lévi-Strauss's structural anthropology was its backbone. This aspect of high-level confrontation explains Deleuze's acceptance of breaking his own rules and quitting his study and his solitude. "We had to circumvent Lévi-Strauss through his disciples, even by force; and here I think that we succeeded. It's clear that when this chapter is finished, we'll have to an ethnologist (Cartry? Your Wolof specialist? Cartry, I think) read it."[87]

Their ethnologist friends were still skeptical about Deleuze and Guattari's three phases—Savages, Barbarians, and Civilized—but they were thrilled to be able to discuss their discoveries with Deleuze. "The fact that our articles were something that he worked from was both pleasant and gratifying."[88] Deleuze benefited from their knowledge of anthropology; they had him read Marcel Griaule and Meyer Fortes, one of Evans-Pritchard's teachers, and Pierre Clastres, whose work on the Guyaki he admired tremendously.[89] Adler and Cartry often started out with short summaries of specific, delicate issues that they sent to Deleuze. "We received these summaries and were often very surprised by their conclusions. The work was serious and often concerned the very sources."[90] Among other ideas that came under discussion was that of the "segmented society," a fashionable notion about traditional Africa at the time. A segmented society was organized on a large scale without a central government. The idea was not new, since it had already appeared in Durkheim's work. "Deleuze was quite interested in this idea, and he asked whether segmented societies should be described locally in a specific ethnic universe alongside statelike formations or whether they were rather the result of major dislocations of very old African states that had left no traces."[91] In fact, Alfred Adler explained Lacan's famous remark, "the only father is a dead father," from an ethnological perspective; for him, there was nothing mysterious about the remark. In his studies of populations in Chad, the only men that could become fathers were initiated sons, which could happen only after the symbolic death of the father. "The expression simply means therefore that you cannot become a father during his lifetime."[92]

In the "Savages, Barbarians, Civilized Men" chapter, the authors find an operator that shapes the three configurations of human history: the processes of coding and decoding, of the territorialization and deterritorialization of fluxes of desire coursing through the social world. The machine is initially territorial, based on valorizing the earth, which is conceived as a primitive whole and the founding pedestal of human history. This is the period when absolute coding marks minds and bodies. Tattoos, excision, incision, cutting, sacrifice, and mutilation were among the many practices referring to "a founding act through which man stops being a biological organism and becomes a full body, an earth, to which organs grab hold, attracted, ironed, survivors of the exigencies of a *socius*."[93]

The split that transforms savages into barbarians happens when a despotic State is created and the State machine imposes its code on its own people. The despot imposes a new alliance that is no longer lateral but vertical, and his people must follow him into the desert. The old code remains but is subjected to new logics enslaving it to the State machine. These first two registers both channel all flux, which remain overcoded. "*Overcoding* is what establishes the essence of the State."[94] One of the major changes ushered in with this historical break is the primacy of reading over orality. Writing is imposed along with the despot and his corps of civil servants. The writing system aligns itself with the voice as its model—here Deleuze and Guattari adopted Jacques Derrida's analyses and his critique of Western logocentrism and phonologism.[95] From this moment on, the law designates without signifying, and we can speak about the arbitrariness of the sign with respect to the signified.

Deleuze and Guattari also use Marxist notions, among others, to describe these two initial phases, but they then draw upon Fernand Braudel's work to demonstrate the forces in play during the age of civilized people, who always used the decoded flux that penetrate state coding. Capitalism is the system best able to respond to the desire for generalized decoding, whence the link with schizophrenia, the subtitle of the book, since both schizophrenia and capitalism seek to free the flux by every means possible. This is the universalizing aspect of capitalism that decodes in order to better set itself on a global scale and respond to the principle of maximizing market laws. "Civilization is defined by decoding and deterritorializing the flux in capitalist production."[96] We could think that as it freed the flux, capitalism would evolve toward a liberating decoding of the flux of desire, but this is not the case. Were this the case, capitalism would be the utopia where humanity is finally liberated. But schizophrenia is the very limit of capitalism, its external limit, and capitalism's job is to inhibit this tendency. "What it decodes on the one hand it turns into rules on the other."[97]

Whence the authors' concern to "schizophrenize," in order to move toward a generalized decoding. Of course the bourgeoisie had taken a decisive step by managing to decode castes, but modern society was struggling with two contradictory forces—on the one hand, an imperious desire to decode on the ruins of the despotic machine, and, on the other, the dream of recoding or reterritorializing the flux and all of contemporary history. "We are oscillating between reactionary paranoid overloads and subterranean, schizophrenic, revolutionary explosives."[98] Deleuze and Guattari make Oedipus a recapitulation of the three historical moments by having it take the place of the imaginary of the old overcodings that are central to capitalist modernity. Things are taken in hand to control the *socius* in the name of a culture of guilt and resentment nourished by the Oedipal myth. The process is furthered by three heroes of codification: Luther, who shifted the object of belief inward; the economist Ricardo, who reterritorialized the means of production within the framework of private property; and Freud, who refolded the essence of desire into a strict framework of privacy. "Instead of great decoded flux, the small recoded streams in mom's bed. Interiority rather than a new relationship with the outside."[99]

FOR A SCHIZOANALYSIS

The book concludes by introducing the potential of schizoanalysis and revisits the two poles of paranoia and schizophrenia, arguing from the outset that Oedipus is located on the paranoid pole. Where psychoanalysis lets us think that incestuous desire emanates from the child, it is in fact "the paranoid father who Oedipizes the son."[100] What follows is a binary development based on the opposition between the negative paranoid pole and the positive schizophrenic pole. While the negative pole tends to locate itself in the masses, in a molar direction, the other pole lets itself be transported toward individuals and molecular particles. The new contrast is thus between a paranoid, molar investment of a subjected group in the first case and, in the second, a schizophrenic, molecular investment leading to a group-subject. Between the two poles runs a transversal line through the body without organs, the immanent substance, as Spinoza saw it. The desiring machines are on the side of the molecular pole, caught in the generalized flows with many connections. They are something like empty signifiers, because they signify nothing and represent nothing more than what is made of them, much as Jacques Monod conceived of the originality of syntheses in molecular biology.

Here we discern a new quality in Deleuze and Guattari's quest: they use binary oppositions during a period that reveled in them—language and speech, signifier and signified, *socius* and unconscious, paradigmatic and syntagmatic, metaphor and metonymy. However, their goal was to move the binary toward multiplicity, dissemination, and generalized fragmentation. The libido is therefore said to be part of the specific energy emitted by desiring machines. While Jacques Derrida was denouncing Western logocentrism, Deleuze and Guattari are attacking Freudian phallocentrism for having anthropomorphized sexuality and considering that there is only one sex—the masculine. In this perspective, the female sex is defined as lack. Ultimately, this perspective leads to purely negative communication, because of castration. The libido finds its common origin in men and women in this absence, and castration becomes its mainspring. Deleuze and Guattari did not think that demanding the rights of subjected feminine sexuality was enough: for them, the libido has be pluralized. "The schizoanalytic formula of the desiring revolution will be first of all, 'to each its sexes.'"[101]

Schizoanalysis is concerned with opening up the endogenous game of the black box of analysis, anchoring it in historical time in a world where the subject is freed from the constraints of the various forms of reterritorialization operating under the yoke of guilt, lack, and the powers of death. "The death wish celebrates the marriage between psychoanalysis and capitalism."[102] Valorizing the processes of production in schizoanalysis places it on the side of *techne*, a micromechanics. Schizoanalysis starts with the claim that desire is in no way a superstructure but rather an integral part of the world of production, of the social arena whose every point it affects. It does so because it makes use of a range of indices: sexuality is merely one limited area for analyzing different types of investments of desire. For Deleuze and Guattari, schizoanalysis is far more powerful than psychoanalysis at elucidating these issues, because it looks beyond the family framework to all forms of sociability and even gives primacy to everything emanating from the social realm broadly understood with respect to investments in the family unit.

Above all, psychoanalysis reflects power relations. Here, Deleuze agrees with Robert Castel's demonstration of "psychoanalysm" as a power relationship that psychoanalysts themselves deny. For Deleuze, presenting transference as the source of this power is merely a deception. He sees a tacit contract based on an exchange of the patient's libidinal flux, which empowers the analyst in exchange for words to express the patient's fantasies. "Like every form of power, it seeks to make the production of desire and the creation of enunciations impotent, in a word, to neutralize the libido."[103]

11

Anti-Oedipus

In the spring of 1972, a bomb dropped in the intellectual and political world. Coming a mere four years after May '68, *Anti-Oedipus* still bore the marks and effects of the period. Daily demonstrations of public unrest kept the events of May '68 fresh in the popular imagination. Political leftism was alive and well and even occasionally managed to surmount divisions, as, for example, on March 4, 1972, when two hundred thousand people attended the funeral of the Maoist Pierre Overney.

In the same year that *Anti-Oedipus* came out, Guattari published *Psychoanalysis and Transversality*, a collection of articles describing his intellectual and political development; Deleuze wrote the preface.[1] In 1971, Guattari's psychiatrist friend Roger Gentis, who had gone to Saint-Alban in 1956 and was one of the founders of GTPSI, had published *Asylum Walls*, which led Maspero to ask him and Horace Torrubia to edit a collection on psychiatry. Guattari's book on transversality immediately came to mind, Gentis recalls. "One of the first books I brought them was Félix Guattari's book on transversality, one of the publications of which I was quite proud, especially since I was less thrilled by what Félix wrote later."[2]

AVOIDING THE SHOALS OF TERRORISM

Anti-Oedipus was a high point in the crystallization of a movement that might have gone awry, as it later did in Italy and Germany, by moving toward terrorism to resolve the ambient stagnation.[3] The Proletarian Left, the organization most prone to terrorism, disappeared in 1973. Was its dissolution an effect of schizoanalysis's cleansing effects on militant paranoia? Any such claim would be baseless, but if the theory of desire helped put an end to the collective death drive of the young militant Maoist move-

ment, it would have served a useful purpose. The war machine of the Proletarian Left and its best-known leader Benny Lévy (alias Victor) was one of
Guattari's favorite targets. In 1972, he wrote in his diary, "The PL has certainly become a big deal! For me, the worst thing is that he used the pseudonym Victor, the name of my miner grandfather from Montceau-les-Mines!
These Maoists are the absolute enemies of the essence of the revolutionary movement: the liberation of desiring energy. . . . Victor is infinitely
cunning."[4]   *Zionist*

Robert Linhart, another Maoist leader, attacked Guattari and the
CERFI group in late 1974 in an article published in *Liberation* entitled "Leftism for Sale?" Underlying the personal attacks, he criticized the deleterious effects of *Anti-Oedipus* and cited the book in the subtitle of his accusation: "The Unexpected Consequences of *Anti-Oedipus*; or, How I Learned
to Be a Good Salesman and to Stop Worrying."[5] *Libération*'s editor in chief,
Serge July, supported him, citing the need for a critique of postleftism's
transformation when Giscard's government used the protests to its advantage. "It's no secret that the famous Giscardian 'change' took its ideas from
the protests. . . . Especially since many leftists are complicit. In addition to
Robert Linhart's article, we need a long discussion about what happened to
the post-left."[6] Robert Linhart saw *Anti-Oedipus* as the source of all the ills
of waning Maoism. The book made it possible to reread Freud in the light of
Taylor's lessons to have proletarians swallow the idea that production satisfies their desires. "Let workers manage to 'get thrilled' by tightening bolts
and they'll become revolutionaries."[7] The CERFI, as the "armed wing" of
Anti-Oedipus, would thus ensure the lowly drudgery of capitalism; the book
was variously described as "profoundly authoritarian," as "paranoid delirium," as "a right-wing book," and as having a "totalitarian agenda"[8] whose
goal was to integrate aging leftists into bourgeois society.

A PUBLISHING BLOCKBUSTER

The press took note of the publication, especially since *Anti-Oedipus* sold
out in three days! *Le Monde* devoted two pages to it. Roland Jaccard, who
introduced the articles, considered the book prophetic in wanting to
schizophrenize society. A friend and former Sorbonne student of Deleuze,
the writer Rafaël Pividal, a professor of philosophy at Paris-VII, wrote the
long introductory article. He applauded the book for continuing the discussion about the relevance of the psychoanalytic discourse of Reich and

Marcuse while also setting it into the historical context of capitalism. He reminded readers that discussing schizophrenia was not an apologia for the illness but a valorization of a machine that, "instead of organizing letters of the alphabet into words, decomposes words to make an alphabet. That's exactly what Picasso did. But Beckett, Kafka and Artaud are three other examples."[9] The review in *Le Monde* reflected the reception of the two authors: Deleuze was applauded or criticized; Guattari tended to go unnoticed. This imbalance grew over time: on occasion, Guattari's name disappeared from references to the book's authors.

François Châtelet, Deleuze's colleague and great friend at Vincennes, talked about his excitement at what he considered the struggle of the new Lucretius, an effort to understand why men fight as if their very salvation depended on it in order to increase their servitude. Marx and Freud provided two answers to this important question, and "these are the questions that Deleuze and Guattari address, not to attack them but to restore the power that the idealist folds want to remove from them."[10] In his luxurious home on rue Clauzel in the ninth arrondissement of Paris, Châtelet organized a big all-night meeting with his friend Deleuze, Guattari, and about thirty other people. "The meeting was very intense. It was like a great Enlightenment salon."[11]

The attacks were occasionally brutal. Kostas Axelos addressed Deleuze:

> Honorable French professor, good husband, excellent father of two charming children, loyal friend, progressive thinker who demands profound reforms in every area where exploitation and oppression exist . . . would you want your children and students to model their "effective life" on your life, or, for example, on Artaud's, who was imitated by so many writers?[12]

André Green, the psychoanalyst, took an openly critical tone; he and the psychiatrist Cyrille Koupernik pronounced Deleuze's remedy worse than the illness. "Ultimately what Deleuze wants to substitute for Oedipus is an inhuman, a-human, proto-personal biological desire, which I find even more frightening. It's the mirror image of the entropy that haunted Freud."[13]

The review in *Le Figaro* was written by François Mauriac's son, Claude Mauriac, who was involved in the struggles of the Groupe Information Prisons alongside Michel Foucault, Jean-Marie Domenach, and Gilles Deleuze. He hailed the publication as an "important book." "It has to be read, reread, meditated on, while we wait for the reactions that it will surely elicit."[14] Madeleine Chapsal reviewed the book in *L'Express*, emphasizing that it was radical in nature and had the revolutionary intention of making a clean, thorough sweep. The book, "full of images and imagination, allows us to dream. Once they've cleared the space, Deleuze and Guattari start unpacking their new ideas. There's something for everyone here."[15]

At *La Quinzaine Littéraire*, Maurice Nadeau organized a debate with the two authors, moderated by François Châtelet, the psychoanalyst Serge Leclaire, the psychiatrist Horace Torrubia, the ethnologist Pierre Clastres, Roger Dadoun, Rafaël Pividal, and a student, P. Rose. The three-hour-long discussions were transcribed, and excerpts of the sixty pages were published. Deleuze and Guattari explained how they had conceived of their joint work. The tone of the discussion was positive and peaceful. Serge Leclaire was indeed a Lacanian, but he issued no direct attack—perhaps because his article "The Reality of Desire" was quoted in *Anti-Oedipus* as a forerunner of the idea of an unconscious-machine.[16]

ANALYSTS JOIN THE FRAY

Lacan was irritated by the book's publication because he had once again failed to secure the approbation of an important philosopher. He instructed the members of the Freudian School to ignore the book and to remain aloof from all the debates about it. Censorship was the rule. Many of his disciples were shocked by his reaction, including Catherine Millot, a young psychoanalyst who was trained as a philosopher, had just joined the Freudian School, and was in analysis with Lacan. "Lacan was really furious and gave instructions forbidding any organized debates about the book in his school. He kept silent and didn't breathe a word about the book in his Seminar. Somewhat later, he referred to it in a text, but he treated Deleuze and Guattari like a Schreberian two-headed eagle."[17] Lacan derided the reviled book by comparing it to the paranoia of Freud's famous Schreber.

According to Catherine Millot, Lacan took *Anti-Oedipus* as "a personal attack that was all the more hurtful because he had made some gestures towards Deleuze, whom he respected."[18] This war machine against psychoanalysis did take him as its prime target, along with his many disciples. Did Lacan change his perspective because of the book's attack? Not in any fundamental way, but it seemed nonetheless to Catherine Millot that after 1972 Lacan insisted increasingly on making Oedipus relative.

The following year, Lacan called his Seminar "The Names of the Father." Was this a response to Deleuze and Guattari? Possibly. Not wanting to be the dupe of Oedipus, we might well be condemned to wandering; after all, hadn't Deleuze and Guattari favored nomadism? Next came the great period of the borromean knots, and Lacan revisited the relationship between the Oedipus myth and structure. He was making reference to Joyce when he suggested that the Oedipus complex was one symptom among many.[19]

In 1975 and 1976, Lacan spent the entire Seminar, "the Sinthome," on James Joyce; his neologistic title referred to symptoms, and, among other things, he analyzed Joyce's literary vocation as a form of redemption through writing.

The psychoanalyst Elisabeth Roudinesco, another member of the school, was a young, disobedient disciple of Lacan who defied his censorship by writing a review of *Anti-Oedipus* in *Les Lettres Françaises*. She had been a student of Deleuze since 1970, the year he started teaching in Vincennes, and she had watched him work out the ideas of the book. She was torn between her admiration for Deleuze and her infatuation with Lacan, but she could not accept the direct assault on psychoanalysis. Her tone was both caustic and affectionate as a result, and her title ironic: "The Drunken Ship of Schizo Docks at Al Capone's."[20] Roudinesco discussed the book's collaborative nature, nicknaming the authors "D. G." and even claiming that "one is the other without it being however a question of being."[21] Roudinesco considered this incendiary book to be an updated version of Reich in its determination to link desire and the *socius*, sexuality and the class struggle. She saw *Anti-Oedipus* as "a very beautiful novel; like *Totem and Taboo* or *Moses and Monotheism*, it's the most beautiful apology possible for the Oedipus complex."[22] But she thought that the authors had missed their mark when it came to Lacan, who was as clear eyed as they were about the Oedipus complex. If the book is meaningful, it is as the novel of Oedipus as the bearer of a different mythology, a mythology of machinic delusion, a reexamination of a mechanized ego. Despite her reservations, Elisabeth Roudinesco recommended the "beautiful book"[23] to analysts and Marxists alike, notwithstanding its hostility to psychoanalysis and the fact that it addressed neither neurosis nor the hysteric. "By eliminating hysteria you're clearly eliminating psychoanalysis. D. G. is frank: we're playing the psychiatric card against psychoanalysis."[24]

Despite Roudinesco's vehement criticism, Deleuze invited his former student for a drink at a bar on the Pont Royal to continue the discussion. Her review in *Les Lettres Françaises* had not sat well with him, and he opened the conversation with an ironic remark. "So Simone Simon, you're attacking me?" Deleuze had thus nicknamed Roudinesco for her striking resemblance to the famous actress. "I answered, 'Yes, I disagree with the Reichism. I don't agree that using drugs will be the solution. We'll end up dealing with the pharmaceutical companies.'"[25] Firmly but kindly, Deleuze answered, "That's all very nice, but for the moment, all you can do is either imitate or criticize your teachers. Start thinking about finding your object."[26]

Psychoanalysts, however, could not avoid feeling that the very core of their practice was coming under fire. André Green rose to the defense of psychoanalysis, first in *Le Monde* and later in a longer article that he published in the *French Psychoanalytic Review*. He analyzed Deleuze and Guattari's work in strategic terms as a reaction or counterattack of philosophy against the Freudo-Lacanians, who had made certain inroads into the world of ideas. He did, however, credit Deleuze and Guattari with the great merit of having gotten beyond the Lacanian idea that the unconscious is structured like a language, and he was delighted to see that affects and drives, the specific concerns of psychoanalysis, were once again being discussed. In his criticism of the Lacanian camp, Green was thinking along the same lines as Deleuze and Guattari: that it was important to valorize an economy of desire rather than the formal logic of the signifying chain. He also recognized that the Freudian tradition made it hard to articulate a relationship between an individual and social structures, and that even if Marcuse had attempted to do so, analysts remained unconvinced. Green wanted to ask the same question that the book did: "What's it for?" We end up with the formula that the revolution must happen but that if it happens without psychoanalysis, it will miss its mark. "You first have to open the eyes of Marx, who was blind to desire, and to blind Freud like Oedipus, and send the complex to hell."[27]

The authors eliminated Oedipus but kept desire, changing it, abolishing lack, frustration, castration, and the law and transforming it into pure desire, an empty signifier that could invest itself everywhere. "We integrated desire into the machine of production and made the machine of production part of desire."[28] André Green disagreed with Deleuze and Guattari on this point, since he thought that they were confusing the experience of satisfaction, which can be imagined as freedom from lack, with desire, which always lacks its object, since it consists of making an absent satisfaction return. The way the authors jettisoned the fear of castration was, for Green, tantamount to a denial of all clinical experience. He remarked that Deleuze and Guattari's notion of desire was somewhat related to the way a pervert operates, making disqualification an integral part of his desire. "The specificity of the object of desire as a person slips behind the quality that it presents and that will be sought in an anonymous, interchangeable way."[29] According to Green, Deleuze and Guattari borrowed fundamentally from the early Freud of the 1895 *Project for a Scientific Psychology*. Consequently, far from being a conceptual advance, *Anti-Oedipus* would be a regression to a pre-Freudian Freud: "*Anti-Oedipus* is Ante-Oedipus."[30]

The book continued to make waves in psychoanalytic circles. Two analysts, Bela Grunberger and Janine Chasseguet-Smirgel, who had already published a book on May '68 under the pseudonym André Stéphane,[31] claiming that the May protestors had not resolved their Oedipus complex, had regressed to the anal stage, and were spending their time throwing "shit" into the streets and writing on walls, attacked again. In a garbled style that they claimed was inspired by Freud, the authors accused the movement of unbridled self-indulgent narcissism, whose frustration fueled a desire for barbarous Nazi-like regressions. In their book, reductive thinking soared to new heights! In 1972, the same two analysts, using the same pseudonym, published a book attacking Oedipus, capitalism, and revolution with similarly reductive results, justifying themselves by the critique of psychoanalysis in *Anti-Oedipus*, which clearly demonstrated the obvious divorce between leftist thinking and psychoanalysis. In Deleuze and Guattari, "we see mom's bed become the bed of capitalism."[32] They accused the authors of denying reality and all authority in favor of a free world of permanent revolution. Both psychoanalysts were openly delighted to celebrate the end of an unnatural marriage between a certain form of leftist thinking and psychoanalysis.

Chasseguet-Smirgel continued her reflection on *Anti-Oedipus* by organizing a study day on June 3, 1973,[33] at which Françoise Paramelle argued that no one escapes Freud and that Deleuze and Guattari were Freudians despite themselves, somewhat like Monsieur Jourdain, who spoke in prose without realizing it. She particularly criticized some of the ideas in the chapter on "psychoanalysis and familialism" and maintained that the definition of schizophrenia as a disorganized, disjunctive flux was wrong, because what the authors described as a way of realizing oneself in the world was in fact a way of closing oneself off from it. She also held that the notion of the unconscious coded by Oedipus was meaningless, since the unconscious is unaware of any code. "The authors think of the unconscious more the way Lacan does when he claims that it is structured like a language."[34] Instead of "Oedipizing," the analyst should challenge the patient's fixations. "We believe that the goal of Freudian psychoanalysis is to de-Oedipize."[35] In Paramelle's view, the authors' many massive interpretations ended up defending Freudian objectives.

SUPPORTERS: GIRARD, LYOTARD, AND FOUCAULT

Much ink flowed as the important intellectual journals reviewed *Anti-Oedipus. Critique* invited Jean-François Lyotard and René Girard to contribute to the discussion. Lyotard admired the torrent that was sweeping away everything in its path. "It's a pantograph that transforms the electrical energy from high-tension wires into turning wheels on tracks, for the traveler into landscapes, dreams, music, and works that are transformed, destroyed, and swept away in their turn."[36] Jean-François Lyotard warned readers against erroneously interpreting the title, since the book is not a destructive polemic but rather an affirmation, a positive, positional act. Above all, the book subverts Marxism, which it does not critique, and sweeps away some cadavers like the proletariat, the class struggle, and surplus value. Lyotard compared Deleuze and Guattari's methods to those of Baudrillard, although he noted some fundamental differences between them. Baudrillard worked on exchange, circulation, and the attempt to construct a Freudo-Marxism, whereas Deleuze and Guattari emphasize productive activities, shifting the core of Marxism and Freudian thinking.

René Girard was more critical of *Anti-Oedipus*, because it neglected the importance of myth and tragedy, but he agreed with Deleuze and Guattari that we should not look to childhood to find the sources of social pathologies. He disagreed about shredding religious belief and considered that the work enunciated, "appearances notwithstanding, a new form of particularly ethereal piety."[37] While he approved of their determination to account for a certain social delusion, he read the delirium through the lens of the mimetic desire underlying all representation and any particular object.[38] Using this model, René Girard rejected all attempts to anchor desire in physiology or in the mind, as well as any pansexualism. For Girard, mimetic desire exists solely in the dialogic relationship and a reciprocal becoming; in this respect, he approached the Nietzschean dimension of Deleuze and Guattari's thinking. "Unlike Freud, who remains bogged down with his fathers and mothers, Nietzsche was the first to detach desire from an object."[39] Girard clearly thought that Deleuze and Guattari had exaggerated the importance of the Oedipus complex, since it remained intact and was even aggrandized. *Anti-Oedipus* is "quite obviously Oedipal to the core since it is completely structured by a triangular rivalry with the theorists of psychoanalysis."[40] Girard did, however, think that the book had some merit for showing how those disciplines seeking a unifying exit from psychoanalytic ideas ran into dead ends. But he also argued that the book merely recapitulated and magnified previous cultural forms rather than taking a definitive step that would make it possible to be done with aporiatic perspectives.

The book also got a lengthy and rather positive review in *Esprit*, where a series of articles discussed its major ideas.[41] Jean Furtos and René Roussillon, both psychoanalysts, expressed their reservations when Deleuze and Guattari ignored the molar level to valorize only the molecular level, judging it more useful to articulate the two levels. The sociologist Jacques Donzelot defended what he found to be an "antisociology."[42] He saw the book as juxtaposing erratic blocks of knowledge that clogged the flux of its writing. *Anti-Oedipus* assaults psychoanalysis using Nietzsche. However, by getting beyond the oppositions between functionalist descriptions and structural analysis and between infrastructures and superstructures, and by ignoring the problem of the State as they did, Deleuze and Guattari managed to avoid many of the usual dead ends of social analyses. Instead of wondering but failing to answer the question, "'What is society?' the authors had the merit of substituting different questions like 'Where do we live?' 'How do we inhabit the earth?' 'How do we live in society?' These concrete questions led to others like 'How do we experience the State?'"[43] The social realm is no longer neutral and prey to internal logics but becomes a site for investments that produce variations. Jacques Donzelot compared Sartre's "group in fusion" with Deleuze and Guattari's "molecular revolutions." Territoriality was the authors' richest idea, he thought, and made it possible to get beyond the distinctions among what were considered marginal and essential elements.

Jean-Marie Domenach, the editor of *Esprit*, concluded the series of articles with a more critical one, even though he recommended that readers read the book as a distraction. For him, the book's inventiveness had a tonic effect and was more amusing than reading Lacan. "Let's let ourselves enjoy this gag for a moment. We don't often have occasion to laugh."[44] But laughing is not the same as agreeing, and Domenach refused to bow before what he considered to be a heavy-handed technique. He emphasized the unexplained expressions that peppered the book. "I know that criticizing a book that defends delusional discourse in the name of logic seems rather pointless."[45] With respect to their theory of desire, why not, but desire is never defined. "I fault the book for not facing the problem, of avoiding the question of suffering. We can use a lovely metaphor, 'desiring machine'; it's harder to say 'suffering machine.'"[46]

In *Les Cahiers du Chemin*, the prestigious but little-known literary review published by Gallimard and edited by Georges Lambrichs, Roger Laporte put his literary talents to work dissecting the book, denouncing it with unusual violence, wondering: "Who are we kidding? Who are they trying to shame?"[47] His answer: "It's the child who remains in each one of us that DG are trying to humiliate,"[48] especially by replacing the mother-father-child triad with the more deeply hidden Papa-Mama-me trio. Roger Laporte felt that the authors' tone reflected less their schizoid tendency than a "paranoid-perverse" language.[49]

Anti-Oedipus made headlines everywhere, but it had virtually no impact on psychoanalytic or psychiatric practices. Surprisingly, perhaps, it never provoked any serious discussion at La Borde, the birthplace of many of its theories but where its publication was a nonevent. Jean Oury confirms, "No. We didn't discuss it."[50] The psychoanalyst Nicole Guillet confessed that she had never even finished the book, even though she was a very close friend of Guattari. "Félix's way of working was fantastic, it was golden for me, it helped me a lot but the way he wrote didn't help me at all in my work, so I never read any of his books all the way through."[51]

Guattari was acutely aware that *Anti-Oedipus* never reached its target public of psychoanalysts despite the coverage. It was illusory to hope that the book would change practice. "Psychoanalysts remained unreceptive. It's completely normal: go ask butchers to stop selling meat for theoretical reasons. Or to become vegetarians! People are constantly demanding it. And they are right to demand high prices, since it works. A bit like drugs. And it also bestows definite social prestige. *Anti-Oedipus* has barely caused any ripples."[52]

The most violent critique other than the one written later by Robert Linhart was a vitriolic attack in 1973 by Michel Cressole, a former student of Deleuze from Vincennes.[53] An elegant homosexual who was confident about his powers of seduction, Michel Cressole wanted to write a book about his teacher. Deleuze was flattered but considered that his student ought to do his own work and refused to take him by the hand to carry out his plan. Because of this misunderstanding, Cressole began to loathe his former idol. He was vengefully derisive, claiming that *Anti-Oedipus* was the bible of a new sect of adepts of schizoanalysis who "resemble these operatic battalions who keep repeating 'let's march" without moving, and merely creating an illusion of movement."[54] According to him, the book did little more to the Marxo-Freudian couple than add a clown claiming to be an artist. The attack led to an epistolary exchange between Cressole and Deleuze that was published in Cressole's pamphlet.

Cressole's tone was bitter and his objective was to destroy Deleuze "as he is spoken of." Referring to a popular song by Sheila, he wrote, "You're out of it dad, like the song says."[55] He denounced Deleuze as the great ringleader of Vincennes, where all kinds of unsavory demands were made by a rigid Master who was suffocating in a little smoke-filled hall. At the same time, Cressole suggested that *Anti-Oedipus* could be used as a "fantastic toy" that two "mad geniuses"[56] had made available for kids. Deleuze's former student ultimately seemed to suggest, in his story of unrequited love, that he promote both himself and the book. "And what if the schizos became your impresarios? Your black worker's coat is already like Marilyn Monroe's pink dress with its pleated bodice, and your long fingernails and glasses are like Garbo's sunglasses."[57] Deleuze wrote a subtle, ironic response to Cressole's brutal, arrogant challenge. "You're charming, clever, mischievous, and even vicious sometimes. You might try to be a bit nicer."[58] Having been accused of using schizophrenics to his advantage, Deleuze, who enjoyed displacements, suggested humorously to his detractor that he had become a happy paranoid, thus pointing out that he had missed the mark.

In response to the attack on his physical appearance, Deleuze corrected the description of his jacket; he also explained his long fingernails:

> At the end of your letter you say my worker's jacket (it's actually a peasant's jacket) is like Marilyn Monroe's pleated bodice and that my fingernails are like Greta Garbo's dark glasses. . . . As you mention my fingernails several times, let me explain. One might say that my mother used to cut them for me and it's to do with the Oedipus com-

plex and castration (a ridiculous interpretation but a psychoanalytic one). One might also note, looking at my fingertips, that I haven't got the normal protective whorls, so that touching anything, especially fabric, causes such irritation that I need the long nails to protect them.[59]

Of course, *Anti-Oedipus* also had its supporters, and Michel Foucault was one of the strongest. He held that this book had a very special status, that it was more than a book: it was a pure event that went beyond the book object with such brilliance that it had to be appreciated for its affective capacity. "*Anti-Oedipus* refers to practically nothing other than its own prodigious theoretical inventiveness, a book, or rather, thing, event, has managed to get the long uninterrupted murmur that has gone from couch to chair to shout itself hoarse."[60] Foucault was enthused by the book and wrote the preface to the 1977 American edition.[61] He saw in *Anti-Oedipus* the development of an art of living along three registers: *ars erotica*, *ars theoretica*, and *ars politica*. The book was a true event of thought. "I would say that *Anti-Oedipus* (I hope the authors will excuse me) is an ethical book, the first ethical book that has been written in France for quite some time."[62] Foucault identified three types of adversaries: professionals of the revolution who professed a form of asceticism in order to have truth prevail; psychoanalysts and semiologists, the technicians of desire, who track the symptoms in the signs; and finally, the true enemy, which is fascism, not only the fascism identified by historians as a political order but also the fascism that lives in each of us. The book's essential merit was to introduce its readers to a nonfascist life. Foucault felt that there were certain fundamental principles that included, above all, the caution against the attractions of power, which implied resisting every form of unitary enclosure, preferring action, thought, and desire by making them proliferate, and freeing ourselves from the category of the negative. A veritable guide for changing daily life, *Anti-Oedipus* was not, however, to be read as a new theory "so often announced: the theory that will encompass everything and is absolutely totalizing and reassuring."[63]

Robert Castel, a sociologist and close friend of Michel Foucault, firmly defended Deleuze and Guattari's ideas. He saluted the book for making a contribution that was "inestimably valuable for a sociology that is critical of psychoanalysis,"[64] which established the relationship between the supremacy of the Oedipal triangle in psychoanalytic theory and practices with the social, political, and religious forms in which psychoanalysis was born and prospered. Robert Castel agreed with Deleuze and Guattari's goal of rearticulating the order of the investment of desires with social practice. For him, Freud may not have been wrong to establish psychoanalysis around the Oedipus complex, but he agreed with the authors' viewpoint when they demonstrated how psychoanalysis reterritorialized within the private sphere "a basic anthropological structure whose genesis was to be sought in the *socius*: this is the fundamental contribution of *Anti-Oedipus*."[65]

LOOKING BACK ON *ANTI-OEDIPUS*

Eight years after *Anti-Oedipus* was published, Deleuze considered it a failure. May '68 and its dreams were long gone, leaving a bitter taste for those who had high hopes but were caught by the stale odors of conservatism. Deleuze expressed his bitterness to Catherine Backès-Clément:

> *Anti-Oedipus* is post '68: it was a time where things were churning, a time of research. There's a very strong reaction today. It's a whole economy of publishing; a new politics imposing conformity. . . . Journalism has taken more and more power from literature. What's more, masses of novels are rehashing the most banal familial themes and endlessly developing a whole papa-mama: it's worrisome when we discover ready-made novels, prefabs, in our family. This is really the year of our historical legacy and in this respect *Anti-Oedipus* was a total failure.[66]

Yet Deleuze introduced *Anti-Oedipus* to his students at Paris-VIII (Vincennes), admitting that not all of the critiques against it were unfounded. Deleuze and Guattari stated in the book: "We are still too competent, and would like to speak in the name of absolute incompetence. Someone asked us if we had even seen a schizophrenic, no, no we've never seen one."[67] Deleuze repeated this conceit to his students, noting with amusement that many had taken the witticism seriously. One particularly aggressive psychiatrist had asked him, "Have you seen any schizos yet?" "I found the question both insulting to Félix, who was working in a clinic where there were many schizophrenics, and to me, because there are few people in the world who haven't seen a schizophrenic. So I answered, 'I? Never,' and she wrote that we'd never seen any schizophrenics. It was very disturbing."[68]

For Deleuze, one of the strong arguments of the demonstration in *Anti-Oedipus* that should have remained intact was that "delirium is a immediately a realm of social-historical investment."[69] The critical axis of familial causality as psychoanalysis practiced it was therefore an essential part of the book's demonstration and amounted to saying that it is not your family that makes you crazy but the world. Deleuze wanted to rectify his argument slightly, in response to many readings of the book that had given too much importance to the schizophrenic angle as intrinsically liberating, in that it experimented with all sorts of very dangerous lines of flight.

Of course, it is appropriate to break down the rigid divisions separating individuals into closed universes and tightly circumscribed zones. Schizophrenia defines itself as an attempt to map possible lines of flight with respect to these segmentations. A line of flight is not intrinsically creative or liberating; each has its specific dangers. It can also be a collapse when it becomes a line of abolition or destruction. That is why the suffering of the psychotic known as a schizophrenic is not aggrandized. Similarly, in terms of world history, societies can undertake dangerous lines of flight. "If I were to assign a content to fascism, it would typically be a line of flight that turns deadly."[70] This theory of lines of flight, which was worked out between 1976 and 1980 and which first appeared in *Dialogue*, was further developed in *A Thousand Plateaus*.

Deleuze also insisted, of course, on the distinction between the clinical entity that follows a line of abolition and death and schizophrenia as a life process. This was an opportunity to reassert both his basic vitalism and his hatred of all morbid affects. The process that he described belonged to a vital line, and nothing negative whatsoever underpinned it. "When I hear that death can be a process, my heart and all my affects bleed."[71] The issue is not to establish some symmetry between life and death as two alternative poles of the process. For Deleuze, the death cult belongs to fascism, which he contrasted with the Spinozan conception that death can only come from without, whence his very detailed critique of the death drive in chapter 4 of *Anti-Oedipus*.

In 1988, when the *Abécédaire* was made with Claire Parnet, Deleuze reexamined something that he considered a misunderstanding about the interpretation of desire in *Anti-Oedipus*. He had not intended to address general longing but rather the transition from an abstract notion of desire to a constructivist approach that addresses the concrete arrangement in which desire expresses itself. "All desire flows from an arrangement. To desire is to construct an arrangement."[72] In contrast, however, Deleuze agreed that the charge against psychoanalysis was legitimate, and he recalled his three major criticisms of psychoanalysis: the unconscious is not a theater but a factory of production, mental illness is not at all what psychoanalysis makes of it since it bears on the entire world, and desire constructs multiple arrangements. With respect to these three major points, Deleuze said that nothing in his position needed to change, and he predicted a rediscovery of the book, which presents a better adjusted conception of the unconscious.

In his conversations with Claire Parnet, Deleuze also referred to the other misunderstandings that led to a reading of the book as a handbook of a cult of spontaneity or schizophrenia. Both of these readings were seriously wrong, and he feared that his Vincennes students might be attracted by some form of self-destructive delirium. "This book is extremely prudent: Don't become wrecks. We were terrified of producing hospital products."[73]

Thirty years after *Anti-Oedipus* was published, Éric Alliez still claims that it is relevant, and he sees in it a shift from Deleuzean biophilosophy to biopolitics, thanks to Guattari's contribution: "by putting the deterritorialization of capital on the plane of immanence to bring it to an absolute and to reach the critical point of liberating immanence in the here and now."[74] By contrast, the sociologist Jean-Pierre Le Goff criticized *Anti-Oedipus* as the source of errors on the political left.[75] He saw it as praising the unconscious and the triumph of anticulture, as a voluntary regression toward the infrasignifier before the division between good and evil has occurred, and therefore as a site of production in its immediacy. He railed against the elitism of the idea that only a happy few have the opportunity to confront the chaos of Being. "Only schizophrenics, delinquents, marginal types and, in another way, artists and revolutionary militants have any chance of reaching it."[76] The rest of humanity would be condemned to wander, impotent and beset by fascistic drives. This equation makes Deleuze and Guattari appear as two enemies of culture who are manipulating the younger generation in order to slaughter it.

In a completely different philosophical register, Jean-Christophe Goddard saw a link between Bergson's *The Two Sources of Morality and Religion* and the theses of *Anti-Oedipus*, which he considered to be a veritable mysticism of mental illness, with psychotics instead of a community of saints. According to Goddard, the book elevated schizophrenia to the position of method, which is obviously not what is usually understood by this term. "Like Spinoza's Christ, the Deleuzean schizophrenic is the philosopher par excellence, and schizophrenia is metaphysical knowledge."[77] Pathological darkness becomes a source of light by freeing a possible contact with the principle conceived as an *élan vital*.

In a rather surprising way, *Anti-Oedipus* has become an important reference for gender studies. In the United States, many currents of thought trying to get beyond sexuality and its male/female duality have found the book useful for countering the totalitarian oppression of both sexes and thereby arguing against Oedipus and castration. In France, the book has been supported by a few Lacanian analysts, such as Jean Allouch, a member of the Lacanian school of psychoanalysis who edited *L'Unebévue* and a series for Epel Publishing, "The Great Classics of Modern Erotology," that distributed North American gay and lesbian studies and queer theory.[78]

Some Lacanian psychoanalysts who "had not been particularly interested in *Anti-Oedipus* when it came out became Foucauldians and Deleuzeans."[79] Far from the lively controversies that ensued when the book was first published, Catherine Millot today acknowledges the merits of the book, for "having argued for an idea of psychosis that is nondeficient. Beyond its idealization of schizophrenia that could seem naive, *Anti-Oedipus* makes more obvious the creative dimension, the freedom, the originality, and the inventiveness of which psychotics are capable, whereas, it has to be said that neurosis and its repression appear inhibited in this respect."[80]

François Zourabichivili insisted that the book had to be read literally as being consonant with the authors' concern with constructing a plane of immanence. Insofar as immanence can only be announced as it becomes, it supposes a particular use of language that bypasses the fashionable classical tropes from the heydays of structuralism, such as metaphor and metonymy, and replaces them with machines. "We are not speaking metaphorically about machines: man *makes machine* as soon as this aspect is repeatedly communicated to the group that he belongs to under very specific conditions."[81] The machine is neither external to man nor a projection from within: it is in a middle space beyond the limits of meaning and belongs to a semantic space that has to be taken literally and is different from the specific meaning, as Zourabichivili points out.

Deleuze and Guattari tested their readers from the opening lines of their book: "It operates everywhere, continuously at times and discontinuously at others. It breathes, heats, and eats. It shits, it fucks. What a mistake to have said *the* id. Machines are everywhere, not at all metaphorically: machines of machines, with their couplings, their connections. A machine-organ is plugged into a machine-source: one emits a flux and the other one cuts."[82] So when Deleuze and Guattari write in the same paragraph that "Judge Schreber has sunbeams in his ass, *Anus solaire*," we should not see a simple metaphor but should read the literal meaning that theorizes its own literalness. To make sure that they were understood, the authors added elsewhere: "Be sure that it works; Judge Schreber felt something, produced something, and can make a theory about it. Something happens: the effects of the machine and not of metaphors."[83] The desiring machine does not therefore refer to a desire operating like a machine. The oxymoron targets a double break with technicist reductions and a phenomenological reading of desire as the subject's tension toward an object or another subject. That's the encounter, the break in the flux that creates the desiring machine and establishes action engendered by thought.

12

Machine Against Structure

Between 1966 and 1969, Deleuze and Guattari were both very close to structuralist authors and works. However, they were also keenly aware of structuralism's dead ends. They challenged every closure on meaning and simple reduction to binary thinking, and at the same time they resisted the processes of temporalization and the pragmatic dimension of language.

A WAR MACHINE AGAINST STRUCTURALISM

As a Lacanian and member of the Freudian School of Paris, Guattari was fully involved in the expansion of structuralism in psychoanalysis. Deleuze, who wanted to move beyond the history of philosophy, was very receptive to the debates in the human sciences and found the clinical and literary treatment of schizophrenics constantly challenging. But neither Deleuze nor Guattari could simply accept the major tenets of the period. Well before they first met in 1969, both were already highly critical of structuralism.

In 1969, when Guattari addressed the Freudian School of Paris, he had already rejected Lacan's tendencies toward formalism and logic. His topic that day was "Machine and Structure,"[1] but it might just as well have been entitled "Machine Against Structure." He was no longer the master's designated successor. Lacan had anointed his son-in-law Jacques-Alain Miller who, with his colleagues from rue d'Ulm, had just begun publishing *Cahiers pour l'Analyse* (*Analysis Notebooks*). Guattari pointed out the impasses and blind spots of the structural grid and argued instead for an idea of machine as an operator destined to think the repressed of structuralism, dwelling at the intersection between the processes of subjectification whereby the subject takes shape and the historical event. This was the first text in which Guattari referred to Deleuze, whom he had not yet met, although he had read and liked *Difference and Repetition*; he also quoted *The Logic of Sense* from the outset to position himself along the lines of a Deleuzean definition of structure. Against structure, defined by its ability to exchange specific elements, the machine depends on repetition in the way that Deleuze understood it—repetition as difference, "as conduct and as a point of view concerning nonexchangeable and nonsubstitutable singularities."[2] Taking Deleuze's theses as his starting point, Guattari felt the need to use the idea of machine to introduce the differentiating element that reintroduced events and movement. "Temporalization penetrates the machine from all sides and we can only situate ourselves with respect to it like an event. The eruption of the machine marks a date, a break that is not homogenous with structural representation."[3] Deleuze and Guattari's positions and discourses were strikingly similar before they ever met. Guattari became the spokesman for a philosophy of the event, which is the most significant philosophical principle in Deleuze's *The Logic of Sense*.

In this originary presentation, we also find an idea derived from "the machine" that became just as important in the Deleuze-Guattari arsenal—the "war machine." Guattari adopted Deleuze's orientation of philosophy, which rejects the idea of representation, and he sets his idea of the machine in this perspective. "The essence of the machine is exactly this *detachment of a signifier* as representing, as 'differentiating' like a causal rupture, heterogeneous with respect to the order of things that is structurally established."[4] To get out of the impasse of structural semiology's panlinguism, Guattari suggested rehabilitating the speech act as signifier. "The voice, as a word machine, cuts and establishes the structural order of language rather than the converse."[5] He therefore completely reverses the structural perspective in which the language system is the only scientific level and where speech is relegated to the realm of pure contingency.

What interests Guattari is the subject, which he conceives as split, ripped, at the intersection, in the in-between, tautly stretched between structure and machine. "The human being is caught in the criss-cross of machine and structure."[6] Guattari respected Lacanian categories while proposing to make them dynamic, and he also adopted Lacan's analysis of partial objects, the object *o*, which he used as a war machine against structural equilibrium: it erupts where it is not expected, as a true "infernal machine" does.[7] The object *o* became that which could be neither reduced to nor assimilated by any structure, and Guattari rebaptized it the "object-machine '*o*'"[8] that prevents circular thinking, deconstructs structural equilibrium, and hampers any attempt at self-representation that decenters the individual "at the edge of himself, at the limit of the other."[9]

Guattari's search for a connection, whether in groups or collective entities, did not simply echo Deleuze's early concerns about the institution and its ambivalent relationship with desire.[10] It also had a productive future in Deleuzo-Guattarism, in the notion of a group-subject and of a collective arrangement of utterances. For Guattari, this critique of structuralism was speculative and eminently political. He wanted to draw lessons from May '68 and reenergize the structures that had been shaken up by those events. Relaunching the revolutionary machine of May '68 was Guattari's properly political question. "The revolutionary project, like the machination of institutional subversion, would have to reveal such subjective potentialities and, at every stage of the struggle, arm them against their 'structuralization.'"[11] In May 1968, institutional structuralism had triumphed at the university,[12] but the period also produced a way of thinking that was in no way structural and that, to the contrary, created a crisis for a paradigm hastily rejected by the very same people who had believed that it had given a voice to a new perspective in modernity: they now claimed that they had never partaken of the structuralist feast.

Deleuze's 1968 and 1969 publications provided Guattari with considerable material for his arguments, because Deleuze's philosophical orientation was not the dominant paradigm of the period. In his thesis, *Difference and Repetition*, Deleuze was vigilant about how structuralism could reduce the event to insignificance. He argued against making structure and event alternatives and instead favored their articulation. "There is no more opposition between event and structure or sense and structure than there is between structure and genesis."[13] Deleuze did, however, acknowledge that structuralism could effectively take account of multiplicities. Its "theater of multiplicities"[14] had nothing to do with the theater of representation. Far from seeking an ideal synthesis of recognition or representation adequate to identity, it was on the trail of the problems that were at the very heart of experimental movements.

Yet, argued Deleuze, structuralism remained a prisoner to the categories of identity and opposition; it failed to pose the right problems. Thus, Saussure-Jakobson linguistics, the lead science of the structuralist paradigm that had transformed the rules of phonology into a heuristic model in their structural aspects, was a prisoner of its binary logics, privileged

negative terms, and "assimilated the differential relations between phonemes to relationships of opposition."[15] According to Deleuze, Saussurian
structuralism mutilated the potentially positive dimension of difference.
To Saussure's linguistics he opposed the work of Gustave Guillaume, a
more marginal linguist whom Deleuze found extremely important. "The
fundamental lesson of Guillaume's work is the substitution of a principle
of *differential position* for that of distinctive opposition."[16] Guillaume's linguistics provided a transcendental exploration of the Idea of the linguistic
unconscious, one that didn't miss its mark this time. In his March 19, 1985,
class on the semiology of cinema, Deleuze expressed his enthusiasm for
Guillaume's work. "What is the signified of power in Guillaume? Movement: what a confirmation! It's a great day! What an encounter!"[17] Deleuze
presented Guillaume as the last of the great linguist philosophers, whose
thesis, which most linguists rejected, was that a word as a minimal significant unit has only one meaning, which he called the "signified of power."[18]
This dimension refers to an idea-matter that preexists discourse but that
cannot be dispensed with. "This was the resurrection of philosophy, which
crept up on linguistics and which linguists hated."[19] Guillaume was a psy-
chomechanic of language, whose ideas about language were quite close to
Deleuze's own goals. Guillaume criticized other linguists for not going
beyond the visible facts. "Guillaume and Deleuze's thinking were similar
in that both claimed that the virtual/powerful was as real as the actual/
effective."[20]

When Deleuze claimed his ontology of difference in his thesis, it led
him to consider quite seriously the theories of those 1960s-era putative
masters of structuralism in all of their facets. He therefore recognized
Freud for having insisted on pregential sexuality consisting in partial
drives; he also credited Lacan for having extended this discovery with his
object *o*. For Deleuze, Lacan also had the merit of dissociating the relationships between real and virtual objects, the latter having the quality of being and not being there where it is. Despite these advances, however, Deleuze believed that psychoanalysis remained a prisoner of a philosophy of
representation of the subject, submitting its theory of repetition to a principle of identity in the past and to analogy and resemblance in the present.

Just as he hailed Lacan's contribution, Deleuze also praised Althusser
and his followers for their work on Marx. "Althusser and his collaborators
are, therefore, profoundly correct in showing the genuine structure in *Capital*, and in rejecting the historicist interpretations of Marxism."[21] Relations

were rather good between Althusser and Deleuze. In 1964, Althusser invited Deleuze to teach at the ENS on rue d'Ulm. Deleuze responded:

> Thank you for your letter and for your offer. Alas, alas. I have not been assigned to Grenoble, which didn't welcome me, I am going to turn around and go to Lyon to exercise the strange function of Professor of Ethics. I will be moving there. So while I would very much like to, I cannot give a course at the School. I am touched that you and the School's students had wished to have me, please tell them so. With all my friendship.[22]

In 1965, Althusser sent Deleuze his books and those of his group. Deleuze's reaction was extremely positive:

> I am touched by your having sent me your three books. You could not have made me happier. I have not yet finished reading them, but already, not only the articles that I've read and admired but everything that I did not know (your explanation of the concept of "problem," a concern we share), the one on fetish and the analysis of the exact role of alienation all seem so important to me that I sense their influence. Of your colleagues, I knew Macherey somewhat and admire him. The three books and your style are impressive . . . (Yes, I believe that these books are quite profound and beautiful. I'd really like to discuss them with you.)[23]

Deleuze's very beautiful text "How Do We Recognize Structuralism?"[24] which was published by his friend François Châtelet in his *History of Philosophy* in 1972 and sent to Althusser, was in fact written in 1968, before Deleuze had met Guattari.

> I am sending you the text on structuralism that I told you about. I had said that my goal was to write a more rigorous easily accessible presentation than what is normally done. But I no longer have even a modicum of the same peace of mind. I have the impression of being in great darkness or of screwing up completely (partially in the last paragraph, "final critiques"). But I'm sending it to you because on the one hand I discuss your work, and on the other because I want you to tell me if it's publishable. Be a friend and read it in a very personal way.

> Writing something bad can always be useful for learning, but pub-
> lishing something bad isn't. Maybe the last part has to be cut.[25]

This was a fundamental text. In it, Deleuze introduced the structural paradigm and tried to identify common criteria amid the various disciplines being explored by examining structural studies in several disciplines—linguistics, literature, anthropology, psychoanalysis, and sociology. The first characteristic was the centrality of the symbolic dimension linking the real and the imaginary: structuralism was credited with the discovery of the third term, and, here as in other areas, linguistics appeared as the lead science. Localization or position was the second criterion; a structural element was meaningful as a function of its location in the structure, and Deleuze paid tribute to the rigor with which Lévi-Strauss had demonstrated this fact. These were the very foundations of the structuralist ambition of becoming a topology, a relational logic. Deleuze felt great sympathy with this way of valorizing what he called the plane of immanence. The third and fourth criteria of structuralism, which made it even more appealing to Deleuze, were the valorization of the differential and the particular. "Every structure is a multiplicity,"[26] and his reading of the structuralist paradigm drew him toward his own ontology of difference, which is obvious when he claimed that "about structure, we will say: *real without being actual, ideal without being abstract.*"[27] He agreed with Lévi-Strauss that the unconscious is always empty and dependent only on its own structural laws. At this point, we are quite removed from the very negative interpretation that took root after Deleuze met Guattari, when they both derided structuralism, calling it the anorexic conception of the unconscious. At this point, structuralism is still presented in a positive light. The fifth criterion was seriality, which makes it possible to introduce movement into structure. This concept was so close to Deleuze's concerns of the moment that he organized *The Logic of Sense* into thirty-four different series. The sixth criterion, entirely fundamental for structuralism, is the principle of the empty slot, the famous zero degree of language and the unconscious. Deleuze pointed out, however, that it is always missing from its place and that this lack is what produces movement. "No structuralism without a zero degree."[28]

In *The Logic of Sense*, we can already see Deleuze's ambivalence toward structuralism: this mixture of fascination for a method that makes it possible for sense to circulate on a surface level around a zero point, an empty placeholder. Deleuze still saw structure as equivalent to a machine, and Guattari's "Machine and Structure" fascinated him all the more so, since Guattari was ahead of the game in his critique of structuralism.

Indeed, in 1969, Deleuze was still saying, "Structure is in fact a machine for the production of incorporeal sense (*skindapsos*)."[29] The linguistic, anthropological, and psychoanalytic studies that revolved around the empty place, which could also be the site of death, the zero value, the floating signifier, all called into question the notion of causality, since cause was not in its place. Deleuze proclaimed that "the importance of structuralism in philosophy, and for all thought, is that it displaces borders."[30] "It is thus pleasing that here resounds today the news that sense is never a principle or an origin, but that it is produced. It is not something to discover, to restore, and to re-employ; it is something to produce by new machinery. It belongs to no height or depth, but rather to a surface effect."[31] This perspective, for Deleuze, was a liberation from transcendence—a valorization of the plane of immanence—and he identified the possible productive machinery of sense that he wanted to see develop and proliferate freely such that preindividual particularities could emerge.

In the chapters, or series, of *The Logic of Sense*, Deleuze scrutinized various structuralist studies, to which he devoted several chapters, while also working out his own metaphysics. He borrowed in particular from Benveniste to distinguish the three possible forms of a proposition: first, the relationship of designating an individuated thing, or the deictic; second, manifestation; and third, signification. Deleuze added a fourth dimension of sense that the Stoics had discovered with the event: " sense, *the expressed of the proposition*, is an incorporeal, complex, and irreducible entity, on the surface of things, a pure event which insists or subsists in the proposition."[32]

Deleuze suggested an approach that drew inspiration in part from the work of linguists by connecting them to his own philosophical orientation; sign and sense were no longer two different strata or alternative perspectives but were indissociably linked. "As Bergson said, one does not proceed from sounds to images and from images to sense; rather one is established 'from the outset' within sense."[33] We are thus plunged into an already-there of sense toward which we regress in an indefinite proliferation demonstrated by Frege in logic and Carroll in literature. What elicited Deleuze's criticism were the possible alternatives of indefinite regression and sterile doubling, a definitive stabilization of sense: "one *or* the other"[34] that still looms over Husserlian phenomenology. The specificity of the pure event is precisely to get beyond all dualities and to open onto the perspective of impossible objects, of paradoxes, absurdities, and oxymorons such as square circles, matter without extension, a mountain without a valley, "objects 'without a home,' outside of being . . . of 'extra being,' pure, ideational events, unable to be realized in a state of affairs."[35] Asserting the paradoxical aspect of regression, Deleuze showed that power could only be serial. He addressed the structuralist distinction between signifier and signified again but gave it another meaning, defining the signifier as every sign insofar as it bears an element of sense and the signified as that which serves as the correlative of that sense: "What is signified, therefore, is never sense itself" but the concept.[36]

With his ever-present concern to proclaim a philosophy of paradox, of the double, of oxymoronic tension, Deleuze insisted on the co-presence of sense and nonsense that do not mutually exclude one another, the false by the true. He reversed the panlinguism of his period; when everyone was proclaiming that everything is structured like a language and that everything starts with language, Deleuze argued that language was less important than the event. "Events make language possible."[37] The beginning does not belong to the language system but to the speech act; in this Deleuze distinguished himself from Saussurian thinking by rehabilitating speech as signifying. "We always begin in the order of speech."[38] With Deleuze, the event becomes the transcendental horizon of languages and makes language possible.

THE HUMANITIES OVERTHROW STRUCTURALISM

The "Deleuze-Guattari arrangement" that began in 1969 inspired each author to take more radical positions. It took a frankly polemical turn by developing one *with* the other in the early 1970s. The opening words of *Anti-Oedipus* reflect the rejection of all structural closure, even if they indicate the lack of pertinence of the subject, the "I," in favor of polymorphous machinic logics. Both authors insisted on the absolute primacy of multiplicities over structuralist binarisms. *Anti-Oedipus* was designed to be a war machine against structuralism, which seriously accelerated the deconstruction of the paradigm that had emerged in 1967 and 1968. Like an infernal machine, it vitiated the paradigm from within.

To the formalism of structural studies, Deleuze and Guattari pro-posed, by their shared authorship itself, an experimental counterpoint. They planned to use the social sciences—anthropology, semiotics, psy-choanalysis, and history—to contest and undo the structuralist paradigm, by rereading the latest work in these disciplines, particularly when they took approaches that were not structuralist. The issue was to have the two of them use the method of "perversion" that Deleuze had defined to get out of the structural enclosure.

According to Deleuze and Guattari, there are all sorts of machines: technical, cybernetic, bellicose, economic, signifying, desiring, and in-stitutional; machines could also be literary. "Machine" became the new term that would unseat the period's buzzwords of "predilection" and "structure." The term became so central that when Deleuze published a new edition of *Proust and Signs* in 1970, he added "The Literary Machine," which included a description of the three machines of Proust's novel. *Anti-Oedipus* began with a chapter on desiring machines, a notion that the au-thors dropped in *A Thousand Plateaus*, because they had achieved their goal of upsetting the idea of structure. In 1980, when *A Thousand Plateaus* came out, the structuralist paradigm was little more than a memory.

OVERTURNING STRUCTURAL SEMIOLOGY

Psychoanalysis "structuralized" by Lacan, the designated adversary of *Anti-Oedipus*, leaned heavily on Saussure. Deleuze and Guattari therefore made a violent critique of the Saussurian theory of the sign, denouncing "the shadow of Eastern despotism. Saussure insists that the arbitrariness of language establishes its sovereignty like the 'masses' that are subjected to general servitude or slavery."[39] In addition, the nonsymmetrical rela-tionship between signifier and signified favored the absolute prevalence of the signifier. The empty slot operating by all sorts of successive folds, which had previously been considered to be something positive, was now considered to depend on a notion of the linguistic field defined by Saussure as transcendence turning around a master signifier.

This linguistics of the signifier was to be replaced by a completely differ-ent linguistics of flux. Guattari's contribution on this point was quite clear, as the preparatory notes for *Anti-Oedipus* attest.[40] In fact, Hjelmslev, the inventor of "glossematics," had initiated an even more formal linguistics than Saussure's, but Deleuze and Guattari had very little to do with glossematics and changed Hjelmslev's ideas slightly to serve their real purpose of using him against Saussurian thinking by creating a truly pragmatic linguistics. To do this, they argued that Hjelmslev was the beginning of the veritable plane of immanence, which corresponded with their hopes for linguistics as "an immanent algebra of languages."[41]

What Deleuze and Guattari borrowed above all from Hjelmslev—and interpreted in their own way—was the distinction between the absolutely reversible planes of expression and content. "Given their functional definition, it's impossible to argue for the legitimacy of calling one of these levels expression and the other content."[42] The distinction had to do with strata, planes of consistency that destroyed Saussure's binarism. In fact, there was to be only a single plane of consistency unfolding in multiple strata. For them, Hjelmslev had the merit of liberating the study of language from its yoke and opening it as much as possible onto a theory of the sign that would embrace everything. Guattari also saw in Hjelmslev's *Essay* the prolegomena of their theory of the collective agent of utterance and the means of getting beyond Saussure's language-speech dichotomy. Hjelmslev was enrolled in Deleuze and Guattari's construction of a semiotic machine against structural semiology. In *Anti-Oedipus*, they remark, "Hjelmselv's linguistics is deeply opposed to the Saussurian and post-Saussurian undertaking. Because it abandons any privileged reference. Because it describes a pure field of algebraic immanence without any overarching transcendent instance, even in the background."[43] The immanent theory of language makes it possible to mold form and substance, content and expression "according to the flux of desire, and cuts these flux according to points-signs or figures-schizes."[44]

Between 1972 and 1980, when *A Thousand Plateaus* was published, Deleuze and Guattari discovered Charles Sanders Peirce, one of the founders of pragmatism, who defined thought as sign.[45] According to Peirce, thought unfolds from a semiotic triangle (sign-object-interpretation) that refers to an indefinite dialogue of interpretations. Arguing this way, Peirce managed to displace linguistics by making it merely a partial subset of general semiology to which the use of the rules of language is subjected. Sense is thus revealed in its practical function. Peirce's other important shift consisted in no longer thinking of the world as physical but as fundamentally semiotic; Deleuze and Guattari, however, rejected this dichotomy of physical and semiotic.

In *A Thousand Plateaus*, the pragmatic approach particularly conveyed an alternative to Saussurian thinking. This time, spoken language prevails as the expression of doing and saying, an elementary unit of language, considered a "precept."[46] Language presents itself as essentially informative, whereas it is first and foremost performative. Deleuze and Guattari also borrowed heavily from John Austin's work[47] on the intrinsic relationships between speech and action in performatives; they also drew from the work of Oswald Ducrot.

During the 1970s, Guattari was already involved in this radical critique of structural linguistics. In 1973, at Columbia University's Reid Hall in Paris, the home to many American universities' study-abroad programs, Sylvère Lotringer invited Guattari to give a course, in which he developed the idea of a micropolitics of desire. From his opening remarks, he was clearly attacking "structuralist analyses [that] try to hide the fundamental duality between content and expression and pay attention only to expression and bracketing content."[48] For Guattari, content is structured by a multiplicity of micropolitical levels before being structured by the rules of language. He also attacked Althusser's ideas. "We consider the insistence on the opposition between science and ideology unfounded, especially in the obsessive manner of the Althusserians. . . . We challenge the validity of a radical epistemological break between a conceptual field that is purely scientific and a purely illusory and mystifying ideology."[49]

Addressing an audience of economists at Dauphine University in Paris during a IRIS colloquium, Guattari likened structuralism to an illness. "There is no reason that the economic sciences should escape the illness that has been ravaging the sciences of language, anthropology, psychoanalysis, etc., for quite some time: namely, structuralism."[50] A little later, in 1979, he attacked Chomsky's dictum that the "depository of pragmatics" collects everything insignificant. Even his chapter's title, "Exiting Language," underscored his hope to propose a line of flight from the popular panlinguism in order to reconnect the study of language to other parts of the social world. He therefore denounced the form of linguistics that adopted the epistemological model of the hard sciences and imitated them to gain legitimacy. This pretension led to ignoring all contingent sociohistorical features. "Everything proceeds as if the *socius* were obliged to bend to language!"[51] On the strength of this rupture and purification, linguists became "imperialists."[52]

Hammering away that there was no language in itself, Guattari drew from historians to show that the process whereby a language becomes homogenous is essentially political.[53] He reiterated this position in *A Thousand Plateaus*. The more or less important stabilization of a language therefore has to do with balances of power and presupposes their historicization. Arrangements are first. "Arrangements of flux and of codes are first with respect to the differentiations of form and structure."[54] In 1979, Guattari was already declaring himself a partisan of a general pragmatics that included various semiologies. He repeated this in *A Thousand Plateaus*, insisting on the political dimension of how language operates.

If Deleuze and Guattari established a correlation with a specific *socius*, these semiotics were not identified with a specific historical moment; the issue was not to oppose a static, purely synchronic structuralism with an evolutionist continuum but rather to show the primacy of mixtures and hybridizations. These arrangements are the very conditions of intelligibility of these regimes of signs. It is the founding event that breaks the flux and starts things moving again in new directions, creating a transition from one regime of signs to another. Two dates—587 B.C. and A.D. 70—the dates of the two destructions of the Temple that forced the Jewish people into exile, are written in an exergue to the "fifth plateau." The Jewish prophet embodied the necessary passage, forced by the destruction of the Temple, from thought to action, inciting the Jewish people to wander. He became the eponymous character of a concrete example of transformational semiotic analysis that could move from a signifying semiotic to a semiotics of subjectification. For Deleuze and Guattari, pragmatics did not merely add a dose of soul to linguistics "but [was] to the contrary, the basic element on which everything else depends."[55]

Schizoanalysis Against Psychoanalysis

In reality, psychoanalysis is familialism with a pseudoscientific discourse. The desiring machine should therefore destroy the Oedipal yoke to free up and schizophrenize the productive forces of the unconscious. In addition to developing arguments that attacked psychoanalytic principles, the two authors also drew on the May 1968 bywords, proclaiming, "We're all schizos! We're all perverts! We're all Libidos that are too viscous or too liquid."[56] The way that analysts constantly convert all unconscious manifestation into a demonstration of Oedipus points to the metaphysics of psychoanalysis that should be submitted to a materialist critique. Promoting a method of disjunction-conjunction, the two authors denounced the psychoanalytic practice of systematically using exclusive disjunctions (either . . . or) that completely ignored schizophrenia and kept it a stranger to Freudian discourse.

The desiring machine must blaze a pathway into structures in order to destroy the master signifier defended by Lacanians. Psychoanalytic interpretation develops from the notion of an initial lack or absence, whereas the subjective breaks, the true breaks of flux, begin instead from something that is brimming over, according to Deleuze and Guattari. Epistemologically missing its object, psychoanalysis was also vilified as an enterprise of normalization and repression that was a continuation of nineteenth-century psychiatry's internments and withdrawals. "Rather than being part of an enterprise of real liberation, psychoanalysis belongs to the broadest enterprise of a general bourgeois repression."[57]

Schizoanalysis tried to reconnect the unconscious to the social and political realms. The Oedipal reading grid was a form of mechanistic reductionism and of simple application. Lacan's structural apparatus sought to repress desire, to work things so that desire would be renounced and thereby perfect the repressive apparatus on the therapeutic level. "By proffering the deforming mirror of incest (ah hah, so that's what you wanted?), desire is shamed, stupefied, cornered such that it is easily persuaded to give 'itself' up."[58]

The desiring machine that was to replace the Oedipal structure took, as its first principle, putting desire back into circulation and making it productive. The hypothetical structural unity of the machine still needed to be undone, however. Difference is located in the molar and molecular machines; desire must be productive, whether production is located at the macro or micro level. However, the structural unity organized around the theory of lack imposes a molar set. "That's the structural operation: it puts lack in the molar set."[59]

Guattari's introduction of this molar-molecular polarity was based in essence on his institutional practice at La Borde. Initially, it was a way of undoing the molar logics of organizational stratification and bureaucratization and making things routine by constantly freeing the molecular flux and their intensities, which could weaken the codes of the molar pole. "The macro-micro distinction is very important, but it belongs more to Guattari than to me. I'm more about the distinction of two multiplicities. That's what I find essential."[60] Guattari suggested contrasting molecular and molar alterity with Lacan's imaginary alterity, which had managed "to linguistify molar sets, refusing the normal geneticism. Everything comes back to structuralism in a linguistic mode. We have absolute, structural and linguistic alterity without any guarantees."[61]

Even if Lacan had the immense merit of discovering, with the object *o*, something on the molecular order that, as a partial object, always escaped or exceeded the structure, he nonetheless remained a prisoner of structure. Defining itself as a materialist enterprise, schizoanalysis opposed the internal games of structure with an external signifying intervention. Above all, schizoanalysis was a mode of experimentation. Like a "mechanic, a micro-mechanic,"[62] what needs to be understood in each individual is not a deeply hidden secret but rather the desiring machines operating in a particular way, along with their errors, accelerations, breaks in the flux, and their becomings. "It's not the pressure lines of the unconscious that count, to the contrary, it's the lines of flight."[63]

Defining the unconscious as a multiplicity of intensities and excesses, Deleuze and Guattari put back into circulation what structuralism had repressed. We might consider, along with Joël Birman, that the clinic defended by Deleuze and Guattari intended to reintroduce the economic problematics of Freudian metapsychology, the dimension of drives that Lacan had eliminated. Deleuze and Guattari were completely opposed to the formalist, purely symbolic conception of an unconscious operating like a structure modeled on linguistics: "they argued in *Anti-Oedipus* that drives run through the unconscious from one end to the other, or, in other words, that no unconscious can exist without intensities."[64] The desiring machine puts the drive and its excesses, mobility and ruptures, its disjunctive capacities, back into circulation. Schizophrenia becomes doubly interesting, because it demonstrates that even with the help of structuralism and Oedipus squared, psychoanalytic discourse is incapable of accounting for and curing it. The schizophrenic is also interesting, because he embodies this figure of unusual impersonality, which Deleuze and Guattari used as a contrast against both desingularized structure and personalism.

POLITICAL ANTHROPOLOGY VERSUS
STRUCTURAL ANTHROPOLOGY

Clearly, the relationship of *Anti-Oedipus* to Lévi-Strauss was far less polemical than it was to Lacan, since *Anti-Oedipus* was essentially taking aim
at psychoanalytic practice. Nonetheless, Deleuze and Guattari were obviously distancing themselves from structural anthropology. They drew
from the work of Edmund Leach, for whom a whole set of empirical, directly observed data were characterized by a lack of structure; Leach did
not mean that there was no structure but simply that structure is the principle of its own imbalance.

Deleuze and Guattari rejected the idea of cold, primitive societies without history and based on the simple reproduction of the same. "The idea
that primitive societies have no history and are dominated by archetypes
and their repetition is particularly weak and inadequate."[65] Even if they did
not consider Lévi-Strauss responsible for the idea, he did decouple "hot"
civilizations and societies that operated along thermodynamic principles
from "cold" societies that functioned in a more mechanical manner, protecting themselves by repetition from all unpredictable elements that
might provoke change.

Deleuze and Guattari also intended to overturn Lévi-Strauss's classical demonstration attributing the universal exchange of women to the desire to avoid closing societies in upon themselves. "Far from being the extension of an initially closed system, a process of opening is primary,
based on the heterogeneity of elements comprising the services and com-
pensating the imbalance by displacing it."[66] Ultimately, Deleuze and
Guattari argue against Lévi-Strauss's claim that the universal incest taboo is an intangible law in every society the world over: the very idea of
this taboo could not be relevant, since "incest does not exist" in many
primitive societies.[67]

The work of Meyer Fortes on territorial logics, the first research regarding the exchange of women, was also useful for their purposes. "The problem is not the circulation of women. . . . A woman circulates by herself. We
are not free to determine what she does, but the legal rights of the offspring
are established to the benefit of a given person."[68] Land is primary, therefore,
with its territorial segments regarding matrimonial exchanges and kinship
structures. Marriage systems and kinship rules are secondary with respect
to territorial codes of the socius. Contrary to Lévi-Strauss's argument,

Deleuze and Guattari claim that "a kinship system is not a structure; it's a practice, a praxis, a procedure and even a strategy."[69]

The very idea that there could be some closure on a kinship structure arises from an error in perspective amounting to detaching matrimonial practices from their political and economic foundations. Pierre Clastres's study of the Guyaki Indians showed that there are no pure nomads, because there is always a sedentary moment of camping that allows nomads to accumulate even in small amounts, to eat, to get married, and so on.[70] The epistemological critique that Deleuze and Guattari make of the proponents of structural anthropology and against all structural semiology is to challenge the priority that structuralist anthropology gives to the realm of exchange and circulation to the detriment of social production and reproduction. Here again, the machine is the strong link, by contrast with the structure: "A soft structure would never operate or make things circulate without the hard machinic element that presides over inscriptions."[71]

All activities run through lived experience to divide it spatially or socially into segments, combining linear, binary, and circular types of segments. But nonstructuralist Africanists such as Meyer Fortes, Evans-Pritchard, and a few others were the ones who showed how the political system of primitive, stateless societies incorporated systems and territorial divisions, using and appropriating a hybrid, flexible system of kinship relations. Deleuze and Guattari did observe some binary thinking at work here, but they contrasted primitive societies, with their flexible divisions, to modern societies and their inflexible divisions. To lend support to their positions, they referred to the reforms of Clisthenes the Athenian, who built a political space in ancient Greece for citizens by overcoding the lineal segments to create a homogenous space. But the two types of spaces are interwoven, and flexibilities exist at the heart of even the most bureaucratic systems, as Kafka showed.[72] By contrast, we can also observe incipient branching and hardening within primitive societies. Every society and every individual experiences these passages of transversal divisions; they create the dominant aspect of politics. "Everything is political, but all politics is both *macropolitics* and *micropolitics*.[73] The micropolitics emerging from these observations and from the preeminence of the political realm becomes a major notion in *A Thousand Plateaus*; it replaces schizoanalysis but functions as its equivalent.

In *Anti-Oedipus*, Deleuze and Guattari contrast structural anthropology with a whole historical and political anthropology that develops according to the biopolarity of the logic of decoding flux and that of recoding processes. While structuralism deals inadequately with primitive societies, functionalism does little better when it asks about the purpose of a given institution and claims to find an answer by identifying its function. Deleuze and Guattari credit ethnologists with being ahead of psychoanalysts, who are mired in questions of meaning. Schizoanalysis goes beyond their false questions by attending to the uses to which things are put. "How it works is the only question."[74]

Deleuze and Guattari raise this question, which leads them to distinguish between Savages, Barbarians, and Civilized Societies, depending on how much the flux is deterritorialized. They construct a real political anthropology, one in which the progressive and discontinuous process of decoding, the collapse of codes, and the liberation of flux play major roles. At every stage, central government structures, whether despotic or feudal, prove unable to resist the forces of decoding that subordinate state-institutional forms in order to subject them. Slowly, various sorts of flux impose their laws. "Flux of properties being sold, of money that flows, of production and of the means of production."[75] The capitalist machine's quality will manage to connect all the decoded flux so that everything plays according to the same rules, forming a system. The history of humanity is not presented as a new teleology insofar as it is moved by the contingency of events that make social becoming bifurcate in one or another direction.

"Clearly, neither capitalism nor the revolution nor schizophrenia have gone the way of the signifier."[76] Civilizations are defined by their degree of codifying or decodifying the flux. A capitalist flux is distinguished from a schizophrenic flux because it is blocked, whereas capitalism recodifies and imposes unbreachable limits. Capitalist modernity was not mistaken in adopting its politics of the "great enclosure," which Foucault analyzed. If capitalism sees in schizophrenia aspects of its own tendency to decode and deterritorialize, it also sees its external limits and can only function "on the condition of stopping this tendency."[77] Like every society within which the tension between two major tendencies exists, to deterritorialize and reterritorialize, capitalism remains fundamentally ambivalent.

Deleuze and Guattari thus envisaged a succession of three social machines, each of which with a dominant element. The first machine, that of savages, is the underlying territorial machine that tries to code flux on the earth's body. Next, the imperial machine of barbarians overcodes the flux on the body of the despot and his bureaucracy. Last, the modern, civilized, capitalist machine decodes the flux and achieves immanence. The history of humanity thus unfolds concretely in a general theory of flux, of multiplicities, and of the primacy of productive machines, thereby rediscovering a dynamic and an axiomatic while also breaking free of purely synchronic, structural readings that valorize the permanent and unchanging and, thereby, make events insignificant.

13

"Minor" Literature as Seen by Deleuze and Guattari

Between 1972 and 1980, along the path from *Anti-Oedipus* to *A Thousand Plateaus*, the 1975 publication of *Kafka* was an important milestone.[1] It was both an extremely original and refreshing reading of a writer whom both Deleuze and Guattari admired tremendously, and, more importantly perhaps, it was an opportunity to experiment with key concepts later developed in *A Thousand Plateaus*. Deleuze and Guattari went from a critical denunciation of psychoanalysis to an affirmation of their own unusual approach. They tested it on a great literary work.

"It's a Rhizome, a Burrow"

Kafka was the first time Deleuze and Guattari used their notion of the "rhizome," which appeared in the book's first lines. "How do we enter Kafka's work? It's a rhizome, a burrow. *The Castle* has 'multiple entrances' organized by unknown laws and principles of distribution. Hotel America with its innumerable doors, main and secondary. . . . We will therefore enter at any point."[2] This principle of multiple possible entries and connections at every point with highly diverse significations, this use of *rhizome*, with its horizontal shoots—unlike a *tree*, which branches hierarchically—led, in 1977, to the eponymous *Rhizome* and provided the introduction to *A Thousand Plateaus*.[3] Particularly useful for describing Kafka's labyrinthine world, the rhizome was also a new weapon against psychoanalytic interpretation. From the opening pages, the adversary was clearly identified: "The principle of multiple entrances alone makes it impossible for the enemy, the Signifier, to introduce itself, and the attempts at interpreting a work that offers itself in fact only to experimentation."[4]

Kafka was a transitional work between two tomes, which introduced the major idea of *arrangement*,[5] which later runs through *A Thousand*

Plateaus. Just as the desiring machine was the key concept of *Anti-Oedipus*, a few years later, *A Thousand Plateaus* can be read as a theory of *arrangement*. Between the two, *Kafka* uses the concept of the machine and describes Kafka himself as a writing machine. But the future shift was already in the works: arrangement was the realization of the machine thanks to the connections that it made possible.

The arrangement and the rhizome, the two basic concepts of Deleuze and Guattari's philosophy, were born of this reading of Kafka: literature allowed them to experiment with their ideas. As was their habit, Deleuze and Guattari took the opposite track from other analyses, readings, and interpretations by Kafka specialists. Where the literary tradition sees Kafka as the expression of a desperate, absurd world confronted with bureaucratic logic and of an obsession that ultimately runs into dead ends of incomprehension, Deleuze and Guattari present a comic, joyful Kafka who is always on the side of desire, confronted with the infernal logic of three different types of bureaucratic machines—Stalinist, Nazi, and liberal American. Their critique was more trenchant than many purely political denunciations.

This study is more than a work about the author Kafka; it is a manifesto against all types of archetypal reading that impose specific interpretations on this or that text: it proclaims experimentation as primary. "We believe only in Kafka's experimentation, neither in interpretation nor significance, only in experimental protocols."[6] The book pursues certain avenues laid out in *Anti-Oedipus*, attacking psychoanalytic reductionism and radically rejecting this archetypal interpretation of Kafka, because it deeply impoverishes the approach to his work and is ultimately based on a misreading of Kafka's November 1919 letter to his father that completely misses the author's irony. In the letter, Kafka blames his father for all of his woes, his inability to live and to write, for all of his failures, apparently "Oedipizing" his entire relationship to the world. For Deleuze and Guattari, however, Kafka's letter means something completely different. The oversized Oedipus is Kafka's way of escaping and freeing himself. Kafka forces himself to do the reverse of what psychoanalysts believe necessary. "Deterritorialize Oedipus in the world instead of reterritorializing himself on Oedipus and in the family."[7] Consequently, Freudians miss the underlying irony of Kafka's willfully enlarged Oedipus.

As in both *Anti-Oedipus* and *Kafka*, the psychoanalytic reading grid is faulted for overemphasizing the Signifier and neglecting the efficiency of the machine—literature in this case. In the stead of this flawed reading, Deleuze and Guattari develop a political theory of literature articulated around a conception of impersonal writing resulting from a collective arrangement. This approach to creation radically changes the status of literature, which, by its ability to affect, is ascribable to a symptomatology, to a true capture of forces transformed into forms. Thus literature proves to be a form of clinical practice.[8]

Deleuze and Guattari resolutely position themselves in the realm of experimentation, opposing literature of the narrow traditional canon in favor of the creative force of a "minor" literature. Their demonstration relies on an analysis of the cultural context of the decadent Hapsburg Empire of the early twentieth century that encouraged centrifugal movements, accentuated the process of deterritorialization, and led to a return to forms of reterritorialization. This extreme tension created a propitious climate for unusual voices to develop, like Kafka's and his contemporaries, such as Einstein, who was teaching in Prague, the physicist Philipp Frank, the twelve-tone composers, and expressionist filmmakers like Robert Wiene and Fritz Lang, not to mention the Prague circle of linguists and Freud in Vienna, who gave birth to psychoanalysis. In this immense, declining empire, German was the official language of power and of the central administration, but other, subordinate languages were also used. Kafka was at the crossroads of several languages: Czech as a Praguer, German as the official language of the Austro-Hungarian empire, and Yiddish because he was Jewish.

According to Deleuze and Guattari, "a minor literature is not the literature of a minor language, but of a minority that writes in a major language."[9] A minor language is therefore defined as a hybrid within a major language. For Kafka, German is the language of literary expression—but a particular German. "In this way, Kafka defines the impasse barring access to writing for the Jews of Prague and making their literature into something impossible: the impossibility of not writing, the impossibility of writing in German, the impossibility of writing otherwise."[10] Kafka had to literally express his alterity and foreignness using the dominant language. "To be like a foreigner in one's own language; this is Kafka's situation in 'The Great Swimmer.'"[11] This externality of the inside make the two processes of territorialization and deterritorialization play out in writing, processes that Deleuze and Guattari develop more fully in *A Thousand Plateaus*. "For the Jews of Prague, the sense was of an insurmountable distance from primitive Czech territoriality."[12] Another aspect of minor literature is that, more than other literatures, it is essentially political: "Each individual affair is immediately plugged into politics,"[13] and in this respect, cannot bend to the restrictive codifications of the Oedipal triangle of psychoanalysis. Finally, minor literature is not the result of an individual subject of utterance but tries to express the voice of an always-absent people—without, however, becoming their spokesperson. It is a literature that uses collective arrangements of utterances.

For Deleuze and Guattari, minor literature possesses the liveliest resources and the most effective forces for unsettling established conventions and powers. There is something immediately challenging about minor literature, although its relationship with major literature does not depend on the Hegelian dialectic whereby the vocation of the minor would be to overturn major literature. To the contrary, the minor sees its emergence as an intensive variable that can transform the major, but this emergence can only be minor, according to Deleuze and Guattari's definition. "Minor is sustained by the existence of the major the way a body without organs calls for the organism."[14]

In this way, Deleuze and Guattari manage to escape what would otherwise be the inescapable dualism to which the major/minor binary leads. Canguilhem's influence is obvious, especially his definition of the "anormal as a constitutive difference between the normal and he pathological which refers less to a model of normality than to an expression of strangeness."[15] In *Anti-Oedipus*, Deleuze and Guattari similarly defined a third term between capitalism and schizophrenia: the schizocreative line of flight, as different simply by its own intensity. What Deleuze and Guattari meant by this major/minor dyad finally was "to articulate three theoretical levels: an ontology of vital force and of becoming, an epistemology of culture engaging a logic of variation, and a political poetry in the form of a theory of domination and of revolutionary-becoming."[16]

Since *Anti-Oedipus*, Deleuze and Guattari had begun to reject Saussurian thinking more radically because of its binary, dualist reading of language, which it considered from the outset as separate from speech.[17] If they had not yet appropriated the contributions of Austin and Searle or Ducrot's pragmatism (they did so in *A Thousand Plateaus*), they were already looking for anything that would deal a different hand and reinstate linguistic polyphony. As a result, Deleuze approached Henri Gobard, a linguist teaching in the departments of psychology and English at Vincennes and for whose 1976 book Deleuze had written the preface.[18] Having learned of Gobard's work while he and Guattari were writing *Kafka*, Deleuze used Gobard's model, which he saw as a possible articulation of social factors with linguistic operations.

Gobard's typology differed from Saussure's dualism, as it was organized around four language functions. He distinguished a vernacular, maternal, or rural language that for Kafka was Czech, the language of his territorial community; Deleuze used this part of his theory. Gobard identified a second *"vehicular* language of exchange, trade, circulation, urban par excellence,"[19] whose function was to wrest one from one's territory, deterritorialize everything by reterritorializing on the basis of economic functions—this language was German, for Kafka. The third linguistic level was the *"referentiary*, the national and cultural (language) that recollected or reconstituted the past."[20] At this level, deterritorialization became cultural reterritorialization, and for Kafka, it was always German, and more specifically, the German of Goethe. Finally, the *"mythic* (language) referring to a spiritual, religious or magical land,"[21] untied to other functions in order to establish a religious reterritorialization—this was Hebrew, for Kafka.

From Haïm-Vidal Sephiha, another linguist, Deleuze and Guattari borrowed a very broad definition of the notion of the intensive,[22] which all become "linguistic elements, however varied they might be, that express the internal tensions of a language."[23] Deleuze and Guattari found in Kafka a multiplicity of these "tensors" (a term adopted from Jean-François Lyotard). As Kafka wrote in his *Diary*, "Not a single word, or practically none, that I write agrees with another, I mean the consonants grate against each other like the sound of metal and the vowels sing like negroes at an exhibit."[24] In a language that always tends toward extremes, the "Kafkaesque process" consists of intensifying German so as to divest it of the significations it harbors.

Metaphor as a representative image yields to metamorphosis, its opposite, because "no proper or figurative sense exist any longer."[25] In this way, the becoming-animals in Kafka have no mythological or archetypal reference and "correspond only to gradients that have been surpassed, to liberated zones of intensity."[26] If, in *The Metamorphosis*, Gregor becomes a cockroach, it is a way for him not only to escape his father but also to succeed where his father failed in "fleeing the manager, the business and the bureaucrats to reach this region where voices only buzz."[27] Instead of structural analogy, Deleuze and Guattari propose a veritable theory of becomings, examples of which abound in Kafka's work. They present becoming-animal as a possible escape, first as a molecular becoming that ultimately integrates itself into a machine, or "rather into a *machinic arrangement* of mutually independent parts."[28]

THE KAFKA EVENT

Guattari had a passion for Kafka, whose *Diary* gives the impression of living as if in a dream. "He paid a lot of attention to his dreams."[29] In the early 1980s, Guattari prepared an anthology of sixty-five dreams and proposed to read them—not through a psychoanalytic lens—to have the specific points found in the expression of these dreams work concretely.

In 1982, several years after *Kafka* was published, Guattari told Jack Lang, then minister of culture, that he wanted to organize something for Kafka's hundredth birthday. Lang was delighted: "Thank you for your note on Kafka. Agreed. Can you take the initiative? Were you to agree to head this up I would be very happy."[30] A committee for Kafka celebrations was created, with Jorge Luis Borges as its honorary president and Guattari as its executive president. Guattari and the art critic Yasha David organized a major exhibit entitled "Kafka's Century" at the Beaubourg Center, from June 7 to October 1, 1984.

Guattari had designed the exhibit with the intention of showing the modern side of Kafka, to bring him into the twenty-first century. He wanted many dimensions to the exhibit: temporary exhibits, video programs, plays, films, and lectures. Guattari's personal notebooks show how carefully he tried to avoid being manipulated by marketing or society types. The exhibit was to be a response to the paradox of Kafka, a secretive author of intimacy and solitude who had given rise to a well-worn adjective. Restoring the paradox required seeing and hearing the many facets of the "Kafka effect." "The greatest intimacy of the Kafka effect also involves the greatest number. That is the wager that we would like to make."[31]

Guattari worked unsparingly to ensure the success of the exhibit. "He invited Jorge Luis Borges to give a talk on Kafka. It was a sublime evening during which the Sightless Seer spoke about his discovery of Kafka. Not that this prevented the Beaubourg administration from refusing to pay his airfare and hotel! So Felix paid from his own pocket!"[32] Guattari had also planned to have a number of symposia and stagings of plays with Jean-Luc Borg's company (*Le Théâtre par le bas*) and with Philippe Adrien, who mounted a production of Kafka's *Dreams* that borrowed heavily from the Deleuzo-Guattarian reading. Later, on March 1, 1988, Guattari invited Philippe Adrien to speak at his seminar on "improvisation," a concept that had been a major inspiration for Adrien's production of *Dreams*.

In 1984, the drama critic Enzo Cormann wrote the dialogue and Philippe Adrien produced the play after many months of improvisations by Adrien's fourteen actors. This was how Cormann met Guattari. Philippe Adrien, the director of the *Théâtre des Quartiers* in Ivry (a suburb of Paris), was giving some training on staging Kafka's dreams and invited Cormann, a writer, to participate. "During the six months that we were preparing the production, Félix came to the theater regularly to watch us work."[33] During this same period, Guattari's friend François Pain was preparing a film based on *Dreams*. When Cormann invited Guattari to dinner with the small troupe, he made a pun without realizing it. "When are you there?" he asked. (*Tu es là quand?*) "Lacan? We'd know about that," answered Guattari.[34] A close friendship developed between the two men. *Dreams* was a hit; it won the 1985 Critics' Prize.[35] In 1983, during the centenary celebrations, Guattari returned to Kafka. "I got trapped in Kafka."[36] He recalled his first patient, the first schizophrenic he treated at La Borde, a young Jewish man who completely identified with Kafka. He spent a lot of time with the difficult young catatonic patient, immured in his silence, and he helped cure his psychosis by having him write. He wrote about Kafka. "My patient's schizophrenia, my own schizophrenic process and Kafka. All of that still communicates in a relationship of influence."[37]

Guattari's handwritten notes are full of analyses of various aspects of Kafka's work. He tested his idea of intensity and of "childhood blocks" in the first chapter of *The Castle*, observing that the castle is not seen from any single angle but through a series of impressions. Different types of registers of intensities follow one upon another, making it impossible to reduce the reading to an Oedipal triangle. Several of these intensive elements are present in all of Kafka's work: "the head was bent, like the form of the contents, and the portrait, like the form of the expression."[38] In a letter to Milena, Kafka describes his childhood terror, a group of linked memories that haunted him during the entire time that he was writing the description of the arrival at the castle: when he was going to school he would pass the bloody stalls of the butcher, which transformed the school into an object of terror. Elsewhere, in Guattari's reflections on *The Metamorphosis*, he remarks on the unfinished aspect of Kafka's work.

It was as if Kafka always wanted to end up with a return to an Oedipal Ithaca but never managed to.... Kafka's literary machine overwhelmed his Oedipus. He didn't manage to overcode his productions. Except perhaps in *The Metamorphosis*.... A schizo bomb explodes the Oedipal compromise. The father finds the courage to throw the apple at Gregor, re-Oedipizing him using violence. The symbol, perhaps, of the apple's fall, of original sin.[39]

14

A Thousand Plateaus
A Geophilosophy of Politics

In 1980, after the polemical, critical phase of *Anti-Oedipus*, Deleuze and Guattari published the more positive second volume of *Capitalism and Schizophrenia*, *A Thousand Plateaus*, which argues for a philosophy of spatial logics. Even today, the book remains deeply original and rich. In it, Deleuze and Guattari radically reject nineteenth-century historicism and its theodicy and teleology, which had prevailed well into the twentieth century. Rather than taking a Hegelian approach to time, they argue for spatial relationships among the many forces manifesting themselves over time.

The two volumes are deeply connected. In *Anti-Oedipus*, the authors want to show that psychosis does not depend on a structural distribution, as the structuralists claim; it is a process. "It's truly a dynamic process-oriented interpretation that is neither personological nor structuralist."[1] The book presents madness as being immediately caught within a field that is sociohistorically invested; the book explores this field by means of a "geoanalysis" that maps micropolitics so as to identify the modes of articulation between the process of subjectification and institutional apparatuses, by making the potential productivity of group-subjects apparent.

The book's title points to its geographical approach: a plateau is like a plane with an endless horizon, an intermediate central zone of intensity. Deleuze liked to say, perhaps to provoke his audience, that the title corresponded to the landscapes of Limousin, specifically the Millevaches plateau he could see from the windows of his house at Saint-Léonard-de-Noblat. Above all, the absence of a defined beginning or end to the plateau corresponded to Deleuze's oft-repeated advice to begin "in the middle." Having destroyed the rigid nature of family institutions in *Anti-Oedipus*, Deleuze and Guattari blazed a new trail by exploring everything having to do with differences and unexplored connections. The book's title was in no way metaphoric but was in fact proclaiming a metamorphosis. "Plateau has a specific meaning in geography, in mechanics and in theater: a plateau of erosion and sedimentation, gears to increase and decrease speed, a stage for performing and filming."[2]

A *Thousand Plateaus* does not refer directly to geography but to physics "in the sense of Bergson's (meta)physics or the geography of the *physis*."[3] Treating information in terms of spatial logic leads to a completely original way of using time. Each plateau in the book has a specific exergual date that refers to the chapter's historical eponymous event; this is a way of recalling the importance of the event for their philosophy using a logic that is no longer chronological or evolutionary.[4]

A *Thousand Plateaus*, like *Anti-Oedipus*, wends through the humanities using an approach that clearly demonstrates its contributions while at the same time expressing a philosophy. In response to Catherine Clément's question about the genre of this new book, Deleuze was unambiguous. "Philosophy, nothing but philosophy, in the traditional sense of the term."[5] The book continues to work out a new metaphysics that would be an ontology of difference drawing from linguistics, anthropology, psychoanalysis, and ethology. The authors' goal was to create functional concepts—a "mechanosphere"—that could change our relationship to the world.

Constructing this "mechanosphere" was part of a method announced in *Rhizome* and used throughout the book. The approach was resolutely constructivist and pragmatic: it starts by demarcating a plane of consistency, a plateau, then establishes two series of points on the plateau, thereby setting up certain asymmetrical connections among some of the points of the various series. This broken line is supposed to function on another plane or connected plateau, where it is attracted to a new line of flight; the network of actions/reactions is indefinite in the rhizome, whose connections have no predetermined finality. Affirming the productivity of this diagonal of thought, of this transversality in action, leads to an unusually dense, dynamic book. "This is the book that I would take with me to a desert island because it's neither inhuman nor superhuman but almost anhuman. It's a multiple machine with multiple becomings."[6]

Indeed, the book's ideas are stupefying. Devoted readers of *Anti-Oedipus* waited eight years for it, and when it came out, it was considered too difficult and confusing; it was generally poorly received. Given its target, *Anti-Oedipus* was an immediate bestseller,[7] whereas A *Thousand Plateaus* was greeted with relative indifference,[8] both because of its density and because it ran against the grain. It was 1980; the "new philosophers" were being celebrated, and the book's concepts were derided for being "as enormous as false teeth." The sophistry that Deleuze and Guattari refined did not, when it was published, create a stir.

The reviews were polite, but the underlying confusion came through. Five years after the book was published, Arnaud Villani, a Deleuze specialist, took up his pen in *Critique* praising it as "essential in its dissection of a space for unusual writing and thinking."[9] In *Le Matin*, Catherine Clément said she was confused but qualified her remarks. "Being baffled is just what was needed."[10] She emphasized the idea of nomadism running through the book and applauded the breakthrough of the many figures of abnormality, of lawless people, and the need to think differently. In his review in *Le Monde*, Christian Delacampagne hailed the two volumes of *Capitalism and Schizophrenia* as "a philosophical treatise without equal in contemporary writing"[11] but warned potential readers that the publication with its commingled world history would present challenges. "The reader will be amazed, impressed, and perplexed."[12]

Libération accorded the book the importance it warranted and before it was published interviewed Guattari, who emphasized the book's political dimension.[13] When the book came out, *Libération* organized a long interview with Deleuze, who explained: "The title *A Thousand Plateaus* refers to these individuations that aren't personal or things."[14] Robert Maggiori remarked that *A Thousand Plateaus* was organized in a paradoxically achronological manner, heteroclitic like an antisystem, or a patchwork, that bore at one and the same time a vision of the world, a totally different philosophical system; Deleuze responded that we are all well aware of the general failure of most systems of knowledge, but above all we recognize that they remain closed in on themselves, locked in their limits. "What Guattari and I are calling rhizome is precisely a case of an open system."[15]

If there is any core notion in the book, it is arrangement. Answering Catherine Clément's question about the unity of this unusually mixed book, Deleuze noted, "It might be the notion of *arrangement* (which replaces desiring machines)."[16] The concept runs through each plateau and, because of its ability to connect the most diverse elements, opens onto a general logic that during those years Guattari often called "diagrammatic." With respect to the abandoned notion of the desiring machine, the concept of arrangement offers the advantage of exiting the realm of psychoanalysis to set all forms of connections into relation, including those in the nonhuman realm, and to release their energies. It is enough to assemble singular and heterogeneous elements and place them in a specific arrangement. It can be the wasp and the orchid; or the horse, the man, and the stirrup; or the horse-man-bow. All combinations are possible between technical machines, animals, and humans. It is always processes of subjectification, of individuation, that are on the horizon. But this goal presupposes detours and reconnections between man and nature, man and *physis*. In fact, pertinent distinctions between nature and artifice no longer exist at the level of the arrangement's links.

Deleuze and Guattari give ethology an extremely important position for restoring the way in which animals construct their arrangements with nature and among themselves. They use the concept quite broadly and without limits, making it ideal for building an open system. The idea of arrangement means putting a set of material relations and a corresponding regime of signs into relationship. An arrangement does not perpetuate itself but is, on the contrary, is always set in motion, always affected by a dose of imbalance, because it is assigned to a field of desire in which it constitutes itself. In this manner, an arrangement plays the same role as the one played by the desiring machine in *Anti-Oedipus*. It is also a way of expressing the fact that desire is only a question of encounters, of ruptures in flux.

Arrangements are not classical binary relations like individual and collective, or signifier and signified, or even sign and sense. Deleuze and Guattari defined two major axes of arrangements, each of which subdivides into two variations: a horizontal axis and a vertical axis. The horizontal axis includes content and expression and has to do with the machinic arrangement of the body, actions, passions, and the collective arrangement of the act of utterance. The vertical axis includes territorialized aspects and points of deterritorialization. This is a far cry from the reigning Althusserian Marxist analyses that made economics the ultimate determinant infrastructure. With arrangements, everything connects among heterogeneous series. Neither mechanical causality nor determinism come into play; connections are made according to the diverse lines of flight of the macropolitical system.

Entirely different—territorial—types of arrangements define the function of the *ritournelle*, or refrain. Birds mark their territory with their song; the same territorializing function existed in ancient Greece and in Hindu systems. But "the ritornello can take on other functions: amorous, professional, social, liturgical and cosmic. It always carries some earth along with it."[17] The rhythms driving the lives of animals and humans are a means of countering chaos and its threats of extinction. This arrangement of an environment responding to chaos gives rise to a "chaos-rhythm or chaosmos."[18] In common language, a refrain is a bit of music that repeats, a theme, a form of the eternal return that also creates time, the "implied time" described by the linguist Gustave Guillaume. Above all, the refrain lends a contradictory dynamic to territoriality. It stretches toward a return to known territory to inhabit it and to expel chaos; this is Mahler's famous *Song of the Earth* and its finale. "The coexistence of two themes: the melody evoking the arrangements of a bird, and the rhythmic theme evoking the deep respiration of the earth, eternally."[19] The refrain also signals the departure for deterritorialization, a change of scenery, a trip, a back and forth between the departure and the return, which sets the tone of an in-between two territories. Its very circularity evokes the fact that there is neither beginning nor end—only infinite variations. "The *ritornello* moves towards territorial arrangement, establishes itself and leaves."[20]

Even if it is usually difficult to distinguish between what belongs to Deleuze or to Guattari, the *ritornello* belongs more to Guattari, a pianist. Moreover, in 1979, Guattari wrote a personal text about the refrain,[21] insisting right away that it conjures away the passage of time, the anxiety of death, the risk of chaos, the fear of losing control expressed by *refrains*, these rhythms that produce inhabited, territorialized time. "Each individual, group, and nation equips themselves with a basic range of talismanic refrains."[22] The ethnologist Pierre Clastres also understood that these refrains were a manner of semiotizing time and pointed to the solitary song of an Indian in the night challenging passing time and the process that "subjects man to the general network of signs."[23] Our complex modern societies have lost this relationship of immediacy with the expression of our anxieties; they even have an illusion of mastery because of their solid machinic material.

The notion of territory can also be misleading, however, like all of Deleuze and Guattari's notions. "Territory is in fact an action that affects the environments and rhythms that 'territorialize' them."[24] This concept is fundamentally tied to pragmatics and therefore expressive rather than passive; this is how there is, in effect, an endogenous relationship between territory and rhythm. "The *ritornello* is the territorialized rhythm and melody become expressive—and they've become expressive because they are territorializing."[25] The authors see this process of territorialization as appropriately contrasted to another pole, a deterritorialization of the *ritornello*, a release into the cosmos to "open the arrangement onto a cosmic force."[26] In every arrangement, the molar line penetrates the system's line of flight thanks to the molecular line of deterritorialization.

Our authors in no way intended to argue for any geographical determinism that made the birth of philosophy in the Greek world inevitable. They simply linked the encounter of the Greek environment and the plane of immanence regarding thought. For the arrangement to take shape, therefore, these two forms of deterritorialization had to meet. For Deleuze and Guattari, Hegel and Heidegger read the birth of philosophy in Greece as historicists. They situated geography on the side of the contingent, by contrast with the school of Vidalian geography and Braudel's emphasis on permanent elements, structures, and the very long duration in geography. For Deleuze and Guattari, geography is "not only physical and human, but mental as well, like the landscape. Geography wrests history from the cult of necessity and emphasizes the irreducibility of contingency. It wrests history from the cult of origins to argue for the power of a 'milieu.'"[27] Their conclusion was that philosophy arose in Greece not out of any necessity but as a pure contingency.

The relationship to territory provides a nationalistic basis to various currents of thought, to philosophical "opinions." Deleuze and Guattari noted the archetypes according to which the French tend to reterritorialize themselves in consciousness, in the *cogito*, unlike the Germans, who did not abandon the Absolute to reclaim the Greek plane of immanence by deterritorializing consciousness. "In the Establish-Build-Inhabit trinity, the French build, the Germans establish, but the English inhabit."[28] Experimentation is first and foremost philosophical and defines what it means to think. It results from the tension between territorialization and deterritorialization. Like the well-known train in the western film, *"philosophy reterritorializes itself three times, once in the past with the Greeks, once in the present with the democratic State, and once in the future with new people and a new land."*[29]

To be free of the Christian axiom of eschatological time, Deleuze and Guattari attack "faciality" in the seventh plateau, dated year zero, the year of Christ's birth. Their critique served to escape eurocentricity, the domination of modern white men over the rest of humanity as the incarnation of progress, and the universal, and, at the same time, to attack phenomenological theses.

Deleuze, as we have seen, always took a different path than that of the phenomenological project. In the 1970s, the phenomenologist Emmanuel

Levinas saw in the human face the injunction of the Other, the foundation of ethics, and the very manifestation of humanity: "To me, the Other's face signifies the unavoidable responsibility preceding any free consent, pact, or contract."[30] For Deleuze and Guattari, by contrast, the face is closely linked to a specific spatiotemporal moment in which it emerges and it cannot therefore claim to be universal. Pursuing the construction of their own metaphysics, Deleuze and Guattari extend the notion of faciality to every form of expression both natural and animal. Wanting go as far as possible in naturalizing the human and in humanizing nature, they reject every form of anthropomorphism. "To the point of saying that if there were a human destiny, it would be to escape the face, undo the face and faceifications, to become imperceptible, clandestine."[31] This is reminiscent of Foucault's saying that he wrote in order to no longer have a face. "Many others, doubtless like me, write so as to no longer have a face. Don't ask me who I am and don't tell me to stay the same: that's an ethics of civil status; it's what determines all of our papers. Let it leave us free when it comes to writing."[32] For Deleuze and Guattari, the issue of faciality belongs to a specific machine of signs that they had already criticized in the fifth plateau, which addresses the regime of signs. This machine wrongfully valorizes simple redundancy and ensures the triumph of the master Signifier. Not only does the entire history of Christianity incarnate the mystical body in the face of Christ, but despotic power also embodies the body of power in its leader. Constantly concerned with keeping the flame of deterritorialization alive, Deleuze and Guattari attack the phenomenological enterprise of faciality, which is a means of enslaving people to the signifier and imposing the law of transcendence.

In 1979, Guattari had already devoted an entire chapter to faciality in *The Unconscious Machinic*, titled "Signifying Faciality, Diagrammatic Faciality."[33] His target there was more capitalism and the micropolitics of closure. "The ultimate paradigm of faciality is 'that's how it is.'"[34] He also attacked Lacan's analysis of the mirror stage, where he gives the face an original role in establishing the ego when it enters the symbolic. Faciality is thus inseparable from power strategies and functions like a "normality signal."[35] It is used to establish a mode of domination based on the primacy of subjectivity and the idea of its autonomy. On the three levels—semiotic, political, and artistic—faceification is a mode of domination: "The face is a politics."[36]

If the face expresses a growth of territorialization, territorialization also includes lines of flight, of resistance that can provide the foundations for a different politics. To do so, however, requires going back to the abstract machine that produced faciality. "Concrete faces are produced by an *abstract faciality machine*"[37] comprising a small binary system that contrasts the white wall of the signifier with the black hole of subjectivity. "The black hole–white wall system would not already be a face, it'd be the abstract machine producing it."[38] In 1980, Deleuze and Guattari were abundantly aware of the risks of certain misunderstandings that they had already experienced with certain interpretations of *Anti-Oedipus*, and thus they warned against the specific dangers of wanting to eliminate the face. "It's no small task to let go of the face. We risk madness: is it just by chance that the schizo loses his sense of face, his own and others, at the same time as he loses the sense of landscape, language and of the dominant significations?"[39] What must be avoided is having the lines of destruction become objects in themselves. Of course, it is possible to point to primitive societies, which, unlike European societies, do not contrast the face with the head, which is seen as being continuous with the body. They do not need the face, which in no way means that they are not human. But Deleuze and Guattari do not argue for a "return to" presignifying semiotics. "We will always fail to imitate the Black, the Indian, and even the Chinese."[40] Regression to the past is a barred road, both sterile and a trap. On the contrary, one has to start from what is—the overcoded face of the capitalist era—to better identify the potential lines of flight. The semiotics of the future that remain to be created is one of "inquiring minds where the points of deterritorialization become operational."[41]

SPATIAL LOGICS

Another important polarization comes into play in the analysis of spatial logics, of the fundamental spatial logics of smooth and striated spaces and nomadic and sedentary spaces. These essentially different spaces exist only through their reciprocal relationships to one another. There is, on one hand, nonpolarized space that is fundamentally open, immeasurable, and peopled with singularities; on the other hand, there is an overcoded, measured, hierarchical space. On one hand, there is the embroidery model, with its central design (striated space); on the other hand, there is the patchwork (smooth space), with its successive additions of fabric and no predetermined limits. Using the patchwork as an example to designate smooth space shows that space is not signifying that it is homogenous.

The opposition is not limited to the terrestrial world, since this binarism also runs through maritime space. "A smooth space par excellence, and yet the one that was confronted earliest on with the exigencies of an increasingly strict striation."[42] There is therefore no simple opposition between a smooth and a striated side, nor is there any overdetermination of the place to describe space, which means that we can travel without moving, while staying in the same place. Indeed, Deleuze describes himself as an "immobile traveler." This tension defines two micropolitical modalities and, at the same time, two esthetics: the haptic specific to the smooth space of contact, touch, and immediacy and the optic art specific to striated space, recalling the vision of things at a distance, to perspective. "Cézanne talked about the necessity *of no longer seeing* the wheat field, of being too close to it, of losing oneself, losing one's bearings in a smooth space."[43] *A Thousand Plateaus* develops above all the micropolitical side that develops from this tension between the striated pole and the smooth pole, with the double polarity contrasting the war machine and the apparatus of capture embodied by the State (plateaus 12 and 13).

Deleuze and Guattari constantly use binary oppositions, but not to argue for a dualistic form of thought. Rather, they use them to destroy them, replacing them by thinking the multiplicities running through pluralized binaries. Where common sense typically thinks of a war machine as a subset of the State apparatus, Deleuze and Guattari insist on the radically different nature of these two poles. The war machine does not belong to the State; what is more, its entire dynamic sets it in opposition to the logic of the State. Created by nomads, war machines were invented to resist, to fight the State apparatus conceived as an apparatus of capture. War machines took shape in a specific smooth space (deserts, steppes, and oceans).

The "Treatise on Nomadology: The War Machine," chapter of *A Thousand Plateaus* lays out this opposition. The chapter's title is a serious and yet ironic reference to Spinoza's political theological treatise[44] that has the status of the "source of a new discipline."[45] Surprisingly, war does not define the war machine. There are three ways to describe it: first, the arithmetic composition of the men comprising it *a contrario* to the territorial organization of the State. Next, "the State apparatus invented a specific type of activity—work."[46] Of course, war machines also involve work, but regulated activity is a free act. Finally, in terms of expression, the State apparatus manifests itself by tools and signs, whereas the war machine defines itself by its weapons.

The State's fundamental question is how to appropriate the war machine to itself, how to capture and force it into serving the State. The war machine, however, tries to resist State logics and to preserve its own specific dynamism. The war machine expresses all of the ambivalence of the line of flight that consists in forcing flight, in exploiting all the lines of deterritorialization. By the exteriority signified by the war machine in relation to the State, the State cannot conceive itself without a relationship to the exterior that feeds it, whereas the war machine exists because of a social arrangement whose originary model is nomadism: whence the "Treatise on Nomadology."[47]

THE PALESTINIANS: THE CASE OF A LANDLESS PEOPLE

Deleuze and Guattari saw the Palestinian cause as a searing, contemporary example of a possible space-time that the PLO would embody. Their sensitivity toward deterritorialized, "landless people" was at the root of their involvement with the Palestinian cause. Guattari was a close friend of Ilan Halévi, a Jewish Israeli writer who represented the PLO at the Socialist International. Halévi came to Paris in 1975, contacted Guattari because of his activities protesting the Algerian War, and easily convinced him to support the Palestinian cause. "He was neither a Third-World supporter nor a Eurocentrist. He was curious about everyone and everything, but he wasn't a voyeur. . . . Félix was one of those internationalists, and it was this initial attitude that determined his position with respect to Palestine and his involvement with the Palestinian thing."[48] Guattari made the CERFI offices available for the first secret meeting between well-known Israelis and Palestinians, which took place in February 1976. Two years later, he was invited to the Occupied Territories to contact militant Palestinians and Israelis who were liaising with the PLO. In 1977 and 1978, Ilan Halévi organized a seminar at Vincennes on the confiscation of Arab lands in Israel, which Guattari followed with passion and assiduity. During one of these discussions, Elias Sanbar, a Palestinian intellectual who knew Halévi and was slightly acquainted with Guattari, was in the hall. He had not been scheduled to speak, but in the heat of the discussion, he improvised lengthy remarks on the guerrilla techniques of the Palestinian underground in the 1930s. "Félix was in the hall and he asked me how I planned to get back to Paris. I said that I was planning to take the metro and he offered to drive me back. A few days later, my telephone rang and someone said to me, 'Hello.

My name is Gilles Deleuze. Can I come see you? I would like to talk with you,' and so he came to my place."[49]

In 1978, Deleuze and Guattari were preparing to write *A Thousand Plateaus* and were absorbed in thinking about war machines, the apparatus of capture. Guattari had convinced Deleuze that he had to get in touch with Sanbar after hearing him speak at Vincennes about the techniques used in nomadic wars. Their meeting led to an intense friendship that lasted until Deleuze's death. "He was always focused on the essential. Nothing was lost. He was always at the core of things. He was someone who asked your questions before you did. It was incredible."[50]

After their initial discussion, Deleuze made his first public statement about the Israeli-Palestinian conflict in an article in *Le Monde*.[51] He adopted his position after the Israeli army's vast operation in southern Lebanon, in which several hundred refugees in the Palestinian camps and Lebanese civilians were killed and which caused tens of thousands of Lebanese to flee toward Beirut. Deleuze strongly defended the Palestinians. "The Palestinians, a people with neither land nor State, are troublesome for everyone."[52] In his article, Deleuze denounced the fact that Palestinians had nothing more than death to look forward to, and he called upon the international community to recognize them as legitimate interlocutors, "since they are in a state of war for which they are certainly not responsible."[53]

In 1979, Guattari, for his part, was helping Ilan Halévi organize a colloquium on Zionism, anti-Semitism, and racism. In 1980, *A Thousand Plateaus* was published and became an important resource for Halévi. "This is an incomparable book, in which, for the first time in a very long time in French letters, philosophers are playing their role, which is to make the world comprehensible, serious."[54]

In 1980, Elias Sanbar planned to create a review dedicated to the Palestinian question. He met with a number of people and explained his well-developed project to each of them, but no one was interested. "I called Deleuze and asked him what to do. He said, 'I don't know, but I'll ask Jérôme Lindon to meet you.'"[55] So Elias Sanbar went to Minuit and met the director, Lindon, who began by explaining the problems of French publishing, adding that Palestine was not really a specialty at that publishing house.

> Next he asked me what I wanted to do with the review and I talked to him for a good fifteen minutes about my plans. I had barely finished when Lindon said, "Minuit will take you. Write me up a single page

that would give the editorial approach of your journal." I immediately sent him something and the next day at 7:15, I got a call. "This is Jérôme Lindon, I read your text; we're on."[56]

The *Review of Palestinian Studies* was born in October 1981.

Shortly after the review was created, Blandine Jeanson, a journalist at *Libération*, told Sanbar that she wanted to publish an article about the new review and asked if Deleuze would write something. Together, Sanbar and Deleuze wrote a long interview entitled "Palestine's Indians," a title they both agreed on.[57] "It was fabulous, fantastic for the review. And this idea of Red Skins grew out of our conversations."[58] In the conversation, Sanbar drew a parallel between the Palestinian situation and the American Indians. "The history of the creation of Israel absolutely repeats the process that gave birth to the United States of America."[59]

In 1982, as the increasingly dramatic fighting in the Lebanese war continued, Deleuze wrote an article acclaiming the Palestinian cause and its leader, Yasser Arafat.[60] "The Palestinian cause is first of all the sum of the injustices that this people has undergone and continues to face."[61] Arafat could only speak about "shame" regarding the massacres of Sabra and Shatila; Deleuze critiqued the interpretation of the Nazi holocaust, an absolute Evil, according to a dehistoricized religious framework. He was extremely radical in his rejection of Israeli politics. "Israel has always been clear about its goal from the start, about emptying the Palestinian territories. . . . It's a genocide when physical extermination is subordinate to geographic evacuation."[62] In order to resist Israel's determination and the international complicity that modestly covered its politics, Deleuze declared that "a great historical personality [needed to be found] about whom one would say, from a Western perspective, that he was a Shakespearean character, and it was Arafat."[63]

Deleuze's position was of course immensely comforting to Elias Sanbar, who was an intellectual militant for the Palestinian cause. Later, during the 1991 Camp David peace negotiations organized by President Clinton, he was part of the Palestinian delegation and given responsibility for the thorny issue of Palestinian refugees.

During those negotiations, I called Gilles and said, "You know, it's very violent for me because I have to negotiate with people who have made my own people miserable." It's not easy and I told him that I'd found an antidote during the negotiations. "Every night, before going to sleep, to justify myself to myself, I read a few paragraphs from Spinoza's *Ethics*," and Gilles answered, "I understand."[64]

In addition to their discussions about poetry, they discussed spatial displacement, the outside-space-and-time created by being uprooted that had made the Palestinians invisible in a way, a form of dissolution in space and over time.

For Sanbar, Deleuze and Guattari's work was essential. "These texts are always with me."[65] When Sanbar published *Figures of the Palestinian* in 2004, he dedicated it "to Gilles Deleuze, in homage to a perfect friendship."[66] "This book was the topic of our final discussion. The last time that I spoke with him, we were discussing this book but we never finished because he had a suffocating coughing fit."[67]

GLOBAL POLITICAL PRAGMATICS

The notion of a war machine is particularly appropriate for thinking about the stateless Palestinian people. Beyond the Palestinian example, however, the function of the war machine is to explore the means of avoiding the creation of a bureaucratic State apparatus to which a population is subjected. This was the core of Deleuze and Guattari's thinking about the ephemeral lives of groups who constantly call themselves into question, just as institutional psychotherapy treated the clinical institution while treating patients. There was also the idea of preserving the efforts by failed and foiled revolutions to transform society. To increase the number of war machines seemed therefore to be a way of creating effective counterweights to avoid these failures. The point was to have them proliferate and multiply infinitely so that official, molar institutions would become unnecessary and disappear, benefiting molecular micronetworks.

The ethnologist Pierre Clastres supported Deleuze and Guattari's ideas.[68] He demonstrated that the State does not "evolve"; it does not arise from the development of productive forces or from the differentiation of political forces. It emerges abruptly, like a pure event, when a community reaches a threshold population of three hundred people. Clastres' other main point was that primitive societies are not only "Stateless" but that they use their war machine to wage war "against the State." They are "societies against the State." War is omnipresent, because war machines control all forms of violence by opposing the State, to maintain the groups' segmentarity, whereas the State must always pacify groups in order to establish itself. The figure of the nomad not only refers to classical nomadism but is also a conceptual persona making it possible to restore the specificity of the war machine. The nomadic is a space for mobilization, not for appropriation. While it can be inhabited, no one establishes himself or herself in this space; one unfolds without capitalizing.

Understood this way and confirmed by ethnologists, the externality of the war machine can also be observed in epistemology, where certain types of science have continued to be subordinate alongside and external to physics. Such a nomad science would have several characteristics, attuned to four different models: a hydraulic model that creates flux rather than solids; a model of becoming and heterogeneity rather than stability; a model that mixes things in an open space; and, finally, a problematic rather than theoretical model. Using this binarity of the nomadic and the sedentary, two scientific traditions have always been cast in opposition: the sciences of repetition on one hand, and, on the other, those of itineration, the ambulatory sciences. Creativity would belong to the nomad sciences, whose objective is to invent problems; the royal sciences would have the job of providing scientific solutions to them. The result would be a potential complementarity that ends up occulting the initial innovative moment, which is quickly overlaid by the procedural efficiency of the solution found by the State science. "Royal science is the only one to have a metric power defining the apparatus of concepts or the autonomy of sciences."[69]

War machines also serve to make meaning circulate, to transgress limits, to use lines of flight in a literal drift to get beyond the enclosures. The war machines have to stay active because they are confronted by the State, which Deleuze and Guattari define as an apparatus of capture. They define social formations as "machinic processes,"[70] preferring these to the Marxist and Althusserian notions of the means of production. They also distinguish primitive societies, whose mechanisms include conjuration-anticipation, from State societies, which are defined by their apparatus of capture: from urban societies defined by their instruments of polarization and nomadic societies by war machines. Where the State directs its efforts toward capitalizing and appropriating itself, the war machine, by contrast, has the "power to transform."[71] The notion of capture, specific to State societies, is rooted in the distant past of Indo-European mythology and designates the pole of sovereignty. The propensity to capture and overcode

State apparatus raises the problem of minorities, who must create war machines to survive.

The issue here is political: keeping multiple resistant micropolitics from disappearing into the State's logic.[72] In the late 1970s, Deleuze and Guattari refer explicitly to the Italian autonomy movement, to Franco Beradi ("Bifo"),[73] to Toni Negri, and to the analyses of the Italian Marxist Mario Tronti of the role of the State apparatus in integrating the working class into capitalist society and the proletariat's need to use its critical strategy only after having been divested of its class position.

To regulate the tension between the two poles (the apparatus of capture and the war machines) and to define a new micropolitics at the crossroads between ethics and politics, Deleuze and Guattari emphasize the social contract, a notion dear to Deleuze. The social contract allows the apparatus of capture to go forward and to subject others to it in an ambivalent manner that cannot be ascribed to a simple dependency, voluntary or imposed. This entire articulation of the self on an increasingly global scale, on a map-world, makes it imperative to define the kind of micropolitics that can integrate spatial logics—a geophilosophy able to localize and reflect upon the multitude of constitutive points of the various life forces of the world rhizome. Whence the necessity of mapping these elements rather than merely plotting them on a given set of conditions, of experimenting and confronting social reality by multiplying access routes.

Guattari continued this work on cartography beyond 1980 in his seminars, on which he based his *Schizoanalytic Cartographies* (1989).[74] Danielle Sivadon organized the seminar schedule, arranged the program and invitations, and deciphered the remarks. "During the first period of 1980–1985, it was essentially Félix talking about his cartographies; during a second period (1985–1992), on rue Saint-Sauveur, we worked more on the basis of guest speakers."[75] Of about one hundred potential guests, a good twenty people came regularly and participated actively in the seminars.

Guattari set the tone at the first session on December 9, 1980. "For me, [this seminar] will only be meaningful if it works. Which is to say quite clearly if the different theoretical arguments that I propose here help people."[76] Arrangement, the key concept of the seminar, came from the just-published *A Thousand Plateaus*. The first issue to be addressed was the collective arrangement of utterance, which served to clarify various hypotheses but also to define what Guattari meant by schizoanalysis. "It's the study of the incidence of machinic arrangements on a given problem."[77]

Here he was embarking on a collective constructivism to test his ideas and show that they are indispensable operators in his practice. Over the years, he mobilized a tremendous range of expertise, realizing the transversality that he had urged. From the very start, Guattari suggests pluralizing the notion of the unconscious. During his presentation, he proposed an idea— acknowledging that it might be a fantasy—of distinguishing between a relative and an absolute unconscious, the latter referring to a consciousness without an object. During the second seminar, he developed the idea by presenting four different unconsciousnesses—subjective, material, territorial or corporal, and machinic—that "would be one range of possibilities, of molecular micro-politics."[78]

He clearly stated that the seminar was fundamentally pragmatic and occasionally directed against the psychoanalytical tradition. "Psychoanalysis has foreclosed the dimension of action (no kidding!). It's enough to mention the transition from 'thought to action' to see, in some way, that we're beyond the realm of analysis. For schizoanalysis, however, the dimension of action becomes completely central."[79] Moreover, paying close, careful attention to contingency and to the singularity of situations urged the rehabilitation of content, the signified, which until that point had tended to disappear beneath the signifying logics. Guattari's own physical experience, his dreams and anxieties, could be examined in this seminar, where everything could be discussed. For example, he describes his first renal colic (he was to have many very serious such episodes) as the physical expression of a threatening black hole related to his fear of the passage of time and of mortality.[80]

In addition to his themes of predilection in psychoanalysis, Guattari welcomed other disciplines into his seminar. In 1983, he invited the ethnologist Barbara Glowzcewski to discuss her work on the dreams of Australian aborigines. Rather than dreams being individual projections, she showed how they translated collective mythic elaborations, linking no fewer than five hundred ethnic groups around a common dream. "The dream is the present and a very distant past. For me, this time that is both the present and very long ago is not a historical time but rather a time of metamorphosis. It's a dynamic time that transforms."[81]

The philosopher Éric Alliez along with the old guard from La Borde, Jean-Claude Polack and Danielle Sivadon, gave several lectures at Guattari's seminar. Their talks on cultural creation led to thinking about spontaneity; Philippe Adrien[82] discussed theatrical improvisation; Yves Buin talked about jazz improvisation in Thelonious Monk's music;[83] and an old CERFI friend, Michel Rostain, discussed improvisation in opera.[84] Guattari also invited his friend Enzo Cormann to lecture on schizotheater. The lecturers were all interested in discerning the traces of subjectification processes wherever they became visible.

In seeking modes of subjectification, or the processes of becoming a subject, Guattari articulates them in relation to territories, environments along the logical lines that he calls "diagrammatics." He raises the same question in *A Schizoanalytic Cartography* and in *A Thousand Plateaus*: "How can we talk about the production of subjectivity today?"[85] Subjectivation, caught between being subjected and the group-subject, depends on machinic arrangements. Yet, more and more, technical-scientific means interfere with humans, and this state of affairs concretizes the analysis of the *socius* as machinic arrangements. "No realm of opinion, thought, images, affects, or narrativity can claim to elude the invasive grip of 'computer support,' databases, or telematics."[86] In a period that he describes as the beginning of Integrated World Capitalism (IWC), Guattari investigates the processes of individuation, the alternative forces of subjectification. Far from being nostalgic about our lost origins, he turns to the unknown beginnings and hopes of innovation, creation, and of new articulations between men and machines.

The philosopher Manola Antonioli correctly emphasizes the pertinence and relevance of Guattari and Deleuze's ideas about spatialized thinking in an era of globalization. "Thought must increasingly consider spaces, dimensions, and territories and acknowledge its essentially *spacing* dimension rather than continuing to meditate solely on history and the history of concepts."[87] During a period marked by the end of certainty, it is appropriate to live differently in our smooth and striated spaces and to abandon the imaginary world of possible closed entities—individual, organic, natural, or governmental—to better understand that they are always open onto the outside, have only a fragmentary reality and an unpredictable becoming. "The opening of 'globalization' will only be possible in a world as an archipelago, with multiple interfaces that increase exchanges, passages, and encounters."[88] According to Manola Antonioli, *A Thousand Plateaus* is a valuable and essentially ethical and political toolbox for this creative approach, which has yet to be fully exploited.[89]

Using the concepts presented in *A Thousand Plateaus*, John Protevi, an American philosopher from Louisiana State University, and the geographer

Mark Bonta together published a book on Deleuze and Guattari's geophi-losophy.[90] What excited Protevi was to find a way to bridge the humanities and the sciences, domains that often remain mutually ignorant. In Deleuze's work, "the geology of morality" chapter was the most suggestive, because "it expresses the desire to create an ontology that can use the same concept to address physical, organic, and social systems."[91] Using the Deleuzo-Guattarian concept of the moment of emitting singularities, he wrote about Hurricane Katrina and linked it to the American notion of changing behavior patterns. In the geophilosophical analyses, the notion of reterri-torializing the very power of deterritorialization worked well for the un-stable zones along the banks of the Mississippi that had been weakened by repeated hurricanes. What was important was to consider the sensitive zones that maximized the possibility of adaptive behavior. Deleuze and Guattari make it possible to work out a sort of political physiology using scientific data in a nonmechanistic perspective. Geography is used here as a nondeterministic resource that cannot be assigned to any simple causes, because the virtual maps of social systems mean that chance and the "emission of singularities" always play a role. John Protevi and his ge-ographer colleague use geomorphological, climatological, and oceano-graphic factors as well as sociotechnical factors to study sociopolitical arrangements.

A *Thousand Plateaus* is therefore a generalized global political pragma-tism whose transversal concepts serve as the foundation on which every-thing else depends. The micropolitics to be built must define the lines of flight running beneath the hard segmentarities to destratify them. Yet "the events of May 1968 remain the micro-political model."[92] Historical teleol-ogy is downplayed in *A Thousand Plateaus* in favor of blocks of becoming anchored as molecular phenomena in their spatial environment realized by May '68. "May '68 in France was molecular and its conditions were all the more imperceptible from a macropolitical perspective. . . . Those who were evaluating things in terms of macropolitics understood nothing about the event because something that couldn't be assigned was escaping."[93]

15

The CERFI at Work

For a few years after it was created in 1967, the CERFI network and researchers were rather somnolent. Although CERFI members were deeply involved in the radical protests, it was only in 1970 that the CERFI itself really "took off." The moment was fortuitous. Having signed two small contracts for a study on creating an educational television station in Côte d'Ivoire and another on the FNAC bookstores, Anne Querrien, the general secretary at the time, happened to run into a woman who worked at the Ministry of Public Works in the stairwell of her apartment building, after having picked up her mail, which included her first copy of *Recherches* (*Research*).[1] "She asked me about it, saying that her boss, Michel Conan, who was responsible for creating a research section at the Ministry of Public Works, would like to see us."[2] The little group was quite enthusiastic about the proposal, as it had begun worrying about its future.

But how could a handful of leftist agitators and promoters of schizoanalysis interest the highest spheres of government? Part of the answer had to do with Michel Conan, an unusual man who was a trained city planner and interested in intellectual issues. He was responsible for reviving public interest in the history of French gardens and architecture. Conan had a generous annual budget of approximately four to five million francs, and he created a broad group of experts in sociology, including organizational sociologists such as Michel Crozier's teams and Marxist urban sociology experts including Christian Topalov. In 1970, two years after the explosions of May '68, Jacques Chaban-Delmas was appointed prime minister, and his government wanted to understand the social unrest; it was willing to spend money on the problem and consult social scientists to find out why institutions were not working, identify frustrated popular aspirations, and propose solutions to get things moving again. The goal was to preserve some semblance of social calm, and it seemed wiser to prevent future unrest than to repair problems after the fact.

Guattari headed a delegation to the ministry to meet with Michel Conan. They explained that the CERFI's surveys were intended to criticize the government and its lack of understanding about necessary social changes. Remarkably, this same government was now offering them contracts and cash to help identify the areas where it could do something in order to better align public decisions with social needs. Given its experience at La Borde, the CERFI was of course prepared to adopt a critical position from within, which was exactly what interested Michel Conan. But the memory of May '68 was still fresh, and the CERFI feared being manipulated or absorbed into the bureaucratic logic: its members had always refused to become civil servants and preferred to remain independent.

The dream of paid collective research suddenly became a reality. The CERFI was going to be able to propose imaginative solutions to the government as a basis for its policies. The first contract, signed in 1971, involved urban planning for the Paris suburb of Evry and the proposed construction of a new psychiatric hospital. The CERFI also won a competitive bid on a major research program about social demands for community facilities. The contract was enormous, both in terms of the number of areas involved and given its million-franc budget. The CERFI had a very small institutional base but a huge intellectual reputation, thanks largely to the support of Guattari, but also to Deleuze and Foucault.

A SELF-MANAGED RESEARCH COLLECTIVE

As a self-managed, independent collective, the CERFI tried to work differently, specifically by practicing its principles of schizoanalysis. During meetings, the current research was discussed in an environment that also took into account each researcher's subjective involvement, libido, and desires. The question of salaries was revisited on a monthly basis, and that heretofore minor issue became more problematic after the enormous budgets allocated to community facilities were deposited in the CERFI bank account.

On Tuesdays, when Guattari was in Paris and could preside over the meeting, the center held its "great mass." Research projects were decided on and their budgets established; the salaries of the small "mafia" of permanent members were reevaluated every two months to take the period's double-digit inflation into account. The core of researchers lived in the

CERFI offices: the small working community had placed its libido in the command post, and psychodramas, crying fits, and arguments abounded. Many people were attracted to the financial manna from heaven, and at the Tuesday meetings, all sorts of projects were proposed, including many that were sheer fantasy. "All the leftists in Paris came with completely bogus projects. Félix supported them blindly. We bought a camera for one person, a motorcycle for another, and we opposed many other requests, which led to a lot of arguments."[3] "We gave money to someone who came to us saying, 'I need five thousand francs for an abortion tomorrow.' 'Send the money back to us when you can, ok, here you go.' And they never came back."[4] The philosophy professor Michel Rostain described how a gang of drug addicts proposed that the CERFI do some research on drugs and managed to get a contract: they got their money. "They were drugged out of their minds. The cops even came to drag them out of our offices where they were living."[5]

The year 1973 was the high point in the CERFI's life. On the strength of its funds and given the stir created by *Anti-Oedipus*, the CERFI paid seventy-five salaried employees a monthly salary of 1,500 francs. Beyond the research for which the group had contracts, the CERFI also financed some internal groups even though they knew that it would not be lucrative. These included François Pain's video group, a sewing group led by the designer Agnès B., who started in the CERFI before making her fortune, and a singing group led by Michel Rostain. Starting in 1972, François Fourquet joined the CERFI; this was particularly significant, because he had just left his job managing La Borde.

The CERFI moved out of its avenue Verzy Avenue office to a small rear courtyard office on rue Buffon in the fifth arrondissement. The room resembled a cellar and had been used to hide people during the Algerian War. Olivier Quérouil, a linguistics student, joined the CERFI in 1970, and Françoise Dolto led a "psycho-club" managed by Nicole Guillet. The goal was to use psychiatric skills without going into analysis, which many thought was too expensive and time consuming. Anne Querrien, Gérard Grass, Olivier Quérouil, Jean-Claude Polack on occasion, and some others created a small group; the idea was to provoke traditional transference through an epistolary mode, and people paid for the right to send ten letters (after an initial free letter) to tell their stories. Olivier Quérouil became the manager of this club before starting to manage the CERFI finances.

In the fall of 1971, the group changed its office once again, this time to a beautiful large apartment at 103 boulevard Beaumarchais owned by the aeronautics industrialist Marcel Dassault, who was probably relatively un-appreciative of the "gang" of protestors. Parisian leftists looking for finan-cial support for every sort of project showed up in the office at one point or another. The semipermanent members—the "mafia"—grew from seven to twenty. Beginning in 1972, the success of *Anti-Oedipus* drew hordes, in-cluding some famous recruits, such as Guy Hocquenghem. The permanent members worked like mad, for in addition to the debates that took place during the meetings, there were surveys and studies to do, reports to be written, and new contracts to be won.

After *Anti-Oedipus* was published, Guattari was overwhelmed by the requests for individual schizoanalysis from potential patients. The office with the CERFI became a means of responding to the growing demand. Guattari asked Anne Querrien, François Pain, and Danielle Rouleau to help him, but not one of them was a doctor or a psychologist. "In the CERFI setting, we met people who told us things that they would have told to a psy-choanalyst and we networked, we branched out."[6] Occasionally, the con-nections had some positive effects, in that certain people blinded by their obsessions of the moment were able to find some pleasure in life once more. But the group in charge was primarily composed of nonspecialists who had never been trained in psychology, and so the new, experimental practice remained precarious. Danielle Rouleau in particular was so overwrought with anxiety that she stopped the experiment. "What struck me was that it worked and could have been a practice. But it implied too much power."[7]

The activity on boulevard Beaumarchais was so intense that many found the move to the suburb of Fontenay-sous-Bois in the fall of 1974 a re-lief. The move was inevitable; neighbors were complaining about the com-motion in the office. As they were leaving boulevard Beaumarchais, the CERFI members were contemplating several different projects. Guattari was returning from a trip to the United States, where he had been intrigued by truly communitarian solutions. They even considered a big project in-volving the renovation of a concrete garage into five floors of collective liv-ing. "Personally I found that prospect terrifying," confessed Florence Pétry.[8] Claude Harmelle, who had been a militant in the National Union of French Students in Dijon and in the BAPU and had joined the CERFI in Paris, pro-posed that everyone put their apartment keys into a hat, an idea based on his conviction that the age of private homes was long gone. "I thought he was quite courageous since he had a very lovely apartment."[9] Ultimately, the solution was more conventional: finding a large house with a garden and terrace in Fontenay-sous-Bois. There was never a true community here, however, as no one lived in the house for more than a few nights. The only real change was that fewer people came to the famous Tuesday meetings, as the new suburban location was harder to get to.[10]

CLARIFYING STATE DECISIONS

The most important issue of the CERFI magazine, *Recherches (Research)*, was the issue introducing a series on public works.[11] It exemplified the claim the group was making for the social sciences. Deleuze and Foucault both managed and wrote for this issue. The journal also printed "militant" articles that were little more than expressions of the researchers' moods, states of mind, personal desires, and frustrations. "To speak about desire and the unconscious, etc., in the social sciences is specific to the CERFI."[12] Regarding public works, the group continued the Lacanian distinction between "demand" and "desire." "We maintain that the request for facilities is determined above all by the supply and the social prestige provided by these public works; knowing what these people wanted was an altogether different issue."[13] Collective desire multiplied into myriad individual desires, including those of the researchers; *Recherches* gave public expression to things that were generally more hidden, repressed, or deemed insignificant and relegated to the corridors of the sociologist's workshop.[14]

François Fourquet and Lion Murard co-authored the issue and acknowledged their intellectual debt to Foucault, Deleuze, and Guattari. The CERFI team also invited Deleuze and Foucault to participate in some of the informal preliminary discussions and published excerpts from Gilles, Michel, and Félix's conversation. Deleuze suggested deconstructing the molar aspect of the idea of public works by distinguishing three specific forms: investment structures, public-service structures, and assistance structures. Taking the road as his example, Foucault distinguished among the functions of the production of production, the production of demand, and the production of normalization. At each level, he identified a corresponding pair of oppositions: the agent of power and the bandit for the first level, the customs agent and the smuggler for the second, and the engineer and the vagabond for the third.

Another significant aspect of the CERFI's evolution was its relationship to Marxism. Up until that time, Marx and Freud were virtually the only theoretical points of reference, whereas the 1973 issue took some distance from Marx. "Our firmness about Marxist principles weakened a bit during our voyage."[15] Under Lion Murard and François Fourquet, the historian Fernand Braudel became an essential resource for understanding market logic and capitalism. The veritable pope of the Annals School in 1973, Braudel had considerable clout with historians.

Shortly after the publication of this collective issue, Fourquet wrote his own book, *The Historical Ideal*, and published it as issue 14.[16] He opened by explaining that his work reflected "a personal crisis and a profound change in my relationship to activism, psychoanalysis, and historical knowledge."[17] Indeed, his book was a critique of militant activism and particularly the activism of Maoist Althusserians such as Robert Linhart, in the name of Sartrean and particularly Nietzschean ideas, to which he added the historian's inspiration borrowed from Fernand Braudel. He concluded: "libido and power are the only things that exist."[18]

Above all, Fourquet wanted to distinguish himself from the CERFI group and its Deleuzo-Guattarian ideas rooted in *Anti-Oedipus* and the defense of a particular militant ideal. Indeed, he pointed out an implicit conception of the militant ideal derived from the ethical ideal, which, to his mind, was little more than an extension of Nietzsche's ascetic ideal in a modern form. He disagreed with this idea, especially because he felt that Deleuze and Guattari were projecting this ethic onto their understanding of the unconscious, distinguishing between a good and a bad unconscious, which he found absurd, since, as Freud had shown, the unconscious ignores time and ethics and is located beyond good and evil. His critique was somewhat veiled but nonetheless decipherable. In 1976, Fourquet made an existential decision in line with his intellectual distancing, by leaving Paris for the Ardèche Mountains, bringing with him the complete works of Nietzsche as companions in his new, more isolated life. He continued working for the CERFI, however, and came back to Paris on a regular basis.

Fourquet's essay aside, *Recherches* wanted to test the notion of a collective arrangement of utterance. It always gave credit to individual authors but favored a collective intellectual effort; it was not enough for the journal to be a mailbox into which articles were dropped off and then cobbled together with little concern for editorial logic. The group set itself an ambitious goal of creating a new collective subjectivity. "Everyone should appropriate the collective subjectivity without losing his or her own. There are times when that can be quite burdensome."[19] Practically speaking, the CERFI did not work in an organized rational manner according to individuals' specific skills or by calling upon outsiders for various projects. There were no directors, secretaries, or professional managers. "The point was basically to be together and create a form of community life."[20] In the immediate aftermath of May '68, this was a way of pursuing an intense utopian existence and forestalling the future. The CERFI respected only the sacred law of the group and its militant interests. Fourquet recalled that they had adopted and transformed the motto of the Companions of Jesus, *Perinde ac cadaver* ("obey like a cadaver") and observed it with the same sense of discipline, understanding it as a call to order: "By militating, militating."[21]

THE ART OF SCANDAL

After *Anti-Oedipus* was published in 1972, Guy Hocquenghem, a former Revolutionary Communist Youth militant, homosexual activist, and founder of the Homosexual Front for Revolutionary Action (*Front homosexuel d'action révolutionnaire*, or FHAR), arrived one day at the CERFI office carrying Deleuze and Guattari's book under his arm, announcing that he had finally found the theory that he needed. He came with a group from the FHAR and asked if the CERFI would let him put out a special issue on homosexualities. He invited the "mafia" to participate, but Anne Querrien was the only one who agreed to do so. This issue turned out to be the review's best known and most provocative, and it even led to legal problems when it was confiscated. In 1973, while the suits were pending, Félix Guattari traveled to Canada for a colloquium. He returned to find his door sealed by the police, who had searched his home and gone through his papers and clothing; another squad had rifled through his office at La Borde.

The March 1973 issue was entitled "Three Billion Perverts."[22] It had not really been produced by the CERFI (which humorously referred to it as the "fag issue") but by the FHAR, although many major figures of French intellectual life lent their support to this "Grand Encyclopedia of Homosexualities" (the issue's subtitle): the list of participants included Deleuze, Guattari, Jean Genet, Michel Foucault, Jean-Paul Sartre, and Jean-Jacques Lebel. Despite the legitimacy that they lent the issue, however, it was, for the authorities, too provocative, and all the copies were eventually confiscated. As the review's director, Guattari was fined six hundred francs for an "affront to public decency." The judges ordered that the copies be destroyed because the issue gave a "detailed description of sexual turpitude and perversion" and was the "libidinous venting of a small group of perverts."

Guy Hocquenghem had obviously been given carte blanche to do what he had wanted to do with his FHAR colleagues, and they had described many shocking homosexual experiences among Arabs, prisoners, and minors. "We used the structure of a review entitled *Recherches* and for an entire year we did whatever we wanted, it was something like group creativity since we were occupying another review. It's very important to be on someone else's playing field."[23]

In his introduction to the issue, Guattari explained that the traditional methods of the humanities had been challenged to undo the forms of censorship that could potentially compromise the success of this encyclopedia of homosexualities. The editors had to get around the concept of objectivity that had generally typified this type of study, as the postwar *Kinsey Report* describing American sexual behavior had done, and it was also necessary to undo the interpretative traps of psychoanalytic interpretation that reduces diverse forms of lived experience to a predefined grid.

In 1973, discrimination against homosexuality and homosexuals was widespread; the issue included a petition protesting the transfer of Jean-Claude Boyer, a high-school teacher in a pilot high school in Saint-Quentin, who had publicly acknowledged his homosexuality and his FHAR membership. Before the sanction had even been issued, Boyer's principal called him a "filthy fag, filthy race. We'll see if your fag union defends you."[24] In his 1974 letter to the court, Guattari explained that he had allowed the FHAR to express homosexual desire to get them out of their ghetto, whether this meant condemning them as pathological or exalting their difference. Standing before the Seventeenth District Court, Guattari defended the fundamentally political nature of the trial. "He called into question a new approach to daily life and desire and the new forms of expression that had erupted since May '68."[25]

The 1973–1974 confrontation with the judicial system was a turning point for the CERFI and for leftist movements in general. The pendulum was swinging in the other direction in an orderly fashion for some and in a confused way for others. "In 1974, the party was over, completely."[26] Long gone were the days when Chaban-Delmas' government was interested in understanding French society in order to improve it. When Valéry Giscard d'Estaing came to power, the CERFI stopped receiving government contracts. In 1975, the Ministry of Public Works and Transport proposed hiring some CERFI researchers, but only those professional researchers who held degrees in their respective fields—which meant only five of the twenty-five employees.[27] Being hired by the government obviously meant the end of the CERFI's independence, as well as unemployment for the majority of the group. "We refused the offer. Michel Rostain and I signed an article in *Le Monde* that definitively shut the doors of the National Center for Scientific Research (CNRS) for me, because we were saying that the notion of career researchers was a bad idea."[28]

In 1974, several things came together—a group that had become enormous, the effects of the censored issue, growing financial difficulties because the big contracts had ended, and the political changes following Mitterrand's defeat and Valéry Giscard d'Estaing's election—to force a change. The decision was made to subdivide the CERFI and to establish financially independent groups. "In 1974, we broke the CERFI into small groups organized like production units, meaning one contract per group. One group: one budget. . . . The slogan was like when we used to say, 'One, two, three Vietnam' during the 1960s. . . . I was saying, 'One, two, three CERFI!' "[29]

To deal with the dwindling budgetary resources, Lion Murard and Michel Rostain took the finances in hand. Until that point, different members oversaw the finances on a revolving basis, although the Tuesday general meetings remained the final arbiters. The new team was determined to reduce spending and balance the budget, which meant making choices about which projects to support. The general Tuesday meetings ended, and Guattari stopped attending regularly. "The CERFI was slowly losing its core, which seemed to be little more than a kind of cashbox draining money from the various groups to support the review."[30] The internal changes also coincided with a move to the Parisian suburb of Fontenay in September 1974.

The CERFI subgroups either had specific activities, like the CERFI music group run by Michel Rostain, or were decentralized, which led to, among other things, the CERFISE (CERFI-Southeast). In 1974, a local CERFI was established in Marseille around Michel Anselme, a pioneer of urban politics in France and a former Maoist militant of the French Marxist-Leninist Communist Party, who had come often to La Borde. At the request of Gaston Defferre, the mayor of Marseille and head of the public housing office, Anselme and his friends took over the first renovation project in one of the housing developments in a Marseille suburb.

CERFI activities also included a video-cinema group run by François Pain. In addition to his conventional activities as a filmmaker (he eventually made a film about La Borde), Pain extended the principle of institutional analysis by proposing apprenticeships to teach institutional staff to film their institutions from within. The group worked in Nantes, in particular, in 1974, in a hospital structure organized into apartments spread throughout the city. Although the psychotherapy center in Nantes claimed to practice institutional analysis, Pain and his "video group" revealed several serious problems.

PUBLISHING SUCCESSES

In 1974 and 1975, the changes at the CERFI included many peripheral activities and publishing activities other than the review. An editorial policy on books was defined, *Recherches* created a new collection entitled *Encres* (*Inks*), and a few particularly successful issues were reprinted in the 10/18 series. This activity reflected Florency Pétry's arrival at CERFI. An activist from the Prison Information Group, she had heard about CERFI and started coming to the famous Tuesday meetings in 1973. Pétry was a trained layout designer; she had been a freelance publisher and had also been involved in consciousness-raising activities organized by the paperback publisher, 10/18, in French universities. "When I joined this CERFI group, I felt that they needed to boost their productivity."[31] In her first meeting with Guattari, he was rather cold and even antagonistic. She wanted the group to be involved in publishing and initially received an unambiguous refusal. But the review was changing and moving more and more toward collective publications. "My personal contribution doubtless was to have seen that it could evolve from a review to a collective book; it took an outsider's perspective to see this."[32] Florence Pétry arrived just at the moment when the reprint of the censored *Three Billion Perverts* was being considered; the second print run of ten thousand copies had sold out immediately. In 1977, shortly after the successes of the reprints, *Recherches* became a full-fledged publishing house and launched the first titles in the *Encres* collection: Félix Guattari's *The Molecular Revolution*[33] and Georges Préli's *La force du dehors* (*The Power of the Outside*). Both books were immediate hits; they confirmed the review's reputation at a halcyon moment when books in the humanities were selling well.[34] Bookstores requested copies of the review, whose print runs easily rivaled those of the books.

Newsstands on the Boulevard Saint Michel stacked copies of Guattari's *The Molecular Revolution* alongside piles of Fourquet's *Historical Ideal*,[35] both sitting right next to *Le Monde*. In *La Quinzaine Littéraire*, Maurice

Nadeau enthusiastically reviewed Guattari's book, which he saw as the emergence of a new voice and way of thinking. Until 1976, however, distribution remained rather unprofessional. Newsstands and bookstores ordered directly from the publisher, who delivered the order and was paid on the basis of sales. Florence Pétry put François Fourquet and Lion Murard in touch with Gallimard's distributor, Sodis, to increase the distribution potential for the CERFI's work.

Publishing some titles in the 10/18 collection—*Power's Public Works: The Historical Ideal* and *The Molecular Revolution*—made the success of *Recherches* even more resounding. At the time, Christian Bourgois played a major role in preparing paperbacks in the humanities and literature. Since the early 1970s, he had accumulated many successes by making bold choices. When he wanted to publish Boris Vian with 10/18, his skeptical friend Pauvert tried to dissuade him. When it was published, Vian's book immediately sold several hundred thousand copies. Ernest Mandel's dryly titled *Treatise on Marxist Economy* sold two hundred thousand copies. Bourgois had a large public of students and young people, and he surrounded himself with student advisors and assistants through whom he was often able to meet certain authors. This was how he met Jean-François Lyotard and Cornelius Castoriadis (whose pseudonym at the time was Chaulieu, "hotspot").

During this period, Deleuze paid an impromptu visit to Bourgois, simply to make his acquaintance. Bourgois had already met Guattari in 1972, after *Anti-Oedipus* had been published and when the CERFI was beginning its large-scale surveys, which interested him considerably. During a lunch meeting between Lion Murard, François Fourquet, Claude Rouot, and Florency Pétry, Bourgois and the CERFI agreed to publish certain *Recherches* titles in paperback. Bourgois was close to Guattari for personal reasons: in the mid-1970s, his first wife, Agnès B., had lived with and then married Jean-René de Fleurieu (the son of Marie-Claire Servan-Schreiber, who became Madame Mendès France), with whom she had two children. "My relationship with Félix was tied to La Borde, to his relationship with Agnès, and to my relationship with Félix's children."[36]

Bourgois respected boundaries, and considered Deleuze and Guattari to be Minuit Editions' authors. But Jérôme Lindon was hostile to the idea of publishing them in paperback, although for friendship's sake he allowed Christian Bourgois to reprint *The Logic of Sense* in 1973 in 10/18, on a one-time-only basis. All the intellectual energy of the Cérisy decades found its editorial outlet in 10/18. "10/18 was about desire in action. I wanted these books to exist and they wanted to bring them to me."[37]

The publishers, Editions *Recherches*, expanded, particularly under Lion Murard and Patrick Zylberman, who involved the publishing house in ambitious projects that provoked some resistance from the group because the editorial politics were increasingly traditional, involving the choice of specific authors. The biggest, most prestigious *Recherches* publications began in 1977, with Theodore Zeldin's five volumes, *The History of French Passions: 1848–1945*. The translation and sale of the rights for this book required a huge investment incommensurate with the CERFI's means. Olivier Quérouil, who managed the center, firmly opposed the idea but was overruled.

Recherches published many books that grew out of CERFI studies. Today we can take the measure of the contribution of each survey. The many publications from 1971 all reflect three particular areas of exploration: madness,[38] the true realm of CERFI expertise that was anchored at the La Borde clinic where most members of the group had been apprentices. The second, very broad area might be termed "world disciplines"—a Foucauldian term describing the examination of past and present State institutions—whose approach was inspired by Foucault, Deleuze, and Guattari and involved the vector of territorial fixation, normalization, or grid disciplines. The CERFI directly opposed the expression of desire and the logics of power using a binary approach, from which Fourquet distanced himself in 1982, when he wrote a summary of CERFI work. At that point, he saw the State as a central institution that did not work alone; its function was to recuperate rather than reprimand. "The first imperative of the Captor-State is to capture, not to dry up, to canalize, or to block; to concentrate, not to block."[39] Yet in the process, dominant and dominated forces are intertwined to such an extent that it becomes impossible to assert any logic external to civil society, as was the case in most of the CERFI's work. That said, because CERFI studies were concrete, valorized experience and because they paid attention to the discourse of the actors, they remained valuable and interesting, even though the paradigm had shown its limits. The third theme of CERFI publications was sexuality. This is unsurprising, given that this current of thought was described as "desiring"; the priority was the satisfaction of desires of all sorts and, consequently, the removal of all obstacles. The grand period for challenging traditions was also propitious for a massive reception of the ideas expressed in the issues on sexual liberation.

Around 1979 and 1980, the critical paradigm of the humanities underwent a profound and generalized crisis. The limits of Marxism and structuralism were becoming increasingly obvious. The political context was changing; the theme of human rights was gaining ground as Soviet dissidents arrived in Europe bringing tales of the Gulag. The extent of the massacres perpetrated by Pol Pot in Cambodia was becoming clear and taking on genocidal proportions. All of this led to serious reevaluations and, above all, to serious doubts about the utopias that had infused the critical studies of the 1960s and 1970s with meaning. The CERFI became unsettled as a result and the fissures were irremediable. The group lost its critical hub and reorganized into small, decentralized groups; the enormous apartment on boulevard Beaumarchais was hardly more than a distant golden age. To survive, the CERFI moved again to a two-room apartment on rue Pleyel in eastern Paris, near La Nation.

At this point, Lion Murard and Patrick Zylberman decided to write to the other CERFI members requesting several thoroughgoing examinations of past positions and suggestions for future positions. Dispensing with a diplomatic presentation, they wrote that the current form of the review "seems to have outlived its useful life."[40] Their dire diagnosis was without recourse: "Moribund. *Recherches* can die a good death, be buried as quickly as possible or change direction—and leadership. Three possibilities, but only the last one warrants serious consideration." The disagreements had grown over the last few years. The first of these was the rejection of the FHAR's positions, which were very explicit and radical. "Our project, which remains to be defined, would take the exact opposite position of Hocquenghem's futurist, fascistic formula, 'We are for the superficial, violence, and sex.'"[41] Lion Murard and Patrick Zylberman wanted an altogether different project, which favored an ethics of responsibility, considering other countries and transcending a particular French self-absorption. "Various voices have bitterly expressed their anger at the misery of this intellectual Lichtenstein which is France, its xenophobia and self-absorption."[42] They proposed a true "revolution inside the revolution," which would no longer make the CERFI a point of reference, stop having Guattari manage, appoint Lion Murard's brother Numa to oversee the editorial group, and link a new group of authors to the review, including Jean-Marie Doublet, François Ewald, Georges Condominas, Marcel Gauchet, and Krzyszof Pomian.

At the end of the 1970s, Patrick Zylberman and Lion Murard disagreed profoundly with Guattari about his refusal to clearly denounce the armed violence advocated by the extreme left in Germany and Italy. In 1978 through 1980, Lion Murard demanded that Guattari explicitly repudiate terrorism. "I added in my text, 'isn't that right, Félix?' Félix called me. He was furious, which I can understand, but it was only an internal note. He threatened to call his lawyers. After twenty years of collaboration, I was rather surprised. Ultimately, I forced myself to rewrite the five objectionable lines."[43] There was no discussion of the text at the plenary meeting, another symptom of the group's disintegration, which aggravated the internal crisis.

In 1980, given this situation, Anne Querrien decided that reorienting the review toward the defense of democratic ideals warranted some discussion at the very least. She was increasingly critical of the relatively undemocratic operations of a review whose director was all-powerful but somewhat detached. Despite her loyalty to Guattari, she was torn, and she agreed with Murard and Zylberman's idea of reorganizing the review. She ultimately wrote a compromise text and in October 1980 received a call from Guattari. He accused her of taking sides with his adversaries and made it clear that he did not want to see her again. "I started shaking like a crazy person and ended up at Saint-Anne," a Parisian psychiatric hospital.[44] We can measure the effects of Guattari's reaction on Anne Querrien when we recall that work and affect were totally integrated among the CERFI group members. Doing research, for those who devoted themselves as she did, required ongoing commitment and limitless devotion that knew no regular working hours. In addition, there were the affective relationships, the analytical work, and transference. Anne Querrien was in analysis with Guattari at the time and would describe the CERFI dysfunctions from the couch. She had already been profoundly frightened by Guattari's comment: "When I see a dead tree and things that are growing back, I look at the things that are growing and don't give a damn about whether or not the tree in the center is dead, because if I were cutting the things that grow back, everything would be dead."[45]

The CERFI never recovered from these internal dissensions. In 1981, Félix Guattari withdrew and turned the direction of the review over to Liane Mozère. From then on, *Recherches* no longer identified itself as the CERFI review. A few issues were published, but the final issue, 49, came out in April 1983. The swan song was symbolically identified as being co-directed by Félix Guattari and Liane Mozère.

When assessing its impact, the collective experience had been rich, but the refusal to create an institutional team had also exacted a heavy toll.

This, however, was part of the CERFI spirit of constantly searching for itself, innovating in response to its own crises. Was the CERFI a group of social-science researchers? A school of thought? An intellectual movement? A juxtaposition of desires? A phalansterist, communitarian experiment? Each individual lived the CERFI in his or her own way, intensely connected to a group where the absence of unifying institutional support made connections all the more vital. The galaxy of planets revolved around their sun Guattari. "It was a stage on which many affects played out, many relationships redefined. . . . I think that that was it, above all, the CERFI, was putting a stage into place."[46] The group's originality had to do with this voluntary entwining of theoretical issues and practical experience, of intellect and affect, of the *socius* and individual desires. There was something heroic about those who tried this way of articulation, as there was nothing obvious about it.

In many areas, the CERFI was innovative and the results of its surveys important. When we consider its investigatory methodology against the mindset of the 1970s, it is surprising to see how much it foreshadowed the pragmatic turn in the humanities of the late 1980s. François Fourquet was surely the person to have most carefully thought about CERFI survey practices in his two major works.[47] Because Fourquet was critical of the idea of disconnecting a subject from the *socius*, and also because he was in search of processes of subjectification, he gave full credit to CERFI researchers and had tremendous ethical respect for their work as a meaningful resource and a privileged space for his investigations.

LISTENING TO THE PLAYERS

In order to write their 1975 *History of Institutional Psychiatry*, François Fourquet and Lion Murard interviewed psychiatrists and administrators who had been instrumental in changing psychiatric practice.[48] "We essentially appear as having set the stage for the utterances that we organized for them in a particular manner; the editing was what we liked most."[49] Fourquet's afterword raises the methodological problems specific to this survey, identifying the two aspects of the research that had made archival documents less important than recorded interviews with participants. The researchers' work essentially consisted in designing a questionnaire and assembling interview excerpts into a final text. Borrowing from journalism and sociology, the authors used a method that helped them avoid making a choice between structure and individuals. "It's not a question of replacing the Structure with the Individual or of saying that individuals make history."[50] Where was the real heart of this history of psychiatry, the driving force that would connect the changes? Fourquet said that he had first thought in terms of "historical matrices." For example, Dr. Aujaleu, the author of a 1960 brochure, inserted his conclusions into a sort of Gaullist grid whose theoretical and practical dimensions affected an individual more than he or she might be aware. Thus there would be complex interactions among Dr. Aujaleu's French grid and Dr. Lucien Bonnafé's Communist matrix and Dr. Georges Daumézon's Protestant grid and the Youth Hostels grid of Dr. Oury and Guattari. "And then that didn't work. Our grids ended up aggravating us. Ultimately, they resembled the *patterns* of American culturalism, with libido thrown into the mix."[51]

In 1980, alone this time, Fourquet published a new survey on national accountability, in which he continued to pursue his thinking about the use of oral sources. He had left Paris for the Ardèche in 1976 and returned permanently to Paris only in 1994. During the intervening years, he shuttled back and forth while pursuing his research for a study of the State. "I went to Paris dressed in a long woolen jacket and clogs and that's how I showed up to see Pierre Mendès France and the others!"[52] As was obvious from his highly unacademic attire, Fourquet felt little need to cultivate any of the professional researcher's critical distance from his subjects, as he was strikingly different from his interviewees. Given how important he considered his oral sources to be, Fourquet succeeded in making the very arid and austere topic of national finances into a compelling story told by the major players. The twenty-six interviews that he conducted between 1978 and 1980 were his major, if not exclusive, source of information. After conducting several interviews, Fourquet would return to the Ardèche. "If the researcher listens well, he discovers magnificent things, whereas scientific discourse typically gives us access to emasculated, anesthetized writing."[53] His work showed that fundamental changes in economic thinking between the prewar Malthusian approach and the postwar planned productivity were linked to greater State control of economic interactions to ensure economic growth. Drawing on his experience in sectoral psychiatry, Fourquet continued working along the same lines as the survey, which "had taught me the extraordinary superiority of contemporary history recounted by the actors themselves over a book that calls itself scientific, and which often muffles the actor's voices in a scholarly rewriting that blends the primary information from the participants with the researchers' commentary making it impossible for the reader to discern between them."[54]

Between the perspective of an ostensibly knowledgeable scholar able to discern bad faith and his interviewees' artificial post-facto justifications and the idea that understanding someone requires listening and assimilating their logic first and foremost, Fourquet was keenly aware that a researcher had to balance both positions, which was not without its difficulties. Wanting and knowing, *socius* and libido, knowledge and power were the creative tensions that kept the CERFI researchers profoundly vital.

16

The "Molecular Revolution"
Italy, Germany, France

In 1976, the Basque country was restless—certainly on the Spanish side of the border, where ETA,[1] the Basque separatist movement, was engaged in an armed struggle against the powers of Madrid. Félix Guattari was dreaming of building a federation of regional protest movements, which could open up secondary fronts and weaken the Nation-State. Despite his extensive network of contacts, he never managed to realize this perilous project, which was located on the cusp between democratic combat and terrorist action.

The Italian May '68: 1977

Guattari and his friends were, however, bathing in a veritable fountain of youth under the Italian sun. Roughly a decade after having been at the heart of the movement of May '68, there they were in the streets of Bologna—awestruck, stupefied—watching their wished-for molecular revolution unfold. This was a movement against all manner of apparatus, expressed in a completely new language with heretofore unheard-of methods. In 1977, when Guattari's essay *Molecular Revolution* came out, Italy witnessed the birth of a movement so radical and violent that France's May '68 seemed like an isolated college-student event in comparison.

Italy in 1977 was undergoing an unprecedented crisis. Economic indicators were hopeless. Each month, the country collapsed a bit more. Two million people were unemployed, and the leaders' projections were not encouraging. In January 1977, as a New Year's wish, the minister of industry himself announced that unemployment would rise in February by 600,000. A 25 percent–per-year inflation rate made the lira plunge; it lost 38.9 percent of its value against the dollar in three years. Paradoxically, in a country that was losing its bearings and its jobs, the broad movement of dissent that broke out did not demand a better distribution of jobs, work for all, or salaries pegged to rising prices. Instead, much less traditionally, protesters wanted to weaken the system's foundation by attacking head on the values of labor, property, and the delegation of power and representation.

The economic and social crisis was widespread, but the political machinery was stymied. The Andreotti government lacked all direction. The large and very influential alternative force that was the Italian Communist Party (PCI) under Beringuer called merely for a national recovery plan, civil order, and an acceptance of austerity. In the name of a necessary "historical compromise," the PCI became a progovernment party. Italian communists had at that time stepped back from the Soviet big brother and had formed a promarket wing favoring a kind of "Euro-Communism." At the same time, their alignment with Italian authorities and the search for an alliance with a party as jeopardized as the Christian Democrats had dramatic effects. The great mass of marginals who were hard hit by the crisis and deprived of all hope were now being given no way out.

This deadlock fed radical reactions, spontaneous irruptions, and violent clashes. Whereas the May '68 movement ultimately spoke in the old Marxist-Leninist tongue, whether in its Trotskyite or Maoist dialect, the Italian dissent a decade later was seeking new inspiration. A whole series of far-left Italian currents found a new language in the theses of Deleuze and Guattari, notably in the 1975 Italian translation of *Anti-Oedipus* and the notion of "desiring machines." The postwar decades of economic prosperity were but a dim memory, and students lacked even the slightest hope of making their diplomas worth anything. Because there was no future, alternative and autonomous currents made the idea of changing life itself the order of the day. They wanted to invent, there and then, new, self-managed spaces and communities prone to liberate the individual in open, collective milieus. When compared to 1968, it seemed that a generational shift was in the works.

Another element in the Italian situation was fueling the radical nature of the conflicts: the persistence of an Italian fascist party, the MSI, which could rely not only on active troops but also had at its disposal a like-minded network at the highest level of the State apparatus able to call out auxiliary forces to suppress any whiff of social dissent. On top of this already explosive situation, there was the strategy of the desperate Christian Democrats, who hoped to manipulate this fascist violence both to intimidate the social movement and to justify an all-out repression of far-left movements. The fascists would carry out repeated bombings; the police would hold the far-left activists responsible and then hold public prosecutions and convictions. The PCI, which benignly watched this unfold, rejoiced at the repression of its rivals.

On December 12, 1969, a bomb exploded on the Piazza Fontana in Milan, killing sixteen people and wounding eighty. For Isabelle Sommier, this was an "original trauma." The next day, the police arrested twenty-seven far-left activists. Other terrorist acts followed: a train derailed on July 22, 1970 (six dead and fifty wounded), a bomb in Brescia detonated during an antifascist demonstration (eight dead and ninety-four wounded), and on August 4, 1974, a bomb detonated in a train (twelve dead and 105 wounded). This "strategy of tension" continued to grow during the 1970s—and with it the number of victims. The P2 Lodge scandal broke out, revealing to the public the high degree of fascist infiltration in the seats of power. Italian leaders were compromising themselves with the worst enemies of democracy, and the PCI was championing "historical compromise" for marginals and dissidents of all stripes. The only path left was the path of radical opposition. When Luciano Lama, the general secretary of the large Italian union group CGIL, turned up at the University of Rome, he was summarily kicked out, which led to clashes among students, police forces, and the PCI security group.

The Italian far left, however, underwent a veritable mutation between 1968 and 1977, which took the form of a creative quest for some and a recourse to terrorism for others. Leninist-like organizations coming out of 1968 had for the most part disappeared from the political landscape.[2] From their ruins arose a movement that vindicated worker autonomy and included many collective movements, especially some particularly powerful ones from some of the largest Italian companies—Fiat, Pirelli, Alfa Romeo, and Policlinico. This movement rejected the traditional forms of delegating power and the right to expression. Many activists from the former Potere Operaio group participated. In 1977, the "Metropolitan Indians," the most creative branch of the movement, insisted on the need to transform relationships between individuals and attacked the system, wielding derision and irony as their principal weapons. They met and moved about in tribes of "Red Skins" through the large cities of Italy, fighting for the liberalization of drugs and "requisitioning empty buildings, the creation of antifamily raids to abduct minors brainwashed by their parents, a square kilometer of green space for each inhabitant, and the return of all animals held captive in zoos to their countries of origin."[3]

As in 1968, these dissident movements did not need to proclaim the need for student-worker alliances. Such alliances already existed between students, young workers, and the numerous subproletarians and unemployed people who identified themselves in the emergence of a movement that put its autonomy at the forefront against any kind of manipulation. The worker's autonomy actions multiplied right up to 1977, and many of them were, in their deeds, against the law and, in their intentions, against political actions: there were occupations of private homes, self-styled reductions in public-service fees, expropriations, and bank robberies. The year 1977 was a boom time for this turbulence, with a "77.62% increase in crimes against property from 1976."[4] Young people, students, workers, and outsiders made up a youthful proletariat that was shaking up the system by praising immediate action to change the life of the outcast. The tension continued to mount between this uncontrollable movement and the desperate powers that be.

This situation had an added aggravation, not present in May '68 and post-1968 France: terrorism, practiced increasingly by a certain number of Italian ultraleft organizations. The Red Brigades (BR), created in 1970, benefited from their presence in the factories, particularly in Agnelli's Fiat plant in Turin. In 1972, they played a central role in impromptu strikes, which unsettled that industrial group; they then seeded panic among the foremen and nonstriking workers by launching the "red scarf" movement. But the BR later turned to terrorism, and their abductions targeted first and foremost magistrates and politicians. Outside the BR, this terrorist branch also included an organization that had been created in 1974, the Proletarian Armed Nucleus (NAP), which brought together far-left activists and former common-law supporters. These two organizations proffered clandestine armed struggle and terrorism. In 1977, not a month went by without abductions, bombings, and assassinations.

Others chose communication and dialogue rather than the path of the Walther P38. Making the best of the 1976 end to RAI's radio monopoly, a profusion of free radio channels took over the airwaves, opening them up to the possibility of countercultural expression. Among the many sites of cultural agitation, Radio Poloare broadcast from Milan to an impressive audience and with the ability to get people into the streets. In December 1976, it transmitted live the riots at the opening of La Scala, and, in March 1977, announced "the death of a woman who had been refused an abortion for medical reasons. In the minutes following, five thousand women took to the streets."[5]

Of all those countercultural radio stations, Radio Alice, launched by the former head of Potere Operaio, Franco "Bifo" Berardi, was one of the most important. Broadcast from Bologna, a university town historically known as a showcase for compromise with the communist municipality, Radio Alice claimed a huge, loyal, and vibrant audience. Bifo was doing his military service at the age of twenty-three when he discovered *Psychoanalysis and Transversality*. Guattari's reflections about psychoanalysis and the way it can change our relationship to the political sphere ignited his activist fire. In the preface to a book about the station, Guattari writes, "Radio Alice goes to the eye of the cultural cyclone—subverting language, publishing the review *A/Traverso*—and it has also plunged directly into political activity that it would like to 'transversalize.'"[6] In 1976, Bifo was arrested for "inciting rebellion." As he put it, "Radio Alice had an incredible international impact. Loads of people listened to it. In the factories, groups of workers would go to their workshops with radios and turn on Radio Alice."[7] In 1977, however, the situation became tenser.

On February 8, 1977, students protesting university reforms were occupying most of Italy's large universities, and at the end of the month a national student-movement gathering was held in Rome and led to violent clashes. On March 11, 1977, a Lotta Continua activist, Francesco Lo Russo, was killed in Bologna by the *carbiniere*; the next day, more than one hundred thousand people demonstrated on the streets of Rome. Gunshots broke out. The city was under siege. In Bologna, the situation was also very tense. "In March 1977, we moved from occupying to creating 'free zones.' We decided that a part of the city would be forbidden to cops and fascists and we set up barricades. The police fired and killed a student."[8] News of the student's death was immediately broadcast in Bologna by Radio Alice, which sparked a gathering of one hundred thousand people.

On March 12, "at 10:25 pm, the police took over the street where Radio Alice was located, an area where until then, nothing had happened. They closed down bars and restaurants, fired tear gas, and stood with pointed guns and bullet-proof vests in front of this 'dangerous lair.'"[9] The radio station was closed, and the *carbiniere* made eight arrests for incitement of delinquency and subversive association, but they were unable to find Bifo. The next day, March 13, Bologna was under siege. Three thousand *carbiniere* and policemen, backed up by armored tanks, occupied the university area under orders from the Christian Democrat prefect. Zanghari, the city's communist mayor, urged the forces of order to exert the highest level of repression. "Between March 11 and 16, a kind of insurrection broke out in Bologna. The entire city center was barricaded, certain neighborhoods were held by students but also by a good number of young workers. An armory had been pillaged."[10] The funeral of the murdered student gave way to violent confrontations. On March 16, the Christian Democrats and the PCI together organized a 150,000-person-strong march protesting the violence, and 15,000 students paraded through the streets of Bologna. A police dragnet arrested three hundred. On May 13, the minister of the interior enacted antiterrorist measures—from then on, those behind bombings would be condemned to life in prison.

Bifo fled to Milan, then Turin, and then crossed the French border, arriving in Paris on May 30 with a burning desire to meet Guattari, whose texts he had so much appreciated. The painter Gianmarco Montesano, a friend of Bifo, and the philosopher Toni Negri introduced him to Guattari. Gianmarco Montesano was a former activist in Potere Operaio and had been instructed by its head to broaden the Italian movement, making it European by creating contacts to develop an alternative leftist network. He had been in Paris for a while and while at the ENS had met Yann Moulier-Boutang, who was working on his *agrégation* in the social sciences. Together they created the group Camarades, which published an information-and-analysis brochure entitled *Matériaux pour l'intervention (Materials for the Intervention)*. Montesano met the sociologist Danièle Guillerm in this group: "When I suggested that Camarades translate things about the movement in Italy and about Radio Alice . . . they proposed that I go speak to Félix about it."[11] The upshot of this meeting was a book on Radio Alice with a preface by Félix Guattari.[12]

At first, Guattari knew fairly little about the Italian situation, except for the antipsychiatry movement, with which he was tightly linked. On a political level, Montesano was his first informant. "My first encounters with Félix were totally self-serving."[13] Beyond the primary motivation to create an efficient, international activist network, a friendly bond quickly formed between them, and Guattari became increasingly interested in the Italian situation. He welcomed Montesano to his home, on rue de Condé, an address open to dissidents and outcasts of every sort. When Bifo, who knew Montesano well, found himself on the lam in Paris, he had little trouble meeting Guattari.

Bifo saw Guattari many times from June 1977 on and quickly became his friend. In Paris on July 7, he went to a friend's house; the Italian police were waiting for him at the door. He was arrested and incarcerated at the Prison de la Santé and then at Fresnes. Guattari and some friends quickly organized a support network to get him released and launched the Center for Initiatives for New Free Spaces (*Centre d'Initiatives pour de Nouveaux Espaces Libres*, CINEL),[14] whose primary objective was to ensure the defense of prosecuted activists. This collective published a journal, found a headquarters on rue de Vaugirard, and immediately rallied its forces to free Bifo.

The trial, whose stakes hung on the Italian legal authorities' request for Bifo's extradition, took place only a few days after his arrest. Although he was being prosecuted for being a host on a free radio station, the extradition request identified him as the head of a gang behind a kidnapping in Bologna. The defense team of French lawyers, including Kiejman, easily revealed the absurdity of the official reasons behind the prosecution. On July 11, Bifo was considered nonextraditable and was welcomed in France as a political refugee. "The afternoon of my release from prison, we wrote up an appeal against repression in Italy to be signed by French intellectuals."[15] Out of prison, Bifo moved into Guattari's home on rue de Condé. He had only just met him but already considered him an "older brother."[16] The two friends scripted the appeal condemning the repression meted out to the movement in Italy, openly pinning the blame on the Christian Democrats and the PCI's policy of historical compromise. This initiative caused a flag-waving national tantrum in Italy. Intellectuals and politicians accused the French of meddling in affairs they knew nothing about, arguing that the French had no right to proffer any lessons to Italians.

BOLOGNA REACTS

To counter this repressive policy and take back the initiative, the entire Italian far left joined together for a great meeting and colloquium in Bologna from September 22 to 24, 1977. The PCI, which governed the city, denounced this assembly as a provocation, with its general secretary, Enrico Beringuer, using the term "plague carriers." Expecting predators, they witnessed instead a three-day gathering of Dantesque proportions for a midsized city like Bologna: eighty thousand people occupied the city in the greatest peace and quiet and without the slightest violence. Given the tension in the air and the size of the crowds, this was a feat indeed. Bifo spent these three days being updated by telephone on what was going on in the city. But the whole Guattari gang was on the Bologna streets, in awe. Every group of the Italian far left was there, from the terrorist wing to the worker-autonomy group, not to mention the "Metropolitan Indians," feminists, homosexuals, and "red dykes." PCI activists were discreet in their home-town, a symbol of the contested historical compromise, making sure that tens of thousands of young people were fed and housed during those three days. A tacit agreement had been struck with the BR so that it would in no way resort to violence. The BR cleverly respected the pact but took advan-tage of this unique occasion, which gave them the right to march in public with impunity, to recruit new members on a massive scale. "This all oc-curred obviously without our knowledge. We hadn't imagined this possi-bility."[17] Over those three days, people marched day and night through the streets of Bologna and debated everywhere, most of all at the sports arena, where thousands came to the "permanent forum" to discuss tactics, strat-egies, and the abolition of labor. From the windows of the Bologna town hall, the powerless PCI bigwigs watched the rainbow-colored flow of humanity. "This was the first time that we had seen a demonstration of twenty thousand young women shouting and making the 'pussy' sign with their hands. It was so beautiful! That was the first time we saw that it was possible! Women Power!" remembers a thrilled Gérard Fromanger.[18]

Guattari became a hero figure in Bologna. He was considered one of the essential sources of inspiration for the Italian left, and he watched the marches with the utmost delight, seeing his thoughts take shape in a social and political force. The day after the gathering, the daily and weekly press put his photo on their covers, presenting him as the founder and creator of this mobilization. Guattari had suddenly become the Daniel Cohn-Bendit of Italy. "When he walked down the streets of Bologna, everyone rushed to greet him, touch him, kiss him. It was crazy. Unheard of. He was Jesus walking on water. I was very happy myself, because I received a few sprin-kles."[19] During these three days, Hervé Maury was also in Bologna in the same hotel as Guattari, Christian Bourgois, and Maria Antonietta Mac-ciocchi: "I was with François Pain like Fabrice at Waterloo, I didn't under-stand a thing. It was a huge party celebrating the pacification of far-left movements and at the same time we were marching toward the prison to liberate comrades and all of a sudden I see some young people pulling guns."[20]

The publisher Christian Bourgois, infuriated by the Italian campaign against the French intellectuals, decided with Yann Moulier-Boutang to go

to Bologna to have it out. He took part in the marches alongside Henri Weber, the leader of the Revolutionary Communist League (LCR).

> We found ourselves in Bologna with tens of thousands of people, tell-
> ing ourselves that we had provoked all of this, with a feeling of fear
> not for ourselves, but that things could degenerate and people would
> become completely irresponsible. I learned a great lesson about Ital-
> ian politics at that point because the Communists were nowhere in
> sight. They were in the hallways of the buildings along the route and
> in the inner courtyards. The police were patrolling the city but were
> staying outside.[21]

Yann Moulier-Boutang was in the French delegation to Bologna. He
was an essential player in creating Franco-Italian solidarity, having early
on made connections with the Italians of the autonomy movement, with
which he identified politically. An activist in the Censier collectives since
1968, he had offered to lodge Italian comrades since 1970. A rather libertarian communist, his leanings were more along the lines of *Cahiers de Mai*, a
weekly publication coming out of the May '68 movement that ran until
1974. In 1972, he organized a meeting at Jussieu with representatives from
Lotta Continua and Potere Operaio. In 1973 and 1974, he mobilized with
immigrant collectives, insisting on the autonomy of their movement: he
had adopted the idea of autonomy from the Italians and it implied taking
the singularity of each group into consideration. This political gesture also
meant that each group would define its own objectives. Starting from this
conception, the social movement was conceived not around a formal unity
but in terms of a connection of multiplicities. While working on this appropriation of the Italy-inspired French movement and acting with Montesano, Yann Moulier-Boutang met Guattari in 1977 and was soon involved
in creating the CINEL to free Bifo. In September, he quite naturally found
himself in Bologna. "I met Félix for the first time at the rue de Condé apartment about this call to go to Bologna."[22] He traveled to Italy with Gérard
Fromanger.

Not all parade participants had the same good intentions. Several
thousand members of the BR had donned ski masks and were wielding
weapons. This demonstration of force definitely helped the Red Brigades
usurp a good part of the movement. The celebration did not degenerate
into violence, but ultimately the challenge of Bologna was a failure be-

cause, beyond the euphoria of the moment, it offered no clear perspective to a movement that imploded on itself, newly confronted by repression and isolation.

THE WALL OF SILENCE IN GERMANY

The dissident movement in Europe was being strenuously repressed. The various governments armed themselves with a sufficient legal arsenal to make their repressive policies as efficient as possible: in France, the antirioters law was passed on June 8, 1970; in Italy, the president of the Italian Republic decreed a law in August 1977 that included new "dispositions concerning public order," strengthening the main legal instrument of Italian repression. The Reale law of 1975 had already allowed police to hold someone in custody indefinitely. Organizations had to be vigilant about the violations of personal freedoms, and the CINEL, which could alert intellectuals at any moment, was eyeing the gathering storm.

Barely two months after the Bologna events, two Germans arrived at the CINEL headquarters, where they were greeted by Guattari and Fromanger. "They told us, 'We'd like you to do for us what you did for the Italians in Bologna, because we are going nuts.' "[23] They were seeking international support for the thousands of alternative communities in Berlin, who were living uncomfortably with a State power that suspected any and every outsider of being part of the Baader gang. Guattari had already committed himself to a trip to Brazil to meet Lula, the Workers' Party leader. He looked to his friend, Gérard Fromanger, to respond to the Germans' request.

Fromanger spoke no German and felt poorly prepared for such a mission. He thought that Félix's proposition was "crazy," but he went all the same, flying to Berlin with Gilles Herviaux, one of his CINEL comrades. During the stopover in Frankfurt, they got a sense of the prevailing climate of terror in Germany—photos of wanted terrorists were posted everywhere. "We got to the Berlin airport. Nobody was there. We were wondering what we were doing there. We almost went back when, several hours later, we saw a guy in the back of the airport with a scarf tied around his neck hanging down to his feet, and a girl with pretty golden hair."[24] Those were their contacts, who shuttled them to central Berlin for a meeting of around sixty people, where they sketched out the groundwork for a large gathering at Frankfurt, at which they expected one hundred thousand people. To get things ready and loosen the stranglehold around the Berlin communities, they would need to bring several thousand people in Berlin together two months later. "In fact, twenty-seven thousand people came to Berlin for three days and three nights, inventing a code called 'Tunix' (Do nothing, don't move)."[25] Members of alternative Berlin groups, constantly suspected of being linked to the Red Army Faction (RAF), could no longer even move about their own neighborhoods. Their wives were insulted and called "dirty whores." If three or more of them were on the street, the police would pull out their machine guns, frisk them, and drag the girls to the station. During those three days, the police suddenly and miraculously disappeared—a breath of fresh air to the Berlin movement. "As a painter, I had invented a little color strategy. Ten thousand little color bombs, hot and cold. Everybody had two or three of them on him, and each time we walked past a tank, splat! In front of the Wall, splat! The tanks were soon covered with all the colors of the rainbow. Depardon took photos. Félix was there, as were Foucault and Deleuze."[26] As in Bologna, Berlin organized a permanent forum in the huge lecture hall of the Polytechnical University, where up to five thousand people could assemble.

In 1977, the CINEL was also on the front lines for the liberation of Ulrike Meinhof's[27] lawyer, Klaus Croissant, who had been imprisoned at the Santé during his visit to Paris. The CINEL had decided, together with the League for Human Rights, to organize a meeting at the Mutalité to defend him. Six thousand people packed the room. But the mobilization failed to prevent the extradition of Croissant by the German authorities.

> We were crammed inside a narrow hallway of the court in Paris as of the early afternoon in front of the door to the courtroom that was carefully packed with plain-clothes policemen. This is where the court had to "publicly" rule on the appeal of the refugee Klaus Croissant to be extradited to Germany. Impossible to get in, so why wait? A lot of beaten-down people discreetly walked away. But this was out of the question for Félix, with his mussed hair, his cheeky humor, and his glasses ready to fly off his face. A few dozen of us held on as he did for many long hours. To not back down, to bear witness, and in the end to learn that the appeal had been rejected. That was Félix. He was always ready to give his all.[28]

The night of the extradition, a small group came to the League for Human Rights headquarters to protest in front of the Santé Prison. Many lawyers, including Jean-Jacques de Félice and Michel Tubiana, were in this group, as was Foucault.

During the CINEL meetings on rue de Vaugirard, a good number of dissidents from the mobilization against Croissant's extradition were starting to adopt the terrorist postures of the Italian Red Brigade and the Baader gang in Germany. The legal expert Gérard Soulier bemoaned this, speaking openly to Guattari about this shift, which he found problematic, confiding that he could not and would not follow suit under any circumstances and threatening that he was ready to quit the CINEL. "Félix told me, 'Don't do that, by no means! It's very important that you stay.' That's when I understood that he was conducting collective psychotherapy. And if there had been no blunders of the Italian/German type, it was because of that. Because it was a venue for catharsis."[29]

Éric Alliez confirms Guattari's very firm position on the question of this terrorist shift, despite Bernard-Henri Lévy's accusation that he had more than a weakness for terrorists' positions: "During those Italian 'somber years,' one had to, for example, go, as I did, to the universities of Rome or Bologna, be on site and speak to potential Red Brigade disciples to dissuade them from taking the plunge. But talking directly with BR members and debating with the assassins themselves, as someone like Guattari did at that time? No, absolutely out of the question."[30] It is true that Guattari did not publicly condemn the Italian Red Brigade or the RAF in Germany in 1977 and 1978. His silence could be explained by the underground work that he was doing to dissuade rather than condemn those tempted to take the terrorist path, explaining how such a choice would be horrible for other people and would lead to self- empoisoning. Guattari played a major role at this level, notably in his rue de Condé apartment, which was an outsiders' drop-in during those years. "The way Félix welcomed and lodged those people! Félix would say, 'Their spying pisses me off.' He'd take in people who were being stalked like animals and tempted by the armed struggle. He'd add, 'We should get a refund from the national health care system.' "[31] According to Jean Chesneaux, another of Guattari's friends in the CINEL mobilizations, "If France was spared Red Brigade– or Red Army Faction–style armed actions, this was largely due to his therapeutic contacts with outsiders and autonomists tempted by direct violence. Félix told me that he hung out with those people because he could keep them from making their Molotov cocktails and instead put them on his psychoanalyst's couch."[32]

THE ITALIAN "SOMBER YEARS"

The Red Brigade's 1978 execution of the Italian council president Aldo Moro heightened repression in Italy and started legal proceedings all over again. The CINEL was again on the front lines as, for example, when Italian legal authorities asked for the extradition of Franco Piperno, who had been arrested in Paris on September 18, 1978, along with Lanfranco Pace, because they were suspected of being linked to Moro's assassination. Given that this warrant led nowhere, a final demand for extradition was justified on the basis of common-law offenses. There was nothing in the files. These Italian activists had never been linked to terrorist groups. In Italy, many well-known personalities, including Leonardo Sciascia, Alberto Moravia, and Umberto Eco, petitioned the Italian magistrates. In France, the CINEL collected signatures against the extradition.[33] Piperno, a former Potere Operaio activist, would have gone to prison instead of becoming what he is today, a professor at the University of Catania and a Nobel Prize–winning physicist.

But the most publicized affair of the late 1970s was the arrest of Toni Negri, another former Potere Operaio director who was not linked to the Red Brigade terrorist network either. A friend of Gianmarco Montesano, Negri, like his friend, was a supporter of worker autonomy. As a philosopher, author, and professor of political and social science at the University of Padua, Toni Negri had the status of a great political leader. He came to Paris in 1977, and thanks to Montesano met Guattari who was then preparing the Bologna gathering. His writings neither defended the Red Brigade nor praised armed violence.

As a leader of the Autonomia group, and more particularly of the Milan Rosso group, Toni Negri was named in an arrest warrant and fled to avoid being arrested, first to Switzerland, where he stayed for three months, and then to Paris in September 1977. He took refuge at Guattari's home. A friendship grew between them, and subsequently he often spent weekends at Dhuizon, near La Borde.

Yann Moulier-Boutang then had Louis Althusser invite Toni Negri to the ENS to teach a seminar on Marx's *Grundrisse*; the seminar was published in 1979.[34] Toni Negri also attended Deleuze's classes at Vincennes. "Listening to Gilles Deleuze was a kind of cleansing of what had been predetermined in my brain. . . . I became a Spinozist after those classes."[35] In 1978 and 1979, Negri foolhardily divided his time between France and Italy, where he was arrested by the Italian authorities on April 7, 1979, along with Oreste Scalzone, another PO leader. Both were accused of being legal frontmen for the Red Brigade and implicated in the assassination of Aldo Moro. They were immediately sent to a "special prison," the Italian equivalent of a maximum-security prison, where Negri remained incarcerated for over four years. At the end of his 1983 trial, the high court of Rome condemned Negri to thirty years of imprisonment and Scalzone to twenty years for subversive action and the creation of armed groups. Of course, the CINEL, with Guattari at the fore, mobilized immediately. "The idea that Negri could be the head of the BR was as ridiculous as if someone had said in 1937 that Trotsky was the head of the KGB."[36]

The CINEL sent activists to visit Toni Negri and Oreste Scalzone in prison. This was an intensely active time for the CINEL, which was facing increasing numbers of demands for extradition and imprisonment. "We incorporated legal experts and lawyers into the CINEL, like Jean-Pierre Mignard, Georges Kiejman, Jean-Denis Bredin, the judge Yves Lemoine, François Loncle from the Socialist Party, and Senator Parmentier. We mobilized and got petitions signed. We challenged well-known individuals and exposed those responsible for bringing the charges."[37]

Immediately after Negri's incarceration but before his trial began, Deleuze defended Toni Negri's innocence to his judges in a letter that was printed in *La Repubblica* on May 10, 1979.[38] He was stunned that someone could be prosecuted and imprisoned without the slightest tangible evidence, and he made the analogy that Carlo Ginzburg used later during the trial of his friend Adriano Sofr, comparing the interrogations to the Inquisition. Deleuze laid out some principles: "First, the courts should hold to a certain principle of identity."[39] In this case, however, the prosecution had no tangible evidence at its disposal to prop up its prosecution. Second, the investigation and preparation of the case must be carried out with a minimum of coherence, according to the principle of disjunction or exclusion, whereas the prosecution "was proceeding by inclusion, by piling up contradictory terms."[40] The Italian press apparently was claiming that Toni Negri possessed the power of ubiquity, since he allegedly had been in Rome, Paris, and Milan simultaneously. Last, Deleuze reacted to the vehement Italian criticisms of French intellectuals concerning the call to Bologna and the charge that they were meddling in others' affairs that did not concern them: "Negri is an important theorist and intellectual in France as well as in Italy."[41] Shortly afterward, when Bourgois published Toni Negri's

Marx Beyond Marx in 1979, Deleuze took up his pen for *Le Matin de Paris* to remind everyone of Negri's innocence. He invited the judges investigating Negri's intentions and his degree of implication in the Moro affair to read his work, which "is literally a proof of innocence,"[42] because the notions he argues confirm that he could only be hostile to such an assassination.

Guattari went to Italy several times to visit Toni Negri in prison and the two men corresponded for more than four years. Above all, this epistolary contact was a great comfort for Negri, who was growing impatient and starting to despair. In May 1980, Guattari visited the prison once more and offered a more regular exchange of letters. Two months later, Toni Negri described his weariness. "I was doing rather badly and am starting to feel a prison fatigue and be in a psychological state that often turns to laziness."[43] At the end of the 1980s, Toni Negri was transferred to the Rebibbia prison in Rome to undergo the first interrogations since his arrest, after seventeen months of incarceration. He had just read the latest book by Deleuze and Guattari. "I've read *A Thousand Plateaus* almost in its entirety. It's an important book. Perhaps the most important I've read in the last twenty years."[44]

In 1983, to help his friend hang on, Guattari suggested that they write a book together on the basis of their correspondence. Toni Negri accepted the offer gladly, since it would help him endure the morbidity of prison life. He also hoped to benefit from the shared writing experience that Guattari had already acquired with Deleuze. "You have more experience than I do working as a couple, and I think you should do the final assembly work."[45]

In June 1983, Toni Negri was freed before being formally condemned, because he had just been elected European deputy for the Italian Radical Party. As he was leaving prison, the political class mobilized to eliminate his parliamentary immunity. Persuaded that he would be sent back to prison, Toni Negri turned to Guattari. In September 1983, a majority of four votes (300 to 296) in the Italian parliament removed his parliamentary immunity. "I left for Corsica in a boat that was most certainly paid for by Félix," he remembers.[46] Helped by Gérard Soulier and Guattari, he arrived secretly in Paris.

He and Guattari then continued the already advanced work on their book. "From 1983 to 1987, my name was Antoine Guattari. He paid for everything. I moved from the place d'Italie to boulevard Pasteur and then to rue Monsieur-le-Prince,"[47] into apartments that Guattari found for him. "Félix looked after me like a brother. He helped me everywhere."[48] Rue de Condé continued to be a hub for the movement. That was where Toni Negri met Daniel Vernet, a journalist for *Le Monde*, Serge July, and Régis Debray. "That was where the 'Mitterrand Doctrine'[49] was conceived. It was not some external position concerning Italy. It was an inside construction."[50]

New Spaces for Freedom was published in 1985.[51] It opened with a defense of "communism," a termed branded with infamy, clarifying that "we conceived of it as a path to a liberation of individual and collective singularities."[52] This break with the traditional Marxist schema claimed that "community and singularity are not in opposition."[53] This essay reaffirmed that what happened was deeply rooted in the 1968 experience, which led to the title of the second chapter—"The Revolution Started in '68."[54] The May '68 movement was not just about political emancipation. It was also the expression of a true will to liberation, both radical and plural.

What some would call the death of the political is only the birth of a new world and new politics: the success of the 1970s reaction and the appearance of a "No Future" tendency linked to the creation of an Integrated World Capitalism (IWC) that neatly slices up the planet. With the IWC, individuals are all the more subjected since they cannot localize power. The world market is presented as an efficient instrument for putting poverty into a "grid" and "enmeshing" marginalization. Despite the global grid overlaying the social universe, the revolution and hence hope are not things of the past.

The book concluded with two personal contributions: one by Guattari on "Liberties in Europe" and another by Negri, "Archaeological Letter." Beyond their shared struggle, we can measure here once more what distinguishes Guattari's open approach to deep questioning and Negri's determination to hold onto the classical revolutionary tradition at any price. Guattari explains that his fight to defend the rights of Bifo, Croissant, Piperno, Pace, and Negri led him to reconsider his judgment "on the importance granted to those supposedly formal freedoms that now seem to me totally inseparable from other 'on the ground' liberties."[55] And Guattari could take satisfaction with the positive role played by organizations like Amnesty International, the League of Human Rights, France Terre d'Asile, and the Cimade in France. He suggested that we talk about "degrees of freedom, or even better, differential coefficients of freedom."[56] This pluralization of our idea of liberty is linked with the concern not to present the State as a monster somewhere outside of society. As Foucault had sketched it out, power is everywhere and first of all in us. We must "make do with it."[57] In his contribution, however, Negri let his ineradicable attachment to Leninism shine through.

If repression and reinforcement were not being used to the same degree in France as they had been in Germany and Italy, it was not thanks to a more robust democratic tradition. Other than for a few marginal incidents, France had simply not lived through the terrorist movements. Nevertheless, the desire to wipe out the leftist menace, the June 1970 antirioter law, and the tough clampdown on some demonstrations in France helped give the international climate of the 1970s the weighty feel of those "somber years."

On September 19, 1979, one of Guattari's best friends, the filmmaker François Pain, was arrested, imprisoned, and prosecuted for events that had occurred more than six months earlier, when he had participated in a metalworkers' demonstration on March 23, 1979, that had culminated in clashes and excesses. François Pain ended up between République and Opéra on the boulevard, which was being ravaged by the independents, shattering shop windows and looting the luxury boutiques. François Pain was walking on the sidewalk in front of a Lancel store when he was hit in the face by a sack. He was photographed, amid a group of ski-masked demonstrators, as he was looking at what had hit him, and the photo appeared in the far-right weekly *Minute*. Already well known to the police for his links with the Italian left and for his activity in support of the free radio stations, Pain was immediately identified and locked up for stealing a bag that the police never found. This was a wonderful opportunity, nevertheless, to make Guattari, through his proxy François Pain, pay for having supported the Italians.

During his interrogation, François Pain was persuaded that he had been arrested because he had just returned from Rome, where he had helped several wanted activists find shelter. "When they showed me the photo of the bag, it was a big relief! I burst out laughing!"[58] The CINEL went into action immediately, and Jean-Pierre Mignard and one of George Kiejman's assistants handled Pain's defense. During one of the CINEL meetings, a heated audience came up with absurd proposals to grab the public's attention. Once, someone at the back of the room yelled, "Some dough for Mr. Pain [Bread]." Guattari answered, "That's great! That's exactly the campaign we're going to lead." François Aubral remembers that at that moment "the guy next to me said, 'Listen, if they keep going like this, he'll stay in prison the rest of his life. I'm Henri Leclerc. I'm defending him.'"[59] Pain was first prosecuted under the antirioter law. His incarceration lasted over four months. His friend Guattari frequently visited him at the Santé Prison and decided to launch, in tandem with the campaign for Pain's liberation, a battle against preventative detention, which would allow the judge to keep Pain in prison for six months before beginning proceedings against him. The National Audiovisual Institute, Pain's employer, intervened in his defense, and the CINEL gathered character references. Pain remembers, "They made me laugh a lot, telling me that Jean-Luc Godard wanted to take the witness stand with a sugar lump stolen from a café and throw it at the judge. The judge would have caught it, and Godard would have said, "He's handling stolen goods! That sugar was stolen!'"[60] The public-opinion campaign worked well, and not a day went by without some article appearing in the press about this affair. Persuaded that he was the real target of the operation, Guattari gave Pain and his girlfriend Marion "a fifteen-day vacation in southern Morocco to make him happy."[61]

At the end of 1979, Guattari was targeted by a police sting that started with a search warrant at La Borde during an investigation of the kidnapping of billionaire Henri Lelièvre by Jacques Mesrine, then public enemy no. 1. The police found nothing, but the daily *L'Aurore* still published an article, "The Leftist Way," signed by Pierre Dumas, supposedly revealing the links between certain crooks and the leftist milieu. That journal also blew out of proportion the case of a certain Charles Bauer, someone Guattari was said to have helped reinstate into normal society at the behest of his friend Pierre Goldman and who had since become Mesrine's accomplice.

FROM COURT JESTER TO FREE RADIO

In March 1980, the weekly *Charlie Hebdo* proposed the idea of presenting the comedian Coluche as a presidential candidate. But, in October 1980, what started out as a gag took another turn. The first polls revealed that around 17 percent of the population intended to vote for Coluche. To carry it off, five hundred elected officials would have to sign a petition for his candidacy. However, what might simply be a formality for large political parties can be quite a hurdle for candidates with no party support. In October 1980, the lawyer Gérard Soulier received a phone call from his friend Guattari. "'You won't believe it,' he said. In fact, Guattari couldn't believe it either. 'I just got a phone call from Gilles Deleuze. Do you know what he told me? He's supporting Coluche's candidacy!'"[62] Gérard Soulier was thrilled.

Not only did he appreciate Coluche's humor, as did many others, but he had been secretly hoping for this candidacy for at least six months. Thus began the famous petition on behalf of the "Candidate for Morons."

A whole series of intellectuals, especially the CINEL network with Jean-Pierre Faye, got behind Deleuze and Guattari, committing themselves to supporting Coluche. "Félix called me and said, 'With Gilles, we've decided to support Coluche's right to his candidacy.' The right said that Coluche would lose in France; the left said that he was going to lose the left vote, and that he still needed his five hundred signatures. I answered, 'Coluche? Who's that?' And he answered, 'He's Père Duchesne.'"[63] Jean-Pierre Faye, who had written a study on Père Duchesne, saw quite clearly how abrasive such a character could be for the French political system. He agreed and actively participated in meetings with Coluche.

To understand this commitment and its strong dynamic, we have to recall the confusing political situation during the fall of 1980, with the re-election of Valéry Giscard d'Estaing for another seven-year term almost certain. It was thought that François Mitterrand was getting ready to repeat his 1974 failure, as he was supposedly unable to alter the destiny of the left. For some activists, not much more than laughter remained, and the Coluche candidacy created a sense of ephemeral energy. "So, Coluche arrived, and he was quite the court jester, because he was talented,"[64] according to Paul Virilio, who met Guattari at that point and became his publisher.

At the end of the 1970s, non-state-accredited radio broadcasting (which means some private radio stations such as Europe 1, Radio Luxemburg, and RMC) was a felony with severe legal repercussions. François Pain, a specialist in this kind of technology, was particularly implicated with his friend Güattari in setting up an alternative radio network that would broadcast without the knowledge of the police. "I created a supply network for transmitters that we smuggled in from Italy."[65] The Italian network was linked to Radio Alice in Bologna, where a particularly efficient technician made excellent transmitters that Pain regularly picked up at the Gare de Lyon.

As soon as the free radio broadcasts were detected, the police jammed them. But they increased in number, proof of the desire to speak out ten years after May '68. Guattari struck up a friendship with a professional who was very involved in the free-radio struggle and who created the Association for Free Airwaves (ALO) in September 1977. The association broadcast a call to liberalize the airwaves that was signed by eighteen personalities, including Deleuze, Guattari, and Foucault. For his part, François Pain managed to organize small associative radio stations into a network following a large 1978 meeting of radio broadcasters. The ALFREDO association grew out of this meeting and brought together this bevy of small networks.[66] Then a majority in the free-radio movement sympathetic to Guattari's positions founded the National Federation of Noncommercial Free Radio Stations.

One of Guattari's sons, Bruno, who was twenty in 1978, became involved in the undertaking. In 1979, while every free-radio attempt was meeting with repression, Bruno took advantage of Jussieu University's neutrality to bring a local radio station to life. Starting from that small success, he broadened his ambitions with Radio Paris 80, for which he supplied the material. When Félix Guattari and François Pain created Radio Libre Paris, which became Radio Tomato in December 1980, Bruno Guattari did the programming.

The repression was getting stronger. The July 1978 law set fines ranging from ten thousand to one hundred thousand francs for any infraction and prison sentences from one month to a year. These measures hardly dampened the determination of those wanting to free the airwaves, and their energy culminated during the great summer 1978 No-Jamming Festival in the Hyères Park. The audience was treated to forty-eight free hours of nonstop music by the best singers of the day, including Jacques Higelin and Telephone. For many small stations, however, the risks were too great, and they had to give up during the fall of 1978 or go underground. As for personalities like Guattari, the powers-that-be would be turned into laughingstocks if they threw them in prison, but they did nevertheless end up in court. A lawyer friend of Gérard Soulier, Michel Tubiana, a future president of the League for Human Rights, pleaded the case for most affairs concerning free radio stations.

> They were often made fun of. More than once, while leaving court, we would have ourselves interviewed with transmitters in a car. I'll always remember what happened in the Seventeenth courtroom. We had brought around forty witnesses to the stand, and the session that started at 1:30 p.m. needed to end by 11:00 p.m. TDF's lawyer, who was leading a civil-action suit, finished her plea by requesting the symbolic one franc in damages. The Seventeenth courtroom was a rather

long room, packed with people. Someone in the back of the courtroom rolled a one-franc coin that ended up dropping at the lawyer's
feet. It was a very funny moment.[67]

Created at the end of 1980, in the middle of the presidential campaign,
Radio Tomato brought together the CINEL activists. "First we broadcast
from Félix's kitchen, then we found a kind of cellar in the basement of the
France Foundation on rue Lacépède."[68] The radio broadcast twenty-four
hours a day, offering cultural programming on film, music, and theater, in
addition to more sociopolitical programs on Monday afternoons. There
were also reports on squatters, and an African man presented *The Argument Tree* at night. The news took up a lot of time, and Gisèle Donnard, a
committed CINEL activist, oversaw this sector, when there were regular
debates on Poland, the war in Lebanon, or on the Israel-Palestine question.
But the quality of the equipment was not high enough to allow for good reception, and the coverage remained weak. Radio Tomato never reached the
audience that it might have.

This airwave experiment corresponds to a practical extension of Deleuze and Guattari's ideas. It is a model of a transversal rhizomatic system
that breaks with State- and market-based vertical logics. As with any rhizome, connections can be made at any point, which makes for rather stunning and always original cartographies, like the one that linked Radio Bastille to its neighbor Radio Onz'Débrouille (Radio "Wefigureitout"), which
collaborated with Radio Fil Rose. "Thanks to this rhizomatic organization
of stations and individuals, the free-radio movement developed as a genuine war machine on the broadcast media field."[69]

When François Mitterrand was elected president of the French Republic on May 10, 1981, he decided to open up the airwaves. Those who had
been speaking from the shadows could finally take full advantage of this
media. However, other problems welled up. Consolidations had to be effec-
tuated to keep on broadcasting. But who would join forces with Radio Tomato? Radio J (Jewish) was originally suggested, but there were too many
pro-Palestinians at Radio Tomato to pull off a friction-free coupling. Tomato finally settled on Radio Solidarnosc, "but there were anti-Semites
there, and that ended in blows. In the end, we found a place for us alone."[70]

A more serious problem weighed on the associative creation of free radio stations when a host of commercial radio stations and their greater resources arrived. As Guattari put it, "On the surface of the aquarium there

are radio-loving minnows, but below, there are fat advertising sharks."[71] To defend his conception of socially experimental radio stations, Guattari invited Jack Lang, the minister of culture with whom he had a good rapport, to a live debate on Radio Tomato with himself, Jean-Pierre Faye, and François Pain. *La Quinzaine Littéraire* published a part of the debate.[72] At the end of 1981, the minister's point of view was close to Guattari's: "Liberty must not be the fox in the chicken coop. . . . Yes to liberty, but on the condition that it not profit the powerful, and that it be a liberty for those who create and have something to say."[73]

The conquest of new liberties also jumped the wall separating the communist world from Western Europe. In the late 1970s, a series of Soviet and eastern European dissidents found refuge in France. The CINEL and the CERFI help distributed the story of their prison-house experience. *Recherches* devoted an issue to them, organized by Natalia Gorbanevsikaia, a Soviet born in 1936 in Moscow.[74]

For Guattari, the CINEL represented the possibility of demonstrating the efficiency of a micropolitics endowed with minimal organizational means and simply linked to action, thereby breaking with traditional schemas. It would have been the political branch of the CERFI, whose activity dealt with the humanities. A bit like the March 22 Movement, CINEL was about assembling personalities from diverse backgrounds around a common goal, thus staving off circular thinking during those "somber years." With no real organization or program but with a regular meeting place, the CINEL "machine" managed to mobilize and raise awareness and also proved its political efficiency during certain crises.

17

Deleuze and Foucault
A Philosophical Friendship

"Perhaps one day this century will be known as Deleuzean."[1] Michel Foucault's lucid remark, made in 1969, has often been repeated. As for Deleuze, "Gilles deeply admired Michel Foucault."[2] Although they saw each other frequently and fought alongside each other for the same political causes, they never really worked together. Yet as the final tributes were being paid to Foucault at La Salpêtrière before a crowd of several hundred mourners, it was Deleuze who stood and read an excerpt from the preface to *The Use of Pleasure*. Some basic disagreements were surely motivated by a certain rivalry as to who incarnated the authority of critical thinking, at least so far as Foucault was concerned, according to Paul Veyne, a close friend of his. "I got the feeling that Foucault saw Deleuze as a rival."[3] Foucault was exasperated to see Nietzsche's works linked so closely to Deleuze's reading and teased Veyne, telling him that what he really liked in Nietzsche was "Deleuze's Nietzsche."[4]

Deleuze, however, was not jealous of Foucault, toward whom he always claimed some closeness. "I never worked with Foucault. But I do think there are a lot of parallels between our work (with Guattari) and his, although they're as it were held at a distance because of our widely differing methods and even our objectives."[5] Regarding their putative rivalry, "I'll say this: the fact that Foucault existed, with such a forceful and mysterious personality, the fact that he wrote such wonderful books, with such style, has never caused me anything but delight."[6] For Deleuze, any rivalry toward Foucault, for whom he felt only admiration, was unimaginable. "Perhaps we met too late. I respected him deeply. The atmosphere changed when he came into a room. There was something different in the air. Things changed. It was atmospheric. Something emanated from Foucault. Foucault's gestures were astonishingly sharp and elegant."[7]

Their story starts in October 1952, in Lille. Deleuze and his friend Jean-Pierre Bamberger were teaching at Amiens High School at the time and attended a lecture by Foucault, who was giving a psychology course at the University of Lille. In the early 1950s, Foucault was quite close to the FCP and Deleuze was on target: "What I heard quite clearly reflected a Marxist perspective."[8] At the end of the conference, Bamberger invited them both to dinner at his place. Their first meeting was icy; it seemed unlikely that they would meet again.

They met again in 1962; it had taken ten years. At that point, Foucault was a professor at Clermont-Ferrand and was finishing his *Raymond Roussel* and *The Birth of the Clinic*. Deleuze had just published *Nietzsche*, which Foucault had liked very much. As Jules Vuillemin had been elected to the Collège de France, a position opened up at the University of Clermont-Ferrand. Foucault suggested that Deleuze might replace Vuillemin; Deleuze came to Clermont and spent the day with Foucault, whom he had not seen since the dinner in Lille. "The meeting went very well, and everybody was happy. The philosophy department approved Deleuze's appointment unanimously and Vuillemin got it approved by the faculty board in a unanimous vote."[9] The promise of collaboration between Foucault and Deleuze within the same philosophy department was stillborn, however, as the Ministry of Universities had already decided to appoint Roger Garaudy, a high-ranking FCP and Politburo member. During this period, Deleuze was posted at the University of Lyon, and he and Deleuze opposed Garaudy, a shared position that brought them closer to one another. "They saw each other regularly when Deleuze traveled to Paris. And without really becoming intimate, they were friendly enough for Foucault to lend his apartment to Deleuze and his wife when he was away."[10]

In the early 1960s, Foucault and Deleuze were working together for Gallimard on an edition of Nietzsche's complete works, which profoundly changed the way Nietzsche had been read in France until then.[11] Both men also participated in the two most important occasions of the "return to Nietzsche": the 1964 conference at Royaumont and the 1972 Cerisy colloquium. Both were close to Pierre Klossowski, who had translated *The Gay Science* in 1954; this was their first major meeting in a philosophical undertaking. Deleuze had met Klossowski through Marie-Magdeleine Davy's circle during the war. When Klossowski published *Nietzsche and the Vicious Circle* in 1969, he dedicated it to Deleuze, in homage to his *Nietzsche and Philosophy*.

Both Deleuze and Foucault worked on Klossowski individually, and each discovered a common object of inquiry inspired directly by his writings.[12] Both philosophers saw in Klossowski's work an extension of the tradition of transgressive literature, crossing fiction with philosophy along the lines of a simulacrum. "The paradoxical *mimesis* that both actualizes and exorcizes makes the simulacrum the point where the relationship between the profane and sacred is inverted."[13] It was important to question the false identity of things and beings by breaking them open in the ways made possible by the simulacrum and the proliferation of masks. Here, the Foucauldian theme of the death of man, which had made *The Order of Things* a success and a scandal, came to the fore. "Klossowski's entire work moves toward a single goal: to assure the loss of personal identity, to dissolve itself."[14] Foucault and Deleuze thus consolidated their Nietzscheism— or anti-Hegelianism—using the simulacrum as a war machine against thought based on identity and representation. Deleuze admired a story in Klossowksi's last essay, *The Baphomet* (dedicated to Foucault), which provided a way out of the moral and theological dilemma between Good and Evil by showing that the two systems are not alternatives but simultaneous, constituting "a grandiose sequel to Zarathustra."[15]

Separately—Deleuze was in Lyon, and Foucault was in Sidi Bou Saïd in Tunisia—both were enthusiastic about May '68. In his seminar on Foucault, Deleuze insisted on the importance of the event for understanding the issues in Foucauldian philosophy, which are theoretical and practical. In 1986, recalling this founding event, Deleuze pointed out its international importance and its contagious energy, which was as hard to describe as to imagine in the desert of the 1980s.[16] For Deleuze, calling into question the various forms of centralization was the agent of this rupture.

During the summer of 1968, when the creation of a university at Vincennes was being considered, Foucault was designated to create the philosophy department. He quite naturally contacted Deleuze, who had to decline temporarily for reasons of ill health. Deleuze was publishing *Difference and Repetition* and *The Logic of Sense* at the time, which Foucault greeted as a philosophical revolution. He was enthused by what he described as a "bolt of lightning that will be named Deleuze: a new way of thinking is possible; thought is possible once more. It does not lie in the future, promised by the most distant of new beginnings. It is here in Deleuze's texts, springing forth, dancing before us, in our midst; genital thought, intensive thought, affirmative thought, a-categorical thought."[17] As early as 1969,

Foucault had clearly understood Deleuze's philosophy as first and foremost a "philosophy of the event," as François Zourabichvili later demonstrated.[18] Foucault showed how the fundamental question posed by Deleuze is that of knowing what thinking is, situating thought within the "affirmative disjunction"[19] of the event and the phantasm. As if echoing Foucault, Deleuze concluded his seminar on May 20, 1986, with the remark, "Only one thing has ever interested Foucault: what does it mean to think?"[20]

THE PRISON INFORMATION GROUP ADVENTURE

In the early 1970s, their philosophical proximity extended to politics, when Foucault created the Prison Information Group (GIP) with Deleuze at his side. The GIP was born out of the dissolution in May 1970 of the GP (Proletarian Left) by Interior Minister Raymond Marcellin. The ruling party was hardening its repressive policy regarding left-wing agitation in the post-1968 period and imprisoning several of the group's militants, including Alain Geismar. In September 1970, the imprisoned militants began a twenty-five-day hunger strike to be granted political-prisoner status, but the strike failed. In January 1971, they began a new hunger strike that elicited greater public support.

Alfred Kastler, Paul Ricoeur, and Pierre Vidal-Naquet requested an audience with Minister of Justice René Eleven and were promised a commission to rule on the conditions of imprisonment. Finally, after thirty-four days without food for some, "the lawyers Henri Leclerc and Georges Kiejman, in a press conference at the Saint-Bernard chapel on February 8, 1971, announced the end of the hunger strike"[21] and the creation of a special detention regime for the prisoners. During the press conference, three well-known intellectuals, Michel Foucault, Pierre Vidal-Naquet, and Jean-Marie Domenach, the director of the journal *Esprit*, announced the creation of the GIP. Initially, the group grew directly out of the Maoist current of thought to protect GP militants being prosecuted by the government and given arbitrary sentences. The former GP members had in fact created a Political Prisoners Organization that was overseen first by Serge July and then by Benny Lévy, but the GP soon became independent.

Without having any prior consultation, Daniel Defert suggested Foucault's name to organize a committee to investigate the general situation in prisons. Foucault accepted, and "at the end of December, he brought together at his home the people he thought would be able either to create or to prepare a commission of inquiry into prisons."[22] The group quickly agreed on their method of inquiry. The lawyer Christine Martineau was finishing a book on work in prisons and, with the help of the philosopher Danielle Rancière, had already designed a questionnaire to distribute to the prisoners: "Our model was Marx's workers' survey."[23] In the end, thanks to Foucault, who had been burned by the popular inquiries led by Maoist militants after 1968,[24] the plans for a commission of inquiry turned into the GIP. The GIP was entirely decentralized (one group per prison). Very quickly, this Parisian model gained ground in the provincial prisons to which the militants had been sent. As a form of organization, it immediately appealed to Deleuze for its practical and effective resistance and because it broke with all forms of centralized bureaucratic machinery, defining itself instead as a microstructure. "The GIP developed one of the only left-wing groups that worked without being centralized. . . . Foucault knew how not to behave like the boss."[25]

Using as an excuse the mounting tension since the September 1971 Clairvaux prison riots, which had culminated in a guard and a nurse being taken hostage by two prisoners, Buffet and Bontens, the minister of justice decided to try to calm the anxious prison guards and punish the prisoners collectively by refusing to let them receive their Christmas parcels that year. The decision fueled further protests in the prisons: in the winter of 1971–1972, thirty-two rebellions broke out, during some of which prisoners destroyed cells and occupied rooftops. On Christmas Eve, the GIP organized a demonstration in front of the Santé Prison in Paris that both Foucault and Deleuze attended. Violent clashes broke out throughout the month of December, notably at the prison in Toul, where fifteen prisoners were wounded.

GIP intellectuals were occasionally asked to go to the provinces. In Nancy, for example, a riot had been strongly quelled and charges had been brought against six of the two hundred rioters. Deleuze, along with Daniel Defert, Hélène Cixous, Jean-Pierre Faye, Jacques Donzelot, among others, made the trip to join the protest demonstration. Foucault could not attend, having been arrested after helping an immigrant who was being beaten up in the metro. In Nancy's central town square, Jean-Pierre Faye was chatting with a journalist from *L'Est Républicain*, who was commenting on how uninteresting the demonstration was. Faye advised him to wait a few minutes longer before judging it. "As soon as I said those prophetic words, the cops rushed us."[26] Deleuze stood up on a bench to speak, was quickly cut off by the police, and said, "Since my boss isn't here, I'm going to speak in his place." As the police were charging, Deleuze was overcome by his respiratory problems and became seriously ill; he lay down on the ground and became semicomatose. Foucault's young friend Jacques Donzelot was extremely concerned and stayed with him. "When he came to, he said to me, 'Oh, are you here with me? How kind of you!'"[27]

At Paris-VIII, when Donzelot defended his thesis on "Policing the Family"[28]—his thesis director was Jean-Claude Passeron—Deleuze proposed that he be part of the jury. "I suddenly got stage fright. I couldn't think of anything to say, so I just said, 'Why do I have to give a formal summary, since you've already read my work?' Deleuze stepped in, saying, 'Don't worry, I'll summarize your thesis for you.' Great!"[29] When the time came to publish the thesis, Deleuze offered to write the preface, but that caused tensions between Foucault and Deleuze. Donzelot had just defended a very Foucauldian thesis, and when he told Foucault that Deleuze was going to write the preface, he got a sharp reply. "I detest that sort of thing, I can't stand it when old men come and put their stamp on young people's work."[30] In the end, so as not to ruffle Foucault, Deleuze wrote an afterword instead of a preface.[31]

On January 17, 1972, the GIP managed to persuade Sartre and Foucault to demonstrate together at a protest against repression in prisons. A small group of public figures aimed to get inside the Ministry of Justice on place Vendôme to hold a press conference. The cream of Parisian intelligentsia sat down in the ministry halls to listen to Foucault, who started to read the declaration made by the Melun prisoners. The police intervened halfheartedly as the demonstrators jeered and yelled "Jail Pleven!" or "Pleven's a murderer!" "The cops push harder. They get mad. Sartre resists. Foucault resists. Faye resists. Deleuze resists and can't stop laughing. But the cops end up winning and manage to throw all of us right back out onto the sidewalk."[32] Finally kicked out of the Ministry of Justice, which was now protected by a three-deep ring of armed and helmeted riot police, the press conference was held in the offices of the *Libération* press agency on rue Dussoubs.

Shortly thereafter, on January 31, 1972, Deleuze wrote a text entitled "What Our Prisoners Expect from Us" for the *Nouvel Observateur*.[33] He listed the prisoners' demands concerning the lifting of censorship, the disciplinary committee and disciplinary wards, using their labor and their conditional liberation, seeing the prisoners' statements as something completely new: not a "public confession" but a "personalized critique."[34] During the demonstrations, Foucault was especially attentive to Deleuze and worried about his health. On December 16, 1972, during confrontations with the police, Claude Mauriac was with Foucault and a small group just after a police charge. "Have you seen Deleuze? I hope he hasn't been arrested. . . . That's how worried Michel Foucault was—he was very pale."[35]

Apart from the actions concerning prisons, the GIP also organized to protest acts of repression and racism. During the spring of 1971, the Jaubert affair broke. Alain Jaubert, a *Nouvel Observateur* journalist, was a witness to police violence during a demonstration by French West Indians. He was carted off in a paddy wagon and beaten up by the special service responsible for crowd control.[36] At a meeting chaired by Claude Mauriac, Foucault announced the creation of an investigative committee. A press conference was held on June 21, 1971. Denis Langlois spoke first, then Deleuze. "An initial group of questions starts with the communiqué released by the Prefecture of Police on May 30. . . . This communiqué is entirely unbelievable because it wasn't written to be believed. There's another goal—to intimidate."[37]

In the fall of 1971, a young Algerian manhandled the female concierge of his apartment building in Goutte d'Or. The concierge's husband saw it happen, retrieved his rifle, and killed the Algerian, claiming that it was an accident. The case cast the mounting racial tensions in the neighborhood into full light, and demonstrations were organized to denounce the racist murder. Foucault created a new investigative committee, whose members included Deleuze, Jean Genet, Claude Mauriac, and Jean-Claude Passeron, among others. On November 27, 1971, Sartre and Foucault led a meeting in the Goutte d'Or in the name of an "Appeal to the Workers of the Neighborhood" signed by Deleuze, Foucault, Michel Leiris, Yves Montand, Jean Genet, Sartre, and Simone Signoret.[38]

These militant actions in 1971 and 1972 gave Deleuze and Foucault an opportunity to start a dialogue about how they defined the new responsibilities of intellectuals with respect to power. It was during the 1972 interview that Deleuze used Guattari's formula: "We are all groupuscules."[39] For Deleuze, the GIP was the expression of a new type of organization that could renew the relationship between theory and practice, setting them in a more concrete, local, and partial framework. "A theorizing intellectual, for us, is no longer a subject, a representing or representative consciousness."[40] Foucault similarly argued that the universal role of intellectuals as

the incarnation of the discourse of Truth was over, because societal demo-
cratization allowed every social group to express its dissatisfactions perfectly well without them. Rather, intellectuals should concentrate on the
struggle against forms of power. Their job is to determine the various loci
of power and to trace their genealogy.

Although the two friends grew closer during these years with respect to
the political sphere, their ideas about political engagement were not exactly the same. "On one hand, Foucault took experience and practices as
his point of departure and conceptualized from there. Deleuze and Guattari invented war machines and then tried them out."[41] Thus Foucault, who
spent time at Saint-Anne and was interested in psychiatry, created the GIP,
then wrote *Discipline and Punish*, and worked on an analysis of power. Deleuze and Guattari, by contrast, produced concepts and machines and then
tested what they produced in social reality. Guattari's ideas were inscribed
within a whole series of social practices linked to Marxism, institutional
psychotherapy, and a series of research groups like the CERFI, which were
experimental sites for the concepts he had worked out with Deleuze.

Despite his reticence with respect to Guattari and his desire to remain
at a distance from his groups, Foucault did let himself be persuaded by Deleuze to be involved in several issues of the CERFI's publications. He contributed to two issues of *Recherches: The Public Works of Power* and *Three
Billion Perverts* in 1973.[42] At the same time, during the 1971–1972 academic
year, Deleuze participated in Foucault's seminar at the Collège de France,
where Foucault was analyzing the nineteenth-century case of Pierre
Rivière, who, at the age of twenty, slit the throats of his mother, brother,
and sister and left his memoirs, which were partially published in 1836.

A Time of Discord

The other period when Foucault and Deleuze were both politically engaged
came in 1977, during the Klaus Croissant affair. On July 11, 1977, the Baader-
Meinhof gang's attorney came from Germany to Paris seeking political
asylum: in his own country he was being treated as a Baader "agent" and as
the terrorists' puppet. As soon as he arrived in Paris, the German authorities requested his arrest and deportation. On September 30, the French
police arrested him.

The attorney Gérard Soulier, a friend of Guattari's who was very active
in the CINEL, learned of the arrest while reading *Le Monde* as he was about

to drop off to sleep. "That woke me up!"[43] He leapt up from the couch, got out the legal directory, and called Jean-Jacques de Felice, Tubiana, and Antoine Compte, who organized a press conference with Henri Noguères, the president of the League for Human Rights. On October 26, 1977, Minister of Justice Alan Peyrefitte declared, "France cannot become a sanctuary for terrorists." In early November, a hearing was held in the tenth chamber of the court of appeal in Paris to rule on the request for deportation; on November 16, 1977, as a small crowd was gathering in front of the Santé Prison along with Foucault and Deleuze, the police charged. Croissant was escorted to the German border.

By this point, the disagreements between the two friends were threatening their friendship. Both joined the demonstration against the deportation of Croissant, but Foucault refused to sign the petition, which already included the names of Deleuze and Guattari, since he thought it was too complacent with respect to the Red Army Faction terrorists and wanted to more carefully and specifically define his support to Croissant.[44] Claude Mauriac remembers calling Foucault "to ask him how he'd reacted to Guattari's phone call about the deportation request for Baader's attorney, Klaus Croissant. We'd had no prior discussion but had both refused to sign the text, agreeing on a definite *no* to deportation but refusing to take responsibility for what the text said about Germany."[45]

Years later, Foucault's American biographer, James Miller, asked Deleuze what had changed their friendship so irrevocably. On February 7, 1990, five years after Foucault's death, Deleuze gave a three-point response.

(1) There's obviously no single answer. One of us could have answered one way one day and another way the next. Not because we are fickle. But because there are many reasons in this area and no single reason is "essential." And because none of them is essential, there are always several answers at once. The only important thing is that I had long agreed with him philosophically and on specific occasions, I no longer made the same evaluations as he did on several points at once. (2) This didn't lead to any "cooling" of relations between us, or to any "explanations." We saw each other less often, as if by the force of circumstances. And from there on, it became more and more difficult to meet up again. It is strange, we didn't stop seeing each other because we didn't get along, but because we weren't seeing each other any more, a kind of incomprehension or distance between us took hold.

(3) I can tell you that I constantly miss seeing him, increasingly so. So what stopped me from calling him? That's where a deeper reason comes into it. Rightly or wrongly, I believed that he wanted greater solitude, for his life, for his thinking; that he needed this solitude, keeping in touch only with the people who were close to him. I now think that I should have tried to see him again, but I think I didn't try out of respect. I am still suffering from not having seen him again, even more so because I don't think there were any external reasons.[46]

This letter says a lot but is also evasive. To better understand this radical break, we have to scrutinize several points of disagreement. In the first place, in 1977, Deleuze and Foucault had diametrically opposed positions regarding the new philosophers: Foucault supported them, but they were violently challenged by Deleuze.[47] In addition to the Croissant affair, they also diverged deeply on the Israeli-Palestinian question. Edward Said spoke with James Miller about this in November 1989. He saw the Middle East conflict as one of the major causes of their disagreement: "He got the information from Deleuze himself,"[48] which Deleuze did not contradict when Miller put the question to him. While Deleuze wrote a long article glorifying Yasser Arafat,[49] Foucault denounced the UN resolution equating Zionism with racism,[50] and in 1978, in the middle of the Lebanese crisis, he attacked the totalitarianism of Syria and the Soviet Union but spared Israeli politics.

In 1981, when the Socialists were voted into power in France, a new political disagreement arose. Deleuze was won over and even excited by the early days of Mitterrand's presidency. He thought it best to demonstrate goodwill and allow the Socialists to carry on with their work. Foucault thought it better to criticize them, just as one would criticize any other party in power, if not more so, because now the communists had become part of Pierre Mauroy's government. When Jacques Donzelot met Deleuze for the last time, it was "in 1981, at the Panthéon. He was following Mitterrand. I ran into him; I was walking the other way. He said to me, 'What's happening is fantastic!' and I answered, no, that Mitterrand was a cynical politician who had been successful. He was thrilled!"[51] Their divergent judgments became obvious when General Jaruzelski staged a coup d'état in Poland in 1981, crushing the dreams of the *Solidarnost* leader Lech Walesa. Foucault and Bourdieu drafted an appeal criticizing the weaknesses of this new Socialist government in the face of a new Stalinesque show of strength. Deleuze was asked to sign but declined; he signed a different appeal written by Jack Lang and revised by Jean-Pierre Faye denouncing the repression in Poland while at the same time praising Mitterrand's actions.

In addition to their political disagreements, Deleuze and Foucault also admitted their many philosophical differences, even if these could not account for the severance of their ties. After expressing great admiration for *Difference and Repetition* and *The Logic of Sense* when they were published, Foucault was perplexed by *Anti-Oedipus* in 1972. While he did write a preface to the 1977 American edition, in which he hailed *Anti-Oedipus* as the first ethical book to be written in a long time, according to Donzelot this was not a true reflection of Foucault's feelings about his friend's book. "Foucault didn't like *Anti-Oedipus* and told me so quite often."[52] Jacques Donzelot wrote his own enthusiastic critique for *Esprit*,[53] something that Foucault was glad not to have to do. For him, the book was "a language effect, like Céline. He [Foucault] took my paper to give it to an American journal, managing in that way to feel justified for not having written anything about it."[54]

In the first volume of his *History of Sexuality*, Foucault settled his accounts with psychoanalysis and with Lacan's theory of lack.[55] He argued against the Freudian conception of desire and strongly refuted the claim that society had become progressively repressive since the classical age. He demonstrated that, to the contrary, discourses about sex were proliferating rather than slowly diminishing. Foucault's criticism of desire and "desirers" caught Deleuze and Guattari in the crossfire. In response, Deleuze wrote Foucault a personal letter that he sent through François Ewald, describing his arguments point by point—the letter was published as "Desire and Pleasure."[56] In it, Deleuze asked if it could be possible to consider as equivalent what pertained, for him, to the "body without organs-desires" and what pertained for Foucault to "body-pleasures." He recalled how virulently Foucault had rejected the concept of desire: "the last time we saw each other, Michel said very kindly and affectionately, something like: I can't stand the word desire; even if you use it differently, I can't stop myself from thinking or feeling that desire equals lack, or that desire is said to be repressed."[57] Deleuze, along the lines of Spinoza, saw pleasures as so many obstacles along the path of the desire to be, of *conatus* (striving), self-accomplishment, or perseverance in being, that could therefore only lead to loss. Pleasure, for him, interrupted the "immanent process of desire."[58]

Wounded by the letter, Foucault did not reply. He saw it as one more reason to break off their friendship. "Soon thereafter, Foucault suddenly decided never to see Deleuze again."[59] To better understand why Deleuze's skepticism so offended Foucault, we need to bear in mind that despite the obvious and immediate public success of his book, which led to a reprint of twenty-two thousand copies after an initial print run of twenty-two thousand, and despite very favorable press reviews, Foucault's circle was disconcerted by the book's central argument questioning the battle against repression. It was hard to understand, after an entire decade of doing just this, how the battle on behalf of the freedom of sexual minorities could be viewed as a deployment of biopower. There were vocal criticisms and expressed incomprehension; Baudrillard's *Forget Foucault* was the final straw, so stunning the weakened philosopher that he abandoned the entire edifice that he had planned. It was only after seven years of silence, after having thoroughly revisited its premises, that he published the second volume of his *History of Sexuality*.

The question of desire was altogether central in the split with Deleuze; after all, questioning desire had initially brought them together.[60] Deleuze and Foucault both thought that Freud and Lacan had failed to really examine desire by reducing it to lack or interdiction. "But if the two philosophers were more closely aligned on behalf of a common cause than before, their differences still remain irreconcilable."[61] In 1983, Foucault was very clear about their disagreement during a long interview with Gérard Raulet, who asked him if he agreed with the idea that there was some similarity between his thought and Deleuze's. "Would this similarity extend to the Deleuzean conception of desire?" Foucault's succinct answer was categorical: "No, that's the point."[62] In fact, they gave different answers to a common line of inquiry. Both were concerned with building a nonfascist life ethic and agreed on the absence of naturalness and the spontaneity of desire ordered into arrangements, but Deleuze and Guattari saw desire as a concatenation of arrangements within a decidedly constructivist perspective. "Deleuze's philosophical stroke of genius is to invent a new vitalism, to seek the conditions not of possibility but of reality between expression and construction."[63] What was also playing out in their different concepts of desire was the way that each appropriated Nietzsche, whom Deleuze used particularly for the way he addressed desire in *The Will to Power*; Foucault was more interested in the question of truth in *The Genealogy of Morals*.

Deleuze's conception of desire was rooted in Nietzsche and also strongly influenced by Spinoza's power of being. Deleuze introduced the power of being into an ontology. In January 1986, in his seminar on Foucault, Deleuze went back to the Foucauldian conception of desire/pleasure, explaining Foucault's refusal of the concept of desire and attachment to the idea of the body and its pleasures as the expression of a sexless sexuality with which he concluded his work *The Will to Knowledge*. According to Deleuze, the will to replace a "molar" conception with sex at its center by a "molecular" approach to multiform pleasures was inspired by Proust's definition of the three levels in *Sodom and Gomorrah*: the great group of heterosexual relations; a second level where same refers to same, man to man and woman to woman; and a third level that is "no longer vertical, but transversal,"[64] in which each man has a feminine aspect and each woman a masculine aspect that do not communicate with each other, whence the absolute need for four terms and molecular arrangements. Pulverizing the theme of guilt, Proust "even talks about local pleasures."[65]

THE TRUTH

The publication of *The Will to Knowledge* created a new disagreement between Foucault and Deleuze about the return of the theme of truth. As Jacques Donzelot recalled, "Deleuze often spoke to me about that, saying. 'Jacques, what do you think, Michel is completely nuts, what's this old idea about truth? He's taking us back to that old idea, veridiction! Oh, it can't be!' "[66] In his letter to Foucault, Deleuze explicitly voiced his concern about seeing this term return in Foucault's work. "The danger is: is Michel returning to an analog of the 'constituting subject' and why does he feel the need to resuscitate the truth even if does make it into a new concept?"[67] For Foucault, it was not a question of revisiting the traditional confrontation between true and false. Talking with Paul Veyne one night about truth in Heidegger and Wittgenstein, Foucault added "literally (because I wrote his sentence down): the question is why truth is so little true?"[68] If it is indeed a question of arousing from its slumbers an old traditional concept, it is "to make it play on a different stage, even at the risk of turning it against itself."[69]

But in his 1977 letter, Deleuze wondered out the means for turning back. Starting from the idea that systems of power are, like those of counterpowers, bearers of truth, Foucault made the question of truth depend on the question of power. Thus the "problem of the role of the intellectual in Michel's thought" was raised, along with "his way of reintroducing the category of truth, since, by completely renewing it and making it depend on power, he can find material in this renewal that can be turned against power. But here, I don't see how."[70] Trying to understand the Foucauldian use of the true in his 1985–1986 seminar, Deleuze perceived a disjunction in Foucault's thought between the realms of seeing and of saying, the visible and the spoken. Starting from this paradoxical tension, the game of truth is played out, for speaking is not seeing. But both philosophers grant the two positions truth. Foucault ends up finding in the objective of truth the function of philosophy: "I can't see many other definitions of the word 'philosophy' besides that one."[71] By contrast, for Deleuze, the importance of an affirmation or a concept is not determined by the truth: "on the contrary, it's its importance and its novelty that determine its 'truth.'"[72]

Crossovers between Foucault and Deleuze exist on many levels: they often used the same authors and sources, but in different and often irreconcilable ways. For example, when Deleuze stopped writing portraits in the history of philosophy, he drew heavily from Stoicism for *The Logic of Sense*. Foucault also drew from Stoic arguments in his very late works. He had already allusively adopted the Stoic outlook of *The Logic of Sense* in stating that it was necessary that utterances be granted their specific "materiality," which would be something on the order of incorporeal materiality. Deleuze and Foucault also had a common enemy in Platonism and made use of the same aspects of Stoicism, such as the primacy of the event. "Foucault and Deleuze also emphasize that the Stoic art of the event seeks to insert the self into the immanence of the world and of time."[73] But they used the Stoics differently. Deleuze's was more of a philosophical history of philosophy wherein the Stoics shifted the entire way of thinking within which "philosophy gets confused with ontology."[74] Deleuze tended to look at the early Stoics, whereas Foucault favored the later Stoics of imperial Rome, the reputed moralists such as Epictetus or Marcus Aurelius.

For both of them, their relationship to the Greeks was mediated by Nietzsche; for Nietzsche, from the Greek age onward, the philosopher is he who affirms life. "The will to power in Nietzsche means the affirmation of life, and no longer judging life as the sovereign-Desire."[75] Foucault's interest in the Greeks in *The Use of Pleasure* was also derived from Nietzsche, but he put forward some very personal propositions: who could be the free man chosen to shepherd the civic community in the Greek city of antiquity?

"Only he who knows how to govern himself is apt to govern others."[76] Deleuze identifies this as Foucault's central idea, which broke with his previous work: this government of self is removed from both knowledge and power to become a veritable "art of the self."[77] However, this strength of subjectification is not primary because it remains dependent on the singularity of the "Greek diagram."

Where Foucault and Deleuze used the Stoics in similar ways, they were also very different if we compare Deleuze's fundamentally affirmative and resolutely Spinozan philosophy and metaphysical approach and Foucault's fundamentally Kantian philosophy, integrating negativity occasionally to the point of skepticism. "For me, his books are great works of skepticism. That is where the truth of Foucault lies, in a modern skepticism linked to a quite mysterious form of engagement."[78] Spinoza was not unimportant to Foucault. "Daniel Defert told me that Foucault had used Spinoza, which was on his bedside when he died. He was in the process of rereading him."[79]

Just as Deleuze adhered closely to Spinoza in his idea of temporality or eternity proper to the *conatus* and eluding *chronos*, Foucault preferred just as strongly the practice of discontinuities and radical rents in the fabric of time. Here, Deleuze favored an ontology of ever-increasing power, whereas Foucault was closer to Kantian criticism. In his 1985–1986 seminar, Deleuze remarked, "there is a neo-Kantianism peculiar to Foucault."[80] During what he called his "little promenade" through Kant, Deleuze paid vibrant tribute to Kant's insight, which he thought extraordinary.[81] According to Deleuze, Foucault found the Kantian gap in his manner of distinguishing between seeing and speaking, which were so different in nature that one could not be reduced to the other. If this gap could not be filled, how could knowledge exist? What Deleuze saw in this Kantian question was an analogy between Kant's situation of being caught between understanding and intuition and Foucault's grappling with the two heterogeneous dimensions of "visible" and "utterable."

Reversing their usual roles, while Deleuzean vitalism—considered dangerous—has often been contrasted with Foucault's neo-Kantianism and credited with being more respectful of established limits, Deleuze called Foucault's positions dangerous on several occasions. He explained what he meant. "Dangerous, yes, because there's violence in Foucault. An intense violence that he mastered, controlled, and turned into courage. He trembled with violence at some demonstrations. He saw what was intolerable. . . . And his style, at least up to the last books that achieved a kind of serenity, is like a lash, it's a whip twisting and relaxing."[82] Deleuze agreed with Paul Veyne that Foucault was a warrior ready to transform the history of thought into a war machine, in a polemilogical approach fascinated by death. Deleuze, for his part, was more on the side of cunning, of ancient Greek intelligence, of the *Metis*, of laughter and a devastating sense of humor.

THE PLAY OF MIRRORS

The philosopher Judith Revel observed the game of mirrors between two philosophers, each of whom went his own way while touching on very similar themes at several moments in their exchanges, a relationship very strong but always oblique. Both had a close relationship to history but each from a different position. The more Kantian Foucault posed the question of the conditions of possibility; Deleuze was concerned with the conditions of reality. In 1968 and 1969, Foucault was delighted to discover the foundations for a politics of difference in Deleuze's work, which echoed his quest for the figure of the other and alterity that had led to his 1961 *History of Madness*. He felt comforted in his positions; Deleuze allowed him to define a way out of structuralism that he would later disown but that he was still ardently defending in 1967. Both philosophers were fascinated by schizophrenia as a way of escaping binary structural codification. "The schizophrenic experience appeared to create a space for narratives that were also manuals for breaking down the code."[83]

In his lectures at the Collège de France in the early 1970s, Foucault developed the idea of the medicalization of society, of the psychiatrization of the social realm, and of the institutionalization of the uses of power, which needed to be countered by anti-institutional uses of knowledge. This position was not far removed from the arguments put forward by Deleuze and Guattari in *Anti-Oedipus* or from the use of institutional psychotherapy at La Borde.[84] Yet what appeared to be a common perspective was not one, in fact, because the horizon of Foucault's enquiry at the time was concentrated on the question of power, whereas Deleuze and Guattari were interested in the processes of subjectivization: group-subjects and collective subjects of enunciation. "Then Foucault turned his attention to subjectivization, which was the case in *Discipline and Punish*, and we thought that they would meet but they didn't."[85]

Judith Revel, who has studied the echoes between the thought of the two philosophers, vouches for the effects of their falling out in the late

1970s when Foucault got involved in ethical issues: "When you look at in-stances from 1977–1978 onward, there are no more references to each other. There's a real silence."[86] On the other hand, regarding the frequent use of spatial metaphors, Foucault and Deleuze, like most of their genera-tion of intellectuals, were very close, which translated a sort of determina-tion on their part to leave Hegelianism and the subjacent philosophy of history behind via spatiality and the logical patterns that it suggested: that of the plane of immanence for Deleuze and Guattari, with its strata and smooth spaces, holes and lines of flight, which enabled a cartography of phenomena. Foucault somewhat similarly defined the general history that he advocated as the possible deployment of a "space of dispersion."[87] As Deleuze emphasized, underlying Foucault's use of the terms genealogy and archeology lies a geology, with its sheets, landslides, and discordances. In fact, Deleuze defined Foucault as a "new cartographer." Of course, De-leuze and Foucault positioned themselves very differently with respect to history, as Deleuze said quite clearly in 1988: "We, Félix and I, always fan-cied a universal history, which he [Foucault] hated."[88]

Two Philosophies of the Event

Foucault and Deleuze both broke free from the philosophy of history in the sense of Hegelian-Marxist teleology to make way for a philosophy of the event. Both were tireless in their different ways as far as their relation to history, historians, and the archive was concerned, in pursuing the sudden appearance of something new, the momentary flashes that upset habits and ready-made thoughts. These moments of crystallization, which were so essential to understanding what was at stake in both social history and the history of thought, were revealed in periods of crisis and change, some-thing that Deleuze himself said when he discussing Foucault's work, begin-ning with its shifts and passages, which reveal moments of crisis whose traversing elucidated the tensions borne by thought between its virtual and actual states. In his attentiveness to the new, Foucault belonged to the French epistemological school of Bachelard and Canguilhem and to Nietz-schean genealogy. Starting from this tradition, he advocates a discon-tinuist approach to time, favoring the radical breaks that he called *épistémè* for a while, although he abandoned the term after *The Order of Things*.[89]

Following Nietzsche, Foucault replaced the quest for temporal origins and causalities with a critical positivism seeking to identify discontinuities by describing their material potentialities. Second, he aimed to identify the singularity of events beyond their acknowledged finality. Finally, eventualization made it possible to make the figure of the conscious subject as well as its illusion of mastering time less important: "Effective history brings out the most unique characteristics and most acute manifestations of events."[90] Foucault contrasted the three Platonic modalities of history with his own deconstructive use of historical myths. History as recognition was replaced by the parodic use of reality, history as continuity by a destructive use of identity, and history as knowledge by a destructive use of truths. From this perspective, history as a total synthesis was seen as a trap, because, according to Foucault, "a possible task remains one of calling into question everything pertaining to time, everything that has taken shape within it, everything that resides within its mobile element, so as to make visible that rent, devoid of chronology and history from which time issues."[91]

Deleuze and Guattari's understanding of the event emphasizes the way it appears suddenly as something new, as a beginning, as its own origin. In *Dialogues*, Deleuze speaks about a "surface flash."[92] In *What Is Philosophy?* Deleuze and Guattari use Péguy's *Clio* to explain that there are two ways of thinking about the event—by recording its effectuation in history and its conditioning or by returning to it, situating oneself within it and passing through all of its components and singularities. In 1980, *A Thousand Plateaus* announced the importance of evenemential scansions, as each of the thirteen plateaus has an inaugural date: "History will never be rid of dates. It is perhaps economy or financial analysis which better demonstrate the presence of the instantaneity of these derisory acts in a total process."[93]

This way of thinking about events was not a form of presentism. On the contrary, philosophy as the creation of concepts must break with its own period. It is fundamentally untimely and inactual according to the Nietzschean conception that Foucault shared. "Act against time, therefore upon time, and hope thereby to plant the seeds of a time to come."[94] Deleuze differentiated history from becoming. The creation of something new was always inactual and constituted a becoming, which certainly needed history and situations in order not to remain completely undetermined, but they elude it at the same time. Becoming breaks out of time and is never reduced to it.

This was the case for May '68, an event that Deleuze, Guattari, and Foucault all experienced intensely. For all three, viewing it only as an historical moment when France was mired in social conflict would be to overlook its essential creativity. It defied the traditional approach of understanding history and even created its crisis. Deleuze and Guattari agreed with this position, since for them, history could not explain what happens. Time creates a crisis in causality beneath which lies a law of pure chance, rendering it ontologically secondary but negating it. In *The Logic of Sense*, Deleuze challenges two approaches to the event: the essentialist Platonic perspective that subsumes the plurality of events under a single pure Event and the circumstantialist approach that reduces the event to a witnessed accident. He insists on the plurality of events as "jets of singularity"[95] and emphasizes that the event itself raises questions: "The event is problematic and problematizing in its own right."[96] In *The Fold*, Deleuze repeats Whitehead's question: "What is an event?" In his view, the event manifests itself as a vibration resounding with infinite harmonics in a vast series, like the rising of something new that is at once public and private, potential and actual, and marked by intensities.

Under these conditions, is it possible to develop a philosophy of the event and bind it within discourse? The event exceeds its discursive expression. Foucault, after *The Archeology of Knowledge*, veered toward a genealogical program that, in *The Order of Things*, his inaugural lecture at the Collège de France, overvalues the discursive level. He laid out a program for calling life, crime, and madness into question by examining of the conditions of the validity of knowledge. It was a matter of restoring "to discourse its character as an event"[97] following relations of discontinuity: "Discourses must be treated as discontinuous practices."[98] In this respect, Foucault presented himself as a contented positivist from *The Archaeology of Knowledge* (1969) onward, concerned with investigating the enunciative foundation for itself, in its positive, actual existence.

Deleuze expresses this excess with respect to the articulation of the event by insisting on its singularity, referring to Duns Scotus and his concept of *haecceity* to define its individuality. Two essential characteristics follow. First, the event is defined by the simultaneous coexistence of two heterogeneous dimensions in a time where future and past continually coincide and overlap while remaining distinct and indiscernible. Second, the event is what happened, so that its emerging dimension is not yet separated from the past, an intensity that comes and is distinguished simply from other intensities. The ideal event, as Deleuze defines it in *The Logic of Sense*, is therefore a singularity or a collection of singularities.

To think the event, Deleuze and Guattari believe that it must follow two distinct temporal modes. First, there is its coming into being within a state of affairs, in present circumstances where it partakes of a particular timeframe called *Chronos*, by virtue of which it fixes things and people to some degree. But at the same time, the event cannot be reduced to its coming into effect, thus the need to envisage a second temporal dimension that Deleuze and Guattari call the time of *Aiōn*, a paradoxical eternity where something incorporeal and ineffectuable exceeds and opens onto the indefinite time of the event, a "floating line that knows only speeds and continually divides that which transpires into an already-there that is at the same time not-yet-here, a simultaneous too-late and too-early, a something that is both going to happen and has just happened."[99]

For Deleuze and Guattari, this insistence on the Event refers to the sphere of action according to the teachings of Spinoza's practical philosophy but also to those of the Stoics.[100] A Stoic path that, in an *élan vital*, consists in being worthy of what happens, of supporting and valuing every glimmer that might be contained in what happens: an event, a speed, a becoming. An *Eventum tantum* can be imperceptible yet change everything:

> Making an event however small is the most delicate thing in the world: the opposite of making a drama or a story. Loving those who are like this: when they enter a room they are not persona, characters, or subjects but an atmospheric variation, a change of hue, an imperceptible molecule, a discrete population, a fog, or a cloud of droplets. Everything has really changed. Great events, too, are made in this way: battle, revolution, life and death. . . . True Entities are events.[101]

DELEUZE, READER OF FOUCAULT

Throughout his career, Deleuze paid very close attention to Foucault's publications and regularly reviewed them. Notably, he wrote two studies in 1970 and in 1975, one on *The Archaeology of Knowledge* and the other on *Discipline and Punish*.[102] And more importantly, in the 1985–1986 academic year, he devoted his entire course to Foucault, publishing *Foucault* the following summer.

That he devoted himself to Foucault's writings immediately after Foucault's death showed the strength of their relationship and Deleuze's struggle to mourn someone who was more than a friend. When asked why he wrote a book on Foucault, Deleuze's answer was quite clear: "It marks an inner need of mine, my admiration for him, how I was moved by his death, and his unfinished work."[103] Deleuze's way of mourning Foucault was to elucidate the particular logic of his thought by seeking its coherence through the crises, leaps, and incessant displacements that it traversed. Following Martial Guéroult's views, Deleuze agreed that each text formed an integral part of the complete works of an author and none could be examined without that context. Everything needed to be conveyed and its logic and movement reconstructed. "A thought's logic is like a wind blowing us on, a series of gusts and jolts. You think you've gotten to port, but then find yourself thrown back out onto the open sea, as Leibniz put it. That's particularly true in Foucault's case."[104] Deleuze therefore retraced Foucault's evolution in his writing, finding both a profound unity and fundamental shifts. All of Foucault's work, according to Deleuze, is articulated around the distinction between seeing and speaking. He is fundamentally dualistic on this matter, deploying two mutually irreducible dimensions: "But for him, the primacy of statements will never impede the historical irreducibility of the visible—indeed, quite the contrary."[105]

Deleuze identified important evolutions in Foucault's work. Until the publication of *The Archeology of Knowledge* in 1969, the major question was that of knowledge. Then, with *Discipline and Punish* and *The Will to Knowledge*, Foucault started working on a new dimension—power. Deleuze wanted to understand what had led him to change from one register to another, suggesting that Foucault's problem was that of the double, and "the utterance is the double of something which is identical to it."[106] Knowledge being the integration of power relations, he therefore played from a double score, that of relations of force, composing power, and that of relations of forms, composing knowledge. Specific singularities arise therefore from an endogenous relationship between knowledge and power.

But this mirroring between knowledge and power leads to a dead end and requires a third axis to recreate a dynamics. Deleuze thought that this third axis was already present, though to a lesser degree, and that it became much more important in Foucault's later work and particularly in his last two books, with the study of modes of subjectification, mistakenly read as the return of the subject. This dimension of subjectification "was present in Foucault, but not as such, it was intermingled with knowledge and power."[107] The question was therefore one of finding out how power and knowledge attempt to take over this third axis of subjectification in order to reappropriate it. Deleuze locates the dynamic in Foucault's thought here, for "the more power tries to conquer subjectification, the more new modes of subjectification form."[108]

Deleuze often read the work of other philosophers through the prism of his own positions and preoccupations. Had he fathered another Deleuzean child in his *Foucault*? This seems to be the opinion of Potte-Bonneville, who sees Deleuze's text as the best introduction to Foucault, encouraging us to read and study his work further. But he also suspects it of hiding aspects of Foucault's thought. "Thus the question of history disappears completely, which is quite strange when discussing Foucault."[109]

When the Foucault specialist Frédéric Gros published a study of Deleuze's reading, he spoke of it as a "metaphysical fiction,"[110] for he did not recognize the Foucault that he knew at all, though he recalls that for Deleuze, understanding Foucault was not a question of providing a scholarly commentary of his work: "For Deleuze, understanding an author, in a way, means discovering the founding principles, laying bare the inherent metaphysics of their thought."[111] It would also mean being able to create an imaginary Foucault, to dream up a metaphysical double. Frédéric Gros does, of course, acknowledge the extraordinary coherence that Deleuze's reading of Foucault's work elucidates: "reading Foucault, Deleuze recognizes how he was marked by his reading of Bergson."[112] Since writing his review in 1995, Frédéric Gros has been able to measure the accuracy of some of the main lines of Deleuze's reading:

> Deleuze's book is a true philosophical work. Everything he says about the relationship between utterances and visibilities shows that he understood something very important, which I later heard in Foucault's last lectures at the Collège de France, that Deleuze could not have had. It was the idea that he was constructing a direct ethics by making correspondences between visible acts and *logoï*, utterances. It is amazing to see how Deleuze, who couldn't have had any knowledge of the Collège de France lectures, was so accurate in his interpretation.[113]

As Robert Maggiori wrote when Deleuze's *Foucault* came out, he does not "explain Foucault, because Foucault explains himself very well in his books, nor does he provide a commentary, of which there are already plenty. Like a miner who respects the rock that resists his pick but knows how to find the treasure in its veins, Deleuze mines Foucault's writings to extract the most productive elements of his thought."[114]

DEATH

The rumor began circulating in Paris during 1984. Foucault was very ill and nobody knew what was wrong with him, although a few people heard that he had been hospitalized. Deleuze was concerned for his friend, whom he had not seen since the late 1970s. "Two weeks before Foucault died, Deleuze called me. He was very worried and wondered if I had any news. 'Do you know what is going on? What has he got?' I didn't know anything except that he was in the hospital. Then Deleuze said, 'Maybe it's nothing. Foucault will leave the hospital and come and tell us that everything is all right.'"[115] According to Didier Eribon, one of Foucault's most heartfelt wishes, knowing that he would not live long, was to reconcile with Deleuze. They never saw each other again. The fact that Daniel Defert asked Deleuze to speak at Foucault's funeral was a sign of how much both men wanted to smooth over their differences, even beyond the separation of death.

Deleuze hated conferences but made an exception for his friend, participating in the international colloquium organized in January 1988 in homage to Foucault. His paper was entitled "What Is a Dispositive?"[116] In his seminar on Foucault, Deleuze referred to Foucault's death in the context of the value he gave to impersonal pronouns and his critique of linguistic personology. In *The Space of Literature*, Blanchot writes of death as an event, coming from beyond the body. "One dies . . ." Foucault reinterpreted this theme and "died according to his interpretation."[117] "Foucault was telling us something that concerned him directly,"[118] that death is not the indivisible, final limit defined by doctors and moralists. One is never done with death: "Foucault lived death like Bichat. That's how he died. He died by taking his place within the 'One dies' and in the manner of 'partial deaths.'"[119]

Beyond their differences and disputes, after the death of both men, can we reasonably speak about a "Foucault-Deleuzeanism"? It would be pointless to coin a term that might miss the singularity of both philosophers, eliminating their disagreements and producing some *faux-semblant* in the name of some ecumenical sterility. Rather, we will describe a "disjunctive synthesis" similar to the relationship between Deleuze and Guattari.

In addition to their shared philosophical heritage, they were also close in the way that they used literature, approaching it in a clinical fashion that set them apart from professional philosophers, whose work was most often limited to academic texts. In *The Logic of Sense*, Artaud's scream deconstructs Lewis Carroll's ingenious surface connections, and Deleuze finds Artaud at the very center of Foucault's inquiries. "The unthought as the double of thought, and at the very end of *The Order of Things*, Foucault reinterprets the theme of the double that he shares with Artaud, Heidegger, and Blanchot."[120] Here Foucault identifies an experience similar to Artaud's, who had reached within thought an element that could not be thought and that becomes a "vital impotence" for the writer.[121]

The theme of the double appears in one of Foucault's first books, written about Raymond Roussel, another writer.[122] On the distortion between seeing and saying, Foucault again finds his inspiration in literature. Roussel formulates the relationship to language, coupling it to the will to push words to their limits, a tendency common to both Foucault and Deleuze. "Break things open, break words open."[123] One of Roussel's writerly strategies was to construct two sentences around a tiny difference that would fundamentally change the overall meaning.[124] For both Foucault and Deleuze, literature is neither an illustration nor a curiosity. It is valuable as an experiment, an act of creation—and since, for Deleuze, philosophy consists in creating concepts, literature accompanies it in its creative work.

We can see in this relationship between Foucault and Deleuze more than shared foundations; Deleuze allowed Foucauldian thinking to develop. Deleuze's "Postscript on Control Societies," published in 1990, follows from Foucault's work.[125] Deleuze, like Foucault, felt implicated by current events and wanted to conceptualize change. Deleuze starts with the historicization proposed by Foucault, who had delineated a model of society founded on sovereignty, in which power reveals itself as the capacity to inflict death. In eighteenth- and nineteenth-century France, a disciplinary model came into being according to the schema of "the great confinement," which led to the generalization of closed universes where discipline affected every part of the social body. Numerous prisons, barracks, schools, and factories were built on the model of the Panopticon. The function of power was no longer to put people to death but to discipline their bodies, make them live, maximize their utility, and let them die.

Foucault had begun to perceive the emergence of a new model, one centered on biopower and the biopolitical control of populations and that seemed slightly out of step with disciplinary concepts. Deleuze began with Foucault's intuitions and expanded them. His 1990 article identified the advent of a new type of society, "societies of control," which emerged after World War II and ended with a general crisis of all forms of confinement: "It's simply a matter of nursing them through their death throes."[126] Deleuze's analysis, which he was already developing in his seminar on Foucault, was prophetic. In this management of life in all its shapes and forms, he rightly foresaw a whole new type of management, based on control and transformation of the legal subject. This legal subject is no longer limited to the person, as it was in the age of humanism, because it implied populations other than human, cereal crops as well as herds of cattle, sheep as well as poultry, and every other living being. In the age of control societies, the legal subject becomes the living, "the living within man."[127]

Imprisonment is no longer needed, "because we know that everybody will be on the highway at a given hour. Probability calculations are much better than prisons."[128] From the 1980s on, Deleuze notes the breakdown of the entire fabric of enclosure, particularly that of factories that were affected by temporary work, by working at home, and flextime. At school, there was less discipline but far more control: "Individuals become 'dividuals,' and masses become samples, data, markets, or 'banks.'"[129] These various transformations destroy the former rigidity of the discipline to pave the way for the microchips and mobile phones that make it possible to constantly control each person, in an open space where outside and inside are no longer useful categories. "The key thing is that we are at the beginning of something new."[130] Fresh forms of subjectification and resistance to control needed new directions.

18

An Alternative to Psychiatry?

Antipsychiatry and La Borde have often been presented as if they were interchangeable—as if the Loir-et-Cher clinic exemplified the French version of the movement. However, according to Jean Oury, La Borde's director, institutional psychotherapy and antipsychiatry are incompatible. At La Borde, psychiatry was practiced and the responsibility for everything that it entailed was accepted. "At about that same period, he [Félix] was fascinated by the antipsychiatrists. That's how La Borde and antipsychiatry became confused in the minds of people who didn't really know anything about it. It always infuriates me."[1] Oury viewed the antipsychiatrists as "very dangerous aesthetes. I liked Basaglia for his impetuous personality, but I didn't like his policies. His patients left in the morning and came back at night and the hospital was in between. Patients literally disappeared. That may be what antipsychiatry is in its concrete form: the hospital does away with its patients, they disappear."[2]

ANTIPSYCHIATRY

Antipsychiatry came into being in Italy when, in 1961, Franco Basaglia decided to abandon the principle of locking up patients with mental disorders, open all hospital departments, and organize general meetings to which everyone could come. Once people adjusted to the new policies, the psychiatrists in his hospital supported him and held more than fifty meetings a week. There were several spectacular recoveries among hospital patients who had been vegetating for close to two decades. Some even improved so much in terms of their mental health that they could go home. After these initial successes, Basaglia decided to look at experimental psychiatric projects elsewhere in Europe. In 1965, he went to La Borde with Giovanni Jervis, another representative of Italian antipsychiatry, but after the visit Basaglia remained critical of institutional psychotherapeutic practices, which he found overly reformist, integrationist, and conformist. At the time, his declared goal was to destroy the institution; the movement that he later created, Psichiatria Democratica, called for the definitive closure of psychiatric hospitals.

In the climate of political radicalization of the 1960s in Italy, the antipsychiatric movement was a force to be reckoned with. Guattari did not agree with Basaglia's more extreme positions. By 1970, he wondered if things weren't "spiraling out of control" and was concerned by the "desperate" character of the enterprise.[3] Guattari also criticized what he considered to be some irresponsible practices, such as refusing to administer drugs on the pretext that they merely covered up a doctor's inability to establish a real relationship with the patient. Eventually, he even wondered whether, despite its good intentions, antipsychiatry might not lead to denying madmen their right to madness. Basaglia's negation of the institution seen this way was a denial in the Freudian sense of the specificity of mental illness.

Antipsychiatry was also well rooted in Britain, with R. D. Laing and David Cooper,[4] whom Guattari met in 1967 on the occasion of two "Study Days on Child Psychosis," organized by the psychoanalyst Maud Mannoni and also attended by Lacan; the symposium led to two issues of *Recherches* (*Research*).[5] Here again, Guattari expressed his reticence about antipsychiatric practices, which he thought were locked into the Oedipal schema that Deleuze and he had wanted to get beyond. Shortly thereafter, he began writing his radical critique of the Anglo-Saxon experiment in antipsychiatry.[6]

The first British experiment in antipsychiatry began with the community that took shape around R. D. Laing at Kingsley Hall in East London in 1965. In this former stronghold of the English labor movement, Laing tried to break down the institutional barriers between those doing the caring and those being cared for. Psychiatrists, nurses, and patients abolished hierarchical relationships and differences in status. Among the group of psychiatrists alongside Laing, David Cooper and Maxwell Jones were the main vital driving forces at Kingsley Hall. The surrounding community was seriously opposed to the experiment and laid siege to the "liberated territory." To make his case, Guattari referred to the case of Mary Barnes, the famous Kingsley Hall resident who wrote a book with her psychiatrist, Joseph Becke, about her experiences. Guattari found that the narrative exposed "the hidden side of British antipsychiatry,"[7] which he saw as a mixture of dogmatic neobehaviorism, familialism, and puritanism in its most traditional form. Mary Barnes, a nurse by profession, took a schizophrenic "trip" to the brink of death. Having barricaded herself into familialism, she denied the surrounding social reality. What did antipsychiatry achieve? It pushed the familialist current to an extreme, instead of framing it in a patient-psychiatrist relationship, it was played out in the collective; this familial emphasis exacerbated all the effects. For Guattari, the cure led in the wrong direction. What Mary Barnes needed wasn't more family: she needed more society.

In Germany, antipsychiatry also found supporters in the Socialist Patients' Collective (SPK) created by Dr. Huber at the University of Heidelberg clinic. Groups of about forty patients and their doctor met for therapy, denouncing the psychiatric institution as an instrument of oppression. The university administration decided to eliminate the protest movement and, in July 1971, using as their excuse the public disorder caused by the patients walking around in the town and its surroundings, as well as several exchanges of gunfire, three hundred policemen armed with machine guns invaded the SPK premises and carried out searches, with helicopters hovering overhead. Doctors and patients were arrested and the SPK forced to disband. Dr. Huber and his wife were imprisoned for several years, and their attorneys were intimidated into dropping their defense.

Guattari found the political dimension of the SPK struggle attractive, but he was not interested in defending their psychiatric practices:

> Something utterly new has happened that has created a way out of ideology, making way for true political struggle. That's what's important about the SPK militants, and not whether they are mixing up social and individual alienation or whether their therapeutic methods are questionable. . . . Like March 22 at Nanterre, the SPK rallied forces for a real fight—and the forces of repression were ready, they saw things for what they were![8]

Guattari and Deleuze went to Heidelberg for the trial in 1972. Pierre Blanchaud, one of Deleuze's students from Vincennes, was in the square facing the university, having come to Heidelberg when he was nineteen to escape from his studies in classics and enjoy the aftermath of 1968. On that particular day he thought he was seeing a ghost: "I could see Deleuze and Guattari right there in front of me! So I shouted, "Deleuze, what on earth

are you doing here?" He replied, "Chance!"[9] This was a joke, obviously, because the militant goal was important enough to bring Deleuze, who hated
traveling, from Paris. In reality, Deleuze and Guattari, along with a group
of Dutch, Italian, and French psychiatrists, were making a show of solidarity with the SPK. On a whim, Pierre Blanchaud followed them to the campus, where a group of students from the far left were calling for mobilization against repression. Pierre Blanchaud admitted to Deleuze that he
was having some financial problems—he was living in near poverty in
Heidelberg.

> Deleuze asked me, "Do I need to leave you some money, then?" And
> he left me four hundred francs, which was a lot at the time. I lived on it
> for two weeks. He said to me, "You can give it back to me when you are
> rich." Many years later, when I got a teaching assistant's job in Ger-
> many in 1983, I wrote him and offered to reimburse him, but he said,
> "No, listen, it's a souvenir of my travels, seeing as I don't travel very
> often."[10]

The "antipsychiatric moment" found supporters in Italy, England, and
Germany but not in France. This exception is certainly due to French progress in the psychiatric sector, the introduction of theories from institutional psychiatry, and clinics such as La Borde. Several groups in France
were advocating antipsychiatry, such as the Asylums Information Group
(GIA), which wanted to unite psychiatric patients and their families against
the psychiatric apparatus: "In our view there is no good, Left-wing psychiatry, unlike bourgeois psychiatry. . . . There are only different degrees of
repressing, marginalizing, stupefying, privatizing and medicalizing madness."[11] Many other small groups arose during that period, such as "Notebooks for Madness," "Guard Rails," "The Margin," "Solongaswe'rehealthy,"
"Breach," "Vouvray," "Psychiatry let loose in Saint-Dizier," or "Itch,"[12] but
they all remained marginal.

At the beginning of the 1970s while traveling in the United States, Guattari met Mony Elkaïm, a Moroccan-born psychiatrist who had acquired an
international reputation for his work in noninstitutional family therapy.
Elkaïm had organized open rehabilitation centers in the South Bronx, one
of the most depressed neighborhoods of New York City. In particular, he
worked with the United Bronx Parents, an association founded in 1966 by
the parents of Puerto Rican school children who were protesting discrimi-

nation. In the same neighborhood, revolutionary militants decided to occupy a floor of the Lincoln Hospital to begin what they called the Lincoln Detox Program for drug addicts. Rather than being given doses of methadone, they received acupuncture and were sent to attend political consciousness–raising seminars. The Lincoln Detox Program believed that the authorities were distributing methadone intentionally to quash revolutionary zeal. The programs initially aroused the suspicion of official institutions, but they were ultimately accepted and helped financially.

Mony Elkaïm was interested in the relationship between mental-health issues and social problems and was working in this area in the United States when he first met Guattari: "I met him at the home of some friends who were living in Manhattan. He was with Arlette at the time and we got along extremely well. I immediately invited him to stay in my apartment in the Bronx State Hospital and I moved elsewhere."[13] Lying on a table in the apartment was an article by Mony Elkaïm, "Antipsychiatry: For an Epistemological Revision," in which Elkaïm criticized the simplistic viewpoint where family and society were by default the cause of mental illness. "Félix said to me, 'You know, our views are quite similar even though we come from very different backgrounds.' At which point he went straight away to the French bookshop in Manhattan, bought *Anti-Oedipus*, and gave it to me."[14] Both men discovered that they saw psychiatric issues as mainly political; their shared perspective ultimately led them on an international adventure.

At the time, Mony Elkaïm was working to make family therapy less strictly familialist by putting it in relation with the social setting, especially in New York, where he was liaising with revolutionary groups such as the Black Panthers and the Young Lords. He was in charge of a group of professional psychiatrists, psychologists, and social workers, but he also recruited people off the street by chance and trained them on the job, thanks to federal funding. Guattari was won over by his new friend and his pioneering work and came back to New York several times to discuss their experiences and visit Manhattan jazz clubs.

THE ALTERNATIVE TO PSYCHIATRY NETWORK

Before going back to Europe in 1974 and 1975, Mony Elkaïm organized a major conference in the Bronx on the theme of "Training Mental Health Workers in Urban Ghettos," with the intention of bringing together different schools of psychiatry. Delegations from New York, Philadelphia, Chicago, and several other major cities in the United States, along with Guattari, Robert Castel, and Giovanni Jervis, attended the conference, which was all the more successful because Mony Elkaïm had gotten funding to cover entry fees and food, and many people from the Bronx came out for a free meal. There was a real party atmosphere.

In 1975, Mony Elkaïm was practicing psychiatry in a poor neighborhood of Brussels when he and Guattari decided to bring alternative-psychiatry projects and dissident psychiatric schools together into an international network. At the time, Mony Elkaïm had an important job working in family therapy. Guattari welcomed his systemic views, which had the merit of seeing therapy in terms of groups rather than desocialized individuals. In Brussels in January, they agreed to form the Alternative to Psychiatry Network. By committing to the network, Guattari wanted to go beyond institutional psychiatry. "With this international network, we've turned the page. We no longer aim to 'reach out . . .'! We want things to come from the interested parties themselves."[15]

The South Bronx project was the model in this area. For Guattari and Elkaïm, it was also a matter of using the network to help the innovators, struggling against repression and conformism, to emerge from their isolation. This was the case especially in northern Italy, the cradle of antipsychiatry, where, in 1969, Giovanni Jervis was about to abandon the experimental project he had begun in Reggio Emilia because of insurmountable political obstacles. The SPK had been ousted by force in 1971. In England, David Cooper had given up and R. D. Laing had become fascinated by India.

Hope was rekindled, however, in Spain at the end of the Franco era. In September 1975, interns from Spanish psychiatric hospitals invited the Alternative to Psychiatry Network to a meeting in Santiago de Compostela to take part in their endeavors and help them resist repression. The meeting was organized in response to a move by the Spanish government to fire twelve interns, two head doctors, and an administrative director who had been found guilty of being involved in innovative reforms. In 1973, they had begun to renew structures in the Consco psychiatric hospital in Santiago de Compostela, where patients were being treated like convicts: "patients in chains, beaten at the slightest provocation, heaped together on beds of straw."[16]

In 1975, Mony Elkaïm managed to get Guattari, Castel, and Franco Basaglia to come, thanks to Castel's help, since Basaglia was reluctant, given his disagreements with Guattari. The initial title, "Alternative to Neighborhood Psychiatry," was quickly rejected as being too limited, and Basaglia's proposition, "Alternative to Psychiatry Network," was adopted.[17] Guattari became very involved in the network, which actively defended Basaglia and the German antipsychiatrists. "Félix was a fantastic militant, he was always ready to help me write a text or letters. He made himself incredibly available at that time and came regularly to Brussels to participate in our activities."[18]

After the inaugural meeting in Brussels, the network organized several other meetings: in Paris (March 1976); Trieste (September 1977); Cuernavaca, Mexico (September 1978); and San Francisco (September 1980). The purpose of these gatherings was to hear about what others were doing elsewhere rather than to create any new form of orthodoxy. In everything he did in the network, Guattari insisted on being open-minded, as there was no unifying scientific authority in a field where efficient practices were a matter of micropolitics. Moreover, their singularity resulted not only from the scale of analysis in small groups but also implied permanent dialogue and an ongoing process of development in relation with the macrosocial scale. No group was to be isolated and cut off from the rest of society in the name of some alternative theory.

The international meetings combined the serious nature of the talks with the more comical aspects of a noninstitutional network whose leaders were often unconventional, like David Cooper, for example, whose book *Psychiatry and Antipsychiatry* played an important role in Mony Elkaïm's intellectual development. Elkaïm also enjoyed the company of Franco Basaglia, with whom he became close friends. "Franco was an exquisitely delicate man. Once when he was passing through Brussels, he stopped by to give me a flower before going off to catch his next plane. Sometimes when I stayed over at his place in Venice or Trieste, he would bring me breakfast in bed and tell me what he had dreamed about the night before."[19]

One of the network's last international meetings took place in San Francisco, a month after Basaglia's death in September 1980. One idea of the meeting was that the Patients Against Psychiatric Assault group would invite the guest speakers to stay at their homes. Elkaïm and Guattari were put in the same room, which turned out to be crawling with cockroaches. "With all those cockroaches, there was no way I could sleep! I stayed up all night perched on a chair!"[20] At dawn, Elkaïm rushed out to find a hotel, over Guattari's protests, since he was afraid of vexing their hosts. During the plenary session, when Elkaïm introduced Guattari, the Italian delegation stood up to leave the hall in protest. Elkaïm lost his temper and asked them for an explanation. Their representatives claimed that someone who gave electroshock treatments (which were indeed used at La Borde) should not be allowed to speak. Elkaïm replied that since Félix was not a doctor, they were fantasizing, at which point they returned to their seats.

ACCUSATIONS OF PEDOPHILIA

The network was less active after 1980 and had only a few more meetings, such as the one in 1983 in Yugoslavia, where Claude Sigala described his experiences caring for problematic children in France, outside of any institutional framework. He had personally borne the brunt of the repression: he had been sentenced to prison in late 1982. After having earned a special diploma in education and studying applied psychology, Sigala worked in institutions for twelve years but found the practices unsatisfying, their compartmentalization upsetting, and the hierarchy frustrating. After meeting Guattari, Fernand Deligny, Roger Gentis, and Maud Mannoni, he decided to start working on alternative approaches.

At the end of 1976, Fernand Deligny and Maud Mannoni sent him two children, and he created Le Coral at Aimargues in southern France near Nîmes. The association consisted of a community of adults and children who cared for children with difficulties in an open setting in which they created a "living place" where the children would be reintegrated, develop their potential, and avoid being shunted off to a psychiatric asylum. The association joined the Alternative to Psychiatry Network, and, in 1982, Sigala organized the first forum of "living places" in Nîmes. The idea caught on, and several "living places" were created in the southeast for psychotic, autistic, and handicapped children. The national health insurance administration recognized the centers, which took their inspiration from Fernand Deligny's work with children but were more overtly political.

In these communities of adults and children, the delicate problem of acceptable relationships and establishing limits came up. Claude Sigala "had been tempted to promote corporeal relations between educators and children as a possible means of forming relationships."[21] This bordered on the taboo subject of pedophilia. Guattari dissuaded Sigala from promoting physical relations, which were likely to compromise and kill the association, which had in fact attracted a number of educators who turned out to be pedophiles. In March 1982, the association was prosecuted, following an accusation made by a very disturbed child who had been placed at Le Coral by the local Social Services department in Le Gard. The boy had fueled rumors in town, because he had run away and, the day after being accused both of raping a little girl from Aigues-Vives and of attempted arson in the local scrubland, he denounced Sigala for raping him. At the end of the year, Sigala was arrested and prosecuted for having hushed up pedophilic practices at the clinic. Le Coral was then accused of being linked to an international network of pedophiles that sold pornographic photographs. None of this remained in the file for the case, but the judge kept Claude Sigala in prison. Segala wrote to Guattari, "You *urgently* need to go and see the file! I am beginning (!) to have had enough. There is NO justification for my imprisonment."[22]

In addition to his friend Guattari, Claude Sigala also had the support of Edgar Morin, Bruno Frappat, the satirical weekly *Le Canard Enchaîné*, and others. "You have to get me out of the can, Félix, by any means. I'm going Crazy and I'm Scared of all this injustice and underhanded crap. You know how much I love Le Coral and the work I've started there. . . . My daughters are being totally messed up by this. . . . My wife is in a panic: there's the real assault."[23] Claude Sigala made his position on pedophilia clear in a text he wrote to Félix Guattari from prison.

> What interests me in sexual minorities is not perversion. . . . I realized right away that pedophiles were attracted to Le Coral not especially because we took in children but because our libertarian, self-managing structure let minors play an important role. We've always been able to set limits concerning respect of the Other. . . . Seeing the pedophile as an individual who stalks a child for sex only is reductive and doesn't have much to substantiate it except in very rare cases. I'm not defending perverts of that sort in any way whatsoever. What I think is more widespread is to see people who love children and give them their freedom. . . . A child needs Love. We don't need to repeat that loving someone doesn't mean possessing them, it means making them happy . . . [24]

Ultimately, Claude Sigala was cleared of the accusations and was able to continue his work at Le Coral, where he organized a second forum in May 1992: the psychiatrist Roger Gentis, Guattari, Maud Mannoni, Edgar Morin, the psychoanalyst Tony Lainé, and the philosopher Cornelius Castoriadis all participated. In the meantime, he published a book for which Guattari wrote the preface.[25] He felt that he and Guattari had a lot in common; twenty days before Guattari died, on August 9, 1992, he suggested they write a book together. "I would like *our* practical and theoretical ideas to be understood by the majority. You know that your books reach a tiny fraction of intellectuals and students. I suggest that we exchange a series of letters that we can then publish in paperback edition."[26]

THE ATTACK ON GOURGAS

Another affair connected to the Alternative to Psychiatry Network occurred in 1977 at Guattari's property at Gourgas, in the Gard region, and affected him deeply. He had bought the large country house at the foot of the Cévennes Mountains near Monoblet in 1967 and let Fernand Deligny use it for a time. The farmhouse was a summer residence for some La Borde people and for CERFI leaders, but more importantly it was a meeting place for the various groups in the protest movement and all sorts of marginal organizations. In 1977, Guattari's friend Louis Ohrant, a militant worker from way back, was living at Gourgas with his wife and three children and managing the property. The antipsychiatric community from the village of Routier in Aude, along with several other communities of the same sort established in the southeast, made it known to Louis Ohrant that they wanted to move to Gourgas. First a delegation came and asked him to vacate the property or at least to move into a small apartment, which Ohrant refused outright. Guattari, the owner of the property, took neither side, and in his "Letters from Afar" preferred an amicable solution. Since a friendly arrangement was obviously out of the question, the Routier community, supported by Parisian militants from the antipsychiatric group Marge, showed up at Gourgas and moved in. Since he did not own the property, Louis Ohrant could not enlist any legal assistance and was forced to leave. The new occupants allowed him to live with his family and two or three friends in a small two-room apartment.

INTERNATIONALIZING THE NETWORK

During the 1980s, the network expanded and took on a more international cast. In December 1986, the Latin-American Alternative to Psychiatry Network met for the third time in Buenos Aires. Guattari spoke about changing paradigms affecting not only broadly psychological practices but also procedures of subjectification in general linked to the revolutions in information, robotics, telecommunications, and genetic engineering. Guattari perceived a shift from a technical-scientific paradigm "to an ethical-aesthetic paradigm, implying moral responsibility, micropolitical engagement, and a creative attitude to each concrete case and each particular situation, which I would relate to the generic theme of resingularizing praxis."[27] Its major social effect would be to make job insecurity more widespread and to end guaranteed work even for civil servants in developed countries.

During this decade, the alternative trend in psychiatry lost two of its great figures when Franco Basaglia and David Cooper died. It did, however, manage to establish a strong and dynamic bastion in Trieste managed by Basaglia's successor, Franco Rotelli. The network began to consider situations in other regions, taking on new projects in Greece, Yugoslavia, Spain, and Latin America. It helped spread information and improve the success of interventions.

Greece was one of the most important new areas for alternative psychiatry. In 1987, psychiatrists from the Trieste team, led by Franco Rotelli, visited a hospital in Thessaloniki. Guattari took advantage of an international antipsychiatry meeting to pay a visit to the service, which had been totally renovated with the help of the Alternative to Psychiatry Network. Two years later, in 1989, a scandal broke out in the press. On Leros, one of the most beautiful islands in the Dodecanese, a psychiatric asylum held 1,200 patients locked up. "A concentration camp with no nursing staff, not even a psychiatrist. The broadcast images were horrifying. Naked bodies, skeletal faces rigid with fear and anxiety peering out from behind bars, and a fetid stench that seemed to permeate the screen."[28] Franco Rotelli decided to set up an international team—Italian, Dutch, Irish, and German—to investigate the situation in Leros. Each group included twelve people, and the team operated under the aegis of the European Economic Community. Guattari left Paris for Athens on October 8, 1989. The file of press cuttings that the journalist Eric Favereau gave him on the plane was truly staggering: patients shut in iron cages behind barbed-wire fences, 85 percent of the patients restrained or in straitjackets. Their treatments were described: blows, water jets to calm them down, and a "waste product of about sixty or seventy deaths a year. No patients discharged in thirty years!"

Form Piraeus, Guattari and his friends went by boat to Kos, stopped over at Kalymnos, and then disembarked from a private launch at Leros on October 9. They arrived at the hospital expecting the worst; in the end Guattari discovered a scandalous but unfortunately common situation. "I have to admit right away that it's no worse here than elsewhere. It is even about the same as most French asylums twenty-five years ago."[29] A visit through the patients' quarters clearly showed that the media had exaggerated and sensationalized the story. "The fact is that there are no longer any naked patients rolling in the mire. There were some, nobody is denying that, but there haven't been any for several months now."[30] One of the psychiatrists from Leros, Lucas Jannis, was a follower of Basaglia and held out great hopes for the arrival of the Italian mission to advance the rehabilitation of the hospital, which was running into considerable resistance.

On the other hand, as Franco Roselli had informed him, one scandal could hide another: Three miles from Athens, Daphni Hospital housed 1,900 people in conditions that were certainly worse than Leros. Guattari began tense negotiations for the group to be allowed to visit, which they did on October 11. They discovered an immense hospital factory with sixteen services divided among thirty-three wards. The doctor in charge, Dr. Savas Tsitouvides, led the visitors through the labyrinth and tried to hide the worst. But he had not reckoned on the vigilance of the team leader from Trieste, who had been working in Athens for a year.

> Chiara Strulti murmured to us, "Ask for Ward 11." Eric Favereau insisted, "And now Ward 11!" There was no turning back; we went to the ward. It was horrific! Ninety-five men, if that word could still be used to describe them—were going round in circles, screaming, some of them were completely naked, some of them were tied up. . . . It was indescribable how they were all piled in together. . . . To cheer me up, Chiara Strulti explained that in another ward they had untied the children who had been strapped up for the last four years![31]

Appraising the work of the Alternative to Psychiatry Network in 1990, Guattari was of the opinion that they had achieved only a few of the goals they had initially set in 1975. The network had not managed to influence national policies for psychiatry except in Italy. Considering the relative conservatism of the 1980s, those "winter years," however, it is exceptional that a network of this sort managed not merely to survive but to build a veritable fortress of resistance to certain practices, thanks to the Trieste team, whose influence spread to the rest of Italy, southern Europe, and Latin America.

In the early 1990s, Guattari saw that the time was right to revive the Alternative to Psychiatry Network, as several recent events seemed likely to ensure its success: the fall of the Berlin Wall in 1989, followed by the fall of other communist regimes, brutally posed the problem of the political use of psychiatry in totalitarian regimes. "It would be a good idea if the Alternative Network, or what's left of it, were present as an interlocutor."[32] Concerned about the essential problem of training, Guattari suggested that the hospital in Trieste, the movement's hub, become an "International Training Center,"[33] a space for professional training and especially for passing on information to nonspecialists, in a manner akin to the Trieste cooperatives.

Starting from the idea that training is not the way to reproduce something, Guattari rather considered training to be autopoeisis, similar to the way that Francisco Varela defined it, meaning that at every level those involved in mental health needed "maximum freedom."[34] For Guattari, the issue was not at all to resurrect the old myth of self-management, which ran the risk of autarky. Real training and relaunching the network necessarily meant linking theory and the experience of individual projects, drawing inspiration from theories of auto-organization.[35]

19

Deleuze at Vincennes

At the end of 1969—the year he met Guattari—Deleuze was offered a teaching position to replace Michel Serres in the philosophy department of the new experimental university at Vincennes that had opened in the fall of 1968. In Lyon, Deleuze had been on the fringes of the May '68 activism, but from 1970 on, he was deep in the heart of the "reactor."

VINCENNES: A RADICAL ENCLAVE

The microcosm at Vincennes was completely unlike traditional academic universities. It was a radical enclave, set in the middle of Vincennes Woods, next to a military firing range. The Ministry of Defense had ceded some land back to the city of Paris for a limited period for a new, experimental university, which was to be built at breakneck speed, so that it could open for the 1968–1969 academic year. The new university, Paris-VIII, was a sort of anti-Sorbonne where multidisciplinarity was the religion; at Paris-VIII, no one taught traditional courses to prepare students for the national examinations, preferring instead to work on developing students' research skills. Lectures were for the most part banned in favor of open group discussions held in small classrooms. Pedantic Sorbonne traditions had no place in this new and resolutely modern university, which used the most sophisticated contemporary technology and methods in the human sciences to transform the humanities subjects of old. University buildings were outfitted with marvelous equipment, making Vincennes a jewel in the crown of a tired Gaullist regime in need of a showcase. The lecture halls were carpeted, television monitors linked every classroom to a central control room, the interiors had been designed by Knoll, and the whole thing was set in the woods, protected from city noise, with only the occasional reverberation of distant gunfire, as army recruits went through their military training.

The most radical May 1968 protesters found refuge at Vincennes, where Maoists filled the halls. All the vital forces of the protests joined in that closed, protected space. Radical politics developed freely, well removed from society, in the middle of the forest, which surrounded the campus like a quarantine fence.

However, for all of its state-of-the-art amenities, Vincennes was at the mercy of the government from the time it opened. Strangled by insufficient budgets that left it virtually destitute, the underfunded university drew more students than it could possibly house. Students soon started smashing the ceilings to see if the police had bugged the classrooms. But Vincennes was kept alive by the collective desire of its members to jealously protect the freedoms they had won: the quality of the exchange of ideas and the free speech, one of the most important spoils of May '68. Behind the ostentation and militant politics of some and the hedonism of others, there were excellent teachers, cutting-edge research, and the ambition to become the most modern humanities faculty in the country. The university very quickly earned an international reputation. Paris may not be France, but Vincennes could have been the world.

The dean of the Sorbonne and English specialist Raymond La Vergnas was responsible for organizing the new university. In October 1968, he presided over a committee of about twenty people, including Roland Barthes, Jacques Derrida, Jean-Pierre Vernant, Georges Canguilhem, and Emmanuel Le Roy Ladurie. A dozen people were selected to form a core group responsible for appointing the entire faculty, from professors to teaching assistants. The grandiose plan was to make Vincennes into a small-scale MIT, an American-style university, a model of modernity, an enclave with an international reputation overtly aiming at multidisciplinarity.

The most spectacular nomination was without a doubt that of Michel Foucault as head of the philosophy department. Foucault was already a star at the time and was able to recruit faculty. He immediately asked Deleuze to join, but ill health prevented him from coming to Vincennes for two years. Michel Serres, whose post Deleuze eventually took, immediately agreed to join the adventure at Vincennes. In the fall of 1968, Foucault approached the ENS on rue d'Ulm via the directors of the journal *Cahiers pour l'Analyse* (*Notebooks for Analysis*) specifically to recruit followers of Lacan and Althusser for Vincennes. He managed to convince Lacan's daughter, Judith Miller, as well as Alain Badiou, Jacques Rancière, and François Regnault. The dominant chord was therefore structuralist and Maoist, although the department was not entirely dominated by the "Maos"—there were other nominees, such as Henri Weber, from the Revolutionary Communist League, and Étienne Balibar, an Althusserian philosopher who was a member of the FCP. Foucault also realized a diplomatic personality would be needed to make the group function smoothly, and for that role he appointed François Châtelet.

Beyond his responsibilities in the philosophy department, Foucault was also involved in getting the entire experimental university up and running. He wanted to replace psychologists with psychoanalysts, so that they could create their own department and take advantage of the available funding. The idea of creating a department of this sort was Jacques Derrida's; Foucault organized it. The psychoanalyst Serge Leclaire became the departmental head, with Lacan's backing. Lacan himself was not at Vincennes, but Lacanian psychoanalysis was overwhelmingly present, transforming psychoanalysis into an official subject of study in the arts curriculum. The entire faculty belonged to the Freudian School of Paris and gave no fewer than sixteen seminars.

At its first general meeting on December 11, 1968, the philosophy department announced the line it wanted to follow. It did not want to "produce guard dogs" but to uphold the ongoing political and ideological struggle and the practice of philosophy that would aid in that endeavor. The department defined its tasks in March 1969, which meant defining the exact nature of the "Philosophical Front" and studying knowledge as a matter of class struggle, thus contributing to "making sure that theoretical Marxist-Leninism dominated among the student masses."[1]

The government had happily conceded this concentration of "revolutionarism" to May '68 and the student movement, but by January 1970, it was alarmed by the way that the department of philosophy was distancing itself from academic norms. The minister of education, Olivier Guichard, denounced the "Marxist-Leninist" character of the philosophy program at Vincennes and the lax attitude toward giving grades. In an interview in *L'Express*, Judith Miller, a Proletarian Left militant, airily declared, "certain collectives have decided to grade students on the basis of written work, others have decided to give a diploma to anyone who thinks they deserve one."[2] The government response to this provocation was swift, and the philosophy department was no longer allowed to award national diplomas. Foucault protested, justifying the extremely political orientation of the Vincennes philosophers.

Foucault left Vincennes in 1970, but not because the government sent him back to teach high school, as was the campus rumor. He had been elected professor at the Collège de France, a high honor, and therefore he relinquished his job as head of department to François Châtelet, the only person capable of steering the unwieldy vessel. Student enrollments dropped as the red sun of the East was setting: 416 in philosophy the first year (1968–1969), 247 in 1970–1971, and 215 in 1971–1972, a drop by half, even while the university grew from 7,900 students in 1968 to 12,500 in 1971–1972.[3]

Infighting

Deleuze arrived at Vincennes during the 1970–1971 academic year, in the midst of the budgetary crisis and internal power struggles among Maoists. The themes of his first seminars were somewhat out of sync with the ambient spirit: "Logic and Desire" and "Spinoza's Logic." The intellectual path of Deleuze's Paris-VIII seminars is particularly rich and closely linked to his publications. During the years 1970, 1971, and 1972, his themes were part of what became *Anti-Oedipus*: codes, flows, coding and decoding, the *double bind*, the libido and work, psychoanalysis and its myths, the body without organs and its intensities, the axiomatic, capitalism, Marx and Freud, and schizophrenia. He had an immediate rapport with his student audience, albeit without any concession concerning the highly philosophical content of his courses. His reputation as a fantastic teacher was well established in Paris even before he came to Vincennes, and he taught to a very large audience right from the start. The little classroom housing his Tuesday seminar overflowed with people; he refused to teach in a lecture hall. Deleuze came to Vincennes in the fall of 1970 and left only when he retired in 1987.

Deleuze was immediately won over by the diversity of his students, which perfectly suited his teaching plan of going beyond classical philosophical texts toward the arts and sciences. Vincennes seemed to Deleuze to have leapt ahead in time: "when I went to another university, I felt as if I had gone backward in time to the nineteenth century."[4] In addition to the students' wide range of abilities and interests, Vincennes also had the particular merit of accepting students who had not finished high school and a large percentage of foreign students attracted by the quality of Deleuze's books and articles and fascinated by his personality. "They came in waves, suddenly there were five or six Australians there, and nobody knew why. There were always Japanese students, fifteen or twenty every year, South Americans, Blacks. . . ."[5]

When Deleuze came to the philosophy department, his close friend François Châtelet was its head, and things were still very agitated. During the entire month of June 1971, and again at the beginning of the new university year in the fall, a very determined strike half-paralyzed the university: short-term administrative and technical staff were protesting against insufficient funding, job insecurity, and low wages. On June 23, 1971, the faculty of the philosophy department signed a statement in support of the strike: François Châtelet and the nine other tenured faculty members, including Deleuze.[6] The movement led to the collective resignation of the University Council and its president, Claude Frioux, on June 11. No formal agreement was reached until November 9, 1971.

In 1974, the philosophy department was shaken by another conflict. This was a period when the neighboring department of psychoanalysis, which was structurally linked to philosophy, was told to toe the line and reorganize under the iron rule of the EFP administration, and thus of Lacan, via his son-in-law, Jacques-Alain Miller, who was appointed head of psychoanalysis at Vincennes in 1974. The journalist Roger-Pol Droit leaked the affair to *Le Monde,* and an article denounced the takeover bid as a cleansing operation reminiscent of Vichy.[7] The family takeover did not please Deleuze or Lyotard, who together drew up a tract, which was distributed in December and published in *Temps Modernes.*[8] Deleuze and Lyotard called this an unprecedented "Stalinian operation" in a university where tradition prohibited private individuals from intervening to nominate or dismiss staff. "All forms of terrorism involve washing: washing the unconscious is no less terrible and authoritarian than brainwashing."[9]

Managed from then on by Jacques-Alain Miller, the department of psychoanalysis at Vincennes supported strictly orthodox Lacanianism. Lacan had warned his students in 1969: "You will find your master." Naively, they thought he was referring to Pompidou, but he meant himself. Psychoanalysis at Vincennes reverted to an ordered structure vanquishing radical politics and reinstating hierarchy. The "putsch" succeeded, and Lacan defined the syllabus according to his view of what Freud would have wanted, namely, the teaching of linguistics: "*linguistics*—which we here know to be the most important thing. . . . Linguistics should be applied to the field of what I call 'the language' in support of its unconscious, where it stems from a purism which takes different forms, precisely because it is formal."[10] In addition to linguistics, there was also logic, topology, and antiphilosophy, "the title I would like to give to the investigation of what academic discourse owes to its supposedly 'pedagogical' mission."[11]

At the same time, the philosophy department was troubled by the question of its part-time faculty. Since everybody had invited their friends to sign up to teach a course, the number of part-time teachers had increased to at least fifty, many of whom never bothered to turn up to teach. The department, headed by Châtelet, decided not to renew the contracts of a good number of teachers who had not honored the terms of their employment. The decision, instigated by Alain Badiou, Jacques Rancière, François Regnault, and Jean Borreil, was made during the reorganization of the department of psychoanalysis. Those who had lost their job called it a Bolshevik coup and alerted Deleuze and Lyotard, who saw it as the start of a witch hunt. "They organized a sort of hunger strike in Deleuze's seminar."[12] The part-time staff started a movement that was supported by Deleuze and Lyotard. Although Châtelet had initially endorsed the decision, he ultimately backed down. But the battle had been long, and the wounds did not heal quickly. Jacques-Alain Miller invited François Regnault, one of the vanquished, to join the department of psychoanalysis, even though he was certainly no professional psychoanalyst. Badiou, Rancière, Linhart, and Weber formed a short-lived section claiming relative autonomy within the philosophy department.

The consequence of these internal quarrels was that the philosophy department divided into clans, and the staff withdrew into their own centers of interest. Châtelet ended up consulting his colleagues by phone before making any decisions, to everyone's great relief. "Then there were two types of meeting: the circus-meeting held in the department and the decision-making meetings held off campus."[13] In one of these meetings, during the twin departmental crises, Gerard Miller's case was discussed. Jacques-Alain's brother was teaching part time in the philosophy department. At one of their meetings, the staffmembers were very wound up about the recent putsch and the atmosphere was tense; they decided to revoke his contract. "Just then, after the vote, Deleuze spoke up, saying, 'I think we've just done something really lousy!' He managed to turn the meeting around, and immediately they reconsidered and renewed Gerard

Miller's contract."[14] Deleuze's attitude shows how much he valued fairness, since there was no love lost between Deleuze and the Lacanian Maoists.

During the 1970s, the reputation of the philosophy department at Vincennes was in crisis, to put it mildly. When they were not giving themselves bad press by squabbling internally, the faculty members were the target of a government who hated them with a vengeance, sometimes openly. A fortnight before announcing Paris-VIII's move from Vincennes to Saint-Denis, on June 16, 1978, Alice Saunier-Seïté, the minister for universities, declared during a dinner debate, "You can't do just anything, we have to put our foot down. It is true that at Vincennes they gave a degree to a horse."[15]

To redress the balance despite this hatred and the waves of students leaving the philosophy department, Châtelet and Deleuze came up with the idea of creating a Polytechnic Institute of Philosophy. The slightly pompous title was odd for Vincennes, but the new "institution" made it possible to award diplomas that gave their holders some degree of social recognition. The idea was to require students to write a thesis on concrete works of art, whether literary, musical, or cinematographic. It is true that the numbers of theses approved by the institute was limited. "No doubt Deleuze had overestimated the creative potential of his students. His idea was always to favor invention and working outside university norms. But most students were obviously more at ease with repetition."[16] Nevertheless, the institute, which was born just prior to the transfer to Saint-Denis, functioned efficiently. A lot of students, many of them foreign, were able to earn a diploma recognized by prospective employers.

Since his arrival at Vincennes, Deleuze was most friendly with his old friend François Châtelet, and the two saw each other often off campus and held each other in high esteem. Yet the authors that interested the two philosophers were different: there was a world of difference between Châtelet's passion for history, Hegel, and political philosophy and Deleuze's philosophical pantheon. In the mid-1970s, they nevertheless decided to teach a class together, along with Jean-François Lyotard and Christian Descamps. "François always used to say that Deleuze was the best philosopher. He admired him greatly and thought that he, more than anyone else in the twentieth century, had come up with a new way of seeing things,"[17] recalls Châtelet's wife, Noëlle, who enrolled in doctoral studies at Vincennes with Deleuze. The viva for her thesis was held in 1973, with a jury made up of her director, Deleuze, Roland Barthes, and Nicos Poulantzas.

Noëlle Châtelet met her husband in 1962: she was nineteen and he was thirty-five. "I remember being astonished by his passion when I was an innocent young boarder. François replied, and it helped me a lot later on, 'I love what you will become.'"[18] In class, Châtelet was like Socrates, a master of *maieutics*, passionate about the transmission of knowledge. A fortnight before he died, he was attached to a life-support machine and could no longer speak properly, but he still insisted on teaching one more class from home. "Suddenly, his voice found new life. His last class was on happiness."[19]

François Châtelet had suffered enormously. Diagnosed with lung cancer caused by smoking, he had a tracheotomy and remained confined to his house for the last two years of his life, bound to his oxygen machines. In 1982, François Châtelet received a letter from his friend Gilles:

> I often think of you at Evreux. After all, you are living proof of the existence of the soul, which is how you held on when your body gave way. I was struck how when you were suffering the worst you stayed so like your usual self: it was the only sign you could give us. You are a marvelous man; Noëlle too, is a marvelous woman (of course I know only too well that my vocabulary is limited). . . . Your students are too attached to you and are missing something, meaning someone, you. May you recover quickly. The different stages of your treatment, your convalescence, your invention of a new way of life, which will keep you safer, you will be able to manage all of that. It started with Normandy, but it also resembles an incredible interior voyage. Fanny and I both send you our love.[20]

In 1983, two years before his death, François Châtelet was in the hospital on the verge of death, and the prognosis on the rehab ward was poor. He received a visit from Deleuze, who helped him decide to accept the tracheotomy and continue living. This was also part of their complicity: suffering, the body gasping for air, their serious respiratory difficulties. "When Gilles went to see François in recovery, he said to him, 'as long as you can still hold a pen, you can still live.' It was the philosopher asking his fellow philosopher to continue. He meant that as long as you can still write philosophy, you must stay alive."[21] During those last two years, Deleuze and his wife went to the Châtelets' nearly every Sunday. "Gilles talked about philosophy with François. Then he said, 'Now let's get onto more serious matters,' and he taught us to play bridge-belote, because he considered that normal belote was beneath us. That was the only time I ever called Gilles 'Gilou.' He was my partner, and Fanny partnered François."[22]

Deleuze wrote a fine testimonial for his friend. As soon as he started teaching again, just after Châtelet's death, he told his students, "the best tribute is to reread his books to gauge their power. His writings are a true work of philosophy."[23] In *Libération*, Deleuze wrote, "He is still a star, not in the sense of a celebrity, but of a constellation."[24] In his article, Deleuze traced the path of his friend's intellectual development from the period when they were students together. He recalled Châtelet's now-forgotten skill as a logician, at a time when people spoke of him as the probable successor to Cavaillès and Lautman, then his passionate interest in history under the influence of Eric Weil, one of the people who introduced Hegel to France. Deleuze expressed his admiration and emotion on rereading his "Fitzgeraldian" novel, *Les années de démolition* (*Demolition Years*) and paid tribute to a great captain of the Vincennes vessel: "the Vincennes philosophy department relied on him. He really is the one who managed this difficult department, and his political skill always drew on his negotiating skills; he drove a hard bargain, with no compromises."[25] Shortly afterward, Deleuze lectured on his friend's work, praising his brilliant philosophy of immanence and the relation between power and acts. "This is where Châtelet was an Aristotelian."[26] The nature of the act in Châtelet's thinking was led by his rationalism, because "the act is reason,"[27] seen as a process and not just a faculty. Deleuze recalled that his friend's first published work was on Pericles.[28] From its hero he drew the lesson that empiricist and pluralist rationalism was developed in the *agora* of a "historical present."[29] The political dimension of his thought was counterbalanced by music. "What Châtelet would have liked more than anything is an opera by Verdi on Pericles."[30]

When Châtelet died, the department of philosophy was more or less taken over by his friend René Schérer, whom he had met when he was preparing for the *agrégation* exams in 1946–1947. When Châtelet was posted to Oran in Algeria in 1948, Schérer, who had gone to Oran the preceding year, welcomed him. Schérer had met Deleuze through Châtelet at the end of the 1940s, and they met up again when he returned to France in 1954. When the University of Vincennes was created, Châtelet asked his friend Schérer to join them.

Until that point, Schérer had felt quite removed from Deleuze's work, but the publication of *Anti-Oedipus* brought them closer. "From then onward I tended to adopt Deleuze's thinking."[31] Their rapprochement was helped by Guattari, by the CERFI, and by Schérer's involvement alongside Guy Hocquenghem on several issues of *Recherches*.[32] When Schérer's position became shaky during the Coral affair, which lasted from 1982 until the case was dismissed in 1985,[33] Deleuze immediately jumped to his defense. After Châtelet's death, Deleuze asked Schérer to captain the ship. "At one point I found myself in charge of the philosophy department. I had gone to see Deleuze, and I don't know why, he acted as if I were more competent than I was in administrative tasks, which he did not like very much; he trusted my opinion."[34] When Deleuze retired in 1987, he and Schérer were so close that Deleuze transferred his research students to him.[35]

Jean-François Lyotard, a former member of the group "Socialisme ou Barbarie" (Socialism or Barbarism), was the other great philosophical figure at Vincennes and close to Deleuze. His relations with Deleuze began with Nietzsche and the 1972 Cerisy conference. "They arrived together and left together and had a very similar reading of Nietzsche."[36] Lyotard welcomed the publication of *Anti-Oedipus* enthusiastically.[37] When Lyotard's *Libidinal Economy* came out, their relationship was at its strongest.[38] At the same time, according to Lyotard's daughter, the philosopher Corinne Enaudeau, "their association was based on a misunderstanding. Lyotard wasn't at all interested in schizoanalysis."[39] She believes that her father was truly political, unlike Deleuze. "There was a real difference of opinion about that. I remember my father coming home angry at Deleuze for passing everything on and not doing anything. He used to imitate him: 'Listen, you know Jean-François, I think I haven't got anything to say about that decision.' Deleuze played at being a child with Châtelet and Lyotard as parents to keep an eye on institutional matters."[40]

Despite a few moments of annoyance, Deleuze and Lyotard were strongly bound, and from 1972 to 1979, their publications were greeted as the expression of a common exigency. They were even considered to be two potential, compatible modalities of a single philosophy of difference. However, when Lyotard brought out *The Postmodern Condition*,[41] the break was final. Deleuze could not stand seeing his friend defend radically relativist positions; Guattari made fun of his rejection of metanarratives. "No more factions, just fads."[42]

It became clear at that time that they were following very different philosophical trajectories, and when Lyotard published *The Differend*[43] he no longer made any reference to works by Deleuze and Guattari. Lyotard no longer followed Deleuze's monism, using instead a dualist approach in the name of Kant, Freud, and especially the analysis of language in British philosophy based on Wittgenstein. They both retained their anti-Hegelianism and their opposition to reconciliatory dialectics, which Lyotard took on in *The Differend*. Despite the deterioration of their relations from 1979 onward, Lyotard continued to hold Deleuze in great esteem, which he expressed when he died. He wrote: "I always thought that he was one of the two geniuses of our philosophical generation."[44] His daughter, surprised to hear her father use this sort of superlative, asked who the other was. He replied that it was Derrida, adding, "each of them had understood the whole of the history of philosophy by age nineteen."[45]

DELEUZE AS TEACHER

Vincennes was above all the place where Deleuze could deploy his exceptional talents as a teacher. He attached enormous importance to his Tuesday seminar and spent most of the week preparing his class. Pierre Chevalier, a family friend who lived with the Deleuzes on rue Bizerte between 1973 and 1983, remembers the care Deleuze took in preparing the seminar for Vincennes. "I saw Gilles set to work on Sunday morning, sometimes on Saturday, polishing the seminar for three days and before he left to teach, there was a physical preparation, as if he were going to take part in a race."[46] He would turn up on Tuesday mornings, no longer needing the little page of notes in his hand because he knew by heart what he was going to say. Yet he gave the impression of thinking on his feet, that his class was a pure improvisation of mental development in harmony with his public. Using this procedure he made his essential points, leaving his students spellbound by the intellectual rigor of his argument. A seminar, according to Deleuze, is "a sort of moving matter akin to music, with each group taking from it what suits them at the time. Not everything suits everybody. Teaching is about emotion. If there is no emotion, there is no understanding, no interest, there is nothing."[47]

Claude Jaeglé has magnificently reproduced the polyphony and different registers of voice that emanated from Deleuze's body as he taught.[48] The attentive silence of his very mixed audience testified to the powerful effect of his dramatic delivery. He raised his public to the lofty heights he lived in and, to make sure everyone was following, he would often ask: "What does that mean?" "Deleuze would hold a concept for a few seconds at the height of a rational development and there would be a pause in the audience's reflective processes; at the heart of this subjective apnea, the transmission of thought occurred."[49] Jaeglé identified several different "characters" that Deleuze deployed when teaching, such as the "rogue," who is not really interested in philosophy. "The rogue produces a sharp, nasal, mischievous tone in Deleuze's voice."[50] One day, Deleuze was surprised to find his classroom door open, and he mockingly explained to his students that the administration had developed a plan of action, complete with strict rules, to prevent them stealing chairs from the neighboring classrooms. "A strange scheme has been implemented. When I arrive, I am supposed to go see a security guard. I give the guard a little badge and he gives me the key to the room, but keeps the badge. After locking the classroom again, I return the key and he returns my badge."[51] Another day, on January 17, 1984, when he was offered a rather insalubrious little classroom in one of the prefab blocks at Paris-VIII (the university was now located at Saint-Denis), he painted a fabulous picture of the very modest room he had been allocated:

> I've been to see the room: it's a palace where we will be very happy. Imagine a little square courtyard, with a little tuft of grass in the middle. All around, single-story buildings, all of them done very smartly in mustard and green. The doors all lead outside, which will save us should there be a fire. The room is quite a bit larger than here, it has a lower ceiling, which will help us concentrate. There are large double glazed picture windows, so there won't be any problems with noise, or heating. We will be quite comfortable there, and if anyone wants to move us on, we'll simply go to the parking lot. We will spend our happiest days there in the fresh air; we'll be free. The only problem is crossing the road to get there. . . . It is a prefab palace with studious halls where nobody lingers. One is struck immediately by the serenity of the atmosphere. Fancy it existing without us even knowing about it.[52]

Similar to the rogue was the "clown," who made fun of repetitions and audibly punctuated the lengthy philosophical chains of reasoning. He was the "rhythmical witness," always asking "whyyyy"? Then there was the "dying man," agonizing on his deathbed to the rumbling and rattling sounds of death. His moaning "aaaaah's" were made in a "senile voice, each word sounding like a gurgle."[53] All of these characters accompanied the seductive, enchanting Deleuze, whose "voice was a charm, an efficient song."[54] He masterfully played all the parts in that philosophical drama before an awed, captive audience.

Among Deleuze's students was Georges Comtesse: a zealot who spoke at length in every seminar to contradict his teacher. The class endured his remarks, but he benefited from Deleuze's courtesy. He came regularly to each seminar and, having read all of his teacher's publications, made Deleuze's concepts and turns of speech his own. He prided himself on accompanying the development of Deleuze's thought by interrogating him and formulating objections to put him to the test.

Elisabeth Roudinesco was one of the students fascinated by Deleuze in the early 1970s. As a member of the Freudian School since 1969, she quite clearly perceived the devastating character of his remarks about psychoanalysis. Deleuze was preparing *Anti-Oedipus* at the time, and she was naturally unable to agree with his radical questioning of the great Signified attacked by the power of flows, the critique of the Oedipus complex, of lack, of the one in the name of multiplicity. At the same time, she was captivated:

> Deleuze was exalted but remained tolerant. He was the most Socratic philosopher you could imagine. Instead of making himself the idol of a religious cult, he fascinated his public like a tender and barbarous midwife delivering the desire of those who came to listen to him. . . . He spoke, without referring to notes, to all and sundry as if the book that he carried within him were written for all time in the depths of his soul.[55]

Elisabeth Roudinesco's admiration, however, did not prevent her from writing an extremely critical review of *Anti-Oedipus* when it came out.[56]

In the early 1970s, Philippe Mengue was part of the crowded Tuesday class. He was a scrupulous analyst of Deleuze's philosophy and worked as a teacher, training future primary-school teachers at the ENS in Le Bourget. He was torn between his Lacanian positions and his fascination with Deleuze and Lyotard. "The first time I met Gilles Deleuze was at the brand-new Vincennes University. What a shock!"[57] He went to the Tuesday seminar, where the ritual was always the same. Deleuze arrived at a room already so packed with students that it was hard to get in the door. The

(ABOVE) **FIGURE 1** Wedding photo, Félix Guattari's parents, Jeanne and Louis, 1939. *Source*: Emmanuelle Guattari, personal collection.

(LEFT) **FIGURE 2** The three Guattari brothers (left to right): Jean, Paul, and Félix, 1932. *Source*: Emmanuelle Guattari, personal collection.

FIGURE 3   Gilles Deleuze (right) with his brother Georges (left) in front of their parents'
summer rental house, Deauville, 1928.   *Source*: Fanny Deleuze, personal collection.

(PREVIOUS PAGE) **FIGURE 4** Gilles Deleuze
(left) with his brother Georges, 1935.
Source: Fanny Deleuze, personal collection.

(BELOW) **FIGURE 5** Félix Guattari standing
between his parents in front of the Mon-Bana
factory, 1935. *Source*: Emmanuelle Guattari,
personal collection.

(ABOVE) **FIGURE 6**   The three Guattari brothers; from left to right: Félix, Jean, Paul. *Source*: Emmanuelle Guattari, personal collection).

(NEXT PAGE TOP) **FIGURE 7**   The three Guattari brothers (left to right): Jean, Paul, Félix, 1953. *Source*: Emmanuelle Guattari, personal collection.

(NEXT PAGE BOTTOM) **FIGURE 8**   La Borde Clinic, 1960s. *Source*: Emmanuelle Guattari, personal collection.

FIGURE 9   Wilfred Burchette, the first journalist to have entered Hiroshima, with his sons at La Borde with Félix Guattari (left), 1965. *Source*: Bruno Guattari, personal collection.

FIGURE 10   Félix Guattari at La Borde. *Source*: Bruno Guattari, personal collection.

FIGURE 11 La Borde Clinic today.

Source: Personal photo.

FIGURE 12　Gilles Deleuze with son Julian, age 1, on the terrace of Mas Rêvéry, 1961.
Source: Fanny Deleuze, personal collection.

FIGURE 13　Gilles and Fanny Deleuze at Félix Guattari's house in Dhuizon on the Vaugoin property in Sologne, near the La Borde Clinic, July 1969. Photo taken by Félix Guattari.
Source: Emmanuelle Guattari, personal collection.

FIGURE 14   Gilles Deleuze, vacation on Skyros, Greece, 1970. Photo taken by Karl Flinker. *Source*: Emmanuelle Guattari, personal collection.

FIGURE 15   Gilles and Fanny Deleuze with their two children, Julien and Emilie, on vacation in Greece, 1970. *Source*: Emmanuelle Guattari, personal collection.

(LEFT) **FIGURE 16** Nicole Guattari, Félix Guattari's first wife, in 1967. *Source*: Bruno Guattari, personal collection.

(BELOW) **FIGURE 17** Arlette Donati, 1970s. *Source*: Bruno Guattari, personal collection.

FIGURE 18   Félix and Nicole Guattari with their daughter, Emmanuelle. *Source*: Emmanuelle Guattari, personal collection.

FIGURE 19   Félix and Nicole Guattari on vacation at the seaside. *Source*: Emmanuelle Guattari, personal collection.

FIGURE 20   Gilles Deleuze and Félix Guattari watching television with Félix's son, Bruno, in Felix's Paris apartment on rue de Condé, 1969. *Source*: Bruno Guattari, personal collection.

FIGURE 21   Gilles Deleuze playing chess at Félix Guattari's house, Stephen Guattari sitting next to him, 1970. Photo taken by Félix Guattari. *Source*: Emmanuelle Guattari, personal collection.

(LEFT) **FIGURE 22**
Gilles Deleuze on the
phone in Félix Guattari's
Paris apartment.
Source: Emmanuelle
Guattari, personal
collection.

(BELOW) **FIGURE 23**
Tomato Radio. Félix
Guattari in the middle.
Franco Piperno on the
left, 1981.
Source: Emmanuelle
Guattari, personal
collection.

Figure 24   Félix Guattari in his office at Dhuizon in the Loir-et-Cher, 1982.

Source: Emmanuelle Guattari, personal collection.

Figure 25   Gilles Deleuze, February 1986. Photo taken by Gerard Uferas.

Source: Previously appeared in *Le Magazine Littéraire* (September 1988): 30.

Figure 26   Félix Guattari. *Source*: IMEC Archives, Félix Guattari collection.

FIGURE 27   Gilles Deleuze, 1986.
Source: Photo taken by Hélène Bamberger/Gamma/Eyedea.

Figure 28 Gilles Deleuze and Félix Guattari, 1980. *Source*: Photo taken by Marc Gantier/Gamma/Eyedea.

Figure 29 Gilles Deleuze and Félix Guattari in 1972, when *Anti Oedipus* was published by Editions de Minuit. *Source*: Photo by Xavier Martin.

place where Deleuze was supposed to sit was already filled with a forest of tape recorders. Deleuze would address his public, "You are very kind. I'm pleased to see so many people here, but all the same, you'll need to leave me a bit of room to put my books down."[58] He always arrived with an armful of books, which he carefully piled on the desk, with pages of notes in them, which he never looked at. In 1973, Philippe Mengue tired of teaching the psychology of education at Le Bourget and told his inspector of his desire to devote himself to metaphysics. He was told that he would be lucky to get a part-time post as a philosophy teacher in the south of France. He took up the offer and left Paris. In 1986, he finished a thesis on sadism, directed by Lyotard, with Deleuze as president of the jury at his viva; he then wrote two studies on Deleuze's philosophy.[59]

Students were drawn to Deleuze's class for a wide variety of reasons. Jean-Michel Salanskis, now a professor of philosophy at Nanterre, had just passed the *agrégation* in mathematics when he became an ardent fan of philosophy thanks to Lyotard's writings and his discovery of *Difference and Repetition*. Richard Pinhas also came to philosophy via Lyotard but sided with Deleuze when the two philosophers stopped seeing eye-to-eye. After Deleuze's death, Pinhas has played a critical role in disseminating his ideas, by maintaining a Web site where a number of Deleuze's Vincennes seminars have been made available in French, English, Spanish, and German. Pinhas attended all of Deleuze's Vincennes seminars between 1970 and 1987, often picking him up from his home to drive him to the university. He also benefited from Deleuze's refusal to consider books sacred: "he gave me quite a few rare texts, annotated copies, books with dedications."[60] To avoid having an unwieldy a pile of books with him, Deleuze would rip out the pages he needed for his class.

The proportion of political militants in his seminar dropped markedly over time. Estimated at about a third in the beginning, the numbers dwindled steadily, making way in the 1980s for a public essentially consisting of apprentice philosophers. During the years he went to the seminar with Deleuze, Richard Pinhas encountered a concrete example of the Greek philosophical tradition of friendship. In the area of philosophical knowledge, Deleuze was in no way imperious, forever repeating that you should simply take what you need for yourself. "I read Spinoza late on, when I was about thirty, and he told me, 'It will come when you really need it, and when that time comes it will really do you good.' He was right, five years earlier, it wouldn't have affected me in the same way."[61]

The German-language student Pierre Blanchaud, who was then only eighteen, was also one of the first regulars at the 1970–1972 seminars. His father, who was self-taught, had talked to him about Deleuze during the summer of 1968, after enthusiastically discovering his *Nietzsche and Philosophy*. Father and son decided to attend Deleuze's Tuesday seminar at Vincennes and Foucault's Wednesday seminar at the Collège de France. "I couldn't understand anything much, but I enjoyed myself. There was a party atmosphere. He spoke in such a kind way! I was really fascinated. I liked him straight away."[62]

During his last years of teaching, from 1984 through 1987, several professional philosophers came to Deleuze's seminar. One of them, François Zourabichvili, became a particularly promising specialist of Deleuze's thought, although his career was tragically cut short in 2006. He attended the last two years of Deleuze's seminar at Vincennes, and when the French University Presses asked him to write a book on Deleuze, they had a few conversations.[63] As a philosophy student at the Sorbonne, Zourabichvili was immediately taken with Deleuze, whose seminar at the time was on Foucault, then Leibniz. "To be in the first ten rows you had to arrive an hour in advance. I was amazed that it was always the same people in front, and I wanted to know what time they arrived. Once I turned up nearly three hours early and there were already five or six people there."[64] He particularly appreciated the insistent way that Deleuze kept returning to the same themes. It was not a kind of chorus, in Deleuze's case, but a means of attaching new dimensions to his initial statement by way of a litany, which worked as a particularly efficient pedagogical tool. Members of the class may not have understood the seminar a particular day, but by virtue of seeing the same theme configured in different ways, they ended up taking it on as their own.

Proust and Signs was the trigger for Zourabichvili's decision to study Deleuze; he was reading it during the first year of preparatory classes for the entrance exam to the ENS in the summer of 1982. "I read it and was stunned, because it was unlike anything I was reading in literary theory. Its content was highly philosophical."[65] Later he felt the same fascination for Deleuze's *Nietzsche*. He read the first two pages over and over, so impressed was he by Deleuze's way of getting to the heart of the matter using concise, efficient sentences that were easy to commit to memory. He got into Deleuze through a stylistic affinity and common interests: he had written his master's thesis on Spinoza.[66] Zourabichvili wanted to write on a contemporary philosopher and therefore chose Deleuze, an obvious choice, as he was attending his seminars from 1985 onward. The Sorbonne, however, was amazed that such a devoted, competent scholar would choose Deleuze, whom they did not consider a true philosopher. The people in his circle thought him at best a brilliant, eclectic commentator or a dandy. "I set myself the challenge of showing that his was a true philosophy. My business was to make the Deleuzean bomb explode inside philosophy."[67]

However, during this last period, philosophers were not the only ones who attended Deleuze's seminar. In 1986–1987, the final year that he dedicated to Leibniz, an employee fighting boredom at the halfway house where he worked regularly sat next to Zourabichvili, having come to Vincennes seeking something to stimulate his thinking. "He enjoyed it; once, the class had been quite arduous it was on the Cartesian *cogito* and Kant. He turned to me and said, 'I don't quite know what it's about, but I really like it.' It's true that you got the impression he wanted to communicate with everyone."[68] When he went to listen to his friend Deleuze at Paris-VIII, Elias Sanbar had a similar experience: "There was a little old lady who came to every seminar, and it was very cold that year. During the breaks, most students went outside to smoke and I stayed behind. I went to see this woman to ask her if she was writing something, why she never missed a single class. She replied: 'Why, *Monsieur*, he helps me to live.' It's true there was something in his thought that helped people to live."[69]

One of the young philosophers of the final period at Paris-VIII, David Lapoujade, attended the Foucault seminar in 1985–1986, and, at the end of the year, Deleuze invited him to his Paris home. Lapoujade became a regular visitor. After four years of regular meetings, Deleuze invited him to Saint-Léonard-de-Noblat, to visit his property in Limousin. The summer days were spent peacefully, going on outings or playing chess or cards. "He devoted a lot of time on his correspondence, because he replied to everybody, in his shaky handwriting."[70] Deleuze also spent some time working; most of the previously unpublished articles included in *Critique and Clinique* were written in Limousin. Otherwise, "Limousin was about family life, resting, playing cards or board games with friends, short trips out in the car."[71] In the main, apart from family, Jean-Pierre Bamberger, Pierre Chevalier, Claire Parnet, and David Lapoujade were the intimates who shared these moments of calm.

In the little classroom at Paris-VIII, a Japanese student, having had to get up very early indeed, sat unfailingly in the seat next to Deleuze every

Tuesday for over ten years. Hidenobu Suzuki came to France from Tokyo in 1974 to improve his French. He knew nothing about philosophy at the time. He enrolled at the New Sorbonne, where he found enough to satisfy his interest in French literature. "One day, a Japanese friend that I used to meet at the Sorbonne gave me Deleuze and Guattari's *Kafka*."[72] He was a passionate fan of Kafka, most of whose works he had read in Japan, and he very impressed by the novelty of Deleuze and Guattari's approach. Some time later, he found out that Deleuze was teaching at Vincennes and decided to go in 1978–1979. The campus was still very active, and there were often untimely interruptions during Deleuze's class. People would turn up to say that they absolutely needed help for their friends in difficulty or ask for financial support for one cause or another. "On nearly every occasion Gilles would pass his hat around the room and pull some notes from his pocket while the hat went round. I thought that was very generous and discovered that he was not at all in an ivory tower."[73] His attitude contrasted strongly with university practice in Japan. Hidenobu, who had been on the far left in Japan, was fascinated to discover how academic research like Deleuze and Guattari's could have a practical application. "Going to his seminars became my passion."[74] Having noticed on the first day that there were many tape recorders around Deleuze, Hidenobu added his own, the very latest Sony model. He became an institution; when someone close to Deleuze expressed regret at not having been to a particular class, he would suggest that they ask the Japanese student to borrow his cassette.[75]

On Tuesday June 2, 1987, the day everybody had been dreading for so long arrived: the final class. For all Deleuze's planning and simultaneous denial of the event—Deleuze considered that there could only ever be a penultimate class, like a penultimate drink—it was an occasion marked by cameras joining the usual pile of tape recorders. The moment was described by Giorgio Passerone, the Italian translator of *A Thousand Plateaus* and representative of the international diaspora fascinated by Deleuze.[76] Passerone, who came from Genoa and was a member of the extreme left-wing Autonomia movement, attended Deleuze's seminars from 1977 onward. "Then I came across *Anti-Oedipus* and decided that it contained a lifeline, so I decided to write my Master's thesis on the idea of difference in Deleuze's thought."[77] While the Italian situation deteriorated, with more and more militants deciding to join the Red Brigades' armed struggle and others losing hope and getting into hard drugs, Passerone applied for a student scholarship, came to France, and attended Deleuze's seminar. "The

Tuesday class always functioned that way, a production-laboratory work-ing around the operator-Deleuze and his task of reading philosophers in a way that unearthed their originality."[78]

Yet the last class ended not only the work that Deleuze had begun on Leibniz but also the cycle of his teaching life, as he chose as his theme har-mony, which he elucidated in the philosophical concept of the "harmony of body and soul." As he often did, Deleuze turned to the creative world to take stock of what an experience of such harmony might be. He referred to the renewal of the notion of harmony in the music of the Baroque age. "We'll need the 'musicians' in the class to make sense of the story of the transformation of the concept of harmony."[79] He called upon the musicolo-gists attending his class, such as Pascale Criton, to unravel the idea of a change in the status of harmony, which was no longer based on regular in-tervals but on chords. This transformation created in Baroque music could be equated to what Leibniz meant by his idea of harmony, which distin-guished three ways of questioning the relation between body and soul: in-fluence, which related to melody; assistance, which corresponded to coun-terpoint; and consensus, which was connected to chords. Deleuze's teaching ended on this open question, without ending as such, because his last class suggested new subjects to explore. He finished the last class by saying, "All this about music has given me new starting points that I would not have discovered without our work together this session."[80]

20

The Year of Combat
1977

Midway between *Anti-Oedipus* (1972) and *A Thousand Plateaus* (1980), Deleuze and Guattari wrote a small, fundamental, programmatic text some hundred pages long entitled *Rhizome*,[1] which insisted on the many possible entries into a work: "no one entry is favored over another . . . so we'll enter from any end."[2] The rhizome is thus conceived as a theory of reception, or of reading, justifying an active role for readers in relation to authors and their presumed intentionality. It is seen as the possible expression of a pragmatic theory of reading: "the rhizome, as a theory of reading, takes the act of reading into account, and makes reception into active production, a true transformation and capture of the work."[3]

The concept itself becomes something of a manifesto regarding their new way of thinking. It has a polemical dimension, as a war machine against the Western tradition of verticality, an alternative to the more hackneyed tree of knowledge. It offers a different way of thinking along horizontal lines, on the plane of immanence, according to a botanical model of rhizomatic plants with proliferating horizontal ramifications. Using this analogy, Deleuze and Guattari wanted to put an end to reasoning that went from the trunk to the branches of a tree, respecting a linear relationship between cause and effect, in favor of a mode of thought with neither a starting point nor final extremity but an infinite number of meaningful connections. They also argue that any break, at any given point, could become meaningful.

Deleuze and Guattari together contest thought based on a single unity that grows a deep taproot to develop a binary logic, preferring ways of thinking through multiplicity, using a "radical-system" produced by the failure to root, following a logic of folds, a theme that Deleuze later developed, based on Leibniz. "The folding of one text onto another, which constitutes multiple and even adventitious roots (like a cutting), implies a supplementary dimension to that of the texts under consideration. In this supplementary dimension of folding, unity continues its spiritual labor."[4] The root-cosmos is opposed to a radical chaosmosis, but it is not a simple question of harvesting the multiple, since it needs to be produced: "The multiple *must be made.*"[5]

Contrasting bulbs and tubers to roots, Deleuze and Guattari, as is their wont, use dualism as the best way to shake up the foundations of binary logic. At the same time, they warn their readers against abusive simplifications like the opposition between good and evil, since the rhizome can be good like the potato and bad like the dandelion. The rhizome leads to a method and several principles. Here again, simplifications have been rife: some readers of Deleuze and Guattari see the rhizome as an excuse for intellectual sloth, sacrificing content for collage. This is a misreading: Deleuze and Guattari advocate an ascetic approach. Making the multiple requires sobriety, contraction, subtraction, and deduction of the facilities of the One, to allow lateral connections producing entirely new areas of relevance.

Connection and heterogeneity are the first of these principles: "any part of a rhizome can be connected with any other and should be."[6] Multiplicity, another principle, is a specific contribution that Deleuze developed in a Bergsonian perspective.

> The distinction between macro and micro belongs perhaps more to Félix than me. My contribution is more that between two types of multiplicities. This is fundamental for me: one of the two types refers to micromultiplicities and is merely a consequence. Even for the problem of thought or science, the idea of multiplicity, as Riemann understands it, seems more important to me than microphysics.[7]

Multiplicity is thus understood as substantive and no longer refers back to the One, as the multiple might. Without object or subject, multiplicity merely has different sizes or divisions: "we will therefore speak of a plane of consistency of multiplicities."[8] To the concept of multiplicity, Guattari adds the possibility of deploying his idea of transversality, whereby branches form in entirely new directions.

Another major principle is the "asignifying rupture. . . . A rhizome may be broken, shattered at a given spot."[9] The fertilizing relation between the wasp and the orchid serves to illustrate the possible multiple arrangements of heterogeneous elements among themselves. In this particular case, both animal and vegetable deterritorialize and reterritorialize to establish a surprising connection between two living beings with no common measure. The rhizome is neither a matter of tracing something already there nor some genealogical ancestry: it is open to novelty, to capture, toward forever new lines of flight, an opening onto an outside.

The other principles of the rhizome concern replacing tracing with mapping and its ability for infinite reproduction, properties that Deleuze and Guattari saw at work in linguistics and psychoanalysis, the two leading structuralist sciences. The result is a very different logic: instead of representing underlying codes, it depends entirely on experimentation; the rhizome innovates and connects heterogeneous fields and shifts reality by multiplying the possible entry points and perspectives. Linguistics and psychoanalysis erroneously impose their respective interpretative grids—rigid models of meaning—on a complex reality. Instead, Deleuze and Guattari proposed a mapping approach like the one that Fernand Deligny used when he had autistic children's teachers draw to help them reconstitute their idiosyncratic wanderings. Deleuze and Guattari even saw the tree's privileged position as a constant of Western civilization, localizing a mode of thought previously considered universal, juxtaposing it with the Oriental relationship to nature that contrasted steppe and garden, desert and oasis, and that used tubers for crops. Jean Haudricourt's work provided Deleuze and Guattari with evidence supporting the opposition between the Oriental replanting of tuber offshoots and the Western sowing of grain-producing plants. This renewed approach to the living world that Deleuze and Guattari suggested (without claiming to inaugurate a new science) was a bending of vision that needed to look along horizontal planes, like those of the plateaus. "We call a 'plateau' any multiplicity connected to other multiplicities by superficial underground stems in such a way as to form or extend a rhizome."[10]

Deleuze and Guattari opened an experimental field using new rules: their essay was a multipurpose toolbox that served initially as a manifesto before becoming the introduction to the second volume of *Capitalism and Schizophrenia*. Their study of experimentation touched all areas. Anne Sauvagnargues insists on its value in the field of aesthetics for rethinking artistic creation as a way of capturing forces and challenging the classical split between art and life, a work and its interpretation.[11] Taking this concept as a starting point makes it possible to define a new way of thinking that was not the quest for *mimesis* between an ostensibly objective reality and the idea gleaned from its representation nor a search for origins or ontological foundations that provide a solid foundation of truth. Instead, what become important are the places where various flux cross and how they meet, the impasses or productive openings of certain lines of flight using a clinical technique. With the rhizome, the continent of scientific knowledge can also be broached, because thinking about thought in terms of liaisons is consonant with neurobiological discoveries.

The multidimensionality of the concept of the rhizome gives us a sense of its powerful relevance. Its cursory presentation in a short text, which was much more accessible than the imposing but often dissuasive *A Thousand Plateaus*, made this propositional rather than polemical pamphlet into a challenge that provoked a counterattack from the parties who felt they had drawn fire from a new flank.

THE "FASCISM OF THE POTATO"

One person understood the compelling nature of *Rhizome* very early on: Alain Badiou, Deleuze's colleague in the philosophy department at Vincennes, where he taught for about thirty years. A former disciple of Sartre and then of Althusser, Badiou led a small group of Maoists at the time and was putting out the journal *Cahier Yenan*, which pledged its support to the "Great Helmsman." For Badiou, the success of *Anti-Oedipus* had created some heavy competition, since Deleuze's seminar had become an event not to be missed in the Vincennes philosophy department. In 1977, he decided that *Rhizome* had taken things a step too far and that Deleuze had become an "enemy of the people." Badiou penned an article in *Cahier Yenan*, "Flux and the Party," attacking *Anti-Oedipus*; he wrote a second article with the particularly evocative title "The Fascism of the Potato," which he signed under the pseudonym Georges Peyrol.

The first article denounced Deleuze and Guattari as proponents of a philosophy of desire "with about the same soporific virtues as opium."[12] They had come to represent the most banal form of moralizing, consisting in laboriously demonstrating that freedom is on the side of good and necessity on the side of evil, all of this to the accompaniment of a "cultural cacophony" and "subversive muscle flexing" leading to no more than a simple return to Kant and with no regard for the teachings of Marxist-Leninism, which remain the standard for "scientific rigor."[13] Behind the playful writing style of *Anti-Oedipus*, Badiou easily unmasks the true identity of the enemies of the people:

> What is the last word of these hateful adversaries of organized revolutionary politics? Read it: to accomplish "this process which has already been accomplished because it carries on" (*Anti-Oedipus*, 459). In other words, let it flow like pus from a wound. Look at them, these old Kantians playing at breaking cultural artifacts. Look at them: time is running out, and they are already gathering dust.[14]

The second document for the prosecution, written under a pseudonym, was designed to show that the positions of Deleuze's colleague and sidekick were "protofascist." What is to be found hiding behind the multiplicity of the rhizome? "The tyranny of revisionism."[15] Badiou understood that *Rhizome*'s target was the One divided into two, the famous dialectical machine for breaking bricks using comrade Lin Biao's strategy: "We can't imagine that Deleuze and Guattari are illiterate. So they must therefore be con men."[16] Their heists served a struggle against dialectics and targeted the legitimate rights of the people. Their reduction of the proletarian One to the One of metaphysics offered tangible proof of their fundamental conservatism: they were attacking the hateful choice of class needed to accomplish the legitimate proletarian revolution. Finally, Deleuze and Guattari invited their readers to confine themselves to the role of passive spectators, as Raymond Aron did, which amounted to a betrayal of the working class: "'Play quietly in your corner' is the watchword of rhizomatic multiplicities."[17] But behind the innocent exterior reminiscent of a children's amusement park, "Deleuze and Guattari are protofascist ideologues. Denial of morality, the cult of natural affirmation, repudiation of antagonism, an esthetics of multiplicity allowing the One of tyranny to persist as an underlying political condition and indelible source of fascination."[18]

The prosecution brooked no appeal. This savage attack was the crowning moment of the years of verbal guerilla warfare against Deleuze led by Badiou and his Maoist troops on the Vincennes campus since the early 1970s. At the height of the conflict, Badiou's "men" would prevent Deleuze from finishing his seminar; he would put his hat back on his head to indicate his surrender. Badiou himself would occasionally turn up at Deleuze's seminar to interrupt him, as he admits in the book he wrote on Deleuze in

1997: "For a Maoist like me, Deleuze, the philosophical inspiration for what I call the 'anarchist-desirers,' is a formidable enemy, all the more so since he works from within the 'movement' and his seminar is a university institution. I've never minced my words; *consensus* is not my strong suit. I myself once led a 'brigade' to intervene in his seminar."[19]

In 1970, Alain Badiou and Judith Miller even created a course together just to monitor the political content of other classes in the philosophy department. Alain Roger, a former student and friend of Deleuze, still remembers Deleuze's pique on the day it was his turn to be inspected by Badiou's "brigade": "I've got to go because I've got Badiou's gang coming."[20] Deleuze reacted extremely calmly to the interventions and avoided direct clashes, even when groups of up to a dozen people bent on picking a fight would show up. "OK Deleuze, it's all very well what you're doing here, but you're just talking all by yourself in front of a captive audience! Look at all your admirers in front of you. They've been struck dumb! They're not saying a word! Is that your approach? Define your approach for us!"[21] Philippe Mengue remembers the virulence of his accusers, who "wanted to make Deleuze contradict himself, turning up with copies of Nietzsche and asking trick questions to try to catch him out."[22] Often the "brigade" would end up imposing the "People's Rule," commanding the students to quit Deleuze's classroom on the pretext of a meeting in Lecture Hall 1 or a rally in support of a workers' struggle. Deleuze reacted calmly, pretending to agree with them and retaliating with irony.

Deleuze was not the only target of Badiou's "brigades." Jean-François Lyotard, another "desirer," also figured on the list of those who had to be disturbed to ensure the salvation of their flocks. Even François Châtelet, the diplomatic chairman of the department since Foucault's departure, was on the list of prey. During the 1970s, however, the Maoist tribunal waned along with the steady decline of troops subscribing to Maoism, and as the years went on, Deleuze's seminar was spared the incursions of the worshippers of the little red book.

When Deleuze died in 1995, Badiou paid him an impassioned tribute. He considered himself the worthy successor to Deleuze's philosophical authority at Paris-VIII, providing that Deleuze's books were reread according to the rules of "proper philosophy." Two years after Deleuze's death, Badiou dedicated a book to him, which aimed to establish how close their relations had been, even if they were purely conflictual.[23] It is true that they had become less polemical in the late 1980s. Even if Badiou was still referring to Stalin and Pol Pot, everyone else had left Maoism far behind by then, and Deleuze had retired in 1987. Badiou began to find some merit in his later books, such as *The Fold*, the essay on Leibniz published in 1988, to which he gave a glowing review in *L'Annuaire Philosophique*. Deleuze, courteous as ever, thanked him warmly, which led Badiou to imagine that together they made "without it being on purpose (on the contrary!) a sort of paradoxical tandem."[24]

When Badiou's *Being and Event* was published in 1988, the two began an exchange of letters comparing their viewpoints; their correspondence lasted from 1992 to 1994 and concerned questions of epistemology and the philosophy of mathematics. Badiou took the initiative, since he wanted to retain some Deleuzean continuity at Paris-VIII—which he managed to do—where large numbers of students wanted to write their thesis on Deleuze. In 1991, when his ex-colleague was finishing *What Is Philosophy?* Badiou suggested scheduling a debate. Deleuze refused, giving a reasoned argument to which Badiou replied in turn. The letters grew into an imposing corpus until late 1994, when both parties agreed to conclude the correspondence. However, Deleuze refused to publish them, and he destroyed the letters, along with all traces of his work in progress, so as to leave only his published work for posterity. Badiou has the complete correspondence at his disposal, but it cannot be published.

In his 1997 homage, Badiou drew a portrait of a Deleuze that was supposed to resemble him but in reality was nothing like the image the Deleuzeans and Guattari held: he produced a sort of pure Deleuze, an essence of Deleuze passed through a filter, an idea of Deleuze without Deleuze. "Which Deleuze?" Badiou asks. The answer: his. Readers were stupefied to learn that Deleuze had proposed a renewed concept of the One, "in its supreme destination, thought is dedicated to the arrival of the One, renamed by Deleuze the One-All."[25] This view was supported by a quotation, taken out of context, which provided the title of his book: "a single clamor of Being for all beings."[26] Badiou thought he could discern in Deleuze's work not a philosophical cry for the liberation of the multiple but the will to develop a metaphysics of the One. Attaining this sublime horizon presupposed separating Deleuze from his many disciples and from all affinity with the sensibilities stemming from 1968. "This 'purified automaton' is certainly much closer to the Deleuzean norm than the bearded 1968 militants bearing the standard of their gross desire."[27]

Badiou's strategy was to return Deleuze to the One, contradicting all of Deleuze's thought, which placed multiplicities at the very core of his philosophical construction: "Their Being, their One and their Whole are artificial and unnatural, always corruptible, fleeting, porous, friable or brittle. . . . For the diversity of the diverse, philosophers substituted the identical or the contradictory."[28] In his December 10, 1985, seminar on Michel Foucault, Deleuze wondered what a dualistic position might consist in and differentiated three types of dualism. The first he considered to be true dualism, which amounted to affirming the existence of two different and incommensurable dimensions. As examples, he used the objective and substantial dualism of Descartes when he differentiates between the substance of mind and that of matter and the subjective dualism of Kant when he distinguishes between receptive and spontaneous cognitive faculties. Added to this true dualism was the use of dualism as a provisional step in attaining the One. In this case, the very movement of division aims at reaching a more fundamental unity. This time Deleuze refers to Spinoza, who distinguishes the attribute of mind from that of extension to attain the unity of substance. In a similar way, Bergson is well known as a master of the duality opposing time and space, matter and memory, or the two sources of morality and religion, but he uses such distinctions methodologically to prepare a reinstatement of a horizon of unity. These ways of thinking remain fundamentally monist, and the collapse occasioned by the tensions of duality always leads to the final triumph of the *élan vital*, ensuring an underlying unity.

The dualism practiced by Foucault and Deleuze was entirely different. And Deleuze attached a primordial importance to it, to the point of claiming that it was what Foucault and he had most in common, even if Foucault did not often use the term "multiplicity," preferring "dispersion" or "dissemination." What is the third form of dualism practiced by Deleuze and Foucault, then? As in Spinoza and Bergson, it was a preliminary step, but the objective was no longer to restore unity but to lead to multiplicities or pluralism. What Deleuze takes from multiplicity is, unlike the adjective "multiple," the fact of becoming a noun, a "multiplicity" rather than a simple attribute. Multiplicity could then be examined in its own right, and Deleuze attempts to do exactly that, in the same way that he aimed to interrogate difference as such in his thesis, *Difference and Repetition*. Multiplicity is the only war machine that could be used not to restore unity but to combat it. "The only way to carry out a critique of Unity is through multiplicity, not by the multiple. I can't destroy unity without substantivizing the multiple."[29]

On the other hand, Badiou was correct in qualifying Deleuze's thought as "ascetic," and he refers to his connection with the Stoics. However, no sooner does he give precedence to the rigor peculiar to Deleuze than Badiou claims that the philosophy of life advocated by Deleuze was in fact a "philosophy of death."[30] How could someone driven by the Spinozan *conatus* and who claimed in 1988 that "Everything I've written is vitalistic, at least I hope it is, and amounts to a theory of signs and events"[31] be motivated by some form of death drive? Against all evidence, Badiou persists: "This identity between thinking and dying is expressed in a veritable hymn to death, where Deleuze slips effortlessly into Blanchot's path."[32]

According to his Paris-VIII students, Deleuze was always courteous, despite the untimely interruptions of Badiou's supporters or, for that matter, of the many schizophrenics who came to the seminar. Only once did he get angry, when he found on his desk a tract by a "death squad" advocating suicide. In his May 27, 1980, class, he claimed that death was an exterior force and could under no circumstances be conceived as a process. "When I hear the idea that death may be a process, my whole heart and all my emotions bleed."[33] The death drive physically disgusted him, and everything in him resisted it so as to allow the forces of life and creativity to triumph.

Continuing in the same vein in his efforts to paint an unrecognizable portrait of Deleuze, Badiou made him into a systemic, abstract philosopher who cared little for individual cases and preferred a system producing concepts that "I would not hesitate to call *monotonous*."[34] It is certain that Badiou's portrait had few similarities, as he himself admitted, with what he called the established *doxa*. To top it all off, Badiou called Deleuze an aristocratic thinker, taking his contempt for debates and discussions as proof of his undemocratic attitude.

During his demonstration, Badiou reduces Deleuze's singularity by assimilating his positions to a simple derivation of Heideggerian ontology. Contrary to his pretensions of wanting to think against his own period, Deleuze would become instead merely a pale reproduction of a century dominated by Heidegger. If Deleuze assimilates philosophy and ontology, then his goal is Being. In this sense, Deleuze would have been spared the radical break of Kant's modernity and would not have partaken in the critical nature of his philosophy. He would have remained a resolutely classical thinker—and Badiou was happy to recognize himself in this attitude. However, he distanced himself from Deleuze when he granted a strategic position to the virtual, since he then became a prisoner of transcendence: "This is also the concept that most sharply separates me from him."[35] Now the philosopher of immanence is on the brink of the most blatant failure of his philosophical enterprise.

It was precisely this question that inaugurated the exchange of letters between the two men, which began in 1993: Badiou wrote to Deleuze to inform him that the category of the virtual maintained a form of transcendence: "Deleuze at once recognized that this was at the heart of our controversy."[36] In his reply, Deleuze insisted on the reality of the virtual. Taking their epistolary arguments as a starting point, Badiou made the most astounding reversal. Using Deleuze's claim that the undecidable nature of a thrown die is attached to a single throw, Badiou contrasted his conception of the irreducible nature of every roll of the dice, each one being ontologically distinct, and concluded that Deleuze was defending multiplicity and the event as rupture, whereas Deleuze would consider himself on the side of unity, continuity, and the eternal return of the same. "For Deleuze, chance is a game of All and it is always replayed as such. For me, there's a multiplicity (and rarity) of chances."[37]

Badiou's reading of *The Fold* lent support to his hypothesis, which amounted to considering Deleuze as backward looking, as playing games with the creases and unfoldings of tradition and with the already-there in a memory that offers a form of subjectification, with Badiou being the only one of the two really receptive to absolute beginnings and true events. Deleuze's extreme sensitivity to all forms of radical creativity in every domain, according to Badiou, did nothing but establish so many experimental fields showing the unfolding of Being. Deleuze joined Badiou in a metaphysical philosophy of Being and its ontological foundation but remained on the sidelines by showing himself incapable of recommending a radically new way of thought. Dubbing himself the rightful heir to the question of Truth, Badiou made Deleuze into a defender of time standing still. Any reader even slightly familiar with Deleuze would be left speechless at Badiou's sleight of hand when, in complete denial of Deleuze's singularity and of his privileged relation to Nietzsche, he presents him as a eulogist of the duty of memory, a defender of the memorial burden who completed his philosophy as "a memorial injunction to forever begin anew."[38] Deleuze an anti-Nietzschean! The scene of this *disputatio* thus set the master of Truth and the event, played by Badiou, against the upholder of memorial tradition and the cult of Falsehood, played by Deleuze. As a diligent Maoist, Badiou remained true to the logic of cleansing, to the *tabula rasa* of the past against those whom he even recently called "renegades."[39]

No serious reader of Deleuze recognizes even the slightest resemblance to him in Badiou's caricature. A deforming-recuperative maneuver of this kind is particularly violent, more so even than a straightforward polemic. The Deleuzeans recognized it immediately for what it was and reacted to the portrait of a pseudo-Deleuze behind which it was easy to see Badiou. The most scathing retort came from Arnaud Villani, a leading expert on Deleuze's writings, who disputed Badiou's methodology itself, which consisted in claiming to discuss the views of another philosopher without taking into account or giving any account of what he actually thought.[40]

According to Villani, Badiou presupposes Deleuze to be "inherently dishonest,"[41] to the extent that he would have knowingly cultivated ambiguity in order to better manipulate and bewitch his disciples. In a special issue of *Futur Antérieur*, Villani argued adamantly against the image of Deleuze as a philosopher fascinated by death. Badiou saw Deleuze as a partisan of the One as opposed to the multiple, using a sort of "one-legged philosophy," wrote Villani, whereas Badiou, on the other hand, as a good disciple of Mao, continued to march on both legs. In the same issue, the Portuguese Deleuzean José Gil reacted to what he called a "nasty book,"[42] correctly identifying Badiou's implacable logic in proving to the reader that where Deleuze had failed he had succeeded and that Deleuze's books should therefore be left on the shelf to allow more time for reading Badiou. A *contrario*, Gil emphasized the endogenous movement of Deleuze's thought and its deviations, such as the decisive moment, in his own view, when he noted the near failure of his ontological project. This was why his meeting with Guattari was crucial: from then on, he no longer worked within concepts but let them "be irrigated until they overflow by the movement that brought them into being, which stems from elsewhere but bears the imprint of where and how fast they proceed."[43]

In the same spirit as Badiou, the philosopher Guy Lardreau published a short pamphlet in 1999 evocatively entitled *Delayed Philosophy*,[44] which aimed to demonstrate how Deleuze had reneged on his promises whereas Badiou had honored them. Lardreau explicitly saw his work as complementary to Badiou's book: "*Deleuze: The Clamor of Being*. This book gives me the freedom to take a sideways look at Deleuze's metaphysics, since it attacks it head on."[45] Of course, Lardreau's bone of contention was with Deleuze's denunciation of the "new philosophers," of which Lardreau was one; Lardreau also had a Maoist past. But Lardreau was also part of the generation influenced by Deleuze's books to the extent that he admitted, in a pastiche of Engels, "in the history of philosophy, we were all Deleuzeans for a moment."[46]

Lardreau denounced Deleuze as an infiltrating tactician who, like a tick, lodged himself under the skin of philosophical works and institutions to corrupt them from within and feed on their blood. "Deleuze's policy was 'infiltration,'"[47] citing as evidence Deleuze's many acts of allegiance to his first teachers Hyppolite, Alquié, Canguilhem, and thus to the academic institution. Deleuze was therefore a "forger," although Lardreau made it clear that no true Deleuzean should be offended, since their hero had, after all, written in praise of the false. Deleuze was quite aware of his successive forcings, and to impose them as the next *doxa*, according to Lardreau, he employed intellectual terrorism and intimidation. If he were faithful to anything, it was to Bergsonism. "Deleuze is badly written Bergson."[48] The mere name of Bergson was enough to disqualify his adversary and relegate him to the spheres of outdated spiritualism and the defense of the established order. "He was only ever interested in doctrines attached to the order of things."[49] The stage was set for Badiou's dialectical materialism and against the outdated spiritualism of the fake modernist Deleuze.

In 1977, Jean Baudrillard published *Forget Foucault*, an attack aimed primarily at the author of *The Order of Things* but that also had Deleuze and Guattari's work in its sights.[50] Baudrillard denounced the thinkers of desire as upholders of the current order who were desperate for power. Like Narcissus, they were prisoners of their own fascinating image, and Foucault was thus the one who, via his knowledge-power-pleasure trilogy, "helped put a power into place which functioned like desire, just as Deleuze established a desire resembling future powers. The collusion is too perfect not to be suspect."[51] Baudrillard attacked the views of *Anti-Oedipus* head on, seeing it as a vain attempt to save both Marxism and psychoanalysis. The Oedipal criticism of psychoanalysis merely exalted the most extreme forms of the axiomatic of desire. As for the defense of "productivity" and "desiring machines," it was a return to the "expurgated axioms of Marxism and psychoanalysis."[52] According to Baudrillard, on the contrary, the only valid logic circulates within the simulacrum, and nothing remains of production and power but illusion. "It has escaped Foucault that power is dying its last death."[53]

THE NEW PHILOSOPHERS: "A BOTCHED JOB"

Most importantly, 1977 was also the year of the great confrontation between Deleuze and the "new philosophers," who shrewdly used the media to put on a show before the largest possible audience, performing a tragicomedy amounting to them disengaging from their involvement in the Maoist proletarian left. Revolutionary eschatology was on its last legs, and it was time for a whole generation to throw off the legacy of '68 in one fell swoop and acknowledge their sins: "Those spoiled kids, those great overgrown children wanted the revolution to come straight away, but no! It didn't happen and they began to shuffle their feet. . . . Poor little lost kittens!"[54] wrote the journalist Pierre Viansson-Ponté. The Mao worshippers—André Glucksman, Christian Jambet, Guy Lardreau, Bernard-Henri Lévy, and many other adepts of the mystical adherence to the Great Helmsman—had discovered the discrete charms of liberalism and a horror of totalitarianism, a concept they claimed to have invented, conveniently overlooking the decisive contributions of people such as Hannah Arendt.

In 1977, Bernard-Henri Lévy published a book so in tune with the spirit of the times that it immediately became a bestseller: *Barbarism with a Human Face*. He denounced May '68 as an image of Evil disguising its Master, seeing in the movement the bleak, lifeless dusk of the twentieth century. "We are experiencing the end of history because we live in the orbit of continued capitalism."[55] Bernard-Henri Lévy massacred Deleuze and Guattari, among others, considering them as expressions of everyday fascism, "barbaric figures." Wrongly assimilating their philosophy to an ideology of desire, he denounced a new form of barbarism: "We know them well, these knights with their light-hearted airs, these fiendishly anti-Marxist and joyously iconoclastic apostles of drifting, bards of the multiple. . . . They have their helmsmen, these sailors of a modern ship of fools, Saint Giles and Saint Félix, shepherds of the great family and authors of *Anti-Oedipus*."[56] Making fascism into a matter of libido on the surface of the social body and at the mercy of fluctuating power relations is part of the "barbarism with a human face" condemned by Bernard-Henri Lévy. The verdict brooks no challenge. "The ideology of desire is a figure of barbarism in the very rigorous sense in which I have defined it."[57]

The pamphlet was delivered by a handsome young man sporting a white shirt, unbuttoned at the neck. "BHL," the darling of Françoise Verny, soon became a brand name and pleased his publishers with his huge print runs. Grasset's golden boy was applauded by a large readership ready to lacerate itself for past errors. The rest was a matter of marketing and networking, shuttling BHL between television studios and press releases.

For Deleuze and Guattari, this bustle was more redolent of the circus than of philosophical speculation, and they found it quite amusing. But when Michel Foucault got involved and became an advocate of the "new philosophers," they could no longer remain silent. Foucault praised Glucksman's *The Master Thinkers* in *Le Nouvel Observateur*,[58] paying tribute to a "great philosophical work." According to Foucault, Glucksman "brings to light at the heart of the most elevated philosophical discourse the runaways, victims, diehards, and righted dissidents—in short, those 'bloody heads' and white ghastly apparitions that Hegel wanted to wipe from the night of the world."[59] Now with the blessing of a Foucault, a true philosopher whom Deleuze held in high esteem, the issue became serious and called for an appropriate response.

Without consulting Deleuze and Guattari, two young philosophers, François Aubral and Xavier Delcourt, were preparing a short critical anthology denouncing "new philosophy."[60] The press attaché for the Gallimard publishing house, Paule Neuvéglise, was looking for an opportunity to promote Aubral before a dreaded appearance on Bernard Pivot's show *Apostrophes*. She had selected him to be one of Philippe Sollers's interrogators on the program *L'homme en question*. Aubral did his duty in a very direct fashion: "Philippe Sollers, you've been a Maoist, a Papist, a feminist, and an antifeminist. Who are you really?"

Deleuze's friend François Châtelet had let him know that a pamphlet was to be published on the "new philosophers," and he was delighted at Aubral's insolence on television. He asked to meet him and invited the two authors of the forthcoming book to dinner. "So we spent the evening starry-eyed at Deleuze's, and Deleuze became the grand sorcerer in relation to this business of the new philosophers."[61] Aubral and Delcourt began by saying how astonished they were that figures such as Deleuze and Châtelet had not spoken out. They let Deleuze know that it would take merely a few words on his part, just a short article to reduce them to dust. "Ah, yes," he said to us, "but you know, they'd just say I was jealous of the younger generation. And I don't want speak to the media, you know I don't go in for that, it's not my sort of thing."[62]

Deleuze went on wondering what he might be able to do and how he might intervene: "We are in a *samizdat* situation. We are in the minority. I need to tell you who these people are. They are always on the side of whoever is in power, no matter what."[63] As the evening went on, Deleuze considered various options with his guests. He thought about writing a short book prefaced by Aubral and Delcourt, but the idea made them laugh. At the end of the evening, Deleuze wished his guests well and warned them what was in store. "He was right because I wasn't familiar with Glucksman the orator, but on the television set as soon as I brought up an intellectual theme, he hit back with concentration camps, Poland . . . and you were dead."[64]

Deleuze thought the best thing to do was to consult Jérôme Lindon at the Minuit publishing house. He was considering writing a few pages as a short booklet, and since there was no question of making any money out of something like that, he asked Lindon to distribute it free to all bookshops, to make it available to customers at the checkout counter. It was no sooner said than done. Jérôme Lindon agreed; the whole thing was to remain a secret. But *Le Monde* got wind of it and immediately published the text in its "Ideas" column on June 19–21, 1977. In the meantime, it was snapped up in the bookshops.

Dated June 5, 1977, Deleuze's text was presented as an interview. An exceptional situation called for an exceptional response, and Deleuze broke with his principle of never wasting time on polemics, which drained his strength of affirmation. But on this occasion, he was caustic, conscious of how dangerous such two-bit philosophers were to thinking itself. To the question: "What do you think of the 'new philosophers'?" Deleuze replied sharply,

> Nothing. I think their philosophy is worthless. I can see two reasons for their worthlessness. First of all, they employ grand concepts as large as craters. LAW, POWER, FAITH, REBELLION, THE MASTER, THE WORLD and so forth. This enables them to come up with grotesque mixtures and simplistic dualities: law and the rebel, power

and the angel. At the same time, the more vacuous the content of their thought, the greater the importance given to the thinker, to the *subject of utterance* in relation to his empty statements.[65]

Deleuze explained that what had changed in the situation and allowed him to intervene was the publication of the "fine, stimulating book" by Aubral and Delcourt.

The affair was serious, according to Deleuze, precisely because it was not serious, and their apology for thought was seductive because it gave the impression that you could do without the complex work of defining precise concepts that were necessary in order to avoid these sorts of dualistic and simplistic dilemmas. "They are spoiling the work that's been done," he commented, in particular the effort he had put in with Guattari. It was time to put things back in their rightful place, and Deleuze identified in the "new philosophers" a carefully orchestrated and engineered phenomenon.[66] What was new was using the logic of marketing in a philosophical area. As Deleuze remarked, someone was bound to have thought of it eventually.

Deleuze identified two major reasons for the triumph of the new philosophers. On the one hand, the relations between journalism and intellectual creation were reversed. The journalistic act created the event, which led to a sort of "minute-thought," since there was no time left for thought to develop. On the other hand, the philosopher "buffoons" were driven by their hatred of 1968. "It's a contest to see who can heap the most dirt on May '68. . . . Their resentment of '68 is all they're trying to sell."[67] The ten-year anniversary of May '68 was approaching, and a part of that generation had turned their backs on their unfulfilled dreams with great delight, in the name of the failure of revolutionary ruptures. Deleuze once more expressed a deeply held conviction in his rejection of the "new philosophers," who were companions of a culture of death.

> What disgusts me is very simple: the new philosophers have made a martyrology of the Gulag and the victims of history. They live off corpses. . . . Those victims had to think and live in a very different way from the people who shed tears in their name, and think in their name, and teach in their name. As a general rule, those who risk their lives think in terms of life, not of death, bitterness and morbid vanity. Resistance fighters like the good things in life.[68]

In the face of dangers that would deaden centuries of philosophical effort, Deleuze offered a hymn to life. The whole of Deleuze and Guattari's project aimed at allowing air to circulate. By contrast, the new philosophers "have rebuilt a stuffy, airless room in a place where a breeze was blowing. It is the negation of all forms of politics and experimentation. In short, what I reproach them with is botching the job."[69]

PART 3

SURPLICES

1980–2007

21

Guattari Between Culture and Ecology

In May 1981, it finally seemed that François Mitterrand would embody the long-nurtured hope of "changing life" through politics. He had represented the left since 1965 and appeared to be the only politician who could challenge General de Gaulle. The thrust of May '68, blunted by the Gaullist triumph in the legislative elections of June 30, finally affected national politics. The uninterrupted postwar domination by the right was over. Mitterrand's 1981 victory thus ended the right's uncontested power, and the elections elicited tremendous enthusiasm in France.

Deleuze and Guattari were also buoyed by the political euphoria. Deleuze attended Mitterrand's jubilant inauguration in the Pantheon on May 21, 1981. Jack Lang's nomination as minister of culture delighted Guattari, as Lang had already demonstrated his sympathy for artists and his desire to change cultural practices profoundly. Guattari even published a quasi-apologetic article in 1983 defending Jack Lang against the vicious campaigns against him. "Finally Jack Lang has come."[1] Guattari was enchanted by Lang's unconventional, enthusiastic, and relatively informal style and his capacity for listening. "Against all evidence, Jack Lang is accused of working to subject culture to state control, as was the case in Eastern Europe. What a peculiar Jdanov, who in truth, encourages the most diverse initiatives, including some extremely surprising ones."[2] Jack Lang made several unusual decisions, including the creation of a music festival that was spectacularly popular. In addition, in May 1981, Guattari won one of his most important battles in liberating the airwaves.

THE HALLS OF POWER

Guattari was an important resource who suggested many ideas to Lang. In August 1981, Guattari wrote to Lang, saying, "We would also like to talk to you about a particularly important topic, which is creating a fourth TV station that would be cultural, devoted to creative, experimental research."[3] In February 1982, Guattari suggested creating a foundation for local initiatives, institutional innovations, social-science research, and cultural activities. Lang told his assistant, Dupavillion, to follow up, commenting, "We should help them . . . it's very important." Guattari's idea was that the decentralization under way might not succeed if it were limited to simply transferring power: thus the idea of creating a third sector "between the capitalist market and government-controlled systems."[4] Jack Lang supported the project and obtained a meeting for a large delegation headed by Guattari, with Jacques Attali, Mitterrand's chief adviser at the Elysée. The foundation was provisionally named the Innovation, Research, Creation Center, or FIRC. Guattari worked tirelessly in government circles to see the project through, meeting with Eric Arnoult and Ségolène Royal: nothing ever came of it. He even met with Jean-Louis Bianco, the general secretary of the president of the republic, hoping to make some headway by proposing that the foundation come under the aegis of a major ministry.

Guattari was actively involved in organizing Kafka's centenary, but he also helped out privately, for example by writing Mitterrand's speech on culture that he gave at the Sorbonne. Jack Lang had Guattari named commander of arts and letters in January 1983. "I am rather indifferent to the symbols of merit and even less able to judge them, so I consider this to be, above all, a gesture of your friendship."[5]

During the 1980s, Lang and Guattari grew friendlier. Lang visited La Borde at Guattari's invitation, and Guattari helped him find a house near Blois. "Thanks again for your hospitality in the Loir-et-Cher. It was magnificent."[6] In 1984, deeply involved in preparing the Kafka centenary, Guattari was invited to lunch with Lang at the ministry. Before the lunch, Guattari wrote to Lang to see how the current projects were faring; most of them were simply stagnating. It was a real show: Lang provided Guattari with entries to several ministries. In 1986, he met with Georgina Dufoix, minister of social affairs and national solidarity. In 1991, Lang proposed to Prime Minister Michel Rocard that Guattari be named to the Economic and Social Council.

At the end of the 1980s, Guattari suggested organizing a universal exhibition to commemorate the bicentennial of the 1789 revolution, on the theme of "Meeting the Fifth World." It would be a large international meeting of representatives from tribal and nomadic minorities from Alaska to the Amazon, China and the Sahara, as well as gypsies from various countries. The goal was not merely to seek justice for oppressed and persecuted populations but also to recognize their contributions to world culture. Despite Jack Lang's very positive commentary—"This project is *fantastic.* Our friend Guattari has a lot of ideas"[7]—the political climate of 1989 did not lend itself particularly well to this kind of event, and the project did not get far. Thanks to his friend Jan-Pierre Faye, who was very close to the Socialist leaders, Guattari finally managed to meet Mitterrand and sat at his table. "Felix spoke up to defend Lang, who was now only a deputy minister relegated to a subministry. Very courageously, starting out strong, my little Félix started talking to the president. 'You should grant culture its full due.'"[8]

Guattari was also involved in creating an international college of philosophy, under Faye's impetus. The idea had arisen because of the situation at the philosophy department at Paris-VIII, which had been moved from Vincennes to Saint-Denis in 1980 and whose diplomas were no longer nationally recognized. [9]"If you see Attali, talk to him now about this possible project, the Philosophical College, where Gilles Deleuze and Félix Guattari will be the soul of Vincennes . . . and where we could invite distinguished international or nonuniversity types to give short or long courses."[10] When Jean-Pierre Chevènement was named minster for national education, Faye suggested the project again and received a favorable reaction from the minister, who told him to arrange a lunch for the two of them, with François Châtelet, Jacques Derrida, and Dominique Lecourt. The lunch led to the creation of an International College of Philosophy, headed by Derrida. Faye was named to lead the college's "High Council," along with Guattari and other experts including René Thom, Vladimir Jankélévitch, Ilya Prigogine, and Isabelle Stengers. However, it quickly became clear that the real power lay in Derrida's hands. The conflict was all the more inevitable since the boringly named high council had no budget and depended entirely on the college, which held the purse strings.

TOUGH TIMES

Despite all of this activity, Guattari's relationship with the Socialists during the 1980s was not without its problems, crises, and irreversible ruptures. Guattari was less and less involved in the Socialist government's politics and had numerous opportunities to manifest his disagreement, which largely explains why many of his projects never took off. In the fall of 1984, Guattari was indignant about the agreement between the Spanish and French governments to extradite Basque ETA nationalists to Spain and broached the topic first with Jack Lang.

> I am *sickened* by these *extraditions* and these *expulsions*. I still cannot believe that the French Socialists have come to this! I know that you are in no way directly responsible for this affair and I can easily imagine your private feelings. Things being what they are, I consider that it is no longer possible to continue a "public" relationship like the one we've had. Please believe that I sincerely regret this and that our friendship endures.[11]

Guattari did not stop at personal and private recriminations; he went on the offensive publicly, and, with Deleuze and Châtelet, wrote an open letter addressed to François Mitterrand, Lionel Jospin (the general secretary of the Socialist Party), and Prime Minister Laurent Fabius that was published in *Le Monde*: "For the Right to Political Asylum, One and Indivisible."[12]

In 1983, the government spokesperson Max Gallo complained publicly about the deafening silence of leftist intellectuals who never lifted a finger to defend the Socialists' policies. This critique at the highest government level led to a lively discussion about the role of intellectuals and their relationships with power. Jean-François Lyotard predicted "a grave for intellectuals,"[13] and Maurice Blanchot, who rarely made public statements, warned against the idea of an eternal rest for intellectuals.[14] This was the situation in which an irritated Guattari intervened both to criticize Max Gallo's remarks, which he deemed a "homily on the softening brains among intellectuals on the Left," and to argue against the idea that intellectuals were natural spokespeople.

Later that same year, a resurgence of racism worried Guattari, who appealed once again for a reaction from the political leadership. "We have the racism we warrant. It is not clear, after May 10 that what we are observing is the status quo. The Socialist government's inability to change the nature of the social fabric has imperceptibly led to a surge in racism."[15] Guattari believed that associations for public utility help people overcome the fears that feed a rejection of others. When the far-right National Front made a dent in the European elections on June 17, 1984, Guattari again criticized the Socialists for losing their bearings because they had not been firmly committed to change. He saw them forced to embark on a path of

> absurd competition with the right about security, austerity, and conservatism. Whereas the appropriate politics could have achieved the necessary economic sacrifices to address the crisis and the changes had it effectively contributed to the arrangement of new modes of collective utterances, instead all hope was disappointed, old corporatisms were back, and old fascistic perversions were gaining ground again.[16]

In the early 1980s, the Initiative Committee for New Spaces of Freedom (CINEL) engaged in several actions intended to clearly demonstrate its international solidarity. It appealed to international public opinion to support the cause of the Sandinistas in Nicaragua against Somoza. The center's headquarters were at Guattari's home in Paris, at 9, rue de Condé. On March 26, 1985, Guattari participated in an international conference on the "collective rights of national minorities in Europe" in Bilbao, Spain. He attacked the disdain with which the subject was treated at a time when national frameworks appeared to be defunct. The upshot was that history was ignoring many minorities. Guattari enumerated them, "Palestinians, Armenians, Basques, Irish, the Corsicans, Lithuanians, Uyghurs, Gypsies, Indians, Australian Aborigines,"[17] seeing in these particular forms of expression a kind of singularity that was to be saved during a period of generalized uniformization but also refusing to consider them as culturally and linguistically isolated groups.

THE ECOLOGICAL REVOLUTION

In the 1980s, Guattari was especially involved in the environmentalist movement. Its leaders had organized large demonstrations in the 1970s, particularly against nuclear energy, and the ecologists won their first election in 1981. Pierre Fournier, who organized the first big ecological demonstration in France, brought together approximately fifteen thousand people in October 1971. In November 1972, he launched the review *La Gueule Ouverte* (*Big Mouth*). A French section of Friends of the Earth had been created in 1971 at the initiative of Alain Hervé, but Brice Lalonde quickly dominated it, claiming to embody the legacy of the "children of May '68."[18] For the first time since 1974, ecology was making its voice heard: René Dumont, the honorary president of Friends of the Earth, won 1.32 percent of the votes in the presidential elections.

In July 1977, at Creys-Malville, forty thousand people protested the construction of the Super-Phoenix supergenerator, despite police restrictions. The demonstration took a bad turn: the police charged, one demonstrator was killed, and about fifty were hurt. Having shown that they could mobilize people, the ecologists got on the ballot in May 1981. Brice Lalonde won 3.9 percent of the vote, representing about one million people. After the elections, Lalonde organized an Ecologist Confederation, which was registered as an association with a decentralized management. In November 1984, at the Clichy meeting, the Ecologist Confederation and the Ecology and Survival organization created by Antoine Waechter in eastern France merged to become the Green Party, which won 3.4 percent of the votes in the European elections of late 1984. Internal dissent, particularly between the left represented by Didier Anger and Yves Cochet and the right led by Jean Briée and Antoine Waechter, weakened the group. Guattari decided to join the Greens at this point in 1985, the year of the *Rainbow Warrior* affair, in which the French Secret Services sank a Greenpeace boat on July 10 off the coast of Auckland, New Zealand. Jean Chesneaux, who later became the honorary president of Greenpeace France, and others organized a small collective protest, "Don't Sink My Boat," with the help of Michel Rocard, the mayor of Conflans-Sainte-Honorine. "We had negotiated with city hall for a boat to demonstrate on the Seine and had naively imagined hundreds of boats waving antinuclear flags, but there were only five. And Guattari was there."[19]

The ecologists were receptive to Guattari's commitment to profound social change and to his critique of the left's politics. He obviously found a home in the left wing of the Greens. After the great student protests of 1986 and the departure of a small group of militants from a slowly dying Unified Socialist Party (PSU),[20] a call was made for a "rainbow" alternative to the traditional leftist parties. The initiative also garnered the support of Renée Dumont and Daniel Cohn-Bendit. Guattari signed the appeal, along with the Green leaders Didier Anger, Yves Cochet, and Dominique Voynet and some non-Greens as well, including Alain Lipietz and some PSU militants, who were inspired by the very powerful German Green Party, the *Grünen*, which had succeeded in creating true associative enclaves within German society and in representing political hope. The signatories of the call for an alternative "to unite transformative social forces in the rainbow of diversity." The December 1986 PSU convention, which imagined its own dissolution, asked outsiders for their reactions to the proposals. Guattari and Daniel Cohn-Bendit responded to their questions, claiming that it was necessary to "encourage what we will call a culture of dissensus, working to deepen specific positions and to resingularize individuals and groups. . . . We should not try to forge some programmatic agreement that ignores differences but rather a collective diagram specifying their practices such that everyone benefits and no one imposes themselves on anyone else."[21] The definition is a synthesis of Guattari's vocabulary and concepts.

The 1988 presidential elections divided the Greens. The left wanted the ex-communist Pierre Juquin as its candidate; Antoine Waechter was a partisan neither "of the right nor the left." Waechter won the bid and took control of the organization by becoming the official Green candidate. He got 3.89 percent of the votes, compared to 2.1 percent for Juquin. Michel Rocard, the recently appointed prime minister, named Brice Lalonde secretary of state and then minister of the environment. In the 1989 European elections, ecologists of all stripes made a major dent by winning 11 percent of the votes and nine seats in the European parliament.

In 1989, Guattari joined another group with ecological leanings, one that had emerged from the Group of Ten, the Science and Culture group, led by, among others, René Passe, Jacques Robin, and Anne-Brigitte Kern, who asked how another left might be imagined. Their first meeting took place at Guattari's home, where they discussed informational change. "For me, he represented transversality and I told him that we should start a journal called *Transversals*. He joined us and wrote about ecosophy for the second issue."[22] Guattari was thus part of the journal's editorial group. "We had many very interesting meetings at Sacha Goldman's house with Edgar Morin, Paul Virilio, Félix Guattari, René Passet, and me."[23] Guattari integrated the environment into his remarks, insisting on the imbalance between North and South, the catastrophic consequences as well as the ethical dimension of the problem. "To be responsible for the responsibility of others, to use Emmanuel Levinas' phrase, doesn't mean giving up our idealistic illusions."[24]

In 1990, Brice Lalonde created Ecology Generation, which planned to locate itself to the left of the Socialist Party but would allow its members to belong to both parties. Several people supported the idea, including Guattari, who was a Green. In fact, Guattari got involved in both organizations, since he was dissatisfied with both Waechter and Lalonde. The Green leaders, however, did not appreciate this double membership and sent Guattari a registered letter telling him to choose, threatening to kick him out of the party. "So it's up to you: if you want to continue to be a member of the Greens, resign from Ecology Generation and send us a copy of your resignation letter by May 14, the date of our next regional Counsel. . . . Unless we hear from you by May 14, we will be forced to consider that you are *de facto* out of the party."[25] Guattari reacted tactically to this ukase, answering that since he had only received the letter on May 13, he couldn't respond by May 14, adding, "I've long found the Greens' organization to be self-absorbed, sectarian, and hyperpartisan, far more concerned about its internal bureaucracy than with social life and the reinvention of new ways of militating."[26] He also added that he was quite critical of Brice Lalonde and claimed to have never intended to remain in Ecology Generation. But, "never having formally joined this association, I can't resign from it."[27]

In early 1992, during the preparations for regional elections, Guattari wrote an article in *Le Monde* about the pettiness of the quarrels between Waechter and Lalonde over the "fuzzy but significant desire of being receptive to 'something else.' . . . It's up to the plural movement of political ecology to give expression to this new aspiration."[28] Somewhat later, Guattari tried to get the militants of the various Green parties to meet, including the Greens and Ecology Generation. After the successful showing in the March 22, 1992, elections, Guattari managed to have a common text adopted by many of the rival militant organizations. Deploring the divisions and sterile polemics, he called for a general meeting of ecologists to unify and mobilize.

This last of Guattari's many battles was waged on the ecological front. Among his handwritten notes is a text dating from a month before his death, entitled "Towards a New Ecological Democracy,"[29] where he observes with satisfaction that a growing percentage of public opinion saw ecologists as the only ones with any new ideas for addressing the essential problems of the period. He regretted only that the two flanks of the movement had aligned themselves too closely with classical models of political parties. "It seems necessary that the living components within each of these movements organize between themselves and together with the associative movement."[30]

In the late 1980s, Guattari invited Paul Virilio, whom he had known since they had both supported Coluche for president, to his home. Virilio was managing a collection at the Galilée publishing house. "I got to his house. We were talking. We were very friendly and I said to him, 'You know, I'd like to publish one of your books in my collection.' He answered, 'Go ahead, there's one lying on the table, no one wants it.' I took a look and took it. He asked me if I'd read it. I said no, but I'll take it."[31] The book was *Schizoanalytic Cartographies*, which Virilio published with Galilée in 1989. It is Guattari's most inaccessible, sophisticated, and logic-based book, and it reflects the activities of the seminar that he gave after finishing *A Thousand Plateaus* in 1980.[32] "It's a little like Guattari's archives, and since he didn't publish much, his archives interested me. I knew that the book would be difficult, but I didn't care much about that."[33] Virilio's impulsive decision to publish the book in a prestigious collection was a moment of enthusiasm. The book never managed to attract a very large public.[34]

Schizoanalytic Cartographies was impressive by virtue of its length. Guattari wanted to add a small piece on ecology. Virilio suggested instead that the ecology part be published separately.[35] "I am instinctive about the beginning of things (like Virilio's collection), and Felix's freshness was important. The text on ecology was as fresh as *Rhizome*."[36] He was right. Published in 1989, *The Three Ecologies* was a success. Guattari defined what he meant by "ecosophy" as the necessary articulation between the political and ethical dimension of the environment, social relationships, and subjectivity. Here, as everywhere, he was concerned with considering modes of subjectification by articulating them from their roots. He observed that technological progress made it possible for people to enjoy more free time but raised the question of how the freedom was used. He also emphasized that the only appropriate analyses were global in an era of global markets. A new paradigm of ethicoaesthetics could encompass the three registers of a mental, social, and environmental ecology. His method—always transversal—sought to demonstrate the potential vectors of subjectification in each case that allowed diverse forms of singularity to develop. Thanks to IT revolutions and to the development of biotechnologies, "new modalities of subjectification are about to see the light of day."[37] Guattari's tone was neither cataclysmic nor lachrymose; rather, he rejoiced in the future workplaces where human intelligence and initiative would be increasingly in demand. He was fascinated with Japan, because that country was able to "graft high-end industries on a collective subjectivity that remained tied to the past, and occasionally to the very distant past (going back to

Shinto-Buddhism in Japan)."[38] Ecosophy, the new discipline, would incorporate this tension.

The Three Ecologies came out in 1989, at a time when the ecologists were busily involved in infighting. Some were arguing for the preservation of the natural environment, leading to the conservative temptation to eliminate technical progress; other committed ecologists were political. "What interested me was that for one of the first times, Felix was describing the three ecologies, meaning, really, the place of a human being in nature with which there has to be an effort to co-evolve."[39] The book also excited Guattari's editor and friend Paul Virilio. "What's important is that ecology is far more than ecology; it's the science of the future. We can't do without it. Ecology will stand as the necessary coherence between the economy in the complex sense of the word and the economy in the ecological sense of the term. The two levels will become one, I am absolutely convinced, and so is Felix."[40]

In *The New Ecological Order*, which came out in 1992, Luc Ferry violently attacked political ecology by trying to reduce Guattari's proposals to a fundamentalist, ultraleftist notion that left no place for human rights, a public space for discussion, or national institutions. Unabashedly confusing the issues, Ferry tried to discredit Guattari's ideas on ecology by linking him with Walther Schoenichen, the author of the Nazi laws on the protection of nature. "For Guattari as for Schoenichen, culture is an ontological reality, not an abstraction: it is part of the being of humans."[41] Ferry completely misunderstood the ecologist struggle, since Guattari had always stated and restated that his ideas were not references to the past.

CHAOSMOSIS

Chaosmosis was published in 1992; it was Guattari's last book.[42] In it, he addressed the idea of the chaosmos that he and Deleuze had already presented. His final work was surely the most accessible and far-reaching of the books that he authored by himself. It was also somewhat of an intellectual testament that he left the year that he died. Its extreme readability had to do with a moment of crystallization and the theoretical and practical experience that he had managed to synthesize. But it was also thanks to the work of his friend, the psychoanalyst Danielle Sivadon. "We rewrote it twice. He had sent the manuscript to Galilée, and it was totally illegible. It had no punctuation or subject. We had to work on two sets of proofs, completely redoing the whole thing."[43]

Guattari wanted to define a new aesthetic paradigm after a process that revisited subjectivity via the machinic. He reasserted the plural, polyphonic nature of his conception of the subject and the importance of the subjectivity that he had encountered in his psychotherapeutic practice. For Guattari, the transversalist method was more effective for considering the often explosive mixture of contemporary subjectivities held hostage to a tension between technological modernity and archaizing commitment. He recalled the criticism of structuralism's reductiveness. "The structuralist current made a serious mistake in claiming to reduce everything about the psyche to the linguistic signifier."[44] He used Daniel Stern's work on infants to understand the emerging character and heterogeneity of subjectivity.[45] In *Chaosmosis*, Guattari discreetly returned to Sartre and the existential question that marked his early work. For him, the consistency of discursive systems was to be sought in their content, "that is, this existential function."[46]

Guattari acknowledged the historical contribution of Freud's thinking, but he wanted to promote an approach that was not organized around the opposition of consciousness and the unconscious but rather where the unconscious was a superposition of different heterogeneous layers of subjectification of variable consistency that produced a flux, which he tried to locate in his schizoanalytic maps.[47] For him, analytic work should not make reference to universals or to predetermined structures but rather to a "constellation of the Universe. Not a universe of general reference but one of realms of incorporeal entities detected at the same time as they are produced. . . . They're given in the instant of creation, like haecceity."[48] This attention to subjectification leads to a rejection of all models that enclose or negate what is new, seeking only regularities and signifying means. Guattari chose process, the irreversible, and singularization. And in order to get beyond binary oppositions, he argued for "the concept of ontological intensity. He implied an ethical-aesthetic commitment to the arrangement of enunciation.[49] Freudian thinking took neurosis as its model, whereas Guattari took psychosis as his model, because in psychosis the other is beyond personal identity, which makes it possible to construct a true heterogeneity.

Drawing on the work of the philosopher Pierre Lévy, Guattari showed that it was impossible to reduce the notion of the machine to mechanical operations. On the one hand, all machines have some part of an "abstract machine," but in the era of robotics and informatics, they have more and more to

do with human intelligence.[50] Like Lévy, Guattari considered that the traditional philosophical "ontological iron curtain" drawn between mind and
matter was no longer pertinent. This gave additional meaning to the other
metaphysics that he and Deleuze had constructed in their work together.

Guattari proposed to extend Francisco Varela's biological notion of
autopoesis, which referred to organisms that engender their own operation and specific limits, to social systems, technical machines, and all
evolving entities once these elements were initially caught in specific arrangements and in becoming. After having again disputed Saussure's division between language and speech, showing the two to be completely intertwined, Guattari defined the new aesthetic paradigm. He began with
the idea that what we perceived in past societies as so many manifestations
of the aesthetic had to do with technical or social imperatives, and he reaffirmed the growing strength of this aestheticizing relationship between
modern human beings and the world. "The aesthetic power to feel seems
about to take precedence in the collective arrangements of enunciations of
our period."[51] This is a sign that modern civilization can only endure by being constantly thrust toward innovation. The process of transformation
continues to raise the question of subjectivity from different angles, however. Subjectivity is no more a natural given than are water or air, so "how
can we work to free it, which is to say, to resingularize it?"[52]

1989: THE COLD WAR ENDS AND THE WALL COMES A-TUMBLING DOWN

Guattari experienced the period of the fall of the Berlin Wall in 1989, the
collapse of communism, and the end of the cold war with the same analytic
acuity. Aware of the risks being created by the multiplication of sectarian
and fundamentalist identities, his optimism and desire for progress toward a better future remained strong. Rather than being discouraged, he
thought that it was now or never for "reinventing politics."[53] The world was
no longer divided between East and West; a process of integration had begun along the lines of world capitalism. In 1987, he wrote an article for
Libération where he described "the new worlds of capitalism."[54] One aspect of postindustrial capitalism or of integrated world capitalism was the
transfer of productive structures of goods and services to productive
structures of signs and subjectivity, meaning the media, surveys, and pub-
licity messages. From these reflections, a final text was written a few weeks

before his death and published posthumously in the October 1992 issue of *Le Monde Diplomatique*.[55] Guattari wanted to shake the growing passivity of a world watching its own destiny on a screen as if it were inevitably escaping its control, whereas the changes taking place would make it possible to create new collective arrangements of enunciations that would affect the entire social fabric. He reiterated the idea that every human being is multiple. "What I plan to emphasize is the fundamentally pluralist, multicentered, heterogeneous character of contemporary subjectivity despite the homogenization that mass mediatization tries to impose. In this respect, an individual is already a 'collective' of different elements."[56] Fordist and Taylorist ideas are already outdated; new collective arrangements of labor need to be invented and conceived on the basis of possible transversalities with the rest of social activities. Guattari insisted on the urgent need to respond to these new challenges, without which the effects of inertia could be cruel and destructive. "If we do not promote a subjectivity of difference, of atypicality, of utopia, our era could slip into horrible conflicts of identity like those now occurring among the people of ex-Yugoslavia."[57]

This allusion to the disastrous implosion of the former Yugoslavia and the risks of a global warlike explosion worried Guattari, who viewed the 1991 Iraq war as a demonstration of American hegemony imposing its solution on the international community. Guattari did not deny that Saddam Hussein bore considerable responsibility for provoking the war, but he pointed out a perversion in the international order that created this disastrous situation: the complicity of major powers in the Iraq-Iran conflict, unresolved Lebanese and Palestinian problems, the policies of the major oil companies, and, "generally, that the relationship between the North and the South continues to be catastrophic."[58]

Deleuze also passionately rejected the war in Iraq. He and his Paris-VIII colleague René Schérer wrote a particularly severe article, "The Filthy War,"[59] which denounced the destruction of the Iraqi nation on the pretense of liberating Kuwait by a Pentagon described as "the organ of State terrorism experimenting with its weapons."[60] They also attacked the French government for doing little more than lining up behind America. "Our government continues to renege on its declarations and rush further and further into a war that it could have opposed. Bush congratulates us as one would congratulate a house servant."[61]

Sacha Goldman encouraged his friend Guattari to begin a multiphase dialogue with Paul Virilio on the aftermath of the Gulf War while the war in the former Yugoslavia was raging. Three sessions were organized on May 4, 1992, June 22, 1992, and August 4, 1992. "The Spanish War was a laboratory. . . . The Gulf War and the war in Yugoslavia are laboratories for what will come later. . . . Given what's just happened in the 1990s, it's the end of weapons of mass destruction that's taking place to the benefit of the media weapons."[62] In the dialogue, Guattari constantly came back to what he considered the major question of modes of changing subjectivity, linking new military technologies and strategies to the "conditions of production of subjectivity to which they are attached."[63] In August, Sacha Goldman sent the transcript of the dialogue to Guattari and Virilio. As he was correcting the text, Virilio got a phone call from Antoine de Gaudeman. "He said to me, 'Paul, have you seen what's happened to Félix?' I said, 'no, is he angry?' Because we'd argued a bit and I thought that he didn't want to do the book with me any more. He said, 'No, he's dead.' "[64]

22

Deleuze Goes to the Movies

On November 10, 1981, Deleuze gave the first lecture of his morning course on cinema; little could he know what would ensue. He devoted three academic years,[1] 250 class hours, and two books to film.[2] This new cycle of studies began immediately after his collaboration with Félix Guattari had drawn to a close. In working on a topic not typically addressed by classical philosophy, was Deleuze taking a respite from philosophy? Not at all. As was often the case, moving into new areas of reflection was the result of both contingent, external factors and the internal necessities of his philosophical reflection.

A Friend of the *Cahiers du Cinéma*

In 1980, Alice Saunié-Seité, the minister of universities, relocated the experimental Paris-VIII university campus from the Vincennes Woods in eastern Paris to the northern Saint-Denis suburb. Because of the move, the campus' grounds and space were more limited. Research and teaching were also affected, but the space crunch led to some productive meetings, including one between the departments of philosophy and film and audiovisual studies.[3] The film department was unusual because it linked theory and practice. Many film directors were invited to the university, including Jacques Rivette, who taught there until 1970. After his departure, the department invited Jean Narboni, associate editor of the *Cahiers du Cinéma*. "They laughed in our faces at the ministry when we asked for film equipment. They acted as if we were dragging the university down, that it was undignified, that there were film schools. But the link between theory and practice was important to us."[4]

A degree program in film was created with a carefully defined curriculum, but thesis directors who had the credentials to direct the doctoral students had to be found. The former March 22 members Guy Fihman and Claudine Eizykman had headed the film department since its creation, and their relations with Jean-François Lyotard had always been excellent, so they asked the philosophy department to oversee research in the film department. Jean Narboni and a few others, including the directors Serge Le Péron and Jean-Henri Roger, were Deleuzeans, as was Dominique Villain, an expert on film esthetics. Since the late 1970s, Guy Fihman and Claudine Eizykman had been teaching film using Bergsonian categories. "As a result, we had a new situation where doctoral students in the film department were being advised by our colleagues from the philosophy department: Jean-François Lyotard, who gave a seminar on the esthetics of the sublime, and Gilles Deleuze, who finally got the opportunity to have his love of cinema and his philosophical interests converge."[5] Although there is no trace in Deleuze's 1966 book on Bergson of his contribution to cinematography,[6] Deleuze did link Bergson and cinema in a piece he wrote on Godard for *Cahiers* in 1976.[7]

There were proposals both serious and less so for doctoral theses, including one request that Deleuze direct a thesis on puppet theater in Lebanon. "Deleuze called me up to say that he had absolutely no expertise in this area, and I told him that I didn't either."[8] Deleuze was on the verge of approving the request simply out of generosity when some Lebanese students told him there had never been any puppet theater in Lebanon and that they suspected that the guy making the request was a cop. "Another time, it was to study the place of workers in Syrian cinema. Deleuze called me again saying that he didn't know anything about this topic and I told him, once again, that I knew as little as he did."[9]

A Brazilian student named André de Souza Parente came to Paris-VIII in 1982, having already read Deleuze and Foucault at the University of Rio and having made a few experimental films. He wanted to earn a doctorate in film studies and enrolled in the film department, but he could not find any accredited professor to direct his research; the film department suggested that Deleuze be his official thesis director. This administrative decision turned out to be a blessing for Parente, who was more passionate about philosophy than about film theory. He attended Deleuze's courses assiduously and wrote his doctoral thesis[10] on "Cinematic Narrativity and Non-Narrativity." Initially reluctant to take him on, Deleuze sent Parente back to the film department, but Pariente insisted on having Deleuze read the thesis. "Once he'd read my thesis, everything changed. He said, 'Not only do I find this extremely interesting, but I'll need you next year,' because he was planning to deal with semiology."[11] Parente defended the thesis in 1988 with Deleuze as his advisor.[12]

Deleuze was a film lover long before he began to write about the cinema. Serge Toubiana, a critic at the *Cahiers du Cinéma*, recalled having seen Deleuze every year since the mid-1970s in the audience of the annual week-long festival of undistributed films organized by *Cahiers* at the Action République cinema. "We felt proud to see him in the crowd that came to view 'our' films every year."[13] According to Toubiana, Deleuze was the only great thinker of the period to "truly love cinema."[14] He very quickly grasped the power of cinema and the need to reflect on this new mode of expression for thinking the world. Consequently, the critics from the *Cahiers du Cinéma* and Deleuze became so deeply enmeshed in discussion that when Deleuze died, Toubiana paid homage to him: "Cinema is the movement of the mind. Cinema *is* Deleuzean."[15]

Deleuze first spoke publicly about cinema in 1974, defending Hugo Santiago's *The Others*, which had created a stir at the Cannes Film Festival and in which Noëlle Châtelet, the young wife of Deleuze's friend François Châtelet, played a role. He praised the film's mobility and its use of the camera, which moved like a rice planter, making many gestures rather than a single planting movement.[16]

In February 1977, after having censored many films the year before, the minister of the interior censored *L'ombre des anges* (*The Shadow of Angels*) by Daniel Schmid. About fifty film directors, critics, and intellectuals signed a petition protesting what they considered a breach of freedom of expression; the decision to censor the film was accompanied by acts of violence. Smoke bombs were set at the Saint-André-des-Arts cinema, to dissuade the few would-be spectators. The film's detractors accused it of being anti-Semitic, which the petition's signers, including Deleuze, refuted.

Deleuze wrote a piece in the February 18 edition of *Le Monde*. He did not deny that films could be anti-Semitic, but he argued that in this specific case the "accusation was inane. It's unbelievable."[17] Certainly there was the issue of a character named the "rich Jew," but the director had explained that he always created something of a disjunction between the faces, the actors, and their discourses. It was pointless to look for signs of this "crazy accusation of anti-Semitism."[18] Deleuze warned against a rising neofascism created by the quiet accumulation of small fears and by equally numerous microfascisms, including the censorship of this film. Deleuze's longtime, loyal friend Claude Lanzmann answered Deleuze's article with a brutal article in *Le Monde*, which made the widening rift between the two quite public. Lanzmann found the film to be unambiguously anti-Semitic. "The legitimate heir to the *Jew Süss* and the *Eternal Jew*, a direct descendant of the zenith of Nazi productions, R. W. Fassbinder and Daniel Schmid's *Shadow of Angels* is an anti-Semitic film certified by the leftist critics in France as being above suspicion."[19] Lanzmann pointed out that the Israeli delegation had walked out of the Cannes Film Festival the previous year in protest against the film's screening and to denounce the "terrorism" of the cinephilic cliques. He attacked Deleuze, who had come to the defense of the unspeakable: "Deleuze blandly concedes that the word 'rich Jew' is very important. Not the word, Deleuze, the thing. Not important, it's fundamental. Without 'the rich Jew'—and Deleuze knows this—there is no film."[20]

During these same years, thanks to Jean Narboni, a bond was forged between Deleuze and the *Cahiers*. Narboni had first learned about Deleuze in 1964, from Barbet Schroeder, who had come to the office announcing that he had just read an extraordinary book: Deleuze's *Proust and Signs*. It took some years, however, for Narboni to connect with Deleuze. In the mid-1960s, the *Cahiers* was going through its Maoist phase, and it took an ultratheoretical Lacano-Althusserian line, with a bit of populism borrowed from President Mao's little red book; it firmly turned its back on bourgeois cinema. The journal's rigid politics led François Truffaut to refuse to have his name appear in the review as of 1970; sales dropped in response.[21] After 1968, a cultural group (*Front Q*) of film and cultural reviews was created including the journals *Tel Quel*, the *Cahiers*, and *Cinéthique*. At the *Cahiers*, this group launched vehement attacks against Yves Boisset, Louis Malle, Jean-Louis Bertucelli, and other so-called bourgeois directors. In 1972, the *Cahiers*, under Pascal Bonitzer, ignored two important films, Jean Eustache's *The Mother and the Whore* and Marco Ferreri's *La Grande Bouffe* (*The Big Feast*). "I felt like we were at an absolute dead end. Great works of art were destined for us but we were incapable of looking at them."[22]

Despite their very strong political allegiance to the revolutionary movement, the *Cahiers* was not living up to its responsibilities, and during the summer of 1973, the editors were asked to demonstrate their loyalty to the militants by helping promote Mao's thinking. The new *Front Q* gave them one year to achieve that goal, but from then on, with the decline of the radical left and of Maoism, things began to change. The *Cahiers* had a very limited stable of film directors; Jean-Marie Straub and Jean-Luc Godard were the only two that they praised unreservedly.

Under Serge Daney and Serge Toubiana, the new team that set up shop at the passage de la Boule Blanche near the Bastille abandoned the old dogmatic line and resumed its "critical function" and its relationship with its public. Straub and Godard were joined by many foreign directors, including Robert Kramer, Hans-Jürgen Syberberg, Manoel de Oliveira, Youssef Shahine, Raoul Ruiz, Akira Kurosawa, Wim Wenders, and Barbet Schroeder. The *Cahiers* also wanted to adopt new theoretical positions and turned to Michel Foucault, Marc Ferro, and Daniel Sibony. The editorial team, including Pascal Bonitzer, Serge Daney, and Serge Toubiana, met with Michel Foucault; their long discussion was published in September 1974. Toubiana put Foucault in touch with René Allio, who later adapted Foucault's study of *Pierre Rivière* for film. In 1975, Daney and Toubiana got back in touch with François Truffaut to ask him for financial support, which he did not give, but he did announce that he would henceforth adopt a position of benevolent neutrality after having lengthily criticized the review's positions since the late 1960s. "He told us that he did not criticize us for our political position but that he resented us for having kept the title *Cahiers du Cinema*, which was part of the Bazin legacy—and for having done what we did with it. He made it clear that we should have changed the title since we'd betrayed Bazin's legacy."[23]

In the summer of 1976, the TV station Antenne 2 programmed six two-hour shows on successive Sundays for Godard's *Six Times Two*.[24] Jean Narboni, like Deleuze, was teaching at Vincennes, and he leapt at the chance to appear on the program, especially since Caroline Champtier had told him that Deleuze really liked Godard and had been impressed by the TV series. He sent Deleuze a letter asking him to write about Godard for the *Cahiers*. Deleuze accepted the idea of an interview, which was recorded at the *Cahiers*' offices, but he then refused to allow the transcript to be published. Instead, he suggested a simulacrum of the interview entitled "Three Questions About *Six Times Two*," and framed four questions. "The 'interview' about *Six Times Two* blew us away. He opened up directions for thinking about Godard that have been repeated, quoted, adopted and stolen ever since, including 'creative stammering,' the lesson of words and things, the politics of borders, the inventions of a foreign language in one's own language, a solitude among people, etc."[25] In the essay, Deleuze described

Godard as a solitary worker somewhat like himself, someone who marked his era without enjoying popular success in his own time, "by following his own line, a line of active flight, a constantly shifting line zigzagging beneath the surface."[26]

Deleuze appreciated Godard's "not a just image, just an image," and he made it a principle for philosophers: "Not just ideas, but just some ideas."[27] For Deleuze, the filmmaker, among other things, raises a valid question when he destroys the notion of the force of labor by suggesting that television viewers should be paid for providing a public service. Godard's other radical shift had to do with questioning the notion of information as a form of commandment. Deleuze went back to André S. Labarthe's remarks from the early 1960s on Godard's manner of replacing transitions with "and" and breaking with linear storytelling by creating false continuities between sequences.

This article eventually led to regular meetings and discussions between Deleuze and Narboni, who saw one another with growing regularity, especially after the publication of *Superpositions*, written by Deleuze and Carmelo Bene, in 1979. The *Cahiers*, and Narboni in particular, who had been stunned by *Notre-Dame of the Turks* at the 1968 Venice Film Festival, championed Bene. In 1971, Bene's second film made the cover of *Cahiers*, and Narboni met Bene during a trip to Paris, although Bene had decided to stop making films by that time to return to the theater. The two men discussed the decision in the company of Jean-Paul Manganara, an Italian literature specialist, and Deleuze, a colleague of Narboni's at Vincennes— Deleuze taught on the floor below Narboni's class. One of Deleuze's students recalls that when Deleuze mentioned his friend Narboni, "he pointed his finger at the ceiling as if some transcendental presence were embodying a higher authority."[28] Both Narboni and Deleuze arrived punctually for their Tuesday morning courses and had time to talk beforehand.

When *Anti-Oedipus* was published in 1972, it shook up the Marxist-Leninist line at the *Cahiers* but did not initially change its tack. Ultimately, the certainties underlying the journal's political positions were affected, and the book nourished a few desiring flux running between the epistemic blocks of the period. Pascal Bonitzer used what he had learned when, during the second half of the 1970s, he focused on film esthetics and wrote a number of studies on the "camera's gaze," the "*hors-champ*" (the area outside the film's field or frame), and deframing. In the fall of 1977, Bonitzer stopped writing long theoretical texts and started making films, clearly expressing his desire for a story. "Why are we so completely bored? Today, we're feeling the lack of stories, good stories more or less everywhere."[29] Bonitzer found Deleuze's writings on cinema particularly refreshing, especially when compared to Christian Metz's semiological theories, which he found useless as criticism. Cinematographic art "expresses itself through films; it is not a language that would express itself by being systematically applied. Deleuze agreed entirely that cinema was a work, and he had a lively, personal understanding of the filmmakers we loved."[30]

Deleuze went regularly to the *Cahiers* and attended the programs organized by Dominique Païni at Studio 43. "He occasionally came with his daughter, Emilie, who had made films herself, and sometimes with his wife, Fanny."[31] Dominique Païni was extremely thoughtful in his film programming and was in the habit of organizing new and old films on a given theme. Among many other topics, he organized programs on the role of canals and rivers in creating the language of French cinema since the silent era. Deleuze directly adopted this theme of lability in *The Image-Movement*, where he argued that water was a signature characteristic of French film; Jean Renoir expressed this motif of waterways and landscapes most intensely.

Jean Narboni was especially struck by Deleuze's capacity to construct classifications and taxonomies, and he amused himself by arguing with Deleuze that the theoretical structure should certainly precede the contents. Narboni considered Deleuze's writing about the impulse-image, affect, the close-up, and the face to be among the most beautiful pages ever written on cinema. Between the originary world of the depths (Stroheim, Bunuel, Nicholas Ray, King Vidor, Losey) and the world of extracorporeal entities (Dreyer, Bresson), Deleuze traced a line "obviously connected to the two others, the line of the brain and of mind, the city-brain. I think that Resnais was ultimately his favorite director."[32]

That Deleuze was close to the *Cahiers du Cinéma* was confirmed in his preface to Serge Daney's book, *Ciné journal*.[33] Deleuze felt that Daney was, like him, someone seeking a profound link between mind and film in a critical tradition like that of Bazin and the *Cahiers*. He applauded the way that Bazin had converted the ambitions of the earliest directors, like Eisenstein or Gance, into a critical optimism that the tragedies of the twentieth century diluted. "Cinema remains linked not to a triumphant collective thought but to a precarious, singular thought that can be grasped and sustained only in its 'powerlessness.'"[34] Deleuze ultimately saw Daney's book as a travel book, though not in the sense of someone seeking exotica but in the Proustian sense of a true dreamer needing to verify his intuitions. "And in your case, we have what you went to ascertain in your travels, that the world really is turning to film, is constantly moving in that direction."[35] The preface was warm even though Deleuze and Daney had met only twice. Both of them wanted to meet again, so Raymond Bellour, who was part of the review *Trafic*, organized a meeting in 1992, two months before Serge Daney died.

Deleuze essentially remained loyal to the Bazinian tradition.[36] His pantheon included the same triad of Rosselini-Renoir-Welles and, like the founding father of the *Cahiers*, Deleuze saw in Italian neorealism the beginnings of modern cinema. As a mixed genre, cinema provided a new way of reaching realism. For André Bazin, a student of Emmanuel Mounier and influenced by phenomenology, "the screen is the transubstantiation of reality, and this phenomenon bears its name: realism."[37] But realism does not mean a simple mimesis of reality, because what the camera finds in the real world is always the "mysterious other" of reality that weakens it while confirming it.[38] In his work on cinema, Deleuze adopted the intellectual legacy of the *Cahiers*. "I don't think that he questioned the big issue of the New Wave. Essentially, he adopted the history of cinema as Langlois, the New Wave, Bazin, the *Cahiers*, Truffaut, and Godard before he conceived it."[39]

This affinity with the *Cahiers* did not preclude other influences. When Deleuze decided to write on cinema, he contacted Michel Ciment, a former student from Louis-le-Grand High School, who had become the editor-in-chief of the film review *Positif*. "He was aware that there had been a long interruption in his relationship with cinema. He needed some documentation and I provided it for him."[40] Deleuze met Ciment several times at the Wepler Brasserie at place de Clichy, where he was advised to read a certain number of books and was given several issues of *Positif* on Losey and Kazan, among others, as well as a general issue on American film, Michel Ciment's passion; in the early 1980s, Ciment had published two books on American cinema that Deleuze made good use of.[41] Ciment, in turn, used Deleuze's *Masochism: An Interpretation of Coldness and Cruelty*,[42] to write a small book on Erich von Stroheim, which came out in 1967.

Deleuze also made reference to *Cinématographe*, another important film review created in the 1970s by Jacques Fieschi, who had worked at *Cahiers* and *La Nouvelle Critique*. *Cinématographe* had links with the professional milieu; its regular contributors included the producer Philippe Carcassonne and the screenwriters Fieschi and Jérôme Tonnerre. It had been created to some extent in reaction to the highly ideological discourse of the *Cahiers* and favored cinema that worked with writing. "It was the beginning of the critique of authors, without ever really saying 'I' but with a particular investment."[43] *Cinématographe* was noted for its dandyism, and although it addressed current film events, it also published pieces on Italian neorealism, Visconti, Godard, and Third World cinema. The pantheon of filmmakers was more or less the same from one review to the other. Michel Ciment considered even Deleuze to be rather "positivistic" in his admiration for Kazan, Losey, and Kubrick, an admiration shared by *Positif.* He remained close to the *Cahiers*, however, and was resolutely on their side in the Hitchcock dispute. "The *Positif* critics, who were more libertarians and surrealists, had hated the way that *Cahiers* presented Hitchcock as the incarnation of redemption on the questions of sin, confession, avowal, and they became rather ridiculously rigid."[44]

The *Cahiers* authors remained loyal Maoists and had thus necessarily turned a blind eye to Scorsese, Altman, Coppola, and many other American filmmakers who were, of necessity, perverted by imperialism. The two journals also made different choices: the Italian Leftist cinema of Antonioni and Visconti, Bunuel, Franju at *Positif*; Hitchcock and Rossellini at *Cahiers*. In the 1960s, the two reviews joined in defense of young filmmakers from Eastern Europe, the Third World, and Canada.

Deleuze's involvement in the world of cinema was such that he even appeared on film in a small role. His friend Michele Rosier proposed that he play Lammenais in his 1974 film on George Sand, *George qui? (George Who?)*; Deleuze appeared in two scenes, one in a salon and another imprisoned in Sainte-Pelagie. In the late 1970s, he briefly considered returning to the screen when Philippe Venault and Raymond Bellour, who had worked on Jules Michelet's *Journal* and had written a script, suggested that he play the part of Michelet.[45]

A New Bergsonian Metaphysics

Deleuze's encounter with the cinematographic world enabled him to reconnect with something outside the realm of philosophy. By showing that cinema heralded a veritable philosophical revolution, he demonstrated that his project remained philosophical and, as he made clear later, his objective was not to write a history of the seventh art.

Deleuze's reflection upon cinema was Bergsonian, and he took Bergson's notions to their limits. "The Bergsonian discovery of a movement-image, and more profoundly, of a time-image, remains, even today, so rich that it's not at all certain that we've drawn all of the implications as yet."[46] Deleuze observed some progress in thinking about cinema in *Matter and Memory*, published in 1896, even though the book predated the official birth of cinema. In *The Creative Evolution*, published in 1907, Bergson renounced the directions in which his initial intuition would have led him. Nearly a century later, Deleuze took up where Bergson had stopped, with Bergson's denunciation of the mechanical illusion of cinema despite his sense that it would lead to a philosophical revolution.

Deleuze adopted Bergson's three ideas about movement. The first was to resolve the confusion between movement and traversed space: movement refers to the indivisible act of moving where space is divisible; movement thus belongs to a different realm—duration. Zeno's famous paradox is well known for illustrating the difficulty of thinking about movement: speedy Achilles can never catch up to the tortoise, which started out earlier, if their respective movements are simply divided spatially. Bergson also believed that movement could not be addressed by dividing the trajectory into static pieces. There is something irreducible about movement that has nothing do with abstract time. If Achilles ultimately leaves the tortoise behind, it is because his movement is incommensurable with that of the tortoise. Each movement is described and proceeds according to its own divisions. Is it not this pure movement, distinct from its spatial underpinning, that cinema expresses?

Bergson's second idea was that there are two ways of reproducing movement using immobile cuts: in terms of the importance of the moments or in terms of ordinary moments defined in terms of their distance from one another. Thinkers in antiquity had considered movement on the basis of privileged moments, whereas for Bergson, this second way of thinking about movement was possible thanks to modern science, which introduced time as a specific variable and required a new metaphysics. "The modern scientific revolution consists in returning movement to ordinary moments rather than to privileged ones."[47] This second manner of defining movement is that of cinematic technology, and Deleuze wondered whether the cinema could be a bearer of this new metaphysics heralded by Bergson. "We would have to say: cinema as metaphysics."[48] We have to consider time in the way that Bergson thinks about it, as an invention. "Time is invention or is nothing whatsoever."[49]

The third Bergsonian idea was that not only are instants immobile slices of movement but also that movement "is a mobile cut of duration, meaning of the Whole or of a whole. This implies that movement expresses something deeper, which is the change in duration or the whole."[50] The temporal perspective must therefore be considered as being specific to the cinematic image, making that image more than an image in motion: it is a movement-image. Deleuze emphasized that the totality in question is not at all a self-enclosed totality. On the contrary, "the Whole is not a closed set; it's Open, a dimension of a being-time that changes and endures and produces something new."[51] This dimension of the Open allows memory to progress in the depths of time. "This is the Open Level. There is the *spirit* of cinema."[52]

In *Matter and Memory*, Bergson even differentiated two types of images: movement-images as a surface phenomenon belonging to actuality and profound memories-images, referring to virtuality. Bergson then goes on to focus on the surface images, where he distinguishes perceptions-images, actions-images, and affections-images. It is the last aspect of affection that indicates the coincidence between subject and object—the source of a particular quality that keeps movement from being a pure translation and becoming a "movement of expression."[53] Between the perception-image and the action-image, the affection-image fills the gap without saturating meaning.

From Bergson, Deleuze also adopts an alternative to the phenomenological approach. At the turn of the century, classical psychology was in the midst of a serious crisis because it could no longer account for the distinction between conscious images and external movements. Two solutions were possible. Phenomenology, according to Husserl, defined the conscious mind as consciousness *of* something, and this way of thinking produced a rich philosophical current. More isolated than Husserl, however, Bergson defined the conscious mind *as* something and, according to Deleuze, went much further than Husserl in salvaging psychology. "My contribution is an attempt to repair Bergson's harsh treatment at the hands of the phenomenologists."[54]

Bergson's contribution was decisive for thinking the image as movement and no less important for thinking the time-image. Bergson distinguished between two types of recognition: immediate recognition born of habit and an attentive recognition that calls upon the past, or memory-image, which, along with the affection dimension, comes to occupy the space between the perception and action. Depending on the situation and what it supposes as a reaction, these memories actualize themselves in images and inform action. The status of the memory-image, however, differs in immediate and in attentive recognition and can play the role of the virtual image in the memory-image as a mode that crystallizes attention. But the memory-image, according to Bergson, is not itself virtual but makes the virtuality of a "pure memory" actual. It is the operator that cannot resurrect the past but remains nonetheless the trace of a former present. This recall, however, often ran into obstacles and failures that intrigued Bergson, because he thought that the inadequacies were the most interesting phenomenon.

These disjunctions in attentive recognition constitute the privileged object of cinema. "Very early on, European cinema addressed a set of phenomena, including amnesia, hypnosis, hallucination, delirium, the visions of dying people, and above all, nightmares and dreams."[55] These memories-images concern the dimension of memory and of the present. The layers of the past seemed to follow each other in a coherent, chronological order. For Bergson, however, "they coexist, to the contrary, from the perspective of the actual present that each time represents either their common limit or the most contracted limit among them."[56] Bergson used the metaphor of the cone to clarify the idea of a point culminating and condensing memories-images required for action in a two-step movement of contraction either in the case of lively attention or dilation in a state of repose.

A metaphysical question arises from this: why does the present pass? This passage of the present is in fact contemporaneous with the present. The past, and the present that it was, are thus contemporaneous, insofar as the present becomes past at the same time that it emerges as present. The present is doubled as it unfolds, therefore, and splits at every moment into a present that it is and a present that it was. These coexisting dimensions are conjugated in singular configurations of the relationships between past and present.[57] This indiscernibility of time's doubling led to what Guattari called the "time crystal" and what Deleuze made into the foundation of the time-image: the image's direct access to time freed from its dependence on movement.

The crystal-image provides cinema a means of direct access to time and, like the crystal ball, the issue becomes more about the function of seeing than about simple perception. Creating new circuits that account for ever-moving reality requires thought, and according to Deleuze, this is what Rossellini did so magnificently in *Europe 51*, where his heroine observes workers entering the factory and says, "I thought that I was watching condemned men." She makes what is more than a merely metaphoric link between prisons and a capitalist enterprise. All of these circuits borne along by cinema have to do with more than psychology: "they are areas of being and of thinking."[58]

For Bergson, thinking consists of setting oneself in one of these areas that contain the question that we cannot formulate while at the same time revealing a previously hidden aspect of being that opens a previously unavailable circuit of thought. This is the "art of thinking"[59] that Deleuze aimed for as he explored contemporary cinema using Bergsonian intuitions.

A CRITIC OF FILMIC SEMIOTICS

When Deleuze began to study cinema in the early 1980s, semiology, the heir to the structuralist paradigm, appeared to provide the most critical stance toward film. Its theoretician, Christian Metz, was actively involved in developing a semiolinguistic reading of film. In 1968, his *Essays on the Meaning of Cinema* opened up an entirely new trend within semiotics.[60]

For Metz, cinema was a narrative language without a tongue: the cinema-image was approximately the same as an utterance. "The filmic shot resembles an utterance rather than a word."[61] If we want to understand the conditions under which this image becomes an utterance, we must define the rules of use: this was what film semiotics set out to do, following in the lines of Saussurian linguistics.

Metz went from being a cinephile to creating a new approach to cinema using a conceptual grid that he refined with his "grand syntagmatic." "My intellectual passion was the linguistic machine itself."[62] In 1964, his first semiological text came out against the sort of film criticism that ignored current linguistics and semiology while at the same time calling increasingly for a specific film language. "I began with Saussure's notion of language. . . . It seemed to me that cinema could be compared to language [*langue*] and not to a tongue [*parole*, or spoken language]."[63]

This extreme formalization of cinematographic language was essentially taken from the work of the linguist Hjelmslev, whose notion of expression, according to Metz, defined the basic unit of filmic "language" very well, whereas codification belonged to a purely formal, logical and relational approach. "In Hjelmslev's sense, a code (= form of the content + the form of expression) is an area of commutability, of signifying differentialities. A single language can therefore have several codes."[64]

Deleuze's approach to cinema was radically different from the approach being taken at Paris-III, the French capital of theoretical film studies at the time. He did not agree that a film image could be defined as a language, because this amounted to ignoring what identifies an image as movement and time. Deleuze viewed Metz as a "Kantian," which was a form of praise, but he added that Metz did not apparently realize it. Kant had relegated the metaphysical Platonic question "what is this?" to the precritical past and replaced it with another question about the conditions of possibility. Instead of the antique couple of the essence behind the appearance, there were facts and the conditions of their possible emergence. Metz was Kantian because he believed that the question of knowing whether or not cinema was part of a universal language, as the pioneers had claimed, was a false problem. His question was, "under what conditions is it possible to consider cinema a language?"[65]

Deleuze praised Metz's for his prudent decision to base his argument on the acknowledged domination of Hollywood cinema as the starting point for narrative cinema. But he diverged from Metz when it came to the price for this. "As soon as an utterance replaced the image, we gave a false appearance to the image because we didn't include movement, its obvious and most authentic characteristic."[66] Everything comes back to language and its rules, and for Metz, the difference between photography and the image-cinema depends on narration. "To go from one to two images is to go from the image to language."[67] Metz's disciples embarked on the same theoretical road, suspending movement in the field defined as semiocriticism.

Metz wanted to construct a "grand syntagmatic," which amused Deleuze. "It really makes me laugh hard when I hear 'The Great Demoiselle is dead!' It's Bossuet speaking!"[68] Still smiling, Deleuze said that he was awaiting the grand paradigmatic after the grand syntagmatic, but Metz agreed that for cinema, the latter was relatively unimportant since it included infinite possibilities.

Instead of Saussurian semiotics, Deleuze proposed another source of inspiration that let him advance his construction of a harmonics of signs along the lines that he had begun with Proust. When he spoke about cinema, what he had in mind was a classification of signs. On November 2, 1982, when he told his students that he was going to reprise and ruminate, "like a cow," the material of his course from the previous year on cinema, he was starting with an intuitive sense that he was working on something important. He had every intention of pursuing his systematic exploration of signs. "I am not saying that if I manage to achieve this classification it will change the world, but it will change me, and that would really be a pleasure for me."[69] Deleuze was not trying to establish the filmic equivalent of Mendelev's table. Instead of Saussure, he used Charles Sanders Peirce, who proposed an entirely different direction for research and pragmatics, one privileging action and uses.[70] Peirce insisted that each level contained prior levels. But what Deleuze found most of all interesting was Peirce's conception of signs as belonging to something other than the logic of language. Peirce's trilogy fundamentally belonged to the movement-image and made it possible to think the film image via its internal logic. Deleuze did not limit himself to Peirce's classificatory "drive": he understood the notion of sign differently, and above all he refused the idea of closing the system with its thirdness. Saussure's model could not work for Deleuze because it was synchronic, denied movement in the name of the law ordering the system, and preferred to take language as its object, excluding speech from the outset.

CINEPHILIC PIONEERS AT THE UNIVERSITY

The birth of the department of film studies at Paris-III dates to 1969, when very few film courses were being offered. It exists thanks to the determination of a single individual, the Artaud specialist Alain Virmaux, assisted by his wife. In 1970, on the advice of Raymond Bellour, Virmaux called the *Cahiers* to recruit some teachers: Jacques Aumont, Pierry Audry, Pascal Bonitzer, and Pascal Kané all accepted his offer to teach even though they had no teaching experience; the enterprise was immediately and spectacularly successful. Students flocked to the classes, and the film critics found themselves lecturing to several hundred people. In 1971, however, the *Cahiers* contingent learned that they would not be rehired, their popularity notwithstanding. They were pugnacious, however, hired a lawyer, occupied the president's office with their students, and won. They wanted to stabilize the department and so they asked the filmmaker René Gilson to head it. Gilson recruited Michel Marie, a militant communist whose skills as an organizer established the academic foundations of the department.

Paris-III won its bid to be recognized and became the epicenter of French university studies of film theory. In 1983, the first nominations for tenured positions were made there. Nearby, at the École des Hautes Études en Sciences Sociales, the structural semiology of cinema as Christian Metz had conceived it was dominant, and Metz gave his course there and continued it at Paris-III as well. Michel Marie, Roger Odin, Jacques Aumont, François Jost, and Marc Vernet were the department stalwarts.

In 1983, when Deleuze's first book on film was published, *The Movement-Image*, university film specialists reacted with consternation and reprobation. "I was terribly resistant. Bergson didn't interest me at all; he was the enemy of the people, I'd read my Politzer when I was little. Later, I thought that he was saying the obvious: to tell us, after three hundred very complicated pages, that the image is moving, thanks, we knew that."[71] Raymond Bellour, who was at the crossroads between these two different currents, found Deleuze's critiques of Metz to be harsh. He greatly admired Deleuze for his contribution to film theory and gave a course on him during the 1989–1990 academic year, but he considered his rejection of the question of narrative overly brutal. He agreed with André de Souza Parente that there are "imaging narrative processes" that allow us to agree that narration is, from the very start, part of the image.

The press warmly welcomed Deleuze's work as an incursion into a new domain. *Le Monde* published a long interview between Deleuze and Hervé Guibert in which Deleuze made it clear that this book was not a history of film but an essay classifying signs and images. He described how much he liked going to specialized movie houses, like the Mac Mahon, where he could see all of Joseph Losey's films. As for his reasons for having written on this subject, he explained that before the war, when he was about ten years old, he often went to the movies. "I have memories of films and actors from this period. I loved Danielle Darrieux, and I like Saturnin Fabre a lot because he frightened me and made me laugh and invented his own delivery."[72] During the postwar years, however, he had almost entirely been absorbed by philosophy. "I came to write about cinema because I'd been struggling for a long time with a problem of signs. Linguistics seemed unsuited to addressing it."[73] Serge Daney wrote a full page in *Libération* about Deleuze's book, also letting Deleuze speak for himself.[74] The *Cahiers du Cinéma* did likewise,[75] and Jérôme Bindé praised the book for demonstrating that the arrival of the seventh art required a true philosophical revolution.[76]

Most film theorists, however, were critical and even caustic about Deleuze's book. In his seminar, Christian Metz accepted that his ideas could be criticized but pointed out that Deleuze and he were not talking about the same thing, which allowed him to avoid any direct confrontation. "Metz wasn't at all a philosopher, he was a grammar specialist, and he was deeply wounded. But he decided not to get involved in the contradictions, so he acted as if he weren't really concerned."[77]

When *The Movement-Image* came out, Metz was no longer the head of a rapidly expanding generalized semiology movement, and he felt increasingly isolated. He withdrew, in response, which made his inner circle, which included Michel Marie, Roger Odin, Marc Vernet, François Jost, and all his seminar regulars, reject Deleuze more volubly. It was only in the 1990s that students started insisting that their teachers teach Deleuze on cinema. This was Jacques Aumont's experience, although he revised his initial negative impressions on the basis of his students' work, especially that of his doctoral student Dork Zabunyan.[78] In the 1990s, Dominique Château was still quite critical and very polemical, seeing Deleuze as a guardian of the philosophical temple: concerned above all with preserving a monopoly on the idea, he had a "cannibalistic [notion] of philosophy."[79] Deleuze's two books on cinema were, to his mind, just a kind of philosophical dressing up of a purely Bazinian conception that ignored Metz's contributions to filmic-linguistic theory. "Deleuze put aside the linguistic issue and reverted to Bazin's (and Bergson's) simplistic ideas."[80]

Among the film theorists, Jean-Louis Leutrat was somewhat unusual for escaping Metz's semiology and establishing a relationship with Deleuze's work early on. Leutrat had been a student in literature in Lyon in the 1960s, and although he had not taken classes with Deleuze, he became familiar with his work when Robert Mauzi, one of his teachers, wrote a lengthy review of *Proust and Signs*. So when Deleuze's books on cinema were published, Leutrat was already familiar with Deleuzean themes, which, for him, provided arguments for resisting the semiological thrust that was carrying film criticism in directions he considered sterile. When Leturat published a book on cinema in 1988, he dedicated it to Deleuze,[81] having taken care to send him the book beforehand for his agreement.

This began an epistolary exchange and led to several meetings between the two.

Leturat knew Deleuze's work well, and he appreciated Deleuze's obvious interest in film because of his numerous film references in *Difference and Repetition*. Deleuze's analysis of Welles' *Citizen Kane* and his claim that "time is no longer subordinate to movement" prefigured the break between movement-image and time-image, which he conceptualized much later. In *Anti-Oedipus*, Deleuze mentioned only Nicholas Ray's *Bigger than Life* and Charlie Chaplin's *Modern Times*. In *A Thousand Plateaus*, published in 1980, he made several technical observations about close-ups and included references to Godard, Eisenstein, Herzog, Hitchcock, Sternberg, Wenders, and Daniel Mann. Several essential ideas were put forth in the works he co-authored with Guattari, including the "dividual" and the major area of virtual exploration; the two books on film have to be considered part of a continuum of Deleuze's philosophical work. "A part of *Time-Image* evolved from the second chapter of *Difference and Repetition*."[82]

Going against the current, Leutrat was one of the rare people to grasp that Deleuze's works on cinema were a coherent part of his entire philosophy. As Deleuze became increasingly popular in film studies, Leutrat was asked more and more often to direct theses or be a member of juries, since he could argue from a solid academic position, given that he had served as the president of Paris-III for five years. When Deleuze retired at the end of the 1987–1988 academic year, he asked Leutrat to advise two of his doctoral students in film, Véronique Tacquin, a Dreyer specialist, and Alain Ménil.[83]

THE 1939–1945 EARTHQUAKE

Deleuze specialists who knew Deleuze's very Nietzschean mistrust of the burden of history were comforted when he said clearly that his work on cinema was about creating a classification of images and signs. However, they were quickly caught off guard by a thesis entirely organized around an extremely trenchant observation of a historical break from which emerged two modes of being for the image: the movement-image before World War II and a time-image after it. Some asked how such a philosopher could be so easily drawn into the very historicism against which he had always argued so vigorously. Was this a necessary concession to a story or to specific narrative constraints in the temporal development of his taxonomy of signs?

We have to take this rupture seriously, beyond any Romanesque constraints, and believe that it is connected to a far deeper questioning of the teleological vision of history reflected in Deleuze's insistent critique of the Hegelian dialectic. For Deleuze, to think modernity implies "renouncing Hegel," as Paul Ricoeur invited his readers to do in his *Time and Narrative*, a work contemporaneous with Deleuze's book. If such a great philosopher had to be abandoned, it is because the triumph of Nazi barbarism in the heart of Europe profoundly shocked our relationship with the world. It was no longer possible to maintain a naïve, linear vision of progressive human history culminating in the reign of Reason. Our relationship to the world must of necessity change, and Deleuze, who was an adolescent when the war broke out, was, in this respect, truly a child of World War II. Consequently, film could become a privileged observatory for him from which to take the measure of the powerful effects of the major tragedy of the twentieth century.

For the first generation of film pioneers, the primary ambition of cinema is to profoundly reconsider our relationship to the world and our thinking about it. Cinema became a mass art when populations became the subjects of cinematographic thinking. Eisenstein and Abel Gance believed that cinema could become the mode of expression of a universal language that would ultimately cut its teeth on the tragedy of history. However, cinema also became a propaganda tool of totalitarian politics, used to manipulate the masses. On this point, Deleuze adopted Serge Daney's analyses of the liberating ambitions of cinema transformed into an enterprise of enslavement.

After World War II, "the grand political staging, State propaganda transformed into *tableaux vivants* and the first human mass manipulations"[84] were called into question, which led to a radical break with cinema as a movement-image. The politics of concentration camps and the cinema that accompanied it, with its chief practitioner Leni Riefenstahl, triumphed over the dreams of liberation borne by cinema. Rather than being a lever to renew thinking, thinking was suffocated. Where there had been some hope of transforming the masses into actors who were responsible for their own history, the cinema ended up contributing to their enslavement, to making them fascists endorsing wholesale brutality. War had always been a vast spectacle, increasingly sophisticated as it modernized and trying less to obfuscate than to demonstrate its lures. Paul Virilio believed that until the Reich collapsed, Goebbels had hoped to rival Hollywood;

both sides of the war, while militarily opposed, had similar images of thought.

At the end of the war, a new alliance between cinema and thought took hold. Just as totalitarianism had shattered Western progressive evolution-ism, the American dream of a fraternal society crumbled in the postwar period. It was, first, the crisis in Hollywood and the collapse of the Ameri-can dream of integration as the melting pot of a single civilization. Then, the technical revolution that made the forms of images proliferate nour-ished a general crisis about the power of images to incarnate the world. In addition to all of this there was the challenge to narrative occurring in the American novel, Dos Passos being an important figure in this. "There is still a totality, but it is dispersive."[85] Twenty years later, in the new Ameri-can cinema of Robert Altman, Sidney Lumet, and John Cassavetes, there is no central character but rather a number of nonhierarchically presented incidents stitched together in a "patchwork story."[86] The surrounding world has become inhuman and unbearable. Barbarian acts swamped all hopes of liberation. It was no longer possible to believe in the world, so cin-ema's new function was to "make it possible to believe in a relationship between humanity and the world."[87]

The link between humanity and the world was thus irremediably de-stroyed between 1939 and 1945 and "had to become an object of belief: it is the impossible, which can only be restored by faith. Belief no longer con-cerns an other or a transformed world."[88] Cinema no longer reflects any supposed reality but becomes the expression of the belief itself in the world, restoring, through illusion and a reenchantment of the world, confi-dence in the existence of a social anchor to human existence. "Christians or atheists, in our universal schizophrenia, *we need reasons to believe in this world*."[89] This break led to a collapse of the sensorimotor organization un-derlying the unfolding of the movement-image. Classical cinema prior to this rupture had been tonal and linked rational breaks in a linear, logical pattern. In this cinema of truth, the sequences externalized an ostensibly true whole. For Deleuze, however, real or fictional made little difference to classical cinema as it sought to achieve truth. Another specific aspect of classical cinema was to give an indirect representation of time, since it de-pended on movement, with its logical links and its externalization in a to-tality produced by editing.

Modern cinema adopted different practices and promised a very differ-ent configuration. Serial rather than tonal, adopting patterns of image sequences and resequences including irrational cuts and disjunctions, cinema no longer makes any claims to being true but presents physical positions similar to a *gestus*, behavior that does not imitate reality but seeks to cast off its constraints as well was those of history.

MOVEMENT-IMAGE AND TIME-IMAGE

Bergson defined three modalities of images: the perception-image, the affection-image, and the action-image. Cinema is first and foremost movement. Deleuze differentiates between four cinematographic currents on the basis of the editing, where everything about movement and its scansion is determined.

The American school composes its images organically, Griffith being the director who carried this to its zenith. The organism under constant threat of implosion: this was the plot of the new nation born of diverse waves of immigrants and whose fragile unity had to be preserved. "The organic whole is always threatened; in *Birth of a Nation*, Blacks are accused of wanting to destroy the recent unity in the United States by benefiting from the defeat of the South."[90]

During the same period, in the Soviet Union, the issue was to show that today's sacrifices were part of a dialectical logic leading to a better world. In the dialectic, division is the motor of historical movement leading toward the future, according to the laws of genetic development. Eisenstein carried this vision to the extreme, showing unity according to a dynamic and force leading inexorably toward movement. Its expression is the pathetic, through which consciousness is revealed to itself as participating in the historical movement. Eisenstein expresses this essential law of the dialectic by virtue of which "the One becomes two and produces a new unity, bringing together the organic whole and the pathetic interval."[91]

In France, filmmakers suggested another approach to the mechanical composition of movement-images in two ways: the "automat-machine" of the clock variety or the steam engine, the thermodynamic machine. "The cinematographic union of man and machine define a human Beast quite different from the animated marionette, and Renoir explored its new dimensions."[92] In addition to this mechanics of solids, there is also a mechanics of fluids illuminating the pronounced taste among French directors for waterways, riverbanks, and the ocean.

In the other dynamic creative center of the period, Germany, expressionism concentrated on light as a vector of intensity in movement. Wegener and Murnau were past masters of this genre, seeking to translate the powers and opacity of the depths to better emphasize the luminosity and play of *clair-obscur*; German expressionism drew its inspiration from non-organic life. "It is vitality as a powerful preorganic germinality."[93]

It was only after 1945 that the crisis of the movement-image became apparent. And it became blindingly clear that action could not change the global situation. The image therefore no longer referred to any organic unity at all but to diverse, dispersed elements. The guiding thread linking images, one to the next, was broken; contingency came to replace logical connections. Goal-oriented action became more like a meandering ramble receptive to all surprises. Finally, a disquieting, hidden power mixed with the communication's foundations seemed to identify with its effects. "The five obvious characteristics of the new image: *the dispersive situation, deliberately weak relationships, a rambling form, the awareness of clichés, the denunciation of the conspiracy.*"[94]

Once again, Deleuze pointed to historical reasons to explain why postwar Italy, with neorealism, was the first to experience the collapse of the movement-image. At the end of the war, Italy was in an ambiguous situation. The government had allied fully with Nazi Germany in dominating Europe but the population had risen up against the fascists. It was on this dangerous ground, among the carpets of dead leaves and shattered illusions, that the new cinema of Rossellini, De Sica, and many others destroyed everything that had previously constituted the glue of the movement-image. In *The Bicycle Thief,* De Sica deconstructed the relationship between action-situation-action linking events, thereby giving contingency full reign. The figure of the forger and of pretense replaced classical cinema's search for truth.

This crisis of cinema-action was translated by replacing the sensorimotor regime with the specific singularity of certain self-sufficient optical and sonorous situations valuable in and of themselves. These produced new signs that Deleuze called "op-signs" and "son-signs," which blurred the boundaries between the real and the imaginary. "This register of exchange between the imaginary and the real was completely obvious in Visconti's *White Nights.*"[95] Italian neorealism was particularly brilliant thanks to Visconti, Fellini, Antonioni, and Pasolini.

Jacques Rancière disagreed about the break between two cinematic ages of classical and modern cinema. "This division may be clear when it is stated, but it becomes less clear once we start examining the two questions that it raises."[96] Rancière agreed that there was a difference in perspective between the movement-image and the time-image but felt that it was suited to the same images that can be examined one by one in terms of affection-image or crystal-images, thereby making the opposition entirely fictive. Rancière regarded Deleuze's break as somewhat like Foucault's separation of the moment of sensorimotor logic.

THE THOUGHT-IMAGE

For Deleuze, the philosophical interest of cinema arose above all from his observation of the automatism of the cinematographic image, which resembles mental operations. He thus discovers a precursor in Epstein, who, at the turn of the century, had tried to construct a "philosophy of cinema."[97] For Epstein, the invention of this new technique was the beginning of a new way of thinking that could change our relationship to the world. Epstein insisted, as Deleuze did later, on this possibility of having direct access to time. "Time, for Epstein, appeared in the cinema like the fourth dimension that is added to the other three spatial dimensions. . . . Time, in cinema, seems to *be in things*."[98] According to Epstein, the camera's automatism was the source of something positive, and the new subjectivity that it created is "riveted," connected to the machine. "The cinematographic image designates the world without intermediary, reaches its pure presence. It is under these conditions that Epstein felt that cinema was essentially poetic, making it possible in fact to rediscover a direct and eminently sensual link with the world."[99] It is unsurprising that Deleuze drew inspiration from Epstein, who was also influenced by Bergson and was similarly concerned about avoiding the phenomenological rift between the order of consciousness and the order of the world.

The image-movement is self-movement, automatic, soliciting the image of thought. This automatic characteristic derives from the techniques of recording and projection but is also present in the contents of what is represented. The fact that the German expressionists depicted the Golem, somnambulists, or other zombies reflects this particular fascination. Robert Bresson also considered a spiritual automaton to be the cinematographic model. Yet this automatism gave new life to the ambition of reaching the mind's unconscious mechanisms. Borrowing Bakhtin's notion of a chronotype that defines a space-time, a temporal-spatial continuum, Deleuze intended to restore a chronotype of thinking that underwent variations whose logic could be understood by philosophy through cinematographic expression. "This space-time is studded with cries."[100] Beneath the layers of discourse, it was the singularity of these philosophical cries that needed to be pursued. Philosophy presupposes an image of the mind that is one of its conditions of possibility, and this refers to a chronotype reverberating with the singularity specific to each thinker.

The encounter between the cinema-image and the image of the mind, for Deleuze, had to do therefore with this spontaneity, this automatism specific to the cinema image. It was this direct relationship to time that marked the second generation of filmmakers. For Robert Bresson, films were also so many ways of representing spiritual automatons capable of finding the automatisms of daily life. "The cinema thus brings out the spiritual automaton in us. What a wonderful idea!"[101] Doesn't this automatism give access to the mind's unconscious mechanisms? So thought the psychiatrist Pierre Janet, at the very end of the nineteenth century, at the moment that cinema was born.

Deleuze responded ironically to Georges Duhamel's critical conception of cinema. Duhamel complained that he could no longer think when moving film images replaced his thoughts. Deleuze found this radical opposition between image and thought inept. "It's precisely because cinema can give life to the spiritual automaton that it has a fundamental relationship to thinking."[102] The connection to philosophical thought occurs both in supraconscious formal logic and in the mind's operations and modes of neuronal transmission.

This last aspect brings Deleuze's inquiry closer to research on neuronal transmission in the cognitive sciences, above all to Gilbert Simondon's work on the brain's topological structure.[103] In this way, Deleuze shifted the question of representative truth, his preferred critical target: the thought-image to which cinema gives us access is in no way the prolongation of some internality or externality whose truth could be projected onto the screen. To the contrary, the image-thought provokes a thought insofar as it creates a disjunction making it possible to perceive the direct relationship to time. "Time appears rather as a force that provokes thought by dissociating it from its image or its 'veridic' self-representation."[104] The complete disintegration of the principle of identity follows from this postulate, and the true can no longer refer to the immutable or to the identical: "What we previously called 'laws' of thinking (the principle of identity, of contradiction and of the excluded third term) thus lose their foundation."[105] Truth is shifted onto the ground of what has moved, of transformations; it refers to inexorable change, to the power of what is false, to the becoming of differentiation. "Here, Deleuze is rewriting Bergson's ontological principle according to which the temporal disjunction between perception and memory informs our freedom of mind and of choice; he casts it into the mold of Nietzsche's claim about the eternal return of difference in repetition."[106] What has always been Deleuze's critical target, in his valorization of what the image-time makes possible, is the split that it authorizes from readymade opinion or *doxa*.

On the screen, what we see are so many overflows or excesses of mastered consciousness. "To think is to learn what a nonthinking body can do, its capacity, its attitudes or postures. It is by the body (and no longer by the intermediary of the body) that cinema weds the spirit, thought."[107] For Deleuze, Antonioni, Cassavetes, Rivette, and Godard went furthest in this corporal expressiveness beyond the spoken word, followed somewhat later by Chantal Akerman, Jean Eustache, Philippe Garrel, and a cinema of postures, of *gestus*, and corporeal positions. Some directors managed to express the possible disjunctions between the attitudes of the mind and body. Antonioni, for example, did not focus on solitude and incommunicability, as has often been said, but on the profound duality of a modern mind completely borne up by the creative potentialities offered by the world confronted with a worn, tired body prey to a sterilizing neurosis. Resnais was also a great explorer of cerebral mechanisms. What cinema reveals is not limited to a world of images; it lets us see an essential dimension of life confronted with duration, the life of the crystals of time. "The crystal is expression. Expression extends from the mirror to the seed."[108] Werner Herzog conjugated the actual and the virtual in these crystal-images, especially in his *Heart of Glass*. So did Andrei Tarkovsky in *The Mirror, Solaris*, and *Stalker*. Max Ophuls also successfully restored the pure crystal. "In the crystal-image, there is this mutual blind and hesitating search for matter and mind."[109] With this crystal-image, Deleuze again echoes Bergsonian inspirations of a temporal interweaving of present and past, because what we perceive through the crystal is precisely this doubling of time. "What we see in the crystal is always the outpouring of life and time in its doubling or differentiation."[110] The crystal gives us access to time in its process of division so that what we perceive is less time in itself than the power it conveys in its process.

Deleuze was fascinated by the eruption of time in the crystal, which made it possible to get beyond a psychological and neuronal explanation of human action. During his landmark lecture, "What Is the Act of Creation?" given on March 17, 1987, at the Femis, the French school of cinematography, he made this quite clear, saying that the philosopher's job was not to reflect on cinema, since filmmakers do not need philosophers to tell them how to think about their practice. He described his contribution not as a way of theorizing cinema but of theorizing "the concepts provoked by cinema."

23

Guattari and Aesthetics
Consolation During the Winter Years

In the mid-1980s, the indefatigable Guattari, ever in search of new ideas, lost his footing. Several events engulfed him, although in his public lectures (the number of invitations kept growing) he appeared unchanged. His inner circle knew that he was sinking into a deep depression and tried vainly to keep him afloat. No single reason triggered his decline, but various things affected him, including many psychological frailties that had never been sufficiently addressed.[1]

Suddenly, it seemed, Guattari was totally bereft of his territory: he lost the rented Dhuizon chateau, located near the La Borde clinic, and its three hundred hectares, eight ponds, and four farms. He was also evicted from his large Latin Quarter apartment on rue de Condé, with its six capacious rooms encircling the formal reception area.

Guattari was far more rooted and settled than he appeared to be, and it was particularly painful for him to mourn these two sites of his private and public identity. He rented a modest house in La Borde near Jean Oury's home and made the rather dark bedroom into his office. This was a particularly inauspicious moment for him to be wrenched from his familiar spaces and their ritornellos, as his dislocations coincided with his mother's death. The haranguer of familial life repeated over and over again how painful his loss was. "He kept saying that he was an orphan."[2]

On top of these personal losses, there was also the somber political climate during these years, with the vestiges of racism once believed to have been definitively eradicated rising to the surface in the form of the right-wing National Front led by Jean-Marie Le Pen. It was a time of lost illusions and withdrawal, a time to tend to one's own garden and stay at home behind locked doors, safely removed from others. The utopia that had perpetually spurred Guattari on dimmed to more of a shimmering mirage. As disappointments continued to mount and disillusionment deepened,

Guattari found it harder to transform existential anxiety into hopeful political projects. In 1978, Gérard Lauzier, an acerbic caricaturist, sketched a bizarre character named "Gilles Guatareuze," a strange hybrid of the two authors, who is being pursued by a hysteric who hails the police in order to have the fellow locked up.[3] The image wounded Guattari. "I know that Lauzier's caricatures affected Félix quite deeply."[4] When François Fourquet met up with Guattari after a long period of aloofness, he immediately perceived his friend's profound distress. "'You know what's happened to me, François. I've been thrown out of the Condé apartment and out of Dhuizon at the same time.' It was something beyond schizo. I felt that he was totally unmoored, literally, a ship that had lost its rudder and no longer knew where to go."[5]

The creative euphoria of collaborating with Deleuze ended in 1980 with *A Thousand Plateaus*. The friendship endured, but the common enterprise was over. In the early 1980s, Deleuze was working on cinema and then became absorbed in his work on *Foucault* and the preparation for his book on Leibniz, which was published as *The Fold* in 1988.[6] During the 1980s, the two each had to find their own pace and personal goals. For Deleuze, connected to the university, this was easier; Guattari was more isolated. Upon returning to La Borde, he went through some difficult moments and was mired in the various disputes of the clinic's board, which accused him of being overpaid for his work. Guattari had worked tirelessly since the 1950s to make La Borde a beacon on the French and international intellectual landscape; these accusations only deepened his sense of isolation and melancholia.

Guattari's psychological structure was a fragile groundwork; his depression was as spectacular for its profundity as for its length. His friend Jean Chesneaux describes two incidents from Guattari's adult life that revealed his pathological relationship to death. The first concerned Pierre Halbwachs, the son of the sociologist Maurice Halbwachs, a militant for all causes who never recovered from his father's death at Buchenwald; the father had sacrificed himself by passing his food rations to his two sons to keep them alive. Pierre Halbwachs was suffering from lung cancer at the time, and his face bore the signs of his impending death. Jean Chesneaux suggested to Guattari that the two visit him. "After the visit, I was completely overcome, knowing that he was going to die. As we were going down the stairs, Felix said to me, 'Why did you ask me to come, Halbwachs is just fine.'"[7] This first denial of death was followed by another. Jean Chesneaux invited Félix to go for a stroll in the Père-Lachaise cemetery. "It's one of the most moving places in Paris. It's pleasant to stroll among the monuments and legends of this cultural haven. I saw him grow pale before we'd walked down two lanes. He spotted a little side door through which he made his escape."[8]

Known for being insatiable and bulimic, Guattari became catatonic, sitting with a pillow pressed to his stomach as if to protect himself from the outside world, watching television programs for days on end. His health problems also worsened; he had excruciating, violent attacks of renal colic. He heaped his suitcases with pills to help dull the pain. He found stones in his urine and had to watch his diet closely and, two years before his death, had several cardiac episodes but was so depressed that he never underwent any of the necessary medical examinations.

JOSÉPHINE

In this state, Guattari went through a particularly difficult relationship. It was 1983. On rue Tournon, Guattari met a beautiful woman, thirty years his junior, and started a love affair that began well but proved deadly. "When he met her, Joséphine was a lovely girl, very pretty, very simple in her manner. Slowly, however, she turned into the wife of a big Parisian intellectual [Guattari] and was spending lots of money and taking enormous amounts of drugs."[9] This disastrous relationship sunk Guattari into a deep depression. The couple married in 1986 and found a superb apartment on rue Saint-Sauveur. Guattari had to borrow money to buy it, but Joséphine continued her sumptuous spending. The costs for feeding her habit rose exponentially, with Joséphine counting on her new husband to buy her drugs. Their intense co-dependency distanced all of Guattari's friends. Joséphine shut the door on any unannounced visitors, making it abundantly clear that the old hospitality for any friend who happened to drop in at any time of the day or night was a thing of the past. Even close friends like François Pain were sent away in no uncertain terms and obliged to keep their distance.

On top of all of this, Joséphine's multiple sexual relationships further vexed Guattari. He confided in François Pain that he was having problems with his new wife. "Félix said, 'You know that it's making me sick. I'm really in deep shit with Joséphine. You have to help me, you've got to go see her.' And he added, 'It's as if you saw me in a ditch after a car crash, and you look on, saying, 'We've got to get him out of there but you don't give me a hand.' "[10] Jean-Jacques Lebel recalls the relationship with Joséphine as a great tragedy that still gives him chills. "I was watching the self-destruction of this man, friend, brother. I am not saying that Joséphine destroyed him. I'm saying that he used Joséphine to destroy himself."[11] Like others, Lebel went as often as possible to Guattari's house. Guattari often called his friends even in the middle of the night, to help him with what had become his intolerable solitude. On rue Saint-Sauveur, friends kept Guattari company as he watched, mouth ajar, the television, which was blasting day and night.

Lebel got a call from Guattari one day and went to see him with along Allen Ginsberg, Edouard Glissant, Paolo Fabbri, and Christian Bourgois, hoping that Félix would feel obliged to put on shoes, wash, go out to buy food, and make a good meal for his friends, as he used to do practically every day. "The dinner was strange," recalls Christian Bourgois, "because Félix's wife appeared like a specter in the middle of the meal and I recall how uncomfortable she made everyone."[12] In fact, Guattari had not prepared anything: Joséphine had simply bought some precooked, plastic-wrapped vegetables, which she threw onto the table along with plastic knives and forks, before retreating to her bedroom on the second floor of the duplex. Anorexic and slender, Joséphine glided between the friends like a shade. Lebel recalls her as a "very slim woman who was deeply withdrawn, who didn't say a word, a cadaverous presence suspended somewhere between life and death."[13] While still with Guattari, Joséphine had a long affair with the writer Jean Rolin, who wrote a story about her after her death by overdose in March 1993.[14]

Guattari was occasionally able to summon his former dynamism, even in this deleterious situation, especially when it was a question of traveling to other countries. But it was not easy to get him moving. In 1988, Éric Alliez worked hard to persuade Guattari that he absolutely needed him in Brazil. "I was calling him constantly from Brazil and we stayed on the phone for ages, and there were lots of silent moments."[15]

Luckily enough for Guattari, despite a certain lassitude for the place to which he had given so much, the universe of La Borde was still there. Jean Oury was well aware that Guattari's condition was serious, and he organized a group of people to help provide some structure for him, including the Blois city counselor Lucien Martin and the psychiatrist Danielle Rouleau. The two met with Guattari and Oury on Thursday afternoons in

GUATTARI AND AESTHETICS **427**

Oury's office throughout the 1980s to talk very freely about things. "It was important, a meeting point that helped him make some headway."[16] Guattari did not discuss his personal problems but reconnected with his practice from the 1960s. During this final period, Deleuze even came regularly to Jean Oury's seminar; he sat silently taking notes in a little black book. Oury found this invaluable, because it meant that the dialogue between them, which had stopped while Deleuze was working with Guattari, was resuming. "At the end of each seminar, Félix was quiet, but the two of them [Deleuze and Oury] remained alone together in the empty hall, seated next to each other and talking for a good hour."[17]

Guattari spent a good part of the week in his small house at La Borde but could invite no one there. He was quite alone, unlike the previous period at Dhuizon, when his friends gathered around the table frequently. His son Bruno lived in the Loir-et-Cher and visited him regularly, providing Guattari with a consoling presence and bringing him food for the weekend. When in 1992 Guattari published his last book, *Chaosmosis*, he dedicated it to his son. "For Bruno, who often came to lift me from the depths of my cave." At the end of the 1980s, this long, dark period drove his daughter Emmanuelle from France to New York, as she could no longer bear the atmosphere on rue Saint-Sauveur and felt that she absolutely had to get away from her father. When she returned in 1991, he was in very poor shape. She brought him the book by Daniel Stern that he had asked for, as he adored reading Stern, who played an important role in *Chaosmosis*. He discussed the book with Emmanuelle and the two of them began a real dialogue, something that had they had never done before. Joséphine had forbidden Guattari's children to set foot in the apartment on rue Saint-Sauveur, so Emmanuelle saw her father on weekends at La Borde. "We took lots of walks. He was really touching."[18] She experienced moments with her father that would never have taken place were it not for his depression. "I would never have met him, it was impossible. The depression created this space."[19] The intellectual machine continued to work, even during the worst times. "He never stopped, even while he was in front of the television. He was always digesting, connecting, working."[20]

TO BE A WRITER

Despite his nearly catatonic state, Guattari remained available and willing to engage in the battles of the moment; few in his wider circle had any idea about his psychological condition. This was when he got actively involved with the ecologists, and he continued to travel, notably to Brazil and Japan. Writing was the one activity above all others that allowed him to compensate somewhat for the practically unbearable suffering. Guattari had always wanted to write, to be a writer. He was a veritable printing press, constantly writing about everything.

In the 1980s, Guattari was a well-known author especially appreciated for the books that he had co-authored with Deleuze. But this left him with a certain bitterness, not only because the public remembered Deleuze's name rather than the names of both authors but also because he had hoped to write a literary work. He wrote many outlines, drafts, and sketches but never really managed to bring any to fruition. He tried his hand at every literary genre—poetry, novels, theater, scripts, memoirs, dreams. "He wasn't a real writer and I think that he suffered because of that. He wanted to write. I think that he was too obsessed by Joyce."[21] In 1975, in a literary work that he wrote critiquing the government's policy of covering Parisian suburbs over with concrete, he referred explicitly to Joyce. "They haven't known where to start since *Finnegan's Wake*! They think that they'll preserve what's most important by destroying as much as possible."[22] After *Kafka*, Guattari started writing a novel enigmatically entitled *33.333*, referring to his personal story and birthday: March 30, 1930. The novel never saw the light of day; it was filled with annotations and very personal observations about his own experience, his entourage, his frequently morbid anxieties, and the parental Oedipal triangle, even though he and Deleuze had violently attacked the Oedipus theory.

In 1986, Guattari signed a collection of poems that also lay gathering dust in his drawers; its title couldn't but suggest the theme of the fold, on which Deleuze was working at the same time.[23] From all of these drafts, a more complete work did emerge, a fragmentary autobiography entitled *Ritournelles*, whose definitive version was completed in 1992 with the help of his painter friend Gérard Fromanger. "He called me and said, 'I've written a terrific text!' He gave it to me, there were three hundred pages and I said, 'OK, that's good, there's some Joyce,' adding, 'there are two hundred pages too many, it's unreadable, repetitive, boring,' and I suggested that we work on it together."[24] Guattari accepted and was all the more enthusiastic since he could not muster the energy to go over his manuscript by himself. Together for six months the two worked very hard, reviewing every line of the manuscript during four-hour sessions either in Paris or in Fromanger's studio in Italy. Fromanger read the text aloud and suggested cutting every passage that a reader might find boring. "I did as Fernand Raynaud did:— Here we are selling beautiful oranges cheap.—We can see that they're oranges!—I delete oranges. I did the same thing to him."[25] At the end of this long travail, only eighty pages were left of the original three hundred, which so entranced Fromanger that he used the text as his inspiration for a huge painting entitled "Chaosmos," which depicted the various colors of the turbulent, violent period of the Gulf War and the attack on the Twin Towers. Just after Guattari died in August 1992, Agnes B. called Fromanger to say that she would publish Guattari's work at her own expense and asked Fromanger to illustrate it. It appeared in two issues of *The New French Review* in 1999.[26] The internal monologue was written in very short sentences constructed like musical phrases in which Guattari recalled memory fragments: the famous lady in black with the weapon and the mirrored armoire standing in front of the bed, his grandfather's death, the figure 33.333, and the various obsessions that gripped him until his death.

Also in 1989, Guattari worked on the theme of *ritornellos*, which had already appeared in *A Thousand Plateaus*. "We've always set musical objects into a relationship with time. It's become obvious that music inhabits time. But what if the reverse were true, that time inhabited music if not in the whole of its development then at least at the core of a certain type of its *ritornellos*?"[27] Guattari started his demonstration with something basically simple—defining the territorialization of many species of birds by their particular ritornello—and then moved on to the complexity of digital recordings, Wagner's leitmotifs, and Philip Glass's repetitive cells before returning again to what was simplest. "The concept of *ritornello* that I'm proposing tends, to the contrary, to cover all types of musical production, like rock, for example, which, for many young people, functions something like an initiation into transnational popular culture."[28] But he was equally willing to consider other possible expressions of these openings that restored noise and silence to music, such as the work of John Cage and Mauricio Kagel and Georges Aperghis' gestural music. "The issue therefore becomes conquering the time of everyday life, its aesthetic *ritornelization* to eliminate its banality and make it singular once again, recreating it and inventing new modes of presence in the world."[29]

While working with Deleuze on this chapter in *A Thousand Plateaus*, Guattari wrote a very long study on Proust entitled "The Ritornellos of Lost Time,"[30] which was published in 1979. He saw *In Search of Lost Time* as an immense rhizomatic map deriving from deterritorialized mental objects. "Vinteuil's little phrase" played the role of expressive material that had concrete effects. Guattari started studying the different arrangements of enunciations of this little phrase throughout the novel. He followed the sonata, which functioned like a ritornello, until it was no longer associated with young girls and even stopped being purely musical. "It's writing itself which becomes musical. Music traverses the notes, the sounds, the walls. . . . The world has become something like a gigantic organ and writing has become music pouring forth from every corner of the sonorous universe."[31]

Guattari's explorations were not limited to writing and literary criticism. He had become friends with the stage director Philippe Adrien following his production of Kafka's *The Dreams*, and he wrote a text for him in January 1985 for a show mixing drama, dance, and the plastic arts. It was entitled *The Moon Master*. Guattari envisioned a troupe of about twelve actors. Georges Aperghis would set the show to music, Daniel Dobels would choreograph a ballet, Adélaïde Vignola would supervise the costumes, and Gérard Fromanger would design the set. Guattari sent the play to Enzo Cormann who, despite his friendship with Guattari, was unconvinced that it should be staged. Guattari wanted to know what he disliked; Cormann answered, "you don't critique delirium."[32]

Guattari suggested on several occasions that they write a play, but Cormann never took him seriously, even though it was a serious request. In 1987, they created a cooperative of French authors,[33] intending to bring a whole series of well-known individuals together for about ten meetings, in order to adopt a text about the kind of artistic creations that should receive support. The plan never panned out, although the two friends did produce a small reading-show together. Guattari sent a good ten plays to Cormann, who kept a single short one entitled *Socrates*, because its facetious tone amused him. He and the actor Arnaud Carbonnier presented the play at the Open Theater during a week of readings by contemporary authors. Guattari and Joséphine sat together in the fourth row. When he created his musical group in 1991, Cormann called it the Grand Ritornello in reference to Deleuze and Guattari's analyses.

Painting, and particularly the work of his friend Fromanger, also caught Guattari's interest. In the 1980s, he wrote "This amazing fresco, *Night, Day*, overwhelms you visually, fascinates you mentally, over twenty-five feet, seven bodies-colors embracing one another in an erotic, morbid dance."[34] Guattari saw Fromanger as the painter of the act of painting, who answered the metaphysical question "what is painting?" with a practical demonstration, a performative. To paint is to make, to paraphrase Austin. Freeing colors of all hierarchical relationships and making them equal, Fromanger, as Guattari saw it, gave priority to expression. Far from deconstruction, his was "processual painting."[35]

In 1986, Guattari wrote a commentary on the series "Cythera, the New City," during an International Contemporary Art Fair (the FIAC). Guattari felt that contemporary art was struggling through a fallow period, although Fromanger, who continued his pictorial quest as if nothing had changed, was somewhat of an exception. "What saves him is surely that his question has never been 'why' but 'how.'"[36] Guattari also associated himself with the painter Merri Jolivet, the son of the composer Andre Jolivet, and wrote a piece about his work for his show in Paris in May 1975. During the 1980s, Imaï Toshimitsu was the most intense painter of what Guattari analyzed as chaosmosis. Toshimitsu had spent his childhood in Kyoto but became a nomadic creator who lived in Montparnasse; in the 1950s he struggled with poverty and hunger until he was recognized. But "behind the Imaï value that the Establishment recognizes, we can still catch a glimpse of the bad boy of the *Beat Generation, Action painting* and *Happenings*."[37]

Guattari also praised the work of the American painter-poet-photographer-sculptor David Wojnarowicz, a Kerouac-like wanderer in revolt who had endured a very disturbed childhood and did whatever it took to survive, including prostitution. A homosexual rebelling against the conformity of American society, Wojnarowicz lived among marginal people and was part of the counterculture; ultimately he was publicly recognized after his 1985 show at the Whitney Biennial. He began by making stencils on New York walls—bomber planes in flames and exploding houses—but he also painted large frescoes in an abandoned warehouse where many dozens of artist friends came to what became a bastion of pictorial creation in New York, East Village Art. The point of the work was to resist the established powers. Guattari clearly saw himself in this artist's revolt against death. Wojnarowicz died of AIDS at the age of thirty-eight, in 1992, the same year that Guattari died.

Guattari also tried his hand in cinema on several occasions. In the early 1980s, he wrote a script for his director friend Robert Kramer, "A Love of UIQ." Although Guattari did not have the same relationship to film as Deleuze did, he did, on several occasions, analyze film production, publishing most of his commentary in a chapter entitled, "Cinema: A Minor Art" in *The Molecular Revolution*.[38] Above all, he responded to invitations to discuss the relationship between cinema and the representation of madness. The theme recurs throughout the history of cinema, but in the 1970s films like Ken Loach's *Family Life* and *Asylum* and Bellocchio's *Fous à délier* (*Untying the Crazies*) were attracting larger audiences. Was cinema a minor art? "Yes, if you make it clear that a minor art is an art that can serve a minority and that the term is in no way pejorative. A major art is in the service of power."[39] Guattari spoke at length during an interview for *Libération* on Terrence Malick's *Badlands*, insisting that the film was, above all, the story of crazy love and of going beyond limits in an ongoing schizo drift.

In December 1973, during a colloquium on "Eroticism and Cinema" in Bologna, Guattari spoke out against those categories that isolate erotic cinema. Because he was a psychoanalyst, Guattari was always in demand. He wrote an article for a 1975 issue of *Communications* on "Psychoanalysis and Cinema,"[40] in which he drew a parallel between psychoanalytic care and cinema and film promoters' fascination with psychoanalysis, citing the hundred-thousand-dollar contract that Goldwyn had offered Freud to write about famous love affairs. Guattari thought that psychoanalysts could learn something about unconscious social investments from cinematographic creation, since filmmakers had to grasp changes in the social imaginary to remain in sync with the public. Moreover, cinema had means beyond speech to transmit intensity and the meaning of relationships; in much the same way that patients use language in analysis, "the semiotic elements of film slide around without ever stabilizing or being rooted."[41]

Guattari conceived of cinema as a specific mode of machinic arrangement with significant effects on public subjectivity. Consequently, he warned against considering commercial cinema as being meaningless, since its unconscious actions were especially deep. "Commercial film is indisputably familialist, Oedipal, and reactionary!"[42] Guattari, like Deleuze, was a fan of Straub and wrote a short piece when *The Death of Empedocles* was released in 1987. He compared this poetic novella and the musical experimentation in *Moses and Aaron* and the *Chronicles of Anna Magdalena Bach* to the beginning of a "speaking-singing" that was meant to convey Hölderlin's metrics.

Architecture was another area that fascinated Guattari, because it connected creativity with social change. In 1988, he wrote an article on architectural enunciation in response to architects who were somewhat confounded by the urban explosions glutting the planet's megalopolises.

"Today, what use would it be to refer to Le Corbusier, for example, in a city like Mexico, which is thundering ahead, completely insane, toward forty million inhabitants! Not even Baron Haussmann could do anything at this point!"[43] Architects could do little more than calmly content themselves with building a few sumptuous monuments, since the object of architecture had exploded. If architecture could be reinvented, it would not be by promoting any particular style or school but by reconsidering "the architectural enunciation" and the profession itself. A professional architect would no longer simply design buildings but "would also help reveal virtual desires of space, places, paths and territories . . . an artist and an artisan of material and relational experience."[44] This redefinition meant shifting toward the project; the architectural contribution would be the ability to perceive the various affects of spatialized utterances on the basis of their scales and functions.

All of these commentaries about artistic and literary creation pay tribute to Guattari's determination to experiment with what he defined elsewhere in theoretical terms as an aesthetic paradigm. He left a "toolbox," more in his theoretical writing than in his own creations, for thinking about art, as Nicolas Bourriaud has written.[45] For Bourriaud, Guattari's conception of subjectivity provided a paradigm for aesthetics that was confirmed by artistic practices of the last three decades. His transversal approach is the only one that can account for Duchamp, Warhol, Rauschenberg, and Beuys. "They all built their work on a system of exchanges with social flux, which undid the myth of the mental 'ivory tower' that Romantic ideology assigned to the artist."[46]

For Guattari, subjectivity was heterogeneous, fundamentally tied to art, which he saw as a leap into existence rather than a distinct realm of aesthetics or a fine point of human activity. "Art, for Guattari, isn't the object of independent analysis, it's the space itself. . . . For [him], artistic practices sketch existential cartographies where subjectivity and sociality find new points of reference, new coordinates, and possibilities of flight."[47]

24

Deleuze Dialogues with Creation

Deleuze presented himself as a pure philosopher and metaphysician. But what distinguished him was that he incorporated the worlds of percepts and affects and literary and artistic creation into his philosophical reflection. This was where he found the sources of his philosophical thinking, and he did not limit himself to being an outside observer. He also worked with artists so as to understand the creative process. For both Deleuze and Guattari, aesthetics was not a separate realm; the philosopher-artist looks at the creative act as being endowed with a special status. Defined as the "creation of concepts," philosophy must be attentive to the process of artistic singularization.

WORKING WITH ARTISTS

We have already seen how important cinema[1] and literature were for Deleuze, in his essays on Proust and Sacher-Masoch and later Lewis Carroll and Antonin Artaud, who were both central figures in his 1969 *The Logic of Sense*. For Deleuze, literature was a testing ground for his philosophical hypotheses. A philosopher of life, he made a fundamental link between life and literature. He believed that a writer or philosopher would ultimately have to address writing and style: "writing has to do with becoming, always incomplete, always in the process of becoming, and which overflows all living material and experience."[2] Writing is, in its essence, always caught up in the act of breaking off, of becoming other—this can be becoming-woman, becoming-animal or vegetable—which is most probably a becoming-minority, through simple proximity. "When Le Clezio becomes-Indian, it's always an incomplete Indian who doesn't know how to raise maize or carve a pirogue."[3] According to Deleuze, literature exists only in the movement of wresting itself from its own past, from its private Oedipal affair. It takes off because of its ability to free itself from the 'I': "We don't write with our neuroses."[4]

Deleuze was fascinated with the ability of American writers to let themselves be deterritorialized. American literature embraced the most impetuous winds of adventure, a minority expressing itself in a majority language—English—based on its past and diverse roots. "Anglo-American literature constantly shows these ruptures, these characters who create their line of flight, who create through a line of flight."[5] In the work of Thomas Hardy, Herman Melville, Robert Louis Stevenson, Virginia Woolf, Thomas Wolfe, D. H. Laurence, F. Scott Fitzgerald, Henry Miller, and Jack Kerouac, "everything is departure, becoming, passage, leap, daemon, relationship with the outside. They create a new Earth."[6]

A collective breath of fresh air and innovative arrangements course through this literature, which is attracted to the idea of the frontier, the imaginary and real conquest of a West that has replaced the Heavenly Jerusalem. Of course, the lines of flight can prove dangerous and even lethal; we need only think of Fitzgerald's alcoholism or Virginia Woolf's suicide. The issue is to get out of the rut, like the prophet who strays from the straight path of obedience. "Of what is Captain Ahab in Melville guilty? Of having chosen Moby Dick, the white whale, instead of obeying the law of the group of fishermen, that deems not all whales fit to hunt."[7] Captain Ahab follows his becoming-whale, which has nothing to do with a simple imitation but rather with a strenuous, coded capture. Each element bears its own deterritorialization, at the end of which "writing always gives writing to those who don't have it, but the latter give writing a becoming without which it would not exist."[8] Rather than literature that hides its own little secret or reveals it only parsimoniously to the reader who is obliged to interpret, Deleuze prefers literature that is entirely oriented toward new experiments, to doing. Anglo-American literature therefore thrilled him. "English or American literature is a process of experimentation."[9]

This literature experiments with lines of flight but does not flee life. On the contrary, it is borne along by the desire to create another reality. It possesses the efficacy of the arrangement, the central concept of *A Thousand Plateaus*, because it is located at the crossroads between interior and exterior, and its thread is defined by the modalities of these conjunctions. "I was saying to myself that the only benefit that I can derive from writing is to see the glass panes separating me from the world disappear."[10] From the outset, then, American literature is a collective arrangement of enunciation in its ability to become the expression of an absent people, to bespeak all of America through its stories. This literature seems to accomplish what Proust wanted to do when he defined the role of literature as the invention of a sort of foreign language conceived as a becoming-other of language. "Every writer is forced to create his/her own language."[11] This position could only make Deleuze extremely sensitive to the issues of switching from one language to another. In 1982, Pierre Blanchaud, a former student and Germanist, described the problems he was having with his publisher about his translation of Kleist's short stories—he refused to simplify Kleist in order to make his stories easier to read in French. Deleuze immediately offered to help him out. "Pierre Blanchaud is one of the rare Kleist translators who has been able to raise the issue of Kleist's style."[12]

Any writer wanting to stray from the beaten path prefers to make his or her language stammer. Beckett, more than any other writer, has developed this method of disclosing inclusive disjunctions. Deleuze provides an extraordinary literary illustration of these stammering series with the famous "I would prefer not to" of Melville's *Bartleby*, on which he comments at length.[13] By its enigmatic quality, its refusal to conform to expectations, and by its escape neither through revolt nor a dialectic reversal of the situation but by taking a line of flight that resembles madness, Bartleby's formula exemplifies the writer's stance. "Every time it occurs, we have the impression of growing madness: not Bartleby's madness particularly, but the madness around him."[14] Deleuze emphasizes how subversive the formula is in its capacity to create a zone of indiscernability and indetermination. The reader expects the eponymous hero to simply accept or refuse what he is asked to do. Yet, every time Bartleby pronounces his magic formula, he plunges everyone around him into great distress, and everything has to start anew. When Deleuze suggests that Melville's oeuvre is haunted by the need to reestablish the link between the inhuman and the human, he is reiterating, albeit implicitly, his own philosophical project of an alternative metaphysics that renews the link between humanity and its chaosmos.

The other dimension is that of the fraternal society freed from paternal power, a humanity called to design its own world, to affirm it as a process, "like a wall of uncemented stones, each stone standing on its own and yet related to the others."[15] In Deleuze's view, the originality of the ritornello, like Bartleby's phrase repeated as a series, is the only possible solution for avoiding the two-fold shoals of the war of specifics, on the one hand, and, on the other, a fusion within a Whole, a Universal that negates singularities. "For Melville and Lawrence, fraternity is the affair of original souls."[16] But that fraternity, founded on pragmatism, whose true hero is Bartleby, leads to failure. Bartleby finds himself confronted with the collapse of the society of brothers, a society that succeeded as poorly as the Soviet society of universal proletarianization.

According to Jacques Rancière, this failure of the society of fraternity confirms the impasse of Deleuze's attempt at liberation; the wall of free stones would express the dead end into which Deleuze leads his reader, defining its direction while "sending him into the wall."[17] Bartleby is thus invested with a Promethean mission similar to the one that Nietzsche assigns to Zarathustra. He becomes the hero of the transition between ontology and politics, but "literature opens no passageways toward a Deleuzean politics. There are no Dionysian politics."[18]

Esprit's director Olivier Mongin knew Deleuze's work from having studied philosophy. He observed in Deleuze's literary studies the development of a geography, of "a mind that moves."[19] For Mongin, guilt was the central issue in Deleuze's reading of Sacher-Masoch, a problem present also in Kant's formal law. "Deleuze drew the lesson that ethical law, which is formal and contentless, makes us guilty. So we enter the European world of permanent guilt, which leads to Kafka."[20] Deleuze's fascination with America led him to seek the idea of a fraternal society free of paternal oversight. "He didn't find it, and he didn't believe in the idea of a Soviet revolution either."[21] Since he did not find this dream society in the New World, his only remaining option was to look at people living in deserts, which he does in *A Thousand Plateaus*. Ultimately, Deleuze explores a place that is neither America nor Europe but the territories of hybrid heterogeneity, of linguistic and cultural mixtures.

The work of Édouard Glissant, a friend of Deleuze and Guattari, is a good example of this hybridity. A writer of mixed Afro-American and French culture born in 1928 in Sainte-Marie, Martinique, Glissant studied philosophy and later ethnology at the Sorbonne; he won the Renaudot Prize in 1958 for his first novel, *La lézarde* (*The Lizard*). When Glissant met Guattari in Paris, he was bowled over by his brilliance and immediately became his friend. "I thought, 'I'm listening to Socrates.' I heard the same wisdom, irony, the same asperity of approach and fundamental benevolence."[22] Édouard Glissant was deeply influenced by Deleuze and Guattari, as their positions bespoke a philosophy that integrated orality. In a concept like the rhizome, Glissant saw a "system of intrusion into identity"[23] recalling a composite identity that he knew so well in the Caribbean. "They think in fractal terms. It's a fractal, nomadic, errant thinking."[24] Glissant used the notion of "quaking thoughts," of a worldquake, in a way similar to Deleuze's linguistic stammering. While Western colonization has made the world racially mixed, Glissant preferred thinking about the values of creolization, the mixture of cultures, individuals, and groups that can produce the unexpected. The Swedish researcher Christina Kullberg finds concepts threading through Glissant's poetry that are quite close to those of Deleuze and Guattari. "The chaos-world in Glissant helps him to describe globalization as mondiality, and his notion of opacity closely resembles Deleuze and Guattari's notion of singularity. What is also essential for him is the theme of diversity that he calls diversality, and the concept of the 'common place' referring to the idea of shared space."[25]

Literature, for Deleuze, is above all experimentation, and he used it to argue against the interpretative approach. As we have already seen, his *Kafka* was in many ways a manifesto of literary experimentation. In writing about literature, Deleuze was not proposing to add a second reflexive, philosophical degree to classical literary criticism but rather to subtract, to make a "surgical amputation,"[26] and thereby to define a critical and clinical space. The eighth plateau in *A Thousand Plateaus* dwells on three short stories centered around the concept of the event in order to answer the often enigmatic question, "What happened?"[27] The novella is defined as a specific genre by virtue of answering this question, whereas the tale answers the question, "What's going to happen?" To argue for this, Deleuze and Guattari took as examples Henry James's 1898 short story "In the Cage," Fitzgerald's 1936 "The Crack-Up," and a French short story published in 1976 by Pierrette Fleutiaux, "Histoire du gouffre et de la lunette" ("Story of the Abyss and the Lunette"). All of Fitzgerald's work reflects the conviction that every life is an entropic process of destruction with breaks that are not necessarily enormous but are more like subtle and supple "microcracks," like those on a dish, that *usually occur when things are going better on the other side.*"[28] Slowly, the imperceptible, tenacious, molecular changes destroy the foundations of the unions, identities, and certainties. In Fitzgerald's short stories, three lines—a cut, a crack, and a rupture—run through every individual.

Various circumstances led to a meeting between Deleuze and Pierrette Fleutiaux. In 1975, Fleutiaux had just returned from the United States and initially moved into a maid's room in the building in the seventeenth arrondissement of Paris where the Deleuzes were living. She then moved into a first-floor studio apartment on the other side of the street, facing the Deleuze's building. Fleutiaux had just published *Histoire de la chauve-souris* (*A Bat's Story*), and Deleuze was intrigued both by the curious couple—she was thirty and her partner and former student was eighteen—and by the plot of the novel, which recounted the delirium of a woman persuaded to hide a bat in her long hair. Deleuze and Fleutiaux quickly became friendly. She read *Anti-Oedipus*, *Kafka*, and *Rhizome*, which deeply influenced her writing with their themes of flux, coding and overcoding, deterritorializing and the "becoming-animal," reminiscent of that which haunted her own long-haired heroine. The psychotic world is never too far away. "I've written a lot of abstract stories, sorts of machinic conjunctures. That also corresponded with what he said about it. He saw things that allowed me to continue in that direction, the machinic fantastic. I see him as a brilliant inventor."[29]

Deleuze and Fleutiaux maintained a silent relationship on either side of the street. When the one opened his window to smoke a cigarette, the other would comb her long hair. Deleuze became a part of Fleutiaux's daily world and a character in her book *We Are Eternal*.[30] In the chapter where he appears, she employs the well-known theme of grass as signifying partnership and communitarianism, contrasted against arborescence, on the side of power. "I was happy to see this grass and watched it while walking down Parisian streets, the grass was our city's dance."[31] The author mentions Deleuze's silhouette in the facing window.

A fan of "minor" genres, Deleuze pays tribute to the novella in *A Thousand Plateaus*. In the 1960s, he had already lent new seriousness to the long underrated genre of the detective story, which subsequently acquired legitimacy. In 1966, when the thousandth volume of the "Black Series" was published, Deleuze hailed the collection's spectacular transformation of the classical detective's quest for truth—either in the French rational manner or in the British clue-hunting style à la Conan Doyle—into a completely different register of a trail of errors and the "power of the false,"[32] employing its trinity of denunciation, corruption, and torture. Deleuze saw the "Black Series" as linking up with the grand tradition, which he traced back to Suetonius and Shakespeare and the theme of the deathly conjunction of the grotesque, terrifying, and deadly.

Deleuze also wrote about the literature of the *poètes maudits* (Baudelaire and Rimbaud, among others) and the tradition of censored literature.

Raymond Bellour has observed the extraordinary affinity between Deleuze and Henri Michaux.[33] In his introduction to the Pléiade edition of
Michaux's work, Bellour describes him as "a variety of multiplicities,"[34]
comprising powerful life experiences as a doctor and a sailor before becoming a writer bent on capturing life forces and their affects in his writing
and painting. Bellour adopted the expression that Deleuze uses for the true
writer as someone who has "made language stammer." In Michaux's use of
fragments, of flux run through with cuts, we seem to have the literary expression most in sync with Deleuze's philosophical themes. "Writing is answering. It's making language, conceived as part of the sensible world, the
place where there is an answer to the events of the sensible world and its
many accidents."[35] Here, Michaux's quest resembles that of the Surrealists—
even if Michaux broke with them—who explored thought through writing
or painting.

As Raymond Bellour points out, in *Foucault*, Deleuze borrowed three
titles from Michaux in one fell swoop, referring to "inside space," the "distant interior," and the "life in the folds."[36] In a dedicatory note to Michaux's
copy of *Difference and Repetition*, Deleuze wrote, "You knew how to say
more in a few pages on schizophrenia and so much better than anything
that's ever been said: the great trials of the spirit."[37] Bellour points out that
among the philosophers, Michaux is the most often cited writer in *What Is
Philosophy?*[38] In one of the book's fundamental chapters on the plane of immanence, Michaux is referred to at the end of a line starting with Epicurus
and moving through Spinoza, indicating that the problem of thinking is a
question of infinite speed. He is then associated with Blanchot and Foucault for the oxymoron of "intimacy as Outside." Bellour argues that Michaux is unique in that he is a writer and a philosopher. Because, for Deleuze,
philosophy has a literary status, he can use Michaux to destabilize philosophical claims. Anne Sauvagnargues also emphasizes that Deleuze and
Michaux were exceptionally close in that both tried to capture vital forces
and affects and both wanted to liberate singularities.[39]

Michaux's work sits at the intersection of literary and pictorial expression, and his work also inspired many lively reflections from Deleuze, who
met the painter Gérard Fromanger in 1971 under remarkable circumstances. Fromanger had just finished a series of paintings that Karl Flinker,
a well-known gallery owner, had promised to show. But as Flinker had
stopped communicating with Fromanger, the painter decided to go to
Flinker's home without forewarning. He went to rue Tournon, running

down from the Senate, walked through the ground-floor exhibit, and went up to Flinker's office on the first floor. Flinker introduced him to the person responsible for the gallery, a certain Fanny, who watched a clash take place between the two men. Flinker explained that he had stopped communicating because he feared Fromanger's leftist entourage—Fromanger was the elected representative of at least three hundred artists. "He told me, 'I'm afraid that you'd lob Molotov cocktails into my gallery, it's going to be a real general assembly day and night and I don't have that kind of time to waste,' but then he went on to say, 'but you're too charming, I'll have to think it over.'"[40] Fromanger got up, letting it be understood that he had gotten the message. Fanny, whom he did not know, accompanied him to the bistro on the other side of the street, where she admitted to being confused by the violence of the relationship between young artists and sellers. "She told me that she couldn't go through that, adding that her husband adored my work and inviting me to dinner at their home. I asked her who her husband was and she answered, 'He's a philosophy professor, he writes books, he's a philosopher.'"[41] That very evening, Fromanger was dining with the Deleuzes, flattered by Deleuze's interest in his work.

Fromanger and Deleuze became fast friends. Deleuze asked Fromanger if he could come to his studio to see his work. This was the beginning of a long collaboration. During these meetings, Deleuze asked the artist how he painted, how he worked, and how he developed his creative process. "Gilles said to me, 'I'm going to ask you dumb-ass questions,' and asked me why I'd put red there. When he asked the question, it made me talk for an hour while he took notes, always encouraging me. 'Oh, good, that's good!' which reconfirmed for me what Leonardo da Vinci said about painting being ideas, having to do with the mind."[42] A couple of weeks later, Deleuze called Fromanger again to ask for a second meeting. "He told me that he still needed some things and that I had to give him a bit more. I was happy, but not truly convinced that I was really giving him anything."[43] Deleuze asked Fromanger how he managed to put things on a canvas that was initially white. "I told him, 'you see it as blank, but in fact it's black.' And his reaction was, 'Ah, fantastic! It's black, black with what?' and I answered, 'It's black with everything every painter has painted before me,' and he said, 'So it's not about blackening the canvas but about whitening it.'"[44] Deleuze went back to this idea virtually word for word in *What Is Philosophy?* "The painter does not paint on an empty canvas, and neither does the writer write on a blank page; but the page or canvas is already so covered with preexisting, preestablished clichés that first you have to erase, clean, flatten, even shred, so as to let in a breath of air from the chaos that brings us the vision."[45]

After one of these working sessions, Fromanger got a phone call from Deleuze inviting him to dinner at his home, saying that the whole family needed his advice on an extremely important affair. Fromanger accepted, delighted. When he arrived, "Gilles was practically dressed in a business suit, their son Julien, who must have been about ten or twelve, was wearing a little tie. I was worried about what was going on and Gilles told me that this was a somewhat special meeting."[46] When it came time for dessert, Gilles turned to the chimney behind him, took the envelope that was sitting on the mantle, and asked Fromanger to open it. Fromanger opened it and found a check for eight thousand francs, which was Fanny Deleuze's first month's salary, and a little letter addressed to Karl Flinker, in which Deleuze explained that, given the relationship that Flinker had with the painter Fromanger, and probably with all other young painters, it would be very difficult for his wife Fanny to continue to work with him, and she had therefore decided to resign as gallery director. Deleuze asked Fromanger if he agreed. "I answered that it wasn't up to me to agree, so he asked me if it was appropriate, and I said yes."[47] So Deleuze took the check and gave it to his son Julien, who ripped it into tiny pieces. Then "Gilles put the ripped up check into the envelope and said to me, 'Gérard, you're the one who's going to put the letter into the mailbox.'"[48]

This story took place very early on in Deleuze and Fromanger's acquaintance, and it sealed a solid friendship. The event was all the more solemn and serious because the Deleuzes were not particularly rich in 1971; this was a real sacrifice. Shortly after this meeting, Deleuze wrote the preface to the catalogue of Fromanger's 1973 exhibit at 9, rue des Beaux-Arts.[49] As a result of working together on how painting engages the thinking process, Deleuze began thinking about colors and emphasizing the disconnection between colors and any explicit meaning. "Colors don't mean anything: green isn't hope, nor is yellow sadness, nor is red gay. Nothing but cold and hot, hot and cold. Art is material. Fromanger paints, meaning that he makes a painting work. Painting-machine of an artist mechanic."[50]

MUSIC, ABOVE ALL

Deleuze also worked with musicians. Typically, he moved into an unfamiliar area after meeting someone who knew about it and from whom he could learn. Deleuze wrote books about cinema, literature, and painting, but never on music. Just before his death in September 1995, he called his friend Richard Pinhas. "Gilles talked about Ravel, about the book on music that he'd like to write and about the book form that he'd like to get beyond."[51]

Deleuze first discussed music in public in 1978, when he was working with Guattari on *A Thousand Plateaus*. Along with Barthes and Foucault, he was attending a seminar on musical time, organized by the Institute for Research and Coordination in Acoustics/Music (IRCAM), directed by Pierre Boulez. Many years later, in January 1996, Boulez paid homage to Deleuze at the Cité de la Musique. He began by saying, "Gilles Deleuze is one of the very rare intellectuals to be deeply interested in music."[52] A small incident occurred on the day of the public discussion. Deleuze started speaking, and someone in the audience stood up, saying that he did not understand. The audience grew restless, and Boulez, exasperated, asked the person to leave the hall. During this exchange, Deleuze sat calmly watching and then resumed reading his prepared text. He commented on the series of five works that Boulez had suggested listening to, in which Deleuze perceived a unity in the series of notes within a nonpulsed time that stood out from the pulsed time. "The question would be understanding what exactly comprises *this nonpulsed time*. This kind of floating time."[53] This time refers to duration, a time freed of measure, "time in the pure state," as Proust had imagined it, composed of heterochronies that neither communicate nor coincide with one another. Deleuze compared this to research in the biological sciences that attempted to articulate disparate molecules. We might speak about sonorous molecules, "sonorous molecules in couples that could traverse layers of rhythm, layers of entirely heterogeneous durations."[54]

This binary opposition between pulsed and nonpulsed times resembles the duality that Deleuze and Guattari developed in *A Thousand Plateaus* between smooth and striated space. Deleuze further developed this thematic resemblance in his 1986 text on Boulez. "From the striated, what then distinguishes itself is a *smooth* or nonpulsed space-time that refers to the chronometry only in overall terms: its breaks are not defined."[55] Boulez had been theorizing his double binarity since the 1960s,[56] and Deleuze found that in his work "the creative fluidity takes priority over the formal norm recognized as necessary for writing and performing the work."[57]

The composer Richard Pinhas, one of the most faithful among the faithful at Deleuze's courses at Vincennes, became a close friend. He was one of the first to introduce synthesizers into French rock music, after having started as a minimalist composer. Pinhas took classes from Deleuze starting in 1971, when Deleuze began teaching at Vincennes, until his retirement in late 1987. Deleuze occasionally asked Pinhas to write short summaries for him on musicological issues. "During that period I was working a lot on analog synthesis and it's a little like what you find at the end of the chapter on 'On Ritornellos,' in *A Thousand Plateaus* on synthetic music."[58] Their exchanges proved mutually productive. Pinhas felt that some of the concepts that Deleuze had worked on inspired his music. "Electronic music is fundamentally based on a sound flux, on its breaks, and on some thinking about the sequences."[59] There was an immediate relationship between Deleuze's thinking about the material and interplay of forces drawn from it and Pinhas's electronic compositions. In addition to all of this were Deleuze's ideas on time and the machinic. "For synthesizers, these were only breaks with connections and repetitions, contrary to today's digital music."[60] Pinhas was amazed: "If I take the last pages in the chapter on the ritornello in *A Thousand Plateaus*, he manages to say in four pages what no musician theorizing even slightly about music could possibly dream of being able to write. That's where his genius lies."[61]

Deleuze's ability to get to the heart of musical creation is all the more surprising in that, unlike Guattari, he started listening to music quite late in his life, listened to very little, and had tastes running to Piaf, Paul Anka, and Claude François. He also liked Ravel's *Bolero*, about which he had planned to write something. One day in 1972, Pinhas brought Deleuze along with him to a recording studio and had him read a text by Nietzsche, accompanied by Pinhas's musical composition. "He was wearing earphones, which amused him a lot. He had also worked a lot on synthesizers."[62] Musical creation for Pinhas was a form of simultaneism similar to the Nietzschean-Deleuzean notion of time as eternity and temporal totality. Beyond the divisions among musical genres, Pinhas considered sound production as a single flux linking Bach, Wagner, Hendrix, Steve Reich, and Philip Glass with different intensities. The logic of sensation that Deleuze defined on the basis of Bacon's work could also be expressed in terms of musical creation, according to Pinhas. "Modulation and rhythm have the same modalities and creative sphere as sensation in the way that Gilles Deleuze defines it: it is irreducibly synthetic and difference at the constitutive level."[63]

In 1975, Pascale Criton, a musician and musicology student, came to meet a friend at the end of one of Deleuze's classes. She opened the door and heard Deleuze drawing an analogy between musical chromatics and what he wanted to signify philosophically. Addressing his audience, he said that it would be interesting to hear from someone who knew something about the issue. Criton was a reserved twenty-one-year-old who was there completely by accident, but she was working on chromatic variation in African cultures. So she spoke up and in a few succinct sentences explained what a specialist might say about the topic. The course was barely over, the hall was emptying out, chairs and tables were being noisily shoved around, and "he looked at me over the rims of his glasses. I turned around to see whom he might be addressing and I finally realized that he was motioning to me."[64] Citron came over to Deleuze, let the last people who were gathered around him leave, and "he took up my remarks on chromatics, asking me to come back to his classes and say more on the subject and to have us listen to music."[65] She agreed, but said that she could not see how she could be useful to him. "At which point he said to me, 'It would be very simple, just have us listen to music or bring along documents and make a short presentation and we could learn a lot about musical chromatics.' This was obviously appealing."[66]

The next week, work began on chromatics. Criton brought a tape recorder so that the class could listen to "Debussy's *The Submerged Cathedral*, Messiaen's *Chronochromie*, and African songs recorded by Gilbert Rouget. Many levels very quickly intertwined. Deleuze was working on notions of war machines and State apparatuses. Chromatics was very close to the war machine!"[67] Beyond the topical contributions on music, Criton was attracted by the texture and rhythm of Deleuze's voice and his way of thinking aloud.

Around the same time, Criton met Ivan Wyschnegradsky, a great Russian musician who had been living in Paris, where he died in 1979. Deleuze was very interested in Criton's work with Wyschnegradsky, who had been a pioneer in what he called ultrachromatics and about whom Criton wrote a book in 1996, dedicated to Deleuze.[68] Deleuze received several versions of the manuscript and wrote to her about it.

> I really believe in your work. . . . It's fascinating, and by the law of serendipitous encounters, marvelous, it happens that I am working on the virtual. So the idea of a sound continuum divided into a partial continuum by the play of intervallic qualities delights me. These qualities may not be defined as yet . . . the process of actualization

that precedes actuality, individuality and sound quality. The pages where you show that in the process of actualization, the limit is indiscernible, just like the passage from level to level are quite beautiful.[69]

Deleuze and Guattari's ideas heavily influenced Criton's compositions. In her piano pieces of the 1980s, she claimed to reach molecular material, to fluidify the material of sound, and she used Guattari's notion of "transcoding" in her work on the musical continuum. Deleuze listened to her attentively. "He didn't pretend to be a musical specialist. It was a laboratory, live, thinking taking form. He used to say to me, 'Is this right?' 'Can I say it this way?'"[70]

In the early 1980s when Deleuze was working on cinema, he kept musical composition in mind. He worked with Criton on Eisenstein's theoretical writings on the harmonies between image and sound. "This belonged to the realm of intermodality, of sensorial transmodality, and we had many discussions and read a lot of theory about it."[71] Over the course of their collaboration, she introduced him to the work of Gérard Griset, a student of Messiaen who had started the "spectral movement" in the mid-1970s, reintroducing temporal processes. Griset had his preferred author, the only philosopher whose writing helped him think about music, and it was Deleuze. When he died at fifty-two, Griset left behind a body of work on theory that Criton showed to Deleuze.

In 1987, Deleuze taught his last course at Vincennes, on harmony, and he told Criton that he wanted to continue working with her on what would have certainly been a book on music. Deleuze's health was deteriorating, however, as was the health of Criton's mother, Dominique d'Acher, who came to the course with her daughter. "I was quite frightened by the timing of these things and months went by when I didn't feel that I could be present for him for a book about music."[72]

Deleuze was excited about creation in film, painting, and music, but he was less interested in theater. His virulent, constant criticism of representation may have created this distance, although a few exceptions led him to consider theatrical productions. Most important was his meeting with Carmelo Bene, who, having started out in cinema, created his own particular genre, in which he staged music, voice, and images as unified components.

Deleuze and Bene met thanks to Jean-Paul Manganaro, an Italian author and translator, who became a close friend of Deleuze. "In 1975, I saw Carmelo Bene in Rome to get him to come to Paris and I made the mistake of asking him who he wanted to see in Paris. He answered, 'Barthes, Deleuze, Klossowski, Lacan, and Foucault.' I didn't know Barthes or Foucault, and I had to get my nerve up to call Deleuze, who was exceedingly kind and cordial. He already knew some of Bene's films."[73] After their meeting, Carmelo Bene and Deleuze had regular discussions about theater that eventually led to *Superpositions* in 1979.[74] The title suggested that, for Deleuze, it was not a matter of imposing an interpretation or a commentary on Carmelo Bene's work but rather of theorizing the subtractive act that Bene himself had undertaken with *Richard III*. The critical/clinical space that Deleuze defined was supposed to be a surgical amputation. Deleuze, who cared little for traveling, agreed to go with Manganaro to Rome to see the play in 1977. Bene had been an actor before becoming a director, and he had been a filmmaker before working in the theater. Deleuze found appealing Bene's ambivalence, his strength in transcending the divisions between author/actor/stage director, which Deleuze called Bene's "actorial machine."

At the heart of Bene's theater, in addition to the question of minor languages, is the theme of variation. "What counts are the relationships between speed and slowness."[75] Here, Deleuze disputed the tragic idea of representing conflicts and contradictions and was delighted by Bene's break from this tradition. Leaving behind the intersubjective dialectic, Bene allowed lines of variations to run according to various modalities and speeds, evolving toward minoritarian becomings. His work also included a long reflection on the body, something close to Deleuze's themes. For Carmelo Bene, theater raises the question of knowing how to be an actor's body without organs and, at the same time, to be a body on stage. The issue was to express "the impossibility of the body to want, to be able: the obstacles, or to use Deleuze's term, the *preventions* that distract and disturb."[76] In his theatrical expression, Bene emphasized the voice and its continuous variations, which are on the order of utterances corresponding to three flux: the actor's on-stage real voice; the recorded voice, and the bent, augmented, and diminished voice based on the actor's real voice.

Regarding the voice, Deleuze paid vibrant tribute to his old friend Alain Cuny, whom he had met at Marie-Magdeleine Davy's home when he was an adolescent.[77] "What the voice reveals is that concepts are not abstract. . . . When the actor's voice is that of Alain Cuny. . . . This may be the most beautiful contribution to a theater of reading. We dream of Spinoza's *Ethics* read by Alain Cuny. His voice is so to speak carried by a wind pushing the waves of demonstrations."[78]

In 1992, Deleuze published an important article entitled "The Exhausted," in the same volume as Beckett's *Quad and Other Plays for Television*.[79] Beckett's world, characters, and disjunctions resemble Deleuze's fascination with Bartleby and his "I would prefer not to." For Deleuze, the absence of possibilities in Beckett's theater makes it part of the theme of exhaustion, which is not mere fatigue, since the tired man still has possibilities even if he cannot realize them, unlike the exhausted man, who has none. "He exhausts himself by exhausting what's possible, and vice versa."[80] According to Deleuze, there are four paths for exhausting the possible: creating exhaustive series of things, drying up the flux of voices, extenuating the potentialities of space, and dissipating the power of the image. "The exhausted is the exhaustive, the dried up, the extenuated, and the dissipated."[81]

Aesthetics, for Deleuze, was hardly a private domain for specialists. It is in each of us as a symbiosis of affects and percepts in very singular combinations, in what he defines as a "logic of sensation," using Francis Bacon. When Deleuze gave an essay on Bacon to Harry Jancovici at the Difference publishing house, he had never met Bacon. His editor Joachim Vital often discussed painting with Deleuze, and while he found his analysis of Bacon particularly passionate and original, he also observed that "he didn't have much baggage in terms of art, and his tastes were controversial."[82] It was all the more surprising therefore for Deleuze to have derived operational concepts from Bacon's work.

No sooner had Deleuze's essay been published than it was sent to Bacon,[83] who found it strikingly acute. "It's as if this guy were watching over my shoulder while I was painting!"[84] Vital, a great Bacon admirer, organized a dinner for Deleuze and Bacon on avenue Trudaine, at the Auberge du Clou restaurant. What was supposed to be a great meeting turned into a disaster.

> The meal was awful, as awful as their discussion. "My dear Gilles," "My dear Francis." They smiled at each other, complimented each other, and smiled again. We were flabbergasted by their platitudes. We tried to salvage the discussion, mentioning Egyptian art, Greek tragedy, Dogen, Shakespeare, Swinburne, Proust, Kafka, Turner, Goya, Manet, Van Gogh's letters to his brother Theo, Artaud, Beckett. Each one tried to take the ball and run with it alone, ignoring the other one. One of the bottles of Bordeaux had turned, which Bacon

took as a personal offense, while Deleuze was carrying on a high-level conversation about the future of the University.[85]

When asked if he had met Bacon, Deleuze answered, "Yes, afterward, after the book. You can feel his power and violence but he's also quite charming. After sitting for an hour, he starts twisting in all directions, like real bacon."[86]

In his own book on Bacon, Michael Pepiatt credited Deleuze for the fact that Bacon had a greater reputation in Paris than he did anywhere else in the world.[87] But even beyond Bacon, Deleuze's study on pictorial art, of access to the "pure figural" through extraction and isolation, was targeting a reflection on esthetics. "Painting should wrench the Figure away from the figurative."[88] In *A Thousand Plateaus*, Deleuze continued studying what he had begun with Guattari on "faceness." He saw Bacon as the painter who undid the faces beneath the overcoded effects to better allow the multiple becomings of heads as prolongations of bodies to appear. What is it that provokes the powerful sensation we feel when looking at a Bacon painting? Essentially, it is his ability to capture the play of forces in the painting that defines its shapes. In Bacon, we find this will to figure life. "Life is the material."

His various experiments allowed Deleuze to construct a transcendental aesthetics of sensation. With his desire to get beyond the opposition between the critical and the clinical, Deleuze worked out a "physics of intensity,"[89] thereby remaining coherent with his early Nietzschean inspiration, pursuing this determination to recapture the forces running through creative experience. Vitalism was at the heart of aesthetics, as Deleuze recalled in his letter to Mireille Buydens, in reply to her book about him. "I think that, in your own way, you've seen what's essential for me, which is 'vitalism,' meaning a conception of life as a nonorganic power."[90] By contrast, however, Mireille Buydens reintroduced into Deleuze's aesthetic a series of contradictory dualisms, such as force and form, and observed in conclusion an "aformalism," thereby misunderstanding Deleuze, as Deleuze remarked to Arnaud Villani. "When I told Deleuze about the problem, he very vigorously disowned it."[91]

According to Villani, the play of oppositions was hardly Deleuze's priority; the body is what he finds fascinating in artists. "To act and react are first, before knowing. An aesthetics of representation has to yield to an *aesthetics* of the active subject,"[92] because his philosophy as a whole leans toward the body as an as yet unexplored force, just as Spinoza had already conceived of it.

THE FOLDS OF IMMANENCE

When he retired from Paris-VIII, Deleuze discovered the concept of the fold, which was consonant with his entire philosophical effort. It resulted from a lengthy study of Leibniz, on whom Deleuze worked for part of the 1979–1980 academic year, returning to him during his final year of teaching in 1986–1987. When Deleuze published his book in 1988,[93] he seemed to be reconnecting with his earliest monographs and their portraitlike style. He both revisited the author, whom he exhumed to make him a contemporary, and sought to resituate Leibniz, the philosopher of the Baroque age faced with the problems of his period.

The collapse of the theological construct in the mid-seventeenth century dramatically opened a new modern era. The construct was built on a closed, monocentric system, and when it encountered the great Copernican-Galilean break, it had to engage with infinity for the first time. The challenge for seventeenth-century philosophers was to think this infinity. Leibniz tried to respond to the two aspects of the problem: he gave an aesthetic response by following the distinct operations of the Baroque to infinity, and he offered an epistemological response that included the event and the verb in the monad, which was a self-enclosed unity that also contained the entire world, despite the absence of any "window to the outside."

The world was thus folded within each soul, differently configured each time. As was his habit, Deleuze distinguished his position from a certain number of the dominant received ideas and interpretations. Whereas Leibniz was taken as a rather smug optimist when he proffered the idea that the world is built from a preestablished harmony, Deleuze demonstrated that, on the contrary, his idea was based on a notion of damnation whereby "the best of all possible worlds stands on the shoulders of the damned."[94]

At a time when theological constructions and rational Enlightenment optimism were both collapsing, Leibniz made it possible for Deleuze to answer a challenge that was all the more urgent for being telluric. In this respect, contemporary efforts to salvage something and rebuild on new foundations "bring us closer perhaps to Leibniz than to Voltaire."[95] In addition, the other metaphysics that Deleuze was trying to work out transcends the division between the subject and the world and reestablishes the bridges between human beings and the cosmos, because the folds everywhere in the universe are in harmony with Leibniz's ideas. "You have to put the world into the subject so that the subject is for the world. This is the twist that comprises the fold of the world and of the soul."[96] These folds are discernable in the foldings of the oldest mountains, such the Hercynian Mountains, and in rivers, plants, and living organisms.

The idea of the fold provides an operator for the transversality that Guattari heralded. The concept is universally appealing because it corresponds to certain uses of daily life. This connection with life is what most thrilled Deleuze. He evoked it in the 1988 *Abécédaire* when describing the many letters he had received from people identifying with this use of the fold, especially the Association of Paper Folders, who published their own review and expressed their appreciation. "We agree. What you are doing is what we're doing. It's a marvel!"[97] When Deleuze published his book, a long list of Leibniz specialists, including Louis Couturat, Bertrand Russel, Martial Guéroult, Yvon Belaval, and above all Michel Serres, had already made Leibniz's work well known during the 1970s and 1980s.

It would be hard to claim, even if Deleuze himself did, that he betrayed Leibniz in the folds of his thought. The Leibniz specialist Michel Fichant agreed with Deleuze's vision. "In rereading *The Fold*, I've realized that Deleuze is far more faithful to Leibniz than we might have thought."[98] By subtitling his book *Leibniz and the Baroque*, Deleuze was not aligning himself with Cassirer's cultural, symbolic reception of Leibniz but was subscribing to the more properly epistemological lineage of the philosophy of mathematics or logic, of Couturat, for example. "What's original, therefore, in Deleuze is that he approaches Leibniz through the Baroque."[99] Bruno Paradis saw things the same way, defining Deleuze's style using a concept that Deleuze had used when describing Foucault's approach—the "diagonal."[100] Indeed, Deleuze found in Leibniz this sense of multiplicities, disparate elements, and distinct domains that can be put into relationship with phenomena of capture of one field in another. Diagonals can sketch lines, fold different knowledges into one another, thereby making mathematics, poetry, architecture, philosophy, and music consonant.

Deleuze was constantly trying to rebuild bridges. In Leibniz, he saw a thinker who made it possible to make the fold of the world pass once more between the folds of the soul and of matter. This notion also avoided the choice between continuities and discontinuities, immobilities and breaks, because the fold bears within itself "at the same time real distinction and inseparability."[101] The fold became the vector of sensible and intelligible intensities mixed together; it referred neither to a beginning nor to an end, nor to heights or depths, but only to a single plane of immanence. Deleuze's goal was to create a concept of the fold that followed all the twists and turns of Leibniz's thinking. "My hypothesis is that the baroque makes folds."[102] Not that the baroque invented the fold, of course: the folds in the sculptures of Greek antiquity are ample evidence of that, but the baroque fold continues infinitely, which is what sets it apart. "A soul could not develop all at once all these folds because they continue to infinity."[103] In the Leibnizian system, Deleuze found a form of vitalism close to his own positions. Leibniz's vitalism consisted in claiming that "the living being is a machine. . . . What contrasts with the mechanical is the machine."[104] The difference between the two is that the machine is part of infinity while the mechanical is finite.

Bernard Cache, a young, recent graduate in architecture from the Lausanne Polytechnical School, came to Vincennes during the 1979–1980 academic year, when Deleuze was starting to discuss Leibniz. "I thought, 'This is it! This is exactly what I'm looking for. I still don't know what it is, but this is it.'"[105] He decided to study philosophy and chose Deleuze as his thesis director. A long dialogue began between them that lasted until Deleuze's death in 1995. The beginning of *The Fold* points out how important Cache found Leibniz's approach to mathematics and geometry. For Deleuze, baroque mathematics began with Leibniz as the realm of variation par excellence. Leibniz's perspectivism was analogous to relativism, but not what we might think of as relativism: "it's not a variation of truth according to the subject but the condition under which the truth of a variation appears to the subject."[106] According to Leibniz, the soul's folds envelop the virtualities of diverse inflections. "The entire world is merely virtuality that actually exists currently only in the folds of the soul expressing it."[107] Cache transformed these principles into material forces by conceiving of manufactured objects based on aleatory models that would allow for the industrial production of modulable nonstandard objects. He started a business called "Objectile Distribution," at Deleuze's suggestion. "One day he said to me that I was talking about objects in a Leibnizian manner using parametrical functions that were in fact objectiles."[108] His business made philosophical principles into a truly unique mode of production, going from the Leibnizian algebraic fold to the geometrical Desarguian fold. For Cache, the issue was a form of neofinalism "that would be a philosophy of denaturation!"[109]

With its many dark interiors and *trompe l'oeils*, exteriorless interiors and interiorless facades, the Leibnizian monad is above all tied to baroque architecture. Baroque space is split into two parts separated by a simple fold. Here we find in particular the binocular vision of Tintoretto and El Greco. We also know that the baroque introduced a new register of light, with chiaroscuro. "Chiaroscuro fills the monad according to a series that we can go over from both directions."[110] This relationship between two levels and intensities of light refers to another split between the infinity of possible worlds and the finitude of real worlds; between the two are the virtual worlds that are actual in the monads that express them without being real. The world is thus "One" for Leibniz but conceived on two distinct levels that we can see in the relationship between the body and the soul, each of which obeys its own laws. The soul expresses the world while the body actualizes it. "These are not two cities, a heavenly and earthly Jerusalem, but the roof and the foundations of the same city, the two floors of the same house."[111]

Concerning musical creation, Leibniz's idea was that the soul sings in harmony with chords, whereas eyes read a single partition and voices follow the melodic line, thereby emphasizing the envelopment through foldings of different operations whose result seeks harmony; most contemporary music expresses this idea. "The same expressive problem continually moves through music, until Wagner or Debussy, and today with Cage, Boulez, Stockhausen, and Berio. The problem is not correspondence but 'fold-in' or 'fold according to fold [*pli selon pli*].' "[112] Deleuze concludes: we remain fundamentally Leibnizian because it is always a matter of folding, unfolding, and refolding.

The theme of the crystal is omnipresent in Deleuze's work, because the crystalline level is the model of the event as the plane of immanence. Christine Buci-Glucksmann,[113] an early student of Deleuze, has pointed out that the crystal has an originary value for building an aesthetics of the virtual. In 1986, she published a book on the baroque[114] and discussed baroque aesthetics with Deleuze, who was working on his book on Leibniz. "We talked about the baroque of the continuous, meaning the model of the Leibnizian fold, Bernini, Italy, the concept, and what I had worked on: the baroque of the void, the rhetoric of the baroque in Naples, Venice, and Spain."[115] Deleuze's death put an end to their fruitful discussions, but Buci-Glucksmann continued to define an aesthetics of the virtual "by trying to work out a third register of the image that was post-Deleuze and which I called the image-flux, different from the image-crystal, which still had some problems; it was an image that is a sort of continuous virtual."[116] Buci-Glucksmann's work was very close to Deleuzean concepts, and she tested them in several creative expressions, for example in her work on Japan.[117] She distinguished several matrices specific to the "Japanese eye," starting with its observations about architecture and urbanism. She saw an initial matrix in the wave effect. "Waves and spirals, like the image's clouds or the folds of the originary are always virtual inflections exactly as Gilles Deleuze and Bernard Cache understood them."[118] Here we are in the realm of multiple variations, lines-universes, inflections that take into consideration the Japanese expression "the spirit of wave" (*l'esprit de la vague*), which is somewhat the reverse of the Western expression "reacting after the fact" (*l'esprit de l'escalier*).

Éric Alliez correctly understood that the construction of this ontology of the virtual was the guiding line of Deleuze's thought.[119]

> Everything happened as if Deleuze had begun by a general submission of all modern philosophy, Kantian and Hegelian, dialectical and phenomenological, Bergson's critique of Einstein: *confusing actual and virtual, reducing mathematical logic for solution cases to the ontological problematic of matter and time.* Insofar as the virtual is the sole object of Deleuzean thought, it can be called the philosophy of becoming, of difference, of immanence or of the event, because it's the virtual that makes it possible to enunciate, from the perspective of a truly transcendental materialism, each of these notions for itself and with the others.[120]

Raymond Bellour, a friend of both Deleuze and Guattari, was dazzled by *Anti-Oedipus* when he read it in 1972, and he interviewed the authors for *Les Temps Modernes*. The interview was too long to be published, but Bellour managed to convince the editor of the *Magazine Littéraire* to showcase *The Fold* when it was published in 1988.[121] Bellour was especially interested in the question of actual and virtual, which had interested Deleuze since his work on Leibniz and until his death. His last, unfinished book project was to have been entitled *Ensembles and Multiplicities*; his final text, "Immanence, a Life," and the piece published as an appendix to *Dialogues*, "Actual and Virtual," were the first two chapters. "It would have been a small book with very short chapters. He wanted to explain the logical ensembles of Russel and Frege and the concept of the virtual. But he killed himself after writing these two texts."[122]

In one of these two final texts, Deleuze returns to his definition of philosophy as a theory of multiplicities that directly poses the problem of the actual and the virtual. "Philosophy is the theory of multiplicities, each of which is composed of actual and virtual elements. Purely actual objects do not exist. Every actual is surrounded by a cloud of virtual images."[123] As for immanence, it includes both of these dimensions without it being possible to say that one belongs to the other. This thematics of the virtual is present in Deleuze's work from the time of his thesis, where he claimed the full reality of the virtual dimension: "The virtual is opposed not to the real but to the actual."[124] Deleuze needed a conception of multidimensional time, which he was seeking in the time-image, taking the time crystal as nonchronological time that makes us see singular becomings. Using the crystal, he valorizes matter organized at the frontiers of the organic and the inorganic, a precipitate of synthesis.

Even if Deleuze's last books did not make much mention of cinema and drew more substantially from literary works—which may have had to do with the fact that during his final years Deleuze was living at home as a recluse—he did quite certainly plan to continue his research on cinema. In 1995, during the last months of Deleuze's life, Raymond Bellour recalls having discussed the question of the virtual, a dimension that is not actual but is nonetheless quite real. "He was preparing a book on the virtual, and I remember having mentioned it to him on the phone in the summer of 1995 when he was in Saint-Léonard-de-Noblat."[125]

25

An Artist Philosophy

Deleuze and Guattari's collaboration culminated in a classical question, which, by arguing for the primacy of "and" over "is," the two authors seemed to have spent their careers avoiding. *What Is Philosophy?* was published in 1991, to the general surprise of the public. Indeed, ever since *A Thousand Plateaus*, Deleuze had been saying that he wanted to work on this theme; his closing words to his final class at Paris-VIII in 1980 were, "Next year, I have to find something new. My dream would be a course on 'what is philosophy?' "[1] His students thought he was joking and broke out laughing. During the 1980s, Deleuze repeated this to his students, saying he had never managed to do the course on philosophy because he was not yet ready to answer that question, which was to him simple in appearance only. He often stressed the importance of the project.[2]

The book had an ambiguous status. Both a very personal project and something of a crowning moment in a philosopher's life, *What Is Philosophy?* was manifestly written by Deleuze alone, but he agreed to a coauthor credit with Guattari, as a tribute to their exceptionally intense friendship, suggesting too that the ideas developed in the book and its language were the fruit of their common endeavors since 1969. *What Is Philosophy?* thus celebrated two decades of collaboration. Its double authorship pays tribute to the arrangement that had made it possible.

TO DO PHILOSOPHY IS TO CREATE CONCEPTS

What Is Philosophy? was publicly received better than *A Thousand Plateaus*, partly because its message clearly concerned the specific function of the philosopher as someone able to create concepts. Here again, Deleuze and Guattari ran against the grain of the 1990s, a decade when everyone purported to create and distribute concepts, especially salesmen. "Concepts" were the hot topic everywhere. Tell me your concept, and I'll tell you who you are. Easier said than done!

Those familiar with Deleuze and Guattari's work were naturally receptive to the message in *What Is Philosophy?* The authors' friend Robert Maggiori wrote a long article accompanying a highly favorable review in *Libération*, based on his interview with the two authors, during which they reiterated the composite nature of the concepts produced by "machinic branching" and showed that their very strong friendship was respectful and reasoned, bespoken by the use of the formal *vous*.[3] Maggiori emphasized that a similar polemical thread ran from *Anti-Oedipus*, where authors targeted psychoanalysis, to this book, which targeted philosophy. "Today's philosophy cannot *assimilate* Deleuze and Guattari's book."[4] He described as "constructivist" the definition of philosophy that, in order to create concepts, had to pull an event out of beings and things, invent conceptual personae, and make sure that they were all connected on the plane of immanence. During the same week that Maggiori's article came out, Roger-Pol Droit also reviewed the book in *Le Monde*. "We've long awaited this book. Deleuze has been announcing it for several years now. Maybe for his whole life."[5] Droit also insisted on the book's untimeliness, its joyful contretemps. "This book can be inexhaustible. It's one of those very rare books that can make useless libraries collapse, it can grab you and get you going."[6] From *Anti-Oedipus* to *What Is Philosophy?* certain concepts appeared while others disappeared. Deleuze and Guattari had accustomed their readers to a particular language that provided a striking contrast with classical philosophical language.

Sylvain Loiseau had started out as a doctoral student in classics before switching to linguistics. He was writing his thesis at Paris-X under François Rastier on the "Semantics of Philosophical Discourse," focusing on philosophy in the 1970s in France. He was working on texts by Lyotard, Derrida, and Foucault, and he included the bulk of Deleuze and Guattari's work in his research. He was therefore able to measure, through their lexicon, the degree to which Deleuze and Guattari had managed to create concepts. Loiseau digitized the texts and made a quantitative analysis of lexical occurrences that allowed him to demonstrate several structuring semantic characteristics: "the opposition/limited/unlimited is a textual constant, especially in *Anti-Oedipus*."[7]

When Deleuze and Guattari spoke about the subject or actor, Loiseau could identify the associated terms, which indicated how the authors attributed functions and semantic roles to them. "Actors have a conflictual relationship with continuity. They must 'get through,' 'destroy the codes,' 'break the limits,' 'scramble things,' and 'demonstrate their autonomy.'"[8] Loiseau pinpointed the moment when Deleuze met Guattari by identifying the changes in linguistic register. In 1968 and 1969, when Deleuze was writing alone, his language was rather classical, semantically speaking, even in *The Logic of Sense*. "*A Thousand Plateaus* is the work that stands out most."[9]

Of course, a philosopher does not create concepts *ex nihilo* in a solitary one-on-one with the blank page; he needs conceptual personae, like the "friend," who would then confirm the Greek origins of philo-sophy. "With the creation of philosophy, the Greeks violently forced the friend into a relationship that is no longer a relationship with an other but with an Entity, an Objectivity, an Essence."[10] Conceptual personae can incarnate themselves in psychosocial figures like the despot, the nomad, the prophet, the traitor, the warrior, and the itinerant, to name those filling the pages of *A Thousand Plateaus*.

Philosophy can call upon an infinite number of conceptual personae, including the idiot. "The idiot is the private thinker, in contrast to the public teacher (the schoolman)."[11] Each of these personae has its "hour of glory," the places where it is rooted, linked to a spatially situated spirit of the times. The idiot appears in a Christian context and emerges on the Slavic, Russian stage; it is a powerful figure in Dostoyevsky. The idiot is also transformed: the new idiot, compared to the old, differs because rather than contenting himself with the obvious, he seeks the absurd.

In the preface to his 1869 *History of France*, Jules Michelet considered himself the product rather than the father of his work, the son thus engendering his father. Deleuze and Guattari similarly consider that the conceptual personae play a major role: the philosopher is merely the envelope. Like *ritornellos*, conceptual personae emerge in an originary place, a territory with its logics of deterritorialization and reterritorialization. Their features are determined by their epoch and by their geographical origins. At the same time, like pure events, they escape the state of things in which they arise and belong to a "determination purely of thinking and thought."[12] This is the only way in which they achieve the status of conceptual personae. Deleuze and Guattari describe what qualifies as being philosophical, which is condensed in the fact of "Laying out, inventing, and creating."[13]

These three linked operations consist in finding a prephilosophical plane on the plane of immanence, of inventing and bringing to life prephilosophical personae, and, finally, of creating philosophical concepts. Writing the history of philosophy amounts to finding this triple gesture and extracting the problem that a given philosopher was working out. The philosopher can both get closest to the true problems and create new concepts during crises: "philosophy thus lives in a permanent crisis. The plane takes effect through shocks, concepts proceed in bursts, and personae by spasms."[14] It is illusory to imagine that we can simply lay out layers of knowledge in the way that erosion deposits layers of sediment on the ground. The criterion, which remains valid, is to be interesting. "A concept must be interesting, even if it is repulsive."[15] Using this criterion, we can find in the history of the most ancient philosophy that which makes a dormant concept "interesting," on the condition that it helps revive different becomings on a new stage, "even at the price of turning the concept against itself,"[16] using the method of perversion dear to Deleuze.

Philosophy is part of invention, but how does it differ from logical science or art? Part II of *What Is Philosophy?* addresses this issue. Science innovates, of course, taking functions rather than concepts as its objects. Confronted, like philosophy, with chaos, it proceeds in the opposite way, by relinquishing infinity to gain in functionality and "*a reference able to actualize the virtual.*"[17] Science must establish its coordinates and fixed limits in order to base its experiments on a plane of reference rather than immanence. The functions that it adopts are composed of "functives" as distinct from concepts. Science and philosophy are similar in that they are two modalities or different types of multiplicities. But a concept can change and become propositional, at which point it is called a prospect. However, at this point, "*the concept loses all the characteristics it possessed as a philosophical concept*: its self-reference, its endoconsistency and its exoconsistency."[18] This remark takes a shot at analytical philosophy, which dominates the North American academic world. By assimilating philosophy to a simple science of logic and confusing concepts and functions, analytical philosophers become the gravediggers of philosophy. "A real hatred inspires logic's rivalry with or its will to supplant philosophy. It kills the concept twice over."[19]

This kind of assimilation arises from a misunderstanding about the concept as a pure sense event, beyond its functionality in a specific state. "The concept is a form or a force; it is never a function in any possible sense of the term."[20] Deleuze and Guattari rip philosophy out of the "fascination-dependency" that long affected it and kept it in the orbit of science. Yet the concept is on the order of the event and by definition avoids being functionalized, since the event is "that part that eludes its own actualization in everything that happens."[21] Being worthy of the event that one must embody requires a certain determination. "Philosophy's sole aim is to become worthy of the event, and it is precisely the conceptual persona who countereffectuates the event."[22] Deleuze and Guattari do not argue that the intrinsic difference between science and philosophy means that the two realms should ignore one another but rather that they should remain distinct and respect each other's specificity, "each according to its line."[23]

AFFECTS AND PERCEPTS

Philosophy and art both involve creativity, but each has different objects. Art is the realm of affects and percepts, which are different from affections and perceptions because they can be preserved and can extend beyond the moment of their sensation. Art's function is to make this conservation and transmission possible beyond the limited moment of the experience. "Sensations, percepts, and affects are those *beings* whose validity lies in themselves and exceeds any lived [experience]."[24] The philosopher creates concepts; the artist creates percepts and affects through architecture, writing, sculpture, painting, and music. This multiform artistic capacity that extends beyond the actual state is central to Deleuze and Guattari's philosophical problematization.

The status of aesthetics is different from that of philosophy, of course, but it is not really seen as a separate realm delimited from the rest of philosophical speculation, because percepts and affects are indistinguishable from thought images and are indeed the very conditions making them possible. They are also the preferred realm within which to experiment with the human creative capacity. Like conceptual personae, affects can play a central role in which certain heroes take their guise.[25] Art is not reserved for humans alone; with Deleuze and Guattari, art once again has an active relationship to the world and to its transformation. "Perhaps art begins with the animal, at least with the animal that carves out a territory and builds a house."[26] Just as philosophy can only live by creating concepts, so too must art always create new percepts and affects. Using different methods and objects, art, logical science, and philosophy share the same perspectives: create a finitude that opens onto infinity and that can reconnect with the surrounding chaos to draw its planes from it. No particular approach has any ascendancy over any other; they are the three variants of thought, and their respective relationship presupposes their intersection on the condition of avoiding any identification or false synthesis.

These three forms of creative expression seek to liberate vital forces wherever they are imprisoned and to rediscover their virtuality by destratifying them. Insofar as there is no determinism on the plane of immanence, every moment and every site can be productive sources of experimentation. Whence the generalized constructivism suggested by a creative *bricolage* that rearranges all forms of vitality and then takes stock of the results. This other metaphysics moves through empiricism: here we again find Deleuze's first works on Hume.[27]

Deleuze and Guattari constantly defend the fundamental gesture of setting the natural, animal, and human world into motion by carefully observing how things happen. This implies a philosophical "style" that constantly seeks new arrangements and concepts able to express the power of creation and translate it into words along artistic-philosophical lines, or an esthetic paradigm whose experimental field would extend beyond art.

In the early 1990s, the research of the biologist Francisco Varela on cognition further extended this artistic model. Varela disagreed with Husserlian phenomenology, finding that it failed to provide access to the structure of experience itself and had become an abstract act of philosophical introspection without any pragmatic dimension. He introduced the notion of "enaction," action embodied as a circular interaction between an organism and its environment, both of which remain strictly independent of each other.[28] To do this presupposed paying particular attention to the most varied arrangement of heterogeneous elements and valorizing the simultaneously appearing emergent phenomena. "There are many relationships between an aesthetics of enaction and a territorial aesthetic as Deleuze and Guattari understand it."[29]

AN AESTHETIC OF LIFE

With Deleuze and Guattari, aesthetics takes on new meaning, touching upon realms of human activity and finding its roots in its lines of flight and deterritorialization. All of the practices and activities that have a relationship to the new, and thus to a form of deterritorialization, can therefore be situated as different modalities of an aesthetic paradigm or of an "artist philosophy." Art, of course, condenses this phenomenon of exhibiting the new: "To create is to reveal oneself."[30]

Mony Elkaïm, the psychiatrist, therapist, and friend of Guattari who worked hard with him on an alternative psychiatric network,[31] expressed his debt to Guattari after his death.

> In the life of one of us, Félix played a crucial role. Acknowledging the productivity of the reference to the open systems far from equilibrium, vulnerable to registers of stable activity and also to instabilities and bifurcations toward other registers of activity, he feared that this reference would become the reigning slogan and that the therapist might forget the ethical and aesthetic aspects of his work. It was through his inspiration that the notion of system, dominated by the ideal of intelligibility, was replaced by that of arrangement, under the sign of heterogeneity.[32]

Elkaïm's tribute gives the measure of how much the concepts and theoretical postures adopted by Deleuze and Guattari were burning social issues. The therapist, with this creative, artistic idea of conjunction, can no longer merely observe analytic categories in a particular situation in the way that "I understand" refers to a readymade interpretative system. The therapist faces the risk of creation, of innovation produced by this particular *bricolage*.

Art and philosophy are in direct contact. Artistic creation is not relegated to some superstructure but constitutes value systems and the source of identity. "Think about the emergence of polyphonic music in the West, a mutant mode of subjectification."[33] Art is considered the resistant realm par excellence; it preserves affects and percepts by defying passing time; it could also be a means of resisting the process of homogenization and a way of lending value to multiplicities. "Art tends toward heterogenesis unlike capitalist homogenesis."[34] The work of art as autopoesis points to a process of autoproduction of the new and could be a possible aesthetic paradigm that could serve as a model for science and philosophy.

In discussing Deleuze's relationship to art, Anne Sauvagnarges distinguishes three successive periods in his work. First, he favored literature. Then, after meeting Guattari, pragmatism led him to the political dimension of artistic creation. Finally, after *A Thousand Plateaus*, he began working out a general semiotics of artistic creation via the image and the study of cinema. While we can identify a greater or lesser insistence on this or that artistic form, the goal, which had been explicit since *Difference and Repetition*, remained constant: to grasp as closely as possible the images of thought, whether they belonged to speaking or to seeing, subject the clinical to the critique and vice versa, and bring the philosopher's analytic observation to the core of the creative act as it happened. For Deleuze, art does not reproduce what is real: it *is* real. "An image doesn't represent a supposed reality; it is its own complete reality."[35]

Deleuze and Guattari shifted the reigning Lacanian distinction of three different levels in the Real-Symbolic-Imaginary (RSI) relationship, where the symbolic order is the most important and the Real-Imaginary poles are virtually antithetical and well removed from one another. On the contrary, they insisted on the reality of the imaginary and on the literalness of utterances as images. Art radically changes the power to affect and to be affected, "such that what we call art or literature consists in a symptomatology of real relations, a 'capture of forces' that proves to be a clinic."[36] The philosopher seizes the expression of forces underlying forms and tries to evaluate their hidden power (an analysis developed along Nietzschean lines). Spinoza enabled Deleuze and Guattari to discern two forms of individuation as two heterogeneous lines: longitude, which is extensive, extrinsic, and concerns the state of forces and signs; and latitude, which is the intensive, intrinsic level concerning affects. It is this double relationship between longitude and latitude that constitutes individuating singularity, or haecceity. Beings do not distribute themselves into grids or boxes according to their different species but on the basis of their specific intensity, meaning their affect. Guattari developed this problem because it emphasized the importance of affect, which broke with Lacan's Signifying master, which assigned everything to the Symbolic and nothing to affect. For Deleuze, affect is the elementary particle of the living. Which is why, referring to ethological studies in the 1988 *Abécédaire*, he describes a tick's mode of being as limited to three affects: the visual stimulus that pushes it to climb to the extreme end of a branch in order to reach light, the olfactory stimulus pushing it to drop onto its prey, and a tactile stimulus leading it to penetrate beneath the skin. "That makes a world."[37]

According to Deleuze and Guattari's theory of becoming (becoming-animal, becoming-intense, becoming-imperceptible), artistic creation functions like the capture of forces. Deleuze and Guattari open a completely different direction than the interpretative tradition, because "the capture of forces makes it possible to substitute the forces-matter relationship for the form-material relationship. By putting heterogeneous forces into contact that produce a new capture, the work associates creator and receiver in a becoming real that takes the mutation of cultures into consideration."[38] By developing this critique of the interpretative approach, Deleuze and Guattari claim a resolutely immanent philosophy. Art is conceived as one force among many, which contrasts with the conception of art for art's sake, of art cut off from its constitutive forces.[39] From this perspective, empiricism was not merely an appetizer for Deleuze, for it is quite persistent in his work, as Philippe Choulet shows. "The Deleuzean initiative consists in decomplexifying empiricism and using it like a war machine, a Trojan horse against idealism and rationalism."[40]

26

Winning Over the West

America wasn't conquered in a day. Disseminators had to do some preliminary groundwork. When Deleuze and Guattari first set foot on American soil in the mid-1970s, American campuses were already partial to French theory.[1] The stars of the moment were Barthes, Foucault, and Derrida, who had been teaching in the United States on a regular basis since 1966. Despite the spectacular stir in France over *Anti-Oedipus*, Deleuze and Guattari were still the poor relations of French theory. Deleuze, who did not enjoy traveling and hated conferences, had not crossed the Atlantic, but an auspicious encounter eventually led to a trip to America for both authors.

LOTRINGER THE FERRYMAN

Sylvère Lotringer's career is remarkable. Jewish, of Polish ancestry, Lotringer was born in Paris in 1938 and became a naturalized French citizen at three months of age. He spent his childhood in occupied France, unwittingly hidden by a Renault factory worker, whom he met again thirty years later. "I have this small distance that allows me to keep my independence. It was the French who saved me but it was also the French who betrayed me. Hence I keep leaving France."[2] When Israel was created in 1948, he left with his parents to settle there, but he stayed only a year before returning to France. He enrolled at the Sorbonne in 1957 and became involved in an extreme-left Zionist organization, Hachomer Hatzaïr. He developed a passionate interest in journals and created his own literary review at the Sorbonne, *L'Etrave*. As of 1959, he began writing regularly in *French Letters*. Initially he majored in psychology but switched to philosophy, the longest course of studies, to avoid being drafted in the Algerian war. Lotringer quickly became a militant activist against the Algerian war and joined the UNEF leaders of the *Letters-Paris* sector.

In 1972, Lotringer obtained a position in Columbia University's Paris program at Reid Hall on rue de Chevreuse near Montparnasse to organize summer university sessions in the humanities and semiotics. He invited high-profile intellectuals such as Catherine Clément, Serge Leclaire, Tzvetan Todorov, Denis Hollier, and several Derrideans. That same year, he discovered—with great enthusiasm—*Anti-Oedipus*. As soon as the book came out, he hired Guattari to teach and invited Deleuze to give several conferences. Guattari and Lotringer became immediate friends; they shared the same interests and peripatetic personalities; both wanted to create something new. In 1974, Lotringer took a sabbatical year in Paris to spend most of his time working with Guattari. He conducted research with the CERFI and later produced an issue of *Recherches* (*Research*) on Saussure. The same year, Lotringer decided to launch *Semiotext(e)* in the United States: the editorial team was set up in Paris and largely comprised American and French students, along with Wlad Godzich, Denis Hollier, Peter Caws, and John Rajchman.

With *Semiotext(e)*, Lotringer created an antiacademic war machine to disseminate the ideas of Deleuze and Guattari in the United States. During this period, Lotringer often went to La Borde to meet with Guattari at his home in Dhuizon. When he returned to the United States in 1975, he decided, along with his friend and colleague John Rajchman, who was also on the editorial board, to organize a large symposium at Columbia University on "Schizoculture" and bring Deleuzo-Guattarian thought to American soil. This project would require bringing over several well-known French intellectuals including, of course, Deleuze and Guattari, but Lotringer and his still relatively unknown journal had neither the institutional nor financial backing for such an undertaking.

Ultimately, the project was realized thanks to Yves Mabin, who was responsible for French assignments abroad and who later became a good friend of Deleuze. He decided to set up a small informal committee to decide which French intellectuals should go to the United States. It had previously been the case that only the American universities took the initiative to invite guests. "The principle was that we wanted these assignments to lead to better coverage of the work of French intellectuals."[3] A list of prospective contributors to an annual review that would have no ideological leanings was compiled. The list contained four professors from the

Collège de France, some twenty directors of study from EHESS, and several university lecturers, all of whom had published articles or books. "This was how I wrote to Deleuze, whom I only knew through his work. Unlike those who believe that intellectuals must serve the state, I've always held the contrary opinion."[4] Yves Mabin asked Deleuze whether he would agree to participate in this assignment in the United States to introduce his work to the American public. Though unexcited by the prospect, Deleuze was intrigued and asked to meet Yves Mabin, who received him in his office on avenue Kléber. "He sat facing me and brought his chair up to my desk. I felt like a defendant in front of police chief Maigret."[5] Deleuze wanted to understand what was behind this curious invitation. "We talked for an hour, and it worked; we instantly took to each other."[6] Deleuze expressed his reluctance about making this sort of trip, but Mabin was firm, adding that he would fail in his mission if Deleuze did not participate; Guattari had already agreed. After much persuasion, Deleuze consented.

Deleuze and Guattari could now accept Lotringer's invitation. The latter was convinced that their philosophical positions were more in sync with American society than with French society. "What appeared to be a utopian theory in France was daily reality in New York."[7] For his symposium on "Madness and Prison," Lotringer went scouting for American homologues of Deleuze and Guattari, but finding none, he invited primarily writers and artists—apart from several intellectuals including Arthur Danto and the psychiatrist Joel Kovel—whose work he felt shared certain things with *Anti-Oedipus*. "I was surprised that someone like John Cage, whose interviews with Daniel Charles I translated, had managed to achieve something rather close to the Deleuzo-Guattarian vision of capitalism."[8] So he invited Cage along with William Burroughs, Richard Foreman, and Ti-Grace Atkins, a renowned feminist. On the French side, he managed to nab Foucault in New York on his return from Brazil as well as Lyotard and Jean-Jacques Lebel, a happenings specialist who introduced Deleuze and Guattari to American artists, singers, and writers he knew and had worked with. Hanging out at the Chelsea Hotel, in the same room as Guattari, Lebel would walk around stark naked. Because he was bilingual, he was appointed the designated host of a radio show that ran for a week during the symposium, broadcasting on WBAI, a leftist New York station. He invited people to start their own discussion forums on the radio, on all possible subjects. "He said: Come on! It's going to be a fabulous free for all. Anyone can come. This is freedom."[9] Hordes of people flocked to the event. Although the Teacher's College amphitheater was huge, Lotringer was overwhelmed. The high cost to rent Columbia University's rooms meant he had to charge a fifteen-dollar entrance fee, and people wanted their money's worth. With his connections at the *Village Voice*, Lotringer managed to get the symposium listed as a "Pick of the Week." "As no one knew what semiotics were, hundreds of people called me the next day asking how much it cost and adding 'could you tell me a bit about semiotics?' "[10] In three days, two thousand people called in about the symposium.

The situation was a pressure cooker on the verge of exploding—which it did. Deleuze's talk went relatively well. He refused a translator, promising to speak slowly and using the blackboard for his drawings. He mostly drew rhizomes, and the public seemed satisfied by his demonstrations. Guattari was next; his talk was simultaneously translated. He quickly provoked a stir that grew increasingly hostile; a good part of the audience started booing him. He was not being attacked for his ideas on power and desire but for being a man. Ti-Grace Atkinson, the leader of the radical feminist movement, had brought her followers, who saw all men as necessarily phallocentric. Guattari exacerbated the situation by speaking about women and desire: "I will always remember Félix leaning over the podium. He picked up his papers and must have gone to sit next to Deleuze and Foucault. It had started off badly and he was furious."[11] Next, Foucault was harassed while speaking about child sexuality. Outwardly attacking the tenets of the Frankfort School, which thought it had taken strides by repeatedly denouncing the power structure's exercise of censorship, he infuriated members of a group claiming to be Marxists,[12] the Larouche Revolutionary Union Committee, which accused him of being paid by the CIA. At the end of the first day, people flooded around Foucault asking him if it were true. Beside himself, Foucault thundered at the audience, denouncing the last talk as illustrating the exaggerations of the 1960s and swearing that he would never set foot in that symposium again.

That night, Deleuze, Guattari, and Foucault met at the Chelsea with John Rajchman and picked apart the symposium's disastrous organization, which had turned the event into a farce. After this apocalyptic beginning, Sylvère Lotringer wondered if Foucault would return the following day for the round table with the psychiatrist R. D. Laing and the radical activist Judy Clark. Foucault was mortified and couldn't sleep that night, but the next day, when an agitator made the same accusation, he answered, " 'I am a CIA agent, Lotringer is a CIA, we are all CIA agents except for you: you are an agent of the KGB!' The guy backed down and the audience laughed aloud."[13] The atmosphere remained tense, however. Two hundred people came in slinging accusations in all directions, assaulting speakers, and creating general mayhem that occasionally led to blows.

In the aftermath, however, there was a "symposium effect" that had positive consequences for Deleuze and Guattari's work and for *Semiotext(e)*. The issue on schizoculture appeared in 1976 and sold five thousand copies in three weeks. A second issue was due to come out, but Lotringer was wary of the success and decided to stop it. Guattari, whose article was to appear in the second issue, was angry. "He was furious and said to me, 'How can you do this? I was the one who helped you put on the symposium.'"[14] The journal *SubStance* was created in 1971 as a sort of echo chamber for French avant-garde thought in the United States, and it published the theses of Deleuze and Guattari on schizoanalysis in its 1974 and 1976 issues and devoted its 1978 issue to Deleuze and Foucault. The English translation of *Anti-Oedipus* followed soon thereafter in 1977, with a glowing preface by Foucault.[15]

HEADING FOR THE FAR WEST

After Lotringer's symposium, the duo continued their American tour under the wing of Jean-Jacques Lebel, who had introduced them to New York's alternative scene. He took them to Lowell, Massachusetts, Kerouac's birthplace, for a Bob Dylan and Joan Baez concert. Allen Ginsburg was on the tour with Dylan and just before intermission, completely stoned, he appeared on stage with his long beard, bells, and harmonium: "The concert was extraordinary. We went through the gates. I fell into Ginsburg's arms and he didn't know who Gilles and Félix were."[16] Then they headed to California.

> We took what they call the "red-eye" flight. Félix and I sat together and Gilles sat with Claire Parnet. Claire fell right asleep and Gilles and Félix talked nonstop for seven or eight hours about their ideas in *Anti-Oedipus* and *A Thousand Plateaus*, which they were working on at the time. It was like an interminable living laboratory, which they left occasionally to live life but to which they quickly returned. I was listening to what they were saying like I might listen to Rimbaud or Nietzsche.[17]

In California they went to listen to Patti Smith in Berkeley. "We went to introduce them. They were moved."[18] That night they drove to San Francisco to meet the poet Lawrence Ferlinghetti, who had built the cabin where Kerouac wrote two of his books. Then they went to visit Henry Miller's house in Big Sur. "Gilles knew Kerouac and Miller's books better than Félix, having theorized about the literature of nomadism and its vanishing point. He said important things about *On the Road* in his conversations with Claire Parnet."[19] Lebel introduced Guattari to the psychoanalytic milieu to meet Arthur Jdanov, the darling of the moment who had managed to bilk money from Hollywood millionaires. "My friend John Lennon was taken in by this Jdanov and his 'Primal Scream,' which consists in reliving the scream of the newborn as it leaves its mother's womb. What a total charlatan!"[20] Lebel was familiar with New York and its shady world and came back several times with Guattari. The first thing Guattari did when he got there was to rent the biggest car available. "What he loved to do was drive down the highway with the radio blasting away."[21]

During one of these trips, Guattari met the former French stage actress Martine Barrat, who was staying at the Chelsea Hotel: she was partial to down-and-out neighborhoods in Harlem and the Bronx and had started taking photographs and making videos. She introduced Guattari to Bronx gang members she knew from her video work. "Félix went with her often to the Bronx. She did things on the girl gangs in the Bronx which I published in *Semiotext(e)*."[22] Guattari was crazy about New York, visited it frequently, and very often met up with Lotringer. In American psychiatry, however, schizoanalysis gained little traction. Invited to the United States in 1974 by the French Cultural Services to explore the state of psychiatry, he traveled from San Francisco to Berkeley, to Stanford, Chicago, Ann Arbor, New Haven, and finally to New York. He was excited about the program, which the economist Pierre Tabatoni and his team had organized, but was perplexed by the state of American psychiatry. "The directions that psychiatry and related disciplines have taken leave me uneasy. I hadn't anticipated finding that behaviorism had [influenced] so much in the humanities or the effects of overspecialization."[23] On the other hand, he was fascinated by *Project One*, one of San Francisco's largest communities, comfortably set up in a closed factory. He stayed there for fifteen days, but what he saw made him rather bitter. "Paradoxically, it seemed to me that its participants haven't lost their fondness for a certain conformity. . . . I found that the solitude and even helplessness that I've seen among many Americans I've met was rather intact in this place."[24]

THE ACADEMY TAKES UP THE BATON

After this heroic period when Deleuze and Guattari's work was first received by America's counterculture of artists and antiestablishment proponents, there was a second burst of enthusiasm among academics, thanks to a Greek-Canadian academic, Constantin Boundas, a philosophy professor at Trent University in Canada. While writing his thesis on Ricoeur in the 1970s, he looked for rigorous poststructuralist philosophy, but his reading of Barthes, Derrida, Foucault, and Lyotard left him unsatisfied. "I was on sabbatical in Paris in 1981 and near my hotel on rue Cujas. I found a lot of Deleuze's books second hand in the Tiers-Mythe bookstore. I bought *Différence et répétition*, took it into my room and five days later had read it without having understood the essentials, but I was nevertheless fascinated and convinced that this was it."[25] Boundas wrote to his thesis director to let him know he was changing subjects to work on Deleuze. He read everything by Deleuze and Guattari that he could get his hands on and met François Laruelle, who encouraged him.

Once back in Canada, he was convinced that he wanted to write on Deleuze, but in 1981, very few of Deleuze's books were available in English.[26] "Deleuze was unknown at that point in philosophy departments. Derrida, Foucault, and Lyotard were already being read, but he wasn't."[27] Boundas then began the enormous and solitary task of translating without any contract, and he translated *Dialogues, The Logic of Sense, Difference and Repetition*, and *Empiricism and Subjectivity*.[28] At the end of the 1980s, Columbia University Press commissioned him to edit a collection of Deleuze's articles. In 1989, during a visit to Paris, he made an appointment with Deleuze to discuss the choice of texts and submit his project outline. The meeting was cordial, but Deleuze insisted on choosing the texts, picking shorter ones from a wide range of publications. When Deleuze mentioned the forthcoming *What Is Philosophy?* Boundas said that Ricoeur was working on a similar subject. Deleuze replied, "Yes, but he is a Christian."[29]

Boundas felt isolated in Canada and sought out other scholars working on Deleuze; he ultimately played a key role in organizing the first meetings among Anglo-American Deleuzeans. In 1991, he had participated in a conference held in Oxford by the British Society of Phenomenology, alongside a number of specialists on the work of Deleuze and Guattari including Ronald Bogue, Paul Patton, Brian Massumi, David Land, Dan Smith, and Eugene Holland.

With the help of his University of Colorado colleague Dorothea Olkowsky and the Canadian Council for Research in the Humanities and Social Sciences, Boundas organized the first international conference of Deleuzeans in May 1992, at the University of Trent: "Gilles Deleuze: Pluralism, Theory, and Practice." The participants came mostly from the United States, Canada, Australia, and England, but there were also French attendees.[30] In 1996, Constantin Boundas organized, again in Trent, the second international Anglo-American conference. Then in May 1999, a third international conference intended to identify the similarities and differences between Foucault, Derrida, and Deleuze on the theme "Rhizome, Genealogy, and Deconstruction" attracted a large number of participants, including many French academics and even Brazilian participants, such as Peter Pal Pelbart.[31] Interest in Deleuze and Guattari's work grew, and the fourth international conference at the University of Trent held in May 2004, "Gilles Deleuze: Experimentation and Intensities. Sciences, Philosophies, Politics, and the Arts" was an even greater success.

Students studying with Deleuze at Paris-VIII also helped disseminate Deleuze and Guattari's work throughout the English-speaking world. Paul Patton, an Australian who enrolled in philosophy in 1975 with a threefold interest in Marxism, Althusser's work, and science, defended his thesis in 1979 under the direction of François Châtelet on "Marxism and the Philosophy of Science: Althusser and Popper." When Patton pushed open the door of the small room where Deleuze taught his Tuesday class, he had not read him and knew him only by reputation:

> I walked into the class and was fascinated, but I didn't have the faintest idea of what was going on. I stayed. He was giving a lecture on *A Thousand Plateaus* and spoke about becomings, animal-becomings, and witches. I didn't see at all what he was getting at and I didn't see the relation to philosophy, but I told myself that it was more like poetry and that attracted me enough to go regularly.[32]

During the 1980s, the craze for Foucault, which had overshadowed Deleuze and Guattari's work, began to die down, which left room for a surge of translations of their work.[33] By the early 1990s, their essential work had been translated into English. In 2001, the Canadian Gary Genosko, a professor of sociology at the University of Lakehead, Ontario, edited three large volumes comprising a fair portion of the studies on Deleuze and Guattari.[34] When, prior to his retirement in 2004, Boundas organized his last conference at Trent on the work of Deleuze and Guattari, the small kernel of twenty researchers had grown to one hundred and fifty, of all nationalities and disciplines: approaches to the work were varied, ranging from speculative propositions of pure philosophy to cultural studies, literature, and art.

Among the initial core of Deleuzean scholars, Eugene Holland, an American, took Deleuze's film course at Paris-VIII in the early 1980s. He started off studying Derrida, who was teaching at Yale at the time. In 1974, he left for San Diego, California, to write his doctorate under Fredric Jameson in the comparative literature department, which was where he first heard about *Anti-Oedipus*. In 1976, Jameson, a Marxist philosopher, gave a lecture that echoed Deleuze's ideas in his chapter on "Savages, Barbarians, Civilized." Holland's Marxist tendencies increased his interest in Deleuze, so he organized a small reading group with other doctoral students: "We spent six months, meeting twice a month, grappling with *Anti-Oedipus* to understand what it held for us."[35] Michel de Certeau was teaching at U.C.–San Diego at the time.[36] As Jameson was leaving San Diego, Holland chose de Certeau and his friend Dick Terdiman to replace him as his thesis directors. Appointed professor in 1985 at Ohio State University, Holland published an introduction to *Anti-Oedipus* in 1999.[37]

Most philosophy departments in American universities favor analytical philosophy and give little credence to "continental" philosophy; as a result, the work of Deleuze and Guattari never received the red-carpet treatment by the philosophical establishment. There were exceptions, however; for example, the Society for Phenomenology and Existential Philosophy regularly presented work on Deleuze at their annual conference. Here, "the interest in Deleuze's work had grown considerably because of renewed interest in Bergson and Spinoza."[38] The continental philosophy of science was the field where Deleuze's ideas spread most widely. Until then, analytical philosophy had monopolized this field of reflection, which considered its continental counterpart a subdomain. Meanwhile, continental philosophy limited itself to post-Heideggerian deconstruction.

The development of scientific thought in chaos theory, genetic theories, and particle physics created new connections with philosophical ontology and Deleuze's theories. The University of Chicago philosophy professor Andrew Cutrofello saw in this an important future for Deleuze's thought and notably for *Difference and Repetition*.[39] Another philosopher and specialist in Deleuze and Guattari's work, Dan Price at the University of Houston, wrote his doctorate in Chicago and began reading their work in the 1980s. Primarily interested in theorizing social and political movement, he spoke of how isolated Deleuzean studies were in a university system largely dominated by analytical philosophy. "Students wanting to work on Deleuze as their primary subject would be strongly discouraged from doing so, as a number of analytical philosophers didn't recognize him as a philosopher."[40]

In film-studies courses, reading Deleuze had become de rigueur, and certain American academics, such as Dudley Andrew, the author of a biography on André Bazin, were key in spreading his ideas. Andrew discovered Deleuze with the English publication of *Proust and Signs* around 1973, when he was a student working on his biography of Bazin. With strong ties to French cinema and particularly to the *Cahiers* film critics—Bazin was the tutelary father of the *Cahiers*—Andrew was naturally drawn to Deleuze's first book on film, which was published in 1983. "I was interested in Bergson, and when I saw that Deleuze started with Bergson, I liked it straight off."[41] Andrew recognized the influence of the *Cahiers*' creator: "Bazin and Deleuze both share this relationship to great authors, to great film makers."[42]

The work of Deleuze and Guattari became a major resource for the younger generation. Julian Bourg, for example, was a student in the late 1980s and early 1990s at a university near Boston known for its work in semiotics. French theory was still in its heyday, and everyone was reading Lyotard, Deleuze, Foucault, and Lacan. Coming from a Catholic background and passionate about social justice, Bourg was interested but uneasy. "I ran into the question of relativism, the critique of the subject and history."[43] When the time came to choose his thesis topic, he decided to examine the relationship between French theory and ethics. He concentrated on Deleuze and Guattari's publications between 1968 and 1972. "I treated it like a road blocked off from ethical questions."[44] Reconstructing the sources and confluences of the river that is *Anti-Oedipus*, Bourg discovered Deleuze's ethical questioning and coherence in his Spinoza-like positions. His thesis was published in 2007 and situated Deleuze and Guattari at the center of what can be called the true philosophy of 1968, that is to say, something very different from what Luc Ferry and Alain Renaut[45] had stigmatized.

Eleanor Kaufman was also a doctoral student in the early 1990s, at Duke University in North Carolina. In the department of theological studies, Ken Surin taught Deleuze; his wife, Janell Watson, worked on Guattari. Duke was one of the first American universities to be interested in Deleuze. "There had long been a great interest in *Anti-Oedipus*, *A Thousand Plateaus*, and *The Logic of Meaning*, which had just been translated into English. There were twenty of us in the research group."[46] Kaufman and several other students organized a conference on Deleuze in March 1993, one of the first in North America apart from Boundas's colloquiums in Canada. It was a huge success.

Kaufman confirmed the impression that Sylvère Lotringer had as early as 1972: the relationship to the world established by the ideas of Deleuze and Guattari would resonate more sharply with American reality than with that of the Old World.

> Particularly with respect to the idea of immanent spaces not organized into a hierarchy. I come from a country of wide-open spaces, which has always helped me understand where I come from, Missouri, the Middle West. I think they're talking about the heartlands of America. There is this vast dimension, and in American literature there are people who don't move, who stay right where they are, like in the books of Herman Melville or Emily Dickinson, people who stay put. Next to the Deleuze of nomadism, there is also a Deleuze who thinks about the state of people who are small and don't move.[47]

The Canadian academic Alain Beaulieu was a pioneer in explaining the connection between phenomenology and Deleuze. He came upon Deleuze's work in Strasbourg in 1997 with his professor, Daniel Payot, and began a thesis the following year in Paris on the relationship between Deleuze and phenomenology, which he saw as particularly ambivalent and subversive. "My background was in phenomenology; I studied philosophy with Jean Grondin at the University of Montreal and spent two years in Germany researching Heidegger."[48]

Early in the game, Columbia University Press played a major role in spreading the work of Deleuze and Guattari, and the University of Minnesota Press, already very active in publishing French theory, maintained an especially strong relationship with Deleuze. Two days after Deleuze's death, Biodun Iginla, a former editor at the University of Minnesota Press, wrote "Saturday, November 4, 1995, I lost the only intellectual father I ever had."[49] In October 1990, when Iginla was taking the reins from Lindsay Waters and Terry Cochran and was becoming Deleuze's editor, the University of Minnesota Press had already published eight of his books. Iginla actively continued this series.[50]

The University of Minnesota professor and philosopher Réda Bensmaïa became friends with Deleuze when he directed a special issue of *Lendemains* on his work.[51] He had already met Deleuze on several occasions, when the press was publishing his works. "Once I even brought his proofs over to him."[52] Their friendship evolved into an active correspondence, traces of which are published in *Negotiations*,[53] in a letter thanking Bensmaïa for the quality of the articles in the issue that he edited.

Also in 1989, the Dartmouth professor and American specialist of French intellectual history Lawrence Kritzman met Deleuze when he started the "European Perspectives" collection at Columbia University Press. *What Is Philosophy?* was the first book published in the collection: "I was very proud of it; I think it's a masterpiece of French thought in the second half of the twentieth century."[54] In 1989, Deleuze received Kritzman at his home on rue de Bizerte. "In general when you meet great thinkers in Paris they talk about what they do, but Deleuze asked me what I was doing."[55]

Deleuze and Guattari now had competent academic exegetes in North America who labored hard to disseminate their work. Among them, Charles Stivale[56] created an important Web site that brings Deleuze and Guattari's texts together with studies on their work and maintains a network of researchers interested in both authors. Brian Massumi, a communications professor at the University of Montreal and the translator into English of *A Thousand Plateaus*, has published his own work on Deleuze and Guattari along with others' articles on their work.[57]

THE AMERICAN CRAZE

From the end of the 1990s on, the number of publications on Deleuze and Guattari in the Anglophone world were subject to something like galloping inflation. From five to six books published between 1998 and 2000, there were ten titles published in 2001 alone. Since 2000, the tendency has continued; comparative literature departments remain very receptive to Deleuze and Guattari's work. According to Dana Polan, who translated *Kafka*, the American Marxist Fredrick Jameson provides a good example, reluctance and reductive tendencies aside, of the possible uses of *Anti-Oedipus* for literary criticism.[58] In 1987, the important journal *Cultural Critique* devoted two issues to minor writers' discourses drawing extensively on Deleuzo-Guattarian concepts and transposing them to the discourse of "subaltern" populations.

Deleuze and Guattari's concepts were also popularized beyond the confines of literary theory, where they provided a useful framework for scientists wanting to rebuild bridges between science and the arts using highly sophisticated technologies. Manuel Delanda, for example, began his career in experimental film, became an artist and computer programmer, and later taught in the philosophy department at Columbia University. Delanda wanted to move beyond the gap between science and the humanities. To do so, he posited Deleuzean ontology as the philosophy of the science of complexity and nonlinear dynamics.[59] Deleuze and Guattari's work was also taken up by a specifically political, antiestablishment faction of the Anglo-American world, for example, by Michael Hardt,[60] a former student of the Italian philosopher Toni Negri, with whom he co-wrote several controversial works of social and political criticism that drew from Deleuze and Guattari's theories.[61] These books set out to defend a form of radical politics fueled by a critique of the capitalist system. Spurred on by the hope of its collapse, those works were largely inspired by a Marxism revitalized by Spinoza and Deleuze and Guattari's concepts.

Though American academics have embraced Deleuze and Guattari's work, albeit somewhat late, in a profound and committed way, the academy was not the only place where their work had an impact. Feminists also showed an interest, though they had initially rejected it brutally, at the infamous 1975 Columbia symposium. "Until the mid-1990s, the relationship between their work and American feminists was dominated by an instinctive mistrust of Deleuze and Guattari's way of "molecularizing" the feminine question."[62] The approach was considered a diversionary tactic from the real, fundamental stakes, which are of a "molar" order. But in the 1990s, the feminist movement became less essentialist, which allowed for a more positive reception of theses on "becoming-woman," on sexual disidentification, on the minority becoming of writing masculine or feminine, and on sexual indetermination and its fundamental ambivalence. Two feminist studies much inspired by Deleuzo-Guattarian theories were published in a volume edited by Constantin Boundas and Dorothea Olkowsky.[63] A step further from academia, Deleuzo-Guattarism was used to celebrate the mechanization of humanity in the name of "cyborg politics," as seen by the feminist Donna Haraway, who in 1985 defined the cyborg as "a cybernetic organism, a hybrid machine and organism, a creature of social reality and of fiction."[64]

Postcolonial studies, a growing field in American academics, also heavily borrowed from Deleuzo-Guattarian ideas, following the lead of Edward Said, the late professor at Columbia University, for whom *A Thousand Plateaus'* "treatise of nomadology" made it possible for him to map the contemporary world and situate the deterritorialized lot of the Palestinians. Another major figure of postcolonial studies, Gayatri Chakravorty Spivak, of Indian origin, has also drawn on Deleuze and Guattari's concepts. Her critique of totalizing systems, her conception of concept as having first and foremost a practical, tactical vocation, her definition of the intellectual, and even her defense of minority literature attest to this proximity.

The Deleuzo-Guattarian concept of the machine served as a war machine against structuralism and found some echoes in the United States among the first electronic networks theorized by Hakim Bey, a friend of Sylvère Lotringer, as "temporary autonomous zones."[65] Bey points out the illegal, rebellious uses of the Web. "The individual work of Félix Guattari had a specific impact on the first American cybercommunities."[66] With their concept of rhizome, Deleuze and Guattari become the great prophets of the Internet, which tangibly sets their notion of the plane of immanence into play, with connections in every directions, dehierarchization, and singular and transversal pathways. Thus, the "Deleuze & Guattari RhizOmat" site offers "pirated" quotes of the two authors triggered by hypertext links.[67] When Deleuzo-Guattarian surfers enact the concepts they have appropriated, they are in sync with the idea of multiplicities, tactics of demultiplication, disjunctive syntheses, machinic demultiplication and production, and even the famous body without organs, which is used to describe the network transformed into a "BwO" zone.

Deleuze's wish for "pop philosophy" favoring practices is manifest in the multiple uses of Deleuzo-Guattarism in America: the transplant was successful. The common ground between the conceptual theses and the singularity of American civilization confirms Sylvère Lotringer's intuition that Deleuze and Guattari did not speak to Americans but were already speaking about America.

27

Around the World

The reputation and influence of Deleuze and Guattari extended well beyond North American shores. From Asia to Latin America and via Europe, their work spread worldwide. Guattari often traveled to promote and discuss his new publications; Deleuze, with few exceptions, observed the effects of his work from his observatory at Paris-VIII, where students came to him from around the world.

In England, there were some Deleuzean institutions, such as the University of Warwick, where Keith Ansell-Pearson and Nick Land, both well known throughout the Anglophone world for their dynamism, were teaching. Deleuze had made his empirical positions clear since his book on Hume; this together with their embrace of pragmatism set them in good standing a priori with a certain number of British scholars. Yet their reception in Great Britain came rather late and was less enthusiastic than it had been on American campuses. In reality, those most likely to be interested in the work of Deleuze and Guattari in a country where empiricism and pragmatism had made a deep impression were more likely to seek another path in French thinking, one more closely affiliated with French theorists who preferred structural logic. However, thanks to English translations that became available in the 1980s, the work of Deleuze and Guattari came to be better known and appreciated. "In England, the 'Deleuzeans' sought neither to comment on his work nor to apply it. Rather, they tried to 'arrange with'—in cinema, sculpture, performance art, and rock music."[1] The Warwick philosopher Keith Ansell-Pearson was clearly committed to Deleuzean positions and even considered Deleuze an "engineer of difference."[2]

Nick Land, who became a myth when he vanished from sight once he stopped teaching, had also been a professor of philosophy at the University of Warwick. He tried to connect the two volumes of *Capitalism and*

Schizophrenia with Norbert Wiener's work in cybernetics and with esotericism and science fiction. In the 1990s, he organized cultural events on themes such as "Virtual Futures," "Afro-Futures," and "Video-Technics," holding both lectures and techno parties at the venerable University of Warwick, which was rather unaccustomed to these sorts of rhythms.

Cultural Studies, a beacon of social-science research in the United Kingdom, did not publish many texts by Deleuze and Guattari, but Lawrence Grossberg, one of the important representatives of this current, began to read Foucault in the late 1970s when he left to teach in Illinois. "This was how I discovered the translation of *Anti-Oedipus* and I started a reading group with a few graduate students and some colleagues from other universities. Charles Stivale, a doctoral student in French at Illinois, was there. We spent an entire year reading Deleuze and Guattari's book line by line."[3] Starting in the early 1980s, Grossberg appropriated the concepts of Deleuze and Guattari to argue against deconstruction and hermeneutics and to emphasize the specifically political dimension of culture by avoiding the shoals of relativism. "I saw in Deleuze (and Foucault) something like a means of getting beyond the limits both of Heidegger's move toward a sort of mysticism in his late work as well as Derridean deconstruction."[4] In the mid-1980s, Grossberg met Meaghan Morris, an Australian cultural-studies specialist who had studied with Deleuze, and invited her to the University of Illinois, where they taught an entire generation of students about British cultural studies and gave them a good grasp of Deleuze and Guattari's work. Grossberg enlisted Deleuze and Guattari in his singular conception of cultural studies as a radical project of political contextualization and discourse analysis. "I see myself more as a pragmatist who uses Deleuzean concepts when necessary to take the context into account."[5]

The Irishman Simon Tormey, part of the young generation in Britain, teaches politics and critical theory[6] at the University of Nottingham, where Philip Goodchild, a well-known Deleuze and Guattari specialist, also teaches.[7] When he discovered their work, Tormey's perception of the world changed radically. "For me, discovering Deleuze and Guattari was like going from a black-and-white world to a world of color."[8] Nothing had prepared Tormey for such a shock: "The depth, the expression, the vibration of their thinking were unimaginable."[9] In the area of artistic creation, Deleuze had become an inspiration for some, including, for example, the British writer Ian Pindar, who was trying to write rhizomatic fictions. The director Benjamin May wanted to stage a "body without organs" with his actors.

Japan: The Chosen Land

Far from the British world, Japan was much more receptive to Deleuze and Guattari's work. The refusal of transcendence and Deleuze and Guattari's immanent thinking resonated somewhat with Japanese Buddhist thought. We have already referred to Hidenobu Suzuki, who recorded Deleuze's lectures at Paris-VIII from 1979 through 1987 and thanks to whom this archive exists;[10] sitting next to him was Kuniichi Uno, Deleuze's future official Japanese translator, who started attending Deleuze's classes in the mid-1970s. After having defended his thesis on Rimbaud, Uno asked Deleuze to direct his thesis on Antonin Artaud, which he defended in 1980. Uno was in France until 1983 and, with Suzuki and several other Japanese students, created a group. "We were in the process of translating *A Thousand Plateaus* and I asked Deleuze, 'why a thousand plateaus?' He answered, 'You know the plateau at Millevaches?' adding, 'It's that for me; I don't know about Félix, but for me, that's it.'"[11] At the time, Kouichi Toyosaki, an important professor in Japan and the translator of *Rhizome*, was supervising these five students. The difficulty of translating certain concepts in the book had necessitated some explanations from the authors. "We had the opportunity of working together with Deleuze and Guattari to discuss the difficult, enigmatic terms and clarify a few points."[12]

In 1983, when Uno returned to Japan, he worked with *Gendai-Shiso*, a contemporary philosophy review that was very receptive to structuralism and French theory. The review helped familiarize the Japanese public with the work of Deleuze and Guattari. In the mid-1980s, they began to be known in Japan thanks to the Japanese publication of *Anti-Oedipus*. Uno had become a professor in the literature department of Rikkyo University in Tokyo; he translated *The Exhausted*, *Foucault*, and *The Fold* and had helped translate *A Thousand Plateaus*. Until 1992, whenever he went to Paris, Uno visited Deleuze at his home. "When I finished translating *The Fold*, he told me that he would have wanted to work more on the relationship between Leibniz and the Orient."[13] *A Thousand Plateaus* was the most popular book by Deleuze and Guattari in Japan, particularly among architects and sociologists. "The body without organs was very meaningful for us Japanese."[14]

Guattari was fascinated by Japan, and he visited eight times. "Sao Paulo and Tokyo were the two cities that most interested Félix."[15] Uno invited Guattari to Japan as soon as he returned, and, later, Guattari was invited by

Akira Asada, who in 1983 published *Structure and Force*, a bestseller on French thought. During his visit, Guattari lectured on schizoanalysis at the University of Kyoto. With Uno's help, Guattari was able to meet the politicized, very militant milieus in Okinawa and visit several psychiatric hospitals. Uno also went to La Borde to see Guattari again in 1984 and 1985 and recorded his interviews for *Gendai-Shiso*, which published a special issue on Deleuze and Guattari. "At the universal exhibit on Design in Nagoya, Guattari addressed a vast audience of around a thousand architects on the way that architecture can change an urban environment."[16]

Guattari was in touch with the best Japanese dancers, photographers, and architects and used his relationships for the benefit of La Borde and its patients. He invited the dancer Turakami to La Borde and even planned to make a film entitled *Black Light* with the photographer Keiichi Tahava, who made the film alone after the death of his friend. Guattari adored walking around Tokyo, with its soaring, gigantic ultramodern skyscrapers alongside small two-story houses in villagelike neighborhoods. He ultimately created a France-Japan association to organize and develop cultural exchanges between the two countries. When cultural events or well-known Japanese individuals were being considered, Guattari advised Christian Descamps, the seminar director at Beauborg from 1984 to 1994.

Guattari's work was translated into Japanese by Masaaki Sugimura,[17] who defined himself as a "68er." Indeed, Sugimura saw Guattari for the first time in May '68, during the occupation of the Odeon. When he returned to Japan in 1970, Sugimura was barred from returning to France for ten years, as he was branded a dangerous Leftist. He then focused on Japanese political issues to reconstruct a new Left in Japan. It was Uno who, invested in translating *A Thousand Plateaus*, one day asked him to translate *The Molecular Revolution*, since no one wanted to deal with a book considered too political. "I started working and found in this book memories of what I had lived through in the 1960s."[18] Deeply involved in protest movements against the Japanese emperor and challenging the very foundations of the imperial system, Sugimura found in Deleuze and Guattari the instruments for conceiving a new type of militant group and the idea of a molecular revolution, which he saw as particularly pertinent for the Japanese context. In the early 1980s, as Deleuze and Guattari's books were beginning to be translated in Japan, "a fashion developed around them. Many Japanese intellectuals proclaimed themselves partisans of their thinking."[19] Indeed, since the end of World War II, Japan was quite receptive to French intellectual currents. Sugimura met Guattari only after having translated *The Molecular Revolution*. They met in Kyoto. "We immediately found each other sympathetic. We talked about May '68 and I found a big brother in Félix. . . . It was a real relief to find in Félix someone who shared my ideas. We were very close for three years, until he died."[20]

Architecture was a central part of Guattari's fascination with Japan. Invited in 1987 by an association of Japanese architects, he became part of a design team that was bidding on a France-Japan symbol.[21] For a 1989 exhibit, he did a study of Shin Takamatsu, one of the most famous Japanese architects.[22] Introducing Guattari's report, Christian Girard claimed, "Guattari opens up the possibility for architects to reconsider the theory behind their practice."[23] Guattari considered Japanese architecture particularly noteworthy with respect to the international modern style. The history of Japanese architecture included several great creators, such as Kenzo Tangue and his student Arata Isozaki, who broke with ambient functionalism and oriented their work toward what Guattari called "processualism."[24] Takamatsu's buildings, like the Kyoto dental clinic built on the model of a baroque locomotive because of its proximity to a railroad line and station, expressed the "becoming-machine" of subjectivity.[25] "This had the effect of transforming the environment, like a sweep of a magic wand, into something like a machinic vegetation landscape."[26]

Japanese sensitivity to the precarious balance of the ecosystem and to ecological concerns was one reason for the positive reception of the ideas in *The Three Ecologies*, Guattari's bestselling book in Japan. Félix Guattari's name "was even used to promote a brand of Japanese whiskey and sake."[27]

BRAZIL: LAND OF HOPE

In the early 1970s, Guattari met Suely Rolnik, a Brazilian Jewish woman whose family had come from Poland and who was enrolled in the social sciences at Sao Paolo University. In January 1970, as the Brazilian dictatorship was becoming more intransigent, she was imprisoned for her Marxist and countercultural activities. In 1971, when she arrived in Paris, she enrolled in Pierre Clastres' sociology courses at Vincennes and went to Deleuze's classes. "My French was still rather poor at the beginning, but the mere timbre of his voice and his attitude, the language that came through the body, the flesh of the words, all of it touched and restored me."[28] Rolnik asked Guattari to go into analysis with him . . . because she felt fine. Guattari seized the opportunity. "He adored that and immediately accepted me as his patient for free, saying, "'We'll start tomorrow at 7 am.'"[29] After a short period of classical analysis on the couch, Guattari started using a schizoanalytic approach, changing Rolnik's lifestyle. He invited her to organize the 1972 Christmas celebrations at La Borde on "The Chinese Revolution" and then quite naturally asked her to organize the March carnival. "That got me completely going again. I organized many workshops with people who finally ended up living at La Borde. There were actors from Julian Beck's Living Theater."[30] At that time, Rolnik was still at Vincennes in the social sciences and then in psychology at Paris-VIII. "One day in 1973, I was at Félix's house and that morning he said, 'I'd like you to stay here because Deleuze is coming to lunch and I want you to meet him.' That's how I met Deleuze."[31]

Employed in the psychiatric services in the Paris region, Rolnik decided to return to Brazil after nine years of exile. She did her doctorate in psychology and then began working in a psychology clinic in Sao Paolo. Deleuze and Guattari had given her exactly what she had been looking for: micropolitics, the relationships between psychoanalysis, politics, and culture in the post-'68 context. Back in Brazil, she worked hard at putting these ideas into circulation among intellectuals. The psychoclinics adopted these ideas rapidly, and they played an essential role in the struggles in the mental-health area even before the fall of the dictatorship. During this same period, Rolnik was also running a seminar with more than eighty people; the training was strongly influenced by Deleuze and Guattari's thinking. It would have been easy, in fact, to create a true school, but Rolnik correctly perceived that this risked betraying the goals of Deleuze and Guattari. Instead, she preferred a pan–Latin American network. Brazilians very quickly adopted *Anti-Oedipus*, which was translated in 1976. In 1981, Rolnik published a book by Guattari entitled *The Political Pulse of Desire*, which reprised a good part of *The Molecular Revolution*.[32]

Guattari went to Brazil seven times and even discussed moving there. In 1982, Rolnik organized a full program of interviews with numerous Brazilian micropolitical movements in the different states and with various people in the psychoanalytic and psychiatric worlds. "It's become the only country where there are such good schizoanalytic theses."[33] She recorded all the discussions, which became some three thousand pages of transcripts on which she set to work. In 1986, this became their shared work and was reprinted six times.[34]

Guattari returned to Brazil at a time when incipient hopes for political change were emerging. Rolnik was very involved in the electoral campaign for the Sao Paolo government of Luis Inacio da Silva, known as Lula, the labor-union candidate and leader of the new Workers' Party. She arranged for Lula to meet Guattari who, during his 1979 trip, had met Jaco Bittar, the labor leader of the oil industry, and several militant workers who were in the process of discussing the creation of a new party. Lula crystallized the hopes of the Workers' Party and won the election. During their meeting, Guattari expressed his hope that this party could invent new instruments for the collective struggle and even a new micropolitical logic.

Guattari maintained his connections with Brazil when he was in Paris thanks to Rolnik's regular updates on the progress of the network in the psych world. Her letters also stressed her total loyalty to his theoretical positions. Indeed, Brazil seemed to be the only country where the schizo-analytic graft really took. It was even "assimilated" in certain academic circles and became part of the MA course work in clinical psychology. Several research centers also examined Deleuze and Guattari's work. This appropriation suggested, among other things, that Brazil's mixed-race society lent itself better than other societies to this labile subjective construction, with its multiple becomings and fundamentally heterogeneous subjectivity. Guattari was seduced not by Brazil's exoticism but because he saw the beginnings of new experiments in subjectification that could provide answers to the political questions being raised in Old Europe. "If you continue to make these changes in Brazil at the same speed at which you've begun, you'll surely manage to affect us in return with these molecular revolutions."[35]

In May 1992, a few months before his death, Guattari was in Brazil, visiting Rio de Janeiro for the publication of the Brazilian editions of *Chaosmos* and *What Is Philosophy?*[36] Editions 34 and the International College of Transdisciplinary Philosophical Research organized a round-table discussion on May 21, 1992, for French and Brazilian researchers. The philosopher Éric Alliez, a friend of Deleuze and Guattari and an expert on their work, had created this center, and it often invited Guattari.

Alliez had first visited Brazil with Guattari during a professional trip organized by Rolnik, and he was as fascinated by Brazil as was Guattari. When he was defending his thesis on temporal logics, directed by Deleuze in 1987, he was invited by the Centro Brasileiro de Pesquisa Fisicao to present his work.[37] The Brazilians were quite interested in the new International

College of Philosophy that had been created in Paris, where Alliez was giving a seminar together with Isabelle Stengers. Believing that an equivalent
institution could be created in Brazil, Alliez was pivotal in making the necessary connections. The spectacular reception of schizoanalysis by Brazilian psychoanalysts also had to do with the fact that Lacan's work was less
well established in Brazil than it was, for example, in Argentina.

After Deleuze's death, Alliez organized an international colloquium in
Rio and Sao Paolo on June 10–14, 1996, to discuss the work of Deleuze and
Guattari, thanks to the Colégio International de Estudos Filosoficos Trasn-
discipnares, which he had helped create.[38] Two philosophers were particularly instrumental in transmitting Deleuze and Guattari: Bento Prado,
who translated *What Is Philosophy?* and who wrote his thesis on Bergson,[39]
and Roberto Machado, who was close to Foucault and who wrote a book on
the genesis of Deleuzean philosophy. In Rio, Norman Madrarasz, a Canadian philosophy professor of Hungarian origin who had spent a decade in
Paris, also identified himself as part of the Deleuzean legacy. In the course
that he gave in Rio, he and his colleague Jorge Vasconcellos taught certain
aspects of Deleuze's thinking and his reading of Nietzsche, among other
things. Vasconcellos thought that if philosophy were to become popular, it
would reach beyond its inner circle of intellectuals to the most disadvan-
taged people. This was the thinking behind the "Filosofia e arte" collection
published by Ciencia Moderna.

MEXICAN BORDERS

Mexico was a far less favorable land for Deleuze-Guattari enthusiasts, despite the country's general receptivity to French theory, thanks to Arnaldo
Orfila, the founder of the Fondo de Cultura Economica and later Siglo 21,
his publishing house. The editorial shift was more advantageous for Braudel and the Annals school—Foucault, Derrida, and Althusser—than it was
for Deleuze and Guattari. Yet a connection had been made, despite everything, with certain Mexican psychoanalytic milieus, thanks to Guattari's
visits. Even since 1975, a Spanish version of Guattari's *Psychoanalysis and
Transversality* had been available, published by the Argentinean Siglo 21
publishing house. The book did not influence psychoanalytical practices in
either Argentina or Mexico, but a small group of Mexican psychiatrists and
psychoanalysts nonetheless decided to discuss its ideas to deepen their

criticism of the psychiatric institutions that Cooper and Basaglia's antipsychiatric positions had previously nourished. Italian antipsychiatry had come to Mexico in 1973,[40] invited by Vian Illich to the Cuernavaca Center for Documentation. Those protesting against psychiatry met in 1976 for the first time in Cuernavaca with Maria Langer, a young Austrian who had fled the Nazis in 1936, first to Spain and then to Argentina, where he created the Argentine Psychoanalytic Association, before moving to Mexico. Also in attendance were Thomas Sachs, Franco Basaglia, and Igor Caruso. Sylvia Marcos organized a second meeting in Cuernavaca in 1978, where Guattari participated in a round-table discussion on psychiatry and antipsychiatry.

To take advantage of Guattari's presence, the alternative psychiatric network of Mexico, the school of psychology's student council, and the director of the school of psychology at the Autonomous University of Nuevo Leon organized a meeting on "Mental Health, Madness, and Society" in Monterey, overseen by two Mexican psychoanalysts, Rodolfo Alvarez del Castillo and Fernando Gonzales. The colloquium was a tremendous success. Addressing an audience of one thousand students, Guattari described the experimental practices at La Borde and the practices of institutional psychotherapy.[41]

Fernando Gonzales, like the other psychoanalysts at the colloquium, had read and appreciated *Anti-Oedipus* and wrote an acerbic critique of the often overly coded grid of psychoanalytic interpretation. "It allowed me to put some distance between myself and the psychoanalytic machine."[42] Gonzales also considered the concept of transversality to be a contribution to his own work, mixing psychoanalysis, history, philosophy, and sociology. "It was thanks to Guattari that I began working at the hospital on institutional intervention in 1978."[43] When Gonzales returned to Mexico in June 1983, the Deleuzo-Guattarian graft had not really taken. "Lacanian thinking was well established. It was the beginning of the importation and total admiration for Lacan."[44] All that remained of Guattari's positions were a few enclaves, such as the master's program in group and institutional social psychology created by Gonzales at the Xochimiko section of the Autonomous University, which enrolled about twenty students per year. In addition to this small group, Guattari's influence was also somewhat palpable in the Mexican Association of Psychoanalytic Group Psychotherapy, which had been created in 1966 and where Jorge Margolis, one of the founders, continues to be active.

A Chilean Who Escaped Pinochet

In the 1970s, a productive meeting took place between Guattari and Miguel Norambuena, a Chilean intellectual fleeing Pinochet's regime. Norambuena had studied at the Beaux Arts School in Santiago and was a militant for the extreme left. Arrested and tortured by the Chilean Army during the 1973 coup d'état, he managed to escape to Switzerland. Twenty-three years old, he had already read and appreciated Cooper's antipsychiatric ideas; he had met Cooper and his companion Marina Zecca in 1976 in Paris and began to work with him. One day, while Cooper and his group were in the middle of a session, Guattari telephoned to persuade him to participate in a meeting at the Mutualité against repression in Italy. The whole group went to the meeting and that evening, at a restaurant, Norambuena happened to be seated across from Guattari, who was talking about the repressive atmosphere. Guattari suddenly turned to him. "'Who're you?' I started telling him my story and he said, 'Listen, your story interests me. The next time you go to see David, come to see me.'"[45]

Miguel Norambuena was quite unwell at the time, having suffered in prison, so he quickly started going to rue de Condé regularly, ultimately becoming a patient of Guattari. At the start of his analysis, Norambuena shed tears for dead Chileans, feeling guilty for being safely in France. Guattari started with him as he usually did, energetically.

> He said, "You're obviously uprooted and you're going to continue to whine about your roots. If you don't get beyond this, I can't help you. But if you experience it like a weed, a rhizome, then I can eventually do something because it can grow back, differently, elsewhere than in your home." I hadn't understood a thing and when I went home that night I looked up rhizome in the dictionary.[46]

During the next session, Norambuena began to understand what Guattari was talking about, and he entered into schizoanalysis with Guattari, which lasted from 1979 to 1986.

The relations between this militant Chilean and Guattari confirm Guattari's repudiation of all forms of terrorism, including military confrontation. Norambuena returned to Chile clandestinely on four different occasions to help his comrades. Each time, Guattari tried to dissuade him from going. "To my great surprise, even for Chile, he was against armed struggle. He was fundamentally opposed to it and spent hours with Chilean comrades that I brought to him seeking his approval. But he ended up dissuading them from deciding to take up arms."[47]

In May 1991, when the political situation was somewhat calmer, Miguel Norambuena went to Chile with Guattari; slightly later, they published a book in Spanish: a collection of lectures that Guattari had given in Chile with an introduction by Norambuena.[48] The theses on schizoanalysis had a definite effect. "Were Deleuze and Guattari to go to Chile today, they wouldn't believe their eyes,"[49] claims Norambuena, who returned to Chile at the end of 2005. Three universities invited him to discuss schizoanalysis, and at each lecture, the halls were overflowing with 150 students. Norambuena now lives in Geneva, where, since 1985, he has been the director of a very unusual psychiatric institution called Le Racard, a nine-bed microstructure where schizophrenics, drug addicts, and other marginals live together and whose organization and psychosocial practices are much inspired by La Borde.

ITALY: A CHOSEN LAND

In Europe, Italy is unquestionably the country where Deleuze and Guattari have been the most read and appreciated. Guattari involved himself in the alternative struggles in Italy in the late 1970s; he was extremely popular and even something of an Italian Cohn-Bendit. His ties with Franco Berardi, or "Bifo"; Toni Negri; Oreste Scalzone; and no small number of other Italian protestors are well known.[50] In Italy, the criticisms of the psychiatric institution were more forceful because of Franco Basaglia's antipsychiatric experiments in Trieste, which crystallized many cultural and political hopes. Einaudi, an important Italian publishing house, translated *Anti-Oedipus* in 1975; the book was immensely successful, accompanying the various mid-1970s radical movements for Italian autonomy.[51] Their successes were spectacular; the backlash was severe: the pendulum swung in the other direction for the alternative movements, which withdrew in the 1980s. If Deleuze recalled these as the "winter years" in France, it was a glacier age in Italy; Deleuzo-Guattarian thinking had identified with a critical radicalness and paid a price for doing so. Einaudi, which owned the rights for *A Thousand Plateaus* and whose translation was ready in 1981, a year after the book had been published in France, ultimately dropped the idea of publishing it.

A *Thousand Plateaus* was finally published in 1987, to general indifference. Academic critics scrupulously ignored the book. Deleuze and Guattari were ignored until the 1990s, when the Italians slowly rediscovered their work. The Heideggerian reading of Nietzsche had long held sway among academics, but Deleuze's very different interpretation eventually became known. A few people adopted his approach, and some, including Tiziana Villani, acted on it: she created the review *Millepiani* in Milan,[52] which explicitly proclaimed its debt to Deleuze and Guattari.

Tiziana Villani was a trained geographer who had moved toward philosophy and was particularly interested in urban planning. Interested in transversality, she defended her doctoral thesis under the direction of Thierry Paquot, the editor in chief of *Urbanisme*, and she organized philosophers, sociologists, urbanists, and art and literature critics for her review. A small collection of books, Heterotopie, was created around *Millepiani*. The public most interested in the ideas of Deleuze and Guattari included artists, architects, and city planners. In other Italian cities, their work is better known thanks to small enclaves; in Trieste, for example, the review *Aut-Aut*, directed by Pier Aldo Rovatti, a philosopher of hermeneutics and friend of Vattimo, encouraged the reception of Deleuze and Guattari's works.

Today in Italy, the two authors have been separated; Guattari is better remembered for his political positions and Deleuze as a more classical but somewhat outdated philosopher. Luca Cremonesi, a doctoral student at the University of Verona, is trying to correct this dichotomy and emphasizes the political dimension of Deleuze's thought. Nonetheless, Italian universities continue to teach Deleuze in a classical manner and read his early work and monographs, most of which have been translated into Italian and serve as introductions to philosophy.

Deleuze also benefited from relationships he developed while teaching at Paris-VIII. For Italy, his contact was Giorgio Passerone, a student who started taking Deleuze's course at Vincennes in 1977. Passerone requested a meeting in June 1980 before deciding on his thesis topic. "He gave me a chapter of *A Thousand Plateaus*, the chapter on the novella, saying, 'You can translate it and go see some Italian publishers.' I rushed to Italy and went to see all the publishing houses."[53] In the fall, Passerone decided on a research topic, which was style, and met with Deleuze regularly. Passerone enrolled as a doctoral student at Paris-VIII and defended his thesis in 1987. That same year, the Italian version of *A Thousand Plateaus*, translated by Passe-

AROUND THE WORLD   **491**

rone, was published; the unpublished preface by Deleuze and Guattari is dedicated to him.[54]

Some young Italian researchers are very interested in Deleuze and Guattari's thought. Giuseppe Bianco, a student in Trieste studying under Pier Aldo Rovatti, recalls: "There was a seminar in 1996 on *The Logic of Sense* that fascinated me."[55] Bianco was searching for a way to get into Deleuze's work but did not find it right away. He ended up telling himself that the key concept and the very heart of this philosophy was in the notion of "multiplicity." Quickly making the link to Bergson, he started working on the reception in the late 1960s of the Bergsonism of the 1920s in order to shed some light not only on Deleuze's link with Bergson but also on an unusual trajectory that was neither phenomenological nor structuralist.

The Italian philosopher Manola Antonioli also worked on Deleuze and Guattari and published several books in France on their thinking.[56] Initially, she found *Anti-Oedipus* and *A Thousand Plateaus* too obscure and difficult to understand. In 1995 and 1996, she nonetheless starting going to 125, boulevard Saint-Germain, where Jean-Claude Polack, who was taking Guattari's seminars, was giving his own seminar. She realized how very contemporary and even prescient the books were, despite the initial impression of being raving fictions. "Above all, I found that *A Thousand Plateaus* became more legible after September 11, 2001, because it was discussing things that weren't yet organized at the time and seemed to belong to the realm of science fiction."[57]

28

Two Deaths

On Friday, August 28, 1992, the regular meeting took place at La Borde. Jean Oury, who ran the clinic, was gone, but Guattari, his second in command, was there, as usual, listening to patients and their various recriminations about the way he assigned responsibilities. There was, among other things, the disparity between assignments and training. Guattari had a team of volunteers look into the problem. One of the patients said, "I would like us to look at condiments. I'm sick of linden. I read a book about this and we could pick the flowers ourselves. The club would have to give us 200 francs to distill them."[1] Guattari answered very seriously that he thought this was altogether possible. "Then he got up and left the room for what seemed like a long time. It was surely at that moment that the doctor examined him. Félix had always been sick. He was used to it, the fatigue, the strain. He came back to the meeting, slipped in as he knew how to do."[2] Another patient talked about the poor organization of cars and pedestrians on the clinic's grounds and asked for better regulation. People started laughing. We found it hard to imagine pedestrian zones in this bucolic setting, but "Félix looked at the guy attentively: 'Yes, the cars are going too fast and it's making us feel uncomfortable walking around at La Borde. He's right about organizing a pedestrian zone,' he said gently. The boy calmed down. The meeting ended. As we were leaving, his joyfulness returned."[3]

That was Guattari's final meeting. He seemed to be in good form that evening; his daughter Emmanuelle recalls their last meal. "What energy! He hadn't talked that much for a long time. He was radiant, bubbly. He said goodbye to me, told me to have a good time, and wore an extraordinary smile. I hadn't seen him smile like that for a very long time."[4] He went back to his little office, where he died of a heart attack during the night. He was sixty-two years old. Guattari had suffered several attacks since 1990: his coronary arteries were blocked, but during his depression, he saw no doctors. He had experienced a cardiac episode during the last meeting at La Borde but preferred to go on as if nothing had happened rather than go to the hospital. His children were at La Borde at the time. That morning, his son, Bruno, was worried because his father was not up early as he usually was. He found his body in his office. On his bedside table lay D. H. Lawrence's *Dogs of Eros* and Joyce's *Ulysses*, in English. At La Borde, the reaction was one of general consternation. "The crazies cried the next morning when O [Oury] told them in the big room that Félix had died. 'Thank you for telling us like this,' they answered. Even if many of them were wandering around that night unable to sleep, they were sufficiently polite and tender to be absolutely silent. The night was calm."[5]

Guattari died as he was coming out of his depression and, after a long catatonic withdrawal, he was again gathering his legendary enthusiasm. A month before the fateful night, he had met Tatiana Kecojevic, a twenty-six-year-old Serbian actress who had fled the war in 1992. Kecojevic lived in London and had come to Paris for a party organized by her friend Sacha Goldman, an advertising specialist. "I met Félix that evening. Since I was from Belgrade, I felt bad, everyone was starting to attack me about what the Serbs were doing. Félix was the only one who saw that the questions were bothering me, and he said, 'But we don't give a damn about all that! Have you seen Paris?' He took me to see Paris that same evening."[6] They exchanged addresses and phone numbers, saw each other again, and a relationship started that made Guattari forget his calamities with Joséphine. Tatiana Kecojevic "fell madly in love with Félix, who called me up, saying 'Old man, I'm in love!' His freshness, his youthful vitality, his youth, his love of life, everything came back."[7] Guattari phoned Gérard Fromanger several times a day to describe his new passion. "He was saying, 'I'll call you back tonight, I hope that this won't end, it's fantastic!' He had decided to leave everything to Joséphine, the apartment, the cars; he'd found a room to live in with her."[8]

Guattari mobilized his entire network of friends to get an acting role for his new girlfriend. Among others, he counted on his new friend, the actor and writer Jacky Berroyer, with whom he had a few plans at the time. He brought Tatiana to all the places where he had lived or been, even to rue d'Aigle in Garenne-Colombes, his childhood home. "He said, 'Tatiana you're young and beautiful, you've got your whole life ahead of you. You should have lots of lovers, but don't leave me!' I was overwhelmed by what he was saying and found his generosity magnificent. I wanted to give him everything that I could possibly give him."[9] Tatiana Kecojevic left for London to organize her move to join Félix in Paris, planning to meet him the following weekend. Guattari left for La Borde. "I remember taking the boat for England and being immensely happy, he gave me tremendous strength. I got to my house and got a phone call to say that he had died."[10] Tatiana Kecojevic returned to France immediately for Félix's funeral along with crowds of his friends.

Joséphine was in the south of France with her boyfriend Jean Rolin, visiting one of his friends. "The day before we left Maussane, like almost every day that week, Joséphine had had a long, joyful phone conversation with F. That evening, when we got back from the restaurant, there was a little note on our key to say that F. had called again."[11] The next day, Jean Rolin's friend told him privately that he had just heard on the radio that Guattari had died. He was supposed to tell Joséphine. Jean and Joséphine drove across France that night to arrive at the mortuary in Blois by the next morning and then went to La Borde.

DEARLY DEPARTED

Gérard Fromanger was chosen to speak at Guattari's graveside, to the crowd of at least fifteen hundred friends who had come to the Père Lachaise cemetery. "I did it. I burst out crying, and there was Tatiana standing in front of me. I named all his mistresses, at least thirty young women. Everyone was crying or laughing. There was a jazz band and huge numbers of people. It was an overwhelming funeral."[12] The author and actor Enzo Cormann read excerpts from *Ritournelles*, Félix's fragmentary autobiography, while standing with a brass quartet in front of the coffin. "First I read a half page alone and then the orchestra accompanied me when I started reading the sentence, 'Do you recognize me?' I asked it, the music started, I sobbed, what *else* could I do?"[13] At the same time, the circle of friends wanted to express how much Guattari always displayed his vitality and enthusiasm, and the burial ended in a sort of party. "It was a rather fabulous souvenir, a very beautiful souvenir. There were songs, poems, speeches and then that evening we celebrated in the Bois de Boulogne, it was strange."[14]

Guattari's entire family was there. His elder brother Jean was surprised and disturbed by the enumeration of his various feminine conquests in front of his brother's tomb but at the same time was transported by the crowd's collective fervor. "Almost everyone threw a flower on his grave. I saw some people throw their wedding rings, their keys, incredible things!"[15] After the funeral, Jean went to Félix's grave every two weeks. Surprising things continued to happen. "On two occasions, I found fresh flowers and the same man. I talked to him, saying, 'Listen, this is very kind. Did you know him?' 'No, I am doing this for a friend who asked me to come regularly.'"[16]

Jack Lang, the minister of culture, and his wife Monique sent a message that was read aloud at the funeral. "Félix has left us. It's hard to believe. His tireless curiosity and his warm gaiety tinged him with something like eternal youth. As we mourn, we want to remember the friend's smile and the thinker's intelligence. We will remember our meetings and our conversations for a long time to come. Our hearts remain warmed by his unforgettable voice."[17]

Deleuze was in Saint-Léonard-le-Noblat with David Lapoujade when he got the news about his friend Félix, who was supposed to have come to see him on August 29, the day he died. He was overcome. He wrote a testimonial that was published in *Chimères*. "Until the end, my work with Félix has been a source of discovery and joy for me."[18] Deleuze also mentioned the inexhaustible richness of the books that his friend Félix had written alone. He noted three important areas of his work: psychiatry and his reflections on group subjects and transversal relationships, his desire to construct a kind of system composed of heterogeneous segments, and his theoretical analyses of literary and artistic production. But he could not discuss the man, who for years had been a part of this bicephalous philosophy, without expressing the essential emotional dimension. "What's so painful about the memory of a friend who has died are the gestures and looks that continue to touch us, that continue to come back to us after his death."[19]

Despite a complicated relationship, the loss was painful for Jean Oury, who had been Guattari's adoptive older brother and for whom Guattari had been so important. Recalling their time together starting in the postwar years, Jean Oury described the death of his alter ego at La Borde. "Today, Félix has left us, abruptly, prematurely. We're all at a loss. We virtually lived together for more than forty years, a gigantic effort remains unfinished."[20]

The Monday, August 31, 1992, front page of *Libération* carried an article entitled "The Thousand and One Lives of Félix Guattari," emphasizing the exceptionally appealing personality of the master of systematic disorganization. "His first name alone sufficed to set Félix Guattari apart.

Direct, jovial, and generous, he was energy, fuel, a network. Someone who, with tremendous verbal alchemy, defined subjectivity."[21] Maggiori quickly penned a long testimonial, "Félix the Rhizome," and arranged for several articles, including one by Jean-Baptiste Marongiu and Marc Ragon, "A Militant for All Seasons," and an interview of Jean Oury by Antoine de Gaudemar, in which Oury claimed that at "sixty years old, he was as he was at fifteen. He never changed: he seemed to be a dreamer but he was in fact extremely attentive, he remembered everything with a false nonchalance and an extraordinary presence. He always kept a youthful simplicity."[22] In the same collection of articles, Paul Virilio paid tribute to their discussion about war, which was interrupted by Félix's death while he was correcting the transcription of their debates. In *Le Monde*, Roger-Pol Droit saluted "An Inventive Provocateur," next to Jean Oury's piece on "A Dialectic of Friendship."[23] Guattari's death also made the front page in other big newspapers, including in Italy, where he was more popular than in he was in France. Even his enemies in the Italian Communist Party put his photo and announcement of the death of "Guattari the Anti-Freud" and "*L'Enfant Terrible*" on the front page of the August 30 edition of its daily *l'Unità*, recalling that the impassioned militant was the veritable banner of the 1977 protest movement in Italy.

Tributes proliferated in the many circles of friends, militants, and artists who had met Guattari. *Chimères*, the review created in tandem with Deleuze, devoted two special issues to Guattari in the summer and winter of 1994.[24] Guattari was a member of the Support Committee for the International Center for Popular Culture created in 1977 by the Center for Studies and Initiatives on International Solidarity. Located on rue Nanteuil, the center organized an evening of tribute to Guattari in January 1994, asking, "What role does international solidarity play in philosophical enquiry?"[25] *Transversales*, the journal run by Jacques Robin, Anne-Brigitte Kern, and Armand Petitjean, to whom Guattari gave much advice, saluted "the friend" and devoted an entire dossier to him in its final 1992 issue.[26]

Jean-Jacques Lebel paid the most spectacular tribute, constructing a baroque "Monument to Félix Guattari" at the Beaubourg Center in 1996. The multiform sculpture engendered public three-hour debates in the foyer of Beaubourg every Thursday for over two months. All of Félix's friends, famous and unknown, came to read texts, improvise comments, play music, or declaim a few verses.

Lebel, recalling Félix's love of cars, dismantled his Renault 25, filled it with soil, and grew hallucinogenic mushrooms in it. A loudspeaker, mounted on an enormous portrait of Félix, projected a recording of Guattari describing Yasha's dream and his desire for a car. "Arriving at Beaubourg, people would ask, hey, is Félix here? Is he alive? It was even more hallucinatory because his voice was blaring everywhere in Beaubourg."[27] Lebel put a slot into the back of the enormous Plexiglas box that the car sat in, so that people could drop letters, poems, and photos. "So many people left messages that I had to empty the box three times, and I had to keep everything because these messages were sent to Félix."[28] Lebel did not ignore Guattari's work. "I put issues of *Chimères* and Félix's writing under the hood where the engine goes."[29] A schizoanalyst's couch, sculpted from texts and objects, sat on the roof, forming part of the car's body. Looming above it all was a twenty-foot-tall slowly revolving heart. Below it, six videos ran constantly. François Pain filmed part of the parade.[30]

GASPING TO DEATH

One person was missing from the crowd. Deleuze was forced to stay connected to his oxygen tanks at home, where he read about the collective outpouring of affection for his friend Félix. "Gilles called me every evening when I was at Beaubourg to ask what had happened that day. He even gave me something to read there."[31] To give Deleuze some material presence, Lebel included numerous tubes in the sculpture. When Deleuze saw the exhibit on TV, he recognized his oxygen tanks. "Over the phone he told me, 'So you put my tubes in.' 'Yes Gilles, I put your tubes in.' And he said, 'That's good, you transformed them.'"[32] "You know, my health is not so good. It's hard for me to breathe, which often keeps me from going out and even speaking. I'm hooked to an oxygen tank like a dog. Illness is obviously awful, even though mine isn't among the most painful."[33] Despite the tanks, he suffered from increasingly violent bouts of suffocation. Deleuze had already seen his friend François Châtelet in the same condition. "It was one of the reasons he gave for leaving, for committing suicide. He wrote me a letter two weeks before his suicide in very shaky handwriting to tell me that he didn't want to live through what François had lived through. I saw him again in his apartment on avenue Niel a few weeks before his death; you could feel that he wanted the suffering to end."[34]

More even than suffering, what Deleuze certainly could not bear above all was that he was less and less able to work, write, and discuss. Toward the end, he had clearly thought about more fragmented, concentrated writing, but his bouts of suffocation were so violent that they made every effort impossible. In September 1995, Deleuze called his friend Richard Pinhas from Saint-Leonard-de-Noblat. "Gilles said, 'I'm having a bad asthma attack.' He hung up, gasping. The phone rang again. Gilles, 'I can barely speak,' metallic but gentle voice. The phone starts buzzing as if an insect artifact were vibrating around his voice, reconstitution machine."[35] In October, Deleuze left Limousin for his Paris apartment. Pinhas called him but he was in such a state that Fanny was unable to hand him the phone. The same thing happened the next day. Finally, Deleuze called him, but only to say that he had to hang up. "I smiled and he bid me farewell. Across Paris, I felt Ariadne's thread separating him, imperceptibly, from life."[36]

Deleuze's friend Yves Mabin was with him during some of his debilitating attacks. "He was absolutely suffocating; that he could stand it for so long is proof of his exceptional courage. He was unusually brave in hanging on to that point."[37] Shortly before killing himself, Deleuze called Yves Mabin, who was not home. Deleuze left a message saying that he would call back. "He called me back on Thursday, and said things that he often said, very affectionately, but I said to myself, why is he calling me to tell me this?"[38] Somewhat worried, Mabin decided to wait until late Saturday morning, when Fanny Deleuze would be back from the market, to avoid disturbing his friend, who usually could not answer the phone himself. That Saturday, November 4, 1995, Fanny told Yves Mabin that Deleuze was dead but did not say that he had just defenestrated himself from their apartment. His circle of friends watched fearfully as it became harder and harder for Deleuze to continue living; they were dreading his death. Yet suicide was so incongruent with Deleuze's embodiment of a vital force and his philosophy of life that certain of his friends tried to see it as a send off, an ultimate final act. That same day, November 4, 1995, Itzhak Rabin, the Israeli prime minister, was assassinated, another tragic death.

For his friends, Deleuze's death was the beginning of a difficult period.

Paris November 5, 1995: the terrible, devastating death of the philosopher Gilles Deleuze. . . . I believe we can only speak philosophically about the death of Gilles Deleuze, who will keep his secret for all eternity. It was certainly not from any despair, or death wish, as he had always found this expression and even the idea of a "death drive," made so popular by psychoanalysis, to be aberrant and contradictory. Deleuze's whole philosophy is a hymn to life, an affirmation of life.[39]

Pierre Verstaeten and Juliette Simont saw Deleuze's act as a final "yes" to death as the follow-up to life by other means: "defending against what happens to us accidentally, *by wanting it.*"[40]

On Monday, November 6, Roggert Maggiori wrote an article in *Libération* paying tribute to the "breath of fresh air" with which Deleuze had infused thinking in this century. "It is impossible to take the full measure as yet of how he swept away everything, shifted everything, philosophical language, the way of doing philosophy, the very definition of philosophy."[41] Maggiori proclaimed Deleuze to be the most philosophical of philosophers. In the same series of articles, Antoine de Gaudemar returned to the theme of exhaustion, which Deleuze had used to describe Beckett's theater. "We cannot help but think of Deleuze himself, exhausted by his serious respiratory problems and finding it increasingly difficult to get around."[42] He added, recalling Deleuze's comments on Empedocles' suicide, that suicide is both an anecdote about a life and an aphorism of thought. The next day, November 7, 1995, *Libération* printed three pages of tributes from Deleuze's students, colleagues, and friends. Alain Badiou published a letter that he had sent to Deleuze in July 1994. Jean-Luc Nancy discussed his own profound distress. "At the moment that Gilles Deleuze takes his leave of us, out of great sadness and respect, we are tempted to keep him as he was, to stop the film, freeze the image."[43] For Jacques Derrida, he would now have to "wander alone"; he expressed how close he was to Deleuze. "Without any doubt and despite all the dissimilarities, Deleuze remains the person whom I always considered to be closest among those of this '*generation.*' I never felt the slightest '*objection*' rise in me, even virtually, against any of his discourses."[44]

Monday evening, two days after Deleuze's death, Laure Adler, who had taken several of his classes at Vincennes, spontaneously paid tribute to Deleuze during her television program, *The Midnight Circle.* She described Deleuze as a "taster of words" to whom she listened with avid delight, getting up early on Tuesday mornings to go to Vincennes. Maggiori compared Deleuze to a carpenter carefully seated at his workbench; Roger-Pol Droit emphasized the specific gesture of Deleuze's thought. "Putting things into motion everywhere. The becomings, the emergences, whereas the history of philosophy more often thought about stable things, permanence."[45]

The November 7 headlines of *Le Monde* also reported Deleuze's death. Roger-Pol Droit's article equated Deleuze's rebellion and intelligence.[46] It published a portrait of Deleuze by Gérard Fromanger and an enumeration of his many experiments by Roger-Pol Droit. That week's *Le Monde of Books* carried several testimonials, showing the many facets of Deleuze's work. Jean-François Lyotard and Frédéric Gros both wrote about his special relationship to the future and his constant flights forward, his manner of living and thinking "trusting only this other time that does not pass away."[47] On Alain Veinstein's program "From One Day to the Next" on France Culture radio, Michel Butel, who had been the director of *L'Autre Journal*, declared that, for him, Deleuze had counted more than anyone else had. "I'd never met anyone so intelligent until I met Deleuze."[48] He recalled his love of life, his refusal of suicide to the point where his action defined a free act that surprised the person committing it. "For me, Deleuze was a little like Samuel Beckett or Che. Without wanting to or realizing it, he paid tribute to friendship, the supreme art of life."[49]

In the fall, Christian Descamps prepared a long article on Deleuze that came out in early 1996 in *La Quinzaine Littéraire*.[50] Yves Mabin, who was working at the Ministry for Foreign Affairs, wrote about the friend he considered a saint.

> One evening, I was dining with the two of them [Gilles and Fanny]. I told Gilles that for me, coming as I do from Brittany, someone who gives something essential to his friends that no one since the beginning of time had ever given was a saint. And that as a result, I thought quite seriously that he was a saint. Gilles smiled, one of those smiles mixing amusement and emotion. Then in one of the most beautiful gestures of love I've ever seen, Fanny stretched out her arms, took Gilles' hands in her long, slender fingers, and said to him, "Yves is right. I also think you're a saint."[51]

Roger-Pol Droit also discussed sainthood in 1998[52] in describing three possible portraits of Deleuze: first, the philosopher who seems to be almost a classical professor but who is already impossible to categorize; then, the philosopher as creator, endlessly attracted to invention; and finally the experimenter who "let himself be altered by outside currents and accepted their excesses. So with Deleuze, thinking is an experience of life rather than of reason."[53] Not that these three portraits were the only possible ones, as so many others could be painted; the final one was that of the sage and refers to the inscription on his gravestone. "Two modified sentences from Nietzsche. One talking about Leibniz: 'Timorous and mysterious in the extreme.' The other referring to the Greeks: "Superficial . . . by their depth.' "[54]

Just before his death, Deleuze's final text was published in the fall 1995 issue of *Philosophy*: "Immanence: A Life."[55] One element of a set conceived on the virtual with a virtually testamentary value.[56]

The philosophical community came together to demonstrate the vitality of Deleuze's philosophy. The academic institutions continued to view him as a pariah: it was the periphery, other countries, that took the initiative. In June 1996, in Brazil, Éric Alliez organized several days of international meetings about Gilles Deleuze in Rio and Sao Paulo, which led to an important publication.[57] In Paris, the International College of Philosophy held a colloquium in January 1997 entitled "Gilles Deleuze: Immanence and Life," including lectures that were later collected and published in an issue of *Rue Descartes*.[58] In 2000, *A Grave for Deleuze*, edited by Yannick Beaubatie,[59] described Deleuze's tremendous attachment to the region around Saint-Léonard-de-Noblat in Limousin, where he spent three to four months every summer at his home, the Mas Révérey. During his last summer, despite being seriously handicapped, he was still able to walk along the Saint-Germain-des-Belles road, a mile or so from Saint-Léonard, on the plateau overlooking the Vienne Valley. Friends in the region and the association of Artists and Writers of Saint-Léonard in Limousin organized two days of discussion on October 25 and 26, 1996, and an exhibit in Limoges entitled "Gilles Deleuze: A Philosopher in Limousin." Elisabeth Lagisquet, who organized this exhibit, insisted on the very strong bond between Deleuze and Limousin, which he called a "profound region." "Perhaps what's needed is a detour through Limousin to try a very particular reading of the work of philosophy, a little bit of hooky, freely, but no less legitimate."[60] Gilles Deleuze was buried on Friday, November 10, 1995, in the new cemetery of Saint-Léonard-de-Noblat.

29

Their Work at Work

Deleuze and Guattari's work continued to be read both internationally and in France after the two authors' deaths. Indeed, their oeuvre drew commentary even before 1995, the year that Deleuze died. This first group of "disciples"—Deleuze and Guattari rejected the notion—included people who had met one or both of the authors or had taken courses at Paris-VIII. However, virtually all of the earliest publications on their work, with the exception of that of Éric Alliez, referred only to Deleuze.

The first major publication was written by thirty-three-year-old Jean-Clet Martin, who intended to lay out the whole of Deleuze's work.[1] Martin lived in Altkirch, near Mulhouse. He had never taken a course with Deleuze but had read his work at an early age. In 1988, he decided to do his research on Deleuze's philosophy. Given that he lived in eastern France, Martin's exchanges with Deleuze were primarily by letter, although he occasionally came to Paris to work with him.

Martin was invited to Deleuze's home in April 1989, late on a stormy afternoon. The day was dark, and Deleuze had not yet turned on the lights in the apartment. "I couldn't see him in the dark, a moment of grace in the shadows. I was having a very hard time making him out, and his voice was becoming inaudible in the complete obscurity, interspersed with rolls of thunder. It was a magical moment for me. His voice was a cry."[2] After this meeting, a philosophical friendship developed between them through the mail and by phone, and Deleuze seemed to appreciate Martin's distinct personality and the fact that he was removed from the tight Parisian cliques. Their discussions were quite productive. In early 1991, Martin sent Deleuze a New Year's card with a reproduction of Van Gogh's sunflowers and a quotation from Malcolm Lowry about strange sunflowers watching from the window. Deleuze wrote back:

Dear friend, your postcard is quite beautiful and Lowry's text, that's exactly what a percept is! In Kafka, a strange horse watches from the window. . . . I haven't written for some time because the move tired me considerably and I've again fallen into a respiratory depression that is hard to bear, and from which I've not yet emerged, even though I'm feeling much better. . . . I've made a lot of progress on the final version of *What Is Philosophy?*[3]

Of the letters that Deleuze wrote him, Jean-Clet Martin selected one for the preface to his book on Deleuze's philosophy. After reading the manuscript, Deleuze reminded Martin that he liked the idea of system in the Leibnizian sense, on the condition that system not be related to the Identical, because what he wanted to do was to construct a philosophy "as a creative activity,"[4] and he insisted on the issue of multiplicity. "You see how important the notion of multiplicity is for me: it's the very heart of it."[5]

Another Deleuze expert, Arnaud Villani, had started out in literature. In the 1960s, he was enrolled in classics and philosophy and received his *agrégation* in classics in 1967 and in philosophy in 1968. Villani then became a philosophy professor at Masséna High School in Nice, where he still teaches *khâgne* courses. He had become interested in Deleuze in 1972 and periodically wrote general articles about his work, the first of which was published in 1980.[6] In 1999, he wrote an essay describing Deleuze's method, in which he included excerpts from his correspondence with Deleuze.[7] In Nice, he also gave summer classes for foreigners on contemporary French philosophy. Over the course of their correspondence, Deleuze warned Villani against his tendency to ignore Guattari.

You must correct the way you tend to overlook Félix. Your perspective remains correct and you can discuss me without Félix. However, *Anti-Oedipus* and *A Thousand Plateaus* are written completely by him just as they are written completely by me, depending on two possible viewpoints. Thus, if you don't mind, I need to point out that you are dealing with me because of what you are doing but it's at all because Félix plays a secondary or "occasional" role.[8]

A New Generation Takes up the Baton

A whole new generation was thrilled by Deleuzo-Guattarism, including a small group of young philosophers at the ENS on rue d'Ulm. They had discovered Deleuze and Guattari and found their work entirely out of sync with their period. Their relationship to it was entirely different from that of the preceding generation, among other reasons because the issues were different. Every person in this small group has become a researcher or teacher at the ENS International Center for the Study of French Philosophy, which is directed by Frédéric Worms, of the previous generation. "I had all of them at the ENS between 1991 and 1995, when I was helping students prepare for their *agrégation* exam."[9]

But unlike Foucault, who created a center and a team that organized the distribution of his work, Deleuze and Guattari's "disciples" were quite free to appropriate their work as they chose. Élie During first read Deleuze during his senior year in high school. He did not understand the meaning of *Foucault* but found the "style" attractive. In *hypokhâgne*, he applied himself more seriously to Deleuze's monographs in the history of philosophy, reading and commenting with a group of five or six students who were planning to study philosophy. Another member of the group, During's friend Thomas Bénatouil, was also accepted at the ENS, where he met David Rabouin, who had been a literature student. Unlike his *khâgne* pals, Rabouin had not really liked Deleuze and Guattari; he had read *Empiricism and Subjectivity*, but the difficult book had not enticed him. It was through Spinoza that he discovered Deleuze. "When we started at the ENS, Thomas Bénatouil and I went to Bernard Pautrat's seminar, who had a decided taste for Spinoza, and both of us wrote our MA theses on Spinoza."[10] A year later, in 1993, Patric Maniglier was accepted at the ENS at rue d'Ulm and joined the small group of Deleuzeans there.

For them, Deleuze was above all a way of doing philosophy differently. Élie During, who became a Bergson expert, tried to construct a theory of local time anchored in physics. After writing his thesis on Spinoza, Thomas Bénatouil earned his doctorate in sociology and then became a specialist on Epictetus and the Stoics.[11] David Rabouin became an epistemologist and wrote his thesis on the philosophy of mathematics during the classical period. Patrice Maniglier studied structuralism and viewed Deleuze as the philosopher of the paradigm, the experimental metaphysics of structural operations.

The many publications and commentary privileging mimesis aggravated Élie During, who recalled Deleuze's remarks that one could not merely refer to the multiple; the multiple still had to be done. For *Critique*, During reviewed two large collective volumes on Deleuze and attacked those portraying themselves as Deleuze's disciples.[12] David Rabouin was a regular contributor to the *Le Magazine Littéraire*, and when the first collection of articles organized by David Lapoujade was published,[13] he and his friends prepared a special issue on Deleuze. They asked very different well-known individuals the joltingly direct question: "Deleuze, for what?"[14] In the presentation, David Rabouin remarked that Deleuzean concepts abounded but had not been sufficiently developed for his work to be well understood. "It's not enough to proclaim, 'long live the multiple,' or to brandish some other pop concept: the only thing that counts is doing something with it, because of an 'external.'"[15]

Anne Sauvagnargues and Guillaume Sibertin-Blanc were close to this small group and in their ENS seminar they paid Guattari's role its due. Anne Sauvagnargues became the first researcher to have a solid university position as an expert in the work of Deleuze and Guattari. In 1997, she was offered a very good teaching job at the ENS but was obliged to enroll in a doctoral program for it. She wanted to work on the relationship between philosophy and art and had been casting about for a contemporary French philosopher. "Deleuze corresponded perfectly. His oeuvre was completed, there hadn't been any true commentator, everything remained to be done and what's more, he thought that art had a real place. It was exactly what I needed."[16] She managed to convince her thesis director, Pierre-François Moreau, but he warned her that he would not be able to recommend her for a job at the Sorbonne on the basis of her work.

Guillaume Sibertin-Blan was enrolled in *khâgne* and *hypokhâgne* classes at Henri IV High School when his future ENS professor, Anne Sauvagnargues, got a job at the ENS and was starting to write her thesis.[17] They met when he enrolled at the ENS, and she helped him prepare for the *agrégation* examination. She also created a small working seminar on Deleuze and Guattari, which interested only four students during the 1998–1999 academic year, including Guillaume Sibertin-Blanc, who needed to take a breather after the *agrégation* examination.

Since 2005, Anne Sauvagnargues and Guillaume Sibertin-Blanc have been giving a seminar called "Readings in Deleuze and Guattari's *A Thousand Plateaus*" as part of the working group "Deleuze, Spinoza, and the Social

Sciences" at the Center for Studies in Rhetoric, Philosophy, and the History of Ideas (CERPHI). Both are proponents of an "externalist" method for making this difficult book more intelligible, which means looking carefully at Deleuze and Guattari's sources to put their utterances and issues into context. "It's a transformation of the history of philosophy, a way of thinking philosophy in its becoming, of claiming that there are no concepts or events outside a certifiable corporeal base, or a certain encounter of powers outside of thinking."[18] Their entire commentary consists in finding the links between Deleuzean texts and the texts with which he was in dialogue in order to measure the differences, emphases, and emergence of new concepts, as well as their disappearance once they had served their purpose. To understand how Deleuzean thinking can be expressed in a few strong propositions means taking the time for this textual and temporal "promenade"; it is a matter of once again grasping the encounters, the disjunctive conjunctions, the rhizomes as semiotic links taken in their specific historical register, which does not require reading things chronologically.

> There are two parts to my method. On one hand, I don't dissociate the intellectual tenor and the material stratigraphy of ideas. On the other hand, I consider that the material stratigraphy, the connection that an author makes with his references, has to do with the intersection of differences. So there is no difference, between idea and society, but a pragmatics of the concept: that's the first idea. The second, I got from Pierre-Francois Moreau for whom there is no key moment in a thinker's biography. That's why you have to go from the static to the dynamic aspect of the system to produce a living image.[19]

This supposes paying close attention to the references of the work being studied, so as to clearly grasp the divergences between the sources and their use and between two notions that seem to say the same things at different points in the gestation of the work but in fact refer to something else depending on context and the spatial-temporal conjunction that it presupposes. "To be interested in the irruption of the new forces you need to identify the curve of a concept in the system, by taking its point of entry into account, its zone of dissipation, the theoretical sectors that it sets into play and the practical connections that result from it."[20]

A New Cultural and Political Radicality

Outside the university world, some collectives and reviews discussed Deleuzo-Guattarian thinking. First among these was *Chimères, a Schizo-analytics Review*, which Guattari created as an extension of his network and seminar and whose birth was decided by Labordian and Guattarian psychiatrists in the kitchen at 125, boulevard Saint Germain. The first issue came out in the spring of 1987, introducing Guattari as the manager and Jean-Claude Polack and Danielle Sivadon as the editors in chief. Initially, *Chimères* was largely concerned with psychiatric issues, always in a spirit of transversality. Somewhat after this, Deleuze accepted the invitation to officially co-direct the review, which claimed to reflect a shared schizoanalytic orientation, but he never had any real intention of getting deeply involved in a collective enterprise, since he loathed such things. Today, the review pursues its mission of promoting cultural agitation.

Chimères was above all Guattari's child, whereas the other reviews draw equally from Deleuze and Guattari and are more directly political, even if the articles are not exclusively about politics. *Futur Antérieur*, for example, was created in 1990 by Jean-Marie Vincent, Denis Berger, and Toni Negri. When it stopped in 1998, there had been forty-three trimestrial issues and ten special issues. A longtime friend of Deleuze, Yann Moulier-Boutang, urged some members of the editorial team to create a political, artistic, and cultural review: *Multitudes* was born in 2000. Faithful to Deleuze and Guattari's spirit of transversality, *Multitudes* intended to publish as much on contemporary art and thinking about the media as on social and political questions including feminism, mixed race, war, racism, ecopolitics, guaranteed income, Europe, and so forth.[21]

Vacarme (Hullabaloo) was another review born of social and political protest and nourished in part by Deleuzo-Guattarian thinking. One of its editorial committee members, Mathieu Potte-Bonneville, discovered Deleuze's work at the very beginning of the 1990s. He was preparing for the *agrégation* and, in 1991, met Pierre Zaoui, a Deleuzean student at the ENS who was taking the exam that same year and was actively involved in organizing meetings and militant actions against unfettered globalization and the Gulf War.

Pierre Zaoui had Mathieu Potte-Bonneville read *A Thousand Plateaus*. "For two years at ENS there was a sort of reflection group of ENS students and others called 'With a Knife Between our Teeth.' "[22] These twenty people

created a little newsletter called *Resistance Notebooks* much inspired by Deleuzean ideas.[23] A few years later, in 1996, at the initiative of Pierre Zaoui,
the small group met again to plan for a review that would be the average
person's echo chamber for new forms of militancy and new social movements: this is how *Hullabaloo* was born in 1997.[24] It would be untrue to say
that the review was entirely Deleuzo-Guattarian, since it was also deeply
influenced by Foucault, but it claimed no intellectual authority for itself. It
was not simply the Deleuzo-Guattarian lexicon that set it apart; above all,
it took a different approach to politics. Its attention to the construction of
arrangements and the way that institutions are always singular and hard to
evaluate from the outside prompted the journal to integrate the ambigui-
ties specific to contemporary social movements that are constantly forced to
negotiate permanent contradictions. "When a political group is forced
to attack pharmaceutical laboratories like Act Up did, it has to negotiate
with them and also to create permanent, shifting alliances. Deleuze makes
this possible because his analyses are operational for judging individual
cases."[25]

Deleuzo-Guattarianism was also the source of a new political radicalness, a sort of war machine against the logics of globalization for Toni Negri and his American friend Michael Hardt, who was teaching comparative
literature at Duke University. In 2000, they presented their analysis in *Empire*, as the realization of a new "Communist Manifesto" adapted to the
conditions of modernity, advocating an alternative utopia in the face of
globalization and uniformity.[26] In 2004, Hardt and Negri attacked the use
of war during periods of globalization, contrasting in binary fashion the
multitude's desire for democracy and the repression imposed by powers
whose logic of sovereignty inexorably led to violence and war. As they saw
it, the "multitude" needed a new science that could destroy sovereignty,
thus renewing the Leninist gesture. To escape the failings of Thermidor,
they argued for a political theory that could reconcile Lenin's centralism
with Madison's constitutionalism. Although they share the spirit of resistance against the logics of control embodied by Deleuze and Guattari,
Hardt and Negri were very attached to a historical teleology and a sense of
history already there, which would simply need new social categories: in
this way they were quite removed from Deleuze and Guattari. They believed that the multitude replaced the notion of the working class, but their
approach largely depends on the same philosophy of history that envisions
revolutionary eschatology.

Manola Antonioli insisted on the force of Deleuze and Guattari's work to elucidate fundamental social changes and to hone a critical perspective and political radicalness. After her book on Deleuze and the history of philosophy,[27] she published a second one in 2004, where she emphasized the productive arrangement between Deleuze and Guattari and the pertinence and lucidity of their concepts for examining the current processes of globalization.[28] She had clearly understood that Deleuze and Guattari were not abolishing history but rather a form of historical teleology that they were replacing with the plurality of spatial logics. Observing that all of their work developed around concepts such as territory, ground, networks, flux, and nomadism, she took it upon herself to explore the "proximity between geography and philosophy that emerges from this work."[29] Antonioli showed in particular the extraordinary contemporaneity of the logics of deterritorialization and reterritorialization that "outline a line of flight towards a future that remains unpredictable."[30]

CRITIQUING THE CRITIQUE

Others distanced themselves from the political orientations of Deleuze and Guattari's thinking. For them, the time had come for grand revisions and for contemplating the end of a certain form of political leftism and the tragic destiny of most utopias. Deleuze and Guattari thus belonged to the past, an emanation of the radical thinking of the 1960s and 1970s that no longer had any intellectual and political relevance.

Philippe Mengue, a former student and one of the first commentators on Deleuze's work, devoted himself to this revisionist effort by raising the question of democracy in a starkly direct manner.[31] A former leftist and *connoisseur* of Deleuze, Mengue sensed a political break in the mid-1980s. "I felt that something was no longer working in our discourse. So at a certain point we are necessarily forced to say to ourselves that there is political rationality."[32] He wanted to show the contradiction between the defense of a theory of the multiple and opposing a plural democracy. Philippe Mengue criticized Deleuze for not considering the mediations specific to politics, which cut him off from political reality. He thought Deleuze displayed visible aristocratic disdain by constantly denigrating opinion, the *doxa*, the press, and the media. "Deleuze takes an antidemocratic Nietzschean position. Nietzsche spat on newspapers, he spits on the media."[33] Mengue clearly makes politics central to Deleuzean thought but protested against reducing the intellectual simply to a warrior's stance incarnating a hypercritical paradigm. "Deleuze ends up necessarily conceiving thought as a nomadic war machine and its act as a guerrilla war."[34]

For Philippe Mengue, overvalorizing minorities as the sole group with a becoming because they are by their essence cut off from the dominant order leads to a radical devalorization of democracy. This makes a rights-based State incompatible with three of Deleuze's philosophy's central themes: immanence, minorities, and becomings. Human rights and the legal-political apparatus are conceived of as transhistorical and therefore transcendent realities. Democracy, defined by its quest for social consensus, would ultimately muzzle minorities in the name of the majority. But according to Deleuze, "only the minor is creative. There is no majority becoming, the only becoming is therefore in the minority. The majority is a halt, an effect of *becomings* and, in return, becomings can only be blocked by the majority."[35] However, Mengue suggested thinking and extending Deleuzeanism against Deleuze by supporting the inflections required by our postmodern moment "by his conception of social heterogenesis and of distinct becomings of history."[36] He saw a future for Deleuzeanism alongside micropolitics and the practices that eschewed the suspicion of the 1960s. Beyond Deleuze, Mengue was attacking a certain form of Deleuzeanism and above all the Guattarian graft of political radicalization as of 1969.

Paul Patton retorted that the three values that Mengue incriminated were in no way antidemocratic.[37] In Patterson's view, the critique of transcendence that would embody the invocation of human rights was motivated by Deleuze's dissatisfaction with what amounts to disincarnated abstractions. If human rights are to progress, it should be more concretely, with the concerned populations, starting with specific situations, inventing laws. Patton also refused Mengue's molar opposition between majority and minority, which was not the conception that Deleuze and Guattari developed, since they saw majority and minority in positions that were neither external nor oppositional but simply noncoincident. As for the opposition between the philosophical concept and opinion, it implied nothing for the public sphere. The resistance to the present that Deleuze and Guattari call for, according to Patton, sought to deepen a future democracy. Likewise, for Arnaud Villani, Mengue's point was totally off the mark: it eliminated a major aspect of Deleuze's thought, which was the dynamic triggered by the line of flight, which has nothing to do with the binarity in which Menge wanted to enclose Deleuzean politics. "Deleuze doesn't criticize democracy because he's some crypto-aristocrat; it's not that democracy goes too far, it's *that it doesn't go far enough.*"[38]

Jacob Rogozinski wrote, among other things, an excellent article on Deleuze in 1988 in *Le Magazine Littéraire*[39] on Mengue's critique. As a high-school student just after 1968, Rogozinski was excited to discover philosophy. "With Deleuze, everything became problematic, worthy of question."[40] Twenty years later, in 1988, he still saluted the fulguration that Deleuze represented in the world of thought. Touched by Rogozinski's article, Deleuze wrote him a short note and dedicated *Leibniz* to him. Yet, for Rogozinski, Deleuze, unlike Lyotard, did not make it possible to think the disasters of the twentieth century. "What's heroic in Deleuze is that he goes to the limits of the radicalism of the 1960s."[41] Today, Rogozinski is particularly severe when it comes to Deleuzeanism. It offers no space for thinking ethics: Deleuze, in a very Spinozan perspective, ignores the desire for evil. Obliterating the question of evil means that he cannot think totalitarianism, political terror, or the major events of the twentieth century: the Shoah, the Gulag, the Khmer Rouge, among others. Giving ethics a place implies giving the subject, the ego, a place; in this respect, Rogozinski observes that Deleuze, like many philosophers of his generation, has what he considers to be a "legicidal" attitude, negating the "I," which should be humiliated and crushed. "His subject is a subject with an 'I,' an anonymous, acephalous subject. He is always opposed to a subject of identity. It's less the subject that is the enemy than the 'I,' the ego. He never thought that there could be an immanent part of the ego so I don't see how we can reach the level of immanence that he talks about."[42]

MODERN MACHINIC THINKING

For the new epistemology of science, which was no longer based on a separation between scientific contents and society, between man and nature, or between objectivity and subjectivity, Guattari and Deleuze's work was a major resource. For the philosopher and sociologist of science Isabelle Stengers, who finished her philosophy studies in 1973 (the year that *Anti-Oedipus* was published), "it was *Difference and Repetition* that made me work."[43] What immediately appealed to her in Deleuze's work was his capacity to get involved and to involve the reader in having typically distinct areas communicate with each other. It was this departitioning that she was looking for in the relationship among the sciences and that she sought in philosophy. In her six volumes of *Cosmopolitiques*, which she published between 1996 and 1997, she ranged over several scientific continents, including the war among the sciences, thermodynamics, time in the work of Prigogine, quantum mechanics, and the faces of emergence.[44] Deleuze and Guattari inspired many of these notions.

Stengers had met Guattari in the 1980s. She invited him to meet with scientists during the years when she was organizing programs at Cerisy with Ilya Prigogine, the 1977 Nobel Prize winner in chemistry. "He did the worst thing imaginable by showing his diagrams. He got going about developments and the scientists understood nothing. It was a missed opportunity."[45] Stengers nonetheless used Deleuzo-Guattarian concepts in her own work and was instrumental in making their work known in Brussels. In the 1980s, she gave a seminar at the Free University of Brussels on Deleuze and Guattari. As of the 1990s, her colleague Pierre Verstraeten, a very active Sartrean, built his introduction to philosophy using *What Is Philosophy?*

Daniel Franco was an early initiate into Deleuze and Guattari's thinking, and when he started teaching at the Free University, he taught a philosophy course on Deleuze for four years. "Deleuze was an extraordinary synthesizer. It's a bit like chasing clouds."[46] Pascal Chabot,[47] the Simondon specialist, also took courses with Isabelle Stengers and Pierre Verstraeten and wrote a book on Deleuze that was published in 1998.[48] For Pascal Chabot, a historian of philosophy initially specializing in Husserlian studies, Deleuze was a "liberator" that let him disintegrate the notion of a base that is essential in phenomenology with his notion of multiplicity. "Deleuze's universe was a breath of fresh air for me."[49]

Pierre Lévy, who became an expert on "intelligent technologies," was deeply influenced by Michel Serres and by Deleuze and Guattari. He had met Guattari in the early 1990s; both were interested in the most modern technology. In these information technologies Lévy even saw the foundations of a cognitive ecology that was not so far removed from Guattari's ecosophy, the basis of a participatory technodemocracy. The question was no longer to think the opposition between man and machines but rather their modes of connection. Lévy considered Warren McCulloch the first person who linked neuronal functioning and logical circuits, thereby establishing the foundations of connectionism. Lévy was inspired by the idea of the rhizome, which in his work became the mode of diffusing knowledge through multiple branchings made possible by the new technologies of intelligence.

The concepts of Deleuze and Guattari also made their way into the new anthropology of science born at the Center for the Sociology of Innovation, which examined the emerging process of scientific and technological innovation, according to Michel Callon and Bruno Latour. The discoveries making it possible to upset social ties are themselves the result of multiple networks involving laboratories, public policy, private finance, and relationships with potential consumers. This anthropology of science put forth a new notion of networks, understood in a very broad sense. "Networks are at one and the same time real like nature, narrated like discourse and collective like society."[50] The term "network" as it was used in the anthropology of science corresponded to a determination to manipulate a notion such that a territorialized vision of society was avoided. In this respect, it is unlike the notion of a field or subfield of institutions that suppose homogenous sets defined by types of actions and specific rules. These networks also mix the human and nonhuman, subject and object.

Bruno Latour returned to this Deleuzo-Guattarian notion to introduce these networks as a double war machine against the idea of structure and interactionism. This powerful operator had some disadvantages, however, since it implied a void at the level of content, leading to an impoverished vision of the world in which we live. Certainly, the apparatus remained detached from all content in order to be able to receive new elements and better follow the most diverse actors, controversies, and configurations. Latour saw himself more in the line of Epicurus, Spinoza, and Nietzsche than of Descartes, Kant, and Husserl, the philosophers of the mind. While contemporary philosophers are relatively useless when it comes to defining a program of investigation in the social sciences, Michel Serres and Gilles Deleuze both played a major role. We can say that the notion of networks was sufficiently close to Deleuze's model of the rhizome, but not entirely like that of the networks in the anthropology of science, where the primary concern, unlike Deleuze's notion, is reterritorialization. In the second place, the notion of the rhizome is too fluid; there are no stopping points, which makes it ill suited to the mechanisms set into place in the encounter between science, technology, and the market.

Michel Callonan and Bruno Latour link the visibility of the scientific fact to the translation chain during the many displacements that make it possible to deduce the initial heterogeneity of discourse, laboratories, and mobilized resources. Above all, this anthropology of science distinguishes itself from the modern project of separation, of a split between the natural world, objects on one hand and subjects on the other. The modern project takes shape with Kant. "Things in themselves become inaccessible while, symmetrically, the transcendental subject distances itself infinitely from the world."[51] Once the break has been established, the attempts to overcome it lead nowhere. The anthropology of science thus seeks another metaphysics, rejoining Deleuze's philosophical quest for an organic link between man and nature. Implied is a critique of Hegelianism that deepens the abyss that it seeks to fill between subject and object. The phenomenological project unfolds in an "insurmountable"[52] tension between object and subject, with quasi-objects "real, discursive, and social,"[53] based on the founding postulate of the anthropology of science. Latour prefers to reverse the usual modern formula that sees an initial purification process splitting that which comes from the subject and that which is extracted from the object, followed by multiplying the intermediaries in order to arrive at an explanation located at the point of contact between the two extremes. Instead, he wants to make the point of splitting/encounter a starting point for research leading toward the extremes of subject/object. "This explanatory model makes it possible to integrate the work of purification like a particular case of mediation."[54]

Deleuze's "Postscriptum on Control Societies" was initially published in 1990 in Michel Butel's *L'Autre Journal* and later reprinted in *Negotiations*.[55] For many analysts of the most contemporary social changes, this essay provides an essential theoretical matrix because it takes both the macrolevel of society and the microlevel of enterprise into account. Bernard Stiegler, for example, uses the essay as his starting point for reflecting on symbolic misery. He deplores the break between politics and aesthetics, whose tragic effect is the collapse of participation in aesthetic creation. He also adopts Deleuze's idea of seeking new arms appropriate to this new control society, which he suggests be described as hyperindustrial. The war is not over, even if it has been transposed. "This war has become essentially aesthetic."[56] In our contemporary period, we need to find, in the manner of Simondon and Deleuze, the processes of individuation that are both psychic and collective, "where *I* and *we* are two faces of the same process, the gap between them also constituting a *dynamic* of the process."[57]

The philosopher Pierre-Antoine Chardel first studied hermeneutics and Derridean deconstruction before turning to Deleuze and Guattari to deal with the new technologies. A humanities professor at the National Institute of Telecommunications, he created an interdisciplinary research group to address ethical, technological, organizational, and social (ETOS) crosscutting questions. In an increasingly standardized society, the question becomes how to preserve multiplicity as a condition of the possibility of creation. "We are hitting upon an ethical question tied to aesthetics, which is to say of aesthetics as the prolegomenon to an ethics, to use a term dear to Ricoeur."[58]

INCREASINGLY CONTEMPORARY

The profusion of articles, books, meetings, and other events marking the 2005 commemoration of the tenth anniversary of Deleuze's death is one sign that Deleuzo-Guattarian is gaining traction and being used in dramatically varied ways. The Beaubourg Center in Paris organized an "Alphabet for Gilles Deleuze" on November 2, 2005, at which many experts, friends, and associates presented an aspect of Deleuze, in alphabetical order, interspersed with audio and filmed documents. It all culminated in a concert by Richard Pinhas. At the French National Library, France Culture organized a huge meeting presided over by Jacques Munier with Clément Rosset, Gérard Fromanger, Anne Sauvagnargues, Toni Negri, and Paola Marrati. A series of books attested to the tremendous fertility of Deleuze's thought in the most diverse areas: art,[59] voice,[60] psychoanalysis,[61] time,[62] the sources of his thinking,[63] not to mention the collections of articles about this or that aspect of his philosophy,[64] the reprints,[65] and the CDs of his classes[66] and seminars.[67]

Architects were particularly receptive to Deleuze and Guattari's work. The urban philosopher Theirry Paquot recalls that Foucault profoundly influenced the community of city planners in the 1980s. "*A Thousand Plateaus* came out in 1980 but didn't really affect this environment immediately."[68] It was only during the 1990s that architects, urban planners, and landscapers started using Deleuzo-Guattarian concepts. "For me, *A Thousand Plateaus* is a magical book with many different topics that must be reread over and over, since each rereading raises a new set of questions."[69] The circulation and appropriation of these ideas was occasionally excessive. The baroque fold was used indiscriminately for everything. All architecture folds, unfolds, and refolds. But more seriously, since the end of the 1990s, the concept of deterritorialization had great heuristic value, even if it was used in ways that were out of sync with the meaning that Deleuze and Guattari had given it. "This concept is most often understood as a form of detachment from the place because of globalization, a kind of delocalization, like industries that move from this or that region to countries where salaries are lower."[70] During a part of his course at the Paris-XI Urban Planning Institute, Thierry Paquot presented the contributions of Deleuze and Guattari because they made it possible to understand the potential existential geography of humans during a period of groundless networks.

The urban philosopher Chris Younès, head of the Philosophy, Architecture, and Urban Network and professor at the Paris School of Architecture at La Villette, studied with Deleuze in Lyon during the 1960s. She and her students took the measure of the significance of his work for urban planning, architecture, and more broadly for urban territories. "I used him a lot in this area of architecture and the city with my students. If there's one philosopher to whom they often refer, it's Deleuze."[71] Her students began reading Deleuze and Guattari on their own and observed several recurrent themes useful for understanding contemporary changes in urbanization. "Three things kept coming back repeatedly: the issue of the fold, rhizomes, and the notion of smooth and striated space."[72] Urban and periurban changes and swings made increasingly central the issues of flux, wandering, and shifts in space in the alternations between deterritorialization and reterritorialization. Moreover, the rhizome inspires the figure of the proliferating city, this whole invisible system that structures urban territories as they expand. The notion of experimentation, of the way that life traverses, is also completely in phase with the ascendency of uses and practices over theoretical constructivism.

The philosopher Jean Attali, an architecture teacher, used Deleuze and Guattari's thought as a toolbox for thinking the city,[73] confirming their international influence on architects. "Schools of architecture in the United States and England responded tremendously to the translation of *The Fold* when it came out in 1993. The philosophical concept helped reinforce interest in nonmetrical geometries, for computer-aided calculations of 'supple surfaces' or aleatory forms."[74] Today, the New York–based architect Peter Eisenman borrows many concepts from *A Thousand Plateaus* and suggests, for example, a broader definition of the notion of diagram.

Deleuze and Guattari's work is also remarkably productive for the epistemology of the body as Bernard Andrieu conceives it. Recently, Andrieu edited an enormous *Dictionary of the Body*, after having published several books, including the neurophilosophy section of the series "What Do I Know."[75] A professor at the University of Nancy, Andrieu continued his university studies in Bordeaux between 1978 and 1984. When he got involved in the epistemology of the humanities, he used Deleuze's work, especially his concept of the "dividual," which he changed to "dividu" to support his vision of the dispersed body and to resist the reductionism of certain currents in the neurosciences. He agreed with Deleuze's argument that the process of individuation started from divided, fragmented bodies rather than the individual as a whole. In Deleuze and Guattari, Andrieu found a philosophy close to biology and the world of the living, a consideration of Being rather than an epistemology of the living, and he considered their contribution as fundamental as that of Merleau-Ponty, Ruyer, or Pradines for countering efforts at reductionism.

The thought of Deleuze and Guattari is operating in philosophical circles, even among philosophers who appear at first glance quite removed from it. For example, Olivier Mongin, the editor in chief of *Esprit*, draws his inspiration from Ricoeur, Lefort, Merleau-Ponty, and Arendt. Yet Deleuze constantly spurs him to think outside established patterns. "There are two authors that I read regularly and who bring me back to philosophy: Ricoeur and Deleuze."[76]

Mongin agrees neither with Deleuze's political radicalness nor his anti-Christianism but finds in him what he particularly appreciates in Ricoeur: receptiveness to things beyond philosophy, a manner of giving philosophical answers to questions that originate outside of philosophy. Olivier Mongin obviously disagrees with Deleuze's rejection of all mediation. "There is no Christ for him, there's no good mediation, even sacrificed. He's an unconventional thinker."[77] Mongin's interest in Deleuze's thinking led him to an asymmetrical parallel: perhaps his oeuvre could be reduced to expressing excess, while that of Ricoeur embodies debt.[78] Beyond the nonencounter between these two philosophers and their different styles, their opposition cannot be reduced to a marginal confrontation between humanism and a theoretical antihumanism. Both stand out from the philosophical tradition, both welcome the nonphilosophical, both engage in aporiatic thinking, everything in a state of tension, giving priority to the "and," thinking together, the in-betweens. Both reject Hegel, neither is satisfied with Kantian formalism, for both Bergson has a special place, and "the agreement between Deleuze and Ricoeur, if we want to find one, essentially has to do with 'being for life' (Spinoza) and a mistrust of 'being for death' (Heidegger)."[79]

Two blind spots remain in Deleuze's Spinozist perspective: tragedy, evil, is no more pertinent than the question asked by Jean Nabert about the "originary affirmation." It remains the case that Deleuze seriously unsettled the genealogical tree, the law of the father, to stop the feelings of lack and guilt in a heroic gesture that leaves us euphoric and, at the same time, give us the power of life in a society founded on fraternal solidarity, a society of alliance rather than of filiation.

30

Conclusion

Between 1969 and 1992, the year of Guattari's death, two authors with very different backgrounds, personalities, and sensibilities collaborated on an exceptional oeuvre. During this long period, a "disjunctive synthesis," or collective arrangement of enunciation—a term that they defined in a portentous way in their first article, published in 1970, on Klossowski—functioned well. It was an improbable marriage of the orchid and the wasp.

Our study may help correct few blind spots that have led to minimizing and even eliminating Guattari's role, leaving only Deleuze's name. We have seen that, before the two met, Guattari was already a purveyor of novel concepts and directions and was a militant for social, political, and psychiatric experimentation at La Borde, in the CERFI, and in the CINEL. Deleuze and Guattari created "war machines" in a completely original manner, testing the validity and limits of their creations in concrete situations. These experiments bear witness to the exceptional and extraordinary nature of their collaboration.

What made their collaboration so productive? Certainly a whole series of reasons that reason alone cannot explain. How do we understand their friendship and mutual fascination, the essential mainsprings of their common enterprise? We can identify several factors, prime among them being their vigilance to always give precedence to movement against everything leading to routine. From this stems their common interest in the taut, complex relationships between the processes of subjectification and institutional logics and their determination to valorize lines of flight and procedures of destratification.

Their gesture is doubtlessly rooted in the same historical realm, the trauma of World War II, which both authors experienced at a moment when they were too young to participate. Their resistance to barbarity was deferred, and we might even imagine their revolt as a displaced effect of the shattering consequences of the values and triumph of Nazism. It was imperative to create new concepts: the trauma of Nazi barbarity made it necessary to carry out the tasks of thinking. To think requires being worthy of an event traversed too early to have been actively involved in it. This is the imperative at the core of the approach to the history of cinema that Deleuze adopted from André Bazin.[1]

Philosophy must not encounter historical tragedy and remain unarmed. On the contrary, it must affirm its function. "Of course, there is no reason to believe that we can no longer think after Auschwitz, and that we are all responsible for Nazism."[2] But the shame of being human, which Primo Levi expressed blindingly well, remains. We are not necessarily responsible individually, but Nazism sullies us all. "There is indeed catastrophe but it consists in the society of brothers or friends having undergone such an ordeal that brothers and friends can no longer look at one other or at themselves without feeling a sense of 'weariness,' perhaps 'mistrust.'"[3] After Auschwitz, we can no longer claim the candor of the Greeks. Here again, it becomes clear that another metaphysics is necessary, a metaphysics reestablishing a relationship with chaos to create out of it vital rather than mortal forces. "This feeling of shame is one of philosophy's most powerful motifs. We are not responsible for the victims but responsible before them."[4]

For Deleuze, the need to change thinking profoundly was imperious, as his correspondence with Dionys Mascolo shows.[5] After Mascolo's *Concerning an Effort of Memory* was published in 1987, Deleuze wrote him to express his admiration for his having so intensely renewed his relationship between thinking and life. In the letter, he also asked Mascolo about his claim that "such a shakeup of the general sensibility cannot help but lead to new dispositions of thinking."[6] Deleuze felt that Mascolo was hiding something about himself, but Mascolo answered that this apparent secret "is nothing other, perhaps, than that of thinking which mistrusts thinking, profoundly. Which is distressing."[7] Mascolo added that he was not trying to be secretive but that this distress is the foundation of possible friendships.

In his answer, Deleuze suggested that Mascolo reverse the order of things; he urged him to consider putting friendship first rather than second, as the founding element rather than the compensatory one. "There is friendship in you as there is in Blanchot, which implies completely reevaluating 'philosophy' because you are the only ones who take the term *philos* literally."[8] The passage through this experience and its memory require that several canonical theses in the history of thought be critiqued. "How could Heidegger's concepts not be intrinsically sullied by their abject re-territorialization?"[9] To prepare the becomings of freedom imposes the necessity of creation. "We lack resistance to the present. The creation of concepts in itself calls for a future form, for a new world and people that do not yet exist."[10]

Avoiding abjection requires experimenting with created concepts: "To think is to experiment, but experimentation is always that which is in the process of coming about."[11] Essentially philosophical, experimentation cannot win acceptance with some past, present, or future territory.

> I've never been touched by those who claim that you have to get beyond philosophy. So long as there is a need to create concepts philosophy will exist, because that's its definition. And we created them as a function of the problems. And problems change. . . . To do philosophy is to create new concepts as a function of the problems being raised today. This last aspect would be: how do problems evolve? As a result of historical and social forces but also the becoming of thinking, which means that we don't pose the same problems and we don't pose them in the same way. There is a history of thought that cannot be reduced to games of influence. There is a whole becoming of thought that remains mysterious.[12]

While Deleuze and Guattari suffered the effects of the trauma of World War II tangentially and after the fact, they participated fully in May '68. Particularly sensitive to the issues of their period, they immediately understood that these events were creating a rupture and starting something new. Guattari's entire postwar path led him to "prepare" for this event, especially the connection that he had already made between politics and psychoanalysis, which led him later to the critique of all bureaucratic efforts. Deleuze was not the revolutionary militant that Guattari was, but May '68 nonetheless laid the groundwork for their eventual meeting and made it profoundly fruitful. Without May '68, they would never have met: the event was this break in the flux necessary for freeing the combination of their creative forces. Neither Guattari nor Deleuze ever repudiated their deep attachment to an *élan vital*.

Anti-Oedipus, the first work they wrote together, was obviously rooted in May '68 and laid out the modalities of renewed thinking about the world.

In 1984, Deleuze and Guattari wrote that only outlaws say that you can get beyond an event; it penetrates people just as it penetrates a society. Responding to the temptation in the social sciences to be reductive: "May '68 was more on the order of a pure event, free of all normal or normative causality. Its history is a succession of simplified instabilities and fluctuations." There was a lot of agitation in 1968, but that is not what counts. What counts is that it was a phenomenon of sense as if a society suddenly saw the intolerable things within it and the possibility of an alternative. It is a collective phenomenon beneath the form: "Give me something that's possible, or I'll suffocate. What's possible doesn't preexist, it's created by the event. It's a matter of life. The event creates a new existence, it produces a new subjectivity."[13]

Two events made their meeting possible, but what made it so productive? How did this bolt of lightning in the heavens of thought announce a new paradigm? For these two thinkers, the issue was to go as far as possible in decentering humanity, in order to better plunge humankind into a living environment and thereby rediscover lost unity. To dehumanize humans in order to better humanize nature: Pierre Montebello calls this "the most human of metaphysics in the cosmos, and the most cosmic of the metaphysics of man since the Copernican revolution."[14] The issue is not to exhume the old metaphysics that attributes too much importance to the same, to the identity of the model, but rather to construct a new metaphysics, bringing a philosophy of nature to the fore and allowing for the development of differences. "Being is in fact on the side of difference neither one nor multiple."[15] This was the sense of Deleuze's quest, a pure metaphysician, as he said of himself, leading his friend Guattari into an adventure begun in the early 1950s. This quest led him to exhume the forgotten, disdained, and vanquished traditions of Tarde, Nietzsche, and Bergson. Because they tried to formulate a new metaphysics that, instead of severing consciousness from nature, would find the element through which, as Bergson believed, consciousness is not conscious of something but is itself the thing—a major shift from Husserl's phenomenological program.

The world, said Nietzsche, is a "world of relations."[16] This conviction threading throughout Deleuze's work is constantly affirmed in *The Logic of Sense*, in the passage from "is" to "and" and the precedence of "and." Similarly, in the 1976 interview by *Cahiers du Cinéma* on Jean-Luc Godard, well beyond valorizing the relationship, the *and* is proclaimed the matrix of diversity and the inauguration of a new metaphysics. "AND isn't even a specific conjunction or relation, it brings in all relations and there are as many relations as ANDs. AND doesn't just upset relations, it upsets being, the verb . . . and so on. AND, 'and . . . and . . . and. . . .' Is precisely a creative stammering. . . . Multiplicity is precisely in the 'and.' "[17]

Under these conditions, thought and matter, dissociated until now in modern thinking, can correlate with each other. As Pierre Montebello points out, this "other metaphysics" sought a different path than the one taken by phenomenology, by turning its back on intentionality in order to rediscover a less mediated, more direct relation between the movement of things and ideas, which must pass through a temporary suspension of consciousness. "To imagine getting beyond man on the line of the crest of the cosmos, carrying humanity to the height of the immanent power that traverses the universe. To rediscover the creative intertwining of being in mankind to illuminate and liberate in exchange human activity and creativity at the heart of nature." This was the ambition of the "other metaphysics."[18]

Notes

INTRODUCTION: BETWIXT OR BETWEEN

1. Robert Maggiori, interview with the author.
2. Jean-Pierre Muyard, interview with the author.
3. Gilles Deleuze, *Présentation de Sacher-Masoch* (Paris: Minuit, 1967). Translated into English by Jean McNeil as *Coldness and Cruelty* (New York: Zone Books, 2001).
4. Jean-Pierre Muyard, interview with the author.
5. Ibid.
6. Félix Guattari, "Machine et structure," *Change* 12 (1969). Reprinted in Félix Guattari, *Psychoanalyse et transversalité* (Paris: Maspero, 1972), 240–248.
7. English quotations are from Gilles Deleuze, *Difference and Repetition*, trans. Paul Patton (New York: Columbia University Press, 1994); Gilles Deleuze, *The Logic of Sense*, trans. Mark Lester (New York: Columbia University Press, 1990).
8. Félix Guattari, autobiographical interview with Ève Cloarec (October 27, 1984), Institut des manuscrits de l'édition contemporaine (IMEC) archives.
9. Gilles Deleuze with Claire Parnet, *L'abécédaire de Gilles Deleuze* (1988), 3 DVDs (Montparnasse: Arte Video, 1997). This was a video produced by Pierre-André Boutang shown on Arte in 1996. See also http://www.langlab.wayne.edu/CStivale/ D-G/ABC1.html.
10. François Fourquet, letter to Gérard Laborde (August 19, 1969), related by François Fourquet.
11. Jean-Pierre Muyard, interview with the author.
12. Félix Guattari, letter to Gilles Deleuze (April 5, 1969), IMEC archives.
13. Ibid.
14. Gilles Deleuze, letter to Félix Guattari (May 13, 1969), IMEC archives.
15. Ibid.
16. Ibid.
17. Félix Guattari, *Psychoanalyse et transversalité*.
18. Félix Guattari, letter to Gilles Deleuze (June 1, 1969), IMEC archives.

19. Félix Guattari created the FGERI in 1965.

20. Félix Guattari, letter to Gilles Deleuze (June 1, 1969), IMEC archives.

21. Gilles Deleuze, letter to Félix Guattari (July 16, 1969), IMEC archives.

22. Ibid.

23. Ibid.

24. Félix Guattari, letter to Gilles Deleuze (July 19, 1969), information provided by François Fourquet.

25. Félix Guattari, some notes on President Schreber, sent to Gilles Deleuze on July 25, 1969, IMEC archives.

26. Robert Maggiori, interview with the author.

27. CERFI, or *Centre d'études, de recherches, et de formation institutionelles*, was a social-science research group created by Guattari in the late 1960s. See chapter 15.

28. This is confirmed in Stéphane Nadaud, *Écrits pour l'Anti-Oedipe* (Paris: Lignes-Manifeste, 2004).

29. Arlette Donati, interviewed by Ève Cloarec (October 25, 1984), IMEC archives.

30. Alain Aptekman, interview with the author.

31. Félix Guattari, "Deleuze and Guattari s'expliquent," roundtable with François Châtelet, Pierre Clastres, Roger Dadoun, Serge Leclaire, Maurice Nadeau, Raphael Pividal, Pierre Orse, and Horace Torrubia, *La Quinzaine Littéraire* 143 (June 16–30, 1972). Reprinted in Gilles Deleuze, *L'île déserte et autres textes. Textes et entretiens 1953–1974*, ed. David Lapoujade (Paris: Minuit, 2002), 301. Translated by Mike Taormina as *Desert Islands and Other Texts (1953–1974)* (New York: Semiotexte, 2003).

32. Ibid., 304–305.

33. References are to the English translation by Hugh Tomlinson and Graham Burchell (New York: Columbia University Press, 1994).

34. Gilles Deleuze, quoted by Robert Maggiori in *Libération* (September 12, 1991). Reprinted in Robert Maggiori, *La philosophie au jour le jour* (Paris: Flammarion, 1994), 374.

35. Ibid., 374–375.

36. Ibid., 375.

37. Ibid., 375–376.

38. Ibid., 376.

39. Félix Guattari, quoted in ibid., 376.

40. Gilles Deleuze, quoted in ibid., 376.

41. Ibid., 377.

42. Gilles Deleuze, *Cahiers du Cinéma* 271 (November 1976). Reprinted in Gilles Deleuze, *Pourparlers* (Paris: Minuit, 1990), 65. Translated as *Negotiations*, trans. Martin Joughlin (New York: Columbia University Press, 1995), 45.

43. *Agencement* was a fundamental theme for Deleuze. It means the temporary (because of the importance of movement and time) encounter of a number of elements (the importance of disparate elements) that create something resembling a context that bears on, for example, the perception of an object. The term has been translated as *assemblage* and also as *arrangement*, a term that Deleuze approved and the one adopted here. Stéphane Nadaud, *Écrits pour l'Anti-Oedipe*, 12.

44. Gilles Deleuze, in *Le Magazine Littéraire* 257 (September 1988), interviewed by Raymond Bellour and François Ewald. Reprinted in Deleuze, *Pourparlers*, 187; translated in Deleuze, *Negotiations*, 136. All quotations from this translation.

45. Félix Guattari, in Robert Maggiori, *La philosophie au jour le jour*, 378.

46. Gilles Deleuze, letter to Kuniichi Uno (October 25, 1982). Reprinted in Gilles Deleuze, *Deux régimes de fous. Textes et entretiens*, ed. David Lapoujade (Paris: Minuit, 2003), 185. Translated as *Two Regimes of Madness* (New York: Semiotexte, 2006).

47. Ibid., 218.

48. Ibid.

49. Ibid., 219.

50. Gilles Deleuze, *L'arc* (1972): 47. Reprinted in Deleuze, *Pourparlers*, 24; translated in Deleuze, *Negotiations*, 13.

51. Gérard Fromanger, interview with Virginie Linhart.

52. Jean-Pierre Faye, interview with Virginie Linhart.

53. Gilles Deleuze, letter to Kuniichi Uno (October 25, 1982). Reprinted in Gilles Deleuze, *Deux régimes de fous*, 219–220.

54. Ibid., 220.

55. Gilles Deleuze, letter to Félix Guattari (undated), IMEC archives.

56. Félix Guattari, *Journal* (November 13, 1971), NRF no. 564 (January 2003), 357.

57. Félix Guattari, *Journal* (October 6, 1972). Quoted in Stéphane Nadaud, *Écrits pour l'Anti-Oedipe*, 490.

58. Félix Guattari, *Journal* (October 13, 1972); quoted in Stéphane Nadaud, *Écrits pour l'Anti-Oedipe*, 496.

59. Gilles Deleuze, *Difference and Repetition*, xxi.

60. Arnaud Bouaniche, "Le mode d'écriture de *l'Anti-Oedipe*, littéralité et transversalité," presentation at the Bordeaux philosophy workshops, Poitiers, Toulouse, organized by Jean-Christophe Goddard (December 2–3, 2005). See Arnaud Bouaniche, *Gilles Deleuze, une introduction* (Paris: Pocket-La Découverte, 2007).

61. Gilles Deleuze, "Pensée nomade" (1972). Reprinted in Gilles Deleuze, *L'île déserte et autres textes*, 353.

62. Ibid., 354.

63. Félix Guattari, *Journal* (October 14, 1972), quoted in Stéphane Nadaud, *Écrits pour l'Anti-Oedipe*, 497.

64. Gilles Deleuze and Félix Guattari, *Kafka. Pour une littérature mineure* (Paris: Minuit, 1975). Translated by Dana Polan as *Kafka: Toward a Theory of Minor Literature* (Minneapolis: University of Minnesota Press), 1986.

65. Ibid., 149.

66. Gilles Deleuze, letter to Kuniichi Uno, "How we worked together" (July 25, 1984). Reprinted in *Deux régimes de fous*, 220.

67. Ibid.

68. Gilles Deleuze, undated letter to Félix Guattari (early 1980s), IMEC archives.

69. Gilles Deleuze, undated letter to Félix Guattari (1981), IMEC archives.

70. Robert Maggiori, interview with the author.

71. Félix Guattari, typed notes on *What Is Philosophy?* IMEC archives.

72. Gilles Deleuze and Félix Guattari, *Rhizome* (Paris: Minuit, 1976), 29.

73. Gilles Deleuze, letter to Félix Guattari (June 24, 1973), IMEC archives.

74. Gianmarco Montesano, interview with Virginie Linhart.

75. Gianmarco Montesano, interview with Virginie Linhart.

76. Michel Butel, interview with Virginie Linhart.

1. FÉLIX GUATTARI: THE PSYCHOPOLITICAL ITINERARY, 1930–1964

1. Jean Guattari, interview with the author.

2. Jean Guattari, interview with Ève Cloarec (November 15, 1984), IMEC archives.

3. Ibid.

4. Ibid.

5. Félix Guattari, interview with Ève Cloarec, IMEC archives.

6. Félix Guattari, notebook no. 3 (November 27, 1952), IMEC archives.

7. Félix Guattari, notebook no. 3 (December 19, 1952), IMEC archives.

8. Félix Guattari, notebook no. 4 (January 13, 1955), IMEC archives.

9. Félix Guattari, interview with Ève Cloarec, IMEC archives.

10. Ibid.

11. Ibid.

12. Félix Guattari, *La révolution moléculaire* (Paris: Encres, Recherches, 1977), 11–12.

13. Félix Guattari, interview with Ève Cloarec, IMEC archives.

14. Ibid.

15. Ibid.

16. Institutional pedagogy as Oury defined it sought to establish rules for living within a school that encouraged students to speak out and teachers and students to help one

another and to work closely together. Oury hoped that this pedagogy might offer a viable alternative to military schools.

17. Félix Guattari, notebook no. 3 (November 14, 1952), IMEC archives.

18. Félix Guattari, interview with Ève Cloarec, IMEC archives.

19. Ibid.

20. Félix Guattari, 1971 Journal, *La Nouvelle Revue Française* 563 (October 2002): 320.

21. Ibid.

22. Félix Guattari, interview with Ève Cloarec (July 10, 1984), IMEC archives.

23. Micheline Guillet (Kao), interview with Ève Cloarec (September 20, 1984), IMEC archives.

24. Ibid.

25. Jean Guattari, interview with Virginie Linhart.

26. Félix Guattari, interview with Ève Cloarec (August 23, 1984), IMEC archives.

27. Félix Guattari, interview with Ève Cloarec (July 10, 1984), IMEC archives.

28. Félix Guattari, notebook no. 4 (November 1953), IMEC archives.

29. Félix Guattari, notebook no. 1 (January 1951), IMEC archives.

30. Félix Guattari, notebook no. 2 (October 4, 1952), IMEC archives.

31. Félix Guattari, notebook no. 2 (October 8, 1952), IMEC archives.

32. Félix Guattari, notebook no. 2 (October 13, 1952), IMEC archives.

33. Félix Guattari, notebook no. 2 (October 24, 1952), IMEC archives.

34. Félix Guattari, "Plutôt avoir tort avec lui," *Libération* (June 23–24, 1990).

35. *Ouvriers face aux appareils, une expérience de militantisme chez Hispano-Suiza* (Paris: Maspero, 1970), 39.

36. Félix Guattari, notebook no. 3 (November 27, 1952), IMEC archives.

37. Félix Guattari, "1971 Diary, [September 10–13]," *La Nouvelle Revue Française* 563 (October 2002): 349.

38. Félix Guattari, interview with Ève Cloarec (August 23, 1984), IMEC archives.

39. Jean Guattari, interview with Ève Cloarec (November 15, 1984), IMEC archives.

40. Félix Guattari, notebook no. 4 (November 26, 1954), IMEC archives.

41. Denis Berger, interview.

42. *La Voie Communiste* 1 (January 1958), BDIC archives.

43. Headlines of *La Voie Communiste* 3 (April–May 1958), BDIC archives.

44. *La Voie Communiste* 20 (February 1961), BDIC archives.

45. See chapter 2.

46. Denis Berger, interview with the author.

47. On March 17, 1960, a telegram signed by Élie Bloncourt, Claude Bourdet, Albert Châtelet, Gilles Martinet, Daniel Meyer, Marcel Prenant, Oreste Rosenfeld,

Jean-Paul Sartre, and Laurent Schwartz was addressed to the president of the French Republic, to the attorney general, and to the minister of the armies demanding the liberation of Gérard Spitzer, published in *La Voie Communiste* 12 (April 1960), BDIC archives.

48. "The Manifesto of the 120," *La Voie Communiste* 16 (September 1960). This was the first publication of this text, which takes a position on insubordination.

49. Michel Cartry, interview with the author.

50. Ibid.

51. Alfred Adler, interview with the author.

52. Ibid.

53. Ibid.

54. Claude Vivien, interview with Virginie Linhart.

55. Ibid.

56. Gérard Spitzer had the aura of a former member of the resistance. His father, a Jewish Hungarian doctor, had been deported, and he joined the Resistance in Grenoble in 1943. When he was fifteen, he was the proletarian sharpshooter (*franc-tireur prolétarien*) responsible for Paris.

57. Interview with Mohammed Boudiaf, *La Voie Communiste* 31 (November–December 1962), BDIC archives.

58. *La Voie Communiste* 23 (June–July 1961), BDIC archives.

59. *La Voie Communiste* 36 (June–July 1963), BDIC archives.

60. Félix Guattari, interview with Ève Cloarec (July 10, 1984), IMEC archives.

61. Ibid.

62. Jean Oury, *Il, donc* (Paris: Matrices, 1978), 25.

63. Félix Guattari, notebook no. 2 (October 2, 1952), IMEC archives.

64. Jean Oury, interview with the author.

65. Félix Guattari, interview with Ève Cloarec (August 29, 1984), IMEC archives.

66. Félix Guattari, notebook no. 3 (March 28, 1953), IMEC archives.

67. Félix Guattari, notebook no. 3 (late September 1953), IMEC archives.

68. Claude Vivien, interview with Virginie Linhart.

69. Félix Guattari, notebook no. 4 (May 1954), IMEC archives.

70. Félix Guattari, "Lacan 1954–55 notebook," class notes (December 15, 1954), IMEC archives.

71. Félix Guattari, "Lacan 1954–55 notebook," class notes (January 12, 1955), IMEC archives.

72. Félix Guattari, "Lacan 1954–55 notebook," class notes (January 20, 1955), IMEC archives.

73. Félix Guattari, "Machine et structure," lecture for the *Ecole Freudienne de Paris*, 1969, published in *Change* 12. Reprinted in Félix Guattari, *Psychanalyse et transversalité* (Paris: Maspero, 1972; repr. Paris: La Découverte: 2003).

2. LA BORDE: BETWEEN MYTH AND REALITY

1. See Anne-Marie Norgeu and Roger Gentis, *La Borde: le château des chercheurs de sens? La vie quotidienne à la clinique psychiatrique de La Borde* (Paris: Érès, 2006).

2. François Tosquelles, in François Fourquet and Lion Murard, *Histoires de la psychiatrie de secteur* (Paris: Recherches, 1975), 22.

3. Hermann Simon, *La psychothérapie de l'asile* (Paris: Société générale d'imprimerie et d'édition, 1933).

4. François Tosquelles, in François Fourquet and Lion Murard, *Histoires de la psychiatrie de secteur*, 68.

5. Ibid., 72.

6. Jean Oury, *Il, donc* (Paris: Matrices, 1978), 73.

7. Including Jean Ayme, Robert Million, Maurice Despinoy, Claude Poncin, Roger Gentil, and Horace Torrubia, among others.

8. The prestigious teacher-training institute on the rue d'Ulm in Paris, referred to henceforth as the ENS.

9. Jean Oury, interview with the author.

10. Ibid.

11. Jean Oury, in François Tosquelles, *Histoires de la psychiatrie de secteur*.

12. Jean Oury (called Odin), *Histoires de La Borde*, in *Recherches* 21 (March–April 1976): 35.

13. Félix Guattari, "La grille," lecture at La Borde training (January 1987), IMEC archives.

14. Jean Oury, interview with the author.

15. Ibid.

16. Jean Oury, *Histoires de La Borde*, 26.

17. Ibid., 31.

18. Jean Oury, "Créativité et folie," transcript of debate with Félix Guattari (July 1, 1983), IMEC archives.

19. See Jean Oury, *Essai sur la conation esthétique*, *Le Pli* (2005).

20. Ginette Michaud, "La notion d'institution dans ses rapports avec la théorie moderne des groupes," thesis for diploma of advanced studies (DES), 1958, quoted in *Histoires de La Borde*, 61.

21. Jean-Claude Polack and Danielle Sivadon-Sabourin, *La Borde ou le droit à la folie* (Paris: Calmann-Levy, 1976), 41.

22. Félix Guattari, interview with Ève Cloarec (August 29, 1984), IMEC archives.

23. Ibid.

24. Félix Guattari, "Sur les rapports infirmiers-médecins" (1955), in Félix Guattari, *Psychanalyse et transversalité* (Paris: Maspero, 1972; repr. Paris: La Découverte: 2003), 11.

25. Jean Oury, *Histoires de La Borde*, 15.

26. Ibid.

27. Ibid.

28. Ibid.

29. Jack Brière, interview with Virginie Linhart.

30. Ibid.

31. Ibid.

32. Jacques Baratier, *Rien, voilà l'ordre* (2004).

33. Jean Oury, interview with the author.

34. Ibid.

35. Michel Cartry, interview with the author.

36. Michel Cartry, interview with the author.

37. Michel Cartry, interview with Virginie Linhart.

38. Michel Cartry, interview with the author.

39. Ginette Michaud, interview with Virginie Linhart.

40. Marie Depussé, *Dieu gît dans les détails* (Paris: P.O.L, 1993), 9.

41. Marie Depussé, in Jean Oury and Marie Depussé, *À quelle heure passe le train . . .* (Paris: Calmann-Levy, 2003), 216–217.

42. Marie Depussé, *Dieu gît dans les détails*, 39.

43. Marie Depussé, interview with Virginie Linhart.

44. Marie Depussé, *Dieu gît dans les détails*; Jean Oury and Marie Depussé, *À quelle heure passe le train. . . .*

45. Marie Depussé, interview with Virginie Linhart.

46. Michel Butel, interview with Virginie Linhart.

47. Ibid.

48. Jean-Claude Polack, interview with the author.

49. Jean-Claude Polack and Danielle Sivadon-Sabourin, *La Borde ou le droit à la folie*. This book contains prefaces by Félix Guattari and Jean Oury.

50. Liane Mozère, interview with the author.

51. François Fourquet, interview with the author.

52. Ibid.

53. Michel Rostain, interview with the author.

54. Lion Murard, interview with the author.

55. François Pain, interview with the author.

3. Daily Life at La Borde

1. Félix Guattari, "La S.C.A.J. Messieurs-Dames," in *Bulletin du personnel soignant des cliniques du Loir-et-Cher* 1 (1957). Reprinted in Félix Guattari, *Psychanalyse et transversalité* (Paris: Maspero, 1972; repr. Paris: La Découverte: 2003), 36.

2. Ibid., 37.

3. Ibid.

4. Jean Oury, interview with the author.

5. Ibid.

6. Jean Oury, *Histoires de La Borde*, in *Recherches* 21 (March–April 1976): 133.

7. Ibid., 142.

8. Nicole Guillet, interview with the author.

9. Ibid.

10. Ibid.

11. Félix Guattari, "La Grille," lecture on "the grid" at La Borde training session (January 1987), IMEC archives.

12. Oscar (Felix Guattari), *Histoires de La Borde*, 226.

13. Jean-Claude Polack and Danielle Sivadon-Sabourin, *La Borde ou le droit à la folie* (Paris: Calmann-Levy, 1976), 40.

14. *Histoires de La Borde*, 247.

15. Liane Mozère, *Le printemps des crèches* (Paris: L'Harmattan, 1992), 109.

16. Félix Guattari, interview with Ève Cloarec (August 29, 1984), IMEC archives.

17. Nicole Guillet, interview with the author.

18. Liane Mozère, interview with the author.

19. Marie Depussé, interview with Virginie Linhart.

20. The initial GTPSI included François Tosquelles, Jean Oury, Roger Gentis, Horace Torrubia, Jean Ayme, Hélène Chaigneau, Philippe Koechlin, Robert Million, Maurice Paillot, Yves Racine, Jean Colemin, and Michel Baudry. This group was later joined by several other psychiatrists, including Giséla Pankow, Jean-Claude Polack, Denise Rothberg, and Nicole Guillet. Information provided by Olivier Apprill.

21. Roger Gentis, *Un psychiatre dans le siècle* (Paris: Erès, 2005), 38.

22. See chapter 18.

23. Félix Guattari, "Introduction a la psychotherapie institutionnelle" (1962–1963), in Félix Guattari, *Psychanalyse et transversalité*, 42.

24. Olivier Appril, interview with the author.

25. Ibid.

26. *Histoire de La Borde*, 273.

27. Félix Guattari, "La Grille," lecture at a La Borde training session, January 1987, IMEC archives.

28. See François Dosse, *Histoire du structuralisme*, vol. 1: *La découverte* (Paris, 1991). Translated as *History of Structuralism*, trans. Deborah Glassman (Minneapolis: University of Minnesota Press, 1997).

29. Félix Guattari, "La transversalité" (1964), in Félix Guattari, *Psychanalyse et transversalité*, 72–85.

30. Ibid., 79.

31. Ibid., 80.

32. Ibid., 84.

33. Jean-Baptiste Thierrée, interview with the author.

34. Ibid.

35. Ibid.

36. Guattari was having an affair with the companion of the psychiatrist Jeangirard, Jacqueline Moulin, then with Ginette Michaud; Micheline was involved with Ben Milard, an Algerian psychiatrist.

37. Micheline Guillet (Kao), interview with Virginie Linhart.

38. Marie Depussé, interview with the author.

39. Nicole Guillet, interview with the author.

40. Her mother, Bérangère, came to work there: her sister Genevieve married the cook René; her other sister, Jeannine, married Ettore Pellandini, and the person in charge of the feasts at La Borde was the wife of the psychiatrist Bidault, Michelle.

41. Marie Depussé, in Jean Oury and Marie Depussé, *À quelle heure passe le train . . .* (Paris: Calmann-Levy, 2003), 214.

42. Bruno Guattari, interview with Virginie Linhart.

43. Ibid.

44. Félix Guattari, interview with Ève Cloarec (August 29, 1984), IMEC archives.

45. Arlette Donati, interview with Ève Cloarec (October 25, 1984), IMEC archives.

46. Félix Guattari, "Journal de 1971" (September 25, 1971), in *La Nouvelle Revue Française* 564 (January 2003): 25.

47. Bruno Guattari, interview with Virginie Linhart.

48. Félix Guattari, "Journal de 1971" (September 2, 1971), in *La Nouvelle Revue Française* 563 (October 2002): 336.

49. Arlette Donati, interview with Ève Cloarec (October 25, 1984), IMEC archives.

50. Ibid.

51. Ibid.

52. Jean Oury, interview with the author.

53. Ibid.

54. Danielle Sivadon, interview with the author.

55. Ibid.

56. Marie Depussé, interview with Virginie Linhart.

57. Félix Guattari, "Journal de 1971" (September 25, 1971), in *La Nouvelle Revue Française* 564 (October 2002): 36.

58. Félix Guattari, interview with Ève Cloarec (October 1, 1984), IMEC archives.

59. Arlette Donati, interview with Ève Cloarec (October 25, 1984), IMEC archives.

60. Jean Oury, in Jean Oury and Marie Depussé, *À quelle heure passe le train* . . . , 243.

61. Ibid., 247.

62. Jean-Claude Polack, interview with the author.

63. Jean Oury, in Jean Oury and Marie Depussé, *À quelle heure passe le train* . . . , 255.

64. Félix Guattari, interview with Ève Cloarec (October 1, 1984), IMEC archives.

65. *Le Moindre Geste*, film by Fernand Deligny, Josée Manenti, and Jean-Pierre Daniel.

66. Josée Manenti, interview with the author.

67. Born in 1913 in Bergues on the Belgian border, Fernand Deligny became a teacher in Nogent, near Paris, in 1936, and then at the Medical-Pedagogical Institute of Armentières. In 1941, he was working at the psychiatric hospital in Armentières in a building that housed young psychotics and young delinquents who were considered unrecuperable.

68. Josée Manenti, "Fernand Delignny . . . ," *Chimères* 30 (Spring 1997): 104.

69. Nicole Guillet, interview with the author.

70. Josée Manenti, interview with the author.

71. Jean Oury, interview with the author.

72. Ibid.

73. François Pain, interview with the author.

74. Fernand Deligny, letter to Félix Guattari (October 9, 1977), IMEC archives.

75. Fernand Deligny, letter to Félix Guattari (October 31, 1977), IMEC archives.

76. Ibid.

77. Félix Guattari, *La revolution moléculaire* (Paris: Recherches, 1977).

78. Fernand Deligny, letter to Félix Guattari (October 31, 1977), IMEC archives.

79. Fernand Deligny, letter to Félix Guattari (April 9, 1978), IMEC archives.

80. Félix Guattari, letter to Fernand Deligny (1979), IMEC archives.

4. Testing Critical Research Empirically

1. Félix Guattari, "La transversalité" (1964). Reprinted in Félix Guattari, *Psychanalyse et transversalité* (Paris: Maspero, 1972; repr. Paris: La Découverte, 2003), 72–85.

2. *Recherches* 6 (June 1967): 316.

3. Guy Trastour, in *Recherches* 1 (January 1966): 2.

4. Editorial, *Recherches* 1 (January 1966): 2.

5. Ibid., 3. The FEGERI founders included many psychiatrists: Jean Ayme, Jean Oury, Gilbert Diatkine, Nicolle Guillet, Claude Poncin, Catherine Poncin, Jean-Claude Polack, Afelio Torrubia, Horace Torrubia, Germaine Le Guillant, Jean-Pierre

Muyard; ethnologists: Michel Cartry, Alfred Adler, Françoise Izard, Michel Izard, Olivier Herrenschmidt; architects: Gérard Buffiere, Catherine Cot, Jacques Depussé, René Poux, Alain Scheidt, Estelle Scheidt, Ametico Zublena; many students; a few economists and sociologists; psychologists; statisticians; educators; and a few writers such as Roland Dubillard, Thomas Buchanan, and Jean Perret. The FGERI was not strictly centralized, and it created many groups in the provinces: the first were created in Blois, Dijon, Lyon, Nancy, Nantes, Nice, Rennes, Strasbourg, and Tours.

6. Félix Guattari, "La causalité, la subjectivité et l'histoire" (1966). Reprinted in Félix Guattari, *Psychanalyse et transversalité*, 175.

7. Ibid., 182.

8. Editorial, *Recherches* 1 (January 1966): 1.

9. See Hervé Hamon and Patrick Rotman, *Génération* (Paris: Seuil, 1987), 1:128.

10. Marc Kravetz, in *Cahiers de l'UNEF* (December 1963). Quoted by Alain Monchablon, *Histoire de l'UNEF* (Paris: PUF, 1983), 150.

11. Guy Trastour, interview with the author.

12. This activity was extended by a mental-health newsletter to ensure that the information and reflection of the work being done by various commissions was connected and to disseminate the results of the university working groups' research.

13. Hervé Hamon and Patrick Rotman, *Génération*, 1:209–210.

14. Ibid., 1:240.

15. Liane Mozère, interview with the author.

16. François Fourquet, interview with the author.

17. Félix Guattari, "Les neuf thèses de l'opposition de gauche" (1996). In Félix Guattari, *Psychanalyse et transveralité*, 108.

18. Ibid., 111.

19. Ibid., 121.

20. Félix Guattari, "Présentation," *Recherches* 6 (June 1967): 4.

21. Ibid., 9.

22. The network included those recruited by the militant action in the UNEF, MGEN, and UEC, and then by the creation of the OG: François Fourquet, Liane Mozère, Hervé Maury, Michel Rostain, Anne Querrien, and Lion Murard all came to train at La Borde.

23. Janet H. Morford, "Histoire du Cerfi. La trajectoire d'un collectif de recherche sociale," *EHESS/DEA* (October 1985): 55.

24. Michel Rostain, in Janet H. Morford, "Histoire du CERFI," 57.

25. Hervé Maury, in Janet H. Morford, "Histoire du CERFI," 75.

5. Gilles Deleuze: The Hero's Brother

1. Michel Tournier, interview with the author. Michel Tournier, *Célébrations* (Paris: Gallimard, 2000), 425.

2. Jean-Pierre Faye, interview with the author.

3. Claude Lemoine, interview with the author.

4. Gilles Deleuze with Claire Parnet, *L'abécédaire de Gilles Deleuze* (1988), 3 DVDs (Montparnasse: Arte Video, 1997).

5. Ibid.

6. Ibid.

7. René Schérer, *Regards sur Deleuze* (Paris: Kimé, 1998), 12.

8. Gilles Deleuze, class at Paris-VIII (June 3, 1980), National French Library video archives.

9. Gilles Deleuze with Claire Parnet, *L'abécédaire de Gilles Deleuze*.

10. Ibid.

11. Ibid.

12. Michel Tournier, interview with the author.

13. Michel Tournier, *Le vent Paraclet* (Paris: Gallimard, 1977), 155.

14. Marc-Alain Descamps, *Marie-Magdeleine Davy ou la liberté du dépaysement* (Paris: Le miel de la Pierre, 2000), 97.

15. Maurice de Gandillac, interview with the author.

16. Gilles Deleuze, "Presentation," *Espace* 1 (1946): 11.

17. Gilles Deleuze, "Du Christ à la bourgeoisie," *Espace* 1 (1946): 93.

18. Ibid., 97.

19. Ibid., 105.

20. Ibid., 106.

21. Michel Tournier, interview with the author.

22. Michel Tournier, *Le vent Paraclet*, 160.

23. Michel Tournier, *Célébrations*, 425.

24. Gilles Deleuze, "Description de la femme. Pour une philosophie d'autrui sexuée," *Poésie* 45, no. 28 (October–November 1945): 28–39.

25. Ibid., 33.

26. Ibid., 32.

27. Michel Tournier, *Le vent Paraclet*, 160.

28. Gilles Deleuze, "Du Christ à la bourgeoisie," 93–106; Gilles Deleuze, "Dires et profiles," *Poésie* 47 (1947).

29. Gilles Deleuze, "Il a été mon maître," *Arts* (November 28, 1964): 8–9. Reprinted in Gilles Deleuze, *L'île déserte et autres textes. Textes et entretiens, 1953–1974*, ed. David Lapoujade (Paris: Minuit, 2002), 109–113. Translated as *Desert Islands*

and Other Texts (1953–1974), trans. Mike Taormina (New York: Semiotexte, 2003).

30. Ibid., 110.

31. Ibid., 112.

32. Gilles Deleuze, quoted by Giuseppe Bianco, "Jean Hyppolite et Ferdinand Alquié," in Stéphan Leclerc, ed., *Aux sources de la pensée de Gilles Deleuze* (Mons: Sils Maria, 2005), 92n2.

33. Jean-Pierre Faye, interview with the author.

34. Kostas Axelos, *Vers la pensée planétaire* (Paris: Minuit, 1964).

35. Gilles Deleuze, "En créant la pataphysique Jarry a ouvert la voie à la phénomenologie," *Arts* (May 27–June 2, 1964): 5. Reprinted in Gilles Deleuze, *L'île déserte et autres textes*, 105–108. Gilles Deleuze, "Un précurseur méconnu de Heidegger, Alfred Jarry," in Gilles Deleuze, *Critique et clinique* (Paris: Minuit, 1993), 115–125.

36. Gilles Deleuze, "Un précurseur méconnu de Heidegger, Alfred Jarry," 115.

37. Ibid., 123.

38. Serge Rezvani, *Le testament amoureux* (Paris: Stock, 1981), 24.

39. Ibid., 126.

40. Olivier Revault d'Allonnes, interview with the author.

41. François Châtelet, *Chronique de idées perdues* (Paris: Stock, 1977), 46.

42. Olivier Revault d'Allonnes, interview with the author.

43. Ibid.

44. Olivier Revault d'Allonnes, interview with the author.

45. Ibid.

46. *Pere Ubu* is the title of Alfred Jarry's 1896 play about a grotesque king and his queen; the play is said to herald the Dada and Surrealism movements. Michel Tournier, *Le vent Paraclet*, 162.

47. Michel Tournier, "Gilles Deleuze: Avez-vous des questions à poser?" *France Culture*, Jean Daive broadcast (April 20, 2002).

48. Alain Aptekman, interview with the author.

49. Serge Rezvani, *Le testament amoureux*, 219.

50. Gilles Deleuze, introduction to Docteur Jean Malfatti de Montereggio, *Études sur la mathèse* (Paris: Griffon d'or, 1946).

51. Ibid., xi.

52. Ibid., xv.

53. Ibid., xx.

54. Gilles Deleuze, introduction to Diderot, *La religieuse* (Paris: Marcel Daubin, 1947).

55. Michel Marié, interview with the author.

56. Michel Marié, *Les terres et les mots. Une traversée des sciences sociales* (Paris: Méridiens-Klincksieck, 1989), 82.

57. Ibid.

58. Claude Lemoine, interview with the author.

59. Ibid.

60. Alain Roger, "Gilles Deleuze et l'amitié," in Yannick Beaubatie, ed., *Tombeau de Gilles Deleuze* (Tulle: Mille Sources, 2000), 36.

61. Alain Roger, interview with the author.

62. Ibid.

63. Ibid.

64. Ibid.

65. Gilles Deleuze, comments on the dissertation of Alain Roger (October 26, 1954).

66. Gilles Deleuze, comments provided by Alain Roger, interview with the author.

67. Alain Roger, "Gilles Deleuze et l'amitié," 40.

68. François Regnault, interview with the author.

69. Michel Ciment, interview with the author.

70. Gilles Deleuze, *Différence et répétition* (Paris: PUF, 1968), 3. Translated as *Difference and Repetition*, trans. Paul Patton (New York: Columbia University Press, 1994), xx. All English translations are taken from this edition.

71. Michel Ciment, interview with the author

72. François Regnault, interview with the author.

73. Ibid.

74. François Regnault, interview with the author.

75. Gilles Deleuze, letter to Maurice de Gandillac, quoted in Maurice de Gandillac, *Le siecle traversé. Souvenirs de neuf décennies* (Paris: Albin Michel, 1998), 357.

6. THE ART OF THE PORTRAIT

1. Gilles Deleuze with Claire Parnet, *L'abécédaire de Gilles Deleuze* (1988), 3 DVDs (Montparnasse: Arte Video, 1997).

2. Ibid.

3. Gilles Deleuze, "Lettre à un critique severe" (1973), in *Pourparlers, 1972–1990* (Paris: Minuit, 1990), 14. Translated as "Letter to a Harsh Critic," in *Negotiations, 1972–1990*, trans. Martin Joughin (New York: Columbia University Press, 1995), 5. All English translations are taken from this version.

4. Gilles Deleuze, *Negotiations*, 6.

5. Thomas Bénatouil, "L'histoire de la philosophie: de l'art du portrait au collage," *Le Magazine Littéraire* (February 2002): 36.

6. René Schérer, *Regards sur Deleuze* (Paris: Kimé, 1998), 12.

7. Jean Hyppolite, *Figures de la pensée philosophique*, vol. 1, *Du bergsonisme à l'existentialisme* (1949; repr. Paris: PUF, 1991), 443–459; Jean Hyppolite, "Vie et philosophie de l'histoire chez Bergson" (1949), 459–467; Jean Hyppolite, "Aspects divers de la mémoire chez Bergson" (1949), 468–488; Jean Hyppolite, "Vie et existence d'après Bergson," (1950), 488–498.

8. Information from Guiseppe Bianco, "Trous et mouvement: sur le dandysme deleuzien. Les cours de la Sorbonne 1957–1960," in Stéphan Leclerc, ed., *Aux sources de la pensée de Gilles Deleuze* (Mons: Sils Maria, 2005), 93.

9. Gilles Deleuze, letter of July 17, 1972, Jean Wahl archive, IMEC. Information from Giuseppe Bianco, "Philosophies du ET. Que se passe-t-il entre (Jean Wahl et Deleuze)?" on the occasion of Jean Wahl Day, organized by Frédéric Worms and Giuseppe Bianco (April 16, 2005), ENS. Giuseppe Bianco, "Jean Hyppolite et Ferdinand Alquié," in Stéphan Leclerc, ed., *Aux sources de la pensée de Gilles Deleuze*.

10. André Cresson and Gilles Deleuze, *David Hume, sa vie, son oeuvre* (Paris: PUF, 1952).

11. Ibid., 41.

12. Michel Tournier, "Gilles Deleuze," *Critique* no. 591–592 (August-September 1996): 699.

13. Gilles Deleuze, *Empirisme et subjectivité* (Paris: PUF, 1953). Translated as *Empiricism and Subjectivity: An Essay on Hume's Theory of Human Nature*, trans. Constantin V. Boundas (New York: Columbia University Press, 1991).

14. Ibid., 106.

15. Gilles Deleuze, letter to Arnaud Villani (December 29, 1986); in Arnaud Villani, *La guêpe et l'orchidée* (Paris: Belin, 1999), 56.

16. Arnaud Villani, "Une généalogie de la philosohie deleuzienne: *Empirisme et subjectivité*," in *Concepts*, "Gilles Deleuze I" (Mons: Sils Maris, 2002), 108.

17. Gilles Deleuze, *Empiricism and Subjectivity*, 22.

18. Ibid., 23.

19. Ibid., 37.

20. Ibid., 38.

21. Manola Antonioli, *Deleuze et l'histoire de la philosophie* (Paris: Kimé, 1999), 30.

22. Ibid., 31.

23. Gilles Deleuze, *Empiricism and Subjectivity*, 40.

24. Ibid., 45.

25. Ibid.

26. Gilles Deleuze's comments, as told by Dominique Séglard, interview with the author.

27. Ibid.

28. *Instincts et institutions*, selected texts with an introduction by Gilles Deleuze (Paris: Classiques Hachette, 1953).

29. Ibid., viii.

30. Ibid., ix.

31. Ibid., xi.

32. Gilles Deleuze, *Empiricism and Subjectivity*, 85.

33. Ibid., 93.

34. Ibid., 103.

35. Ibid., 87–88.

36. Gilles Deleuze, *Différence et répétition* (Paris: PUF, 1968). Translated as *Difference and Repetition*, trans. Paul Patton (New York: Columbia University Press, 1994). All English translations are taken from this edition.

37. François Châtelet, *Histoire de la philosophie*, vol. 5: *Les lumières* (Paris: Hachette, 1972), 65–78. Reprinted in Gilles Deleuze, *L'île déserte et autres textes. Textes et entretiens 1953–1974*, ed. David Lapoujade (Paris: Minuit, 2002), 226–237. Translated as *Desert Islands and Other Texts (1953–1974)*, trans. Mike Taormina (New York: Semiotexte, 2003).

38. Gilles Deleuze, *L'île déserte et autres textes*, 226.

39. Patricia de Martelaere, "Gilles Deleuze, interprète de Hume," *Revue Philosophique de Louvain* 82 (February 1984): 224.

40. Arnaud Villani, "Une généalogie de la philosophie deleuzienne: *Empirisme et subjectivité*," 120.

41. Gilles Deleuze, *Negotiations*, 138.

42. Olivier Revault d'Allonnes, interview with the author.

43. Marc-Alain Descamps, interview with the author.

44. Rafaël Pividal, interview with the author.

45. Giuseppe Bianco, "Philosophies du ET. Que se passe-t-il entre (Jean Wahl et Deleuze)?"

46. A few traces of these classes exist can be found in the ENS-Fontenay Saint-Cloud archives in the ENS-LSH library in Lyon. On Bergson: 19 typed pages, published by Frédéric Worms, ed., *Annales bergsoniennes II. Bergson, Deleuze, la phénoménologie* (Paris: PUF, 2004), 166–188; On Rousseau: 27 typed pages; on Kant, 24 typed pages; on Hume, 38 typed pages.

47. Gilles Deleuze, "Jean-Jacques Rousseau précurseur de Kafka, de Céline et de Ponge," *Arts*, no. 872 (June 6–12, 1962): 3. Reprinted in Gilles Deleuze, *L'île déserte et autres textes*, 73–78.

48. *Doctorat d'études supérieures* (DES), a doctoral-level degree.

49. Giuseppe Bianco, "Trous et mouvement: sur le dandysme deleuzien. Les cours de la Sorbonne 1957–1960," 95.

50. Gilles Deleuze, "*Descartes, l'homme et l'oeuvre*, par Ferdinand Alquié," *Cahiers du Sud* 337 (October 1956): 473–475.

51. Ibid.

52. Ferdinand Alquié, in Gilles Deleuze, "La méthode de dramatization," in *L'île déserte et autres textes*, 148.

53. Ibid., 149.

54. Gilles Deleuze, "Jean Hyppolite, logique et existence," *Revue Philosophique de la France et de l'Étranger* 7–9 (July–September 1954): 457–460. Reprinted in Gilles Deleuze, *L'île déserte et autres textes*, 18–23.

55. Ibid., 20.

56. Ibid., 24.

57. Alain Roger, interview with the author.

58. François Regnault, interview with the author.

59. Gilles Deleuze, "De Sacher-Masoch au masochisme," *Arguments* 21 (1961). After this first study, Deleuze developed his work on Sacher-Masoch in 1967. Gilles Deleuze, *Présentation de Sacher-Masoch* (Paris: Minuit, 1967). Translated into English by Jean McNeil as *Coldness and Cruelty* (New York: Zone Books, 2001).

60. The fashion for Sade has grown since the 1930s. Several important studies have been written, including Pierre Klossozski, "Elements d'une étude psychanalytique sur le marquis de Sade," *Revue de Psychanalyse* (1933); Pierre Klossozski, *Un si funeste désir* (Paris: Gallimard, 1963); Maurice Blanchot, *Lautréamont et Sade* (1947); Simone de Beauvoir, *Faut-il brûler Sade?* (1955); Georges Bataille, *La littérature et le mal* (1957); Jacques Lacan, "Kant avec Sade," *Critique* 191 (1963); Michel Foucault, "De Sade à Freud," *Critique* 195–196 (1963); *Oeuvres complètes de Sade* (1967); Roland Barthes, *Sade, Fourier, Loyola* (1971).

61. Gilles Deleuze, letter to Arnaud Villani (December 29, 1986). In Arnaud Villani, *La guêpe et l'orchidée*, 56.

62. Ibid., 11.

63. Anne Sauvagnargues, *Deleuze et l'art* (Paris: PUF, 2005), 44.

64. Gilles Deleuze, *Présentation de Sacher-Masoch*, 15.

65. Theodor Reik, *Le masochisme* (Paris: Payot, 2000).

66. Gilles Deleuze, "De Sacher-Masoch au masochisme."

67. Gilles Deleuze, *Présentation de Sacher-Masoch*, 30.

68. Ibid., 57.

69. Ibid., 99.

70. Ibid., 51.

71. Gilles Deleuze, *La philosophie critique de Kant* (Paris: PUF, 1963), 23. Translated as *Kant's Critical Philosophy: The Doctrine of the Faculties*, trans. Hugh Tomlinson (Minneapolis: University of Minnesota Press, 1985).

72. Gilles Deleuze, interview and remarks assembled by Jean-Noël Vuarnet, *Les Lettres Francaise* (February 28–March 5, 1968). Reprinted in Gilles Deleuze, *L'île déserte et autres textes*, 192.

73. Gilles Deleuze, "L'idée de genèse dans l'esthetique de Kant," *Revue d'Esthetique* 2 (April–June 1963). Reprinted in Gilles Deleuze, *L'île déserte et autres textes*, 79–101.

74. Gilles Deleuze, "Sur quatre formules poétiques qui pourraient résumer la philosophie kantienne," *Philosophie* 9 (Winter 1986). Reprinted in Gilles Deleuze, *Critique et clinique* (Paris: Minuit, 1993).

75. Gilles Deleuze, *La philosophie critique de Kant*, 23.

76. Ibid., 54.

77. Gilles Deleuze, *Difference and Repetition*, chap. 2, "Repetition for Itself," 70–128.

78. Guillaume Sibertin-Blanc, interview with the author.

79. Vincent Descombes, *Le même et l'autre* (Paris: Minuit, 1979), 178.

80. Manola Antonioli, *Deleuze et l'histoire de la philosophie*, 87.

81. Jean-Clet Martin, *Variations. La philosophie de Gilles Deleuze* (Paris: Payot, 1993), 34.

82. Gilles Deleuze, *Logique du sens* (Paris: Minuit, 1969). Translated as *The Logic of Sense*, trans. Mark Lester with Charles Stivale (New York: Columbia University Press, 1990), 103.

83. Gilles Deleuze, *Proust et les signes* (Paris: PUF, 1964). Translated as *Proust and Signs*, trans. Richard Howard (Minneapolis: University of Minnesota Press, 2000).

84. On the unity of the plan to work on "the image of thought," which is the thread running through *Nietzsche and Philosophy, Proust and Signs*, and *Difference and Repetition*, see Arnaud Bouaniche, *Gilles Deleuze, une introduction* (Paris: Pocket-La Découverte, 2007), 45–52.

85. Gilles Deleuze, *Proust et les signes* (1970 edition), 7.

86. Ibid., 21.

87. Ibid., 9.

88. Ibid., 190.

89. Ibid., 186.

90. Ibid., 190.

91. Robert Mauzi, *Critique* 225 (February 1996): 161.

92. Jean-Claude Dumoncel, interview with the author.

93. Jean-Claude Dumoncel, *Le symbole d'Hécate. Philosophie deleuzienne et roman proustien* (Orleans: HYX, 1996), 60.

94. Gilles Deleuze, *Proust et les signes*, 69.

95. Ibid., 71.

96. Ibid., 73.

97. See Dork Zabunyan and Gilles Deleuze, *Voir, parler, penser au risque du cinéma* (Paris: Presse de la Sorbonne nouvelle, 2006).

98. Gilles Deleuze, interview with Jean-Noel Vuarnet, *Les Lettres Françaises* (February 28–March 5, 1968). Reprinted in Gilles Deleuze, *L'île déserte et autres textes*, 193.

99. Gilles Deleuze, *Proust et les signes*, 184n1.

100. Ibid., 137.

7. NIETZSCHE, BERGSON, SPINOZA: A TRIO FOR A VITALIST PHILOSOPHY

1. Prospectus of the Société francaise d'études nietzschéennes, cited by Jacques Le Rider, *Nietzsche en France. De la fin du XIXe siècle au temps présent* (Paris: PUF, 1999), 185.

2. Jean Wahl, *La pensée philosophique de Nietzsche des années 1985–1888* (Paris: La Sorbonne, CDU, 1959); *L'avant-dernière pensée de Nietzsche* (Paris: La Sorbonne, CDU, 1961).

3. *Nietzsche, 1844–1900. Etudes et témoignages du cinquantenaire*, ed. Martin Flinker (1950).

4. Gilles Deleuze, *Nietzsche et la philosophie* (Paris: PUF, 1962). Translated as *Nietzsche and Philosophy*, trans. Hugh Tomlinson (New York: Columbia University Press, 1983). Quotations taken from this English translation.

5. Gilles Deleuze, *Nietzsche and Philosophy*, 2.

6. Ibid., 3.

7. Friedrich Nietzsche, *La généalogie de la morale*, trans. H. Albert (Paris: Mercure de France, 1900), II, para. 2.

8. Gilles Deleuze, *Nietzsche and Philosophy*, 21.

9. Ibid., 69.

10. Gilles Deleuze, "La méthode de dramatization," *Bulletin de la Sociéte Française de Philosophie* 3 (July–September 1967): 89–118. Reprinted in Gilles Deleuze, *L'île déserte et autres textes. Textes et entretiens 1953–1974*, ed. David Lapoujade (Paris: Minuit, 2002), 131–162. Translated as *Desert Islands and Other Texts (1953–1974)*, trans. Mike Taormina (New York: Semiotexte, 2003).

11. Jean Wahl, "Nietzsche et la philosophie," *Revue de métaphysique et de morale* 3 (1963): 353.

12. Ibid., 373.

13. In his June 6, 1963, letter to Jean Wahl, Deleuze suggested inviting eleven people: France: Beaufret or Polin, Delay, Foucault or Laplanche, Gabriel Marcel, Jean Wahl; Germany: Heidegger, Fink, Lowith; Switzerland: Starobinski, Hanks Barth; Italy: Vattimo.

14. Michel Foucault, "Nietzsche, Freud, Marx," in *Cahiers de Royaumont*, no. 6 (Paris: Minuit, 1967). Reprinted in Michel Foucault, *Dits et écrits* (Paris: Gallimard, 1994), 1:564–579.

15. Gilles Deleuze, "Conclusions sur la volonté de puissance et l'éternel retour," in *Cahiers de Royaumont*, no. 6; Also in Gilles Deleuze, *Nietzsche* (Paris: Minuit, 1967), 275–287. Reprinted in Gilles Deleuze, *L'île déserte et autres texts*, 163–177.

16. Ibid., 165.

17. Gilles Deleuze, *Nietzsche* (Paris: PUF, 1965), in the "Philosophers" collection. It contains an introduction to Nietzsche's life, a presentation of his philosophy, a dictionary of his principal characters, and an anthology of extracts from his work.

18. Gilles Deleuze and Michel Foucault, "Introduction générale," in *Oeuvres philosophiques complètes de Nietzsche* (Paris: Gallimard, 1967), v. Reprinted in Michel Foucault, *Dits et écrits*, 1:561–564.

19. Ibid., 561.

20. Ibid.

21. Gilles Deleuze, "L'éclat de rire de Nietzsche," interview with Guy Dumur, *Le Nouvel Observateur* (April 5, 1967). Reprinted in Gilles Deleuze, *L'île déserte et autres textes*, 178–181.

22. Gilles Deleuze, interview with Jean-Noel Vuarnet, *Les Lettres Françaises* (February 28–March 5, 1968). Reprinted in Gilles Deleuze, *L'île déserte et autres textes*, 191–192.

23. Pierre Klossowski, *Nietzsche et le cercle vicieux* (Paris: Mercure de France, 1969).

24. Jean-Michel Rey, *L'enjeu des signes* (Paris: Seuil, 1971); Bernard Pautrat, *Versions du soleil* (Paris: Seuil, 1971); Sarah Kofman, *Nietzsche et la métaphore* (Paris: Payot, 1972).

25. This Cerisy Decade was republished in two volumes: *Nietzsche aujourd'hui?* vol. 1: *Intensités*; vol. 2: *Passion*. It included contributions from Bernard Pautrat, Jean-Luc Nancy, Pierre Klossowski, Jean-François Lyotard, Gilles Deleuze, Sylviane Agacinski, Rodolphe Gasché, Eric Clemens, Roberto Calasso, Jacques Derrida, Jean-Michel Rey, Jean-Noël Vuarnet, Pierre Bardot, Léopold Flam, Philippe Lacoue-Labarthe, Jean Mourel, Édouard Gaède, Sarah Kofman, Éric Blondel, Jeanne Delhomme, Karl Liwith, Paul Valadier, Eugen Biser, Richard Roos, Heinz Wismann, Eugen Fink, and Norman Palama.

26. Gilles Deleuze, "Pensée nomade," in *Nietzsche aujourd'hui?* 1:159–174. Reprinted in Gilles Deleuze, *L'île déserte et autres textes*, 351–164.

27. Ibid., 351.

28. Ibid., 354.

29. Ibid., 359.

30. Jacques Le Rider gave some figures in *Nietzsche en France. De la fin du XIXe siècle au temps present* (Paris: PUF, 1999). *Genealogy of Morals*, the most widely read work, sold 269,000 copies in the OPC edition (1971) and 105,000 in the 1985 Folio edition for a

total of 385,000 copies. *Thus Spoke Zarathustra*: 191,000 copies; *The Gay Science*: 183,500 copies. The Cerisy Decade on Nietzsche corresponded with the year that *Anti-Oedipus* was published, so it is not surprising to see the aspect of political protest borne in Nietzschean thought revisited and opening toward lines of flight and toward a nomadism of thought to be deterritorialized and decoded.

31. Nietzsche, *Genealogy of Morals*, II, para. 17.

32. See Jean-Clet Martin, *Variations. La philosophie de Gilles Deleuze* (Paris: Payot, 1993), esp. "Nomadologie," 51–71.

33. Manola Antonioli, *Deleuze et l'histoire de la philosophie* (Paris: Kimé, 1999), 52.

34. See Gilles Deleuze and Félix Guattari, *A Thousand Plateaus*, trans. Brian Massumi (Minneapolis: University of Minnesota Press, 1987), chap. 12, "Treatise on Nomadology—The War Machine."

35. At the time, he was responsible for teaching (*chargé d'enseignement*), which meant that he had not yet written his doctoral thesis (*thèse d'état*).

36. Gilles Deleuze, letter to Jean Wahl (December 16, 1964), Jean Wahl archives, IMEC, from Giuseppe Bianco.

37. Gilles Deleuze, letter to François Châtelet (1996), Châtelet archive, IMEC.

38. Jeannette Colombel, "Deleuze-Sartre: Pistes," in *Deleuze épars*, ed. André Bernold and Richard Pinhas (Paris: Hermann, 2005), 41.

39. Ibid., 41.

40. Chris Younès, interview with the author.

41. Alain Roger, interview with the author.

42. Jeannette Colombel, "Deleuze-Sartre: Pistes," 42.

43. Chris Younès, interview with the author.

44. Ibid.

45. Joë Bousquet, *Traduit du silence* (Paris: Gallimard, 1941).

46. "My wound existed before me—I was born to embody it!" wrote Bousquet, and Deleuze observed: "The wound is something that I receive in my body, in a particular place, at a particular moment, but there is also an eternal truth of the wound as impassible, incorporeal event." Gilles Deleuze and Claire Parnet, *Dialogues* (Paris: Flammarion, 1997), 80. Translated as *Dialogues II*, trans. Hugh Tomlinson and Barbara Habberjam (New York: Columbia University Press, 2002; rev. ed., Columbia University Press: New York, 2007), 65.

47. Chris Younès, interview with the author.

48. Ibid.

49. Ibid.

50. Gilles Deleuze, *Le bergsonisme* (Paris: PUF, 1966). Translated as *Bergsonism*, trans. Hugh Tomlinson and Barbara Habberjam (New York: Zone Books, 1997).

51. Gilles Deleuze, "Bergson, 1859–1941," in Maurice Merleau-Ponty, ed., *Les philosophes célèbres* (Paris: Lucien Mazenod, 1956), 292–299. Reprinted in Gilles Deleuze, *L'île déserte et autres textes*, 28–42.

52. Ibid., 31.

53. Ibid., 32.

54. Ibid., 37.

55. Ibid., 39.

56. Ibid., 41.

57. Gilles Deleuze, "La conception de la différence chez Bergson," in *Les etudes bergsoniennes* (1956), 4:77–112. Reprinted in Gilles Deleuze, *L'île déserte et autres textes*, 43–72.

58. See Giuseppe Bianco, "L'inhumanité de la différence. Aux sources de l'élan bergsonien de Deleuze," in *Concepts, Gilles Deleuze* (Mons: Sils Maria, 2003), esp. 68–73.

59. Gilles Deleuze, "La conception de la différence chez Bergson," 54.

60. Ibid., 57.

61. Ibid., 72.

62. Gilles Deleuze, ed., *Bergson. Mémoire et vie* (Paris: PUF, 1957).

63. Anne Sauvagnargues, "Deleuze avec Bergson. Le cours de 1960 sur *L'évolution créatrice*," in *Annales besonniennes* II, *Bergson, Deleuze, la phénoménologie*, ed. Frédéric Worms (Paris: PUF, 2004), 153.

64. Gilles Deleuze, "Cours sur le chapitre III de *L'évolution créatrice* de Bergson," in *Annales besonniennes* II, *Bergson, Deleuze, la phénoménologie*, ed. Frédéric Worms (Paris: PUF, 2004), 169.

65. Ibid., 170.

66. Ibid., 186.

67. Gilles Deleuze, *Le bergsonisme*.

68. Georges Politizer, *La fin d'une parade philosophique, le bergsonisme* (1929; repr. Paris: Pauvert, 1968).

69. Ibid., 11.

70. Frédéric Worms, interview with the author.

71. Gilles Deleuze, *Le bergsonisme*, 1.

72. Henri Bergson, *Essai sur données immédiates de la conscience* (Paris: PUF, 1889). Translated as *Time and Free Will: An Essay on the Immediate Data of Consciousness*, trans. Frank Lubecki Pogson (Kessinger Publishing, 1996).

73. Gilles Deleuze, *Le bergsonisme*, 31.

74. Ibid., 51.

75. Ibid., 100.

76. Henri Bergson, *L'évolution créatrice* (Paris: Alcan, 1907), 155. Translated as *Creative Evolution*, trans. Arthur Mitchell (New York: Dover, 1998).

77. Ibid., 315.

78. Elie During, interview with the author.

79. Frédéric Worms, interview with the author.

80. Ibid.

81. Ibid.

82. Gilles Deleuze, *Dialogues II*, 15.

83. Gilles Deleuze and Felix Guattari, *Qu'est-ce que la philosophie?* (Paris: Minuit, 1991), 49. Translated as *What Is Philosophy?* trans. Hugh Tomlinson and Graham Burchell (New York: Columbia University Press, 1994), 48. Quotations are from this edition.

84. Ibid., 60.

85. Gilles Deleuze, *Spinoza et le problème de l'expression* (Paris: Minuit, 1968). Translated as *Expressionism in Philosophy: Spinoza*, trans. Martin Joughin (New York: Zone Books, 1997).

86. See Ferdinand Alquié, *Servitude et liberté chez Spinoza* (Paris: CDU Sorbonne, 1959). Reprinted in *Leçons sur Spinoza* (Paris: La Table ronde, 2003).

87. Gilles Deleuze, *Spinoza textes choisis*, Collection Philosophes (Paris: PUF, 1979). This is part of the same series as the *Nietzsche* volume published in 1965, and like the former, it contains an introduction to the author's life and philosophy and an index of the principal ideas, followed by an anthology of excerpts.

88. Gilles Deleuze, "Spinoza et nous," *Revue de synthèse* 89/91 (January 1978). Reprinted and expanded in Gilles Deleuze, *Spinoza. Philosophie pratique* (Paris: Minuit, 1981), 164–175.

89. Gilles Deleuze, "Spinoza et les trois Éthiques," in Gilles Deleuze, *Critique et clinique* (Paris: Minuit, 1993).

90. Guillaume Sibertin-Blanc, interview with the author.

91. Thomas Bénatouil, interview with the author.

92. Ibid., 21.

93. Ibid., 22.

94. Gilles Deleuze, class at Paris-VIII (February 17, 1981), National Library sound archives.

95. Spinoza, *Ethique* (Paris: GF-Flammarion, 1965), book 1, definition 6, p. 21.

96. Gilles Deleuze, *Spinoza et le problème de l'expression* (Paris: Minuit, 1968), 18.

97. Ibid., 15.

98. Ibid., 51.

99. Spinoza, *Ethique*, book 4, 4, demonstration, p. 224.

100. Gilles Deleuze, *Spinoza et le problème de l'expression*, 108.

101. Ibid., 119.

102. Ibid., 134.

103. Spinoza, *Ethique*, book 3, 2, sc., p. 137.

104. Gilles Deleuze, *Spinoza et le problème de l'expression*, 221.

105. Ibid., 234.

106. Ibid., 240.

107. Jean-Claude Dumoncel, interview with the author.

108. Gilles Deleuze, "Spinoza et nous," 168.

109. François Zourabichvili, "Deleuze et Spinoza," in *Spinoza au XXe siècle*, ed. Olivier Bloch (Paris: PUF, 1993), 240.

110. Ibid., 238.

111. Gilles Deleuze, interview with Raymond Bellour and François Ewald, *Le Magazine Littéraire* 257 (September 1988).

112. Gilles Deleuze, *Spinoza. Philosophie pratique*, 43.

113. Ibid., 59.

114. Gilles Deleuze, class lecture (March 17, 1981), Vincennes, National Library sound archives.

115. Ibid.

116. Gilles Deleuze, "Spinoza et les trois 'Éthiques,'" in *Critique et clinique*, 172.

8. An Ontology of Difference

1. Gilles Deleuze, *Difference and Repetition*, trans. Paul Patton (New York: Columbia University Press, 1994), xix.

2. Ibid., 59.

3. Ibid., 67.

4. Ibid., 128.

5. Ibid., 66.

6. Gilles Deleuze, *Logique du sens* (Paris: Minuit, 1969). Translated as *The Logic of Sense*, trans. Mark Lester with Charles Stivale (New York: Columbia University Press, 1990), 129–130.

7. Gilles Deleuze, *Difference and Repetition*, 208.

8. Gilles Deleuze, *Le pli. Leibniz et le baroque* (Paris: Minuit, 1988). Translated as *The Fold: Leibniz and the Baroque*, trans. Tom Conley (Minneapolis: University of Minnesota Press, 1992).

9. Gilles Deleuze, *Difference and Repetition*, 208.

10. Ibid., 227.

11. Ibid., 158.

12. Ibid., 29.

13. Ibid., 55.

14. Ibid., 41.

15. Ibid., 120.

16. Ibid., 198.

17. Ibid., 303.

18. Ibid., 304.

19. Guillaume Sibertin-Blanc, interview with the author.

20. Gilles Deleuze, *Difference and Repetition*, 304.

21. Gilles Deleuze, *The Logic of Sense*, 179.

22. Alain Beaulieu, "Husserl," in *Aux sources de la pensée de Gilles Deleuze 1*, ed. Stéfan Leclerq (Mons: Sils Maria, 2005), 84.

23. Paul Virilio, *Voyage d'hiver* (Paris: Parentheses, 1997), 47.

24. Gilles Deleuze, *The Logic of Sense*, 21.

25. Ibid., 97.

26. Ibid., 102.

27. Ibid., 102.

28. Diogenes Laertius, quoted by Gilles Deleuze, *The Logic of Sense*, 142.

29. Ibid., 146.

30. Victor Goldschmidt, *Le system stoïcien et l'idée de temps* (Paris: Vrin, 1953).

31. Gilles Deleuze, *The Logic of Sense*, 155.

32. Ibid., 130.

33. Zourbachvili, interview with the author.

34. Gilles Deleuze, *Negotiations, 1972–1990*, trans. Martin Joughin (New York: Columbia University Press, 1995), 169.

35. François Zourbachivili, *Le vocabulaire de Deleuze* (Paris: Elipses, 2003), 43.

36. Gilles Deleuze, afterword to Herman Melville, *Bartleby* (Paris: Flammarion, 1989). Reprinted in Gilles Deleuze, *Critique et clinique* (Paris: Minuit, 1993), 89–114.

37. Gilles Deleuze, *The Logic of Sense*, 148.

38. Joë Bousquet, quoted by Gilles Deleuze, *The Logic of Sense*, 148; Gilles Deleuze, *Negotiations*, 65.

39. Alain Beaulieu, "Gilles Deleuze et les stoïciens," in *Gilles Deleuze, héritage philosophique*, ed. Alain Beaulieu (Paris: PUF, 2005), 50.

40. He did not designate an object that was present but one that was both past and to come, thus breaking the impact of negativity in disjunctive propositions such as, "Or as Chrysippius said, 'If you have never lost something, you have it still; but you never lost horns, ergo you have horns.'" Gilles Deleuze, *The Logic of Sense*, 137. Deleuze used these paradoxical propositions to create some movement in the operations of logic.

41. Gilles Deleuze, interview with Raymond Bellour and François Ewald, *Le Magazine Littéraire* (September 1988). Reprinted in Gilles Deleuze, "On Philosophy," in *Negotiations*.

42. Alain Beaulieu, "Gilles Deleuze et les stoïciens," 63.

43. Gilles Deleuze, *Michel Foucault* (Paris: Minuit, 1986), 92.

44. Gilles Deleuze, *Critique et clinique*, 110.

45. Gilles Deleuze, *Spinoza, philosophie pratique* (Paris: Minuit, 1981), 170.

46. Gilles Deleuze, *The Logic of Sense*, 143.

47. Gilles Deleuze and Felix Guattari, *Qu'est-ce que la philosophie?* (Paris: Minuit, 1991). Translated as *What Is Philosophy?* trans. Hugh Tomlinson and Graham Burchell (New York: Columbia University Press, 1994), 73.

48. Gilles Deleuze, *Difference and Repetition*, 110.

49. Ibid., 254.

50. Gilles Deleuze, *Nietzsche et la philosophie* (Paris: PUF, 1967). Translated as *Nietzsche and Philosophy*, trans. Hugh Tomlinson (New York: Columbia University Press, 1983), 39.

51. Bernard Andrieu, "Deleuze, la biologie et la vivant des corps," in *Concepts, Gilles Deleuze* (Mons: Sils Maria, 2002), 94.

52. Ibid., 92.

53. Gilles Deleuze, *The Logic of Sense*, 87.

54. Ibid., 87.

55. Anne Sauvagnargues. *Deleuze et l'art* (Paris: PUF, 2006), 87–88.

56. Bernard Andrieu, interview with the author

57. Gilles Deleuze, *Difference and Repetition*, 105.

58. Ibid., 106.

59. Gilles Deleuze, *The Logic of Sense*, 187.

60. Ibid., 205.

61. Ibid., 207.

62. Ibid., 211.

63. Gilles Deleuze, *Difference and Repetition*, chap. 2, n. 3, p. 313.

64. Gabriel Tarde, "La variation universelle," in *Essais et mélanges sociologiques* (Paris: Stock and Masson, 1895), 391.

65. Gabriel Tarde, *Les lois de l'imitation* (Paris: Alcan, 1890).

66. Gilles Deleuze and Felix Guattari, *Mille plateaux*, 267. Translated as *A Thousand Plateaus*, trans. Brian Massumi (Minneapolis: University of Minnesota Press, 1987).

67. Gilles Deleuze, Paris-VIII class (January 7, 1986), National French Library sound archives.

68. Gilles Deleuze and Felix Guattari, *Mille plateaux*, 267.

69. Gilles Deleuze, Paris-VIII class (January 7, 1986), National French Library sound archives.

70. Eric Alliez, preface to *Oeuvres de Gabriel Tarde*, vol. 1: *Monadologie et sociologie* (Paris: Synthélabo, 1999), 11.

71. Ibid., 11.

72. Ibid., 25.

73. Gilles Deleuze, *Difference and Repetition*, 246.

74. Gilbert Simondon, *L'individu et sa genèse physico-biologique* (Paris: PUF, 1964).

75. Pascal Chabot, interview with the author.

76. Ibid.

77. Simondon's thesis was published as *L'individu et sa genèse physico-biologique*. The review by Gilles Deleuze was "Gilbert Simondon, l'individu et sa genèse physico-biologique," *Revue Philosophique de la France et de l'Étranger* 156, nos. 1–3 (January–March 1966): 115–118. Reprinted in Gilles Deleuze, *L'île déserte et autres textes. Textes et entretiens 1953–1974*, ed. David Lapoujade (Paris: Minuit, 2002), 120–124. Translated as *Desert Islands and Other Texts (1953–1974)*, trans. Mike Taormina (New York: Semiotexte, 2003).

78. Ibid., 120–121.

79. Ibid., 123.

80. Ibid., 124.

81. Anne Sauvagnargues, "Gilbert Simondon," in *Aux sources de la pensée de Gilles Deleuze I*, 196–197.

82. Gilbert Simondon, *L'individu et sa genèse physico-biologique*, 260.

83. Gilles Deleuze, *Difference and Repetition*, 215.

84. Ibid., 185.

85. Ibid.

86. Ibid.

87. Ibid., 215.

88. François Chomarat, "Geoffroy Saint-Hilaire," in *Aux sources de la pensée de Gilles Deleuze I*, 181.

89. Raymond Ruyer, "Le psychologique et le vital," *Bulletin de la Société Française de Philosophie* (November 26, 1938): 159–195.

90. Gilles Deleuze, "Réponses à une série de questions" (November 1981), in Arnaud Villani, *La guêpe et l'orchidée* (Paris: Belin, 1999), 130.

91. Gilles Deleuze, letter to Jean-Clet Martin (June 13, 1990). In *Variations. La philosophie de Gilles Deleuze* (Paris: Payot, 1993), 7.

92. Alain Beaulieu, "Gilles Deleuze et le stoïciens," in *Gilles Deleuze, héritage philosophique*, 52.

93. Gilles Deleuze, *Difference and Repetition*, 35.

94. See chapter 20.

95. Gilles Deleuze, *Difference and Repetition*, 35.

96. Ibid., 36.

97. Pierre Montebello, interview with the author.

98. Pierre Montebello, *L'autre métaphysique* (Brussels: DDB, 2003).

99. Ibid., 8.

100. Ibid., 10.

101. Ibid., 12.

102. Gilles Deleuze, "Bergson, 1859–1941," in *Les philosophes célèbres*, ed. M. Merleau-Ponty (Paris: Mazenod, 1956). Reprinted in *L'île déserte et autres textes*, 33.

103. Pierre Montebello, *L'autre métaphysique*, 113.

104. Gabriel Tarde, *La logique sociale* (Paris: Institut Synthélabo, 1999), 231.

105. Gabriel Tarde, *Monadologie et sociologie*, 44.

106. Friedrich Nietzsche, *Oeuvres complètes, Fragments posthumes* XIV, 14, (93).

107. Gilles Deleuze, *Difference and Repetition*, 284–285.

108. Gilles Deleuze, *Le pli*, 105.

109. Whitehead, *La fonction de la raison et autres essais* (Paris: Payot, 1969), 156. The English original was titled "The Function of Reason" and was given as a Louis Clark Vanuxem Foundation Lecture at Princeton University (March 1929).

110. Arnaud Villani, "Deleuze et Whitehead," *Revue de Métaphysique et de Moral* (April–June 1996): 247.

111. Ibid., 256.

112. Gilles Deleuze, "L'immanence: une vie," *Philosophie* 47 (September 1995): 3–7. Reprinted in Gilles Deleuze, *Deux régimes de fous. Textes et entretiens (1975–1995)*, ed. David Lapoujade (Paris: Minuit, 2003), 360.

113. Jean-Christophe Goddard, *Fichte. L'émancipation philosophique* (Paris: PUF, 2003), 8.

114. Ibid., 15.

9. THE FOUNDING RUPTURE: MAY 1968

1. Jean-Pierre Muyard, interview with the author.

2. Hervé Hamon and Patrick Rotman, *Génération* (Paris: Seuil, 1987), 1:473.

3. Félix Guattari, interview with Virginie Linhart, IMEC archives, 1984.

4. Ibid.

5. Ibid.

6. Anne Querrien, interview with the author.

7. Jean-Jacques Lebel, interview with Virginie Linhart.

8. Ibid.

9. Ibid.

10. Ibid.

11. Jo Panaget, interview with the author.

12. Jean-Marie Doublet, interview with the author.

13. Recorded debate of the Young Hispano group with Félix Guattari (June 29, 1968). Transcription provided by Jo Panaget.

14. Félix Guattari, "La contre-révolution est une science qui s'apprend," *Tribune du 22 Mars* (June 5, 1968). Reprinted in Félix Guattari, *Psychanalyse et transversalité* (Paris: Maspero, 1972; repr. Paris: La Découverte, 2003), 211.

15. Félix Guattari, "Extraits de discussion" (June 23, 1968). Reprinted in *Psychanalyse et transversalité*, 217.

16. Ibid., 221.

17. Ibid., 223.

18. Jean-Claude Polack and Danielle Sivadon-Sabourin, *La Borde ou le droit à la folie* (Paris: Calmann-Levy, 1976), 54.

19. See chapter 18.

20. Jean Oury, interview with the author.

21. Ibid.

22. Danielle Sivadon, interview with the author.

23. Jean-Claude Polack, interview with Virginie Linhart.

24. Ibid.

25. Gilles Deleuze, comments related by Chris Younès, interview with the author.

26. Jeannette Colombel, "Deleuze-Sartre. Pistes," in *Deleuze épars*, ed. André Bernold and Richard Pinhas (Paris: Hermann, 2005), 43.

27. Claude Lemoine, interview with the author.

28. Gilles Deleuze with Claire Parnet, *L'abécédaire de Gilles Deleuze* (1988), 3 DVDs (Montparnasse: Arte Video, 1997).

29. Gilles Deleuze, letter to François Châtelet (1969), Châtelet collection at IMEC.

30. See the introduction, above.

31. Félix Guattari, "Interview on *Anti-Oedipus*," *L'Arc* 49 (1972). Reprinted in Gilles Deleuze, *Negotiations, 1972–1990*, trans. Martin Joughin (New York: Columbia University Press, 1995), 13.

10. "PSYCHOANALYSM" UNDER ATTACK

1. See R. Crémant (Clément Rosset), *Les matinées structuralistes* (Paris: Laffont, 1969).

2. Louis Althusser, "Freud et Lacan," *La Nouvelle Critique* 161–162 (December 1964–January 1965).

3. See the introduction, above.

4. Félix Guattari, autobiographical interview with Ève Cloarec, IMEC archives.

5. Ibid.

6. Ibid.

7. Félix Guattari, "Journal 1971" (October 6, 1971), *La Nouvelle Revue Française* 563 (October 2002): 349–350.

8. Gilles Deleuze, "De Sacher-Masoch au masochisme," *Arguments* 21 (1961).

9. Gilles Deleuze, *Presentation de Sacher-Masoch. Le froid et le cruel*; followed by *La Venus à la fourrure* (Paris: Minuit, 1967).

10. Jean Laplanche, *Problématiques 1, l'angoisse* (January 23, 1973 class) (Paris: PUF, 1980), 296.

11. Jean-Paul Chartier, "La rencontre Lacan-Deleuze ou une soirée de Lacan à Lyon à l'automne 1967," *Le Croquant* 24 (Winter 1998–1999): 25.

12. Ibid., 26.

13. Jacques Lacan, "Place, origine et fin de mon ensignement." Cited in ibid., 44.

14. Ibid., 64.

15. Ibid., 28.

16. Ibid., 29.

17. Ibid.

18. Gilles Deleuze, *Difference and Repetition*, trans. Paul Patton (New York: Columbia University Press, 1994), 17.

19. Ibid., 19.

20. Ibid., 102.

21. Ibid.

22. Jacques Lacan, *Le seminaire*, livre XVI: *D'un autre à l'autre* (1968–1969) (Paris: Seuil, 2006), 134.

23. Ibid., 218.

24. Ibid.

25. Ibid., 227.

26. Sophie Mendelsohn, "J. Lacan-G. Deleuze. Itinéraire d'une rencontre sans lendemain," *L'évolution psychiatrique* 69 (April–June 2004): 365.

27. Gilles Deleuze, *Difference and Repetition*, 108.

28. Jacques Lacan, *De la psychose paranoïaque dans ses rapports avec la personnalité* [On the Relationship Between Paranoid Psychosis and Its Relationship to Personality] (Paris: Le François, 1932; repr. Paris: Seuil, 1975).

29. Gilles Deleuze, "Les bonnes intentions sont forcément punies," in *La logique du sens* (Paris: Minuit, 1969), 236–244. Translated as "Good Intentions Are Inevitably Punished," in *The Logic of Sense*, trans. Mark Lester with Charles Stivale (New York: Columbia University Press, 1990), 202–209.

30. Ibid., 208.

31. Ibid., 211.

32. Ibid., xiii.

33. Ibid., 127.

34. Ibid.

35. Ibid., 133.

36. Antonin Artaud (1948), quoted by Gilles Deleuze in *The Logic of Sense*, 342n8.

37. Gilles Deleuze, preface to Louis Wolfson, *Le schizo et les langues* (Paris: Gallimard, 1970), 5–23. Reprinted in Gilles Deleuze, *Clinique et critique* (Paris: Minuit, 1993), 18–33.

38. Michel Foucault, *Raymond Roussel* (Paris: Gallimard, 1963). Translated as *Death and the Labyrinth: The World of Raymond Roussel*, trans. Charles Ruas (New York: Continuum, 2007).

39. Gilles Deleuze, preface to Louis Wolfson, *Le schizo et les langues*, 15.

40. Serge Cottet, "Les machines psychanalytiques de Gilles Deleuze," *Revue de Psychanalyse* 32 (February 1996): 15–19.

41. Gilles Deleuze, preface to Louis Wolfson, *Le schizo et les langues*, 23.

42. Catherine Clement, *Vies et légendes de Lacan* (1981; repr. Paris: Le Livre de poche, 1986), 35.

43. Jacques Lacan, *Le séminaire*, livre XX: *Encore* (1973–1974) (Paris: Seuil, 1975), 118. Translated as *On Feminine Sexuality, the Limits of Love and Knowledge*, trans. Bruce Fink (New York: Norton, 1998).

44. Catherine Millot, interview with the author.

45. Félix Guattari, "Machine et structure," lecture for the Freudian School of Paris, 1969; reprinted in *Change* (1972) and in Félix Guattari, *Psychanalyse et transversalité* (Paris: Maspero, 1972; repr. Paris: La Découverte, 2003).

46. Deleuze finds the answer "forceful and rigorous. It raises all sorts of problems. The easiest one is that you should study the type of schizophrenic or paranoid machine.... You'd have to show that like all machines, the schizophrenic machine has/is inseparable from (a) a type of production that here is properly schizophrenic, to be defined, and (b) from a type of transcription or recording.... There are a few indications, good ones as I recall, on the production of a schizophrenic table in a recent book of Michaux. You should reread this: and your experience at La Borde should provide all sorts of joyful and detailed analyses on the following points: schizophrenic production; the very particular way in which use and consumption enter into relationship with the production in schizophrenia; the very specific modes of recording.... And in all of that, you have to define a specifically schizophrenic economy. Second, another connected question: you begin your letter by recalling that the manifestation-subjacence no longer plays out for the schizophrenic. If that amounts to saying that the complex has invaded the mind at the cost of loss of reality, or even at the cost of the collapse of symbolism—age, sex, etc.—so be it. But that is only partially true, as Lacan recalled in his thesis, since there is a whole system of transformations that intervene so that homosexuality, for example, isn't "manifest," etc. Third, this is where the hardest part starts. You define machine by a break or rather by the existence of several breaks.... Finally, I'm more concerned about the

coherence of your concept of antiproduction." Gilles Deleuze, letter to Félix Guattari (July 29, 1969), IMEC archives.

47. Félix Guattari, in Stéphane Nadaud, *Écrits pour l'Anti-Oedipe* (Paris: Lignes/Leo Scheer, 2005), 98. Translated as *The* Anti-Oedipus *Papers*, trans. Kélina Gotman (New York: Semiotexte, 2006).

48. Ibid., 102.

49. Ibid., 148.

50. Ibid., 152–153.

51. Ibid., 154–155.

52. Ibid., 203.

53. Ibid., 212–213.

54. Ibid.

55. Ibid., 272.

56. Gilles Deleuze and Félix Guattari, *Anti-Oedipe* (1972), 99. Translated as *Anti-Oedipus*, trans. Robert Hurley, Mark Seem, and Helen R. Lane (London: Continuum, 2004).

57. Gilles Deleuze, Paris-VIII class (February 12, 1973), reprinted and expanded in "Beneath a Few Sign Regimes," in Gilles Deleuze and Félix Guattari, *A Thousand Plateaus*, trans. Brian Massumi (Minneapolis: University of Minnesota Press, 1987).

58. Gilles Deleuze and Félix Guattari, *Anti-Oedipe*, 319.

59. Michel Foucault, *Histoire de la folie à l'âge classique* (Paris: Gallimard, 1971). Translated and abridged as *Madness and Civilization: A History of Insanity in the Age of Reason*, trans. Richard Howard (London: Tavistock, 1965). Unabridged edition: *History of Madness*, ed. Jean Khalfa, trans. Jonathan Murphy and Jean Khalfa (London: Routledge, 2006).

60. Gilles Deleuze and Félix Guattari, *Anti-Oedipe*, 59.

61. Gilles Deleuze, interview on *Anti-Oedipus* with Catherine Backès Clément, which first appeared in *L'Arc* 49. Reprinted in Gilles Deleuze, *Pourparlers* (Paris: Minuit, 1990), 29. Translated as *Negotiations*, trans. Martin Joughlin (New York: Columbia University Press, 1995), 13–24.

62. Gilles Deleuze and Félix Guattari, *Anti-Oedipe*, 220.

63. Claude Lévi-Strauss, *Mythologiques, le cru et le cuit* (Paris: Plon, 1964). Translated as *The Raw and the Cooked*, trans. John Weightman and Doreen Weightman (New York: Harper & Row, 1969).

64. Gilles Deleuze and Félix Guattari, *Anti-Oedipe*, 325.

65. Ibid., 34.

66. Ibid., 16.

67. Ibid., 36.

68. Gilles Deleuze, "Capitalisme et schizophrenie," interview with Vittorio Marchetti in *Tempi Moderni* 12 (1982). Reprinted in Gilles Deleuze, *L'île déserte et autres textes*.

Textes et entretiens 1953–1974, ed. David Lapoujade (Paris: Minuit, 2002), 323. Translated as *Desert Islands and Other Texts (1953–1974)*, trans. Mike Taormina (New York: Semiotexte, 2003).

69. Gilles Deleuze, Paris-VIII class (May 28, 1973).

70. Ibid.

71. Ibid.

72. Ibid.

73. Gilles Deleuze, Paris-VIII class (May 14, 1973).

74. Gilles Deleuze and Félix Guattari, *Anti-Oedipe*, 27.

75. Ibid., 54.

76. Ibid., 30.

77. Ibid., 97.

78. Ibid., 106.

79. Ibid., 160.

80. Marie-Cécile Ortigues and Edmond Ortigues, *Oedipe africain* (Paris: Plon, 1966).

81. Alfred Adler and Michel Cartry, "La transgression et sa dérision," *L'Homme* (July 1971).

82. Ibid, quoted in Gilles Deleuze and Félix Guattari, *Anti-Oedipe*, 189.

83. Marcel Griaule, "Remarques sur l'oncle utérin au Soudan," *Cahiers Internationaux de Sociologie* (January 1954).

84. Alfred Adler, interview with the author.

85. Gilles Deleuze, letter to Félix Guattari (April 5, 1970), IMEC archives. "A" is Alfred Adler; "Z" is Andras Zempléni.

86. Gilles Deleuze, undated letter to Félix Guattari, IMEC archives.

87. Ibid.

88. Michel Cartry, interview with the author.

89. Pierre Clastres, *Chroniques des indiens Guayakis* (Paris: Plon, 1972).

90. Michel Cartry, interview with the author.

91. Ibid.

92. Alfred Adler, interview with the author.

93. Gilles Deleuze and Félix Guattari, *Anti-Oedipe*, 169.

94. Ibid., 236.

95. Jacques Derrida, *De la grammatologie* (Paris: Minuit, 1967); Jacques Derrida, *L'écriture et la différence* (Paris: Seuil, 1967). Translated as *Of Grammatology*, trans. Gayatri Spivak (Baltimore, Md.: The Johns Hopkins University Press, 1976); and *Writing and Difference*, trans. Alan Bass (London: Routledge, 1978).

96. Gilles Deleuze and Félix Guattari, *Anti-Oedipe*, 291.

97. Ibid., 292.

98. Ibid., 310.

99. Ibid., 322.

100. Ibid., 327.

101. Ibid., 352.

102. Ibid., 400.

103. Gilles Deleuze, "Quatre propositions sur la psychanalyse" (1973), in Gilles Deleuze and Félix Guattari, *Politique et psychanalyse* (Paris: Bibliothèque des mots perdus, 1977). Reprinted and revised in *L'île déserte et autres textes*, 382. During this colloquium, which was the first meeting of the Milan Psychoanalysis and Politics conference in May 1973, Guattari gave a lecture on "The Desire Struggles in Psychoanalysis," which has been reprinted in Gilles Deleuze, *Deux régimes de fous. Textes et entretiens, 1975–1995*, ed. David Lapoujade (Paris: Minuit, 2003), in which he emphasizes the political value of *Anti-Oedipus*.

11. *ANTI-OEDIPUS*

1. Félix Guattari, *Psychanalyse et transversalité* (Paris: Maspero, 1972; repr. Paris: La Découverte, 2003).

2. Roger Gentis, *Un psychiatre dans le siècle* (Paris: Érès, 2005), 128.

3. See chapter 16, below.

4. Félix Guattari, *Journal*, notes (April 1, 1972), IMEC archives.

5. Robert Linhart, "Gauchisme à vendre?" *Libération* (December 7, 1974).

6. Serge July, in *Libération* (December 7, 1974).

7. Robert Linhart, "Gauchisme à vendre?"

8. Ibid.

9. Rafaël Pividal, "Psychanalyse, schizophrénie, capitalisme," *Le Monde* (April 28, 1972).

10. François Châtelet, "Le combat d'un nouveau Lucrèce," *Le Monde* (April 28, 1972).

11. Noëlle Châtelet, interview with the author.

12. Kostas Axelos, "Sept questions à un philosophe," *Le Monde* (April 8, 1972). While Axelos had been a very close philosopher friend of Deleuze since the mid-1950s, their relationship quickly broke apart because of these questions. "After these questions in *Le Monde*, we no longer saw one another. We called, but I understood that it was over." Kostas Axelos, interview with the author.

13. Cyrille Koupernik, "Un délire intelligent mais gratuit," *Le Monde* (April 28, 1972).

14. Claude Mauriac, "L'Oedipe mis en accusation," *Le Figaro* (April 1, 1972).

15. Madeleine Chapsal, "Oedipe connais plus," *L'Express* (March 27–April 2, 1972).

16. Serge Leclaire, "La réalite du désir," in *Sexualité humaine* (Paris: Aubier, 1970).

17. Catherine Millot, lecture on *Anti-Oedipus*, Pompidou Center, "Abécédaire for Gilles Deleuzes, Revue Parlées," November 2, 2005.

18. Ibid.

19. Catherine Millot, interview with the author.

20. Elisabeth Roudinesco, "Le bateau ivre du schizo débarque chez Al Capone," *Les Lettres Françaises* (April 18, 1972). Reprinted as "Oedipe et la schizophrénie," in Elisabeth Roudinesco, *Un discours au réel* (Paris, 1973), 195–204.

21. Elisabeth Roudinesco, *Un discours au réel*, 195.

22. Ibid., 199.

23. Ibid., 203.

24. Ibid.

25. Elisabeth Roudinesco, interview with the author.

26. Elisabeth Roudinesco, *Généalogies* (Paris: Fayard, 1994), 54.

27. André Green, "Réflexions critiques," *Revue Française de Psychanalyse* 36, no. 3 (1972): 494.

28. Ibid.

29. Ibid., 495–496.

30. Ibid., 497.

31. André Stéphane, *L'univers contestionnaire* (Paris: Petite Bilbiothèque Payot, 1969).

32. André Stéphane, "La fin d'un malentendu," *Contrepoint* 7–8 (August–November 1972): 244.

33. Janine Chassegnet-Smirgel, ed., *Les chemins de l'Anti-Oedipe* (Toulouse: Privat, 1974).

34. Ibid., 73.

35. Ibid.

36. Jean-François Lyotard, "Capitalisme énergumène," *Critique* (November 1972): 925. Reprinted in Jean-François Lyotard, *Des dispositifs pulsionnels* (1973), 7–52.

37. René Girard, "Système du délire," *Critique* (November 1972): 961.

38. René Girard, *Mensonge romantique et vérité romanesque* (Paris: Grasset, 1961). Translated as *Deceit, Desire, and the Novel: Self and Other in Literary Structure* (Baltimore, Md.: The Johns Hopkins University Press, 1966).

39. René Girard, "Système du délire," 965.

40. Ibid., 976–977.

41. Jean Furtos and René Roussillon, "L'Anti-Oedipe. Essai d'explication," *Esprit* (December 1972): 817–834.

42. Jacques Donzelot, "Une anti-sociologie," *Esprit* (December 1972): 833–855.

43. Ibid., 849.

44. Jean-Marie Domenach, "Oedipe à l'usine," *Esprit* (December 1972): 856.

45. Ibid., 857.

46. Ibid., 863.

47. Roger Laporte, "Gilles Deleuze, Félix Guattari: Capitalisme et schizophrénie, L'Anti-Oedipe," *Les Cahiers du Chemin* 16 (October 15, 1972): 96.

48. Ibid., 97.

49. Ibid., 104.

50. Jean Oury, interview with the author.

51. Nicole Guillet, interview with the author.

52. Félix Guattari, *La revolution moléculaire* (Paris: Recherches, 1977), 31.

53. Michel Cressole, *Deleuze* (Paris: Editions Universitaires, 1973).

54. Ibid., 91.

55. Ibid., 103.

56. Ibid., 104.

57. Ibid., 105.

58. Gilles Deleuze, "Lettre à un critique severe," in Michel Cressole, *Deleuze*. Reprinted in Gilles Deleuze, *Pourparlers* (Paris: Minuit, 1990), 11. Translated as *Negotiations*, trans. Martin Joughlin (New York: Columbia University Press, 1995), 3. Quotations from this edition.

59. Ibid., 5.

60. Michel Foucault, "Cours au Collège de France du 7 janvier 1976," in *Dits et écrits* (Paris: Gallimard, 1994), 3:162–163.

61. Michel Foucault, preface to Gilles Deleuze and Felix Guattari, *Anti-Oedipus: Capitalism and Schizophrenia* (New York: Viking, 1977), xi–xiv. Reprinted in *Dits et écrits*, 133–136.

62. Michel Foucault, *Dits et écrits*, 134.

63. Ibid.

64. Robert Castel, *Le psychanalysme* (Paris: Maspero, 1973; new ed., Paris: Champs-Flammarion, 1989), 83.

65. Ibid., 275.

66. Ibid., 274.

67. Gilles Deleuze and Félix Guattari, *Anti-Oedipe*, 456.

68. Gilles Deleuze, Paris-VIII class (May 27, 1980), National Library sound archives.

69. Ibid.

70. Ibid.

71. Ibid.

72. Gilles Deleuze with Claire Parnet, *L'abécédaire de Gilles Deleuze* (1988), 3 DVDs (Montparnasse: Arte Video, 1997), letter D.

73. Ibid.

74. Eric Alliez, "L'Anti-Oedipe—trente ans et quelques après," *Radical Philosophy* 124 (March–April 2004).

75. Jean-Pierre Le Goff, *Mai 68. L'héritage impossible* (Paris: La Découverte, 1998).

76. Ibid., 343.

77. Jean-Christophe Goddard, *Mystique et folie. Essai sur la simplicité* (Brussels: Desclée de Brouwer, 2002).

78. Ibid., 45.

79. Catherine Millot, interview with the author.

80. Ibid.

81. Gilles Deleuze and Félix Guattari, *Anti-Oedipe*, 464.

82. Ibid., 7.

83. Ibid.

12. Machine Against Structure

1. Félix Guattari, "Machine and Structure," 1969 lecture, printed in *Change* 12 (1972): 240–248.

2. Gilles Deleuze, *Difference and Repetition* (1968), trans. Paul Patton (New York: Columbia University Press, 1994), 1.

3. Félix Guattari, "Machine and Structure," in *Psychanalyse et transversalité* (Paris: Maspero, 1972; repr. Paris: La Découverte, 2003), 241.

4. Ibid., 243.

5. Ibid.

6. Ibid.

7. Ibid., 244.

8. Ibid.

9. Ibid.

10. *Instincts et institutions*, ed. Gilles Deleuze (Paris: Classiques Hachette, 1953).

11. Félix Guattari, "Machine et structure," in *Psychanalyse et transversalité*, 248.

12. See Francois Dosse, *Histoire du structuralisme*, vol. 2: *L'institutionalisation: à la conquête de l'université*, 173–182. Translated as *History of Structuralism*, vol. 2: *Institutionalization: Conquering the University*, trans. Deborah Glassman (Minneapolis: University of Minnesota Press, 1997).

13. Gilles Deleluze, *Difference and Repetition*, 191.

14. Ibid., 192.

15. Ibid., 204.

16. Ibid., 205.

17. Gilles Deleuze, Paris-VIII class (March 19, 1985), National Library sound archives.

18. The "signified of power" according to Gustave Guillaume is the unconscious dynamic that organizes polysemism in a given lexeme. The meaning of a word in discourse is therefore always an arrangement between the spoken word (signified of power) and the context.

19. Gilles Deleluze, Paris-VIII class (March 19, 1985), National Library sound archives.

20. Pierre Blanchaud, interview with the author.

21. Gilles Deleuze, *Difference and Repetition*, 191.

22. Gilles Deleuze, letter to Louis Althusser (October 29, 1964), Althusser archives, IMEC.

23. Gilles Deleuze, letter to Louis Althusser (February 28, 1966), Althusser archives, IMEC.

24. Gilles Deleuze, "A quoi reconnaît-on le structuralisme?" in *Histoire de la philosophie*, vol. 8: *Le XX siècle*, ed. François Châtelet (Paris: Hachette, 1972), 299–335. Reprinted in Gilles Deleuze, *L'île déserte et autres textes. Textes et entretiens 1953–1974*, ed. David Lapoujade (Paris: Minuit, 2002), 238–269. Translated as *Desert Islands and Other Texts (1953–1974)*, trans. Mike Taormina (New York: Semiotexte, 2003).

25. Gilles Deleuze, letter to Louis Althusser (February 24, 1964), Althusser archives, IMEC.

26. Gilles Deleuze, "A quoi reconnaît-on le structuralisme?" 247.

27. Ibid., 250.

28. Ibid., 261.

29. Gilles Deleuze, *La logique du sens*, 88. Translated as *The Logic of Sense*, trans. Mark Lester with Charles Stivale (New York: Columbia University Press, 1990), 71. Quotations from the English text.

30. Ibid., 71.

31. Ibid.

32. Ibid., 19.

33. Ibid., 28.

34. Ibid., 32.

35. Ibid., 35.

36. Ibid., 37.

37. Ibid., 181.

38. Ibid.

39. Gilles Deleuze and Félix Guattari, *Anti-Oedipe* (Paris: Minuit, 1972), 245.

40. Félix Guattari, in Stéphane Nadaud, *Écrits pour l'Anti-Oedipe* (Paris: Lignes/Leo Scheer, 2005), 98. Translated as *The* Anti-Oedipus *Papers*, trans. Kélina Gotman (New York: Semiotexte, 2006).

41. Louis Hjemslev, *Prolégomènes à une théorie du langage* (Paris: Minuit, 1968), 11.

42. Ibid., 85.

43. Gilles Deleuze and Félix Guattari, *Anti-Oedipe*, 288.

44. Ibid.

45. Charles Sanders Peirce, *Ecrits sur le signe* (Paris: Seuil, 1978). See *Collected Papers of Charles Sanders Peirce*, vols. 1–6, ed. Charles Hartshorne and Paul Weiss; vols. 7–8, ed. Arthur W. Burks (Cambridge, Mass.: Harvard University Press, 1931–1935, 1958).

46. Gilles Deleuze and Felix Guattari, *Mille plateaux* (Paris: Minuit, 1980), 95.

47. John Austin, *Quand dire, c'est faire* (Paris: Seuil, 1970). Originally *How to Do Things with Words* (Cambridge, Mass.: Harvard University Press, 1975).

48. Félix Guattari, "Pour une micro-politique du désir," (1975), in *La révolution moléculaire* (Paris: Recherches, 1977), 241.

49. Ibid., 274.

50. Félix Guattari, "La valeur, la monnaie, le symbole," in *La révolution moléculaire*, 291.

51. Félix Guattari, *L'inconscient machinique* (Paris: Recherches, 1979), 23.

52. Ibid., 24.

53. Michel de Certeau, Dominique Julia, and Jacques Revel, *Une politique de la langue* (Paris: Gallimard, 1975).

54. Félix Guattari, *L'inconscient machinique*, 13.

55. Gilles Deleuze and Félix Guattari, *A Thousand Plateaus* (Minneapolis: University of Minnesota Press, 1987), 184.

56. Gilles Deleuze and Félix Guattari, *Anti-Oedipe*, 59.

57. Ibid., 80.

58. Ibid., 142.

59. Ibid., 366.

60. Gilles Deleuze, "Réponse à une série de questions" (November 1981), in Arnaud Villani, *La guêpe et l'orchidée* (Paris: Belin, 1999), 131.

61. · Félix Guattari, in Stéphane Nadaud, *Écrits pour l'Anti-Oedipe* (November 14, 1970), 185.

62. Gilles Deleuze and Félix Guattari, *Anti-Oedipe*, 404.

63. Ibid., 405.

64. Joël Birman, "Les signes et leurs excès. La clinique chez Deleuze," in *Gilles Deleuze, une vie philosophique*, ed. Éric Alliez (Paris: Les Empêcheurs de Penser en Rond, 1998), 485.

65. Ibid., 177.

66. Gilles Deleuze and Félix Guattari, *Anti-Oedipe*, 176.

67. Alfred Adler and Michel Cartry, "La transgression et sa dérision," *L'Homme* (July 1971).

68. Meyer Fortes, in "Recherches voltaïques" (Paris: CNRS, 1967), 135–137.

69. Gilles Deleuze and Félix Guattari, *Anti-Oedipe*, 173.

70. Pierre Clastres, *Chronique des indiens Guayakis* (Paris: Plon, 1972).

71. Gilles Deleuze and Félix Guattari, *Anti-Oedipe*, 222.

72. See chapter 13.

73. Gilles Deleuze and Félix Guattari, *Mille plateaux*, 260.

74. Gilles Deleuze and Félix Guattari, *Anti-Oedipe*, 213.

75. Ibid., 265.

76. Ibid., 291.

77. Ibid., 292.

13. "Minor" Literature as Seen by Deleuze and Guattari

1. Gilles Deleuze and Félix Guattari, *Kafka. Pour une littérature mineure* (Paris: Minuit, 1975).

2. Ibid., 7.

3. Gilles Deleuze and Félix Guattari, *Rhizome* (Paris: Minuit, 1977). See chapter 20.

4. Gilles Deleuze and Félix Guattari, *Kafka*, 7.

5. Deleuze defined "arrangement" in, among other places, his discussions with Claire Parnet, in *Dialogues*, where the term *assemblage* is used to translate *arrangement*. "What is an assemblage? It is a multiplicity which is made up of many heterogeneous terms and which establishes liaisons, relations between them, across ages, sexes and reigns—different natures. Thus, the assemblage's only unity is that of co-functioning: it is a symbiosis, a 'sympathy.'" Gilles Deleuze and Claire Parnet, *Dialogues* (Paris: Flammarion, 1997), 69.

6. Gilles Deleuze and Félix Guattari, *Kafka*, 145–157.

7. Ibid., 14.

8. Ibid., 19.

9. Giles Deleuze, *Critique et clinique* (Paris: Minuit, 1993).

10. Gilles Deleuze and Félix Guattari, *Kafka*, 29.

11. Ibid., 29, reference to Kafka's letter to Brod (June 1921), *Correspondance, 1902–1924* (Paris: Gallimard, 1984), 394.

12. Ibid., 48.

13. Ibid., 30.

14. Ibid.

15. Anne Sauvagnargues, *Deleuze et l'art* (Paris: PUF, 2005), 140.

16. Georges Canguilhem, *Le normal et le pathologique* (Paris: PUF, 1966).

17. Guillaume Sibertin-Blanc, "Pour une littérature mineure: un cas d'analyse pour une théorie des normes chez Deleuze" (March 12, 2003), UMR 8163, Lille University 3,

Savoirs textes, langage study group led by Pierre Macherey, "La philosophie au sens large." Text available online.

18. See chapter 12.

19. Gilles Deleuze, "Avenir de la linguistique," preface to Henri Gobard, *L'alienation linguistique (analyse tetraglossique)* (Paris: Flammarion, 1976). Gilles Deleuze, *Deux régimes de fous. Textes et entretiens, 1975–1995,* ed. David Lapoujade (Paris: Minuit, 2003), 61–65.

20. Ibid., 61.

21. Ibid.

22. Ibid.

23. Haïm-Vidal Sephiha, "Introduction à l'étude de l'intensif," *Langages* 18 (May–June 1970): 104–120.

24. Gilles Deleuze and Félix Guattari, *Kafka,* 41.

25. Franz Kafka, *Journal* (December 13, 1910) (Paris: Grasset, 1913), 17.

26. Gilles Deleuze and Félix Guattari, *Kafka,* 40.

27. Ibid., 24.

28. Ibid., 25.

29. Ibid., 68.

30. Félix Guattari, "Les rêves de *Kafka,*" IMEC archives. Reprinted as "Kafka, le rebelle," *Le Magazine Littéraire* (December 2002).

31. Jack Lang, letter to Felix Guattari (August 30, 1982), IMEC archives.

32. Félix Guattari, notes, *Kafka* notebooks, IMEC archives.

33. Enzo Cormann, "Comme sans y penser," *Chimères* 23 (Summer 1994).

34. Translator's note: *Tu es là quand* is a homonym for *Tu es Lacan* ("you're Lacan") and for *tuer Lacan* ("to kill Lacan").

35. This play was produced in Bologna by the painter Gianmarco Montesano, a friend of Guattari.

36. Félix Guattari, "Kafka," Jean Daive program on France Culture (August 24, 2003), INA archives.

37. Ibid.

38. Félix Guattari, "Notes sur les intensités et la fonction 'Blocs d'enfance' [the first chapter of *The Castle*]," handwritten notes, IMEC archives.

39. Félix Guattari, "Notes on *The Metamorphosis,*" handwritten notes, IMEC archives.

14. *A THOUSAND PLATEAUS*: A GEOPHILOSOPHY OF POLITICS

1. Gilles Deleuze, Paris-VIII class (May 27, 1980), French National Library sound archives.

2. Arnaud Villani, "Géographie physique de *Mille plateaux,*" *Critique* 455 (April 1955): 333.

3. Ibid., 345.

4. November 20, 1923, is followed by A.D. 587 and then November 28, 1947, year zero, 1874, 1933 . . . These scansions have the effect of disorienting time and freeing it of rules so that *Chronos* yields to *Aïon*.

5. Gilles Deleuze, "Une tentative d'agencement entre les saviors et la pratique quotidienne," interview with Catherine Clément, *Le Matin* (September 30, 1980).

6. Isabelle Stengers, interview with Virginie Linhart.

7. Anti-Oedipus sold 63,000 copies between 1972, when it was published, and early 2007.

8. *A Thousand Plateaus* sold 30,500 copies between 1980 and 2007, its difficulty notwithstanding.

9. Arnaud Villani, "Géographie physique de *Mille plateaux*," 331.

10. Catherine Clément, "L'expression nomade de la modernité," *Le Matin* (September 30, 1980).

11. Christian Delacampagne, "Deleuze et Guattari dans leur machine délirante," *Le Monde* (October 10, 1980).

12. Ibid.

13. Petites et grandes machines à inventer la vie," Félix Guattari, interview with Robert Maggiori, *Libération* (October 32, 1980).

14. Gilles Deleuze, "Entretien sur *Mille plateaux*," interview with Christian Descamps, Didier Eribon, and Robert Maggiori, *Libération* (October 23, 1980). Reprinted in Gilles Deleuze, *Pourparlers* (Paris: Minuit, 1990), 11. Translated as *Negotiations*, trans. Martin Joughlin (New York: Columbia University Press, 1995), 26.

15. Ibid.

16. Gilles Deleuze, "Une tentative d'agencement entre les saviors et les pratiques quotidiennes," interview with Catherine Clément, *Le Matin* (September 30, 1980).

17. Gilles Deleuze and Félix Guattari, *Mille plateaux* (Paris: Minuit, 1980), 384.

18. Ibid., 385.

19. Ibid., 418.

20. Ibid., 396.

21. Félix Guattari, "Le temps des ritournelles," in *L'inconscient machinique* (Paris: Recherches, 1979), 109–153.

22. Ibid., 109.

23. Pierre Clastres, *La société contre l'état* (Paris: Minuit, 1974), 107ff.

24. Gilles Deleuze and Félix Guattari, *Mille plateaux*, 386.

25. Ibid., 389.

26. Ibid., 433.

27. Ibid., 92.

28. Ibid., 101.

29. Ibid., 106.

30. Emmanuel Levinas, *Autrement qu'être ou au-delà de l'essence* (The Hague: Nijhoff, 1974), 141.

31. Gilles Deleuze and Félix Guattari, *Mille plateaux*, 209.

32. Michel Foucault, *L'archéologie du savoir* (Paris: Gallimard, 1969), 28. Translated as *The Archaeology of Knowledge*, trans. A. M. Sheridan Smith (London: Routledge, 2002).

33. Félix Guattari, *L'inconscient machinique*, op. cit. p. 75–108.

34. Ibid., 77.

35. Ibid., 78.

36. Gilles Deleuze and Félix Guattari, *Mille plateaux*, 209.

37. Ibid., 207.

38. Ibid.

39. Ibid., 230.

40. Ibid., 231.

41. Ibid., 233.

42. Ibid., 598.

43. Ibid., 615.

44. Spinoza, *Oeuvres, III. Traité théologico-politique*. (Paris: PUF, 1998).

45. Guillaume Sibertin-Blanc, "Deleuze, Spinoza et les sciences socials: lectures de *Mille plateaux* de Deleuze et Guattari," CERPHI seminar at ENS (May 13, 2006).

46. Gilles Deleuze, Paris-VIII class (November 6, 1979), National Library sound archives.

47. See Guillaume Sibertin-Blanc, "Etat et généalogie de la guerre: l'hypothèse de la 'machine de guerre' de Gilles Deleuze et Félix Guattari," *Asterion* 3 (September 2005).

48. Ilan Halévi, "Un internationaliste singulier," *Chimères* 23 (Summer 1994): 120.

49. Elias Sanbar, interview with the author.

50. Ibid.

51. Gilles Deleuze, "Les gêneurs," *Le Monde* (April 7, 1978). Reprinted in Gilles Deleuze, *Deux régimes de fous. Textes et entretiens, 1975–1995*, ed. David Lapoujade (Paris: Minuit, 2003), 147.

52. Ibid.

53. Ibid., 149.

54. Elan Halévi, "Un internationaliste singulier," 123.

55. Ibid.

56. Ibid.

57. Gilles Deleuze, "Les indiens de Palestine," interview with Elias Sanbar, *Libération* (May 8–9, 1982). Reprinted in Gilles Deleuze, *Deux régimes de fous*, 179–184.

58. Elias Sanbar, interview with the author.

59. Elias Sanbar, "Les Indiens de Palestine," 181.

60. Gilles Deleuze, "Grandeur de Yasser Arafat" (written in September 1983), *Revue d'Études Palestiniennes* 10 (Winter 1984). Reprinted in Gilles Deleuze, *Deux régimes de fous*, 221–225.

61. Ibid., 221.

62. Ibid., 222.

63. Ibid., 223.

64. Elias Sanbar, interview with the author.

65. Ibid.

66. Elias Sanbar, *Figures du Palestinien. Identité des origines, identité de devenir* (Paris: Gallimard, 2004).

67. Elias Sanbar, interview with the author.

68. Pierre Clastres, *La société contre l'état*.

69. Ibid., 463.

70. Gilles Deleuze and Félix Guattari, *Mille plateaux*, 542.

71. Ibid., 545.

72. Every struggle takes place through all of these undecideable propositions and is built on revolutionary connections against the *conjugations of the axiomatic*. Ibid., 591.

73. See chapter 16.

74. Félix Guattari, *Cartographies schizoanalytiques* (Paris: Galilée, 1989).

75. Danielle Sivadon, interview with the author.

76. Félix Guattari, seminar presentation (December 9, 1980), IMEC archives.

77. Ibid.

78. Félix Guattari, seminar presentation (January 13, 1981), IMEC archives.

79. Félix Guattari, seminar presentation (April 28, 1981), IMEC archives.

80. "One day, a scene that crystallized everything. I was on the train that I always took on Thursdays and was going to the dining car; the waiter came over and said, 'Sir, I'm shaking your hand because this is the last time that I'll be here, I'm retiring. My God! Frightening!'" Félix Guattari, seminar presentation (December 8, 1981), IMEC archives.

81. Barbara Glowczewski, "Espaces de rêves," in Félix Guattari seminar (January 18, 1983), MEC archives.

82. Philippe Adrien, Félix Guattari seminar (March 1, 1988), IMEC archives.

83. Yves Buin, Félix Guattari seminar (November 15, 1988), IMEC archives.

84. Michel Rostain, Félix Guattari seminar (January 10, 1989), IMEC archives.

85. Félix Guattari, *Cartographie schizoanalytique*, 9.

86. Ibid.

87. Manola Antonioli, *Géophilosophie de Deleuze et Guattari* (Paris: L'Harmattan, 2003), 9–10.

88. Ibid., 26.

89. Manola Antonioli, "La machination politique de Deleuze et Guattari," in *Gilles Deleuze, héritage philosophique*, ed. Alain Beaulieu (Paris: PUF, 2006), 73–95.

90. Mark Bonta and John Protevi, *Geophilosophy: A Guide and Glossary* (Edinburgh: Edinburgh University Press, 2004).

91. John Protevi, interview with the author.

92. Philippe Mengue, *Gilles Deleuze ou le système du multiple* (Paris: Kimé, 1994), 227.

93. Gilles Deleuze and Félix Guattari, *Mille plateaux*, 264.

15. THE CERFI AT WORK

1. "Architecture et programmation, psychiatrie," *Recherches* 6 (June 1967).

2. Anne Querrien, interview with the author.

3. Lion Murard, interview with the author.

4. Michel Rostain, in Janet H. Morford, "Histoire du CERFI," DEA for EHESS (October 1985): 139.

5. Ibid., 178.

6. Anne Querrien, interview with the author.

7. Ibid.

8. Florence Pétry, *Recherches* editor in chief, interview with the author.

9. Ibid.

10. After three years, in February 1978, the CERFI moved back to the twelfth arrondissement of Paris to an office on rue Pleyel.

11. "Généalogie du Capital. 1. Les équipements du pouvoir," *Recherches* 13 (December 13, 1973).

12. François Fourquet, "L'accumulation du pouvoir ou le désir d'Etat," *Recherches* 46 (September 1982) : 15.

13. Ibid.

14. The companion of the *Le Monde* journalist Daniel Vernet, Marie-Thérèse Vernet-Stragiotti, was criticized for spending too much time as a couple, territorializing herself too much. This story exemplifies the major battle of the period against all forms of enclosure in couples. Daniel Vernet's companion had the nerve to schedule her vacation with Daniel just before the issue for which she was responsible was finished! Two members of the "mafia" called her in the day before her departure. Things got serious because Thérèse had agreed to write the final report, but her commitment was considered compromised by her "petit bourgeois" attitude.

15. François Fourquet and Lion Murard, presentation, *Recherches* 13 (December 1973): 1.

16. François Fourquet, *L'idéal historique*, *Recherches* 14 (January 1973). Reprinted in UGE (Paris: 10/18, 1976).

17. Ibid., 7.

18. Ibid., 8.

19. Anne Querrien, in Janet H. Morford, "Histoire du CERFI," 139.

20. Ibid.

21. François Fourquet, in ibid., 75.

22. *Trois milliards de pervers, Recherches* 12 (March 1973).

23. Guy Hocquenghem, interview with Jean-Pierre Joeker and Alain Sanzio, *Masques* (March 1981): 16.

24. Text signed by F. Châtelet, H. Weber, D. Bensaïd, G. Deleuze, J.-F. Lyotard, R. Schérer, G. Lapassade, F. Guattari, R. Lourau, F. Lourau, G. Hocquenghem, M. Juffe, R. Barjonnet, and C. Hennion.

25. Felix Guattari, "Trois milliards de pervers à la barre" (1974), in *La révolution moléculaire* (Paris: Recherches, 1977), 118. Translated as *Molecular Revolution: Psychiatry and Politics (Peregrines)* (New York: Puffin, 1984).

26. Anne Querrien, interview with the author.

27. The five included François Fourquet, Lion Murard, Liane Mozère, Michel Rostain, and Anne Querrien.

28. NRS employees are civil servants.

29. Michel Rostain, in Janet H. Morford, "Histoire du CERFI," 111.

30. Anne Querrien, in ibid., 112–113.

31. Florence Pétry, interview with the author.

32. Ibid.

33. Félix Guattari, *La révolution moléculaire.*

34. *Recherches* 22, *Co-ire* (1976), by René Schérer and Guy Hocquenghem, sold seven thousand copies in a year and a half. Issue 25, *Le petit travailleur infatigable* (1976), by Lion Murard and Patrick Zylberman, had two editions printed—a first edition of four thousand copies and a second edition of 4,500 copies—all of which were sold.

35. François Fourquet, *L'idéal historique.*

36. Christian Bourgois, interview with the author.

37. Ibid.

38. With Fernand Deligny's *Cahiers de l'immuable*, no. 18–20–24 in 1975 and 1976; *Psychiatrie: le secteur impossible*, no. 17 (March 1975); *Histoires de La Borde*, no. 21 (April 1976); *L'asile*, no. 31 (February 1978); and *Déraisonances*, no. 36 (March 1979).

39. François Fourquet, "L'accumulation du pouvoir ou le désir d'État," *Recherches* 46, (September 1982): 64.

40. Lion Murard and Patrick Zylberman, typed text given to the author by Lion Murard; he was speaking to the CERFI to Anne, Liane, Félix, Michel, François, Numa, Olivier, Claude H., Georges, Claude R. Gérard, Luc, Philippe, Florence, and Françoise.

41. Ibid.

42. Ibid.

43. Lion Murard, interview with the author.

44. Anne Querrien, interview with the author.

45. Félix Guattari, quoted by Anne Querrien in Janet H. Morford, "Histoire du CERFI," 163.

46. Félix Guattari, in ibid., 218.

47. François Fourquet and Lion Murard, *Histoire de la psychiatrie du secteur* (Paris: Recherches: 1980); previously published as *Psychiatrie: le secteur impossible? Recherches* 17 (March 1975). François Fourquet, *Les comptes de la puissance. Histoire de la comptabilité nationale et du plan, Recherches* (Paris: Encres, 1980).

48. Dr. Aujaleu, Dr. Pierre Bailly-Saslin, Dr. Lucien Bonnafé, Dr. Georges Daumezon, Félix Guattari, Dr. Robert-Henri Hazemann, Mrs. Laurenceau, Ms. Mamelet, Dr. Mignot, Dr. Jean Oury, Dr. Danielle Sabourin-Sivadon, Dr. Paul Sivadon, Dr. Horace Torrubia, Dr. François Tosquelles, and Dr. Charles Vaille.

49. François Fourquet and Lion Murard, "Présentation," *Histoire de la psychiatrie du secteur*, 6.

50. Ibid., 314.

51. Ibid., 316.

52. François Fourquet, *Les comptes de la puissance.*

53. François Fourquet, interview with the author.

54. François Fourquet, *Les comptes de la puissance*, xi.

16. THE "MOLECULAR REVOLUTION": ITALY, GERMANY, FRANCE

1. *Euskadi Ta Askatasuna* (ETA), "Basque Homeland and Freedom."

2. Poetere Operaio dates from 1969 but dissolved itself in 1973. The leaders of this organization, which had a true influence in its time, included, among others, Toni Negri, Oreste Scalzone, Franco Piperno, Nanni Balestrini, and Sergio Bologna. Lotta Continua, created at the same time, also dissolved itself a bit later, in November 1976.

3. Fabrizio Calvi, *Italie 77, le mouvement, les intellectuels* (Paris: Seuil, 1977), 29.

4. Isabelle Sommier, *La violence politique et son deuil. L'après-68 en France et en Italie* (Rennes: PUR, 1998), 102.

5. Fabrizio Calvi, *Italie 77*, 34.

6. Félix Guattari, preface to *Collectif A Traverso. Radio Alice, radio libre* (Paris: Editions Jean-Pierre Delarge, 1977), 6.

7. Franco Berardi ("Bifo"), interview with Virginie Linhart.

8. Ibid.

9. Les Untorelli, *Recherches* 80 (November 1977): 19.

10. Franco Berardi ("Bifo"), interview with Virginie Linhart.

11. Gianmarco Montesano, interview with Virginie Linhart.

12. *Collectif A Traverso. Radio Alice, radio libre.*

13. Gianmarco Montesano, interview with Virginie Linhart.

14. Along with Félix Guattari, CINEL members included the lawyer Gérard Soulier, the painter Gérard Fromanger, Yann Moulier-Boutang, Eric Alliez, Jean-Pierre Faye, Jean Chesneaux, and Gilles Deleuze.

15. Franco Berardi ("Bifo"), interview with Virginie Linhart.

16. Ibid.

17. Ibid.

18. Gérard Fromanger, interview with the author.

19. Ibid.

20. Hervé Maury, interview with the author.

21. Christian Bourgois, interview with the author.

22. Yann Moulier-Boutang, interview with Virginie Linhart.

23. Gérard Fromanger, interview with the author.

24. Ibid.

25. Ibid.

26. Ibid.

27. Ulrike Meinhof was considered the mastermind of the RAF. Born in 1934 in Oldenburg, she studied philosophy, sociology, and pedagogy in the 1950s, then became a journalist and participated in the liberation of Andreas Baader on May 14, 1970, as well as several bombings.

28. Jean Chesneaux, *L'engagement des intellectuals 1944–2004. Itinéraire d'un historien franc-tireur.* (Toulouse: Privat, 2004), 259–260.

29. Gérard Soulier, interview with the author.

30. Bernard-Henri Lévy, interview with Eric Conan, Denis Jeambar, and Renaud Revel, *L'Express* (January 10, 2005).

31. Eric Alliez, interview with the author.

32. Jean Chesneaux, interview with the author.

33. Ibid.

34. Toni Negri, *Marx, au-delà de Marx* (Paris: Christian Bourgois, 1979).

35. Toni Negri, "Surpris par la nuit," radio broadcast with Alain Veinstein on *France Culture* (April 23, 2002), INA archives.

36. Yann Moulier-Boutang, interview with Virginie Linhart.

37. Gisèle Donnard, interview with Virginie Linhart.

38. Gilles Deleuze, "Lettera aperta ai guidieri di Negri," *La Repubblica* (May 10, 1979). Reprinted in Gilles Deleuze, *Deux régimes de fous. Textes et entretiens, 1975–1995*, ed. David Lapoujade (Paris: Minuit, 2003), 115–159.

39. Ibid., 156.

40. Ibid., 157.

41. Ibid., 158.

42. Gilles Deleuze, *Le matin de Paris* (December 13, 1979). Reprinted in Deleuze, *Deux régimes de fous*, 161.

43. Toni Negri, letter to Félix Guattari (Trani, July 18, 1980), IMEC archives.

44. Toni Negri, letter to Félix Guattari (Rome, November 28, 1980), IMEC archives.

45. Toni Negri, letter to Félix Guattari (Rebbibia, Rome, July 10, 1982), IMEC archives.

46. Toni Negri, interview with the author.

47. Ibid.

48. Toni Negri, interview with Virginie Linhart.

49. The "Mitterand Doctrine" concerns commitments made by President François Mitterrand in 1985 to not extradite former activists with links to the far left who had broken with their "somber years" past.

50. Toni Negri, interview with the author.

51. Félix Guattari and Toni Negri, *Les nouveaux espaces de liberté*, "Communists Like Us?" (New York: Semiotexte).

52. Félix Guattari and Toni Negri, *Les nouveaux espaces de libertés*, 7.

53. Ibid., 12.

54. Ibid., 15.

55. Ibid., 98.

56. Ibid., 103.

57. Ibid., 108.

58. François Pain, interview with the author.

59. François Aubral, interview with the author.

60. François Pain, interview with the author.

61. Ibid.

62. Gérard Soulier, interview with the author.

63. Jean-Pierre Faye, interview with the author.

64. Paul Virilio, interview with the author.

65. François Pain, interview with the author.

66. ALFREDO is a combination of ALO ("Association for Freedom of the Waves") and the Italian FRED ("Federation of Italian Associative Radio Stations").

67. Michel Tubiana, interview with the author.

68. Gisèle Donnard, interview with the author.

69. Mathieu Dalle, "Les radios libres, utopie deleuzo-Guattarienne," *French Cultural Studies* 17, no. 1 (February 2006): 67.

70. François Pain, interview with the author.

71. Félix Guattari, *Libération* (August 27, 1981).

72. "Entretien avec Jack Lang sur les radios libres," in *La Quinzaine Littéraire* (November 16–30, 1981).

73. Ibid.

74. "Nous, dissidents," in *Recherches* 34 (October 1978).

17. DELEUZE AND FOUCAULT: A PHILOSOPHICAL FRIENDSHIP

1. Michel Foucault, "Theatrum Philosophicum" (1970), in *Dits et écrits* (Paris: Gallimard, 1994), 2:76. In English translation in Michel Foucault, *Language, Counter-Memory, Practice: Selected Essays and Interviews*, ed. Donald F. Bouchard (Ithaca, N.Y.: Cornell University Press, 1977), 165–197.

2. Fanny Deleuze, interview with the author.

3. Paul Veyne, interview with the author.

4. Ibid.

5. Gilles Deleuze, "Fendre les choses, fendre les mots" (1986), in *Pourparlers* (Paris: Minuit, 1990), 117. Translated as "Breaking Things Open, Breaking Words Open," in *Negotiations, 1972–1990*, trans. Martin Joughin (New York: Columbia University Press, 1990), 85.

6. Ibid., 117.

7. Gilles Deleuze with Claire Parnet, *L'abécédaire de Gilles Deleuze* (1988), 3 DVDs (Montparnasse: Arte Video, 1997).

8. Gilles Deleuze, in Didier Eribon, *Michel Foucault* (Paris: Flammarion, 1989), 83.

9. Ibid., 162.

10. Ibid., 163.

11. See chapter 7.

12. Michel Foucault, "La prose d'Actéon" (1964), translated as "The Prose of Acteon" in *Aesthetics, Methods, Epistemology*, ed. James D. Faubion (New York: The New Press, 1999); Gilles Deleuze, "Klossowski ou les corps-langages" (1965), translated as "Klossowski or Bodies-Language" in *The Logic of Sense* (Translated as *The Logic of Sense*, trans. Mark Lester with Charles Stivale (New York: Columbia University Press, 1979).

13. Philippe Sabot, "Foucault, Deleuze et les simulacres," *Concepts* 8 (2004): 6.

14. Gilles Deleuze, *The Logic of Sense*, 283.

15. Ibid., 299.

16. Gilles Deleuze, Paris-VIII seminar (January 28, 1986), National Library sound archives.

17. Michel Foucault, "Theatrum Philosophicum," in *Dits et écrits*, 2:98; *Language, Counter-Memory, Practice*, 165–197.

18. François Zourabichvili, *Deleuze. Une philosopie de l'événement* (Paris: PUF, 1994).

19. Michel Foucault, "Theatrum Philosophicum," in *Dits et écrits*, 2:85; *Language, Counter-Memory, Practice*, 185.

20. Gilles Deleuze, Paris-VIII seminar (May 20, 1986), French National Library sound archives.

21. Philippe Artières, Laurent Quéro, and Michelle Zancarini-Fournel, *Le groupe d'informations sur les prisons. Archives d'une lutte 1970–72* (Paris: IMEC, 2005), 28.

22. Daniel Defert, "L'émergence d'un nouveau front: les prisons," in *Le groupe d'informations sur les prisons*, 317. Around twenty people gathered at Foucault's home for the meeting, including Daniel Defer, Casamayor, Jean-Marie Domenach, Louis Joinet, Frédéric Pottecher, Christian Revon, Jean-Jacques de Felice, Christine Martineau, Danielle Rancière, and Jacques Donzelot.

23. Ibid., 318.

24. Notably by the Bruay-en-Artois affair of 1972. Near the miners' quarters in Bruay, the naked, mutilated body of a teenage girl named Brigitte Dewèvre, a miner's daughter, was found. Pascal, the judge, quickly decided to charge the solicitor Pierre Leroy. The Maoist daily *La Cause de Peuple* considered that only a bourgeois pig could have committed such a crime and a popular tribunal was formed in the name of necessary popular justice.

25. Gilles Deleuze, Paris-VIII seminar (January 28, 1986), French National Library sound archives.

26. Jean-Pierre Faye, interview with the author.

27. Jacques Donzelot, interview with the author.

28. Jacques Donzelot, *La police des familles* (Paris: Minuit, 1977).

29. Jacques Donzelot, interview with the author.

30. Michel Foucault, reported by Jacques Donzelot, interview with the author.

31. Deleuze wrote a handsome afterword entitled "L'ascension du social." Gilles Deleuze, "L'ascension du social," afterword to Jacques Donzelot, *La police des familles*, 213–220.

32. Alain Joubert, *Michel Foucault, une journée particulière* (Lyon: Aedelsa Editions, 2004), 15.

33. Reprinted in Gilles Deleuze, *L'île déserte et autres textes. Textes et entretiens 1953–1974*, ed. David Lapoujade (Paris: Minuit, 2002). Translated as *Desert Islands and Other Texts (1953–1974)*, trans. Mike Taormina (New York: Semiotexte, 2003), 204–205.

34. Ibid., 286.

35. Claude Mauriac, *Mauriac et fils* (Paris: Grasset, 1986), 388.

36. The companie républicaine de sécurité, or CRS.

37. Gilles Deleuze, Paris-VIII archives, BDIC.

38. See Didier Eribon, *Michel Foucault*.

39. Gilles Deleuze, "Les intellectuels et le pouvoir," *L'Arc* 49 (March 4, 1972). Translated as "Intellectuals and Power," in Michel Foucault, *Language, Counter-Memory, Practice*.

40. Ibid., 289.

41. Judith Revel, interview with the author.

42. See chapter 15.

43. Gérard Soulier, interview with the author.

44. Much later on it became known that this democratic figure and state attorney was, in fact, a Stasi agent.

45. Claude Mauriac, *Mauriac et fils*, 294.

46. Gilles Deleuze, letter to James Miller (February 7, 1990). In James Miller, *Michel Foucault* (Paris: Plon, 1993), 346.

47. See chapter 20.

48. James Miller, *Michel Foucault*, 345.

49. Gilles Deleuze, "Grandeur de Yasser Arafat," *Revue d'Études Palestiniennes* 10 (Winter 1984): 41–43. Reprinted in Gilles Deleuze, *Deux régimes de fous* (Paris: Minuit, 2003), 221–225. Translated as "The Grandeur of Yasser Arafat," *Discourse* 20, no. 3 (Fall 1998): 30–33.

50. Michel Foucault, *Le Monde* (October 17–18, 1986). Reprinted in *Dits and écrits*, 2:96.

51. Jacques Donzelot, interview with the author.

52. Ibid.

53. See chapter 10.

54. Jacques Donzelot, interview with the author.

55. Michel Foucault, *La volonté de savoir* (Paris: Gallimard, 1976). Translated as *The History of Sexuality, Vol. 1: An Introduction*, trans. Robert Hurley (New York: Pantheon, 1978).

56. Gilles Deleuze, "Désir et plaisir" (on Foucault's *La volonté de savoir*), in *Magazine Littéraire* 325 (October 1994): 59–65. Reprinted in Gilles Deleuze, *Deux régimes de fous*, 112–122. Translated as "Desire and Pleasure" in Gilles Deleuze, *Two Regimes of Madness: Texts and Interviews, 1975–1995*, ed. David Lapoujade, trans. Ames Hodges and Mike Taormina (New York: Semiotexte, 2006), 122–134.

57. Ibid., 118–119.

58. Ibid., 119.

59. James Miller, *Michel Foucault*, 345.

60. David Rabouin, "Entre Deleuze et Foucault: penser le désir," *Critique* 637/638 (June–July 2000), 475–490.

61. Ibid., 485.

62. Michel Foucault, interview with Gérard Raulet, "Structuralisme et post-structuralisme," *Telos* 16, no. 55 (Spring 1983), 195–211. Reprinted in Michel Foucault, *Dits et écrits*, 4:445.

63. Eric Alliez, interview with the author.

64. Gilles Deleuze, Paris-VIII seminar (January 21, 1986), French National Library sound archives.

65. Ibid.

66. Jacques Donzelot, interview with the author.

67. Gilles Deleuze, "Désir et plaisir," in *Deux régimes de fous*, 113.

68. Paul Veyne, "Le dernier Foucault et sa morale," *Critique* 471/472 (August–September 1986): 940n1.

69. Hervé Couchot, "Philosophie et vérité: quelques remarques sur un chassé-croisé," *Concepts* 8 (2004): 29.

70. Gilles Deleuze, "Désir et plaisir," in *Deux régimes de fous*, 118.

71. Michel Foucault, introduction to his seminar at the Collège de France (January 11, 1978), public recording, quoted by Hervé Couchot, "Philosophie et vérité," 39n1.

72. Hervé Couchot, "Philosophie et vérité," 43.

73. Thomas Bénatouil, "Deux usages du stoïcisme: Deleuze et Foucault," in Frédéric Gros and Carlos Lévy, *Foucault et la philosophie antique* (Paris: Kimé, 2003), 31.

74. Gilles Deleuze, *The Logic of Sense*, 179.

75. Gilles Deleuze, Paris-VIII Foucault seminar (May 6, 1986), French National Library sound archives.

76. Ibid.

77. Michel Foucault, *L'usage des plaisirs* (Paris: Gallimard, 1984), 90. Translated as *The Use of Pleasure: The History of Sexuality, vol. 2*, trans. Robert Hurley (New York: Random House, 1985).

78. Matthieu Potte-Bonneville, interview with the author.

79. Judith Revel, interview with the author.

80. Gilles Deleuze, Paris-VIII Foucault seminar, BNF audio archives.

81. "Kant is the first to have defined the human being in relation to the split which divides each one of us." Kant brought about the development of modern philosophy by differentiating two heterogeneous dimensions and by insisting on the irreducible disjunction between receptivity and spontaneity, between intuitions and concepts, and by making finiteness into a constitutive principle: "With Kant, something came to light which could not be seen beforehand." Ibid.

82. Gilles Deleuze, "Un portrait de Foucault," interview with Claire Parnet (1986), in Gilles Deleuze, *Pourparlers*, 140. Translated as "A Portrait of Foucault" in Gilles Deleuze, *Negotiations*, 103.

83. Judith Revel, "Foucault lecteur de Deleuze: de l'écart à la différence," *Critique* 591/592 (August–September 1996), 734.

84. See chapter 2.

85. Judith Revel, interview with the author.

86. Ibid.

87. Michel Foucault, *The Archeology of Knowledge*, trans. A. M. Sheridan (London: Tavistock, 1972), 10.

88. Gilles Deleuze, interview with Raymond Bellour and François Ewald, *Le Magazine Littéraire* (September 1988): 24.

89. "Necessarily, we must dismiss those tendencies that encourage the consoling play of recognitions. We need to break into pieces everything that enables the consoling game of recognitions. Knowledge, even under the banner of history, does not depend on 'rediscovery' and it emphatically excludes the 'rediscovery of ourselves.' History becomes 'effective' to the degree that it introduces discontinuity into our very being—as it divides our emotions, dramatizes our instincts, multiplies our bodies and confronts them with themselves. . . . This is because knowledge is not made for understanding, but for cutting." Michel Foucault, "Nietzsche, généalogie, histoire" (1971), in *Dits et écrits*, 2:147–148. Translated as "Nietzsche, Genealogy, History," in Michel Foucault, *Language, Counter-Memory, Practice*, 154 (translation slightly modified).

90. Ibid.

91. Foucault, *Les mots et les choses* (Paris: Gallimard, 1966), 343. Translated as *The Order of Things: An Archaeology of the Human Sciences* (New York: Vintage, 1970), 331.

92. Gilles Deleuze, *Dialogues*, 80.

93. Gilles Deleuze and Felix Guattari, *Mille plateaux* (Paris: Minuit, 1980), 103. November 20, 1923, is linked to galloping inflation in Germany after 1918: "The curtain falls on 20 November 1923," wrote J. K. Galbraith in *Money: Whence It Came, Where It Went*, rev. ed. (New York: Houghton Mifflin, 1995).

94. Friedrich Nietzsche, *Untimely Meditations*, trans. R. J. Hollingdale (Cambridge: Cambridge University Press, 1983).

95. Gilles Deleuze, *The Logic of Sense*, 53.

96. Ibid., 54.

97. Michel Foucault, *L'ordre du discours* (Paris: Gallimard, 1971), 53.

98. Ibid., 55.

99. Gilles Deleuze and Félix Guattari, *Mille plateaux*, 320. Translated as *A Thousand Plateaus* (Minneapolis: University of Minnesota Press, 1987), 262.

100. "Not being inferior to the event, becoming the child of one's own events." Gilles Deleuze, *Dialogues*, 62–63.

101. Ibid., 49.

102. Gilles Deleuze, "Un nouvel archiviste" (1970) and "Ecrivain non: un nouveau cartographe" (1975). Revised versions printed in Gilles Deleuze, *Foucault*, trans. Sean Hand (New York: Continuum, 2006), 11–30, 31–51.

103. Gilles Deleuze, interview with Didier Eribon (1986), in *Pourparlers*, 129. Translated as "Life as a Work of Art," in *Negotiations*, 94.

104. Ibid.

105. Gilles Deleuze, *Foucault*, 43.

106. Gilles Deleuze, Paris-VIII Foucault seminar (December 17, 1985), French National Library sound archive.

107. Gilles Deleuze, Paris-VIII Foucault seminar (May 6, 1986), French National Library sound archive.

108. Ibid.

109. Mathieu Potte-Bonneville, interview with the author.

110. Frédéric Gros, "Le Foucault de Deleuze: une fiction métaphysique," *Philosophie* 47 (September 1995): 53–63.

111. Ibid., 54.

112. Ibid., 63.

113. Frédéric Gros, interview with the author.

114. Robert Maggiori, "Gilles Deleuze–Michel Foucault: une amitié philosophique," *Libération* (September 2, 1986).

115. François Regnault, interview with the author.

116. Gilles Deleuze, "Qu'est-ce qu'un dispositif?," in *Michel Foucault philosophe* (Paris: Seuil, 1989), 185–195. Translated as "What Is a Dispositive?" in *Michel Foucault Philosopher*, ed. and trans. T. Armstrong (New York: Routledge, 1991).

117. Gilles Deleuze, Paris-VIII Foucault seminar (November 26, 1985), French National Library sound archive.

118. Ibid.

119. Ibid.

120. Gilles Deleuze, Paris-VIII Foucault seminar (April 22, 1986), French National Library sound archive.

121. Ibid.

122. Michel Foucault, *Raymond Roussel* (Paris: Gallimard, 1963).

123. Raymond Roussel, *Comment j'ai écrit certains de mes livres* (Paris: UGE 10/18, 1977).

124. For example, Roussel would generate from the sentence "Les lettres du blanc sur les bandes du vieux billard [The white letters on the cushions of the old billiard table]" the punning and homonymic sentence "Les lettres du blanc sur les bandes du vieux

pillard [Letters by a white man about the hordes of the old plunderer]." He would then write a story linking these two concepts.

125. Gilles Deleuze, "Postscript on Control Societies," in *Negotiations*, 178.

126. Ibid.

127. Gilles Deleuze, Paris-VIII Foucault seminar (April 8, 1986), French National Library sound archive.

128. Ibid.

129. Deleuze, "Postscript on Control Societies," in *Negotiations*, 180.

130. Ibid., 182.

18. An Alternative to Psychiatry?

1. Jean Oury, in Jean Oury and Marie Depussé, *A quelle heure passe le train* . . . (Paris: Calmann-Lévy, 2003), 223.

2. Jean Oury, interview with the author.

3. Félix Guattari, "Guérilla en psychiatrie," *La Quinzaine Littéraire* 94 (May 1970). Reprinted in Félix Guattari, *Psychanalyse et transversalité* (Paris: Maspero, 1972; repr. Paris: La Découverte, 2003), 263.

4. See R. D. Laing, *The Politics of Experience* (London: Tavistock, 1967); David Cooper, *Psychiatry and Antipsychiatry* (London: Tavistock, 1967).

5. *Recherches* 7, "Enfance aliénée I" (September 1967); and *Recherches* 8, "Enfance aliénée II" (December 1968).

6. Félix Guattari, "Mary Barnes ou l'Oedipe antipsychiatrique" (1973), in *La révolution moleculaire* (Paris: Recherches, 1977), 125–136. Translated as "Mary Barnes's 'Trip,'" in *The Guattari Reader*, ed. Gary Genosko (Cambridge, Mass.: Blackwell, 1996), 46–54.

7. Ibid., 127; 47.

8. Félix Guattari, *La révolution moléculaire*, 152–153.

9. Pierre Blanchaud, interview with the author.

10. Ibid.

11. PIA brochure, "Psychaiatrie, la peur change de camp in Gardes Fous." Reprinted in Alain Joubert, Jean-Claude Salomon, Nathalie Weil, and Ian Segal, *Guide de la France des luttes* (Paris: Stock, 1974), 371.

12. "Cahiers pour la folie," "Garde-fous," "Marge," "Tankonalasanté," "Brèche," "Le Vouvray," "Psychiatrie en liberté de Saint-Dizier," and "La Gratte," among others.

13. Mony Elkaïm, interview with Virginie Linhart.

14. Ibid.

15. Félix Guattari, *La révolution moléculaire*, 149.

16. Ibid., 155.

17. See Mony Elkaïm, ed., *Réseau-alternative à la psychiatrie, Collectif International* (Paris: 10/18, 1977).

18. Mony Elkaïm, interview with Virginie Linhart.

19. Ibid.

20. Ibid.

21. Jean-Claude Polack, interview with the author.

22. Claude Sigala, letter to Guattari (January 22, 1983), IMEC archives.

23. Ibid.

24. Claude Sigala, letter to Félix Guattari (February 4, 1983), IMEC archives.

25. Claude Sigala, *Vivre avec* (Paris: Editions du Coral, 1987).

26. Claude Sigala, letter to Félix Guattari (August 9, 1992), IMEC archives.

27. Félix Guattari, "Un changement de paradigme," third meeting, Latin-American Alternative to Psychiatry Network, Buenos Aires (December 17–21, 1986), typescript, IMEC archives.

28. Félix Guattari, diary entry (September 27, 1989), Paris. "Le Journal de Léros," typescript, IMEC archives, published in *Chimères* 18 (Winter 1992–1993): 36.

29. Félix Guattari, diary entry (October 9). *Chimères* 18 (Winter 1992–1993), 44.

30. Félix Guattari, diary entry (October 10). *Chimères* 18 (Winter 1992–1993): 46.

31. Félix Guattari, diary entry (October 11). *Chimères* 18 (Winter 1992–1993): 51.

32. Félix Guattari, typescript, "The Alternative to Psychiatry Network" (1990), IMEC archives.

33. Félix Guattari, handwritten letter to Maria Grazia and Franco about the Alternative to Psychiatry Network, IMEC archives.

34. Ibid.

35. See Francisco Varela, *Autonomie et connaissance* (Paris: Seuil, 1989).

19. DELEUZE AT VINCENNES

1. Preliminary instructions for teaching philosophy (March 1969), "Vincennes," BDIC Archives.

2. Judith Miller, interview with Madeleine Chapsal and Michèle Manceaux, *L'Express* (March 16, 1970). Her statement provoked an immediate reaction. On April 3, 1970, she received a letter from the ministry ending her secondment to the university and sending her back to teach high school.

3. See Charles Soulié, "Le destin d'une institution d'avant-garde: histoire du département de philosophie de Paris-VIII," *Histoire de l'Éducation* 77 (January 1998): 57.

4. Gilles Deleuze with Claire Parnet, *L'abécédaire de Gilles Deleuze* (1988), 3 DVDs (Montparnasse: Arte Video, 1997).

5. Ibid.

6. "Vincennes" archives, BDIC.

7. Roger-Pol Droit, *Le Monde* (November 15, 1974).

8. Gilles Deleuze and Jean-Francois Lyotard, "A propos du département de psychanalyse à Vincennes," *Les Temps Modernes* 342 (January 1975): 862–863. Reprinted in Gilles Deleuze, *Deux régimes de fous* (Paris: Minuit, 2003), 56–57.

9. Ibid., 57.

10. Jacques Lacan, "Peut-être à Vincennes," *Ornicar?* 1 (January 1975): 3.

11. Ibid., 5.

12. Jacques Rancière, interview with the author.

13. Ibid.

14. Ibid.

15. Alice Saunier-Seïté, reported in *Ouest-France* (June 19, 1978). Reprinted in Pierre Merlin, *L'université assassinée: Vincennes 1968–1980* (Paris: Ramsay, 1980), 82.

16. René Schérer, interview with the author.

17. Noëlle Châtelet, interview with the author.

18. Ibid.

19. Ibid.

20. Gilles Deleuze, letter to François Châtelet (May 3, 1982), IMEC archive.

21. Noëlle Châtelet, interview with the author.

22. Ibid.

23. Gilles Deleuze, seminar (January 7, 1986), University of Paris-VII, National Library sound archives.

24. Gilles Deleuze, "Il était une étoile de groupe," *Libération* (December 27, 1985): 21–22. Reprinted in Gilles Deleuze, *Deux régimes de fous*, 247.

25. Ibid., 249.

26. Gilles Deleuze, *Péricles et Verdi. La philosophie de François Châtelet* (Paris: Minuit, 1998), 8. Translated as "Pericles and Verdi: The Philosophy of Francois Chatelet," *The Opera Quarterly* 21, no. 4 (Autumn 2005), 716–724.

27. Ibid., 9.

28. François Châtelet, *Périclès* (Paris: Club français du livre, 1960).

29. Deleuze, *Péricles et Verdi*, 20.

30. Ibid., 25.

31. René Schérer, interview with the author.

32. See chapter 15.

33. René Schérer, interview with the author.

34. Ibid.

35. The many doctoral students Schérer inherited from Deleuze included Yvonne Thoros, Jean-Clet Martin, and Giorgio Passerone.

36. Christian Deschamps, interview with the author.

37. See chapter 10, above.

38. Jean-François Lyotard, *L'economie libidinale* (Paris: Minuit, 1974). Translated as *Libidinal Economy*, trans. Iain Hamilton Grant (Indianapolis: Indiana University Press, 1993).

39. Corinne Enaudeau, interview with the author.

40. Ibid.

41. Jean-François Lyotard, *La condition postmoderne* (Paris: Minuit, 1979). Translated as *The Postmodern Condition: A Report on Knowledge*, trans. Geoff Bennington and Brian Massumi (Minneapolis: University of Minnesota Press, 1984).

42. "Plus de vagues, des vogues," Guattari, quoted by Jean Chesneaux, interview with the author.

43. Jean-François Lyotard, *Le différend* (Paris: Minuit, 1983). Translated as *The Differend: Phrases in Dispute*, trans. Georges van den Abeele (Minneapolis: University of Minnesota Press, 1988).

44. Jean-François Lyotard, *Libération* (November 5, 1995). Reprinted in Jean-François Lyotard, *Misère de la philosophie* (Paris: Galilée, 2000), 194.

45. Jean-François Lyotard, quoted by Corinne Enaudeau, interview with the author.

46. Pierre Chevalier, "Gilles Deleuze: avez-vous des questions à poser?" Radio France Culture (April 20, 2002), program by Jean Daive and Clotilde Pivin, INA archives.

47. Gilles Deleuze with Claire Parnet, *L'abécédaire de Gilles Deleuze*, letter P for "Professor."

48. Claude Jaeglé, *Portrait oratoire de Gilles Deleuze aux yeux jaunes* (Paris: PUF, 2005).

49. Ibid., 18–19.

50. Ibid., 24.

51. Gilles Deleuze, in "Gilles Deleuze: avez-vous des questions à poser?"

52. Gilles Deleuze, seminar (January 17, 1984), French National Library audio archives.

53. Claude Jaeglé, *Portrait oratoire de Gilles Deleuze aux yeux jaunes*, 32.

54. Ibid., 33.

55. Elisabeth Roudinesco, *Généalogies* (Paris: Fayard, 1994), 53.

56. See chapter 10.

57. Philippe Mengue, in Yannick Beaubatie, ed., *Tombeau de Gilles Deleuze* (Tulle: Mille Sources, 2000), 49.

58. Gilles Deleuze, quoted by Philippe Mengue, interview with the author.

59. Philippe Mengue, *Gilles Deleuze ou le système du multiple* (Paris: Kimé, 1994); Philippe Mengue, *Deleuze et la question de la démocratie* (Paris: Kimé, 2003).

60. Richard Pinhas, interview with the author.

61. Ibid.

62. Pierre Blanchaud, interview with the author.

63. François Zourabichvili, *Deleuze. La philosophie de l'événement* (Paris: PUF, 1994).

64. François Zourabichvili, interview with the author.

65. Ibid.

66. François Zourabichvili, *Spinoza: une physique de la pensée* (Paris: PUF, 2002); François Zourabichvili, *Le conservatisme paradoxale de Spinoza: enfance et royauté* (Paris: PUF, 2002).

67. François Zourabichvili, interview with the author.

68. Ibid.

69. Elias Sanbar, interview with the author.

70. David Lapoujade, interview with the author.

71. Ibid.

72. Hidenobu Suzuki, interview with the author.

73. Ibid.

74. Ibid.

75. The full set of recordings is available in the audiovisual hall of the French National Library: 177 classes, 400 hours, between 1979 and 1987. Inventory published by Frédéric Astier, *Les cours enregistrés de Gilles Deleuze: 1979–1987* (Mons: Sils Maria, 2006).

76. Giorgio Passerone, "Le dernier cours?" *Le Magazine Littéraire* 257 (September 1988): 35–37.

77. Giorgio Passerone, interview with the author.

78. Giorgio Passerone, "Le dernier cours?" 36.

79. Ibid.

80. Gilles Deleuze, Paris-VIII seminar (June 2, 1987), French National Library audio archives.

20. The Year of Combat: 1977

1. Gilles Deleuze and Félix Guattari, *Rhizome* (Paris: Minuit, 1976). Reprinted as the first chapter in Gilles Deleuze and Félix Guattari, *Mille plateaux* (Paris: Minuit, 1980).

2. Gilles Deleuze and Félix Guattari, *Kafka. Pour une littérature mineure* (Paris: Minuit, 1975), 7–8.

3. Anne Sauvagnargues, *Deleuze et l'art* (Paris: PUF, 2005), 120.

4. Gilles Deleuze and Félix Guattari, *Rhizome*, 15; *A Thousand Plateaus*, 6.

5. Ibid., 17; 7.

6. Ibid., 18; 8.

7. Gilles Deleuze, "Réponse à une série de questions" (November 1981), in Arnaud Villani, *La guêpe et l'orchidée* (Paris: Belin, 1999), 131.

8. Gilles Deleuze and Félix Guattari, *Rhizome*, 24; *A Thousand Plateaus*, 9.

9. Ibid., 27; 10.

10. Ibid., 63; 24.

11. Anne Sauvagnargues, *Deleuze et l'art*, 181–183.

12. Alain Badiou, "Le flux et le parti," *Cahier Yénan* 4 (1977): 26.

13. Ibid., 38.

14. Ibid., 40–41.

15. Georges Peyrol (i.e., Alain Badiou), "Le fascisme de la pomme de terre," *Cahier Yénan* 4 (1977): 43.

16. Ibid., 44.

17. Ibid., 50.

18. Ibid., 51–52.

19. Alain Badiou, *Deleuze. La clameur de l'être* (Paris: Hachette, 1997). Translated as *Deleuze: The Clamor of Being*, trans. Louise Burchill (Minneapolis: University of Minnesota Press, 2000).

20. Reported by Alain Roger, interview with the author.

21. Reported by Philippe Mengue, interview with the author.

22. Ibid.

23. Alain Badiou, *Deleuze. La clameur de l'être*.

24. Ibid., 12.

25. Ibid., 19–20.

26. Gilles Deleuze, *Difference and Repetition* (Paris: PUF, 1968), 304.

27. Alain Badiou, *Deleuze. La clameur de l'être*, 22; 12.

28. Gilles Deleuze, *The Logic of Sense* (New York: Columbia University Press, 1990), 268.

29. Ibid.

30. Alain Badiou, *Deleuze. La clameur de l'être*, 24.

31. Gilles Deleuze, *Negotiations* (New York: Columbia University Press, 1995), 144.

32. Alain Badiou, *Deleuze. La clameur de l'être*, 24.

33. Gilles Deleuze, Paris-VIII seminar (May 27, 1980). IMEC archives.

34. Alain Badiou, *Deleuze. La clameur de l'être*, 26.

35. Ibid., 69.

36. Ibid., 70.

37. Ibid., 115.

38. Ibid., 98.

39. Alain Badiou, *Le siècle* (Paris: Seuil, 2005). Translated as *The Century* (London: Polity Press, 2007).

40. "Without doing so, it is not 'two in one,' Badiou on Deleuze, but one split in two, Badiou on Badiou." Arnaud Villani, "La métaphysique de Deleuze," *Futur Antérieur* 43 (April 1998): 56.

41. Ibid.

42. José Gil, "Quatre méchantes notes sur un livre méchant," *Futur Antérieur* 43 (April 1998): 71–84.

43. Ibid., 77.

44. Guy Lardreau, *L'exercise différé de la philosophie. À l'occasion de Deleuze* (Paris: Verdier, 1999).

45. Ibid., 60n7.

46. Ibid., 15.

47. Ibid., 44.

48. Ibid., 62.

49. Ibid., 63.

50. Jean Baudrillard, *Oublier Foucault* (Paris: Galilée, 1977). Translated as *Forget Foucault* (New York: Semiotexte, 2007).

51. Ibid., 24.

52. Ibid., 37.

53. Ibid., 54.

54. Pierre Viansson-Ponté, preface to J. Paugam, *Génération perdue* (Paris: Laffont, 1977), 15–16.

55. Bernard-Henri Lévy, *Le barbarisme à visage humain* (Paris: Grasset, 1977). Translated as *Barbarism with a Human Face* (New York: Harper & Row, 1979).

56. Ibid., 20.

57. Ibid., 140.

58. Michel Foucault, "La grande colère des faits," *Le Nouvel Observateur* (May 9–15, 1977): 84–86.

59. Ibid.

60. François Aubral and Xavier Delcourt, *Contre la nouvelle philosophie* (Paris: Gallimard, 1977).

61. François Aubral, interview with the author.

62. Gilles Deleuze, quoted by François Aubral, interview with the author.

63. Ibid.

64. François Aubral, interview with the author.

65. Gilles Deleuze, "A propos des nouveaux philosophes et d'un problème plus général," supplement to *Minuit* 24 (May 1977). Reprinted in Gilles Deleuze, *Deux régimes de fous* (Paris: Minuit, 2003), 127.

66. "Clavel is reminiscent of Dr. Mabuse, an evangelical Dr. Mabuse; Jambet and Lardreau are Spöri and Pesch, his two assistants (they want to catch Nietzsche and 'bring him in'). Benoist is the messenger, Nestor. Lévy is first impresario, then script girl, jovial host, disk-jockey. . . ." Gilles Deleuze, *Deux régimes de fous*, 129.

67. Ibid., 131.

68. Ibid., 132.

69. Ibid., 133.

21. GUATTARI BETWEEN CULTURE AND ECOLOGY

1. Félix Guattari, "Enfin Jack Lang vint . . ." *Le Quotidien de Paris* (March 18, 1983). Also in *Le Nouvel Observateur*, "Plaidoyer pour un 'dictateur.'"

2. Ibid.

3. Félix Guattari, letter to Jack Lang (August 22, 1981), IMEC archives.

4. Félix Guattari's notes regarding a foundation, sent to Jack Lang (February 13, 1982), IMEC archives. The foundation was supposed to respond to the concern for creating a democratic, decentralized institution to establish the necessary connections among nonprofit associations. "A right to research ought to be proclaimed. Workers in a company, institutions, mothers in the same neighborhood should be able to become promoters of research."

5. Félix Guattari, letter to Jack Lang (January 26, 1983), IMEC archives.

6. Jack Lang, letter to Félix Guattari (January 6, 1983), IMEC archives.

7. Jack Lang, comments on the letter from Félix Guattari (April 14, 1984), IMEC archives.

8. Jean-Pierre Faye, interview with the author.

9. See chapter 19.

10. Jean-Pierre Faye, letter to Félix Guattari (October 26, 1981), IMEC archives.

11. Félix Guattari, letter to Jack Lang (September 26, 1984), IMEC archives.

12. Excerpts from the Open Letter, entitled "Quelle Europe veut-on construire?": "The extraditions and expulsions of Basques who have sought refuge in France creates a profound and potentially irreversible rift in the trust that we had in you, despite the uncertainties, and in the government of François Mitterrand. . . . Until now, political asylum was considered a fundamental right. . . . What kind of Europe are we creating with these procedures? The Europe of freedom or of social control and security raised to the level of a supreme cult?" *Le Monde* (October 18, 1984).

13. François Lyotard, "Tombeau des intellectuals," *Le Monde* (October 8, 1983). Reprinted in François Lyotard, *Tombeau des intellectuels et autres papiers* (Paris: Gallimard, 1984).

14. Maurice Blanchot, "Les intellectuels en question. Ébauche d'une reflexion," *Le Débat* 29 (March 1984).

15. Félix Guattari, "On a le racisme qu'on mérite," *Cosmopolis* (November 1983). Reprinted in Félix Guattari, *Les années d'hiver* (Paris: Barrault, 1985), 39.

16. Félix Guattari, "La gauche comme passion processuelle," *La Quinzaine Litteraire* (July 1984). Reprinted in Félix Guattari, *Les années d'hiver*, 53.

17. Félix Guattari, "Le cinquieme monde nationalitaire," conference at Bilbao (March 26, 1985). Reprinted in Félix Guattari, *Les années d'hiver*, 71.

18. Raymond Pronier and Vincent Jacques Le Seigneur, *Génération verte. Les écologistes en politique* (Paris: Presses de la Renaissance, 1992), 27.

19. Jean Chesneaux, interview with the author.

20. The GOP, *Gauche Ouvrière et Paysanne* (Worker and Peasant Left), with Marc Hergon, Alain Rist, Alain Lipietz, Alain Desjardin, and Gerard Peurière.

21. Félix Guattari and Daniel Cohn-Bendit, "Pavane pour un PSU défunt et des Verts mort-nés" (October 1986), IMEC Archives.

22. Jacques Robin, interview with Virginie Linhart.

23. Ibid.

24. Félix Guattari (April 1990), IMEC Archives.

25. Letter from the Greens Executive Secretariat to Félix Guattari (May 7, 1991).

26. Félix Guattari, letter to the Greens Executive Secretariat (May 13, 1991), IMEC Archives.

27. Ibid.

28. Félix Guattari, "Une autre vision du futur," *Le Monde* (February 15, 1992).

29. Félix Guattari, "Vers une nouvelle démocratie écologique" (July 1992), IMEC Archives.

30. Ibid.

31. Paul Virilio, interview with Virginie Linhart.

32. See chapter 14.

33. Paul Virilio, interview with Virginie Linhart.

34. See "A Geophilosophy of Politics," in Félix Guattari, *Cartographies schizoanalytiques* (Paris: Galilée, 1989).

35. Félix Guattari, *Les trois écologies* (Paris: Galilée, 1989).

36. Paul Virilio, interview with Virginie Linhart.

37. Félix Guatari, *Les trois écologies*, 62–63.

38. Ibid., 63.

39. Jacques Robin, interview with Virginie Linhart.

40. Paul Virilio, interview with Virginie Linhart.

41. Luc Ferry, *Le nouvel ordre écologique* (Paris: Grasset, 1992; repr. Paris: Livre de poche, 1998), 176.

42. Félix Guattari, *Chaosmose* (Paris: Galilée, 1992).

43. Danielle Sivadon, interview with the author.

44. Félix Guattari, *Chaosmose*, 16.

45. Daniel Stern, *Le monde interpersonnel du nourrisson* (Paris: PUF, 1989).

46. Félix Guattari, *Chaosmose*, 87.

47. Félix Guattari, *Cartographies schizoanalytiques*.

48. Félix Guattari, *Chaosmose*, 33.

49. Ibid., 49–50.

50. Pierre Lévy, *Les technologies de l'intelligence* (Paris: La Découverte, 1990).

51. Félix Guattari, *Chaosmose*, 141.

52. Ibid., 187.

53. Félix Guattari, "Réinventer la politique," *Le Monde* (March 8, 1990).

54. Félix Guattari, "Les nouveaux mondes du capitalisme," *Libération* (December 22, 1987).

55. Félix Guattari, "Pour une refondation des pratiques sociales," *Le Monde Diplomatique* (October 1992).

56. Ibid.

57. Ibid.

58. Félix Guattari, "Le courage d'une politique," *Lettre d'Information de Génération Écologie* 6 (January 28, 1991).

59. Gilles Deleuze and René Schérer, "La guerre immonde," *Libération* (March 4, 1991).

60. Ibid. Reprinted in Gilles Deleuze, *Deux régimes de fous* (Paris: Minuit, 2003), 351.

61. Ibid., 351.

62. Paul Virilio, "Le concept de guerre," typed transcription of dialogue with Guattari (August 4, 1992), IMEC archives.

63. Félix Guattari, ibid. August 4, 1992 dialogue.

64. Paul Virilio, interview with Virginie Linhart. See chapter 28.

22. DELEUZE GOES TO THE MOVIES

1. These years were 1981–1982, 1982–1983, and 1984–1985.

2. Gilles Deleuze, *Cinéma 1. L'image-mouvement* (Paris: Minuit, 1983); *Cinéma 2. L'image-temps* (Paris: Minuit, 1985). Translated as *Cinema I: The Movement-Image*, trans. Hugh Tomlinson and Barbara Habberjam (Minneapolis: University of Minnesota Press, 1986) and as *Cinema II: The Time-Image*, trans. Hugh Tomlinson and Barbara Habberjam (Minneapolis: University of Minnesota Press, 1989).

3. The film department at Vincennes was created as an arts department in the fall of 1968, but the high numbers of students enrolling forced the department to split up into subdisciplines.

4. Jean Narboni, interview with the author.

5. Guy Fihman, "Deleuze, Bergson, Zénon d'Elée et le cinéma," in Olivier Fahle and Lorenz Engell, ed., *Le cinéma selon Deleuze* (Paris: Presses de la Sorbonne nouvelle, 1997), 66.

6. Gilles Deleuze, *Le bergsonisme* (Paris: PUF, 1966). Translated as *Bergsonism*, trans. Hugh Tomlinson and Barbara Habberjam (New York: Zone Books, 1988).

7. Gilles Deleuze, "Trois questions sur *Six fois deux*," *Cahiers du Cinéma* 271 (November 1976). Reprinted in Gilles Deleuze, *Pourparlers* (Paris: Minuit, 1990), 55–56. Translated as *Negotiations*, trans. Martin Joughlin (New York: Columbia University Press, 1995), 37–45.

8. Jean Narboni, interview with the author.

9. Ibid.

10. He wrote a thesis for a *Diplôme d'études avancées* (diploma of advanced studies), a latter-day doctorate less demanding than the national doctorate (*doctorat d'état*), which typically took ten years to write and was extremely long.

11. André de Souza Parente, interview with the author.

12. He first published something in France on this topic in 2005, when he was the director of the Research Center for the Culture and Technology of the Image at the Federal University of Rio de Janeiro: *Cinéma et narrativité* (Pairs: L'Harmattan, 2005). The work had already been published in Brazil with a preface by Raymond Bellour.

13. Serge Toubiana, "Le cinéma est deleuzien," *Cahiers du Cinéma* 497 (December 1995): 20.

14. Ibid.

15. Ibid., 21.

16. Gilles Deleuze, "Un art de planteur," in *Deleuze, Faye, Roubaud, Touraine parlent de "Les Auters," un film de Hugo Santiago, écrite en collaboration avec Adolfo Bioy Casares et Jorge Luis Borges* (Paris: Christian Bourgois, 1974). Reprinted in Gilles Deleuze, *L'île déserte et autres textes* (Paris: Minuit, 2002), 401–403. Translated as *Desert Islands and Other Texts*: 1953–1974, trans. Mike Taormina (New York: Semiotexte, 2003).

17. Gilles Deleuze, "Le juif riche," *Le Monde* (February 18, 1977). Reprinted in Gilles Deleuze, *Deux régimes de fous* (Paris: Minuit, 2003), 123. Translated as *Two Regimes of Madness: Texts and Interviews, 1975–1995* (New York: Semiotexte, 2006).

18. Ibid., 124.

19. Claude Lanzmann, "Réponse à Gilles Deleuze. Nuit et Brouillard," *Le Monde* (February 23, 1977).

20. Ibid.

21. *Cahiers* sales dropped from 15,000 in 1968 and 1973 (subscriptions plus newsstand sales) to 3,403! See Antoine de Baecque, *Cahiers du cinéma, histoire d'une revue* (Paris, 1991), 2:225.

22. Serge Toubiana, interview with the author.

23. Ibid.

24. *Six fois deux/Sur et sous la communication* was a series of TV shows broadcast in 1976 that included a warning stating that it was not like other programs. Jean-Luc Godard developed his thoughts on communication and especially on the production,

transmission, and reception of information on TV. The six programs each included two parts: the first was theoretical, discussing an aspect of the production and consumption of images; there was then a response in the form of an interview with an individual offering a subjective viewpoint.

25. Jean Narboni, "Gilles Deleuze . . . une aile de papillon," *Cahiers du Cinéma* 497 (December 1995): 94.

26. Gilles Deleuze, "Trois questions sur *Six fois deux*," *Cahiers du Cinéma* 271 (November 1976). Reprinted in Gilles Deleuze, *Pourparlers*, 56; translated in Gilles Deleuze, *Negotiations*, 38.

27. Ibid., 57; 38.

28. Jean Narboni, interview with the author.

29. Pascal Bonitzer (1977), quoted by Antoine de Baecque, *Cahiers du cinéma, histoire d'une revue*, 2:296.

30. Pascal Bonitzer, interview with the author.

31. Dominique Païni, interview with the author.

32. Jean Narboni, "Gilles Deleuze . . . une aile de papillon," 25.

33. Gilles Deleuze, "Lettre à Serge Daney: optimisme, pessimisme et voyage," preface to Serge Daney, *Ciné journal* (Paris: Cahiers du cinéma, 1986). Reprinted in Gilles Deleuze, *Pourparlers*, 97–112; translated in Gilles Deleuze, *Negotiations*, 68–79.

34. Ibid., 101; 71.

35. Ibid., 110; 78.

36. See Dudley Andrew's bibliography in *André Bazin* (Paris: Cahiers du cinéma, 1983).

37. Antoine de Baecque, *Cahiers du cinéma, histoire d'une revue*, 1:58.

38. André Bazin, *Qu'est-ce que le cinéma?* (Paris: Cerf, 1976). Translated as *What Is Cinema?* trans. Hugh Grey (Berkeley: University of California Press, 1967, 1971).

39. Serge Toubiana, interview with the author.

40. Michel Ciment, interview with the author.

41. Michel Ciment, *Kubrick* (Paris: Calmann-Levy, 1980); Michel Ciment, *Les conquérants d'un nouveau monde: essais sur le cinema américain* (Paris: Gallimard, 1981).

42. Gilles Deleuze, *Masochism: An Interpretation of Coldness and Cruelty*, trans. Jean McNeil (New York: G. Braziller, 1971).

43. Alain Ménil, interview with the author.

44. Michel Ciment, interview with the author.

45. Raymond Bellour, interview with the author.

46. Gilles Deleuze, *Cinema 1. L'image-mouvement*, 7.

47. Ibid., 13.

48. Gilles Deleuze, Paris-VIII course (December 1, 1981), French National Library sound archives.

49. Henri Bergson, *L'évolution créatrice* (Paris: PUF, 1998), 341. Translated as *Creative Evolution*, trans. Arthur Mitchell (New York: Dover, 1998).

50. Gilles Deleuze, *Cinema 1. L'image-mouvement*, 18.

51. Paola Marrati, "Deleuze. Cinéma et philosophie," in *La philosophie de Deleuze* (Paris: PUF, 2004), 251.

52. Alain Ménil, "Deleuze et le bergsonisme du cinéma," *Philosophie* 47 (September 1995): 49. See also Alain Ménil, *L'écran du temps* (Lyon: PUL, 1992).

53. Gilles Deleuze, *Cinema 1. L'image-mouvement*, 97.

54. Gilles Deleuze, Paris-VIII course (January 5, 1982), French National Library sound archives.

55. Gilles Deleuze, *Cinema 2. L'image-temps*, 95.

56. Ibid., 130.

57. The past that is contemporary with the present gives the virtual image or the mirror image. "According to Bergson, the "paramnesis" (illusion of *déjà vu* and *déjà vécu*) only makes this evidence tangible." Ibid., 106. Pure virtuality does not need to actualize itself insofar as it is interwoven into the actual present image. It does not depend on a psychological state of consciousness but solely on the temporal dimension. But it is a matter of a particular temporality—not chronological temporality that can be divined in a crystal ball: "cronos not Chronos." Ibid., 107.

58. Gilles Deleuze, Paris-VIII course (June 7, 1983), French National Library sound archives.

59. Ibid.

60. Christian Metz, *Essais sur la signification au cinéma* (Paris: Klincksieck, 1969).

61. Ibid., 118.

62. Christian Metz, interview with Marc Vernet and Daniel Percheron, *Ça, Cinéma* (May 1975): 26.

63. Christian Metz, interview with Raymond Bellour, *Semiotica* 4, no. 1 (1971): 242.

64. Ibid., 266.

65. Gilles Deleuze, Paris-VIII course (February 26, 1985), French National Library sound archives.

66. Gilles Deleuze, *Cinema 2. L'image-temps*, 41.

67. Christian Metz, *Essais sur la signification au cinéma*, 53.

68. Gilles Deleuze, Paris-VIII course (March 5, 1985), French National Library sound archives.

69. Gilles Deleuze, Paris-VIII course (November 2, 1982), French National Library sound archives.

70. Charles Sanders Peirce, *Écrits sur le signe* (Paris: Seuil, 1978).

71. Jacques Aumont, interview with the author.

72. "Portrait du philosophe en spectateur," interview with Gilles Deleuze by Hervé Guibert, *Le Monde* (October 6, 1983).

73. Ibid.

74. Gilles Deleuze: "Cinéma 1, Première," *Libération* (October 3, 1983).

75. "La photographie est déjà tirée dans les choses," interview with Gilles Deleuze by Pascal Bonitzer and Jean Narboni, *Cahiers du Cinéma* 352 (October 1983).

76. Jérôme Bindé, *Le Nouvel Observateur* (October 21, 1983).

77. Jacques Aumont, interview with the author.

78. Dork Zabunyan, *Gilles Deleuze. Voir, parler, penser au risque du cinéma* (Paris: New Sorbonne Presses, 2006).

79. Dominique Château, *Cinéma et philosophie* (Paris: Nathan, 1996), 107.

80. Ibid., 142.

81. Jean-Louis Leturat, *Kaléidoscope* (Paris: PUL, 1988).

82. Ibid., 146.

83. Alain Ménil, *L'écran du temps*, 1988.

84. Serge Daney, *La rampe* (Paris: Gallimard, 1983), 172.

85. Gilles Deleuze, Paris-VIII course (May 4, 1982), French National Library sound archives.

86. Ibid.

87. Gilles Deleuze, *Cinema 2. L'image-temps*, 222.

88. Ibid., 223.

89. Ibid.

90. Ibid., 48.

91. Ibid., 59.

92. Ibid., 64.

93. Ibid., 76.

94. Ibid., 283.

95. Ibid., 17.

96. Jacques Rancière, *La fable cinématographique* (Paris: Seuil, 2001), 146.

97. Jean Epstein, *L'intelligence d'une machine. Écrits sur le cinéma, 1, 2* (Paris: Seghers, 1974).

98. Suzanne Hème de Lacotte, "Epstein et Deleuze, cinéma et image de la pensée," *Chimères* 57 (Fall 2005): 76–77.

99. Ibid., 79.

100. Gilles Deleuze, Paris-VIII course (October 30, 1984), French National Library sound archives.

101. Ibid.

102. Gilles Deleuze, Paris-VIII course (October 30, 1984), French National Library sound archives.

103. Gilbert Simondon, *L'individu et sa genèse physico-biologique* (Paris: PUF, 1964).

104. D. N. Rodowick, "La critique ou la vérité en crise," *Iris* 23 (Spring 1997): 8. See also D. N. Rodowick, *Gilles Deleuze's Time Machine* (Durham, N.C.: Duke University Press, 1997).

105. Ibid., 14.

106. Ibid., 22.

107. Gilles Deleuze, *Cinema 2. L'image-temps*, 246.

108. Ibid., 100.

109. Ibid., 101.

110. Ibid., 102.

23. GUATTARI AND AESTHETICS: CONSOLATION DURING THE WINTER YEARS

1. See chapter 1.

2. Arlette Donati, interview with Ève Cloarec (October 25, 1984), IMEC archives.

3. "Mad drama. 5 policemen wounded at Saint-Tropz. Gilles Guatareuze called the police to have his mistress interned. The least surprising wasn't seeing the famous theoretician of antipsychaitry running after the police chief of Saint-Tropez pleading, 'You aren't going to put her at La Borde or with the nice people, right! They could screw up and let her escape! They could screw up and let her escape! No, no, a serious place, right? A padded cell and everything.'" Gérard Lauzier, "Unbutton Your Brain," *Tranches de Vie* 4 (1978); reprinted in *Le meilleur des années 70* (Paris: Dargaud, 2001).

4. François Fourquet, interview with Virginie Linhart.

5. Ibid.

6. Jonathan Strauss, "The Fold," *Yale French Studies* 80 (1991): 227–247, translates pages 5–9 and 38–53 of the French text. Gilles Deleuze, *The Fold: Leibniz and the Baroque*, trans. Tom Conley (Minneapolis: University of Minnesota Press, 1993).

7. Jean Chesneaux, interview with the author.

8. Ibid.

9. Danielle Sivadon, interview with the author.

10. François Pain, interview with the author.

11. Jean-Jacques Lebel, interview with Virginie Linhart.

12. Christian Bourgois, interview with the author.

13. Jean-Jacques Lebel, interview with Virginie Linhart.

14. Jean Rolin, *Joséphine* (Paris: Gallimard, 1994), 20.

15. Eric Alliez, interview with the author.

16. Jean Oury, interview with the author.

17. Marie Depussé, interview with Virginie Linhart.

18. Emmanuelle Guattari, interview with Virginie Linhart.

19. Ibid.

20. Ibid.

21. Marie Depussé, interview with Virginie Linhart.

22. Félix Guattari, "L'amateur amate," IMEC archives. Published in Marc Pierret, *Le divan romancier* (Paris: Christian Bourgois, 1975).

23. Félix Guattari, "Crac en plan pas un pli" (April 1986), typed text, IMEC archives.

24. Gérard Fromanger, interview with the author.

25. Gérard Fromanger, interview with Virginie Linhart.

26. Félix Guattari, "Ritournelles," *La NRF* (January 1999): 338–374; (April 1999): 314–329.

27. Félix Guattari, "Les ritournelles Essere," handwritten notes (May 1999), IMEC archives.

28. Ibid.

29. Ibid.

30. Félix Guattari, "Les ritournelles du temps perdu," in *L'inconscient machinique* (Paris: Recherches, 1979).

31. Ibid., 308.

32. Enzo Cormann, "Comme sans y penser," *Chimères* 23 (Summer 1994): 25.

33. The original group included Denise Bonal, Enzo Cormann, Roland Dubillard, Jean-Claude Grumberg, Félix Guattari, Jean Jourdheuil, Romain Weingarten, and Jean-Paul Wenzel.

34. Félix Guattari, "Gérard Fromanger, la nuit, le jour," *Eighty Magazine* 4 (August 1984). Reprinted in Félix Guattari, *Les années d'hiver* (Paris: Barrault, 1992), 249.

35. Ibid., 256.

36. Félix Guattari, "Cythère, ville nouvelle," FIAC 1986, Grand Palais (October 24–November 2, 1986), handwritten notes, IMEC archives.

37. Félix Guattari, "Imaï, peintre de la chaosmose," typed text, IMEC archives.

38. Félix Guattari, "Le cinéma: un art mineur," in *La revolution moléculaire* (Paris: Recherches, 1977), 203–238.

39. Félix Guattari, "Le cinema doit devenir un art mineur," *Revue Cinématographique* 18 (April 1976). Reprinted in *La revolution moléculaire*, 205.

40. Félix Guattari, "Le divan du pauvre," *Communications* 23 (April 1975).

41. Ibid., 233.

42. Ibid., 237.

43. Félix Guattari, "L'énonciation architecturale" typed text, IMEC archives.

44. Ibid.

45. Nicolas Bourriaud, "Le paradigme ésthetique," *Chimères* (Winter 1994): 77–94.

46. Ibid.

47. Olivier Zahm, "Félix Guattari et l'art contemporain," *Chimères* (Summer 1994): 48.

24. DELEUZE DIALOGUES WITH CREATION

1. See chapter 22.

2. Gilles Deleuze, *Critique et clinique* (Paris: Minuit, 1993), 11. Translated as *Essays Critical and Clinical*, trans. Daniel Smith and Michael Greco (Minneapolis: University of Minnesota Press, 1997).

3. Ibid., 12.

4. Ibid., 13.

5. Gilles Deleuze, *Dialogues II*, trans. High Tomlinson and Barbara Habberjam (New York: Columbia University Press, 36).

6. Ibid., 48.

7. Ibid., 42.

8. Ibid., 44.

9. Ibid., 49.

10. Henry Miller, *Sexus* (Paris: Buchet-Chastel), 29.

11. Marcel Proust, *Correspondance avec madame Strauss*, letter 47 (Paris: Livre de poche, 1972), 110–115; quoted by Gilles Deleuze, *Critique et clinique*, 16.

12. Gilles Deleuze, *Critique et clinique*, 138n4.

13. Gilles Deleuze, afterword to Herman Melville, *Bartleby* (Paris: Flammarion, 1989); reprinted in *Critique et clinique*, 89–114.

14. Gilles Deleuze, *Critique et clinique*, 91.

15. Ibid., 110.

16. Ibid., 112.

17. Jacques Rancière, *La chair des mots* (Paris: Galilée, 1998), 203.

18. Ibid., 202.

19. Olivier Mongin, interview with the author.

20. Ibid.

21. Ibid.

22. Edouard Glissant, "Philosophie de la mondialité," *France Culture* (July 25, 2003).

23. Ibid.

24. Ibid.

25. Christina Kullberg, interview with the author.

26. Anne Sauvagnargues, *Deleuze et l'art* (Paris: PUF, 2005), 19.

27. Gilles Deleuze and Félix Guattari, *Mille plateaux* (Paris: Minuit, 1980), 235–252.

28. Gilles Deleuze and Félix Guattari, *Mille plateaux*, 243.

29. Pierrette Fleutiaux, interview with the author.

30. Pierrette Fleutiaux, "Le philosophe, d'lourès, le philosophe," in *Nous sommes éternels* (Paris: Gallimard, 1990), 679–692.

31. Ibid., 681.

32. Gilles Deleuze, "Philosophie de la série noire," *Arts et Loisirs* 18 (January 26–February 1, 1966): 12–13. Reprinted in Gilles Deleuze, *L'île déserte et autres textes* (Paris: Minuit, 2002), 117.

33. Raymond Bellour dedicated the preface to the *Complete Works of Henri Michaux*, to, among others, Gilles Deleuze and Félix Guattari. Henri Michaux, *Oeuvres complètes* (Paris: Gallimard, 1998).

34. Ibid., xiii.

35. Ibid., xiv.

36. Gilles Deleuze, *Foucault* (Paris: Minuit, 126).

37. Henri Michaux, *Oeuvres complètes*, 3:xxxix.

38. Raymond Bellour, in Eric Alliez, ed., *Gilles Deleuze. Une vie philosophique* (Paris: Synthélabo, 1998), 537–543.

39. Anne Sauvagnargues, *Gilles Deleuze et l'art*, 200–208.

40. Gérard Fromanger, interview with the author.

41. Ibid.

42. Gérard Fromanger, interview with Ève Cloarec.

43. Ibid.

44. Ibid.

45. Gilles Deleuze and Félix Guattari, *What Is Philosophy?* trans. Janis Tomlinson and Graham Burchell (New York: Columbia University Press, 1996), 205.

46. Gérard Fromanger, interview with the author.

47. Ibid.

48. Ibid.

49. Gilles Deleuze, "Le froid et le chaud," in Gérard Fromanger, *Le peintre et le modèle* (Paris: Baudard Alvarez, 1973). Reprinted in Gilles Deleuze, *L'île déserte et autres textes*, 344–350.

50. Ibid., 344.

51. Richard Pinhas, *Les larmes de Nietzsche. Deleuze et la musique* (Paris: Flammarion, 2001), 24.

52. Pierre Boulez, quoted by David Rabouin, *Le Magazine Littéraire* (February 2002): 40.

53. Gilles Deleuze, "Rendre audibles des forces non audibles par elles-mêmes" (1978), in *Deux régimes de fous* (Paris: Minuit, 2003), 143.

54. Ibid., 144.

55. Gilles Deleuze, "Occuper sans compter: Boulez, Proust et le temps" (1986), in *Difference and Repetition*, trans. Paul Patton (New York: Columbia University Press, 1994), 274.

56. Pierre Boulez, *Penser la musique aujourd'hui* (Paris: Gonthier, 1963).

57. Mireille Buydens, *Sahara. L'ésthetique de Gilles Deleuze* (Paris: Vrin, 1990), 154.

58. Richard Pinhas, interview with the author.

59. Ibid.

60. Ibid.

61. Ibid.

62. Richard Pinhas, "Deleuze Variations," *France Culture* (April 21, 2002).

63. Richard Pinhas, *Les larmes de Nietzsche. Deleuze et la musique*, 200.

64. Pascale Criton, interview with the author.

65. Ibid.

66. Ibid.

67. Pascale Criton, "L'invitation," in André Bernold and Richard Pinhas, eds., *Deleuze épars* (Paris: Hermann, 2005), 56.

68. Pascale Criton, preface to Ivan Wyschinegradsky, *La loi de la pansonorité* (Geneva: Contrechamps, 1966).

69. Gilles Deleuze, letter to Pascale Criton (December 2, 1993).

70. Pascale Criton, "Deleuze Variations," *France Culture* (April 21, 2002).

71. Pascale Criton, interview with the author.

72. Ibid.

73. Jean-Paul Manganaro, interview with the author.

74. Carmelo Bene and Gilles Deleuze, *Superpositions* (Paris: Minuit, 1979).

75. Ibid., 113.

76. Jean-Paul Manganaro, preface to Carmelo Bene, *Notre-Dame des Turcs* (Paris: POL, 2003), 17.

77. Gilles Deleuze, "Ce que la voix apporte au texte," in *Deux régimes de fous*, 303–304.

78. Ibid., 303–304.

79. Gilles Deleuze, *L'epuisé* (Paris: Minuit, 1992).

80. Ibid., 57.

81. Ibid., 78.

82. Joachim Vital, *Adieu à quelques personnages* (Paris: La Différence, 2004), 228.

83. Gilles Deleuze, *Francis Bacon. La logique de la sensation* (Paris: La Différence, 1981). Translated as *The Logic of Sensation*, trans. Daniel W. Smith (Minneapolis: University of Minnesota Press, 2003).

84. Francis Bacon, quoted by Joachim Vital, *Adieu à quelques personnages*, 228.

85. Joachim Vital, quoted in ibid., 236–237.

86. Gilles Deleuze, "La peinture enflame l'écriture," comments from Hervé Guibert, *Le Monde* (December 3, 1981). Reprinted in Gilles Deleuze, *Deux régimes de fous*, 170–171.

87. Michael Pepiatt, *Bacon. Anatomie d'une énigme* (Paris: Flammarion, 2004).

88. Gilles Deleuze, *Francis Bacon. La logique de la sensation*, 17.

89. Anne Sauvagnargues, *Gilles Deleuze et l'art*, 260.

90. Gilles Deleuze, "Letter-preface," in Mireille Buydens, *Sahara. L'esthétique de Gilles Deleuze*, 5.

91. Arnaud Villani, "De l'esthétique à l'esthésique: Deleuze et la question de l'art," in Alain Beaulieu, ed., *Gilles Deleuze, héritage philosophique* (Paris: PUF, 2005), 105.

92. Ibid., 100.

93. Gilles Deleuze, *Le pli. Leibniz et le baroque* (Paris: Minuit, 1988).

94. Gilles Deleuze, *Libération* (September 22, 1998), remarks from Robert Maggiori. Reprinted in Gilles Deleuze, *Pourparlers* (Paris: Minuit, 1990), 220. Translated as *Negotiations*, trans. Martin Joughlin (New York: Columbia University Press, 1995), 162.

95. Ibid.

96. Gilles Deleuze, *Le pli*, 37.

97. Gilles Deleuze with Claire Parnet, *L'abécédaire de Gilles Deleuze* (1988), 3 DVDs (Montparnasse: Arte Video, 1997).

98. David Rabouin, interview with the author.

99. Ibid.

100. Bruno Paradis, "Leibniz: un monde unique et relatif," *Le Magazine Littéraire* 257 (September 1988): 26.

101. Ibid., 129.

102. Gilles Deleuze, Paris-VIII class (October 28, 1986).

103. G. W. Leibniz, *La monadologie* (Paris: Belin, 1952), para. 61.

104. Gilles Deleuze, Paris-VIII class (October 28, 1986).

105. Bernard Cache, interview with the author.

106. Gilles Deleuze, *Le pli*, 27.

107. Ibid., 32.

108. Bernard Cache, interview with the author.

109. Bernard Cache, "Objectile: poursuite de la philosophie par d'autres moyens?" in *Gilles Deleuze. Immanence et vie* (Paris: PUF, 1998).

110. Gilles Deleuze, *Le pli*, 45.

111. Ibid., 161.

112. Ibid., 187.

113. Christine Buci-Glucksmann, "Les cristaux de l'art: une esthetique du virtuel," in *Gilles Deleuze. Immanence et vie*.

114. Christine Buci-Glucksmann, *La folie du voir. De l'esthétique baroque* (Paris: Galilée, 1986).

115. Christine Buci-Glucksmann, interview with the author.

116. Ibid.

117. Christine Buci-Glucksmann, *L'ésthetique du temps au Japon. Du zen au virtuel* (Paris: Galilée, 1986).

118. Ibid., 97–98.

119. Eric Alliez, "Sur la philosophie de Gilles Deleuze: une entrée en matière," in *Gilles Deleuze. Immanence et vie*, 49–57.

120. Ibid., 56–57.

121. Gilles Deleuze, "Un philosophe nomade," *Le Magazine Littéraire* 257 (September 1988).

122. David Lapoujade, interview with the author.

123. Gilles Deleuze, "Actual and Virtual," in *Dialogues II*, 148.

124. Gilles Deleuze, *Difference and Repetition*, 208.

125. Raymond Bellour, interview with the author.

25. AN ARTIST PHILOSOPHY

1. Gilles Deleuze, University of Paris-VIII course (June 3, 1980). National French Library, sound archives.

2. In 1991, Deleuze wrote to his philosopher friend Mikel Dufrenne, who, like Deleuze, had been suffering from a serious respiratory deficiency since 1988. "Dear Mikel, Thank you for your note, at the end of the *Esthetics* flyer. Alas, I will not be able to contribute to this issue because, having finally finished the book that I was dreaming of as being my final book, *What Is Philosophy?* I want to stop for at least two or three years and truly retire. It's also necessary because the winter was very difficult in terms of my health: long suffocations, tied like a dog to my oxygen tank, painless but a lot of respiratory panic. Ongoing Convalescence. All of these plaints less to complain than to communicate with you, in the hope that your own health has held steady." Gilles Deleuze, letter to Mikel Dufrenne (April 25, 1991), in *Revue d'Esthétique* 30 (1996): 57.

3. Robert Maggiori, "Une bombe sous la philosophie," *Libération* (September 12, 1991). Reprinted in Robert Maggiori, *La philosophie au jour le jour* (Paris: Flammarion, 1995), 374–381.

4. Ibid., 379.

5. Roger-Pol Droit, "La création des concepts," *Le Monde* (September 13, 1991).

6. Ibid

7. Sylvain Loiseau, interview with the author.

8. Ibid.

9. Ibid.

10. Gilles Deleuze and Felix Guattari, *Qu'est-ce que la philosophie?* (Paris: Minuit, 1991). Translated as *What Is Philosophy?* trans. Hugh Tomlinson and Graham Burchell (New York: Columbia University Press, 1994), 3. Quotations are from this edition.

11. Ibid., 62.

12. Ibid., 70.

13. Ibid., 77.

14. Ibid., 82.

15. Ibid., 83.

16. Ibid.

17. Ibid., 118.

18. Ibid., 137–138.

19. Ibid., 141.

20. Ibid., 144.

21. Ibid., 156. See chapter 17.

22. Ibid., 160.

23. Ibid., 161.

24. Ibid., 164.

25. So, for example, Deleuze and Guattari do not consider jealousy in Proust to derive simply from disappointed love, but as finality: "and if we must love, it's so that we can be jealous." Ibid., 175.

26. Ibid., 183.

27. Gilles Deleuze, *Empiricism and Subjectivity: An Essay of Hume's Theory of Human Nature* (New York: Columbia University Press, 1991).

28. See Francisco Varela, Evan Thompson, and Eleanor Rosch, *L'inscription corporelle de l'esprit* (Paris: Seuil, 1993).

29. Mony Elkain and Isabelle Stengers, "Du marriage des hétérogènes," *Chimères* 2, no. 21 (Winter 1994): 150.

30. Ibid., 153.

31. See chapter 18.

32. Mony Elkaim and Isabelle Stengers, "Du mariage des heterogènes," 159.

33. Félix Guattari, "Entretien avec Olivier Zahm, April 28, 1992," *Chimères* 2, no. 21 (Summer 1994): 50.

34. Ibid., 51.

35. Gilles Deleuze, "Portrait d'un philosophe en spectateur," interview with Hervé Guibert, *Le Monde* (October 6, 1983). Reprinted in Gilles Deleuze, *Deux régimes de fous* (Paris: Minuit, 2003), 199.

36. Anne Sauvagnarges, *Deleuze et l'art* (Paris: Presses universitaires de France, 2005), 58.

37. Gilles Deleuze with Claire Parnet, *L'abécédaire de Gilles Deleuze* (1988), 3 DVDs (Montparnasse: Arte Video, 1997).

38. Anne Sauvagnarges, *Deleuze et l'art*, 107.

39. "Art is never an end, it is only an instrument for tracing the lines of life, meaning all the real becomings, that don't happen simply *in* art, all of these active flights, that don't consist in making *in* art, in taking refuge in art, these positive deterritorializations that don't want to reterritorialze themselves in art, but rather to bring art along with them, towards the regions of the asignifyng, of the asubjective and of the faceless." Gilles Deleuze and Felix Guattari, *A Thousand Plateaus* (Minneapolis: University of Minnesota Press, 1987), 230.

40. Philippe Choulet, "L'empirisme comme aperitif. Une persistance de Deleuze," in *Deleuze épars*, ed. Andre Bernold and Richard Pinhas (Paris: Hermann, 2005), 93–111.

26. Winning Over the West

1. François Cusset, *French Theory* (Paris: La Découverte, 2003).

2. Sylvère Lotringer, interview with the author.

3. Yves Mabin, interview with the author.

4. Ibid.

5. Ibid.

6. Ibid.

7. Sylvère Lotringer, "No Comment," *Chimères* 37 (1999): 14–15.

8. Ibid., 15

9. Sylvère Lotringer, interview with Virginie Linhart.

10. Sylvère Lotringer, interview with the author.

11. Sylvère Lotringer, interview with Virginie Linhart.

12. This labor committee was Marxist in appearance only and was in fact a small group of the extreme Right whose objective was to create confusion in the American radical Left.

13. Sylvère Lotringer, "No Comment," 16.

14. Sylvère Lotringer, interview with the author.

15. Gilles Deleuze and Félix Guattari, *Anti-Oedipus* (New York: Viking, 1977).

16. Jean-Jacques Label, "Gilles Deleuze: Avez-vous des questions?" *France Culture*, hosted by Jean Daive (April 20, 2002).

17. Jean-Jacques Lebel, interview with Virginie Linhart.

18. Ibid.

19. Ibid.

20. Ibid.

21. Ibid.

22. Ibid.

23. Félix Guattari, "Notes sur mon voyage aux États Unis" (September–October 1974), IMEC archives.

24. Ibid.

25. Constantin Boundas, interview with the author.

26. *Anti-Oedipus* was published in 1977, *Masochism* by Brazilier in 1971, and *Proust and Signs* by Brazilier in 1972.

27. Constantin Boundas, interview with the author.

28. Of the three books translated by Constantin Boundas, only *Empiricism and Subjectivity* was published (New York: Columbia University Press, 1991). Boundas later edited Mark Lester and Charles Stivale's translation of *The Logic of Sense* (New York: Columbia University Press, 1990).

29. Gilles Deleuze, reported by Constantin Boundas, interview with the author. This collection of texts was published as *The Deleuze Reader,* ed. Constantin Boundas (New York: Columbia University Press, 1993).

30. Constantin Boundas and Dorothea Olkowski, eds., *Gilles Deleuze and the Theater of Philosophy* (New York: Routledge, 1994). This first Deleuzean conference galvanized researchers interested in his work; only twenty researchers attended, but they were particularly interested in pursuing their exchanges. This was also an occasion to launch new initiatives: Charles Stivale made the contacts necessary to publish an issue of *SubStance* devoted to *A Thousand Plateaus* in the mid-1990s.

31. The bulk of the conference papers were published in a special issue of *Angelaki* 5 (August 2000).

32. Paul Patton, interview with the author. Patton convinced several students to take Deleuze's course during this period. It was the beginning of a small colony of assiduous Australians attending Vincennes. When he returned to Australia in 1981, Patton began translating *Rhizome* into English and spent five years translating Deleuze's *Différence et répétition*, published in 1994. Paul Patton also edited a critical reader with French and Anglophone specialists: Paul Patton, ed., *Deleuze: A Critical Reader* (New York: Blackwell, 1996).

33. Gilles Deleuze, *Nietzsche and Philosophy* (New York: Columbia University Press, 1983); Gilles Deleuze, *Kant's Critical Philosophy* (Minneapolis: University of Minnesota, 1984); Gilles Deleuze and Félix Guattari, *Kafka* (Minneapolis: University of Minnesota Press, 1986); Gilles Deleuze, *The Movement-Image* (Minneapolis: University of Minnesota Press, 1986); Gilles Deleuze, *Dialogues* (New York: Columbia University Press, 1987); Gilles Deleuze and Félix Guattari, *A Thousand Plateaus* (Minneapolis: University of Minnesota Press, 1987); Gilles Deleuze, *Foucault* (Minneapolis: University of Minnesota Press, 1988); Gilles Deleuze, *Bergsonism* (New York: Zone Books, 1988); Gilles Deleuze, *Spinoza: Practical Philosophy* (San Francisco: City Lights Books, 1988); Gilles Deleuze, *Cinema 2: The Time-Image* (Minneapolis: University of Minnesota Press, 1989).

34. Gary Genosko, ed., *Deleuze and Guattari,* 3 vols. (London: Routledge, 2001).

35. Eugene Holland, interview with the author.

36. See François Dosse, *Michel de Certeau, le marcheur blessé* (Paris: La Découverte, 2002).

37. Eugene Holland, *Deleuze and Guattari's* Anti-Oedipus (New York: Routledge, 1999).

38. Andrew Cutrofello, interview with the author.

39. Andrew Cutrofello, *Continental Philosophy: A Contemporary Introduction* (New York: Routledge, 2005).

40. Ian Price, interview with the author.

41. Dudley Andrew, interview with the author.

42. Ibid. Deleuze is being used increasingly in cinema studies. The Harvard professor David Rodowick, the author of an excellent book on film theory (see chapter 22), organized a large international conference at Harvard on Deleuze in May 2005, "Afterimage of Gilles Deleuze's Film Philosophy," on the tenth anniversary of his death and the twentieth anniversary of the publication of *Cinema 2*. We should also mention Dudley Andrew's colleague at Yale, John MacKay, who teaches early cinema and especially Vertov, and who gives a seminar on Deleuze every year.

43. Julian Bourg, interview with the author.

44. Ibid.

45. Julian Bourg, *Forbidden to Forbid: May '68 and the Return to Ethics in Contemporary France* (Montreal: McGill-Queen's University Press, 2007).

46. Eleanor Kaufman, interview with the author.

47. Ibid.

48. Alain Beaulieu, interview with the author. Published in 2004, Beaulieu's thesis, *Gilles Deleuze et la phénoménologie* (Mons: Sils Maria, 2004), consisted in closely following Deleuze's almost amorous struggle with phenomenological ideas. Each of Deleuze's key concepts was, according to Beaulieu, a way of positioning and distinguishing himself with respect to phenomenology in order to construct his own approach. He hoped to elucidate the Deleuzean conceptualization on its own ground and the questions it answers, which end up echoing those of phenomenology while offering another perspective.

49. Biodun Iginla, "Gilles Deleuze – In Memoriam (1925–1995): A Personal Note," *Iris* 23 (Spring 1997): 191.

50. Gilles Deleuze, *The Fold: Leibniz and the Baroque* (Minneapolis: University of Minnesota Press, 1993); Gilles Deleuze, *Essays Critical and Clinical* (Minneapolis: University of Minnesota Press, 1997); Gilles Deleuze, *Francis Bacon* (Minneapolis: University of Minnesota Press, 2004). Iginla was a former student of Deleuze at Paris-VIII in 1975 before continuing in comparative literature at the University of Minnesota. The rhizome "often helped me in my career as an editor. Biodun Iginla, "Gilles Deleuze—In Memoriam (1925–1995): A Personal Note," 193. Tom Conley advised him to read *Anti- Oedipus* in 1973, even before he had started taking Deleuze's

course. "It became my bible." Ibid., 194. In his opinion, Foucault's prophecy had already come true. "In a sense, this century is already Deleuzean. For example, he had already theorized the distinction between actual and virtual at least two decades before the cybernetic and technoevangelists began talking about the distinction between real life (RC) and virtual reality (VR)." Ibid., 195.

51. Réda Bensmaïa, ed., *Lendemains* 53 (1989).

52. Réda Bensmaïa, interview with the author.

53. Gilles Deleuze, "Lettre à Réda Bensmaïa sur Spinosa," in *Pourparlers* (Paris: Minuit, 1990), 223–225. Translated in *Negotiations* as "Letter to Réda Bensmaïa, on Spinoza," 164.

54. Lawrence Kritzmann, interview with the author.

55. Ibid.

56. Charles Stivale, *The Two-Fold Thought of Deleuze and Guattari* (New York: Guilford Press, 1998).

57. Brian Massumi, *A User's Guide to Capitalism and Schizophrenia: Deviations from Deleuze and Guattari* (Cambridge, Mass.: The MIT Press, 1992); Brian Massumi, *Parables for the Virtual: Movement, Affect, Sensation* (Durham, N.C.: Duke University Press, 2002); Brian Massumi, ed., *A Shock to Thought: Expressions After Deleuze and Guattari* (New York: Routledge, 2001). "Deleuze of America: the third excluded. This is to say, the affirmation: our possible impossible. To read Deleuze, between sincerity and cynicism, is to experience an apprenticeship of thought as a practice of reopening. A vanishing point, a refractory pragmatism." Brian Massumi, quoted by Elie During, in *Le Magazine Littéraire* (February 2002): 56. The Australian academic Ian Buchanan also became a prolific expert on Deleuze's work, which he first likened to that of Michel de Certeau's concerning the concept of the plane of immanence. Ian Buchanan, *Michel de Certeau: Cultural Theorist* (London: Sage, 2000). A professor at the University of Tasmania, he directed a group publication on Deleuze's work (Ian Buchanan and John Marks, eds., *Deleuze and Literature* [New York: Columbia University Press, 2001]) and he has since become an orchestrator of Deleuzeanism on the British front; he teaches at Cardiff and is the editor at Edinburgh University Press.

58. Fredrick Jameson, *Fables of Aggression: Wyndham Lewis* (Berkeley: University of California Press, 1979).

59. See Manuel Delanda, *Intensive Science and Virtual Philosophy* (New York: Continuum International Publishing Group, 2002); Manuel Delanda, *New Philosophy of Society: Assemblage Theory and Social Complexity* (New York: Continuum, 2006).

60. Michael Hardt, *Gilles Deleuze: An Apprenticeship in Philosophy* (Minneapolis: University of Minnesota Press, 1992).

61. Michael Hardt and Toni Negri, *Empire* (Cambridge, Mass.: Harvard University Press, 2000).

62. François Cusset, *French Theory*, 163.

63. Elizabeth Grosz, "A Thousand Tiny Sexes: Feminism and Rhizomatics"; and Rosi Braidoti, "Toward a New Nomadism: Feminist Deleuzean Tracks, or Metaphysics and Metabolism," in *Gilles Deleuze and the Theater of Philosophy*, ed. Constantin Boundas and Dorothea Olkowski (New York: Routledge, 1994).

64. Donna Haraway, quoted in François Cusset, *French Theory*, 270.

65. Hakim Bey, *The Temporary Autonomous Zone: Ontological Anarchy, Poetic Terrorism* (New York: Autonomedia, 1991).

66. François Cusset, *French Theory*, 265.

67. Ibid., 266.

27. AROUND THE WORLD

1. Hugh Tomlinson and Robert Galeta, *Le Magazine Littéraire* (September 1988): 60.

2. Keith Ansell-Pearson, ed., *Germinal Life: The Difference and Repetition of Deleuze* (New York: Routledge, 1999); Keith Ansell-Pearson, ed., *Deleuze and Philosophy: The Difference Engineer* (New York: Routledge, 1997).

3. Lawrence Grossberg, interview with the author.

4. Ibid.

5. Ibid.

6. Simon Tormey, *Anti-Capitalism: A Beginner's Guide* (New York: Oneworld, 2000).

7. Philip Goodchild, *Deleuze and Guattari: An Introduction to the Politics of Desire* (London: Sage, 1996); Philip Goodchild, *Gilles Deleuze and the Question of Philosophy* (New York: Associated University Press, 1996).

8. Simon Tormey, interview with the author.

9. Ibid.

10. See chapter 19.

11. Hidenobu Suzuki, interview with the author.

12. Kuniichi Uno, interview with the author.

13. Ibid.

14. Ibid.

15. Hidenobu Susuki, interview with the author.

16. Kuniichi Uno, interview with the author.

17. He translated *La révolution moléculaire* in 1988, followed by *Les trois écologies, Psychanalyse et transversalité*, and *Les années d'hiver*.

18. Masaaki Sugimura, interview with Virginie Linhart.

19. Ibid.

20. Ibid.

21. The "Les paravents" project.

22. Félix Guattari, "Les machines architecturales de Shin Takamatsu," in *Transfigura-tion*, exhibition catalogue, Europalia 89, Japan in Belgium, 99–107. Reprinted in *Chimères* (Winter 1994): 127–141.

23. Christian Girard, *Chimères* (Winter 1994): 128.

24. Félix Guattari, "Les machines architecturales de Shin Takamatsu," 130.

25. Ibid., 131.

26. Ibid., 134.

27. Masaaki Sugimura, interview with Virginie Linhart.

28. Suely Rolnik, interview with the author.

29. Ibid.

30. Ibid.

31. Ibid.

32. Félix Guattari, *Pulsation politique du désir* (Soulina, 1981). Félix Guattari and Suely Rolnik, *Micropolitica, cartografías do desejo* (Petropolis: Vozes, 1986). Translated as Félix Guattari, *Micropolitiques, les empecheurs de penser en rond* (Paris, 2007).

33. Suely Rolnik, interview with the author.

34. Félix Guattari and Suely Rolnik, *Micropolitica, cartografías do desejo*.

35. Félix Guattari and Suely Rolnik, *Micropolitica, cartografías do desejo*, 4th ed., 311.

36. Félix Guattari, *Caosmos-um novo paradigma estético* (Rio: Ed. 34, 1992); Gilles Deleuze and Félix Guattari, *O que é a filosophia?* (Rio: Ed. 34, 1992).

37. Éric Alliez, *Les temps capitaux* (Paris: Le Cerf, 1999).

38. Papers given at the colloquium were published in Éric Alliez, ed., *Gilles Deleuze. Une vie philosophique* (Paris: Synthélabo, 1998).

39. Bento Prado, *Presencia a camp transcendantal, consciencia e negatividade na filosofia de Bergson* (EDUSP, 1989).

40. Roberto Machado, *Deleuze e la filosofia* (Rio: Graal, 1990).

41. Guattari returned to Mexico and gave a lecture at the National Autonomous University of Mexico in October 1981 entitled "Les temps machiniques et la question de l'inconscient." Reprinted in Félix Guattari, *Les années d'hiver* (Paris: Barrault, 1986), 125–137.

42. Fernando Gonzalez interview with the author. See *La guerra de la memorias. Psicoanalisis, historia e interpretacion* (Mexico City: Universidad Iberoamericana, 1998), esp. chap. 2 on Freud and the psychoanalytic interpretation machine.

43. Ibid.

44. Fernando Gonzalez, interview with the author.

45. Miguel Norambuena, interview with the author.

46. Ibid.

47. Ibid.

48. Félix Guattari, *Cartografía del deseo* (Buenos Aires: La Marca, 1995).

49. Miguel Norambuena, interview with the author.

50. See chapter 16.

51. "The '77 Movement with its 'emarginati,' its metropolitan Indians, newspapers (Attavers), its free radio stations (Radio Alice) finds a veritable book-tool in *Anti-Oedipus*." Giorgio Passerone, *Le Magazine Littéraire* (September 1988): 61.

52. The editorial committee comprised Roberto Callegari, Marco Dotti, Ubaldo Fadini, and Francesco Galluzi.

53. Giorgio Passerone, interview with the author.

54. Gilles Deleuze and Félix Guattari, "Préface pour l'édition italienne de *Mille Plateaux*," reprinted in Gilles Deleuze, *Deux régimes de fous* (Paris: Minuit, 2003), 288–290. Translated as Gilles Deleuze, *Two Regimes of Madness: Texts and Interviews, 1975–1995* (New York: Semiotexte, 2006).

55. Giuseppe Bianco, interview with the author.

56. Manola Antonioli, *Deleuze et l'histoire de la philosophie* (Paris: Kimé, 1999); Manola Antonioli, *Géophilosophie de Deleuze et Guattari* (Paris: L'Harmattan, 2003).

57. Manola Antonioli, interview with the author.

28. TWO DEATHS

1. Marie Depussé, *Dieu gît dans les détails* (Paris: POL, 1993), 143.

2. Ibid., 144.

3. Ibid.

4. Emmanuelle Guattari, interview with Virginie Linhart.

5. Marie Depussé, *Dieu gît dans les détails*, 145.

6. Tatiana Kecojevic, interview with Virginie Linhart.

7. Gérard Fromanger, interview with the author.

8. Ibid.

9. Tatiana Kecojevic, interview with Virginie Linhart.

10. Ibid.

11. Jean Rolin, *Joséphine*, (Paris: Gallimard, 1994), 48.

12. Gérard Fromanger, interview with the author.

13. Enzo Cormann, "Félix Guattari," *Chimères* 2, no. 2 (Summer 1994): 30.

14. Patrick Farbias, interview with Virginie Linhart.

15. Jean Guattari, interview with the author.

16. Ibid.

17. Jack and Monique Lang, text read at the funeral on September 14, 1992, IMEC archives.

18. Gilles Deleuze, "Pour Félix," *Chimères* 18 (Winter 1992–1993): 209.

19. Ibid.

20. Jean Oury, "Pour Félix," *Chimères* 18 (Winter 1992–1993): 208.

21. Robert Maggiori, *Libération* (August 31, 1992): 32.

22. Jean Oury, *Libération* (August 31, 1992): 35.

23. Roger-Pol Droit and Jean Oury, *Le Monde* (September 1, 1992).

24. *Chimères* 1, no. 21 (Winter 1994) and no. 23 (Summer 1994).

25. With the participation and speeches by Jean-Paul Gay, Michel Benasayag, Gisèle Donnard, Ilan Halévi, François Lautier, Bernard Ravenel, and René Schérer.

26. Anne-Brigitte Kern, Sacha Goldman, Gilles Deleuze, and Jean Oury, "Félix Guattari," *Transversales* 18 (November–December 1992).

27. Jean-Jacques Lebel, interview with Virginie Linhart.

28. Ibid.

29. Ibid.

30. *Monument to Félix Guattari*, a film by Jean-Jacques Lebel and François Pain, produced by François Pain, National French Library audiovisual archives.

31. Jean-Jacques Lebel, interview with Virginie Linhart.

32. Ibid.

33. Gilles Deleuze, letter to Jean-Pierre Faye (March 15, 1991). In Jean-Pierre Faye and Henri Maccheroni, *Dialogue et court traité sur le transformat* (Paris: Al Dante/L'enseigne des Oudin, 2000), 67–68.

34. Noelle Châtelet, interview with the author.

35. Richard Pinhas, *Les larmes de Nietzsche. Deleuze et la musique* (Paris: Flammarion, 2001), 19.

36. Ibid., 26.

37. Yves Mabin, interview with the author.

38. Ibid.

39. René Schérer, "L'écriture, la vie," *Revue des Lettres, Sciences et Arts de Corrèze* 99 (1996). Reprinted in *Regards sur Deleuze* (Paris: Kimé, 1998), 10.

40. Pierre Verstraeten and Juliette Simont, "Vol de l'aigle et chute profonde," in *Gilles Deleuze* (Paris: Vrin, 1998), 16.

41. Robert Maggiori, "Un courant d'air dans la pensée du siècle," *Libération* (November 6, 1995).

42. Antoine de Gaudemar, "Le geste d'un philosophe," *Libération* (November 6, 1995).

43. Jean-Luc Nancy, "Du sens dans tous les sens," *Libération* (November 7, 1995).

44. Jacques Derrida, "Il me faudra errer tout seul," *Libération* (November 7, 1995).

45. Roger-Pol Droit, on "Le cercle de Minuit" (November 6, 1995), INA Archives.

46. Roger-Pol Droit, "La rébellion et l'intelligence d'un philosophe," *Le Monde* (November 7, 1975).

47. Jean-François Lyotard, "Le temps qui ne passe pas," *Le Monde* (November 10, 1975).

48. Michel Butel, "Du jour au lendemain," France Culture (November 7, 1995), INA Archives.

49. Ibid.

50. Christian Descamps, "Pour Deleuze le minoritaire," *La Quinzaine Littéraire* (February 1.–15, 1996).

51. Yves Mabin, "Gilles, l'ami," *La Quinzaine Littéraire* (February 1–15, 1996).

52. Roger-Pol Droit, "Saint Deleuze," in *La compagnie des philosophes* (Paris: Odile Jacob, 1998), 299–312.

53. Ibid., 301.

54. Ibid., 302.

55. Gilles Deleuze, "L'immanence: une vie," *Philosophie* (September 1995): 3–7.

56. See chapter 8.

57. Éric Alliez, *Gilles Deleuze. Une vie philosophique* (Paris: Synthélabo, 1998).

58. *Rue Descartes* 20, *Gilles Deleuze. Immanence et vie* (May 1998). Articles by José Gil, Alain Badiou, Françoise Proust, Éric Alliez, Guy Lardreau, René Schérer, Toni Negri, Christine Buci-Glucksmann, Lucien Vinciguerra, Jean-Clet Martin, Danielle Cohen-Levinas, and Bernard Cache.

59. Yannick Beaubatie, ed., *Tombeau de Gilles Deleuze* (Tulle: Mille Sources, 2000).

60. Elisabeth Lagisquet, "Pourquoi parler de Gilles Deleuze en Limousin?" in *Un philosophe en Limousin*. Gilles Deleuze, published by the association, Saint-Léonard en Limousin, "ses artistes et écrivains" (1996), 6.

29. THEIR WORK AT WORK

1. Jean-Clet Martin, *Variations. La philosophie de Gilles Deleuze* (Paris: Payot, 1993).

2. Jean-Clet Martin, interview with the author.

3. Gilles Deleuze, letter to Jean-Clet Martin (January 19, 1991).

4. Gilles Deleuze, "Lettre-préface" (June 13, 1990), to Jean-Clet Martin, in *Variations*, 7.

5. Ibid., 8.

6. Arnaud Villani, "Modernité de la pensée philosophique. II," *Revue de l'Enseignement Philosophique* 2 (December 1992–January 1993); Arnaud Villani, "Deleuze et la philosophie microphysique," in *Philosophie contemporaine. Annales de la faculté de lettres de Nice*, no. 9 (Nice: Les Belles Lettres, 1995); Arnaud Villani, "Géographie physique de *Mille plateaux*," *Critique* 455 (1985): 331–347.

7. Arnaud Villani, *La guêpe et l'orchidée* (Paris: Belin, 1999).

8. Gilles Deleuze, letter to Arnaud Villani (August 1, 1982), in *La guêpe et l'orchidée*, 125–126.

9. Frédéric Worms, interview with the author.

10. David Rabouin, interview with the author.

11. Thomas Benatouil, *Faire usage. La pratique du stoïcisme* (Paris: Vrin, 2006).

12. Éric Alliez, ed., *Gilles Deleuze, une vie philosophique—rencontres internationales, Rio De Janeiro, São Paulo, 10–14 Juin 1996* (Paris: Synthélabo, 1998); Keith Ansell-Pearson, ed., *Deleuze and Philosophy: The Difference Engineer* (London: Routledge, 1997).

13. Gilles Deleuze, *Desert Islands and Other Texts: 1953–1974*, trans. Mike Taormina (New York: Semiotexte, 2003).

14. "L'effet Deleuze. Philosophie, esthétique, politique," *Le Magazine Littéraire* (February 2002).

15. David Rabouin, interview with the author.

16. Anne Sauvagnargues, interview with the author.

17. Published as *Deleuze et l'art* (Paris: PUF, 2005).

18. Anne Sauvagnargues, interview with the author.

19. Ibid.

20. Anne Sauvagnargues, *Deleuze et l'art*, 12.

21. *Multitudes* (Summer 2006). Yann Moulier-Boutang, editor.

22. Mathieu Potte-Bonneville. Interview with the author.

23. This short lived and very disparate group dissolved very quickly and its members got involved in various militant actions in the battle against AIDS, in Act Up, and in support groups for Algerian intellectuals and for unemployed and marginal types. Mathieu Potte-Bonneville, interview with the author.

24. *Vacarme* 34 (Winter 2006). Stany Grelet, editor.

25. Mathieu Potte-Bonneville, interview with the author.

26. Michael Hardt and Antonio Negri, *Empire* (Cambridge, Mass.: Harvard University Press, 2000).

27. Manola Antonioli, *Deleuze et l'histoire de la philosophie* (Paris: Kimé, 1999).

28. Manola Antonioli, *La géophilosophie de Deleuze et Guattari* (Paris: L'Harmattan, 2004).

29. Ibid., 12–13.

30. Ibid, 252.

31. Philippe Mengue, *Deleuze et la question de la démocratie* (Paris: L'Harmattan, 2003).

32. Philippe Mengue, interview with the author.

33. Ibid.

34. Philippe Mengue, *Deleuze et la question de la démocratie*, 32.

35. Ibid, 104.

36. Ibid, 204.

37. Paul Patton, "Deleuze et la démocratie," lecture at an international colloquium organized by Manola Antonioli and Pierre-Anoine Chardel, "Gilles Deleuze, Félix Guattari et le politique" (January 14–15, 2005), Paris-VIII.

38. Arnaud Villani, "Comment peut-on être deleuzien?" in *Deleuze épars*, ed. André Bernhold and Richard Pinhas (Paris: Hermann, 2005), 82.

39. Jacob Rogozinski, "La fêlure de la pensée," *Le Magazine Littéraire* 25 (September 1988): 46–48.

40. Ibid., 46.

41. Jacob Rogozinski, interview with the author.

42. Ibid.

43. Isabelle Stengers, interview with the author for *L'empire du sense. L'humanisation des sciences humaines* (Paris: La Découverte, 1995; repr. 1997), 35.

44. Isabelle Stengers, *Cosmopolitiques* (Paris: La Découverte, 1996–1997).

45. Isabelle Stengers, interview with Virginie Linhart.

46. Daniel Franco, interview with the author.

47. Pascal Chabot, *La philosophie de Simondon* (Paris: Vrin, 2003).

48. Pierre Verstraeten and Isabelle Stengers, eds., *Gilles Deleuze* (Paris: Vrin, 1998).

49. Pascal Chabot, interview with the author.

50. Bruno Latour, *Nous n'avons jamais été modernes* (Paris: La Découverte, 1991), 15.

51. Ibid., 76.

52. Ibid., 79.

53. Ibid., 87.

54. Ibid., 107.

55. Gilles Deleuze, *Pourparlers, 1972–1990* (Paris: Minuit, 1990). Translated as *Negotiations, 1972–1990*, trans. Martin Joughin (New York: Columbia University Press, 1995).

56. Bernard Stiegler, *De la misère symbolique. 1. L'époque hyperindustrielle* (Paris: Galilée, 2004), 41.

57. Ibid., 96.

58. Pierre-Antoine Chardel, interview with the author.

59. Anne Sauvagnargues, *Deleuze et l'art*.

60. Claude Jaeglé, *Portrait oratoire de Gilles Deleuze aux jeux jaunes* (Paris: PUF, 2005).

61. Monique David-Ménard, *Deleuze et la psychanalyse* (Paris: PUF, 2005).

62. Yann Laporte, *Gilles Deleuze, l'épreuve du temps* (Paris: L'Harmattan, 2005).

63. Stéfan Leclercq, ed., *Aux sources de la pensée de Gilles Deleuze* (Mons: Sils Maris, 2005).

64. Alain Beaulieu, ed., *Gilles Deleuze. Héritage philosophique* (Paris: PUF, 2005); André Bernold and Richard Pinhas, eds., *Deleuze épars*.

65. Gilles Deleuze and Félix Guattari, *Qu'est-ce que la philosophie?* (Paris: Minuit-poche, 2005). Translated as *What Is Philosophy?* (New York: Columbia University Press,

1994). Jean-Clet Martin, *La philosophie de Gilles Deleuze* (Paris: Payot, 2005); Catherine Clément, ed., *Gilles Deleuze* (Paris: Arc/Inculte, 2005).

66. Gilles Deleuze, *Cinema*, 6 CDs (Paris: Gallimard, 2006).

67. In addition, in 2005 several university events included the work of Deleuze and Guattari. On January 14–15, Manola Antonioli, Pierre-Antoine Chardel, Ivan Lapeyroux, and Hervé Reynauld organized an international colloquium on Deleuze, Guattari, and politics, at Paris-VIII. On December 2–3, Jean-Christophe Goddard organized two study days on *Anti-Oedipus* at the University of Poitiers.

68. Thierry Paquot, interview with the author.

69. Ibid.

70. Ibid.

71. Chris Younès, interview with the author.

72. Ibid.

73. Jean Attali, *Le plan et le détail. Une philosophie de l'architecture et de la ville* (Nîmes: Jacqueline Chambon, 2001).

74. Ibid., 216.

75. Bernard Andrieu, *Le dictionnaire du corps en sciences humaines et sociales* (Paris: CNRS, 2006).

76. Olivier Mongin, interview with the author.

77. Ibid.

78. Olivier Mongin, "L'excès et la dette. Gilles Deleuze et Paul Ricoeur ou l'impossible conversation?" in *Paul Ricoeur, cahiers de l'Herne*, ed. François Azouvi and Myriam Revault d'Allonnes (Paris, 2004), 271–283.

79. Ibid., 282.

30. Conclusion

1. See chapter 22.

2. Gilles Deleuze and Félix Guattari, *Qu'est-ce que la philosophie?* (Paris: Minuit-poche, 2005). Translated as *What Is Philosophy?* (New York: Columbia University Press, 1994), 106.

3. Ibid., 107.

4. Ibid., 108.

5. "Correspondence Dionys Mascolo–Gilles Deleuze," *Lignes* 33 (March 1998): 222–226. Reprinted in Gilles Deleuze, *Deux régimes de fous* (Paris: Minuit, 2003), 305–310.

6. Dionys Mascolo, *Autour d'un effort de mémoire* (Paris: Maurice Nadeau, 1987), 20.

7. Dionys Mascolo, letter to Gilles Deleuze (April 30, 1988), in Gilles Deleuze, *Deux régimes de fous*, 306.

8. Gilles Deleuze, letter to Dionys Mascolo (August 6, 1988), in Gilles Deleuze, *Deux régimes de fous*, 307.

9. Gilles Deleuze and Félix Guattari, *What Is Philosophy?* 109.

10. Ibid., 108.

11. Ibid., 111.

12. Gilles Deleuze and Claire Parnet, *L'abécédaire* (Paris: Pierre-André Boutrang, 1988).

13. Gilles Deleuze and Félix Guattari, "Mai 68 n'a pas eu lieu," *Les Nouvelles Littéraires* (May 3–9, 1984). Reprinted in Gilles Deleuze, *Deux régimes de fous*, 215–216.

14. Pierre Montebello, *L'autre métaphysique* (Paris: Desclée de Brouwer, 2003), 12.

15. Gilles Deleuze, "Bergson, 1859–1941," in *Les philosophes célèbres*, ed. Maurice Merleau-Ponty (Paris: Mazenod, 1956). Reprinted in Gilles Deleuze, *L'île déserte et autres textes* (Paris: Minuit, 2002), 33.

16. Friedrich Nietzsche, *Oeuvres completes. Fragments posthmes*, XIV, 14, 93.

17. Gilles Deleuze, "Trois questions sur *Six fois deux* (Godard)," *Cahiers du cinéma* 271 (November 1976). Reprinted in Gilles Deleuze, *Pourparlers, 1972–1990* (Paris: Minuit, 1990). Translated as *Negotiations, 1972–1990*, trans. Martin Joughin (New York: Columbia University Press, 1995), 44.

18. Pierre Montebello, *L'autre métaphysique*, 305.

Index

EUROPEAN PERSPECTIVES

A Series in Social Thought and Cultural Criticism

LAWRENCE D. KRITZMAN, EDITOR